The Nineteenth-Century Symphony

The Nineteenth-Century Symphony

Edited by D. Kern Holoman

UNIVERSITY OF CALIFORNIA, DAVIS

Schirmer Books
AN IMPRINT OF SIMON & SCHUSTER MACMILLAN
New York

PRENTICE HALL INTERNATIONAL
London   Mexico City   New Delhi   Singapore   Sydney   Toronto

Schirmer Books
An Imprint of Simon & Schuster Macmillan
1633 Broadway
New York, NY 10019

Library of Congress Catalog Card Number: 96-24580

Printed in the United States of America

Printing number
1 2 3 4 5 6 7 8 9 10

Library of Congress Cataloging-in-Publication Data

The nineteenth-century symphony / edited by D. Kern Holoman.
        p. cm. — (Studies in musical genres and repertories)
    Includes index.
    ISBN 0-02-871105-X (alk. paper)
    1. Symphony—19th century. I. Holoman, D. Kern, 1947-
II. Series.
ML 1255.N5 1996
784.2'184'09034—dc20   96-24580
                                                             CIP
                                                             MN
This paper meets the requirements of ANSI/NISO Z39.48–1992 (Permanence of Paper).

Contents

Preface

Professor Todd begins his preface to *Nineteenth-Century Piano Music*, the first volume that appeared in this series, by suggesting that over the century the piano "became essentially the instrument of choice."[1] Perhaps. But it is equally reasonable to think of the nineteenth-century symphony orchestra as the listening experience of choice for an ever-growing proportion of the ticket-buying public. Certainly the symphony itself was a fabulous sensual experience: rich with the passions of Romanticism, loud, colorful, and—given its enthusiastic embrace of the era's notion of progress—consistently modern. Whether the venue was a makeshift scaffolding out of doors or one of the several acoustically perfect orchestra halls that are themselves triumphs of the era's philharmonic enterprise, symphonies got performed—and listened to—more than ever before.[2]

The philharmonic societies that sprang up all over Europe and in due course reached distant new worlds descended in part from the academy concerts and subscription series of the Enlightenment, in part from the princely chapels. In Paris the Société des Concerts du Conservatoire (est. 1828) gathered professors, students, and the public specifically to essay the symphonies of Beethoven; in Leipzig the venerable Gewandhaus Concerts, too, enjoyed interlocking personnel with the new Conservatory there (from 1843). Vienna, Berlin, London, and eventually New York were large enough to sustain rival orchestras (and back in Paris, for that matter, there were eventually four concert societies—those of the Conservatoire, Pasdeloup, Colonne, and Lamoureux—giving their concerts simultaneously, on Sundays at 5:00). Frankfurt had its Museum Concerts (est. 1808); Cologne its Gürzenich Concerts (est. 1857); Munich its amateur Wilde Gung'l (from 1864; conducted from 1875 by Richard Strauss's father, Franz) and professional Kaim Orchestra (from 1893). The Hofkapelle in the tiny town of Meiningen became, under Duke Georg II, the nineteenth century's answer to Mannheim, numbering among its conductors von Bülow (1880–85) and Richard Strauss (1885–86) and among its favored guests both Brahms and Wagner. Brahms's Fourth was premiered there in 1885, as was, in the same year, Strauss's First Concerto for French horn.

Meanwhile the instrument makers—at once handcraftspersons in the old manner and starry-eyed avatars of the new industry—assiduously plied their trade. Romanticism in symphonic music is in part defined by the new orchestral chromaticism they made possible, first in the wood-wind and only slightly later with workable valving strategies for horns and trumpets.[3] By midcentury the tuba was capturing the long-contested spot at the bottom of the brass choir; pedal harps and the English horn and other outrigging wind, plus all manner of experimental percussion, trans-formed the Haydn/Beethoven orchestra into music's equivalent of a three-ring circus (this latter also a product of the era). Virtuoso players worked hand in hand with the luthiers to perfect the instruments and compose the tutors—Arban, Klosé, Tulou, and the like—that went with them. More than one composer-writer hurried to meet the demand for treatises on the new craft now being called orchestration.

In short, the symphony orchestra and the symphonic genre nour-ished each other, opening broad new vistas to the intellectual spirit and new markets to the entrepreneurial, habitually flinging the next new chal-lenge before the imagination of composers, builders, players, and (above all) listeners. This confluence of high art and the marketplace is much at issue in our volume, as are the other cultural underpinnings—politics, philosophy—of the compositional contract. Another common theme in the chapters that follow is the matter of narrative and allusion in musical discourse: the repertoire embraces so much heroic struggle and birth-to-death rhetoric that by the time of Tchaikovsky's mottoes, Richard Strauss's tales, and Mahler's neuroses the symphony begins to read like so much code. The overarching spirit, of course, is Beethoven's, and the Ninth Symphony (to say nothing of a composer's subconscious desire to match Beethoven's total) a proposition sine qua non. Open this book any-where, and you are within a few paragraphs of Beethoven.

Where, then, might one begin an approach to this substantial and singu-larly nuanced repertoire, and how might it be treated in a single volume of accessible length? The authors' debate on the matter resulted in the plan to begin with Schubert and his response to Classicism, alongside an evaluation of the symphonic contributions of Weber and Spohr, two com-posers arguably well beyond the grip of the Classical style. We elected to conclude our attention to the Viennese component of the symphonic repertoire with Mahler's Fourth (1900), then enjoyed wedging Elgar's two symphonies (1908, 1910) and Sibelius's (1899–1924) in anyway. With regret we omitted the works of the Norwegian composer Carl Nielsen (1892ff.) and developments in America that culminated in the sym-phonies of Charles Ives (1898ff.).

We leave the concerto and most of the vocal/orchestral repertoire to other volumes, though with Brahms and Mahler in particular that line is hard enough to draw. And we are able to allude only in passing to the century's other great orchestral repertoire, that of the theatre. In fact, opera and ballet so involved most of the principals of our story—composers, performers, listeners—that my opening proposition, like Professor Todd's, may itself need arguing.

Our fourteen authors traverse, then, the wide spectrum of approach that characterizes current musicology, a discipline in what might be thought of as the flower of self-discovery. Traditional modes of archival research and analysis have in recent years significantly enhanced what we know of even the most familiar of the composers treated here—Brahms, say, and Mahler and Tchaikovsky—such that a central purpose of these essays is the taking of stock and the positioning of new research within the context of inherited knowledge and attitudes. Where the music is lesser known and the historical terrain less well understood, the issue is to refocus our attention on works that were, at least at the time, central: that is the goal, for example, of Ralph Locke's superb essay on the French symphony, which posits some answers to the intriguing question "What *about* French music between the *Fantastique* and the *Faune?*"

Always there is the issue of how new music was negotiated by the public, which as often as not in the nineteenth century had something to do with a descriptive program. It is at the core of Kenneth Hamilton's treatment of Liszt, Bryan Gilliam's of Strauss, and my own of Berlioz; and it forms a central component of our present understanding of such diverse composers as Schumann, Bruckner, and Mahler as well. Michael Beckerman quite wrestles with Dvořák and his programs, sensing—now that we know a good deal about the relationship between "Hiawatha" and the *New World*—that there must be programs everywhere and frustrated that he cannot establish what they are. However that may be, asking this once-forbidden sort of question seems a mark of the good common sense to be found herein.

Many of our chapters—Spohr, Schumann, Mendelssohn, Bruckner, Mahler, among others—are by authors whose work first focused on a particular composer at the time of their doctoral dissertations and who have since become the English-language authorities on their subject. Brian Newbould's assessment of Schubert struggling to master progressive symphonic structure brings with it the particular expertise of one who has himself rendered Schubert's unfinished sketches and drafts into performable texts. James Hepokoski has been intrigued by the failure of the sonata in late-century and the corresponding need to theorize practices that used to thought of as the "dissolution" of tonality. Here he brings his considerable experience to bear on Elgar and Sibelius, composers of what might be termed the expanded canon.

But the canon of nineteenth-century symphonies is no longer an especially compelling concept. What the big orchestras play, nowadays, to stay in the live-concert business is only a fraction of the listening experience available to us as we form our assessment of the genre: practically all of it is now available on compact discs. It will be the ongoing work of these authors and their successors to construct enveloping understandings of all we can now know.

The nineteenth-century symphony had begun with Beethoven's works and their reception, a discovery that left Berlioz and all who shared his sentiments thunderstruck:

> In an artist's life one thunderclap sometimes follows swiftly on another, as in those outsize storms in which the clouds, charged to bursting with electric energy, seem to hurl the lightning back and forth and blow the whirlwind.
> I had just had the successive revelations of Shakespeare and Weber. Now at another point of the horizon I saw the giant form of Beethoven rear up. The shock was almost as great as that of Shakespeare had been. Beethoven opened before me a new world of music, as Shakespeare had revealed a new universe of poetry.[4]

Symphonies and symphony concerts went on to follow the courses charted by the early Romantics—ever bigger, ever more intricate of design and purpose—until at length they collapsed under their own weight, along with the rest of the culture, in 1914. (Ravel's *La Valse* [1920] affords a terrifying retrospective.) And collapse may not be too strong a word, for afterward there really was a sea change, such that despite every effort to the contrary the symphony as a living genre in fact began to wane.

—D. Kern Holoman

Notes

1. *Nineteenth-Century Piano Music,* ed. R. Larry Todd (New York, 1990), vii.

2. I treat this same subject matter at greater length in my introduction to the nineteenth-century chapters of *Performance Practice: Music After 1600,* ed. Howard Mayer Brown and Stanley Sadie (London: New Grove Handbooks in Music, 1989), 323–45.

3. The foundational study of the modern orchestra's emergence remains that of Adam Carse, *The Orchestra from Beethoven to Berlioz* (Cambridge, 1948).

4. *The Memoirs of Hector Berlioz,* trans. and ed. David Cairns (corrected ed. London, 1990), 65.

Acknowledgments

The present volume was long of genesis, part of an initiative first proposed by Maribeth Anderson Payne and R. Larry Todd that has since resulted in the eight volumes listed on p. ii. Jonathan Wiener carried the project through the reorganization of Schirmer Books as a division of Macmillan Library Reference USA. At the University of California, Davis, editorial support was provided by Thomas A. Young and Michael Malone; Malone prepared the majority of the musical examples using *Score*, a computer program developed at Stanford by Leland Smith. Seminars at the University of California, Davis, and Duke University worked through the book in manuscript and offered numerous corrections and improvements. Jonathan Elkus and John Palmer lent valuable professional expertise during the final stages of production.

Permission to reproduce the illustrations has been graciously extended by

Bildarchiv der Österreichische Nationalbibliothek

Royal College of Music, London

Mary Flagler Cary Music Collection in the Pierpont Morgan Library, New York

The Collection of Robert Owen Lehman, on deposit at the Pierpont Morgan Library, New York

The Kaplan Deposit at the Pierpont Morgan Library, New York

Musée Berlioz, La Côte-St.-André

Richard Macnutt

International Gustav Mahler Gesellschaft, Vienna

Newberry Library, Chicago

To all these the authors, editor, and general editor extend their deep thanks.

Contributors

Michael Beckerman, Professor of Music History at the University of California, Santa Barbara. His books *Janáček as Theorist* (1994) and *Janáček and Czech Music* (1995) have been published by Pendragon Press, and *Dvořák and His World* (1993) was published by Princeton University Press.

David Brodbeck, Associate Professor of Music at the University of Pittsburgh, is the editor of the series Brahms Studies (University of Nebraska Press, 1994–) and author of a forthcoming Cambridge Handbook on Brahms's First Symphony. Among his other publications are studies of Schubert's dances and the sacred music of Mendelssohn.

Clive Brown's book on performing practice, *Classical and Romantic Performance Practice*, is to be published by Oxford University Press. In addition to *Louis Spohr: A Critical Biography* (Cambridge University Press, 1984), he has published editions of music by Weber, Spohr, and Beethoven. His edition of Beethoven's Fifth Symphony (Breitkopf & Härtel, 1995), contains a number of new readings. Brown, an active violinist, is Reader in Music History at University College, Bretton Hall, University of Leeds.

Bryan Gilliam is Associate Professor of Music at Duke University. He has published articles on Bruckner, Strauss, and Kurt Weill and is the author of *Richard Strauss's "Elektra"* (Oxford University Press, 1991). He is editor of *Richard Strauss and His World* (Princeton University Press, 1992), *Richard Strauss: New Perspectives on the Composer and His Work* (Duke University Press, 1992), and *Music and Performance during the Weimar Republic* (Cambridge University Press, 1994). Gilliam is currently writing a biography of Strauss for Cambridge University Press.

Kenneth Hamilton is a pianist and lecturer at the University of Birmingham, England. He is the author of *Liszt's Sonata in B Minor* (Cambridge

University Press, forthcoming) and a contributor to the *Cambridge Companion to the Piano*. As a pianist he has broadcast internationally on radio and television, with particular emphasis on the nineteenth-century virtuoso repertoire.

Stephen E. Hefling, Associate Professor of Music at Case Western Reserve University, has also taught at Stanford and Yale. He has published numerous articles on Mahler's works and served as an editor for the *Kritische Gesamtausgabe*, and is currently editing a volume of the series Mahler Studies for Cambridge University Press. Also an authority on historical performance practice, Hefling is the author of *Rhythmic Alteration in Seventeenth- and Eighteenth-Century Music: Notes Inégales and Overdotting* (Schirmer Books, 1993).

James Hepokoski is Professor of Musicology at the University of Minnesota. He is the author of *Jean Sibelius: Symphony No. 5* (Cambridge University Press) and three books on Verdi's late operas: *Giuseppe Verdi: "Otello," Giuseppe Verdi: "Falstaff"* (both Cambridge University Press), and *Musica e Spettacolo: "Otello" di Giuseppe Verdi* (G. Ricordi). A co-editor of the journal *19th-Century Music*, Hepokoski has also published work on Debussy, Strauss, Dvořák, and Ives.

D. Kern Holoman, Professor of Music at the University of California, Davis, is the author of the *Catalogue of the Works of Hector Berlioz*, volume 25 of the *New Berlioz Edition* (Bärenreiter, 1987), and *Berlioz* (Harvard University Press, 1989). He is the conductor of the UC-Davis Symphony Orchestra and former Dean of Humanities, Arts, and Cultural Studies at the Davis campus.

Joseph C. Kraus is Associate Professor of Music Theory at the University of Nebraska, Lincoln. His articles on the music of Tchaikovsky and Mozart have appeared in *Music Theory Spectrum*, the *Journal of Musicological Research*, and the *Mozart-Jahrbuch*. During an extended visit to Russia he studied sketch materials at the Tchaikovsky State House–Museum in Klin.

Ralph P. Locke is Professor of Musicology at the Eastman School of Music, University of Rochester, where he is the senior editor of the series Eastman Studies in Music. He is the author of *Music, Musicians, and the Saint-Simonians* (University of Chicago Press, 1986) and a co-editor of *Cultivating Music in America: Women Patrons and Activists since 1860* (University of California Press, forthcoming).

Brian Newbould, Professor of Music at the University of Hull, is the author of *Schubert and the Symphony: A New Perspective* (Toccata Press, 1992). His completions of several works left unfinished by Schubert (including the Seventh, Eighth, and Tenth Symphonies) have been widely performed and recorded, and he has edited several other works of Schubert.

J. Stephen Parkany studied Bruckner with Robert Bailey and Larry Todd, then Anthony Newcomb and Joseph Kerman. An oboist and choral baritone, he has taught at Amherst College and Victoria University, New Zealand.

Linda Correli Roesner is the editor of Schumann's Symphony No. 3 in F♭ Major Op. 97 in the new Schumann complete edition, *Robert Schumann: Neue Ausgabe sämtlicher Werke*, Serie I, Bd. 3 (Schott, 1995). She has also edited the four Schumann Symphonies for Edition Eulenberg. Her edition of Brahms's Violin Concerto for the new Johannes Brahms complete edition is in preparation.

R. Larry Todd, Professor of Music at Duke University, is the general editor of the series Studies in Musical Genres and Repertoires, and edited the volume of the series devoted to nineteenth-century piano music. He has written extensively about the music of the nineteenth century, especially the music of Mendelssohn, and most recently has edited the volume *Schumann and His World* (Princeton University Press, 1994).

CHAPTER ONE

Schubert

Brian Newbould

The chronological epicenter of Franz Schubert's symphonic career may be placed about twelve years after that of Beethoven's, but Beethoven's symphonies were the product of a man aged thirty to fifty-four, while Schubert's date from his fourteenth to thirty-first years. Can it then be supposed that Beethoven, the older man, was more rooted in Classical tradition, while the younger symphonist responded to new currents and reached for new horizons with the adaptability of youth, more readily embracing the emergent Romanticism?

In truth, Schubert anticipated the dawn of Romanticism more tangibly in that genre he had made his own, the lied, than in the instrumental media in which Beethoven had already occupied the high ground. Although Schubert's symphonic swan song, the "Tenth" Symphony sketched on his deathbed in 1828, is a pioneering work that bursts the bonds of tradition as radically—though in its own terms—as any Beethoven symphony had done, his symphonic youth was a humble, even cautious apprenticeship in which he went back for the most part beyond Beethoven to his eighteenth-century forebears for models. Of course, lieder by their nature seem to espouse what with hindsight we see as Romantic ideals, since one measure of the new spirit was its openness to extramusical infiltration, while the piano became the Romantic instrument par excellence. But at the same time, perhaps because the smaller form posed less daunting structural quandaries to a teenager and left its composer free of the harmonically straitening problems of orchestral composition in the age of valveless brass instruments, Schubert tried his toes in the inviting waters of harmonic innovation sooner in song than in symphony, there anticipating the coloristic enrichment that was another feature of post–Classical development.

There are strong grounds for a holistic view of Schubert as a Classical composer who approached Romanticism in his songs, and to some extent in later instrumental works, rather than as a Romantic who was slow

ILLUSTRATION 1.1. Schubert in 1821. Portrait by Kupelwiesser. Bildarchiv der
Österreichische Nationalbibliothek.

to slough off Classical habits in his instrumental thinking. The typical
Classical composer was, after all, one who ventured and remained loyal to
all or at least most media, a criterion met by not only Haydn, Mozart, and
Beethoven but also Schubert—as well as the majority of their less illustri-
ous contemporaries. The specialist was largely a Romantic phenomenon
(consider Chopin, Wagner, Paganini, a host of Italian opera composers
from Rossini to Verdi, Wieniawski, Meyerbeer, and Hérold). Mendelssohn
and Schumann, perhaps through reverence for Mozart and Beethoven re-

spectively, affected some Classical versatility while simultaneously indulging an up-to-the-minute taste for the extramusical, be it Italian, vernal, Scottish, Lutheran, or Rhenish; and Brahms, much later, favored a new Classicism of all-media breadth and absolutism warmed by a passion for the new harmonic and tonal riches unlocked by the Romantics, not to mention modernist notions of texture and articulation, as well as a freedom and subtlety of phraseology that for all its Romantic overtones is fundamentally Classical. Brahms cherished Classical instruments, too, in preference to their technologically more advanced offspring, though he gave them an eloquently Romantic voice.

Brahms was one of the chief beneficiaries of Schubert's symphonic legacy. Schubert himself took from Haydn and Mozart, in his first five symphonies at least, but was not impervious either to the pre-*Eroica* Beethoven. What appears to be his earliest attempt at a symphony, a D-major fragment of 1811 now catalogued as D. 2b, comprises a short slow introduction and a few measures of *allegro* that are clearly based on the corresponding part of Beethoven's Second. One does not blame the fourteen-year-old composer, whose school friend Josef von Spaun noted his strong attachment to that particular Beethoven work, for leaning on it, consciously or no, to guide his first steps in the genre.

The first symphony known to have been completed, No. 1 in the familiar canon, followed in 1813 when Schubert was sixteen. It is a fluent, well-wrought, even voluble essay, though on the whole more impressive for its technical assurance than for its inventive magic. The debt to the slow movement of Mozart's "Prague" Symphony in Schubert's slow movement is well concealed until Mozart's chromatic ascent in quicker notes at the end of his third measure—studiously avoided by Schubert in the early stages—creeps in with charming, and revealing, effect toward his last cadence (Ex. 1.1). It is interesting that the only reminiscence of the *Eroica* in Schubert's entire oeuvre is a double echo—in the second subjects of both outer movements—of what Beethoven had borrowed from a pre-*Eroica* work, the theme from his ballet *Prometheus*. The energetic tuttis of the First Symphony have an exuberance peculiar to them, in that

EXAMPLE 1.1.

a. Mozart, Symphony No. 38, movt. 2, m. 3

b. Schubert, Symphony No. 1, movt. 2, m. 124

Schubert thought better in later works of scoring the trumpets at such late Baroque, un-Classical altitudes.

Spaun relates that Schubert's school orchestra at the Stadtkonvikt in Vienna, where he studied from the age of eleven, played a symphony and an overture every night after supper, and that the young boy came to know many of Haydn's and Mozart's works as a violinist in this milieu. Schubert's particular favorites, Spaun tells us, were Mozart's Symphony No. 40 in G Minor and Beethoven's Second. Six of Schubert's thirteen attempts at a symphony were in the key of Beethoven's Second, D major, perhaps because he had learned from that work that this key minimizes, for technical reasons, the inadequacies of the valveless horn and trumpet in orchestral use.

For his own Second Symphony (1814–15) Schubert turned from D, however, to B♭ major and composed a work more structurally venturesome than his First, and more generalized in its debts. Here he develops a Beethovenian sense of dissonance. The dactylic rhythm that dominates the finale, and which is not absent from the central development for a single measure, lends itself, alternately, to frothy exhilaration and dark Beethovenian rhetoric.

If the finale of the Second Symphony is Schubert's finest symphonic movement so far, the finale of the Third Symphony (1815), back in D major, is no less impressive. A racy tarantella, displaying less of solo timbres than of corporate exultation, it adopts and adapts in its coda a strategy doubtless learned from the first-movement coda of Beethoven's Second— a highly charged and exploratory "excursion" from and back to the home key, subjugating thematic process to harmonic adventure. An innovative feature of the first movement is the interrelating of slow introduction to *allegro* through a common idea that is secondary in both cases (Ex. 1.2). Genial and polished from beginning to end, the Third Symphony is especially compact and "of a piece"—as one might expect of a work that was composed, for the most part, within an eight-day period. It is, if you like, Schubert's "Linz" Symphony, but only because it "goes" with the élan and finesse of the Mozart (which was likewise composed at breakneck speed) and not because of any more specific connections.

EXAMPLE 1.2. Schubert, Symphony No. 3, movt. 1, mm. 4, 35

The Fourth may then be taken as Schubert's Sturm und Drang symphony, which is to say that it is an evocation of a minor-key genre familiar from notable examples in Haydn and Mozart: the title *Tragic* (Schubert's afterthought) should lead us to expect no more than that. This is no Goethe tragedy, nor the heroic struggle from minor to ultimate major pioneered in Beethoven's Fifth. Schubert simply enjoys exploring the shades of darkness, in contrast to the shades of light with which the Third Symphony was concerned, and the different range of key relationships opened up when one takes a minor rather than major key as the starting point.

The Sturm und Drang was of course a late-eighteenth-century phenomenon, and Schubert must have known and relished some of Haydn's Sturm und Drang symphonies. He kept his gaze pointedly on the eighteenth century when later in the same year he revived the genre of "chamber symphony," stripping back the orchestra to something like its size and constitution before a woodwind eightsome and a pair each of horns, trumpets, and drums became the norm in late Haydn. Perhaps this Fifth Symphony is so successful because it pays homage to Mozartian scale and manners with no suggestion of pastiche. True, Schubert forsakes his home key of B♭ to cast his minuet in G minor, the key betraying a palpable debt (as do the notes themselves) to the minuet of his favorite Mozart symphony, No. 40 in G Minor. But all in all, Schubert's restraint here acts like the self-imposed limitations in Brahms or Stravinsky, releasing priceless nuggets of fresh, personal invention. Schubert wins the ear from the outset, delaying the arrival of the most lovable of his symphonic themes by a mere four-measure preface. Self-effacing though this preface sounds—a mere formality enabling the violins to trip their way down to the first note of the theme?—it moves center stage at the beginning of the development section, being thus integrated into the symphonic design. If the four-measure preface of Schubert's previous symphonic movement, the finale of the *Tragic*, sowed the seed in his mind, it here germinates with a new and heady fragrance.

Beethoven had left his mark here and there on Schubert's first four symphonies, but in the Fifth there is hardly a trace. Was there, then, a growing determination on Schubert's part to fix his sights on pre-Beethovenian models? If so, he soon sensed it was not a way forward, and a number of faltering steps followed in the critical years ahead, before the symphonic maturity of the "Unfinished" and "Great" could be attained. First, passing his twenty-first birthday in 1818, Schubert ventured a work that now presents a more absorbed influence of Beethoven, especially in its superb scherzo (a term he used for the first time in a symphony), and somewhat incongruously reflects elsewhere the pleasure Schubert took in elements of Rossini's style.

So well assimilated is the debt to Beethoven in the scherzo of the Sixth Symphony that one may not at first trace the manner of structuring its central spans to the equivalent movements of Beethoven's First. Equally the rhythm of Beethoven's theme (Ex. 1.3a) may go unnoticed in Schubert's (Ex. 1.3b), as the contour of Mozart's perky finale tune in the F Major Piano Concerto, K. 459, seems to have driven its invention, too. (Mozart's theme is shown transposed to C major in Ex. 1.3c.) Whatever Schubert owes here, he repays with dividends, at least until he drops the tempo and, unfortunately, the creative temperature for a trio whose rotating harmonies and bland scraps of melody can find no convincing purpose. This is, incidentally, the sole instance in his symphonies of Schubert's marking a trio to be played at a different tempo from its framing minuet or scherzo. Conductors take note.

EXAMPLE 1.3.
a. Beethoven, Symphony No. 1, movt. 3, mm. 1–4

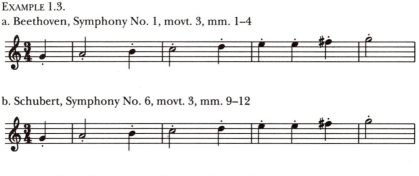

b. Schubert, Symphony No. 6, movt. 3, mm. 9–12

c. Mozart, Piano Concerto, K. 459, movt. 3, mm. 1–4 (transposed to C)

Realizing perhaps that this Sixth Symphony—strangely, the only one publicly performed in his lifetime—provided no clear pointers to the way ahead (although modern ears find the prophecies of the "Great" in the finale tantalizing), Schubert soon set about sketching a symphony in piano score, something he had never done before. This new symphony was aborted, however, after fragments of only the first and last movements were penned. Now catalogued as D. 615, it comprises a venturesome slow introduction (Ex. 1.4) indebted to that of Haydn's Symphony No. 104 but going well beyond the model, and an *allegro* exposition that never really takes wing, while the finale fragment is a delightful retrospect of middle-period Schubertian charm.

More than two years then elapsed before Schubert tried again, in the winter of 1820–21. Still working in piano score, he constructed an altogether more sizable and imposing fragment. D. 708A has parts of all four movements sketched, and the music is more tonally and texturally

EXAMPLE 1.4. Schubert, Symphony D. 615, movt. 1, mm. 1–7

daring and arresting than anything he had conceived in a symphony before. It is not known why Schubert abandoned this sketch, unorchestrated, with only the third movement well enough shaped that it can be completed by deduction, but perhaps his realization that in a D-major work the horns, trumpets, and drums could not have contributed to the big chords of A♭ and C♯ (in the finale), which clearly require an orchestral tutti, was a deterrent.

That might explain, too, why later in 1821 he reverted to his old habit of composing directly into full score when he began his Seventh Symphony. This time he completed the structure of his symphony, writing in all the measures, but in two-thirds of them only a single instrument is notated. The Seventh Symphony is, then, mapped out from beginning to end, though after the fully composed first 110 measures the texture remains skeletal, with only one to seven of the fourteen staves filled. Schubert needed no more paper, only ink, to complete the work; yet he never did. Having begun it in August, he kept an appointment with his friend Schober to work on a new opera in September. The first act of *Alfonso und EstRella* is dated 20 September, and he continued work on the opera until toward the end of the year. He may well have felt uncomfortable about returning to the Seventh Symphony after that, for his style was now developing fast, and in not many months he would be ready to give the world the "Unfinished."

The Seventh leaves the eighteenth-century concept of symphony far behind. It runs to about forty minutes and employs the largest orchestra Schubert ever called for in a symphony, including three trombones (absent from Nos. 1 to 6) and four horns (as against two in the symphonies that followed). Still affected by Rossini in some of its themes (Exs. 1.5–6), it looks forward to both the "Unfinished" and the "Great" in its introduction, transitions, developments, and codas. It also ventures formal strategies not to be adopted in Nos. 8 and 9. The first movement lacks a repeat of the exposition, and the first subject is omitted from the recapitulation in both the outer movements. The finale, on the other hand, does have an exposition repeat, and Schubert took the trouble to compose every detail of the short section that leads back to the opening and is heard just once, and for that purpose only.

EXAMPLE 1.5. Schubert, Symphony No. 7, movt. 1, mm. 1–5

EXAMPLE 1.6. Schubert, Symphony No. 7, movt. 4, mm. 1–7

At the end of this singular orchestral sketch, Schubert pens in his final double bar with a decisive hand and adds "Fine" with a flourish. "Finished" the work probably was, in his mind, for although the overall absence of details of harmonization, textural elaboration, and instrumental filling out seems to leave the composer well short of the finish line, in fact such additions would have been for him a matter of relatively routine (though still creative) craft—provided that he returned to complete the job with little delay. Its completion by another hand in another century is a different matter, but the point of such an effort is that it makes a fascinating and rewarding transitional work available to listeners, not just musicologists gifted with the ability to hear with their eyes. Careful use of analogy helps one in the task: for example, Schubert composed an overture in 1819, only two years earlier, that shows us how he handled an orchestra of exactly the same constitution in exactly the same keys (E minor turning to E major).[1]

ILLUSTRATION 1.2. Part of Schubert's original sketch for the Seventh Symphony, showing melodic fragments for clarinet, flute, first violins, and clarinet again. Royal College of Music, London.

The "Unfinished" Symphony: No. 8 in B Minor, D. 759

Of all the enigmas of incompletion in Schubert's symphonic oeuvre, none is more teasing than the case of the Symphony No. 8 in B Minor, the "Unfinished." It followed the Seventh in September 1822, and Schubert stamped his newly won symphonic mastery on every page of its first two movements, a broad *allegro moderato* in triple time in which lyrical and dramatic elements find perfect fusion, and a sublimely poetic *andante con moto*. A piano sketch of a third movement stops after giving the melody line of the trio's first section. Although there is no trace of a finale, it is widely accepted that the big entr'acte from *Rosamunde* (1823) was originally conceived to conclude the symphony. Put briefly, the grounds for this supposition are that Schubert assembled his incidental music for *Rosamunde* in great haste, that most of it accordingly consisted of adaptations of other music of his own already composed, that the entr'acte is too big to serve credibly in this context, and that it is in B minor, is in sonata form (typical of symphonic finales rather than theatrical interludes), and uses the same orchestral forces. The conjectured reasons for abandonment are covered elsewhere,[2] but it should be noted that Schubert's decision to pass the completed two movements to Anselm Hüttenbrenner, as a representative of the Styrian Music Society in Graz, would seem to suggest either that he would have been happy to have those two movements performed on their own or that he might have resumed work on the symphony if Hüttenbrenner had subsequently signaled to Schubert his view of the work or intention to perform it, which apparently he did not.

In the rare and somber key of B minor, the "Unfinished" inhabits an emotional world of its own. A keen-sighted imagination backed by well-practiced technique penetrates beyond the visions of earlier years to reveal melodic profiles, textural formations, and harmonic and orchestral hues new to symphonic thinking. A few examples must suffice. After the introductory theme in cellos and basses has cadenced, a hushed, eloquent string "accompaniment" awaits its woodwind theme. It is to the oboe and clarinet in unison that Schubert assigns this theme—a color combination firmly and consistently avoided by composers up to this time, but aptly intensifying the poignant strength of this theme. When the same theme has run its course and Schubert concludes his first paragraph with powerful chordal punctuation, he entrusts the function of transition (from first key to second, and from first theme to second) to a tiny four-measure passage consisting almost entirely of a held unison in horns and bassoons. Thus a process that is traditionally time consuming is compressed so that the colors of the contrasting keys and themes are drawn into closer juxtaposition.

When the introductory theme descends to new depths at the beginning of the development section, the vast textural hollow that results looks more like Shostakovich than Schubert (Ex. 1.7). And the gathering of tension from this point forward, achieved both by asking the players to give more and by adding other instruments, with the trombones tellingly present, is a highly dramatic outcome of the essentially lyrical motivation, as is the shock harmonic diversion at the apex of the crescendo.

EXAMPLE 1.7. Schubert, Symphony No. 8, movt. 1, mm. 118–25

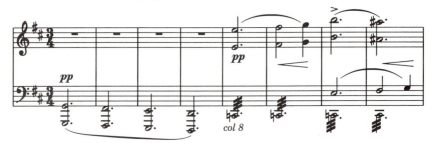

The "Great" C-Major Symphony: No. 9, D. 944

For nearly a hundred years after Sir George Grove mooted the idea in the *Times* in 1881, the Schubert literature contained allusions to a "Gastein" Symphony written in 1825 but subsequently lost. Letters between Schubert and members of his circle referred to a symphony being begun when he was on holiday at Gmunden and Gastein in that year, but it was not thought possible that any of the known symphonies were written in 1825. The myth of the "Gastein" endured until discredited in the last quarter of the twentieth century, when documentary and archival research, coupled with the study of paper types and patterns of paper use by the composer, led to the conclusion that the "Great" C-Major Symphony, thought to have been written in 1828, was in fact composed in 1825 and is the "missing" Gastein symphony.[3] The date of 1828 on the autograph is explained by John Reed as an alteration of the figure "1825" by the composer himself to make the work more saleable to a publisher three years after its composition. Schubert made some revisions in 1826 and more perhaps up to the summer of 1827. But not beyond: a surviving set of parts that accords with the final version of the work has been dated not later than August of that year.[4]

The "Great" C-Major Symphony—the *große Symphonie* he had for some time aspired to write—was the only symphony Schubert completed in the last ten years of a symphonic career spanning fewer than twenty. If the "Unfinished" had seemed to embody an awakening of Romantic impulses in the symphony, as the "Quartettsatz" in C minor of 1820 had in the string quartet, the "Great" is not perhaps a predictable sequel. The seeds of its style are to be found rather in the Sixth and Seventh Symphonies, while its scale—alien to early Schubert as to the Haydn/Mozart tradition he had until not long ago embraced—places it alongside the "grand" symphonies of Beethoven: the *Eroica*, Seventh, and Ninth. But it lacks the quasi-programmatic provenance of the *Eroica* and the specific extramusical allusions of a vocal text that take Beethoven's Ninth strictly outside the Classical symphonic tradition. Its generic model is arguably Beethoven's Seventh, which Schubert knew and admired, and it can legitimately be regarded as the last great Classical symphony.

With Beethoven's Seventh, too, it shares an immense kinetic energy. One is as much a celebration of rhythm as the other, but the brilliance of Beethoven's A-major key (tending to necessitate high horn parts) is replaced by an orchestral weight and sonority to which the trombones, absent from Beethoven, contribute in many memorable ways. This richness and power affects not only the vast, driving outer movements. The scherzo makes explicit the firmly grounded solidity implied in the sketched scherzo of the Seventh Symphony, while its trio has a sustained fervor and amplitude of texture quite new to the symphonic trio; and the slow movement works the full orchestral resource toward one of the most powerful orchestral climaxes of all time.

In the spirit of late Beethoven, Schubert pioneers a remarkable and unique structure for his first movement, crowning a career-long interest in the integration of a slow introduction into the first movement proper. In his First Symphony he had reintroduced the opening *adagio* at the beginning of the recapitulation. In the Third Symphony he fashioned an important secondary idea of his *allegro con brio* from an unassuming detail of the initial *adagio maestoso*. Now, in the Ninth, he recalls the opening *andante* theme (Ex. 1.8) to conclude the *allegro ma non troppo*, as climax to a strenuous coda; but material from that theme, especially its second measure, also insinuates itself into the exposition, development, and recapitulation, acting as sole thematic concern of substantial portions of each. Such cross-fertilization of introduction and main movements, mooted by Beethoven in the first movement of his Op. 13 Piano Sonata ("Pathétique"), reaches its Classical *ne plus ultra* in the "Great."

EXAMPLE 1.8. Schubert, Symphony No. 9, movt. 1, mm. 1–8

The "Tenth" Symphony

The "Unfinished" and "Great" are, then, the contrasting twin peaks of Schubert's early symphonic maturity—early, in that Beethoven had produced no symphonies at all when he reached a comparable age. The poetic intensity of the one and sonorous splendor of the other both find an echo in the symphony Schubert planned and partially executed in the weeks before his death in 1828 (Ill. 1.3). But other concerns likewise take hold of his fertile imagination in this often meager piano sketch: there are structural experiments here to out-Beethoven Beethoven, and an exploitation of contrapuntal device—never before so extensively applied in a Schubert symphony—that opens new expressive frontiers.

That Schubert had sketched this twilight "Tenth" Symphony came to light only in the 1970s. It was dated to September–October 1828 by analysis of the paper type and by linking its contrapuntal proclivities with Schubert's documented decision to seek counterpoint lessons with Simon

ILLUSTRATION 1.3. The house in Kettenbrückengasse, Vienna, where Schubert sketched his Tenth Symphony and died. Bildarchiv der Österreischische Nationalbibliothek.

Sechter at about this time.[5] He went to one lesson, on 4 November, and died on 19 November. Apart from the double counterpoint, canon, fugal writing, and combination of themes in the scherzo-finale of what appears to be a three-movement work, there were counterpoint exercises already worked on the piece of paper Schubert took for his slow movement.

In his first movement Schubert began the development with a change of tempo, which Beethoven had done only in order to refer back to a slow introduction, not the case here. This strategy, like the reduction in the number of movements from four to three, reflects an appetite for radical rethinking of traditions that Beethoven tended to indulge in the third-period piano sonatas and string quartets, not the symphonies.

The second movement combines echoes of the pathos of "Der Leiermann" in *Die Winterreise* (1827) with prophecies of the Mahler of *Kindertotenlieder* (1905). It presents a bleak, sparsely filled emotional landscape, but Schubert added, as an afterthought, after completing his finale, a consoling major-key theme that haunts all who hear it. This theme (Ex. 1.9) appears once only in the sketch: its addition was possibly his last creative act. Would he have allowed such a conspicuously beautiful theme to be heard only once? Probably not, but then why did he not indicate a reprise of it later in the movement? In a private way perhaps he did, for he crossed out his coda. There was nothing in this coda that he could have wished to change unless he had decided to incorporate the reprise of this newly added theme, for which there is no suitable location in the music that precedes the coda.

EXAMPLE 1.9. Schubert, Symphony No. 10, movt. 2

As in the case of the Seventh Symphony, only a modern performing version can salvage this music for the ear of posterity. But such a version must necessarily be much more speculative than a realization of the Seventh. Apart from the structural dilemma posed by the second movement, and structural uncertainties in the first movement, the spare textures of the second movement are without precedent in Schubert's orchestral oeuvre, as is the sprightly counterpoint of the movement that follows it.

What Schubert attempted in the third movement is a fusion of scherzo characteristics with rondo form, of which there is an interesting though remote precedent in the finale of Beethoven's Piano Sonata in G Op. 14, No. 2. But the deft contrapuntal complexities, culminating in a Brucknerian combination of the two themes, are unique and forward looking—not that Bruckner, Mahler, or any of their contemporaries could have known what a remarkable pioneer Schubert became in his dying days.

In fact, it was only in the second half of the nineteenth century that Schubert's other symphonies became at all widely disseminated, and even then their progress was patchy. A few of the early symphonies had private performances in Schubert's presence. The Sixth had two public performances in his native city in 1828 (after his death) and 1829. Apart from that and a performance of two movements of the Ninth in 1839, made palatable by having an aria from Donizetti's *Lucia di Lammermoor* sandwiched between them, the Viennese public heard nothing of their own symphonist until Hellmesberger gave the Ninth complete in 1850. Breitkopf had published the orchestral parts in 1840 and the score in 1849, yet performances of this work were spasmodic for some time yet (Paris and New York, 1851; London, 1856; Vienna again, 1857; only in 1897 was the second French performance scheduled).

The "Unfinished," hoarded by Hüttenbrenner for some forty years, saw the light of day only in 1865. Except for performances of No. 4 in Leipzig in 1869 and No. 6 there soon after, it is not certain that the earlier symphonies were performed until they appeared in London one by one, in the 1860s and 1870s, and in the first-ever Schubert cycle in 1881. Brahms then edited the symphonies for the Breitkopf complete edition in the 1880s and 1890s.

It was only with the advent of broadcasting in the twentieth century that the symphonies gained a secure place in the repertoire and in public affections. Nineteenth-century composers, however, took the trouble to study them, even when they could not hear performances. Schumann longed to write symphonies like Schubert's Ninth, which he sent to Mendelssohn in Leipzig, asking him to conduct it there.[6] Berlioz found the same work "worthy of a place among the loftiest productions of our art." Bruckner admired and learned from Schubert, as did Brahms. Both absorbed into their own vocabulary Schubert's technique of juxtaposing keys a third apart, but both, too, were affected by his pioneering harmonic idiom, his flair for orchestral coloring, and his mode of travel between successive keys (not only a third apart) by a magical variety of modulations, shifts, and shocks. While Dvořák valued the "Unfinished" and "Great" especially, he also pleaded for more performances of the earlier symphonies: "the more I study them, the more I marvel." Sullivan, who traveled to Vienna with Grove and came back with copies of the early symphonies, assimilated something of Schubert's idiom into his own style, in the Savoy operas and elsewhere.

The unfinished symphonies, other than the "Unfinished" itself, impinged less on succeeding composers of the century, except that Mendelssohn came by the sketch of No. 7 before it passed into the hands of Grove and the Royal College of Music in London. A performing version of it was made by the English composer J. F. Barnett, performed at the Crystal Palace, and published in piano score in 1884, though the score and parts were subsequently lost. None of the other sketched works was known of in the nineteenth century. The work that most remarkably peers into the future, the Tenth Symphony, never itself became a part of that future until 1982, more than a century and a half after Schubert's death.

If that death had been averted until the 1830s or beyond, who knows what further symphonic exploits Schubert's eleventh-hour preoccupations would have helped to shape? One thing is certain: they would have differed from the known exploits of the ensuing decades—those of Berlioz, Mendelssohn, Schumann, Berwald, and Liszt—and would have enriched the subsequent history of the symphony in the nineteenth century in ways beyond our capacity to imagine.

Notes

1. A "realization" of the sketch by the author of this chapter has been widely performed and recorded, as have his performing version of the Tenth Symphony, completion of the "Unfinished," and orchestration of the fragments D. 615 and D. 708a. All of these works are included in the Philips CD album *Schubert: The Ten Symphonies* performed by the Academy of St. Martin in the Fields under Neville Marriner. The Seventh is also available on a Harmonia Mundi disc played by the

Berlin Radio Symphony Orchestra under Gabriel Chmura, and the completed "Unfinished" is issued by Virgin Classics in a recording by the Orchestra of the Age of Enlightenment under Sir Charles Mackerras. The score of the Seventh is published by the University of Hull Press (1992), and that of the Tenth by Faber Music.

2. In my *Schubert and the Symphony: A New Perspective* (London, 1992).

3. See John Reed's interpretation of the relevant documents in *Schubert: The Final Years* (London, 1972), 71–92; Otto Biba's archival study "Franz Schubert und die Gesellschaft der Musikfreunde in Wien," in *Schubert-Kongress Wien 1978: Bericht*, ed. Otto Brusatti (Graz, 1979), 22–36; and papyrological evidence presented by Robert Winter in "Paper Studies and the Future of Schubert Research," in *Schubert Studies: Problems of Style and Chronology*, ed. Eva Badura-Skoda and Peter Branscombe (London, 1982), 209–75.

4. The dating is that of Otto Biba, with corroboration by Robert Winter. See Biba, "Schubert's Position in Viennese Musical Life," *19th-Century Music* 3 (1980): 107.

5. Winter, "Paper Studies," 255.

6. Schumann found the score among Schubert's posthumous manuscripts at the home of Ferdinand Schubert, the composer's brother, in 1838, and sent it to Leipzig, where Mendelssohn was conductor of the Gewandhaus Orchestra (see *Neue Zeitschrift für Musik* 13 [1840]). Schumann then attended Mendelssohn's Leipzig performance, after which he wrote enthusiastically to Clara, on 11 December 1839, "[I] had nothing left to wish for, except . . . that I could write such symphonies myself" (F. G. Jansen, *Robert Schumanns Briefe: Neue Folge* [Leipzig, 1904], 175).

Selected Bibliography

Brown, Maurice J. E. *Schubert Symphonies*. BBC Music Guide. London, 1970.

Carner, Mosco. "The Orchestral Music." In *Schubert: A Symposium*, ed. Gerald Abraham. London, 1947. Rev. ed. London, 1969.

Gal, Hans. *Franz Schubert and the Essence of Melody*. London, 1974.

Kunze, Stefan. *Franz Schubert: Sinfonie h-moll: Unvollendete*. Munich, 1965.

Laaff, Ernst. *Franz Schuberts Sinfonien*. Wiesbaden, 1933.

McNaught, William. "Franz Schubert." In *The Symphony*, ed. Ralph Hill. London, 1949.

Newbould, Brian. *Schubert and the Symphony: A New Perspective*. London, 1992.

———, ed. *Franz Schubert: Symphony No. 7 in E (D. 729)*. Realization, full score with preface. Hull, 1992.

Reed, John. *Schubert: The Final Years*. London, 1972.

Schubert, Franz. *Drei Symphonie-Fragmente*. Facsimile sketches of D. 605, D. 708a, and D. 936a. Kassel, 1978.

Smith, A. B. *Schubert, I: The Symphonies in C Major and B Minor*. Musical Pilgrims Series 15. London, 1926.

Tovey, Donald Francis. *Essays in Musical Analysis*, vol. 1, *Symphonies I*. London, 1935.

CHAPTER TWO

Weber and Spohr

Clive Brown

The symphonies of Carl Maria von Weber and Louis Spohr are peripheral to the modern concert repertoire, but for quite different reasons. Much of Weber's best music has never lost its popularity; several of his overtures are regularly played, and his position among the leading composers of the nineteenth century is assured. His two symphonies, however, are early works, generally regarded as unrepresentative of their composer's genius, and were rarely performed even in his own lifetime. Spohr's symphonies, though not all of them rank among his finest compositions, are fully mature compositions that constitute an important strand in his creative output and occupied a prominent place in the symphonic repertoire of the mid-nineteenth century, when Spohr was regarded as a leading composer. Spohr's music, unlike Weber's, disappeared almost entirely from concert programs within a half century of his death and has only seriously begun to claim renewed attention since the mid-1980s.[1] Weber's symphonies, although marginal both in the composer's output and in the symphonic tradition, are engaging works, rich in traits that foreshadow his achievement in other branches of composition; Spohr's, especially his earlier ones, are highly individual compositions of considerable artistic worth, and they throw a revealing light on the development of the nineteenth-century symphony.

Spohr (b. 1784) and Weber (b. 1786) were subject to many similar musical and intellectual stimuli; they belonged to the generation of German musicians whose early experience coincided with the mature achievements of Haydn and Mozart and whose passage into adulthood was accompanied by the appearance of Beethoven's mold-breaking symphonic compositions. But unlike their younger contemporaries Mendelssohn and Schumann, Spohr's and Weber's musical proclivities had been essentially determined before they were exposed to the music of Beethoven's second and third periods. Any reactions to Beethoven's later works, positive or negative, that may be detected in their music are largely superficial; the fundamental characteristics of their styles, already apparent in youthful works, were not significantly affected by Beethoven's example. Although both composers admired Beethoven's First and Second Symphonies, seeing them as worthy additions to the Classical canon, they became increasingly estranged from those that followed.

Weber commented on Beethoven to Nägeli in 1810: "The passionate, almost incredible inventive powers inspiring him are accompanied by such a chaotic arrangement of his ideas that only his earlier compositions appeal to me; the later ones seem to me hopeless chaos, an incomparable struggle for novelty, out of which break a few heavenly flashes of genius proving how great he could be if he would tame his rich fantasy."[2] Spohr's recorded comments on Beethoven—for instance, that he was "wanting in aesthetic feeling and a sense of the beautiful,"[3]—are equally ambivalent and have often been quoted. Nevertheless, both composers championed Beethoven's music as performers and conductors, without confining themselves to the works that they wholeheartedly appreciated.

Among the most prominent stylistic features that sharply distinguish their music from Beethoven's are a pronounced tendency to exploit chromaticism in melody and harmony for expressive effect, a liking for self-contained lyrical melodies, the use of figures derived from virtuoso instrumental idioms, sectional construction depending on contrast or repetition rather than organic development of germinal ideas, the use of a rich orchestral palette, and an emphasis on orchestral color for its own sake.

Although the Viennese Classical tradition was a major source of inspiration for German composers whose styles were formed in the 1790s and early 1800s, they were also subject to other powerful influences. It is significant that Spohr recalled a time in his youth (about 1800–1801) when he valued Cherubini more than Mozart and that Weber sought to prepare the ground for German opera in Prague with a succession of French operas by Cherubini, Spontini, Isouard, Boieldieu, and Dalayrac.[4] Both Spohr and Weber were undoubtedly exposed to a considerable repertoire of French operas at an early stage in their development.[5] They would also have been familiar with a range of North German Singspiele by Hiller, Reichardt, and others. Spohr's activities as a violinist and Weber's as a pianist gave them an intimate knowledge of the music of such composers as Viotti, Rode, Kreutzer, Dussek, Prince Louis Ferdinand, and Field. The amalgamation of these influences, largely unfamiliar to the modern listener, with elements acquired from the Viennese Classical tradition, generated a distinctive and, in its turn, powerfully influential musical language.

Weber

Symphony No. 1 in C Op. 19, J. 50
Symphony No. 2 in C, J. 51

Weber's symphonies, both in C major, resulted from a sojourn in Carls-ruhe in 1806–08, where he was the guest of Grand Duke Eugen Friedrich Heinrich von Württemberg-Öls. They were composed between the mid-dle of December 1806 and the end of January 1807 for the duke's modest but efficient court orchestra. Their scoring for an orchestra of one flute, two oboes, two bassoons, trumpets and horns, timpani, and strings was evidently determined by the forces available in Carlsruhe. The special prominence given to the flute, oboe, and horn parts doubtless reflects both that the duke was a keen amateur oboist and that there were accom-plished woodwind players in the orchestra, though it may also indicate the early development of Weber's interest in instrumental color, so evi-dent in his later orchestral writing. Only the First Symphony, issued by An-dré in 1812, was printed in Weber's lifetime. The Second was published by Schlesinger in the 1840s.

A few years after their composition Weber expressed his misgivings about the published symphony, candidly highlighting its weaknesses. He wrote apologetically about the structural peculiarity of the first movement to its dedicatee, his friend Gottfried Weber, in 1834,[6] and two years later, in a letter to the influential critic Friedrich Rochlitz, he observed: "I am not really very pleased with anything in it except the minuet and possibly the *adagio*. The first *allegro* is a wild fantasy movement, perhaps in over-ture style, in disjointed sections, and the last could have been better worked out." The extent of his retrospective dissatisfaction, perhaps even embarrassment, with the symphonies is implied by his evidently disingen-uous statement to Rochlitz that he had composed them when he was six-teen years old, and his avowal: "God knows, I would write many things dif-ferently now in my symphonies."[7]

Weber's own condemnation has been echoed by subsequent writers, even those who were otherwise highly sympathetic to the composer. The symphonies have generally been dismissed as immature and of limited musical worth. Weber's pupil Julius Benedict commented that the First Symphony "shows much less of Weber's individuality than might be ex-pected. He follows as strictly as possible the example of Haydn, but in the working out of the different subjects is far behind the Father of the Sym-phony." Referring to the Second Symphony he further observed:

> The same desire to follow Haydn in the structure, style, and elaboration of the themes is manifest in every movement; but the whole composition seems written to order, and various

> beauties scattered everywhere suffer from interpolations and episodes which have no direct bearing on the principal subject, and are all too frequently stiff and awkward—giving evidence that this branch of the art, even had he continued to attempt it, did not belong to Weber's sphere.[8]

Even the devoted nineteenth-century Weberian F. W. Jähns, while recognizing the attractive qualities in some movements, was dismissive of Weber's constructional ability. John Warrack has appreciatively drawn attention to Weber's "dark-hued instrumental textures" in the slow movements and "a Schubertian note" in the *andante* of the First Symphony and the opening movement of the Second Symphony, but he is broadly in sympathy with Jähns's critical assessment, remarking that the symphonies have a "negative merit in that they show Weber's talents to lie in a different sphere."[9]

Much of this criticism seems well founded. Certainly, in the structurally more ambitious first movements Weber's inability to achieve symphonic coherence is all too evident, but these works also possess something both appealing in their own right and interesting as a foretaste of features that were to make Weber so much more successful in other fields of music. Benedict's statement that Weber modeled himself closely on Haydn is not unreasonable as far as structure in its broadest sense is concerned, but it can scarcely be justified in respect of the material. The themes, their harmonic treatment, and the sensitive, colorful scoring clearly reveal Weber's stylistic kinship with Spohr and other "early Romantic" pioneers. Many passages display a style and spirit entirely at odds with that of Haydn, nor is Beethoven's influence evident, despite Gottfried Weber's opinion that in the First Symphony Weber's style "approaches that from Beethoven's earlier or middle period."[10] Weber's use of expressive chromaticism, as for instance in the *andante* of the First Symphony (Ex. 2.1), sharply distinguishes him from Haydn or Beethoven.

The second subject of the first movement in the Second Symphony is also entirely characteristic. Its effectiveness depends rather more on detail and the beauty of the moment than on the appropriateness of the material within a larger scheme; in this respect the differences of scoring and of tonal direction between the appearances of the subject in the exposition and recapitulation are particularly instructive (Ex. 2.2). Weber constantly employed chromatic inflections and orchestral color on the small scale to achieve his overall effect; the conclusion of the *adagio* of the Second Symphony, with its atmospheric background of *pp* horns and *ppp* trumpets accompanying a sentimental Romantic cliché in the bassoons (Ex. 2.3), is typical of such detail.

Weber (along with many of his contemporaries) certainly found difficulty in reconciling his musical aims and temperament with the more extended formal schemes inherited from the Classical masters and developed by Beethoven; he generally regarded "sonata form" as a ready-made vessel into which to pour his ideas. The mercurial juxtaposition of what Jähns described pejoratively as "heterogenous elements, pathetic, wild, and naïve, even reminding one of foreign folk song"[11] in the first movement of the First Symphony, however, seems to be more a conscious attempt to create something striking and individual than the result of ineptitude in handling a received form. As Joachim Veit has argued, negative criticism of Weber's symphonies has too often been based on comparison with Classical models that Weber was not interested in following.[12] It was partly Weber's artistic nature, not merely his inexperience, that kept him from composing symphonies in the Classical tradition; his natural bent inclined him to the picaresque rather than to the pursuit of connected musical argument. The tendencies that made his symphonies "unsymphonic" were, in the fullness of time, to contribute a vital ingredient to his success as a dramatic composer.

EXAMPLE 2.1. Weber, First Symphony, movt. 2

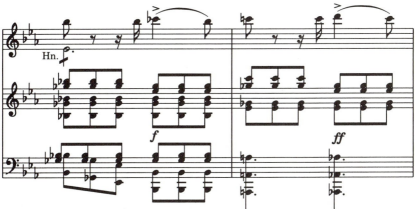

EXAMPLE 2.2. Weber, Second Symphony, movt. 1

a.

In the recapitulation, after six measures that are melodically and harmonically the same as the first six measures of Ex. 2.2a (but where the melody is played by the bassoon), the music continues as in Ex. 2.2b.

(continued)

b.

EXAMPLE 2.3. Weber, Second Symphony, movt. 2

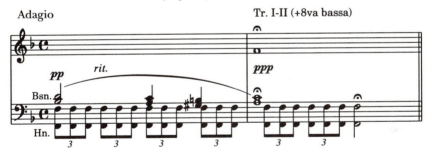

Spohr

Symphony No. 1 in E♭ Major Op. 20

Symphony No. 2 in D Minor Op. 49

Symphony No. 3 in C Minor Op. 78

Symphony No. 4 in F Major Op. 86, *Die Weihe der Töne*

Symphony No. 5 in C Minor Op. 102

Symphony No. 6 in G Major Op. 116, *Historische Symphonie*

Symphony No. 7 in C Major Op. 121, *Irdisches und Göttliches im Menschenleben*

Symphony No. 8 in G Minor Op. 137

Symphony No. 9 in B Minor Op. 143, *Die Jahreszeiten*

Symphony No. 10 in E♭ Major Op. 156 (withheld from publication)

Spohr's symphonies, spanning the years 1811 to 1857, occupy a central place in their composer's output, especially after the mid-1820s. His First Symphony reveals a somewhat undigested mixture of styles but is already distinctive of its composer. The Second Symphony (1820) shows Spohr in assured command of his own idiom, while by the time of the Third Symphony (1828) his style had essentially reached its fullest maturity. The subsequent works reflect changing notions of the structure and function of the genre that produced some particularly effective results in the Fourth, Fifth, and Seventh Symphonies (1832, 1837, and 1841), but there was little corresponding stylistic development. Spohr's later symphonies, despite many appealing qualities, indicate an increasing tension between the innovative and conservative aspects of his artistic nature, sometimes resulting in a degree of expressive and formal constraint that compromises their overall artistic success. His influence on younger contemporaries during the 1820s and 1830s, however, was undoubtedly considerable, and he anticipated many features in the music of Mendelssohn, Schumann, and even Brahms, as well as a host of minor composers.

In a review of Spohr's concert overture *Die Tochter der Luft* (The daughter of the air), Schumann highlighted the expressive element, which was perhaps Spohr's most powerful contribution to the vocabulary of nineteenth-century music, observing that "in his elegiac violins, his sighing clarinets we recognized once more the noble, suffering Spohr."[13] As early as 1804 Rochlitz, referring to Spohr's D-Minor Violin Concerto Op. 2, noted that his predilection seemed to be for the "grand and for a soft dreamy melancholy."[14] The Concert Overture in C Minor Op. 12, of 1807, elicited the observation that Spohr's music exhibited a "character of spirited yet temperate seriousness and an agreeable mixture of gloomy and tender melancholy"; the reviewer further observed, "If one should call this Romantic the present critic would not object."[15]

Terms such as "passionate melancholy" or "noble melancholy" were often used subsequently to describe the predominant characteristic of Spohr's style. Many of his contemporaries were powerfully moved by this element in his music. The composer and influential theorist Moritz Hauptmann (1792–1868) described his first hearing, in about 1809, of Spohr's Overture Op. 12 in terms reminiscent of a passage from the literary writings of Wackenroder or Jean Paul: "After hearing that overture I cried, cried again the whole way home, cried at home by the pailful, and cried for several days afterwards. I see myself even now, sitting alone weeping like mad in a delirium of joy and despair. Nothing in later life can compare with this. . . . In those days Spohr was my idol."[16]

Symphonies Nos. 1–3

Spohr's early works primarily reflected his activities as a solo violinist, though an attempt to write an opera on Weisse's *Kinderfreund* in early childhood hinted at grander ambitions. The profile of his output during the years 1805–10, however, shows his growing determination to make his mark as a composer-violinist rather than merely as a violinist-composer. He seems to have concluded at an early stage that, as he declared in his "Aufruf an deutsche Componisten" (1823),[17] a composer's reputation was established through success in the theater, for by the end of 1810 he had already completed three operas, the third of which, *Der Zweikampf mit der Geliebten* (The duel with the beloved), enjoyed a modest success in Hamburg in November 1811. As director since 1805 of the musical establishment in Gotha (where there was no opera house), Spohr must already have entertained the idea of symphonic composition, yet apart from the overtures to his operas, the Overture Op. 12 remained his only work for orchestra alone until 1811.

His reluctance to essay a symphony probably stemmed from his consciousness that certain genres, especially the string quartet and symphony, had been given a particular weight by the achievements of the Viennese Classical masters and were not to be attempted lightly. Spohr was one of the first North German musicians to champion Beethoven's op. 18 quartets—as early as 1803—and despite serious reservations about developments in Beethoven's style after the period of the Second Symphony, Spohr's writings show him to have retained a lively awareness of the magnitude of Beethoven's achievements. His early music reveals a positive if often superficial response to Beethoven's example.

In Spohr's Symphony No. 1 in E♭ Op. 20, written for the Frankenhausen Music Festival of 1811, this is particularly evident in the scale and design of the scherzo: following the example of the scherzo in Beethoven's *Eroica*, it is an unusually extended movement, running to 605 measures. (Spohr soon concluded that it was too long and asked the publisher to delete the first two repeats in the unsold copies.)[18] Such outward parallels are not, however, matched by any deep-reaching stylistic affinity. The range and frequency of modulation in Spohr's scherzo, for instance, is greater than in any of Beethoven's, and the nature of the harmonic and melodic idiom throughout is quite different. The impact of Mozart is far stronger, and Spohr himself confessed that at this time he was still inclined to draw his inspiration too directly from Mozartian models. This can clearly be seen in resemblances between Spohr's First Symphony and Mozart's Symphony No. 39, in the same key; the kinship becomes immediately apparent in the first movement's portentous slow introduction, leading to a more relaxed triple-meter *allegro*. But the differences are as striking as the similarities. Spohr's chromaticism is more intensive, and many passages from the *allegro* show the influence of Cherubini and composers of the French violin school in melody (Ex. 2.4a) and harmony (Ex. 2.4b), though already assimilated into Spohr's increasingly individual idiom. French influence was also perhaps responsible for the inclusion of three trombones in all the movements except the *larghetto*.

EXAMPLE 2.4. Spohr, First Symphony, movt. 1
a.

b.

A reviewer in the *Allgemeine musikalische Zeitung* enthused that he had not heard a symphony "for many years which possesses so much novelty and originality without singularity or affectation, so much richness and skill without bombast or artifice," and the First Symphony quickly gained a place in the repertoire. Nevertheless, Spohr turned his attention to other genres of composition. His association with Beethoven in Vienna between 1812 and 1815 may have reinforced his unwillingness to risk comparison in a field where Beethoven was preeminent, but his concentration on opera, concertos, and chamber music—not to mention his unsettled career—probably had more to do with it.

The composition of his Symphony No. 2 in D Minor Op. 49 in 1820 was prompted by an invitation from the London Philharmonic Society to perform with them for the 1820 season and to compose an overture.[19] On arrival in London he persuaded the directors to program his First Symphony, but also, inspired by the excellence of the orchestra, completed his Second Symphony "in a spirit of the greatest enthusiasm"[20]—and in a period of some three weeks.

The Symphony No. 2 shows the considerable development of Spohr's style since the composition of the First. Mozartian influences have been almost entirely submerged, and the diverse stylistic elements that are still to some extent perceptible in the earlier work have been subsumed into a highly distinctive personal idiom. Nobody who is familiar with Spohr's music would fail to detect his fingerprints in almost every bar. Those who are not may find the music full of reminiscences, but these are almost entirely reminiscences derived from knowledge of later music by younger composers. Many later works of composers whose youthful admiration for Spohr is well attested contain echoes of this symphony: Mendelssohn's First Symphony Op. 11, for instance, is hardly conceivable without it. Sterndale Bennett specifically identified Spohr's Second Symphony as one that held a particularly strong place in his early experience,[21] and many lesser composers who were coming to maturity in the 1820s and 1830s such as Kalliwoda, Gade, and G. A. Macfarren seem to have drunk at the same source. Some years after Spohr's death Macfarren observed that "few if any composers have exercised such influence on their contemporaries as Spohr did, and many living writers may be counted among his imitators."[22]

The Second Symphony provides an illuminating example of Spohr's fondness for intensive concentration on small motivic units. The initial twenty-two bars of the first movement contain all but one of the thematic ideas that pervade the movement (Ex. 2.5a and b); an additional important idea, a rising fourth followed by a falling sixth, appears for the first time in the second subject (Ex. 2.5c). Scarcely a bar of the first movement is without one of these ideas or a derivative. The *larghetto* is luxuriantly harmonized with pronounced dominant thirteenths over a tonic pedal, chains of expressive suspensions, and enharmonic modulations. Spohr uses these features together with a masterly command of orchestral color to create a characteristic mood of gentle yearning. The scherzo, one of his best, has a Beethovenian five-part form (two appearances of scherzo and trio followed by a coda), but the trio's richer orchestration on its

EXAMPLE 2.5. Spohr, Second Symphony, movt. 1

a.

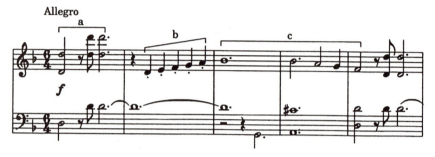

b.

c.

second appearance is unusual. A typical chromatic passage for wind and timpani in the coda builds up tension before the final outburst from the full orchestra (Ex. 2.6). The D-major finale, whose principal theme, warmly harmonized, anticipates the amiable flow of some later nineteenth-century D-major symphonic finales (e.g., Brahms and Dvořák), provides an engaging but distinctly lightweight conclusion to the symphony.

EXAMPLE 2.6. Spohr, Second Symphony, Scherzo: Presto

The eight years that elapsed before Spohr returned to symphonic composition were eventful. He accepted the post of Hofkapellmeister in Kassel in 1822, where he was to remain for the rest of his life. There he completed three more operas, the first of which, *Jessonda* (1823), a full-scale grand opera with continuous music, was hailed in terms almost as extravagant as those for Weber's *Der Freischütz* (1821). In 1825 he composed his enormously successful oratorio *Die letzten Dinge* (The Last Judgment).[23] After the death of Weber in 1826 and Beethoven in 1827, Spohr was widely hailed as the greatest German composer of the day.

The Symphony No. 3 in C Minor Op. 78, written in the first months of 1828, added fresh laurels to Spohr's brow. It is a richer, more full-bodied work than its predecessor, especially in its treatment of the orchestra.

In the Second Symphony Spohr had handled his orchestra rather like a large chamber ensemble, but in the Third, though still sensitive to the timbre of individual instruments, he seems to have aimed for a more homogeneous sound. It was probably this aspect of his orchestration that led Samuel Sebastian Wesley to assert that Spohr "excelled Mendelssohn in his ability to produce a marvellous tone from his orchestra."[24] In many ways Spohr's orchestral sound provided a model for later German composers. Schumann aimed to emulate it but failed; Joachim, Brahms, and numerous of their contemporaries owed a direct or indirect debt to Spohr's example.

The Third Symphony is revealing of Spohr's limitations as well as his strengths. The outer movements illustrate the problem that many Romantic composers seem to have experienced in generating organic development from their material. In the first movement Spohr sidestepped the problem (exacerbated by the derivation of the second subject from the first; Ex. 2.7a–b) by employing a procedure with which he had earlier ex-

EXAMPLE 2.7. Spohr, Third Symphony, movt. 1

a.

b.

perimented, most notably in the Octet Op. 32 of 1814: instead of a conventional development section he brought back a version of the introductory common-time *andante grave* notated in the $\frac{6}{8}$ time signature of the *allegro* in long note values. In the finale he resorted to a device that was to become, almost axiomatically, the last resort of a composer who was short of inspiration for development: a fugal exposition. Despite Mendelssohn's opinion that Spohr was the best fugue writer of the day,[25] this is a rather inflexible example with eleven entries of the theme at precise four-bar intervals. The finale as a whole, however, is a highly effective movement that, unlike those of the first two symphonies, has the musical weight to balance the first movement. Spohr's approach suggests a belated recognition of one of the fundamental changes that Beethoven had wrought in the concept of the symphony, though Mozart's "Jupiter" Symphony was perhaps a more direct inspiration. Spohr's pejorative comments about the last movement of Beethoven's Fifth illustrate how little sympathy he had for Beethoven's triumphalism.

The two middle movements of Spohr's Third Symphony are highly characteristic of their composer. The *larghetto* has a dreamy Romantic atmosphere and contains some striking orchestral effects, particularly when, for the second subject (in C major), Spohr uses unison violins, violas, and cellos accompanied by irregularly placed chords from the wind section (Ex. 2.8).[26] In order to bring this back at an appropriate pitch in

EXAMPLE 2.8. Spohr, Third Symphony, movt. 2

the recapitulation, Spohr arranged its return in D♭ major. Spohr treated the harmonically rich and tonally adventurous scherzo and trio as a continuous entity; the capricious trio signals a change of mood but not an interruption of the musical argument.

Symphonies Nos. 4–6

The failure of the three operas with which Spohr attempted to repeat the success of *Jessonda* (1824, 1827, 1830), coupled with the serious discouragement of further opera composition caused by the closure of the Kassel Hoftheater after the 1830 revolution, initiated a significant change in Spohr's output. At the time of Weber's death the main focus of their creative activity had seemed remarkably similar, each having completed two symphonies and seven operas. During the second half of Spohr's career symphonic composition seems, to a certain extent, to have served him as a proxy for the composition of opera. By 1830 he had composed nine operas and three symphonies; the years 1831 to 1857 saw only one more opera and seven more symphonies, of which five had some programmatic content.

The first of Spohr's program symphonies was written in the immediate aftermath of the failure of his opera *Der Alchymist* (1830) and the closure of the Kassel Hoftheater. Spohr was too deeply despondent to consider any further operatic projects at that time, but following the unexpected death of his friend and operatic collaborator Carl Pfeiffer, he conceived the idea of writing a cantata based one of Pfeiffer's poems, "Die Weihe der Töne" (the consecration of sound; generally known in English as "The Power of Sound"). After some preliminary work, however, he decided to use the poem as the basis for a symphony, No. 4 in F Major Op. 86.

Spohr adhered closely to the content of the poem and instructed in the first edition of the score that "for the understanding of the present symphony the listener requires, apart from the contents list (which must be printed on the program), a knowledge of the poem itself, whose content the composer has attempted to reproduce in music." He requested that the poem should be either distributed or recited before the performance. Although the main outline of a conventional symphony is still apparent (as in Berlioz's almost contemporaneous *Symphonie fantastique*), the shape is modified to a considerable extent by the scheme of the poem.[27]

The first movement, illustrating the first two of the poem's nine verses, is closest in form to a conventional symphonic movement. The "deep silence of nature before the creation of sound" is evoked in the *largo* introduction, which leads straight into a sonata-form *allegro*, whose first theme grows out of a motto phrase that pervades the introduction; this seems, as in Beethoven's "Pastoral" Symphony, to be an awakening of joyful feelings. The second subject is more descriptive: strings characterize the

rustling breezes of the poem, while flutes, oboe, clarinet, and horns provide a stylized imitation of bird song for more than forty measures (Ex.
2.9). Chromatic rumblings in the bass herald the development section,
which portrays a storm (not described in the poem); structural coherence
is maintained by the presence of the motto phrase. The recapitulation is
regular, and distant echoes of the storm are heard in the coda.

EXAMPLE 2.9. Spohr, Fourth Symphony, Allegro

Verses three to five, describing the role of music as lullaby, dance, and love song, are illustrated in the *andantino* second movement. Spohr treats each in a separate section with its own time signature ($\frac{3}{8}$, $\frac{2}{4}$, and $\frac{9}{16}$ respectively). After each idea has made its appearance, the composer combines them in a manner reminiscent of the supper scene in Mozart's *Don Giovanni*. A symphonic parallel can be found in the *réunion des themes* in movt. 3 of Berlioz's *Harold in Italy*—which Spohr's symphony predates by three years.

The sixth and seventh verses deal with music to inspire courage in war and give thanks for victory. Spohr gives a more narrative shape to this idea. The first section, a marchlike piece entitled "Departure for Battle," evokes a departing army (the last twenty-three bars are a continuous diminuendo); a contrasting middle section portrays "the anxious feelings of those left behind"; the march returns *pianissimo*, as if from a distance, rising in crescendo to a triumphant climax. The movement concludes with a hymn of thanksgiving for victory, which Spohr treats as a contrapuntal chorale prelude on an "Ambrosian Song of Praise." Here, too, there is a parallel with *Harold in Italy*: this time to the Pilgrims' March, though Spohr's treatment is much more self-consciously archaic than Berlioz's.

The finale, loosely based on Pfeiffer's last two verses, opens with a funeral chorale, "Begrabt den Leib" (Bury the body), which leads into a final *allegretto* "Consolation in Tears," where the melodic profile and harmonic tensions are redolent of the final movement of Tchaikovsky's *Pathétique* (Ex. 2.10).

The success of the Fourth Symphony, which was to remain among Spohr's most popular works, seems to have strengthened his interest in the idea of linking musical ideas to a specific program. Within a short time he was at work on a fantasy in the form of a concert overture, inspired by Ernst Raupach's mythical tragedy *Die Tochter der Luft* (based on a drama by Calderón); this was performed in Kassel and at the Leipzig Gewandhaus in the spring of 1837. Shortly afterward, however, Spohr decided to use this work as the basis for the first movement of a new symphony that he had been invited to write for the Concerts Spirituels in Vienna (where *Die Weihe der Töne* had roused considerable interest). The Symphony No. 5 in C Minor Op. 102 gained a rapturous reception at its Vienna premiere on 1 March 1838, where "none of the innumerable beauties went unnoticed, each movement received the deserved tribute to his mastery; indeed, the richly fantastic scherzo was so universally electrifying that it had to be repeated."[28]

A notable feature of this symphony is Spohr's employment of a thematic link between the outer movements, reflecting both his pioneering use of leitmotiv and reminiscence in opera and his experimentation with motivic development in multimovement instrumental works (most notably in the Nonet of 1814). The melody stated at the beginning of the *an-*

EXAMPLE 2.10. Spohr, Fourth Symphony, movt. 3

dante introduction to the first movement (Ex. 2.11a) is developed in the central portion of the following *allegro* (Ex. 2.11b) and is also transformed to provide the second subject of the finale (Ex. 2.12). The use of material from the introduction to the first movement in place of a conventional development section recalls Spohr's procedure in the Third Symphony, but here his treatment of the idea is quite different. In place of the earlier work's more or less literal repetition, Spohr now uses the initial theme as the germ of an extended rhapsodic melody, spun out to more than forty

EXAMPLE 2.11. Spohr, Fifth Symphony, movt. 1

a.

(*continued*)

EXAMPLE 2.11. (*continued*)

b.

Allegro

EXAMPLE 2.12. Spohr, Fifth Symphony, movt. 4

Presto

measures and accompanied, Tchaikovsky-fashion, by fragments of the
first subject. In the finale the theme is one of three principal melodic
ideas that seem to compete for supremacy; the other two ideas, after being separately stated, are combined in the development section in a skill-
ful fugato. The middle movements are a fine *larghetto* in A♭, whose scoring
is given particular richness by the use of trombones, and a vigorous
scherzo in C major with a charmingly contrasted D♭-major trio.

Rhythmic vitality and freedom in the treatment of phrase lengths is
a notable feature throughout the Fifth Symphony, and for the most part
Spohr successfully avoided falling into the individual but predictable patterns that increasingly gained him the reputation of a "mannerist." The
Symphony No. 5 as a whole is among Spohr's finest orchestral works, reflecting the full technical mastery of his maturity, but also richly invested
by a powerful creative imagination and vigor that seems less evident in his
later works.

The *Historische Symphonie* is one of Spohr's most curious, and it
raised considerable controversy among his contemporaries. Spohr's impulse to compose it seems to have arisen partly out of the growing vogue
for "historical concerts," in which a range of music from Baroque to nineteenth-century was performed (usually in chronological order), and
partly out of Spohr's increasing alienation from the musical culture of his
time. His distaste for much of the new music that was popular with the
public is clear from his correspondence at this time. A visit to Kassel by
the virtuoso Ole Bull in January 1839 prompted him to compose a con-
certino for violin and orchestra entitled *Sonst und Jetzt* (Then and now), in
which a *tempo di menuetto antico,* displaying the noble singing quality of the

violin, is contrasted with a tarantella-like *vivace*, dominated by technical fireworks. Spohr's sympathies were undoubtedly with the former, for despite the technical demands of his own violin writing, he had always striven to subordinate mere brilliance to musical substance.

The *Historische Symphonie*, No. 6 in G Major Op. 116, composed in the summer of 1839, was a more developed manifestation of his concern with changing musical styles and tastes. Each of its four movements was intended to represent a different period. The scheme is as follows:

I	*Largo grave; Allegro moderato;* Pastoral Bach and Handel period, c. 1720
II	*Larghetto* Haydn and Mozart period, c. 1780
III	Scherzo Beethoven period, c. 1810
IV	Finale: *Allegro vivace* Modern period, c. 1840

Spohr did not intend accurate stylistic imitations, but rather attempted to evoke the general spirit of each period though the use of characteristic forms and direct allusions to themes or gestures from particular works or composers. Spohr's own style, thinly disguised, is apparent throughout. As Schumann observed, "He remains the master as we have always known and loved him. In fact, these forms to which he is not accustomed bring out his individuality even more strongly, just as one with a particularly characteristic bearing often reveals himself most clearly when he assumes a disguise."[29]

The first three movements all suffer to some extent from a lack of stylistic conviction. The *larghetto*, evoking the spirit closest to Spohr's heart, is the most satisfying, and the scherzo, conspicuously lacking Beethoven's boldness despite its initial three-note timpani solo, the weakest. It is the finale, however, with its superfluity of percussion and loosely connected, trivial ideas, that is the most problematic. Here Spohr seems to have intended to satirize everything he most disliked about modern music.

At the Sixth Symphony's London premiere the finale was hissed. One critic, assuming that Spohr's target was the "present French and Italian schools of instrumental writing," considered that the audience "did not see the joke, and consequently treated as earnest that which the composer could only have meant as a severe, but not unfair, piece of ridicule."[30] Another considered that there were perhaps composers in the room who "endured a sense of personal ridicule."[31] Mendelssohn, too, found little sympathy with Spohr's intention: after trying the work in Leipzig he wrote diplomatically that he would rather Spohr had crowned the symphony with a movement in his own style "like the overture to *Faust* or so many of your magnificent, spirited overtures."[32]

Symphonies Nos. 7–9

Three years after the composition of the *Historische Symphonie* Spohr essayed another approach to program music with his Symphony No. 7 Op. 121, entitled *Irdisches und göttlisches im Menschenleben* (The earthly and divine in human life). It was entirely in the spirit of the times that he should try to grapple with ethical and philosophical concepts in an instrumental composition, though the subject of goodness and innocence corrupted by human weakness and passion, which lies at the root of this work, is not very different from the central issue in several of his operas, particularly *Faust* and *Pietro von Abano*. Formally, this is the most radical of his symphonies. Not even the outlines of the Classical symphony are to be detected in its three movements, each prefaced by a four-line verse:

> *Kinderwelt* (The child's world),
>> *Adagio; Allegretto*
> *Zeit der Leidenschaften* (The time of passions),
>> *Larghetto; Allegro moderato*
> *Endlicher Sieg des Göttlichen* (Final victory of the divine),
>> *Presto; Adagio*

Another peculiarity of the symphony is its scoring for "double orchestra." The first orchestra, a large chamber ensemble of flute, oboe, clarinet, bassoon, two horns, two violins, viola, cello, and bass, seems to be associated with the spiritual side of human nature; the second, a full orchestra with trombones (though without a second oboe or bassoon), with humankind's basic passions—in Freudian terminology, the superego and the id.

The two instrumental bodies are in equilibrium in the first movement, which Schumann, in his wholly enthusiastic review, described as being as "full of variegated dreams as is a happy life of childhood." In the turbulent second movement, "full of unrest and thoughtfulness . . . so troubled, so enticing, so treacherous, and yet so full of longing desire," Spohr seems concerned to depict the tension between these two aspects of human personality such that the first orchestra appears to be under the influence of the second. Schumann thought the last movement to "depict mankind still imprisoned in the path of error; the better voice becomes louder and more pressing, till the inward warning sounds again triumphantly, and idle endeavor and struggle find an end in sweet and holy peace."[33] Here the second orchestra is given increasingly distinct material of a calming nature, which gradually dominates the turbulent C-minor *presto*, and the two orchestras are united in the concluding fifty-bar *adagio*, based on a figure resembling the Dresden Amen (Ex. 2.13).

Between the composition of the Seventh and Eighth Symphonies Spohr turned for the last time to opera with *Die Kreutzfahrer* (The crusaders, 1844). Though it achieved only a succès d'estime, it may partly have assuaged his need for dramatic expression in the symphony, for his Symphony No. 8 in G Minor Op. 137, composed for the London Philhar-

EXAMPLE 2.13. Spohr, Seventh Symphony, movt. 2

monic Society's 1848 season, reverted to a Classical form and has no explicit extramusical associations. It is a prime example of Spohr's later tendency to produce works so full of his stylistic mannerisms that they seem to lack individuality in their own right. Like most of his music it is beautifully crafted and contains much attractive material; on the small scale, too, there are many engaging features, such as the use of string harmonics with low clarinets, bassoons, and horns in the coda of the first movement, the unusual writing for trombones in the richly scored slow movement, and the agile violin solo in the trio of the third movement. In this late phase of Spohr's style the qualities in his music that appealed to Brahms's artistic nature are often apparent, but Brahmsian structural logic is altogether lacking. Hans von Bülow's reaction to the new work was typical of many: after hearing it for the first time he wrote to Raff that it contained "some beautiful parts, but nothing new."[34] A decade later Bülow neatly alluded to Spohr's self-repetition when he wrote in his humorous "Prophetic Musical Calendar" for 1859: "Spohr composes his Eighth Symphony yet again without realizing it."[35]

Indeed, many of the comments applicable to the Eighth Symphony also fit the Symphony No. 9 in B Minor Op. 143, which Spohr wrote in the early months of 1850. Although he chose a programmatic idea, *Die Jahreszeiten* (The seasons), and divided the work into two parts, the usual four-movement symphonic scheme is barely disguised. The first part (Winter—transition to Spring—Spring) and the second (Summer—introduction to Autumn—Autumn) are in reality each divided into two linked sections, and the overall structure is thus a sonata-form *allegro*, a scherzo, a slow movement, and a sonata-rondo finale. Like the Eighth Symphony, the Ninth contains much attractive music, skillfully presented, but adds nothing significant to Spohr's symphonic canon. The mixture of disappointment and respect with which the symphony was received is nicely encapsulated in an English review that ended, "Spohr has taught us, by previous essays, to expect so much, that the announcement of a new symphony from his pen is almost tantamount to the promise of a new *chef d'œuvre* for the art. That we have been disappointed on the present occasion cannot be denied; but, if 'Homer nods' at intervals, why not Dr. Spohr?"[36] The Eighth and Ninth Symphonies are typical of the late compositions that prompted J. C. Lobe's comment in 1859: "With each new work he himself tore a flower from the well-deserved wreath of his fame."[37]

Spohr's important contribution to the musical vocabulary and experience of the period was essentially complete by the 1830s. His increasing alienation from much of the musical culture of the middle nineteenth century left its mark on his later music. He felt himself to have outlived his own age and was seen in the same light by others. He found it difficult to respond positively to his disenchantment with the direction of musical developments, so forcibly shown in the satire of the finale of the Sixth Symphony. With the Seventh Symphony he took his earlier interest in experimentation to its furthest limit, producing his last significant symphony. After that he appears to have sought refuge in repeating more familiar patterns, and the last symphonies reflect his hardening conservatism. Having composed a Tenth Symphony in 1857, which still displays his usual technical skill, he, too, seems to have realized that he had nothing new to say and suppressed it, along with several other works written about the same time.

Notes

1. This revival of interest is particularly evident in a rapidly increasing number of recordings, which provide an opportunity to reassess the value and significance of his work. Two complete series of recordings of the Spohr symphonies are currently being issued on CD.

2. Letter of 1 May 1810. Given in *Carl Maria von Weber: Writing on Music*, ed. John Warrack, trans. Martin Cooper (Cambridge, 1981), 15.

3. *Louis Spohr: Lebenserinnerungen*, ed. Folker Göthel (Tutzing, 1968) 1:180; see also Clive Brown, *Louis Spohr: A Critical Biography* (Cambridge, 1984), 97–99.

4. John Warrack, *Weber*, 2d ed. (Cambridge, 1976), 155ff.

5. Brown, *Spohr* (Cambridge, 1984), 10ff.

6. Letter of 9 March 1813. Given in Jähns, *Verzeichniss*, 64.

7. Letter of 14 March 1815. Given in Jähns, *Verzeichniss*, 65.

8. Sir Julius Benedict, "Weber," in *The Great Musicians*, ed. Francis Hueffer (London, 1881), 139, 160.

9. Warrack, 59, 58.

10. *Allgemeine musikalische Zeitung* 12 (1810): 502–03.

11. Friedrich Wilhelm Jähns, *Carl Maria von Weber in seinen Werken: Chronologisch-thematisches Verzeichniss seiner sämmtlichen Compositionen* (Berlin, 1871), 64.

12. Joachim Veit, "Zum Formproblem in den Kopfsätzen der Sinfonien Carl Maria von Webers," in *Festschrift Arno Forchert zum 60. Geburtstag*, ed. G. Allroggen and D. Altenburg (Kassel, 1986), 184–99.

13. *Neue Zeitschrift für Musik* 6 (1837): 181.

14. *Allgemeine musikalische Zeitung* 7 (1804–05): 201ff.

15. *Allgemeine musikalische Zeitung* 11 (1808–09): 185.

16. Moritz Hauptmann, *The Letters of a Leipzig Cantor*, trans. and ed. A. D. Coleridge (London, 1892) 1:13.

17. *Allgemeine musikalische Zeitung* 25 (1823): 458.

18. Letter from Spohr to Peters, printed in *Allgemeine musikalische Zeitung*, n.s. 2 (1867): 315.

19. Overture in F, WoO 1 (unpub.; performed by the BBC in 1984 in an edition prepared by Clive Brown).

20. Letter of 1820, pub. in Edward Speyer, *Wilhelm Speyer der Liederkomponist* (Munich, 1925), 49.

21. J. R. Sterndale Bennett, *The Life of Sir William Sterndale Bennett* (Cambridge, 1907).

22. *The Imperial Dictionary of Universal Biography*, xiii, 104.

23. The success of *Der Freischütz* is seen as a significant landmark in the history of German opera; it is less well known that Spohr's *Jessonda* made almost as powerful an impact, though its popularity declined rapidly after Spohr's death, and it disappeared from the German repertoire after the First World War. *Die letzten Dinge* was extensively performed (especially in England) well into the twentieth century.

24. Conversation recorded in C. H. H. Parry's diary, 6 January 1866.

25. Robert Schumann, *Erinnerungen an Felix Mendelssohn Bartholdy*, ed. G. Eismann (Zwickau, 1947), 68.

26. The first edition of the score omits the composer's metronome mark for the *larghetto*, which has caused some modern conductors seriously to miscalculate the tempo. In common with Spohr's other *larghetti*, the tempo should be fairly but not excessively slow; in fact, the first edition parts contain the metronome mark: $\quarternote = 50$.

27. For a reproduction of the poem see Folker Göthel, *Thematisch-bibliographisches Verzeichnis der Werke von Louis Spohr* (Tutzing, 1981), 145–47.

28. *Allgemeine Theaterzeitung* 32 (1838): 196.

29. Schumann, *Neue Zeitschrift für Musik* 14 (1841): 53.

30. *The Musical World* 13 (1840): 225.

31. *Atlas* 15 (1840): 236.

32. Letter in the Deneke collection (Bodleian Library, Oxford), MS. M. Deneke Mendelssohn c. 42, 15.

33. *Neue Zeitschrift für Musik* 16 (1842): 36.

34. Hans von Bülow, *Briefe und Schriften*, ed. M. von Bülow (Leipzig, 1895–1908) 1:146.

35. Ibid. 3:245.

36. *Musical World* 25 (1850): 766.

37. Johann Christian Lobe, *Musikalische Briefe: Wahrheit über Tonkunst und Tonkünstler von einen Wohlbekannten* (Leipzig, 1860), 232.

Selected Bibliography

Berrett, Joshua, ed. *Louis Spohr, 1784–1859: Three Symphonies.* The Symphony, 1720–1840, ed. Barry S. Brook and Barbara B. Heyman, series C, vol. 9, Symphonies Nos. 4, 6, and 7. New York, 1980.

Brown, Clive. *Louis Spohr: A Critical Biography.* Cambridge, 1984.

———, ed. *Selected Works of Louis Spohr,* vol. 6, Symphonies Nos. 1, 2, and 5. New York, 1987.

Heussner, Horst. "Die Symphonien Louis Spohrs." Ph.D. dissertation, University of Marburg, 1956.

Tenschert, Roland. "Die Sinfonien Webers." *Neue Musik-Zeitung* 48 (1927): 481–85.

Veit, Joachim. "Zum Formproblem in der Kopfsätzen der Sinfonien Carl Maria von Webers." In *Festschrift Arno Fochert zum 60. Geburtstag,* ed. Gerhard Allroggen and Detlef Altenburg, 184–99. Kassel, 1986.

Warrack, John. *Carl Maria von Weber.* 2d ed. Cambridge, 1976.

CHAPTER THREE

Schumann

Linda Correll Roesner

Writing in 1839 in the *Neue Zeitschrift für Musik*, Robert Schumann concluded his largely negative and even pessimistic review of several recently published symphonies with the thought that Beethoven's death obliged a new generation to create a new norm for the symphony so that it might flourish again.[1] His condemnation earlier in the article of the then-prevailing state of the symphony in Germany could not have been more complete: "For the most part the more recent symphonies decline intellectually into the overture style—the first movements, that is to say; the slow [movements] are only there because they cannot be left out; the scherzos are scherzos in name only; the finales no longer know what the preceding movements contained." The composer-critic castigated German symphonists for excessive thematic allusions to Beethoven's symphonies while failing to sustain or to master the great symphonic form, "where in rapid succession the ideas appear [ever] changing and yet are linked through an inner, spiritual bond."[2]

The year 1839 was a momentous one in Schumann's career, for it was during his sojourn in Vienna that winter that he unearthed the symphonies of Franz Schubert and persuaded Schubert's brother Ferdinand to send the "Great" C-Major Symphony, D. 944, to Leipzig for performance at the Gewandhaus under Mendelssohn's direction. (The concert took place on 21 March 1839.) Schumann's account of his discovery of this work and his enthusiastic appraisal of it appeared in the *Neue Zeitschrift für Musik* of 10 March 1840. Although this celebrated article is not in any sense a review, it is clear that Schubert's C-Major Symphony fulfilled all of Schumann's hopes for a viable post–Beethovenian symphonic direction. Several attributes of Schubert's symphony that Schumann singles out for specific comment are later examined anew in his own symphonic writing: Schubert's handling of the individual instruments as well as the orchestral masses, "which often speak simultaneously, like human voices [*Menschenstimmen*] and chorus"; the breadth of form; the poetic idea of the symphony as novel.[3]

Schumann's reaction as critic to the symphonies of composers writing in the 1830s as well as to the symphonies of Schubert must be viewed not only in the context of the shadow of Beethoven but also from the standpoint of Schumann's own symphonic aspirations. Until quite recently it was customary to pigeonhole chronologically the compositions of the first decade or so of Schumann's career: piano music through 1839; the "song year" 1840; the "symphony year" 1841; the "chamber music year" 1842. Reexamination of Schumann's piano music of the 1830s in light of his autobiographical and critical writings, however, has led to a reevaluation of the role of these works in his emergence as a symphonist,[4] and it seems logical to assume that the challenge of large-scale composition, particularly the dimensions of symphonic form, could not have been so successfully met in 1841 with the composition of the Symphony No. 1 in B♭ Major Op. 38 had the composer not been constantly thinking about and working with the problem of large-scale form after Beethoven.[5]

The gradual shift in musical aesthetics during the decade of the 1840s is a point to be borne in mind in a discussion of Schumann's symphonies, for the progression toward a complete unification of the musical work of art—the aesthetic of the "total artwork" that would dominate intellectual and artistic thought in the second half of the nineteenth century—coincided exactly with Schumann's activity as a symphonist. The question of how Schumann's symphonic œuvre fits into this aesthetic trend is a focus of the present study. The related topic of the structural role played by an underlying poetic/symbolic/programmatic idea is also addressed.[6] The discussion confines itself to Schumann's symphonies, because it is clear from his writings that the symphony conveyed a dimension and a weight of tradition largely absent from other orchestral genres.[7]

Symphony No. 1 in B♭ Major ("Spring") Op. 38

Schumann's First Symphony (the "Spring") was sketched in only four days, 23–26 January 1841. During the course of the next few months, however, it underwent considerable revision. In Schumann's lifetime Op. 38 was his most popular and most frequently performed symphony, and therefore it is perhaps not surprising that of all four of the mature symphonies Op. 38 comes closest to the letter—as well as the spirit—of the German-Austrian symphonic tradition.[8]

The first movement of Op. 38, while it undeniably courts the symphonic tradition, contains enough anomalies of structure to suggest that Schumann intended to strike out in a new direction. Some of these may indeed be programmatically motivated. Although in all four mature symphonies Schumann pursues the ideal of the unified work of art, the two symphonies of 1841—the B♭-Major and the D-Minor—are considerably less subtle in this regard than the two later ones, the C-Major and the E♭-Major. The unifying element in Op. 38 is the "motto" theme of the introduction to the first movement that announces the "beginning of spring" (Ex. 3.1). Melodically and especially rhythmically this theme dominates the first movement: introductory fanfare, principal area of the exposition, closing area of the exposition, the entire development section, the extensive coda. Later in the symphony it forms the basis for the first trio of the third movement and is also suggested near the end of the finale (mm. 312ff.).

EXAMPLE 3.1. Schumann, Symphony No. 1 in B♭ Major Op. 38, movt. 1, mm. 1–2

Besides setting the tone (figuratively and literally) and providing the melodic material for the first movement, the motto and the introduction proper play a decisive role in defining the movement's sonata structure. Tonalities hinted at in the introduction also affect the unfolding of the entire symphony.

One striking—for Schumann—aspect of the first movement of the "Spring" Symphony is its adherence to the classical sonata-form procedure in which a polarity, or conflict, set up between the tonic key and another key—usually the dominant in classical works in major keys—is resolved toward the end of the movement in favor of the tonic. Normally this tonal conflict takes place in the exposition, where strong tonic definition in the principal tonal area is countered with strong definition of the new key in the secondary area and followed up with a highlighting of the new key, often after a brief modulatory departure, in the closing area of the exposition. In the first movement of Op. 38 Schumann maintains the Classical tonal polarity (he even adopts the traditional dominant), but shifts the responsibility for defining the tonic from the principal area of the exposition to the introduction. The introduction thus becomes fully integrated with the following *allegro*, and not merely because of its "motto" theme.

The definition of B♭ major in the introduction to the first movement is threefold and increasingly emphatic: the opening fanfare in the horns and trumpets, harmonized *fortissimo* by the entire orchestra (mm. 1–4); the *fortissimo* return to B♭ major (m. 12) after a brief turn to minor tonalities; the crescendo on the dominant of B♭ major (mm. 31ff.) as the introduction accelerates to the tempo of the ensuing *allegro molto vivace*. The principal theme of the exposition thus arrives riding a strong tonic wave, but after its first four measures the tonic focus becomes sharply and, I think, deliberately weakened. The second phrase on the submediant (mm. 43–46) ends with a half cadence on the dominant, but then a sudden drop to the subdominant, E♭ major, shifts the tonal focus by tonicizing that key. The repeat of the opening period (mm. 47–54) in this tonicized E♭ major thus ends with a half cadence on its dominant, B♭, which is of course the tonic key of the exposition but which no longer sounds like it. At this point (m. 55) B♭ major is abandoned as the transition to the secondary tonal area begins.

In contrast to the rapid falling away from the tonic in the principal area of the exposition, the secondary tonal area, F major, is defined with increasing clarity. Its first phrase begins "out of key"—on the mediant, A minor (mm. 81–84)—but the harmonic treatment of the continuation makes it clear that this was a momentary diversion. The secondary area of the exposition borders on textbook classic: a more lyric theme sets forth the new key (mm. 81–95); the theme's sixteenth-note accompaniment figure is then employed to expand the theme and extend its tonal compass (mm. 96–117) until an emphatic return to F major coupled with the rhythmic pattern of the motto (mm. 118ff.) closes the exposition.

The strong tonic emphasis of the introduction compensates for the tonally weak principal theme, which, thematically as well as tonally, functions like a quasi-development of the opening motto. This developmental quality of the principal theme is reinforced when Schumann inserts the theme in its entirety into the middle of the development section, beginning it in D major and reorchestrating it (mm. 178–93).[9] But it is Schumann's handling of the retransition and the beginning of the recapitulation that demonstrates conclusively that it is the introduction itself, not the "principal" theme of the exposition derived from it, that structurally defines the tonic and the return to the tonic. The development section culminates in a retransition that commences on the tonic $^6_4$ (m. 290) and incorporates, four measures later, the *fortissimo* return in the brass of the introductory motto in double augmentation over a dominant pedal. As in the introduction itself, the brass fanfare is followed by a triumphal statement of the motto in the tonic by the full orchestra. Thus the brass motto, unharmonized in the introduction but fully harmonized here, serves as both retransition and recapitulation, eliding the two areas of the traditional form.[10] The principal theme of the exposition, never needed for tonal definition even in the exposition, is simply omitted from the recapitulation, which continues with the transition from the exposition (mm. 317ff.).

Could Schumann's treatment of the principal area of the exposition have been inspired by the poetic idea of the movement? The motto of the introduction announces the "beginning of spring" (*Frühlingsbeginn*), and a short while later the motto theme is taken up in the principal area of the exposition, where the rigidly regular phrase structure supports a series of tonicizations, suggesting that the myriad voices of nature are responding to spring's call in a succession of new "tones" as spring advances through the valley.[11] When this passage later appears in toto in the development section (mm. 178ff.), new "voices" take up the call in new keys and a new orchestration with solo woodwinds and triangle. Although the orchestration confirms that these *Stimmen* are undeniably *Naturstimmen*, Schumann may have wished the effect to be similar to the orchestral effects that he admired in Schubert's C-Major Symphony and that inspired his allusion to *Menschenstimmen* in his article on the Schubert work.

Whether or not the structure of the first movement reflects the work's avowed program, later in the movement a seeming interpolation can be shown to have symbolic origins and through them a vital connection with the poetic idea of the movement and the symphony. Near the end of the coda, at measure 437, a seemingly new cantabile theme appears: its rhythm reveals it as a transformation of the motto (Ex. 3.2). It culminates (mm. 460–67) in a vivid reference to Schumann's song "Widmung," evoking Rückert's words "mein guter Geist, mein bessres Ich!" (my good spirit, my better self!) (Ex. 3.3).[12] "Widmung" is the first song

EXAMPLE 3.2. Schumann, Symphony No. 1 in B♭ Major Op. 38, movt. 1, mm. 437–51

EXAMPLE 3.3a. Schumann, Symphony No. 1 in B♭ Major Op. 38, movt. 1, mm. 460–67

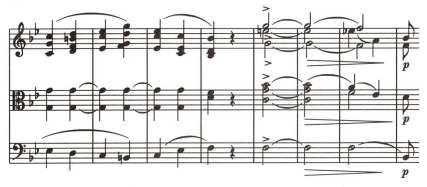

EXAMPLE 3.3b. Schumann, "Widmung" Op. 25, movt. 1, mm. 37–39

in the collection *Myrthen* Op. 25, presented to Clara Schumann by Robert on their wedding day, 12 September 1840. *Myrthen*—myrtles, the traditional German bridal wreath—may also be said to embody an image of spring; thus the symbolism is twofold: a dedication to Clara and a further reference to spring itself.[13] (This reference to "Widmung" and other, more subtle references to the song in the second and third movements— 2, mm. 110–13; 3, mm. 353ff.—do not appear in Schumann's sketches.)

Op. 38 is the only one of Schumann's symphonies explicitly to adopt in a recognizably traditional design the Classical tenet of tonal polarity and resolution in movements in sonata form. The first movement modifies the points of tonal definition, but even these are intact in the finale. Clearly Schumann considered it desirable in his first mature symphony to acknowledge the tradition. His inclination in large-scale form, however, was to use tonalities intellectually for their "referential" value rather than merely for their functional properties, which he tended to employ mainly as rhetoric. In Op. 38 this referential use of key can be seen in the composer's pairing of D (D minor or D major) with the tonic Bb.[14] The emphasis on D is prominent from the opening bars of the symphony, where the fanfare in the horns and trumpets begins on D. When the motto/fanfare is later echoed at the start of the exposition, it begins on Bb.[15] Allusions and references to D appear again and again during the course of the first movement: the turn to D minor in m. 5 and the recapitulation of the passage, *fortisissimo*, in mm. 311–16; the emphatic cadence on D major in mm. 19–21; the appearance in the development section of a new—and welcome—countermelody in D minor (mm. 150ff.); the interpolation in the development section of the entire principal theme, beginning in D major (mm. 178ff.; in the sketch Schumann inserted a double bar and a two-sharp key signature here); the "out-of-key" entrance of the secondary theme in the recapitulation, beginning on D minor before turning to the Bb tonic (m. 344ff.). The most prominent cyclic links in Op. 38 occur between the first movement and the third, where the first trio is based overtly on the motto. Not surprisingly, the third movement returns to the B♭/D pairing of the first movement.

When referential tonalities are employed together with thematic means of integration within and between movements, large structures are created "artificially," often despite the presence of recognizable but structurally insignificant shells of traditional forms. In the three symphonies that follow Op. 38, Schumann intensified his quest for total integration of the musical material. And in each of these works he approached this ideal from a different perspective while at the same time investing them with links to the works that preceded them.

Symphony No. 4 in D Minor Op. 120

The D-Minor Symphony Op. 120, sketches for which were begun in May 1841 but set aside and not finished until August,[16] was completed in score on 9 September 1841 and presented to Clara Schumann on her birthday, 13 September, together with the proof sheets of the first printed orchestral part of Op. 38 and the newly published Rückert Lieder Op. 37 (the "Liebesfrühling" collection, which contains songs by both Clara and Robert). After an unsatisfactory premiere in December 1841, the composer did not actively seek to have the symphony published and appears to have abandoned it.[17] In 1851, however, he returned to the work, revising it somewhat and completely reorchestrating it.[18] In this form it was published in 1853 as Symphony No. 4 Op. 120; in the meantime the two much later symphonies had appeared as Nos. 2 and 3.[19]

The 1851 version of the D-Minor Symphony is in many ways problematic because stylistically the symphony remained a work of 1841. The heavier orchestration of the 1851 version, although uniquely suited to Schumann's late musical style of dense textures, markedly slower harmonic rhythm, and increased rhythmic flexibility, seems inappropriate when grafted onto the fast harmonic rhythm and short-breathed phrases characteristic of Schumann's style of the early 1840s.[20] It seems clear that what interested Schumann at the time of composition was the possibility of totally unifying a large-scale work by infusing all of the movements—none of which in Op. 120 is entirely complete in itself—with common thematic threads, harmonic motives, and tonal gestures and at the same time linking them physically by doing away with the breaks between them.[21] In 1841 such an approach to the symphony was indeed unusual.[22] In 1851, by which time Schumann had explored the possibilities of total integration with supreme subtlety and mastery of form, the potential of his effort of ten years earlier may have been what drew him back to the abandoned score.[23]

Like Op. 38, Op. 120 employs a "motto" theme in the introduction to the first movement. The motto (Ex. 3.4) provides just one of many unifying threads that run through the symphony.[24] It supplies the thematic basis for the entire first movement (Ex. 3.5). It is incorporated bodily into

EXAMPLE 3.4. Schumann, Symphony No. 4 in D Minor Op. 120, movt. 1, mm. 2–3

EXAMPLE 3.5. Schumann, Symphony No. 4 in D Minor Op. 120, movt. 1, mm. 29–32

the Romanze (mm. 12ff.) and then expanded in melodic compass to form the D-major middle section of the Romanze (mm. 26ff.). The trio of the scherzo directly recalls the D-major section of the Romanze, and the scherzo theme itself is a melodic inversion of the motto. Finally, in the form in which it appeared as the main theme of the first movement, the motto reappears in the transition to the finale and later as a counterpoint to the first theme of the finale, a theme that derives from a motive generated in the development section of the first movement (Ex. 3.6).[25]

EXAMPLE 3.6a. Schumann, Symphony No. 4 in D Minor Op. 120, movt. 4, mm. 17–18

Schumann may have felt that this intensive, one could say unsparing, use of a unifying motive was necessary to carry out his plan of suggesting four movements in one. In employing a motto, however, he was also relying on a technique that he had perfected in the 1830s in works

EXAMPLE 3.6b. Schumann, Symphony No. 4 in D Minor Op. 120, movt. 1, mm. 121–24, cf. mm. 171–74.

for solo piano. The real breakthrough in Op. 120 comes not from such obvious unifying devices as the motto, but from the bold experimentation with the large-scale form itself.

Structurally, the break with traditional procedures of the first movement and the conception of the finale as both a continuation of the first movement and culmination of the work as a whole was unprecedented in 1841.[26] Unlike the exposition of the first movement of Op. 38, the principal area of the exposition of Op. 120 does indeed define the tonic key, D minor. But after the cadence in the tonic in measure 42 (measure numbers refer to the 1851 version), the remainder of the exposition departs from traditional paths. In a procedure that he would later employ often in movements in sonata form, Schumann deliberately deemphasizes the secondary area of the exposition, tonally and thematically. The principal theme dominates the entire exposition. When the new key, the "traditional" relative major, F major, is reached (m. 59) it does not function in a sonata-like manner as a well-defined contrasting key, but sounds instead like a lengthy cadential prolongation. The arrival in F is not articulated until the very end of the exposition (m. 83). Since the idea of tonal conflict is so utterly diminished in the exposition, complementing the seemingly obsessive monothematicism, Schumann saw no need in 1841 to repeat the exposition in the Classical manner.[27]

The development section assumes much of the role of defining the structure in the first movement of Op. 120. After the sudden drop to ♭VII at the beginning of the development,[28] an extensive motivic development of the movement's theme leads to a rhetorical pause, complete with fermata, on the dominant of F major (mm. 145–46). At this point a lyric theme marked *dolce*—the first lyrical moment in the symphony—enters *piano* in this generously prepared, "real" F major (Ex. 3.7). In his 1841 autograph score Schumann further set off the entrance of the lyric theme

EXAMPLE 3.7. Schumann, Symphony No. 4 in D Minor Op. 120, movt. 1, mm. 147–54

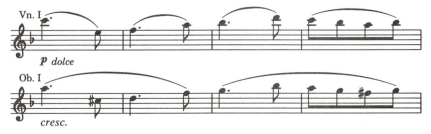

with a double bar and the designation *animato*. Although the fourth measure of the new theme incorporates the motto, and in the 1841 version of the symphony the theme was contrapuntally combined with the movement's principal theme, this lyric moment is clearly intended to contrast with the main theme and its D-minor orientation, which was so carefully established in the exposition.[29] Schumann's choice of the "traditional" relative major for the entrance of the lyric theme—the true "second subject"—certainly is not fortuitous. The lyric theme provides such an inviting respite from the rhythmically incessant main theme that it completely overshadows a newly generated motivic aspect of the main theme—punctuating chords in a dotted rhythm, or suggesting a dotted rhythm (see mm. 121–22 [Ex. 3.6b], 171–74)—that will become a key link between the first movement and the finale.[30]

After a repeat at the minor third of much of the development section (mm. 175–248 = mm. 101–74), the retransition begins on the dominant of B♭ (mm. 277ff.) with mysterious *pianissimo* string tremolos that progress via a sequence featuring diminished-seventh chords to a pedal on the dominant of D (mm. 285ff.).[31] Thus prepared, the tonic key, D, enters at measure 297. But the tonic is D major, not D minor, and the theme that is "recapitulated" is not the principal theme, but instead the lyric theme from the development section. "Recapitulation" is hardly a fitting term for this return to the tonic, since the lyric theme is never presented in its original form, but rather continues to evolve through a succession of transformations. (The principal theme does return with a new motivic continuation in the coda, mm. 337ff., where again the punctuating chordal motive is prominent, mm. 349ff.)

The appearance of the major mode of the tonic toward the end of the first movement of Op. 120 can be viewed not as a reprise, or even a return, but as an arrival at a new level of the symphonic argument. (In many ways the movement is a prototype for the much more ambitious finale of the C-Major Symphony Op. 61.) After the digression of the two middle movements of the symphony—a "digression," however, that expands the tonal and melodic compass—the finale will take up exactly where the first movement leaves off.

   In addition to their thematic extension of the motto, the two middle movements are structurally significant from the standpoint of tonal reference. The ostensibly A-minor Romanze projects its middle section in D major (mm. 27ff.). This passage is later recalled in the trio of the third movement, in B♭ major (mm. 65ff.). The scherzo, which is in D minor, does not come to a full close, but instead ends in B♭ major with the trio material. The linking of D and B♭ is, I believe, Schumann's way of paying homage to Beethoven in a D minor symphony that otherwise diligently avoids references to the Ninth Symphony. Moreover, it almost certainly refers back to Schumann's own pairing of these two keys in Op. 38. In Op. 120 B♭ major is suggested as early as the introduction to the first movement (mm. 7–9, 15–16), but with the exception of the striking allusion to the dominant of B♭ at the start of the retransition (mm. 277ff.), Schumann waits until the trio of the third movement to link the two keys definitively. Then, at the beginning of the *Langsam* transition to the finale, B♭ major and D minor are, for a moment, fused.

   Schumann conceived the finale of Op. 120 as a true culmination, rather than a lighter-weight windup. The fact that the thematic/motivic, harmonic, and structural connections with the first movement are integrated into the finale (rather than serving merely as reminiscences) indicates that he intended the finale to carry on the symphonic discourse of the opening movement. Furthermore, the revisions he undertook in 1851 were clearly meant to intensify the relationship between the two movements. For example, at the beginning of the finale Schumann added the principal theme of the first movement as punctuation to the motive from the development section of the first movement that serves as the opening idea of the finale; he omitted entirely the extraneous melody of the original second phrase of the finale; he reorchestrated the section beginning at measure 265 in the development section of the first movement so the chordal theme would be played by the full brass choir (instead of primarily by the woodwinds) and thus later be evoked by the closing theme of the exposition of the finale (mm. 67ff.). And he set up a rhythmic parallel, complete with fermata, between the passage preparing the entrance of the lyric theme in the first movement and the last two measures of the transition/introduction to the finale, thus propelling the listener forcibly back to the development section of the first movement, in which the opening motive of the finale was first heard, and at the same time forging a link with the lyric theme of the first movement, which otherwise is physically absent from the finale. (Compare mm. 144–46 of the first movement with mm. 15–16 of the *Langsam* transition to the finale.)

   Although it can be convincingly argued that in the one-movement form of Op. 120 the finale functions as recapitulation of the first movement,[32] the situation seems more complex. The motivic and thematic links are ingeniously constructed and undeniably reinforce the idea of recapitulation. But the "arrival" in D major in the first movement, with its ongoing expansion of the lyric theme, makes an indelible impression and appears to be the true point of departure for the finale. The D minor of the exposition of the first movement is recalled and then dispensed with in the *Langsam* transition/introduction. The finale itself (*Lebhaft*) is firmly in D major. It even has a Classical exposition: clearly defined tonal areas in the tonic and the dominant, a real second subject (mm. 39ff.) that nonetheless shares the dotted rhythmic pattern of the principal thematic idea, and a closing area that reinforces the new key (mm. 67ff.).

But mainly it is the wealth of new thematic ideas in this bright D-major finale that gives the impression not of recapitulation but of ongoing, joyful expansion. Although every new thematic gesture can be shown to relate to an already established rhythmic pattern or melodic contour, the thematic material nonetheless seems fresh. The second subject is particularly poignant because it has links to Schumann's biography. This melody (Ex. 3.8) is one of Schumann's "emblem" themes, a term I use to

EXAMPLE 3.8. Schumann, Symphony No. 4 in D Minor Op. 120, movt. 4, mm. 39–42

characterize melodic ideas that recur from work to work. Its symbolic association with Clara seems certain.[33] In March 1841 Schumann wrote in the *Ehetagebuch* that his next symphony would be called "Clara" and that in it he would paint her portrait with flutes, oboes, and harps (see above, note 24). Although there are no harps in Op. 120 (the 1841 autograph score does include a staff for guitar in the Romanze, but it is blank), in the 1841 score the *dolce* second subject of the finale—the emblem theme—features solo woodwinds without any doublings in the strings: clarinet (cf. mm. 39ff. of the 1851 version), oboe (cf. mm. 44ff.), and flute (cf. mm. 52ff.).

After a brief development section, the symphony's final arrival in D major (mm. 129ff.) becomes the sole province of the second subject. This parallels the arrival in D major in the first movement while simultaneously completing the symphonic argument. As we have seen, in the first movement the arrival in D major featured the lyric theme (the "real" second subject) first presented in the development section. But instead of functioning in a recapitulatory fashion, the theme continued to evolve. In the finale the second subject, already complete, simply claims the tonic key. An extensive coda (mm. 172ff.) then brings the symphony to a close.

Symphony No. 2 in C Major Op. 61

A crucial four and a half years separated the first version of the D-Minor Symphony and the C-Major Symphony, sketched in December 1845 when Schumann's recovery from the nervous breakdown he suffered in the middle of 1844 was nearly complete. During these years Schumann immersed himself in the large forms. In 1845, together with Clara, he intensified the study of counterpoint, which had engaged him throughout his career. Most significantly, beginning in 1845 he began to compose away from the piano and to "conceive and work out everything in my head."[34] Thus the intellectual approach that we have observed in conjunction with the composer's creative conception of form in the large dimension is now applied to the thematic material itself. As a result the integration of the thematic material of a work, always an important aspect of Schumann's music, becomes increasingly more subtle and powerful.

Schumann's last two symphonies, C Major Op. 61 (1845–46) and E♭ Major Op. 97 ("Rhenish," 1850), attain the cumulative sweep that was clearly the objective of the D-Minor Symphony by discarding the four-movements-in-one format in favor of multimovement designs with real *adagio* movements. In both symphonies the slow movement is the penultimate one (as in Beethoven's Ninth) and is fused thematically, tonally, and structurally with the finale. In both symphonies this pairing of slow movement and finale causes the weight of the work as a whole to fall toward the end, heightening the impact of the slow movement on the overall design. In the introspective C-Major Symphony, the *adagio espressivo* forms the emotional core. In the E♭-Major Symphony, outgoing, even exuberant, the *Feierlich*, with its dense contrapuntal textures and vivid ecclesiastical imagery, is the intellectual high point.

The sophisticated thematic evolution of the C-Major Symphony Op. 61 moves far beyond the motto derivations of Op. 38 and even Op. 120. The thematic structure of the entire work unfolds out of the opening measures of the introduction to the first movement.[35] Going hand in hand with the thematic unification of the symphony is a tonal plan that might be unique in the history of the symphony: the tonic of each of the movements is C major, but until the tonic-affirming finale, C major is treated equivocally, established only near the respective ends of the first three movements and giving the impression that the tonic was attained in these movements only by great strength of will.

Schumann's motivation for implementing this tonal plan seems to have been symbolic, autobiographical, and even novelistic. For in Op. 61 Schumann reaches back almost ten years, to the C-Major Fantasie Op. 17. The first movement of Op. 17, which Schumann described to Clara Wieck in 1838 as "a deep lament for you," employs the same tonal "program" that he later elaborates over the course of four movements in Op. 61.[36] In the first movement of Op. 17 the tonal goal, C major, is postponed repeat-edly until the end, where it appears simultaneously with the definitive form of a reference to the sixth song from Beethoven's cycle *An die ferne Geliebte*, "Nimm sie hin denn, diese Lieder, die ich dir, Geliebte, sang" (Take them then, these songs that I sang to you, beloved).[37] In Op. 61 the definitive form of the same reference to "Nimm sie hin denn, diese Lieder" crystallizes near the end of the finale (mm. 394ff.) and coincides with the final arrival at the tonal goal C major (Ex. 3.9).

EXAMPLE 3.9a. Beethoven, *An die ferne Geliebte* Op. 98, No. 6, mm. 9–10

EXAMPLE 3.9b. Schumann, Fanatasie in C Major Op. 17, movt. 1, mm. 296–97

EXAMPLE 3.9c. Schumann, Symphony No. 2 in C Major Op. 61, movt. 4, mm. 394–97

It cannot be coincidental that both of these deeply personal works cite the same theme at a comparable place in the overall design. Schu-mann's course of action makes the symbolic significance of C major in both works difficult to ignore: C undoubtedly stands for Clara, and both works are in the nature of a declaration for and dedication to her.[38] In Op. 17 the tonal goal substitutes for Schumann's real-life goal, to be united with his beloved. In Op. 61 the tonal goal, which Schumann him-self suggested symbolizes the victory of the spirit over darkness and de-spair, may be intended as a tribute to Clara for her love and support dur-ing the period of nervous breakdown, certainly a trying time in their marriage.[39]

But the referential use of C major as a long-postponed tonal goal and the quotation from *An die ferne Geliebte* are not the only gestures that serve to dedicate—unofficially—Op. 61 to Clara.[40] Two subtle messages to the recipient of "these songs" also appear. In the *adagio espressivo* at mm. 94–96 and again at mm. 98–100 the reprise of the *adagio* theme contains a melodic elaboration not present earlier (Ex. 3.10). Is it only accidental that this new turn in the melody is the "emblem" theme that I postulate to

EXAMPLE 3.10. Schumann, Symphony No. 2 in C Major Op. 61, movt. 3, mm. 38–39; mm. 94–96

have an association with Clara? And at measures 336–39 in the finale Schumann inserts a reference to the passage in the coda of the first movement of the "Spring" Symphony (mm. 460ff.) that quotes the song "Widmung" from *Myrthen* Op. 25, the collection of songs dedicated to Clara Schumann and presented to her by her husband on their wedding day (Ex. 3.11; cf. Ex. 3.3). Although in Op. 61 the allusion to "Widmung" is almost subliminal, filtered as it were through the reference in Op. 38, this phrase, which appears only once in the finale of Op. 61, seems inessential to both the thematic and the structural unfolding of the movement. Thus its role as "message" takes on added meaning.

EXAMPLE 3.11. Schumann, Symphony No. 2 in C Major Op. 61, movt. 4, mm. 336–43; cf. Ex. 3.3a

In Op. 61 Schumann skillfully manipulates the symphonic tradition to suit not only his poetic/symbolic purpose but also his aesthetic position. The sonata-allegro form of the first movement, although present on the surface, totally lacks the tonal polarity that defines traditional sonata style: tonal conflict is minimized in the exposition, and any emphasis on the second tonal area is postponed until the end of the exposition; the thematic material is fully integrated so that thematic continuity is assured. In Op. 61, owing to the tonal program, even the tonic emphasis customary at the beginning of the exposition is played down. The muting of the tonic with subdominant inflections that characterizes the introduction is carried into the exposition, where it is aided by the prominent second-beat accents. The "secondary tonal area" oscillates between E♭ major and its dominant before arriving very late at the "traditional" dominant, G major, where the first strong cadence of the movement occurs at measure 100, almost at the end of the exposition. After a constantly modulatory development section, the beginning of the recapitulation (mm. 245ff.) again features the subdominant leanings of the principal area of the exposition. Since the parallel with the exposition is strictly maintained, it is not until near the end of the recapitulation (m. 303) that the tonic, C major, becomes established.

Symbolic postponement of the tonal goal is also a feature of the second movement, where the approaches to C major during the course of the movement become increasingly stronger but are repeatedly thwarted: the first definitive cadence in the tonic does not appear until the end of the movement.

In addition to their unorthodox treatment of the tonic, the first two movements of Op. 61 are characterized by unusually restless harmonic movement. (Only the two trios of the second movement provide a degree of tonal stability.) The paired *adagio espressivo* and finale, however, arrest this incessant motion in order to project a false tonic, counteract it with the real tonic (*adagio espressivo*), and then unequivocally affirm the long-delayed tonic goal (finale).

The tonal plan and the form of the *adagio espressivo* provide convincing evidence that in Op. 61 Schumann set out deliberately to evoke the symbolism of the Fantasie Op. 17. In form the movement recalls the unusual final movement of Op. 17, *Langsam getragen*. Both movements abandon early on what seems to be the tonic key in favor of a strong projection of another key that appears to usurp the tonic role. In Op. 17 this "false" tonic is F major, the subdominant. In Op. 61 it is E♭ major.[41] Both movements unfold in such a way that their second halves strictly parallel their first halves, but with a few imaginative changes in harmony the "false" tonic is supplanted by the real.[42] In Op. 17 the form of the *Langsam getragen* reinterprets the parallel form of the first movement and brings the *Fantasie* to a close by reaffirming the tonal goal of the first movement. In Op. 61, on the other hand, Schumann indicates that although the symbolic tonal goal has been approached more decisively than in the first two movements, once again it has not been fully achieved: in the coda of the *adagio espressivo* C major is clouded by inflections of the subdominant minor (mm. 118ff.), and the movement avoids a tonic-affirming perfect cadence.

It is left to the finale to set forth unequivocally the tonic key, which it does with the aid of every rhetorical gesture in the Classical arsenal. From the opening flourish on a C-major scale to the "Classical" tonal contrast of the exposition—a sonata-rondo with the second subject (a transformation of the theme of the *adagio espressivo*) firmly in the dominant—the key of the finale is never open to question. Even as the movement progresses and it becomes increasingly clear that its scope is broad, its form innovative, and its purpose narrative, symbolic, retrospective, heroic, ecumenical, the tonal treatment remains exaggeratedly traditional.[43] The symphony's intricate thematic evolution, which culminates in the "Beethoven" theme at the point of tonal recapitulation in the finale (mm. 394ff.), would have considerably less emotional and structural impact if the tonal designs of the first three movements had been more traditional. This final arrival in the tonic (as in Op. 120, the term "recapitulation" is hardly appropriate) carries with it the weight of the entire symphony, as Schumann makes clear when he incorporates, mottolike, the thematic material from the introduction to the first movement (mm. 445ff.), interweaving it with the constantly expanding "Beethoven" theme.

Symphony No. 3 in E♭ Major ("Rhenish") Op. 97

Schumann's last symphony was composed in November and early December 1850, shortly after the composer's move to the Rhine city of Düsseldorf to assume the directorship of the Düsseldorf Allgemeine Musikverein. Like the "Spring" Symphony Op. 38, the "Rhenish" originally had a program rich in pictorial imagery, which the composer suppressed before publication.[44] Nonetheless, one of his reasons for seeking to interest the Bonn publisher N. Simrock in the work was to see it published in the Rhineland, because "perhaps here and there [it] reflects a bit of local color."[45] The primary sources confirm that the Rhineland in general and Cologne Cathedral in particular provided the inspiration for the symphony. The "solemn ceremony" of the suppressed title for the fourth movement, however, cannot be demonstrated to reflect Schumann's direct impression of a specific event. Although it has often been assumed that Schumann was present in Cologne Cathedral on 12 November 1850 for the elevation of the Archbishop Johannes von Geißel to Cardinal, his diary shows that he was home in Düsseldorf, sick, on that day. Furthermore, there is no evidence that he ever attended a High Mass in the cathedral, although he visited it twice as a tourist in the fall of 1850. Thus the fourth movement, an acclaimed polyphonic tour de force with unmistakable ecclesiastical connotations, accompanies a "solemn ceremony" in Schumann's imagination only.[46]

In Op. 97 the tonal interconnections and intricate thematic relationships that characterize the earlier symphonies become ever more subtle when coupled with the full breadth and contrapuntal complexities of the composer's late style. Without resorting to even a hint of a motto, Schumann develops the entire symphony out of a complex of motivically related themes.[47] The unifying motives are intervallic ("germ" motives: the perfect fourth in both ascending and descending form; the sixth, usually major, sometimes minor), rhythmic (particularly dotted and double-dotted figures), and tonal (the striking introduction of B major at three important points of articulation in the first, fourth, and fifth movements).

In the (introductionless) first movement the first three measures of the principal theme present the perfect fourth, the major sixth, and the dotted rhythmic figure that is embedded in almost every theme in the symphony. The driving figure in eighth notes in the middle strings is an important component of the principal theme and serves to enhance not only the rhythmic continuity of the movement but also the interrelationship of the themes: the eighth-note figure becomes melodic beginning in measure 25, forming a middle, "contrast" period of the principal area while harmonically foreshadowing G minor, one of the paired keys of the "secondary" area; later it is deployed in another melodic form in the closing area of the exposition (mm. 143ff.). In the development section it is related to the second subject through contrapuntal combination beginning at measure 239.

In the exposition of the first movement of Op. 97 both the principal theme and the second subject (mm. 95ff.) emerge out of the descending perfect-fourth motive. As if to emphasize this thematic unity, there is no compartmentalization of "principal" and "secondary" themes into separate areas of the exposition. Rather, principal and secondary areas are essentially treated as one unified discourse, and thematic gestures characteristic of one are incorporated into the area normally associated with the other. For example, in the principal area beginning at measure 47 a rhythmic pattern that will soon be associated with the second subject is "previewed," juxtaposed with statements of the characteristic rhythm of the principal theme (mm. 43ff., 49ff.). In the "secondary area" proper (mm. 95ff.), tonal conflict is deemphasized by oscillation between G minor, the relative minor of the dominant, and the dominant, B♭ major. B♭ major is reserved not for the "second subject" but for a forceful interjection of the principal theme (mm. 111ff.). Thus here as elsewhere in late Schumann the traditional idea of tonal conflict, although present in the abstract, ceases to be structurally meaningful.

In the first movement of Op. 97 (and throughout the entire symphony) the themes are never presented as cut-and-dried entities, but as fluid constructions that continually change: a new melodic continuation, a slight rhythmic alteration, a strategically placed counterpoint, a phrase overlap, and so forth. As the movement progresses, the interrelationships within the thematic complex are intensified, so that the recapitulation functions not as a reprise but as a continuation and further elaboration. Indeed, the manner in which the development section and recapitulation are elided emphasizes the continuity. (See mm. 367ff., the "retransition," where the head motive of the principal theme in the horns enters in the tonic over a dominant pedal.[48] When the actual "recapitulation" is finally reached in m. 411 via four measures of augmented-sixth chord, the complete principal theme, entering *fortisissimo* on a tonic $^6_4$, is still poised over the dominant pedal.) With its substantially recomposed recapitulation, the movement elaborates and advances the conceptual approach of Op. 120 and Op. 61.[49] But in Op. 97, perhaps because the integration of the material is so complete, the composer did not consider it necessary to employ radical formal designs in order to stress the arrival at a new stage of the symphonic journey (cf. the outer movements of Op. 120 and the finale of Op. 61, where Schumann emphasizes the idea of arrival by refusing to recapitulate the principal theme of the movement). Figure 3.1 gives an idea of the sophisticated thematic integration of Op. 97.

Although the first movement of Op. 97 rivals the finale of Op. 61 in dimension, Op. 97 is end-oriented, like Op. 61 and, on a smaller scale, Op. 120. As in those two symphonies, this is owing in part to the unfolding of the thematic material over the course of the entire symphony. But perhaps the most important factor in the work's end orientation is simply the existence of the impressive fourth movement. The solemn Eb-minor tonality, the imposing presence of trombones for the first time in the symphony, the intricate polyphony, the rhythmic complexities—every detail in the musical language of the fourth movement proclaims that here is where the weight of the symphony falls. The fourth movement is then essentially continued in the finale, but with complete thematic transformation and metamorphosis of mood, as if the "solemn ceremony" of the original title of the fourth movement had suddenly emerged out of doors.[50]

Schumann jotted down his first ideas for themes of the fifth movement (and, by extension, the fourth) while he was sketching the third. Preliminary sketches of the outline of the fourth-movement theme as it later appears in the major mode beginning at measure 271 of the fifth movement, and of the theme that enters at measure 27 of the fifth movement (labeled "Th. IIa" by Schumann), are interspersed with the third-movement draft (see the example in Fig. 3.1).[51] Intervallically the third bar of "Th. IIa" (m. 29 of the finale) in this preliminary sketch corresponds exactly with what was to become the countersubject of the fourth movement. Significantly, this melodic shape, which begins with the motive of the ascending perfect fourth, had already appeared in the second movement, where it formed the contrasting B period of the scherzo (mm. 17ff.) and again in the third movement, where it was used as a cadential gesture (mm. 9–10, passim). Not until the fourth movement, however, does it really come into its own, first appearing as a closing gesture (mm. 6ff.), but then developing into what is virtually a countersubject as the movement progresses (see mm. 23ff.). When this countersubject from the fourth movement reemerges at the beginning of the development section of the fifth movement (mm. 99ff.) and is developed in conjunction with themes of the fifth movement proper, the long span of continuity is assured,[52] and Schumann's reason for revising the third measure of "Th. IIa" becomes clear: to eliminate a conspicuous redundancy.

Figure 3.1

I.

P

The important 8th-note rhythm ♫♫♫ in the middle strings becomes melodic in mm. 25ff, forming a "contrast" period of the principal area and harmonically foreshadowing one of the paired keys of the secondary area, G minor. At mm. 77ff this 8th-note figure forms the transition. At mm. 143ff, with a slight melodic alteration, it appears in the closing area of the exposition; and in this form, with a new continuation, it begins the development section (see mm. 185ff).

Foreshadows the rhythm of the second subject and relates it to the rhythm of the principle theme.

This new, chromatic dimention of the second subject (cf. the "motto" of Op. 120) is extensively developed.

The chromatic dimension evolved in the development is later expanded diatonically in the retransition.

Its quarter-note movement is later incorporated into the new expansion of the principal theme that serves as the transition in the recapitulation. Here the quarter-note movement that orginally emerged out of a melodic inversion and subsequent chromatic expansion of the second subject (mm. 213ff) is re-integrated with the second subject via a direct link with the rhythm of the principal theme, thus revealing an additional relationship between "principal" theme and "second subject."

The double-dotted variant of the rhythm of the principal theme later becomes an important point of articulation when it reappears in the horns at the beginning of the retransition (m. 367) with the melodic intervals of the principal theme. (The double-dotted figure in the finale, mm. 287ff, refers back to m. 367 of the first movement.)

Note the increased emphasis on the major 6th (mm. 367ff). In the coda the major 6th becomes more prominent still (mm. 563ff), but the rhythmic pattern returns to simple dots.)

II.

The Scherzo theme (a) features the ascending perfect 4th (cf. mm. 213ff of the 1st movement) and the major 6th.

This characteristic figure (the b theme of the Scherzo) later is incorporated into the IIIrd movement (mm. 9ff) and appears, transformed, as the main theme of the IVth movement (and the "countersubject" derived from it).

The Trio theme (c) is punctuated by theme b.

The coda combines the perfect 4th with the major 6th (cf. the coda of the 1st movement, m. 563) and prepares for the emphasis on the major 6th in the IIIrd movement.

III.

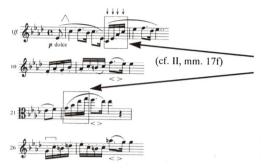

(cf. II, mm. 17f)

The major 6th is echoed at the beginning of the IIIrd movement.

This seemingly innocuous figure embedded in the IIIrd-movement themes will later become the apotheosis-like climax of the IVth movement (mm. 52ff), a trumpet fanfare in the Vth movement, and the climax of the development section of the Vth movement (mm. 130ff).

IV.

(cf. I, m. 367, m. 563; tonally cf. I, m. 281)

V.

P

"Th. IIa"

First Sketch (**F-Pn**, ms. 329, fol. 10ᵗ)

preliminary sketch for V, 271ff [IV], sketched during the composition of III, (**F-Pn**, ms 329, fol 10ᵗ)

(cf. III, mm. 1, 21, 34; IV, mm 52ff)

"S"

The "second subject," a variant of "Th. IIa," provides very little definition of the new key (A-flat major).

(the "countersubject" of the IVth movement, here in the Vth movement developed along with Vth-movement motifs)

(cf. IV, m. 52; I, m. 281)

(cf. mm. 57ff)

This leads directly into an imitative statement in augmentation (mm. 271ff) of the IVth-movement theme that then melds with an allusion to the dotted pattern of the principal theme of the Ist movement (mm. 280ff).

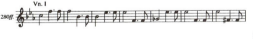

(cf. the double-dotted figure in I, mm. 367ff)

cf. I, mm. 1ff)

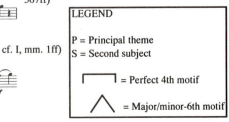

LEGEND

P = Principal theme
S = Second subject

⌐   ⌐ = Perfect 4th motif

∧ = Major/minor-6th motif

The complete thematic integration of Op. 97 makes possible a tonal link that Schumann exploits with striking results. At measure 52 in the fourth movement a sudden drop from the plagal cadence in E♭ minor to the key of the ♭VI, B major, heralds, *forte*, a gesture in the brass and winds that has unmistakable connotations of apotheosis. For eight long measures in the slow tempo of the fourth movement, E♭ minor, resonating softly in the strings, alternates with B major, *forte* and *fortissimo* in the brass and winds. An augmented-sixth chord serves as the conduit between the two keys. Finally B major resolves, via a Neapolitan-sixth chord, to the dominant of E♭ minor (m. 59), and the movement comes to a close. Thematically the apotheosis-like figure incorporates both the perfect-fourth and major-sixth motives; it relates specifically to a figure embedded in third-movement themes (see the examples in Fig. 3.1). But the striking appearance of B major refers all the way back to the development section of the first movement (mm. 281ff.). There a statement in B major of a rather extensive segment of the principal theme directly follows the first appearance in a minor key of the opening phrase of the same theme (in A♭ minor, mm. 273ff.), and resolves, via augmented-sixth chords (mm. 299ff.), to E♭ minor (m. 311)—whereupon the entire passage is repeated in sequence.[53]

The final link in this B-major chain appears in the fifth movement, where B major forms the climax of the development section and begins the retransition (mm. 130ff.). As in both earlier appearances, B major is approached from A♭ minor and resolves via an augmented-sixth chord to the dominant of E♭ (E♭ major in the finale; see mm. 136ff.). The melodic material at measure 130 of the finale vividly recalls the apotheosis-like theme of the fourth movement. Earlier in the finale the figure had appeared as a trumpet fanfare (m. 60), but it is characteristic of the deft—Mahlerian—thematic interplay in this symphony that it is not until measure 130 that the seemingly straightforward fanfare becomes an event of major proportions.

The spectacular coda of the finale of Op. 97 sums up not only the myriad interrelationships of this symphony but also Schumann's aesthetic ideal. All of the thematic and motivic threads are drawn together, and everything does indeed relate to everything else, "the ideas . . . [ever] changing and yet . . . linked through an inner, spiritual bond."[54] In the coda these ever-changing ideas crystallize in a new, chorale-like metamorphosis of the theme of the fourth movement (mm. 255ff.; see Fig. 3.1) that serves to cement the relationship between the fourth and fifth movements and the opening measures of the symphony.

Op. 97 is probably Schumann's most "objective" symphony. Although it avowedly projects images of the Rhineland, it does not have the intimate biographical connotations that pervade Op. 61 and that reside in but do not overwhelm Op. 120 and Op. 38. As a body of works, Schumann's symphonies illustrate the composer's approach to the genre as a tradition to be cherished, but also as an ideal to be constructed and examined anew with each successive work.[55] Schumann never followed formulas. The degree of structural creativity attained and sustained in these four works is impressive by any standards, but particularly when considered in the context of a continuing symphonic tradition after Beethoven.

Notes

1. *Neue Zeitschrift für Musik* 11, no. 5 (16 July 1839): 18 (review of works by Preyer, Reissiger, and Lachner).

2. Ibid., 11, no. 1 (2 July 1839): 1.

3. Ibid., 12, no. 21 (10 March 1840): 81–83 (English translation in Robert Schumann, *On Music and Musicians*, ed. Konrad Wolff, trans. Paul Rosenfeld [New York, 1946], 107–12). Schumann observes that it would be necessary to copy out the entire symphony in order properly to convey the novelistic character that pervades it (ibid., p. 83). Earlier in the article (p. 82) he refers to "this heavenly length of the symphony, like a thick novel in four volumes possibly by Jean Paul." The concept of instruments speaking as human voices is brought up again in Schumann's review of Mendelssohn's Symphony in A Minor Op. 56: *Neue Zeitschrift für Musik* 18, no. 39 (15 May 1843): 156.

4. Reinhard Kapp, *Studien zum Spätwerk Robert Schumanns* (Tutzing, 1984), argues convincingly that many of Schumann's early piano works are orchestral music in disguise and as such are vehicles for solutions to the problems of large-scale orchestral writing (pp. 31, 39, 47, passim). Akio Mayeda's important study, *Robert Schumanns Weg zur Symphonie* (Zurich, 1992), had not appeared by the time of this writing.

5. An early effort, the "Jugendsymphonie," or "Zwickauer Symphonie," in G minor dates from 1832–33. See Jon W. Finson, *Robert Schumann and the Study of Orchestral Composition: The Genesis of the First Symphony, Op. 38* (Oxford, 1989), 2–17; Gerald Abraham, "Schumann's Jugendsinfonie in G Minor," in *Slavonic and Romantic Music: Essays and Studies* (New York, 1968), 267–80; Mosco Carner, "The Orchestral Music," in *Schumann: A Symposium*, ed. Gerald Abraham (London, 1952), 187–90. A study score of the symphony, ed. Marc Andreae, was published in 1972 (Edition Peters, Nr. 8157). In his influential study of Schumann's symphonics ("Orchestral Music," pp. 176–244), Mosco Carner argued that Schumann's approach to composition was fundamentally unsuited to symphonic form because it was dominated by small-scale, additive thought processes. The symphonic form Carner used as his point of reference, was, of course, Beethoven's.

6. Schumann did not live long enough to become embroiled in the controversy over "absolute" music versus "program" music that, fanned by the writings of the Viennese critic Eduard Hanslick, raged during the second half of the nineteenth century and came to a head in the early decades of the twentieth. Schumann's writings, however, demonstrate that he took for granted the underlying poetic meaning of any given work.

7. See Michael Struck, "Am Rande der 'grossen Form': Robert Schumanns Ouvertüren und ihr Verhältnis zur Symphonie," in *Probleme der symphonischen Tradition im 19. Jahrhundert*, ed. Siegfried Kross with Marie Luise Maintz (Tutzing, 1990), 239–78.

8. Robert Schumann, *Tagebücher*, vol. 3, *Haushaltbücher: 1837–1856*, ed. Gerd Nauhaus (Leipzig, 1982), 172–73. The symphony was begun immediately after Schumann had abandoned his sketch of a symphony in C minor. Schumann's entries in his *Haushaltbuch* show that the poetic association of the B♭ major symphony with springtime was part of the basic conception of the work: 23 January, "Frühlingssymphonie angefangen" ("Spring symphony begun," p. 172). In the autograph full score (**US-Wc** ML96.S415 Case) the work bears the title "Frühlingssymphonie" and each of the movements is also titled: 1, "Frühlingsbeginn" (Spring's beginning); 2, "Abend" (Evening); 3, "Frohe Gespielen" (Merry playmates); 4, "Voller Frühling" (Full spring). Schumann withdrew the titles before publication. See Linda Correll Roesner, "Studies in Schumann Manuscripts" (Ph.D. dissertation, New York University, 1973), 1:346–65; Finson, *Orchestral Composition*, 65–91; Roesner, "Einige quellen- und textkritische Bemerkungen zur B-Dur-Sinfonie, Op. 38," in *Schumanns Werke: Text und Interpretation*, ed. Akio Mayeda and Klaus Wolfgang Niemöller (Mainz, 1987), 89–100. See the extensive list of performances on the flyleaf of Schumann's autograph score (**US-Wc**), published, together with the sketches, in an excellent facsimile edition by the Robert Owen Lehman Foundation (New York, 1967). Finson, *Orchestral Composition*, 36–64, deals extensively with Schumann's indebtedness in Op. 38 to Schubert's "Great" C-Major Symphony.

9. Finson considers this the "recapitulation" of the principal theme (*Orchestral Composition*, pp. 43ff.).

10. Akio Mayeda's thought-provoking study of the sketches for Op. 38 stresses Schumann's multidimensional handling of form and content in the first movement of the symphony, in particular the deliberate blurring of the functions of the motto and the principal theme (the "Motto-Thema-Doppeldeutigkeit"); see Akio Mayeda, "Die Skizzen Robert Schumanns als stilkritische Erkenntnisquelle," in *Robert Schumann: Ein romantisches Erbe in neuer Forschung*, ed. Robert-Schumann-Gesellschaft Düsseldorf (Mainz, 1984), 120–35.

11. A poem by Adolph Böttger inspired the symphony (see Robert Schumann, *Tagebücher*, vol. 2, *1836–1854*, ed. Gerd Nauhaus [Leipzig, 1987], 143, 510 [n. 446]). It ends with the line "Im Tale blüht der Frühling auf" (In the valley spring bursts forth). Mosco Carner observes that the rhythm of the poem exactly fits the rhythm of the motto ("Orchestral Music," p. 193). The regular, rather short-breathed phrases frequently incorporating harmonic excursions are typical of Schumann's style in the early 1840s (see, e.g., the first movement of the Piano Quintet Op. 44), but the unusually early and conclusive abandonment of the tonic in Op. 38 suggests an extramusical explanation. In a letter to the Berlin conductor Wilhelm Taubert, Schumann provides some details about the poetic idea of the symphony, but then equivocates by stating that the poetic images came to him only after he had written the work: "Könnten Sie Ihrem Orchester beim Spiel etwas Frühlingssehnsucht einwehen; die hatte ich hauptsächlich dabei, als ich sie schrieb im Februar [*sic*] 1841. Gleich den ersten Trompeteneinsatz, möcht' ich, daß er wie aus der Höhe klänge, wie ein Ruf zum Erwachen—in das Folgende der Einleitung könnte ich dann hineinlegen, wie es überall zu grüneln anfängt, wohl gar ein Schmetterling auffliegt, und im Allegro, wie nach und nach alles zusammen kommt, was zum Frühling etwa gehört. Doch das sind Phantasieen, die mir *nach* Vollendung der Arbeit ankamen." (If in performance you could [only] instill some longing for spring into your orchestra; such [longing] was paramount in me

as I wrote [the symphony] in February [*sic*] 1841. Right at the start I would like the first trumpet entry to sound as if from on high, like a call to awaken—in the following bars of the introduction I could then suggest how everything begins to green, even how a butterfly flys up, and in the *allegro* how everything that, let us say, belongs to springtime gradually comes together. But these are fantasies that occurred to me *after* completion of the work.) *Robert Schumann's Leben: Aus seinen Briefen*, ed. Hermann Erler, 2 vols. (Berlin, [1886]), 1:293.

12. Robert Haven Schauffler was the first to draw attention to this reference: *Florestan: The Life and Work of Robert Schumann* (New York, 1945), 399.

13. Robert presented Clara with proof sheets of the first printed orchestral part of Op. 38 on her birthday in 1841: 13 September, the day after their first wedding anniversary. (See Clara's entry in the *Ehetagebuch*, the "marriage diary" that the Schumanns kept jointly [*Tagebücher* 2: 186]. For an English translation of the marriage diary, see *The Marriage Diaries of Robert & Clara Schumann: from their wedding day through the Russia trip*, ed. Gerd Nauhaus, trans. Peter Ostwald [Boston, 1993].)

14. See Linda Correll Roesner, "Schumann's 'Parallel' Forms," *19th-Century Music* 14 (1991): 265–78. The concept of the "double-tonic complex," identified and eloquently presented by Robert Bailey in his studies of Wagner's compositional process (e.g., in the commentary to the Norton Critical Score *Prelude and Transfiguration from Tristan and Isolde* [New York, 1985], 116–21), becomes increasingly important in defining the structure of Schumann's large-scale works, particularly the works composed after 1845. Reinhard Kapp refers to the same phenomenon in Schumann's late works as Schumann's "Bitonalität" and views it as part and parcel of the composer's drive toward total unification (*Spätwerk*, 175–78). In Op. 38 the direction is clearly discernible.

15. Schumann's revision of the pitches of the motto, often cited as an example of the composer's inexperience with orchestration, is rather more complex than is generally acknowledged. The sketches reveal that originally both the introductory motto and the principal theme of the exposition began on D. Schumann later revised the motto/fanfare to begin on B♭ but retained the original pitches of the principal theme. Later still, in a revision undertaken in the autograph score, the composer began the principal theme of the exposition on B♭. Finally, after hearing the work in rehearsal, he reinstated the original pitches of the motto—beginning on D—because when it began on B♭ the sixth and seventh notes, G and A (stopped notes on the natural horns in use at the time), produced a muffled, comic effect. However, the composer retained the revised B♭ opening of the principal theme. The revisions clearly show that the limitations of the natural horns were not the only factors that influenced Schumann's conception of the motto theme. Some kind of interplay between B♭ and D seems to have emerged early in the compositional process. This leads one to question the propriety of "restoring" the "original" B♭ opening of the fanfare simply because it can be played on the valve horn without difficulty (Gustav Mahler and, in our own time, Erich Leinsdorf experimented with this).

16. *Tagebücher* 3:184, 192–93.

17. However, he made a halfhearted attempt to interest the publisher Peters in the work in 1843. See Rufus Hallmark, "The Sketches for *Dichterliebe*," *19th-Century Music* 1 (1977): 133.

18. A discussion of the symphony in the context of Schumann's late works appears in Linda Correll Roesner, "Ästhetisches Ideal und sinfonische Gestalt: die

d-Moll-Sinfonie um die Jahrhundertmitte," in *Schumann in Düsseldorf: Werke, Texte, Interpretationen*, ed. Bernhard R. Appel (Mainz, 1993), 55–71.

19. In a note on the verso of the title page of the first edition, Schumann called attention to the period of time that had elapsed between Op. 120's origin and its publication. Apparently he attempted at that time to have the symphony renumbered (as No. 2) in accordance with its chronological position, but the publisher refused (unpublished letter of 21 April 1853 from Breitkopf & Härtel to Schumann, in Krakow, Biblioteka Jagielonska; copy in Düsseldorf, Robert-Schumann-Forschungsstelle). See the preface to my edition of the symphony (Edition Eulenburg, forthcoming 1997).

20. A score of the "1841" version—actually a conflation of both versions—was edited by Johannes Brahms and Franz Wüllner and published by Breitkopf & Härtel in 1891 as a supplement to the old Schumann Gesamtausgabe (series 1, no. 4a). In 1982 C. F. Peters published an edition prepared by the conductor Marc Andreae (available in rental only). In recent years the 1841 version of the work has been performed by major orchestras (e.g., the London Philharmonic under Kurt Masur, the Cincinnati Orchestra under Jesús López-Cobos in Andrae's edition). A critical edition of the 1841 score will appear in *Robert Schumann: Neue Ausgabe sämtlicher Werke* (Mainz, 1991).

21. The idea of a symphony in one movement was part of Schumann's initial conception of work, as can be seen in Clara Schumann's entry for 31 May 1841 in the *Ehetagebuch*: "[Robert] hat gestern eine Symphonie wieder begonnen, welche aus einem Satze bestehen, jedoch Adagio und Finale enthalten soll" (Yesterday [Robert] again began a symphony, which [will] consist of one movement, but which will nonetheless contain [an] *adagio* and [a] Finale) (*Tagebücher* 2:166).

22. Mendelssohn's Symphony No. 3 in A Minor Op. 56, completed in January 1842 and first performed in March 1842, was also intended to be played without breaks between the movements, but unlike Schumann's Op. 120, the individual movements are complete entities. Schumann's 1843 review of Mendelssohn's Op. 56 (*Neue Zeitschrift für Musik* 18, no. 39 [15 May 1843]: 155–56) clearly indicates his preoccupation with the ideal of total unity: "In der Grundlage zeichnet sich die Symphonie Mendelssohn's noch durch den innigen Zusammenhang aller vier Sätze aus; selbst die melodische Führung der [*sic*] Hauptthema's in den vier verschiedenen ist eine verwandte; man wird dies auf eine erste flüchtige Vergleichung herausfinden. So bildet sie denn mehr als irgend eine andere Symphonie auch ein engverschlungenes Ganze; Charakter, Tonart, Rhythmus weichen in den verschiedenen Sätzen nur wenig von einander ab. Der Componist wünscht auch selbst, wie er in einer Vorbemerkung sagt, daß man die vier Sätze ohne lange Unterbrechung hintereinander spiele." (Fundamentally Mendelssohn's symphony is conspicuous for the inner relationship of all four movements; even the melodic contour of the main theme in each of the four separate [movements] is a related [idea]; one will discover this on a first, cursory comparison. Thus, more than any other symphony it also forms a tightly knit whole; character, tonality, rhythm in the different movements vary only slightly from one another. As he mentions in a prefatory remark, the composer even wishes the four movements to be played without long pauses between them.)

23. See the discussion of the violin and piano sonatas Op. 105 and Op. 121 and the Piano Trio Op. 110, in Roesner, "Ästhetisches," 61–67.

24. This theme seems to have had particular significance for Schumann, since reminiscenses of it appear in both of his later symphonies. In Op. 61 the thematic material in the strings in the introduction to the first movement bears a strong resemblance to the motto idea of Op. 120 in mood as well as in thematic contour (see especially mm. 23ff.). In Op. 97 the chromatic extension of the secondary theme of the first movement that appears in the development section at mm. 213ff. is exactly the same as the Op. 120 motto, minus the first three notes. Schumann also employed this theme as a fugue subject in two sketches dating from 1845 or 1846 (see Roesner, "Ästhetisches," p. 60). Eric Sams, drawing on a comment that Schumann wrote in mid-March 1841 in the *Ehetagebuch* that his next symphony would be called "Clara" and that in it he would portray her with flutes, oboes, and harps (see *Tagebücher* 2:154), suggests that the theme may be an encipherment of the name Clara ("Schumann and the Tonal Analogue," in *Robert Schumann: The Man and His Music*, ed. Alan Walker [London, 1972], 400).

25. This contrapuntal combination was not in the 1841 version of the work.

26. Reinhard Kapp suggests that Liszt's hearing of Schumann's D Minor Symphony at its December 1841 premiere (Liszt and Clara Schumann performed Liszt's *Hexameron* on the same program) may have influenced his own essays in one-movement form: "Robert Schumann: Sinfonie Nr. 4 d-Moll, Op. 120," *Neue Zeitschrift für Musik* 143 (1982): 55.

27. The repeat signs at the end of the exposition in both first movement and finale were a very late addition to the 1851 autograph score of Op. 120 (**D-B** Mus. ms. autogr. R. Schumann 17), inserted in 1853 when Schumann was readying the score for publication. Their presence is puzzling, since they contradict the structural argument, particularly in the first movement. Did Schumann believe that the heavier orchestration of the 1851 version demanded that the symphony also be made "grander" in length?

28. This drop down a whole step is one of the motives that links the opening movement to the finale. It reappears at the same place—the beginning of the development section—in the finale. A detailed motivic analysis of Op. 120 appears in Egon Voss's "Einführung und Analyse" in the Goldmann-Schott miniature score of Op. 120 (Mainz, 1980), 173ff.

29. See Roesner, "Ästhetisches," pp. 68–69. The 1841 autograph score (**A-Wgm** A-292 [Nachlaß Brahms]) reveals that both passages where the lyric theme appears are on replacement leaves glued to the stubs of the original leaves. This suggests that the contrapuntal combination of the two themes replaced another version of the passage. See also Rufus Hallmark, "A Sketch Leaf for Schumann's D-Minor Symphony," in *Mendelssohn and Schumann: Essays on their Music and its Context*, ed. Jon W. Finson and R. Larry Todd (Durham, NC, 1984), 41.

30. See Voss, "Einführung und Analyse," 176ff.; Kapp, "D-moll," 55; Maria Rika Maniates, "The D Minor Symphony of Robert Schumann," in *Festschrift für Walter Wiora zum 30. December 1966*, ed. Ludwig Finscher and Christoph-Hellmut Mahling (Kassel, 1967), 444ff.

31. Repeats of large blocks of material for structural balance and harmonic color are typical of Schumann in this period of his career; cf. the first movement of Op. 38. Kapp regards the extensive transposed repetition beginning at mm. 175ff. as analogous to the repetition of the exposition in a traditional sonata form ("D-moll," 56).

32. See Voss, "Einführung und Analyse," 194 (Voss considers the *Langsam* introduction/transition to be one of the main elements of recapitulation); Kapp, "D-moll," 55ff.

33. The earliest work to which I have been able to trace it is the F-minor *Concert sans orchestre* Op. 14 (1836), in the Quasi Variazioni on an Andantino of Clara Wieck (variation 4, mm. 16ff.). It appears in Schumann's unpublished *Brautbuch*—a notebook he kept during the period of his engagement to Clara Wieck and inscribed to her—with the date 20 October 1839 and the remark "klang mir schön" (sounded beautiful to me). Other works in which the melodic gesture appears include the third movement of the String Quartet Op. 41, No. 1 (movement 1, mm. 6ff.); the Piano Concerto Op. 54 (movement 2, mm. 11ff.; movement 3, mm. 255ff.); the Romanze (mm. 45ff.) of the Concerto for Four Horns and Orchestra Op. 86; both sonatas for violin and piano (Op. 105, movement 3, mm. 76ff.; Op. 121, movement 1, mm. 224ff.), and the C-Major Symphony Op. 61 (see below).

34. The large forms include the String Quartets Op. 41; Piano Quintet Op. 44, and Piano Quartet Op. 47; Piano Concerto Op. 54 (first movement composed as an independent fantasy in 1841, the other movements added in 1845), and the oratorio *Das Paradies und die Peri* Op. 50. Schumann may have employed contrapuntal discipline as an aid in combating the mental depression that had all but incapacitated him since returning from a concert tour to Russia in May 1844; see *Tagebücher* III, 378ff., and Peter Ostwald, *Schumann: The Inner Voices of a Musical Genius* (Boston, 1985), pp. 191ff. *Tagebücher* 2:402 (in an appendix to Tagebuch 18): "Erst vom Jr. 1845 an, von wo ich anfing alles im Kopf zu erfinden und auszuarbeiten, hat sich eine ganz andere Art zu componiren zu entwickeln begonnen." (Not until 1845, at which time I began to conceive and to work out everything in my head, did an entirely different manner of composition begin to develop.)

35. Anthony Newcomb discusses this thematic evolution in detail: "Once More 'Between Absolute and Program Music': Schumann's Second Symphony," *19th-Century Music* 7 (1984): 233–50.

36. "Eine tiefe Klage um dich." Robert and Clara Schumann, *Briefwechsel: Kritische Gesamtausgabe*, ed. Eva Weissweiler, 2 vols. to date (Basel, Frankfurt-am-Main, 1984–), 1:126. Op. 17 was composed in 1836 during the period when Robert Schumann and Clara Wieck were competely cut off from one another by Clara's overpossessive father, prohibited even from exchanging letters. On Schumann's "novelistic"content, see Linda Correll Roesner, "Tonal Strategy and Poetic Content in Schumann's C-Major Symphony, Op. 61," in *Probleme der symphonischen Tradition im 19. Jahrhundert: Internationales Musikwissenschaftliches Colloquium Bonn 1989*, ed. Siegfried Kross with Marie Luise Maintz (Tutzing, 1990), 295–305.

37. See Roesner, "Parallel," 273ff.; Charles Rosen, *The Classical Style: Haydn, Mozart, Beethoven* (New York, 1971), 452.

38. Cf. a similar symbolic use of C major in the *Davidsbündlertänze* Op. 6, discussed in Roger Fiske, "A Schumann Mystery," *Musical Times* 105 (1964): 577–78, and Peter Ostwald, *Schumann*, 131.

39. Cf. the finale of Beethoven's Fifth Symphony. In a letter of 2 April 1849 to the Hamburg music director D. G. Otten, Schumann referred to the circumstances under which he wrote Op. 61: "Die Symphonie schrieb ich im Dezember 1845 noch halb krank; mir ist's, als müßte man ihr dies anhören. Erst im letzten

Satz fing ich an mich wieder zu fühlen; wirklich wurde ich auch nach Beendigung des ganzen Werkes wieder wohler. Sonst aber, wie gesagt, erinnert sie mich an eine dunkle Zeit." (I wrote the symphony in December 1845 when I was still half sick; it seems to me that one must hear this in it. Not until [writing] the last movement did I begin to feel myself again; actually, after finishing the entire work my health did improve. But otherwise, as I said, it reminds me of a dark time.) Robert Schumann, *Briefe: Neue Folge,* ed. F. Gustav Jansen (Leipzig, 1904), 300 (see also pp. 262, 319). Newcomb, "Once More," pp. 234ff. discusses the "plot archtype" of Op. 61 and its perception by various writers. Op. 61 was one of Clara's favorite works, as she wrote in her diary after a performance of the symphony in Zwickau in July 1847: "Mich erwärmt und begeistert dies Werk ganz besonders, weil ein kühner Schwung, eine tiefe Leidenschaft darin, wie in keinem andern von Roberts Werken! ein ganz besonderer Charakter und eine ganz andre Emfindung waltet hier vor, als z.B. in der 'Peri.' . . . Diese beiden Werke gehören jedes in seiner Art zu meinen liebsten musikalischen Genüssen." (This work in particular enthuses and enraptures me because it contains a bold dash, a deep passion as in none of Robert's other works! An entirely distinct character and an entirely different feeling prevail here, than, for example, in the 'Peri.' . . . These two works, each in their own way, number among my most treasured musical pleasures.) Berthold Litzmann, *Clara Schumann: Ein Künstlerleben: Nach Tagebüchern und Briefen,* 3 vols., 2d ed. (Leipzig, 1906), vol. 2, *Ehejahre,* 135.

40. The symphony bears a dedication to King Oskar I of Sweden and Norway. The monarch acknowledged the dedication with the gift of a silver snuff box.

41. In the Fantasie, E♭ major was the "diversionary" key of the first movement (see Roesner, "Parallel," 273–78). The use of E♭ major as a diversion in the Fantasie almost certainly was in the composer's mind when he deployed the key in a similar role in the C-Major Symphony (secondary area of the exposition of the first movement; several points of articulation in the scherzo; false tonic of the *adagio*; a major point of articulation in the finale, mm. 280ff., where an interim version of the *An die ferne Geliebte* theme enters after three rhetorical pauses).

42. Analysis of Op. 17, movt. III appears in Roesner, "Parallel," 276–78; analysis of Op. 61, movt. III in Roesner, "Tonal Strategy," 300–301.

43. Note, e.g., the none-too-subtle references to the finale of Beethoven's Ninth symphony at mm. 410ff. and especially mm. 544ff. ("alle Menschen"). Detailed analyses of the finale appear in Newcomb, "Once More," 243–48; Carl Dahlhaus, "Studien zu romantischen Symphonien," in *Jahrbuch des Staatlichen Instituts für Musikforschung Preußischer Kulturbesitz,* ed. Dagmar Droysen (Berlin, 1973), 110–19; Roesner, "Tonal Strategy," 301–05. Schumann's sketches for the movement are discussed in Jon W. Finson, "The Sketches for the Fourth Movement of Schumann's Second Symphony, Op. 61," *Journal of the American Musicological Society* 39 (1986): 143–68.

44. In Schumann's autograph score (**D-B** Mus. ms. autogr. R. Schumann 12) only the fourth movement is titled: "Im Character der Begleitung einer feierlichen Ceremonie" (In the character of an accompaniment to a solemn ceremony)—a title that has occasioned endless speculation in the Schumann literature with regard to which particular ceremony is being depicted. (A summary of the literature and an interpretation of the extant evidence appears in *Robert Schumann: Neue Ausgabe sämtlicher Werke. 3 Symphonie op. 97,* ed. Linda Correll Roesner

[Mainz, 1995], 179–182.) A hitherto-unpublished letter (ibid., p. 179) from Schumann to the Konzertdirection Köln, however, indicates that Schumann wished a program describing the pictorial content of each of the movements to be distributed at the symphony's second performance, in Köln on 25 February 1851 (the program apparently has not survived). Reinhard Kapp, in his commentary ("Einführung und Analyse") to the Goldmann-Schott miniature score of Op. 97 (Mainz 1981, 190) suggests that a review in the *Rheinische Musik-Zeitung* of the Düsseldorf premiere—actually a programmatic interpretation of the individual movements, providing each with a Rhineland scenario—originated in Schumann's inner circle and was authorized by the composer (see the facsimile, ibid., 189).

45. Letter of 19 March 1851 to the firm of N. Simrock, in Erler, *Robert Schumann's Leben* 2:138–39.

46. *Tagebücher* 3:539, 544; Litzmann, *Clara Schumann* 2:227; *Tagebücher* 3:544. The fourth, expanded edition of Wilhelm Josef von Wasielewski's *Robert Schumann: Eine Biographie*, ed. Waldemar von Wasielewski (Leipzig, 1906), 455, 458, is apparently the source of the account that Schumann was present at the archbishop's elevation to cardinal. The reviewer J. C. H., writing in *Signale für die musicalische Welt* 9, no. 8 (February 1851): 74, called the fourth movement a "halo floating over the whole"; Theodor Uhlig, in an extensive review of the published symphony (*Neue Zeitschrift für Musik* 36, nos. 11 and 12 [12, 19 March 1852]: 117–20, 129–33), found the church music character of the fourth movement disturbing and inappropriate for the "secular" symphony, opining that although Schumann's intent was not to depict a "literal elevation of the soul," the composer had nonetheless "entered the delicate sphere of aesthetic speculation" (p. 132).

47. Analyses of Op. 97 appear in Peter Gülke, "Zur Rheinischen Sinfonie," *Musik-Konzepte: Sonderband Robert Schumann* 2 (December, 1982): 237–53; Reinhard Kapp, "Einführung und Analyse," 207–32. Schumann's sketches for Op. 97 are discussed in Roesner, *Studies* 1:204–76, and in the Appendix to *Robert Schumann: Neue Ausgabe sämtlicher Werke. 3. Symphonie op. 97*, 287–302. A complete facsimile of the draft (**F-Pc** Ms. 329, Ms. 334) is included as a supplement to this edition.

48. A rather blatant allusion to the entrance of the horns in the tonic over a dominant pedal in the recapitulation of the first movement of Beethoven's *Eroica*. Other allusions to the *Eroica* in Op. 97 include the key (E♭ major), the triple meter, and the prominence of the perfect fourth.

49. Schumann's revisions in the recapitulation of the first movement of Op. 97 are discussed in Roesner, *Studies* 1:241–45.

50. See also Donald Francis Tovey, *Essays in Musical Analysis*, vol. 2, *Symphonies (II), Variations and Orchestral Polyphony* (London, 1935), 55.

51. **F-Pc** Ms. 329, fol. 10r.

52. Cf. the use in Op. 61 of the theme of the *adagio espressivo* as the second subject in the exposition of the finale and its subsequent development.

53. This A♭-minor–B-major progression is preserved in the fourth movement, since A♭ minor is suggested by the plagal cadence that precedes the sudden emergence of B major. In the A♭-minor appearance of the principal theme in the development section of the first movement, the ascending sixth of the theme's second bar becomes a minor sixth for the first time, a form in which it will not be heard again until the beginning of the fourth movement. This is another subtle link in the symphony's cumulative form.

54. See note 2.

55. Schumann shares this approach with Mahler. See Reinhard Kapp's discussion of structural solutions in Schumann's symphonies reexamined and reconstructed in Mahler's symphonies: "Schumann-Reminiszenzen bei Mahler," *Musik-Konzepte Sonderband Gustav Mahler* (July 1989): 325–61.

Selected Bibliography

Andreae, Marc. "Die vierte Symphonie Robert Schumanns, ihre Fassungen, ihre Interpretationsprobleme." In *Robert Schumann: Ein romantisches Erbe in neuer Forschung,* ed. Robert-Schumann-Gesellschaft Düsseldorf, 35–41. Mainz, 1984.

Boetticher, Wolfgang. *Robert Schumann: Einführung in Persönlichkeit und Werk.* Berlin, 1941.

———. *Robert Schumann in seinen Schriften und Briefen.* Berlin, 1942.

Carner, Mosco. "The Orchestral Music." In *Schumann: A Symposium,* ed. Gerald Abraham, 176–244. London, 1952.

Dahlhaus, Carl. "Studien zu romantischen Symphonien." *Jahrbuch des Staatlichen Instituts für Musikforschung Preußischer Kulturbesitz 1972* (1973): 104–19.

Edler, Arnfried. *Robert Schumann und seine Zeit.* Laaber, 1982.

———. "Ton und Zyklus in der Symphonik Schumanns." In *Probleme der symphonischen Tradition im 19. Jahrhundert: Internationales Musikwissenschaftliches Colloquium Bonn 1989,* ed. Siegfried Kross with Marie Luise Maintz, 187–202. Tutzing, 1990.

Finson, Jon W. *Robert Schumann and the Study of Orchestral Composition: The Genesis of the First Symphony, Op. 38.* Oxford, 1989.

———. "Schumann, Popularity, and the Ouverture, Scherzo, und Finale, Opus 52." *Musical Quarterly* 69 (1983): 1–26.

———. "The Sketches for Robert Schumann's C Minor Symphony." *Journal of Musicology* 1 (1982): 395–418.

———. "The Sketches for the Fourth Movement of Schumann's Second Symphony, Op. 61." *Journal of the American Musicological Society* 39 (1986): 143–68.

Gülke, Peter. "Zur Rheinischen Sinfonie." *Musik-Konzepte Sonderband Robert Schumann* 2 (December 1982): 237–53.

Hallmark, Rufus. "A Sketch Leaf for Schumann's D-Minor Symphony." In *Mendelssohn and Schumann: Essays on Their Music and Its Context,* ed. Jon W. Finson and R. Larry Todd, 40–51. Durham, NC, 1984.

Kapp, Reinhard. "Lobgesang." In *Neue Musik und Tradition: Festschrift Rudolf Stephan zum 65. Geburtstag,* ed. Josef Kuckertz, Helga de la Motte-Heber, Christian Martin Schmidt, and Wilhelm Seidel, 239–49. Laaber, 1990.

———. "Das Orchester Schumanns." *Musik-Konzepte Sonderband Robert Schumann* 2 (December 1982): 191–236.

———. "Robert Schumann: Sinfonie Nr. 4 d-Moll, Op. 120." *Neue Zeitschrift für Musik* 143/6–7 (1982): 54–56.

———. "Schumann-Reminiszenzen bei Mahler." *Musik-Konzepte Sonderband Gustav Mahler* (July 1989): 325–61.

———. *Studien zum Spätwerk Robert Schumanns*. Tutzing, 1984.

———. "Tempo und Charakter in der Musik Schumanns." In *Schumanns Werke: Text und Interpretation,* ed. Robert-Schumann-Gesellschaft Düsseldorf, 193–222. Mainz, 1987.

Lichtenhahn, Ernst. "Sinfonie als Dichtung: Zum geschichtlichen Ort von Schumanns 'Rheinischer.'" In *Schumanns Werke: Text und Interpretation,* ed. Robert-Schumann-Gesellschaft Düsseldorf, 17–27. Mainz, 1987.

Mayeda, Akio. "Aspekte der Schumannschen Instrumentation: Am Beispiel der ersten Sinfonie, Op. 38." In *Festschrift Hans Conradin,* ed. V. Kalisch, 83–96. Bern, 1983.

———. *Robert Schumanns Weg zur Symphonie.* Zürich, 1992.

———. "Die Skizzen Robert Schumanns als stilkritische Erkenntnisquelle." In *Robert Schumann: Ein romantisches Erbe in neuer Forschung,* ed. Robert-Schumann-Gesellschaft Düsseldorf, 119–39. Mainz, 1984.

Nauhaus, Gerd. "Final-Lösungen in der Symphonik Schumanns." In *Probleme der symphonischen Tradition im 19. Jahrhundert: Internationales Musikwissenschaftliches Colloquium Bonn 1989,* ed. Siegfried Kross with Marie Luise Maintz, 307–20. Tutzing, 1990.

Newcomb, Anthony. "Once More `Between Absolute and Program Music': Schumann's Second Symphony." *19th-Century Music* 7 (1984): 233–50.

Oechsle, Siegfried. "Schubert, Schumann und die Symphonie nach Beethoven." In *Probleme der symphonischen Tradition im 19. Jahrhundert: Internationales Musikwissenschaftliches Colloquium Bonn 1989,* ed. Siegfried Kross with Marie Luise Maintz, 279–93. Tutzing, 1990.

Ostwald, Peter. *Schumann: The Inner Voices of a Musical Genius.* Boston, 1985.

Roesner, Linda Correll. "Ästhetisches Ideal und sinfonische Gestalt: Die d-Moll-Sinfonie um die Jahrhundertmitte." In *Schumann in Düsseldorf: Werke, Texte, Interpretationen,* ed. Bernhard R. Appel, 55–71. Mainz, 1993.

———. "Einige quellen- und textkritische Bemerkungen zur B-Dur-Sinfonie Op. 38." In *Schumanns Werke: Text und Interpretation,* ed. Mayeda and Niemöller 89–100. Mainz, 1987.

———. "Studies in Schumann Manuscripts: With Particular Reference to Sources Transmitting Instrumental Works in the Large Forms." Ph.D. dissertation, New York University. 2 vols. 1973.

———. "Tonal Strategy and Poetic Content in Schumann's C-major Symphony, Op. 61." In *Probleme der symphonischen Tradition im 19. Jahrhundert: Internationales Musikwissenschaftliches Colloquium Bonn 1989,* ed. Siegfried Kross with Marie Luise Maintz, 295–305. Tutzing, 1990.

Sams, Eric. "Schumann and the Tonal Analogue." In *Robert Schumann: The Man and His Music,* ed. Alan Walker, 390–405. London, 1972.

Schmid, Manfred Hermann. *Musik als Abbild: Studien zum Werk von Weber, Schumann und Wagner.* Tutzing, 1981.

Schumann, Robert. *Briefe, Neue Folge.* 2d ed. Ed. F. Gustav Jansen. Leipzig, 1904.

———. *Gesammelte Schriften über Musik und Musiker.* 5th ed. Ed. Martin Kreisig. 2 vols. Leipzig, 1914.

———. *3. Symphonie op. 97.* Ed. Linda Correll Roesner. *Robert Schumann: Neue Ausgabe sämtlicher Werke.* Serie I: Orchesterwerke. Werkgruppe 1: Symphonien. Bd. 3. Mainz, 1995.

————. *Robert Schumann's Leben: Aus seinen Briefen.* Ed. Hermann Erler. 2 vols. Berlin, [1886].

————. *Tagebücher.* Vol. 1. *1827–1838.* Ed. Georg Eismann. Leipzig, 1971. Vol. 2. *1836–1854.* Ed. Gerd Nauhaus. Leipzig, 1987. Vol. 3. *Haushaltbücher: 1837–1856.* Ed. Gerd Nauhaus. Leipzig, 1982.

Schumann, Robert, and Clara Schumann. *Briefe und Notizen Robert und Clara Schumanns.* 2d ed. Ed. Siegfried Kross. Bonn, 1982.

————. *Briefwechsel: Kritische Gesamtausgabe.* Ed. Eva Weissweiler with Susanna Ludwig. 2 vols. to date. Basel and Frankfurt am Main, 1984– .

————. *The Marriage Diaries of Robert & Clara Schumann: from their wedding day through the Russia trip.* Ed. Gerd Nauhaus. Trans. Peter Ostwald. Boston, 1993.

Struck, Michael. "Am Rande der 'großen Form': Schumanns Ouvertüren und ihr Verhältnis zur Symphonie (mit besonderer Berücksichtigung der Ouverture zu Shakespeare's *Julius Cäsar* Op. 128." In *Probleme der symphonischen Tradition im 19. Jahrhundert: Internationales Musikwissenschaftliches Colloquium Bonn 1989,* ed. Siegfried Kross with Marie Luise Maintz, 239–78. Tutzing, 1990.

Wasielewski, Wilhelm Josef von. *Robert Schumann: Fine Biographie.* Dresden, 1858. 4th ed., ed. Waldemar von Wasielewski. Leipzig, 1906.

CHAPTER FOUR

Mendelssohn

R. Larry Todd

Felix Mendelssohn's symphonies and concert overtures have long enjoyed a secure position in the nineteenth-century canon, even if some would judge them to inhabit an ethereal realm in the shadow of Beethoven's magisterial oeuvre. But this familiar repertoire affords an insufficient view of Mendelssohn's overall contribution to orchestral music. The standard ten compositions—five symphonies and five overtures (*A Midsummer Night's Dream, Calm Sea and Prosperous Voyage, The Hebrides, The Fair Melusine,* and *Ruy Blas*)—should be augmented by the Trumpet Overture Op. 101 (1826) and the impressive, if studious, group of thirteen early string sinfonie (1821–23) that preceded the abrupt emergence of the composer's mature style in the overture for *A Midsummer Night's Dream* (1826). Three minor occasional works—the March Op. 108 for the painter Peter Cornelius (1841) and two works for wind orchestra, the *Ouvertüre für Harmoniemusik* Op. 24 (1824, rev. 1839) and the *Trauer-Marsch* Op. 103 for Norbert Burgmüller (1836)—require only brief mention. To be sure, Mendelssohn wrote fluently for the orchestra beyond the genres of symphony and the overture, and a discussion of his orchestral music is incomplete without recalling, for example, the pellucid scoring in the finale of the Violin Concerto Op. 64 (1845), the virtuosic treatment of the orchestra in the incidental music to *A Midsummer Night's Dream* (1844),[1] or the carefully calculated orchestration of the fugal textures in the overture to *Elijah* (1847), especially admired by Edward Elgar.[2] Still, the symphony and the independent concert overture were the two orchestral genres in which Mendelssohn excelled, and they are the focus of this chapter.

Student Works: The String Sinfonie

We do not know when Mendelssohn began to write for orchestra. His earliest substantial efforts are the thirteen string symphonies written for performances at the composer's Berlin residence, of which the first datable sinfonia, No. 4, was completed in September 1821. Sinfonia No. 8 (November 1822), was rescored for full orchestra, and thus it stands as a kind of Mendelssohnian Symphony No. 0, predating by some two years his Symphony No. 1 in C Minor Op. 11. But Mendelssohn also had occasion to write for full orchestra in his series of singspiele, including *Die Soldatenliebschaft* (1820), *Die beiden Pädagogen* (1821), *Die wandernden Komödianten* (1822), and *Die beiden Neffen* (1823).[3] In *Die beiden Pädagogen*, composed between January and March 1821—presumably a few months before the first string sinfonia—we can examine the twelve-year-old's efforts to manage the complexities of an orchestral score.

This early attempt was a carefully measured and cautious one. From Carl Friedrich Zelter, the director of the Berlin Singakademie, Mendelssohn had received a thorough grounding in figured bass, chorale, canon, and fugue in the Bachian tradition, and had been introduced to the music of Haydn and Mozart as well. By 3 February 1824, the pupil's fifteenth birthday, Zelter could proclaim him a member of the brotherhood of Mozart, Haydn, and Bach. Beethoven, conspicuously absent in this list, was just beginning to influence Mendelssohn significantly.[4] Though the assimilation of Beethoven's music became a crucial issue for the young composer during the 1820s, in 1821 his principal stylistic sources remained the rich contrapuntal heritage of J. S. Bach and the refined classicism of Haydn and Mozart; the latter is especially evident in *Die beiden Pädagogen*, a work that reveals Mendelssohn's intimate knowledge of the Mozart operas, including *The Marriage of Figaro* and *Don Giovanni*.

The overture to *Die beiden Pädagogen* is scored for a Classical doublewind orchestra, supplemented by horns, trumpets, and timpani; the string ensemble is generally divided into four parts, again pointing to eighteenth-century models. Structurally, the overture is cast in a simple ternary sonata-form mold. Its monothematic exposition and false return of the tonic near the beginning of the development suggest Haydn's influence, though a few turns of phrase, including an energetic string passage near the opening, possibly recall the overture to Mozart's *Marriage of Figaro*. Much of the overture is dominated by the strings; the brass and timpani are rarely employed, and the woodwinds only timidly color the neutral string texture, with occasional, brief solos for oboe and clarinet.

By October 1821 Lea Mendelssohn-Bartholdy was able to report that her son had recently composed six symphonies "nach Art der Alten, ohne Blaseinstrumente," that is, "in the old manner," for strings alone;[5] seven additional string symphonies were completed by the end of 1823.[6]

Eyewitness accounts by the theorists Heinrich Dorn and Adolf Bernhard Marx, who attended performances of the sinfonie, reveal a second obsolescent feature in their performance practice: they were evidently heard with Mendelssohn providing a continuo accompaniment at the keyboard,[7] recalling the Baroque practice that had been observed as recently as the 1790s, when Haydn directed his "London" symphonies from the keyboard.

Some scholars have argued that the impressionable Mendelssohn was emulating the eighteenth-century North German symphonic school of C. P. E. Bach,[8] whose string symphonies were still being performed by Zelter in Berlin.[9] Several stylistic features of Mendelssohn's sinfonie indeed suggest a debt to Emanuel Bach, often overlooked because of the more decisive influence of his father. Among these features we may cite forceful unison openings with marked disjunct motion (nos. 2, 3, 5, 6, 7); unpredictable interruptions, sometimes accompanied by sudden shifts in dynamics (5, 7); and extended sequential passages and suspension chains (several examples)—all common features of Emanuel Bach's four-part string symphonies, including the set of six published in 1773 (Wotquenne 182). Other "archaic" features of Mendelssohn's sinfonie include the severe monothematicism and spinning out of thematic material from an initial motivic kernel; crossing of the violin parts; preference for a three-movement plan (sometimes with the second and third movements linked by a transition or *attacca* sign); trio-sonata textures in the slow movements; and, in the first few sinfonie, the occasional use of binary as opposed to fully fledged ternary sonata form.

A good example of Mendelssohn's revival of an antiquated style is the slow movement of No. 2, where he establishes a trio-sonata texture not unlike a passage from Emanuel Bach's third *Prussian* Sonata (Wot. 48): the two have a similar treble figure imitated one bar later in the same register against a bass line (Ex. 4.1). But Mendelssohn's movement is a veritable canonic study, and here the irrepressible influence of J. S. Bach emerges. In the first part of the movement (mm. 1–19) a more or less strict canon unfolds in the violins. In the middle part (mm. 20–44) the canonic pair shifts to the viola and bass; in addition, the mirror-inverted form of the subject now appears against its "prime" version. In the final portion (mm. 45–63), the prime and mirror are contraposed in the violins, and at the compressed space of half a measure.

By 1821 the writing of fugues had become an avocation for the twelve-year-old; as he later admitted to J. C. Lobe, Mendelssohn preferred the "finely woven voices, the polyphonic movement, and here my early studies in counterpoint with Zelter and my study of Bach may have had their principal impact."[10] In the sinfonie, Mendelssohn refined his contrapuntal skills in four- and five-part writing. No fewer than eight sinfonie contain fugues or fugato passages (5–9, 11, 12, and the unnum-

EXAMPLE 4.1a. Mendelssohn. *Sinfonia* No. 2 in D Major, movt. 2, mm.1–4

EXAMPLE 4.1b. C. P. E. Bach, Sonata in E Major, Wot. 48/3, movt. 2, mm. 1–3

bered *Sinfoniesatz*), often in an erudite display. Not only do the fugal subjects divulge a familiarity with Bach's *Well-Tempered Clavier* and common Baroque fugal subjects (e.g., the finale of No. 12, similar to Handel's "And with His Stripes" in *Messiah*), but they are deployed in a range of learned, academic devices, including augmentation, stretto, and mirror inversion. What is more, Mendelssohn also explored fugues with multiple subjects—as "though the composer officially wished to demonstrate how diligently he had studied and mastered his subject through counterpoint."[11]

Three fugal subjects (11:3, 12:1, and the *Sinfoniesatz*) illustrate Mendelssohn's full immersion in Bachian chromatic counterpoint. Two (12, *Sinfoniesatz*) are coupled with slow introductions in dotted-rhythmic style, in a revival of the French overture. On the other hand, most of the remaining fugues are incorporated into sonata-form or rondo finales (5:3, 6:3, 7:3, 8:4, 11:4), and offer formal amalgams whose models are found in the fugal finales of Haydn and Mozart. Truly astonishing is Mendelssohn's variety of formal solutions for these fugal finales. No. 11:3, in sonata form, may be taken as one example. It begins with a robust, compact figure in F minor built up into a clearly articulated eight-bar period. To this is then added some imitative counterpoint, a foreshadowing of the subsequent fugal exposition that begins in earnest in measure 41 after a pause on the dominant. In a nod to Baroque counterpoint, Mendelssohn presents a five-part fugato on the austere subject of a descending chromatic tetrachord. But further on in the exposition, after the modulation to the mediant (m. 107), we hear a lyrical contrasting theme in a homophonic style, as the movement resumes its sonata-form plan by alluding to the Classical style. At the end of the exposition, the fugal subject is reemployed as the closing theme in the mediant. Then, in the development, Mendelssohn unexpectedly introduces a fresh, five-part fugal subject. Not surprisingly, the new subject is designed to combine with the original fugal subject, a task Mendelssohn accomplishes in the recapitulation.

Such a hybrid of fugue and sonata has its roots in a distinguished eighteenth-century tradition (e.g., Haydn's String Quartets Op. 20 and Symphonies Nos. 13 and 70, and Mozart's String Quartet, K. 387). The *ne plus ultra* of this tradition, of course, was the finale of Mozart's "Jupiter" Symphony, well known to Mendelssohn, who heard a performance in Leipzig in 1821. In the finale of Sinfonia No. 8, he attempted to imitate Mozart's consummate blending of fugal and sonata-form principles by devising four distinct thematic subjects that could play various roles in a ternary sonata form yet could be combined in a tour de force coda.[12]

Given his conservative training, Mendelssohn's attraction to the "Jupiter" Symphony is understandable enough, though in some works his emulation of Mozart was not limited to contrapuntal techniques. Indeed, several sinfonie suggest that the high Classical style of Mozart and Haydn acted as a kind of counterweight to the domineering influence of J. S. Bach. Thus, in Sinfonia No. 6 Mendelssohn introduced a minuet, thereby expanding the three-movement pattern of the earlier symphonies to the Classical paradigm of four movements. Occasionally, he alluded more or less clearly to particular Classical models: thus, the minuet of No. 7 resembles that of Haydn's String Quartet in D Minor Op. 76, No. 2; and in the finale of No. 6, Mendelssohn appears to have turned to the finale of Mozart's "Prague" Symphony. Somewhat more novel effects obtain in Nos. 9 and 11, where Mendelssohn introduced scherzi in lieu of minuets, and where he incorporated two Swiss melodies he had recorded during his 1822 sojourn in Switzerland. In the scherzo of No. 9 a yodel melody (trio, marked "La Suisse") and rustic drone effects bring the music stylistically close to the sound world of Beethoven's "Pastoral" Symphony. In the scherzo of No. 11 (*Schweizerlied*), Mendelssohn added a percussion complement of timpani, triangle, and cymbals, delaying their entrance, however, until toward the end of the movement, where they recall Haydn's employment of a Janissary style in the slow movement of the "Military" Symphony.

Sinfonie Nos. 1–7 are scored for four-part strings, though in Nos. 6 and 7 Mendelssohn tentatively began to work with a five-part texture by dividing the cello and double bass. In Nos. 9–11 he explored five-part textures by dividing the violas instead of the bass; and in No. 9, by dividing the violas and the bass line, he achieved a six-part texture. This progression from four to five and six parts shows his proclivity toward increased complexity, a trend that culminated in the 1825 finale of the Octet—another blending of sonata and fugue, one that Mendelssohn prescribed was to be performed in a symphonic style.

The string sinfonie represent the summation of Mendelssohn's student work with Zelter. Two traditions—Bachian counterpoint, with its involved, chromatic part writing, and the high Classical style of Haydn and Mozart, with its balanced, articulated phrase structures—are juxtaposed in these youthful efforts, yielding curious stylistic admixtures. But the two traditions continued to shape the evolving style of Mendelssohn, whom Schumann labeled the Mozart of the nineteenth century, and whom we recognize for signal contributions to the Bach revival.

Symphony No. 1 in C Minor Op. 11

Mendelssohn's first published symphony, Op. 11 in C Minor, did not appear in print until 1834, although the autograph dates from ten years before (March 1824) and there is titled sinfonia 13, demonstrating that he had originally viewed the work as an extension of the string symphonies. Opus 11 was performed at the Mendelssohn home on 14 November 1824 (the birthday of the composer's sister, Fanny) and in 1825, and again in Leipzig in 1827, when it was reviewed by G. W. Fink, editor of the influential *Allgemeine musikalische Zeitung*.[13] It was in the portfolio of compositions Mendelssohn brought in 1829 to London, where it was heard at a Philharmonic concert on 25 May, with a newly made orchestration of the scherzo from the Octet substituting for the minuet. In 1830 Mendelssohn released a piano duet arrangement of the work, and in 1834 the parts appeared.

The first symphony is an energetic work in which Mendelssohn strove to break away from the academic character of the string symphonies (though the conspicuous fugato in the development and coda of the finale is one exception to this observation). The dynamic opening theme, with its dramatic interruptions and accentuated diminished-seventh sonorities, suggests the storm music from Weber's *Der Freischütz*, the Berlin premiere of which Mendelssohn had attended in 1821, as well as the influence of Beethoven, increasingly evident in Mendelssohn's music of the mid 1820s. The serene *andante* shows an exploration of mediant relationships; its monothematic structure and balanced phrases recall the late symphonies of Mozart and Haydn. Of special note is the menuetto, barred in $\frac{6}{4}$ meter, which Mendelssohn borrowed from his Viola Sonata of February 1824. For the symphony he extensively revised the minuet and prepared a new trio, brimming with the new enthusiasm he must have felt for Beethoven's music. The scherzo of Beethoven's Fifth, with its celebrated transition to the finale, served as a model for Mendelssohn's transition to the return of the minuet, as the softly dampened string textures in A♭ and *pianissimo* timpani strokes of Example 4.2 clearly reveal. And the finale of Op. 11, with its resilient concluding stretto in C major, again seems inspired by Beethoven's symphony.

EXAMPLE 4.2. Symphony No. 1 in C Minor Op. 11, movt. 3 (Trio), mm. 86–92

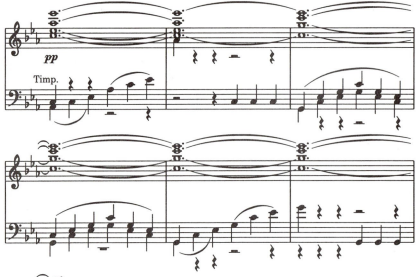

The "Reformation" Symphony:
No. 5 in D Major Op. 107

Mendelssohn did not return to the symphony until 1829, when he began work on what he called his *Kirchensinfonie*, that is, the "Reformation" Symphony. (There is some evidence that he composed two toy symphonies in 1827 and 1828, but these are lost.[14]) The stimulus for the new symphony was the tercentenary of the Augsburg Confession, celebrated throughout Protestant Germany on 25 June 1830. By May 1830 Mendelssohn had completed the work, but for a variety of reasons that remain unclear, it was not performed in June. Some two years later, in 1832, F.-A. Habeneck rehearsed the symphony at the Conservatoire in Paris, but Mendelssohn failed to achieve a French performance, and the premiere was postponed until 15 November 1832 in Berlin, after he had effected some revisions. Then, for reasons again unclear, Mendelssohn rejected the symphony as a "jugendliche Jugendarbeit" (childlike juvenilia) and in 1838 instructed his friend Julius Rietz to burn the manuscript.[15] But the work was preserved and published posthumously in 1868 as Symphony No. 5 Op. 107, and thus, like Schubert's "Unfinished" Symphony (published in 1867), entered the symphonic repertoire only in the second half of the nineteenth century.

The "Reformation" Symphony was Mendelssohn's first symphonic foray into programmatic music. Judith Silber Ballan has demonstrated how it shows the unmistakable influence of Beethoven and responds to the critical writings of A. B. Marx, who during the 1820s developed the thesis that Beethoven had brought instrumental music inexorably to program music and that music could not only represent fundamental ideas (*Grundideen*) but also depict a kind of narrative.[16] Mendelssohn's symphony impresses as a celebration of the Reformation and of Luther's "triumph" over the abuses of the Catholic Church. (The scherzo-like second movement is the one whose programmatic significance is at best vague, and that remains the weak link in the chain of four movements.) The affirming finale, a kind of symphonic fantasy on the Lutheran chorale "Ein' feste Burg ist unser Gott," offers a parallel to the celebratory finale of Beethoven's Ninth. (One other tie to the Ninth is Mendelssohn's use, at the end of the third movement, of a thematic recall from the first.) The mournful slow movement of the "Reformation" Symphony, with its descending sigh figures and recitative-like passages, brings to mind the slow-movement lament of Beethoven's Piano Sonata Op. 110. And finally, the opposition of two distinct styles of music in the outer movements— Palestrinian counterpoint to suggest Catholic church music, and the homophonic chorale to suggest Protestant congregational worship—resembles in a way Beethoven's opposition of French and English music in *Wellington's Victory*, a composition, curiously enough, highly prized by Marx for its narrative strategies.

By citing "Ein' feste Burg," Mendelssohn effectively brought the genre of the symphony near the realm of church music, achieving a generic hybrid that he would explore more extensively in the *Lobgesang* Symphony of 1840. From this perspective the "textless" "Reformation" Symphony bears comparison to the extended series of texted chorale cantatas he composed between 1827 and 1832, several of which were based on standard Protestant hymns, including "Christe, Du Lamm Gottes" (1827), "Vom Himmel hoch" (1831), and "Ach Gott, vom Himmel sieh' darein" (1832). The symphony is related, too, to Mendelssohn's larger-scale psalm settings that followed the chorale cantatas. Four of these (Psalms 42 Op. 42; 95 Op. 46; 114 Op. 51; and 98 Op. 91), unfold a tonal chain with two descending thirds, i–VI–iv–I, the same plan employed in the symphony (D–B♭–g–D). Like the psalms, Mendelssohn treated the "Reformation" Symphony as a unified cycle; perhaps the clearest evidence of this approach is the tonal link between the third movement, in G minor, and the finale, which begins by introducing "Ein' feste Burg" in G major before reestablishing the tonic D major.

The first movement of the "Reformation" contains two specific allusions to Catholic church music that bear further scrutiny (Ex. 4.3). The more celebrated, the Dresden Amen (marked by an ascending line of the fifth), has attracted attention because Wagner later incorporated it in the Grail Theme of *Parsifal* (before Mendelssohn, Karl Loewe and Ludwig Spohr had employed it as emblematic of Catholic church music). The other allusion, in the opening measures (D–E–G–F♯), ties Mendelssohn's symphony to the famous "Jupiter" motive that had been used by Haydn,

EXAMPLE 4.3. Symphony No. 5 ("Reformation") in D Major Op. 107 movt. 1, mm. 33–36

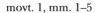
movt. 1, mm. 1–5

Mozart, and Fux in the eighteenth century and by many Baroque composers before them. Its original function had been as a psalm intonation in sacred chant, but by presenting the figure in a rising point of imitation and with carefully controlled dissonance treatment, Mendelssohn probably intended to revive the style of sixteenth-century Palestrinian polyphony, viewed by the nineteenth-century Leipzig jurist Justus Thibaut as embodying church music in its purest form. Not only was Mendelssohn familiar with Thibaut's book *Über Reinheit der Tonkunst* (On purity in music, 1825), but he explored Palestrinian counterpoint in two contemporary motets, *Tu es Petrus* Op. 111 (1827) and the remarkably historicist *Hora est* (1828), for sixteen voices (four choirs) and continuo.

The "Italian" Symphony: No. 4 in A Major Op. 90

Like the "Reformation" Symphony, the "Italian" Symphony failed Mendelssohn's unrelenting critical scrutiny and remained unpublished at his death in 1847; not until 1851 was it issued as Symphony No. 4 Op. 90. It was conceived during the Italian sojourn of 1830 and 1831, though its official premiere, conducted by the composer, was delayed until 13 May 1833, to fulfill a commission by the London Philharmonic. Three additional English performances by Ignaz Moscheles and Cipriano Potter occurred during Mendelssohn's lifetime, but curiously he never authorized a performance on the Continent. Recent research has examined how in July 1834, after the English premiere, Mendelssohn rewrote the last three movements; but when it was published in 1851, the score for the 1833 performance was chosen as the basis of the edition.[17] In short, the "Italian" Symphony we know today does not represent the "Fassung letzter Hand," and a new edition of the work is greatly needed in order to assess Mendelssohn's revisionary zeal and his final intentions for the work.

For Julius Benedict, the symphony was "warmed with the balmy air of a southern clime"; it conveyed no less than the "complete epitome" of Mendelssohn's "varied impressions as experienced during his Italian travel."[18] Surely the bright, resilient opening, in which the theme, doubled in octaves in the violins, is supported by an energetic wind tremolo on the tonic $^6_4$, remains one of Mendelssohn's most vivid scorings. Italianate warmth is felt, too, in the second theme, doubled in thirds (and reinforced at the octave). But the symphony is nevertheless rooted in the Germanic tradition: in letters sent to Berlin from Italy Mendelssohn remained distinctly critical of the music he encountered there. Tovey detected in the opening movement traces of Beethoven's Seventh, and the unexpected intrusion of a fugato in the development—a fugato on a new theme—is characteristic of Mendelssohn's indulgence in Germanic counterpoint.[19]

Of the other movements the second and fourth stand out for their evocative, programmatic qualities. The slow movement, with its chant-like opening intonation and modal flavor (D minor, with lowered seventh scale degree) is heard in an archaic (for 1833) style and almost certainly was intended to evoke a sacred procession such as Mendelssohn witnessed in Italy. (In 1831 he recorded detailed descriptions of Roman Office services during Holy Week, which included the antiphonal chanting of psalms.)[20] Mendelssohn's attempt to write in a *stile antico* was likely influenced by the extraordinary scene of the armored men in the second act of Mozart's *Die Zauberflöte*, where the chorale "Ach Gott vom Himmel sieh' darein" is intoned in unison against a walking bass line and accompaniment in species counterpoint. In Mendelssohn's example, a modally inflected melody is given by the strings against a detached, walking bass line, in simple two-part harmony (Ex. 4.4). Each phrase of the melody is repeated with an expanded wind accompaniment, producing an antiphonal effect. A second, contrasting theme in the dominant major returns us to conventional tonal harmony; the two themes then alternate, yielding the scheme A-B-A-B-A.[21] In the concluding measures Mendelssohn fragments the first phrase of A and allows the movement to conclude with the bass line alone, *pianissimo*, as if to suggest the passing by of the procession, an effect that bears comparison to the close of the "Marche des pèlerins" in Berlioz's nearly contemporaneous *Harold en Italie*.[22]

EXAMPLE 4.4. Symphony No. 4 ("Italian") in A Major Op. 90, movt. 2, mm. 1–5

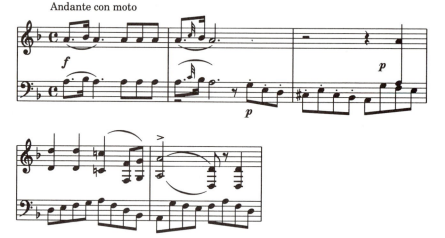

Mendelssohn himself labeled the finale a saltarello, thus divulging the inspiration for the movement to be the popular folk music he heard in Italy; a letter from Rome, dated 17 January 1831, includes this description of the dance: "Later there was dancing, and you should have just seen how Louise Vernet danced the saltarello with her father [Horace Vernet, the French painter]. Whenever she had to stop, just for a moment, to take up the large tambourine, begin beating on it, and relieve us, who could hardly even move our hands any more, then I would have liked to be a painter—this would have made a splendid picture!"[23] A few years later, during her 1839–40 sojourn in Italy, Mendelssohn's sister, Fanny Hensel, also encountered the dance. Her musical impressions of it were preserved in the piano piece "Il Saltarello romano," published in 1846 as Op. 6, No. 1. Its key (A minor), melodic design around the fifth scale degree, and characteristic skips place it stylistically close to the "Italian" Symphony (Ex. 4.5a–b).

According to W. S. Rockstro, who studied composition with Mendelssohn in 1845, the winding, conjunct subject entering in G minor in m. 122 was meant as a tarantella (Ex. 4.5c), a dance traditionally associated with tarantism.[24] Now Mendelssohn would have known the finale of Carl Maria von Weber's Fourth Piano Sonata Op. 70, which, though published

EXAMPLE 4.5a. Fanny Hensel, "Il Saltarello romano" in A Minor Op. 6, No. 4, mm. 1–6

EXAMPLE 4.5b. Mendelssohn, Symphony No. 4 ("Italian") in A Major Op. 90, movt. 4, mm. 7–8

EXAMPLE 4.5c. Mendelssohn, Symphony No. 4 ("Italian") in A Major Op. 90, movt. 4, mm. 122–126

in 1823 without a title, was commonly understood by Weber's circle to represent a tarantella. (Weber's autograph clearly labeled it as such.) Here, for example, is an account by Weber's student Julius Benedict, a close friend of Mendelssohn: "The last movement, a wild fantastic Tarantella with only a few snatches of melody, finished in exhaustion and death. None but Weber himself could give the true picture of this fierce struggle of reason against the demon of insanity which this fine composition so graphically describes."[25] In Mendelssohn's saltarello finale the unexpected intrusion of the tarantella results in a confusion in form that in turn engenders a delightful unpredictability in the music. What begins as a saltarello in A minor gives way to a tarantella in G minor that yields, in the end, not to an unambiguous return of the saltarello but rather to a juxtaposition of the two over the tonic $^6_4$. Just before the *forte* end, Mendelssohn inserts a diminuendo to *pianissimo*, perhaps symbolizing, as Michael Tusa has proposed in his discussion of Weber's finale, not "exhaustion and death" à la Benedict, but rather the "abatement of hysteria" associated with the tarantella. Whatever its programmatic meaning, Mendelssohn's finale impresses as original, vibrant music; one can only wonder why this exemplary score did not measure up to the composer's rigorous standards.

The *Lobgesang* Symphony: No. 2 in B♭ Major Op. 52

After abandoning work on the "Italian" Symphony Mendelssohn gave some thought to composing a symphony in B♭ major, for which a few sketches from around 1838 and 1839 survive.[26] Then, in 1840, he was commissioned to compose a major work for the Leipzig quadricentenary of the invention of moveable type. The *Lobgesang* Symphony Op. 52 eventually emerged as a three-movement orchestral sinfonia (which reused some of the earlier symphonic sketches) joined to nine vocal movements requiring chorus and soloists;[27] the texts, chosen principally from the Bible, concern the praise of God and mankind's progress from darkness to enlightenment (through the dissemination of God's word, its implied agent being the Gutenberg Bible). By introducing texts into the work, Mendelssohn was responding to Beethoven's Ninth Symphony, and we may profitably group the *Lobgesang* with other nineteenth-century texted symphonic experiments such as Berlioz's *Roméo et Juliette* (1839) and Liszt's *Faust* Symphony (1854). But in contrast to Beethoven's celebrated finale, in which an extended, quasi-operatic finale is built up on Schiller's ode, Mendelssohn's "finale" is constructed as a full-fledged cantata on sacred texts. Further, the introduction of texts in the *Lobgesang* enabled Mendelssohn to bridge the gap—more directly than in the "Reformation" Symphony—between the symphony and religious music.

In consultation with his friend Karl Klingemann, Mendelssohn decided to title the new work a *Symphonie-Cantate*, thus acknowledging a new type of generic hybrid. To link the sinfonia and cantata together he designed a recurring trombone invocation. Heard at the very outset of the work, it comprises a step and third spanning two fourths (F–G–F–B♭, and B♭–C–E♭–D, Ex. 4.6) and is related to the psalm intonation, F–G–B♭–A, that Mendelssohn had recently used in his setting of Psalm 42 Op. 42 (1837) and that would have been known to him in transposed form as the "Jupiter" motive. After figuring prominently in the development and close of the first movement, the intonation is worked into the trio of the second movement, where it appears in counterpoint to a freely composed wind chorale, a harbinger that the textless symphony will become a texted cantata. Though absent in the final movement of the sinfonia, *adagio religioso*, this intonation is given new life by the revelation of God's word in the opening choral movement of the cantata ("Alles was Odem hat, lobe den Herrn": All that has breath, praise the Lord). And at the end of the cantata, the trombone intonation is brought back with the opening measures of the symphony to conclude the composition, reaffirming the unity of the whole.

EXAMPLE 4.6. Symphony No. 2 (*Lobgesang*) in B-flat Major Op. 52, movt. 1, mm. 1–2

Maestoso con moto

The overall design of the *Lobgesang* thus comprises a symphony of instrumental praise followed by a cantata that gives vocal utterance to that praise. There are other structural parallels between the textless and texted parts (see Fig. 4.1). The three movements of the sinfonia form a descending tonal chain (B♭–g/G–D) with links between the movements (a short instrumental recitative between 1 and 2; harmonic and melodic

Sinfonia, no. 1

Maestoso	**Allegro**	**Allegretto**	**Andante religioso**
motto	(recitative)	Trio (chorale)	
B♭ — B♭		g / G / g D	

Cantata, nos. 2–10

2			3	4	5 ⌐ 6 ⌐
Allegro	**Moderato**	**Recitative, Allegro**		**Andante**	**Allegro**
motto					
Chorus (organ)	Sopr., Chor.	Tenor		Chorus	Sopr. duet Tenor
B♭ — B♭ g —				g E♭ c	

(tonal descent by thirds)

7	8	9	10	
Allegro	**Chorale**	**Andante**	**Allegro**	**Maestoso**
Chorus (organ)	*Nun danket alle Gott* a cappella, orch.	Sopr./Ten.	Chorus fugue (organ)	motto
D G B♭ — B♭ — B♭				

(reversal of *Sinfonia*)

Figure 4.1. Mendelssohn, Symphony No. 2 (*Lobgesang*) Op. 52. Structural Diagram

ties between 2 and 3). In a similar way, the through-composed cantata presents a highly structured tonal progression, now coordinated with the textual progression from darkness to light as God's word is promulgated. After the initial chorus of praise (No. 2, B♭), the next four numbers inaugurate a tonal descent by thirds, to G minor (Nos. 3 and 4, for tenor and chorus), E♭ major (No. 5, duet for two sopranos), and C minor (No. 6, for tenor). No. 6, cast in Mendelssohn's most dissonant vein, marks the midpoint of the cantata, the turning from darkness to awakening and enlightenment: "Wir wandelten in Finsterniss. Er aber spricht: Wache auf!" (We wandered in the darkness. But He speaks: Awaken!). In a dramatic recitative the question "Hüter, ist die Nacht bald hin?" is posed three times, in successively ascending transpositions. The answer, given by a soprano solo, prepares the lifting of the darkness in the ensuing, radiant D-major chorus (No. 7, "Die Nacht ist vergangen"). In No. 8 Mendelssohn introduces the chorale "Nun danket alle Gott" in G major, first a cappella and then with orchestral accompaniment. Nos. 9 and 10, a duet for soprano and tenor and closing fugal chorus, return us to the tonic B♭ major, and with the final appearance of the trombone intonation, full circle to the opening. Mendelssohn's plan is thus made clear: the tonal descent of Nos. 3–6 to represent mankind's ignorance of the Word is balanced by the enlightening ascent of Nos. 7–9, which reverses the tonal order of the three movements of the sinfonia. (The chorale in No. 8 is a counterpart and textual clarification of the textless chorale melody in the second movement of the sinfonia.)

During Mendelssohn's lifetime the *Lobgesang* remained one of his most popular works, though later its reputation declined considerably, owing in part to its unusual mixture of genres. In many ways, the dramatic structure and large-scale tonal plan of the *Lobgesang* looked forward to the oratorio *Elijah*, while its use of a stylized psalm intonation and responsorial techniques between soloist and chorus recalled Mendelssohn's earlier psalm settings. And its first three movements, though symphonic in character, were nevertheless unlike other German symphonies of the time. Ultimately the generic synthesis of the *Lobgesang* failed to impress the later nineteenth century, held under the sway of the Wagnerian music drama and its synthesis of symphonic and dramatic elements.

The "Scottish" Symphony: No. 3 in A Minor Op. 56

Mendelssohn's remaining symphony, the "Scottish" (No. 3 Op. 56), required some fourteen years from gestation in 1829 to completion in 1842 and publication in 1843 with a dedication to Queen Victoria. (In 1844–45 Mendelssohn took up plans for a new symphony in C major, but was unable to proceed beyond a few pages in score and some sketches.)[28] Its early stage overlapped with that of the "Italian" Symphony, so that a full reconstruction of the chronology of the "Scottish" is difficult.[29] Its inspiration, as the composer revealed in a letter, was a visit to Holyrood Palace in Edinburgh, and its associations with Mary, Queen of Scotland:

> In the deep twilight we went today to the palace where Queen Mary lived and loved. One can see there a little room, with a winding staircase before the door. They climbed up there, found Rizzio in the little room, took him and murdered him in a dark corner three rooms away. The chapel below is now roofless. Grass and ivy thrive there and at the broken altar where Mary was crowned Queen of Scotland. Everything is ruined, decayed, and the clear heavens pour in. I think I have found there the beginning of my "Scottish" Symphony.[30]

As with the "Italian" Symphony, Mendelssohn refrained from providing a programmatic sketch, though a cautious interpretation permits some observations about the second, third, and fourth movements (Ex. 4.7). The scherzo, featuring a pentatonic melody, was clearly conceived in a dance-like folk idiom and reflects the folk music Mendelssohn heard in Scotland in 1829. The slow movement, with its recurring, processionlike passages

EXAMPLE 4.7. Symphony No. 3 in A Minor ("Scottish") Op. 56
movt. 2, mm. 9–12

movt. 3, mm. 34–35

movt. 4, mm. 182–87

in dotted-note style, is in a majestic style appropriate for Queen Mary; the descending tetrachord supporting this style invokes a dirge or lament.[31] The finale, which Mendelssohn described as *allegro guerriero*, suggests a struggle that reaches its climax in the dissonant fugato of the development; eventually the contest is resolved in the A-major postlude.[32] For W. A. Lampadius, "one could fancy the last struggle which gave to Queen Elizabeth her complete victory over her unfortunate rival."[33]

When the symphony was premiered in Leipzig on 3 March 1842, Mendelssohn emphasized its through-composed, cyclic form by deliberately withholding the movement tempo markings from the program. But "this method of representation was not favorable to the understanding of the piece,"[34] and so he eventually prefaced the first edition with an explanatory note: "The individual movements of this symphony must immediately follow one another, and not be separated by the customary long pauses. For listeners the contents of the individual movements can be given on concert programs as follows: Introduction and Allegro agitato; Scherzo assai vivace; Adagio cantabile; Allegro guerriero and Finale maestoso."[35]

A critic of the *Allgemeine musikalische Zeitung* found all four movements "very closely related to one another" and "bound by an inner connection."[36] Indeed, Mendelssohn's chief concern seems to have been the organic unity of the symphony, by means of which a germinal idea, announced in the opening measures, was reused throughout the work in a variety of transformed guises. In this regard, the "Scottish" Symphony bears comparison with Robert Schumann's contemporaneous Fourth Symphony, which, sketched in 1841 and revised in 1851, was not only through-composed but also depended on a cyclical thematic approach (see chapter 3). In the "Scottish" Symphony, the germinal idea is a triadic figure that unfolds the tonic A-minor sonority in second inversion (E–A–B–C; Ex. 4.8). First given by the winds and violas in the slow introduction, the figure is embellished to become the opening theme of the *allegro* (E–F–E–A–B–C), and then reworked into the accompaniment to the second theme. The return of the slow introduction at the end of the

EXAMPLE 4.8. Symphony No. 3 in A Minor ("Scottish") Op. 56
movt. 1, mm. 1–4

movt. 1, mm. 64–67

(*continued*)

EXAMPLE 4.8. (*continued*)
movt. 1, mm. 125–129

movt. 4, mm. 396–99

first movement reintroduces the figure, and in the following scherzo it is redeployed in a pentatonic configuration (C–F–G–A). Finally, in the celebratory conclusion of the finale, the figure is recast in A major (E–F♯–A–B–C♯).

The brooding, melancholy affect of the symphony is representative of the Scottish—better, Ossianic—manner that Mendelssohn developed in a variety of works; in particular, the symphony has a marked stylistic affinity with the earlier *Hebrides (Fingal's Cave)* Overture, and with Niels Gade's concert overture *Nachklänge von Ossian* (Echoes of Ossian), a derivative composition completed and performed in Leipzig in 1840, not long before Mendelssohn resumed work on the "Scottish" Symphony.[37] Particular features of the manner include the darkly hued scoring (e.g., the opening of the symphony, in which the theme is colored by the low winds and violas, without the violins),[38] open-spaced chords and drone effects (finale, mm. 36lff.), and rough-hewn harmonic progressions (first movement, mm. 209ff. and 427ff.). All of these pieces, too, show new approaches to form. Thus, the first movement of the "Scottish" Symphony includes three themes in its exposition and an extended coda paralleling the development; the entire movement is framed by the slow introduction. This flexible approach recalls Gade's concert overture, and its mottolike quotation from Ludwig Uhland's poem "Freie Kunst" (Free art): "Formel hält uns nicht gebunden, / Unsre Kunst heisst Poesie" (Formulas do not constrain us, Our art is named poesy).

Concert Overtures

Robert Schumann treated Mendelssohn's concert overtures as "the crown and sceptre of all instrumental composers of the day"; for Schumann, these works effectively compressed "the idea of the symphony . . . within a smaller space."[39] The programming of overtures along with symphonies was a common practice during Mendelssohn's early days in Berlin, but most of the overtures heard in the concert hall were borrowed from operas or had been composed for a particular occasion (e.g., Beethoven's *Egmont* Overture and Weber's *Jubel* Overture). What Mendelssohn essentially accomplished was to give greater autonomy to the overture as an independent genre and to test its ability as purely instrumental music to express extramusical ideas. After composing one nonprogrammatic overture, the so-called Trumpet Overture (Op. 101, 1826), he conceived the ideas in rapid succession for three programmatic works, *A Midsummer Night's Dream, Calm Sea and Prosperous Voyage,* and *The Hebrides* (Opp. 21, 27, and 26, in 1826, 1828, and 1829), all of which, however, were withheld in publication in full score until 1835.[40] Two other programmatic overtures, *Zum Märchen von der schönen Melusine* (Op. 32) and *Ruy Blas* (Op. 95), were composed in 1833 and 1839.

Throughout his career Mendelssohn remained reluctant to disclose the programmatic ideas of his instrumental music, in marked contrast to Berlioz, who, for example, continued to refine and revise the printed program of the *Symphonie fantastique.* Mendelssohn maintained that music offered a more precise language of emotions than did the language of words, and that ultimately, words were inadequate to describe purely instrumental music. But he was nevertheless a composer of programmatic music; if considerably more conservative than Berlioz, Liszt, and others in setting limits for programmatic ideas, he did not recoil, as Friedrich Niecks observed early in the twentieth century, from touching the unclean thing.[41]

The rarely heard Trumpet Overture dates from March 1826, barely a few months before the seventeen-year-old composed his astonishing overture to *A Midsummer Night's Dream.* The Trumpet Overture was performed in Berlin in April 1828 and revised in April 1833, when Mendelssohn added trombone parts. The London premiere was heard on 10 June 1833, with the composer conducting; later that year, at a music festival in Düsseldorf, he pressed it into service as an overture to Handel's oratorio *Israel in Egypt.* But then the work was set aside and not published until 1867, as Op. 101. In many ways it may be viewed as a preparatory study for Mendelssohn's next three overtures. The opening trumpet fanfare, as Eduard Devrient observed,[42] is rhythmically similar to one used in the *Hebrides* Overture, and the development section is devoted to a coloristic treatment of the orchestra, by which dabs of wind color are contraposed against a neutral backdrop of strings, a technique further explored in *A Midsummer Night's Dream* and the *Hebrides.* The use of mediant relationships in the development foreshadows the *Hebrides*; finally, the trumpet fanfare, which returns (reharmonized) in the development, just before the reprise, during the reprise, and at the conclusion, functions like a motto and anticipates the cyclical treatment of the famous four wind chords that open *A Midsummer Night's Dream.*

In the case of the more celebrated overture from 1826, inspired by Mendelssohn's reading of the Schlegel Shakespeare translations,[43] the composer himself penned a sketch of its program in 1833 for the publishers Breitkopf und Härtel;[44] and in 1842 Mendelssohn reused ideas from the overture in his incidental music for Ludwig Tieck's production of the play in Berlin, so that it is relatively easy to match the network of musical motives in the overture with dramatic elements in the play. Thus, the scurrying E-minor music for the strings was intended for the fairies, and by 1882 had become so associated with Mendelssohn that it could be parodied in Sullivan's *Iolanthe.* Mendelssohn also included bright, regal E-major music for the court of Theseus and Hippolyta, a lyrical contrasting theme for the lovers (its chromatic descent, according to A. B. Marx, suggested their wanderings),[45] boorish figures for Bottom and the Tradesmen, and hunting calls for Theseus's party in the forest. To draw these various motives into focus, Mendelssohn conceived wonderfully imaginative nuances from a Classical double-wind orchestra (augmented only by an ophicleide, to suggest Bottom): for example, the wind chords in successively expanding registers, the division of the violins into four parts for the fairies' music, the use of a solo contrabass in the development, and the magical rescoring of the wind chords at the conclusion, with the added timpani roll on the dominant pitch B, "one of the most consummate subtleties to be found in any orchestration," in the view of Tovey.[46]

The rich tapestry of motives, which required a modification and expansion of the sonata form, appears to be a response to Marx's call for "characteristic" music, so that the overture can convey fundamental ideas, or *Grundideen,* that capture the essence of the play. Tying the motives together is a common descending tetrachord, initially hidden and thus implicit in the opening wind chords (E–D♯–C♮–B), then made explicit through a series of transformations (e.g., the fairies' music, E–D♮–C♮–B, and Theseus's music, E–D♯–C♯–B). Describing the tonally ambiguous progression I(vi?)–V–iv–I, the wind chords act as the agent of metamorphosis that transports us from the real world to that of the fairies; as Franz Liszt mused, they resemble "slowly drooping and rising eyelids, between which is depicted a charming dream world of the most lovely contrasts."[47]

In *Calm Sea and Prosperous Voyage* Mendelssohn discovered his extramusical inspiration in two short poems of Goethe from 1795 that contrasted the deathly stillness ("Todesstille fürchterlich") of a vessel becalmed at sea with the rejuvenation of the vessel and its sailors as they

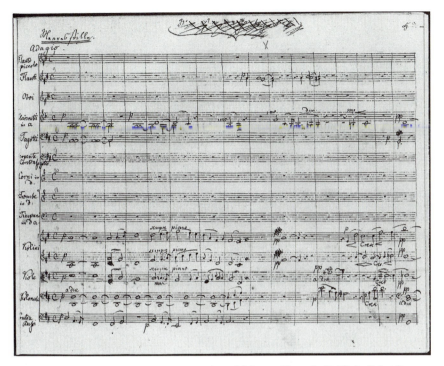

ILLUSTRATION 4.1. Autograph manuscript of *Meeresstille und glückliche Fahrt* Op. 27. The Mary Flagler Cary Music Collection in the Pierpont Morgan Library, New York. Cary 62.

greet the reviving winds and prepare to continue their voyage. (The poems were occasioned by Goethe's own experience of being becalmed off the coast of Capri in 1787.) Musically, the overture is indebted to Beethoven's texted cantata, for chorus and orchestra, on the same poems (Op. 112): the two works share the key of D major, static, open-spaced chords for *Calm Sea*, and a gradually accelerating transition leading to *Prosperous Voyage*. But Mendelssohn went considerably beyond Beethoven's modest setting. First, he enlarged the orchestra to include a piccolo, third trumpet, serpent, and contrabassoon, so that the expanded range could suggest more vividly the vast expanse of the ocean. Furthermore, he indulged in a kind of poetic license by extrapolating from Goethe's poem a conclusion in which the vessel arrives safely in the harbor, an event only hinted at in the last line: "Schon seh' ich das Land" (Already I see land). In the coda of the overture the dramatic passage for timpani and three trumpets was meant to depict welcoming cannon volleys from the shore and answering fanfares from the ship. Finally, stressing the organic cohesion of his composition, Mendelssohn again used an interconnected series of motives, all of which derive ultimately from the opening bass motive of *Calm Sea*, D–A–G–F♯, and its characteristic rhythm ( ).

ILLUSTRATION 4.2. Autograph manuscript of *Die Hebriden* (1830). The note at the bottom of the page was later added by the composer Charles Gounod. The Collection of Robert Owen Lehman, on deposit at the Pierpont Morgan Library, New York.

The *Hebrides* remains Mendelssohn's most elusive overture; he revised the work extensively and pondered several different titles (starting with *Die Hebriden* in 1829; then, in the early 1830s, *Ouvertüre zur einsamen Insel, The Isles of Fingal,* and finally, in 1835, *Fingalshöhle*), but appears to have left no detailed comments about the programmatic meaning of the overture. Some critics have taken it to be a naturalistic seascape inspired by the Scottish sojourn of 1829, during which Mendelssohn meticulously recorded pen-and-ink drawings of the rugged Scottish wilderness. But the progressive reference to Fingal and Fingal's Cave raises the possibility that he was thinking as well of the Ossianic poems, still popular in Germany even though in the eighteenth century they had been debunked by Samuel Johnson as a literary forgery of the Scotsman James Macpherson. The widespread German reception of Ossian as a primitive yet noble body of literature that rivaled the epic poetry of classical Greece could account for Mendelssohn's extraordinary efforts to write in a rough-hewn, uncultured style, and to remove vestiges of counterpoint (artful music) in favor of sea gulls, as he put it.[48]

In Germany, not infrequently, the overture was reviewed with references to Ossian: for Julius Benedict, the trumpet fanfares at the close of the exposition represented a distant Ossianic battle; Schumann referred to a Leipzig performance of the overture with the title *Ossian in Fingalshöhle*; and Henry F. Chorley noted the "fresh, Ossianic, sea-wildness of the overture."[49] Moreover, it was the primary influence on Niels Gade's frankly programmatic overture *Nachklänge von Ossian*. Whatever its meaning, the overture shares approaches to thematicism, flexible treatment of form, and orchestration with *A Midsummer Night's Dream* and *Calm Sea and Prosperous Voyage*. Thus, all the thematic material is derived from a cell-like motive heard in the first few bars (F♯–D–C♯–D–B–F♯); the traditional divisions between the exposition, development, and reprise are deemphasized, in order to strengthen the organic quality of the music; and in the orchestration Mendelssohn favors nuance and understatement (there are few *forte* passages in the score, and it ends, like its two predecessors, *piano*).

The fourth programmatic overture, *Zum Märchen von der schöne Melusine*, was based on the popular German fairy tale of the half-human, half-mermaid Melusina and her knight-lover Raimund. In 1824 the Austrian playwright Franz Grillparzer offered a libretto on the subject to Beethoven, but not until the 1830s was it set to music as a romantic opera by Conradin Kreutzer; Mendelssohn's overture was the result of his unsatisfactory reaction to a performance of the opera in Berlin in 1833.[50] A cursory glance at Kreutzer's overture shows why: there are two subjects, an undulating one for Melusina and a brisk march theme for Raimund, but they are insipid and are strung together without any cogent sense of thematic development or elaboration (Ex. 4.9a–b). Mendelssohn's solu-

EXAMPLE 4.9.

a. Conradin Kruetzer, *Melusina*, Overture

b. Conradin Kreutzer, *Melusina*, Overture

(*continued*)

EXAMPLE 4.9. (*continued*)

c. Mendelssohn, Overture to *Die schöne Melusine* in F Major Op. 32, mm. 1–4

d. Mendelssohn, Overture to *Die schöne Melusine* in F Major Op. 32, mm. 68–71

tion was to adjust the sonata form to accommodate the enchanted realm of Melusina, a realm of imagination and poetry, and the practical world of Raimund and his knightly deeds. The two are presented in alternation, so that the exposition is actually a double exposition, and the development and reprise are binary as well; the two realms ("halb ideal, halb real," as one review of Kreutzer's score put it)[51] are thus sharply delineated (Ex. 4.9c–d) yet intersect as well, for their essential motives are interconnected. Melusina's music is characterized by a flowing, ascending triadic figure that prefigures a similar motive in Wagner's *Rheingold*. Raimund's music, in the parallel minor, is marked by a robust, descending triadic figure; a second, lyrical subject suggests his longing for Melusina. Robert Schumann called attention to some delicacies in Mendelssohn's orchestration, notably the *pianissimo* trumpet calls near the beginning (a device also used in the *Hebrides*), but read into the piece imagery of pearls, magic castles, and deep seas, an interpretation that the composer dismissed as too fanciful. When asked about the meaning of the overture, he was reported to have mused, "Hmm, a *mésalliance*."[52]

A dramatic work also occasioned Mendelssohn's final overture, *Ruy Blas*, after the 1838 play by Victor Hugo. The overture was quickly written in a few days to accompany a production of the play in 1839; Mendelssohn also composed a short Romanze for a chorus of peasant women in act 2.[53] The play, concerning the decadence of seventeenth-century Spanish court life, left Mendelssohn unimpressed. Ruy Blas is a servant, secretly in love with the queen, who is made to play the role of the grandee; at the end, after his illicit passion is revealed, he poisons himself and dies in the queen's arms. Though Mendelssohn hurriedly composed the overture as an exercise of his compositional facility and left it for posthumous publication (as Op. 95), the work contains some effective music, including the colorful second theme and piquant amphibrachs (♩♩♩) of the closing section. What is more, the overture is a remarkably taut structure. The opening, thrice-stated wind intonation serves as a unifying motto, reappearing before the second thematic group in the exposition and reprise. Its descending tetrachord bass line (C–B♭–A♭–G) is reharmonized (C–B♭–A♮–G, mm. 13–16) and accompanies the first theme of the exposition (C–B♮–A♭–G, mm. 33–38) before it emerges *fortissimo* as a chromatic tetrachord (C–B♮–B♭–A♮–A♭–G, mm. 64–67), the traditional symbol for a lament (Ex. 4.10).

EXAMPLE 4.10. Overture to *Ruy Blas* in C Minor, Op. 95
a. mm. 1–4

b. mm. 64–66

Throughout his career Mendelssohn worked principally within the confines of the Classical, double-wind ensemble, preferring to extract subtle blends of color and nuances from familiar means rather than exploring bold new approaches to scoring and instrumental combinations, as did his contemporary Berlioz in the *Grand Traité d'instrumentation et d'orchestration modernes* (1843). Mendelssohn's efforts as an orchestral musician were inextricably tied to his incessant activities as one of the premier conductors of the time, primarily at the famed Gewandhaus in Leipzig, but also at the Philharmonic in London, and at numerous music festivals in Germany. His brief ascendance to the forefront of German music during the 1830s and 1840s coincided with the rise of the orchestra as a common municipal institution. His art served to underscore the educational role of the orchestra in European music culture and, indeed, considerably hastened the formation of the orchestral concert-hall canon so familiar to us today.

Notes

1. Thus Tovey's remark about the flute solo in the opening scherzo to the incidental music for *A Midsummer Night's Dream*: "Listeners who wish to appreciate what this involves may be recommended to pronounce two hundred and forty

intelligble syllables at the uniform rate of nine to a second without taking breath." Donald Francis Tovey, *Essays in Musical Analysis* (London, 1935; rpt. 1981), 411.

2. William H. Reed, *Elgar As I Knew Him* (London, 1936), 84–86.

3. Of these only *Die beiden Pädagogen* has been published: *Leipziger Ausgabe der Werke Felix Mendelssohn Bartholdys*, ed. Karl-Heinz Köhler, series 5, vol. 1 (Leipzig, 1966).

4. See my article "A Mendelssohn Miscellany," *Music & Letters* 71 (1990): 52–64, and the literature cited therein.

5. Letter of 19 October 1821 from Lea Mendelssohn-Bartholdy to Henriette Pereira Arnstein (Mendelssohn Archiv, Deutsche Staatsbibliothek, Berlin).

6. *Leipziger Ausgabe*, ed. Hellmuth Christian Wolff, series 1, vols. 1–3 (Leipzig, 1965–72).

7. A. B. Marx, *Erinnerungen aus meinem Leben*, vol. 1 (Berlin, 1865), 111–12; Heinrich Dorn, *Aus meinem Leben*, vol. 3, *Erinnerungen* (Berlin, 1872), 49.

8. See, among others, Wulf Konold, "Mendelssohn's Jugendsymphonien," *Archiv für Musikwissenschaft* 46 (1989): 1–41, 155–83.

9. At the Ripienschule, organized in 1807 to promote older instrumental music.

10. J. C. Lobe, "Gespräche mit Mendelssohn," *Fliegende Blätter für die Musik* 1 (1855): 280–96, trans. in *Mendelssohn and His World*, ed. R. Larry Todd (Princeton, 1991), 198.

11. *AmZ* 30 (1828): col. 63 (review of the piano fugue Op. 7, No. 5).

12. For further details see my "Mozart according to Mendelssohn: A Contribution to *Rezeptionsgeschichte*," in *Perspectives on Mozart Performance*, ed. R. Larry Todd and Peter Williams (Cambridge, 1991), 167ff.

13. *AmZ* 31 (1827): cols. 156ff.

14. They were written for Christmas. See Sebastian Hensel, *Die Familie Mendelssohn 1729 bis 1847* (Berlin, 1911), 7th ed., 2:206–25.

15. Letters of 11 February and 26 June 1838. See Max Friedländer, "Ein Brief Felix Mendelssohns," *Vierteljahrsschrift für Musikwissenschaft* 5 (1889): 483–89.

16. On Marx's influence, see Judith Silber Ballan, "Marxian Programmatic Music: A Stage in Mendelssohn's Musical Development," in *Mendelssohn Studies*, ed. R. Larry Todd (Cambridge, 1992), 149–61.

17. See J. Michael Cooper, "'Aber eben dieser Zweifel': A New Look at Mendelssohn's 'Italian' Symphony," *19th-Century Music* 15 (1992): 169–87.

18. Jules Benedict, *Sketch of the Life and Works of the Late Felix Mendelssohn Bartholdy* (London, 1850), 21.

19. In the coda Mendelssohn brings back the fugato subject, thus linking the coda and development sections, a device possibly influenced by the first movement of Beethoven's *Eroica* Symphony.

20. See his letters of 4 April and 16 June 1831, in Mendelssohn, *Reisebriefe aus den Jahren 1830 bis 1832*, ed. Paul Mendelssohn Bartholdy (Leipzig, 1878), 100ff. and 129ff.

21. The effect is somewhat reminiscent of the *Heiliger Dankgesang* movement in Beethoven's String Quartet Op. 132, with its alternation of modal (Lydian) and tonal (D-major) passages.

22. It is unlikely that Berlioz knew the "Italian" Symphony in 1834, though he later conducted it in London.

23. Trans. from the corrected German text in Felix Mendelssohn Bartholdy, *Reisebriefe von 1830/31*, ed. Peter Sutermeister (Zurich, 1949), 199.

24. As reported by Donald Tovey in *Essays in Musical Analysis* (London, 1935–39, rpt. 1981), 393–94.

25. Julius Benedict, *Weber* (London, n.d.), 155; see also Michael Tusa, "In Defense of Weber," in *Nineteenth-Century Piano Music*, ed. R. Larry Todd (New York, 1991), 162–63, 166–68.

26. See Eric Werner, "Mendelssohniana," *Die Musikforschung* 28 (1975): 21; and Douglass Seaton, "A Study of a Collection of Mendelssohn's Sketches and Other Autograph Material, Deutsche Staatsbibliothek Berlin 'Mus. Ms. Autogr. Mendelssohn 19'" (Ph.D. dissertation, Columbia University, 1977), 111ff.

27. On the early version of the *Lobgesang*, premiered with some five hundred performers in Leipzig on 25 June 1840, and Mendelssohn's subsequent revisions for a performance on 3 December, see Seaton, "Study," 180ff., and the preface to Seaton's new edition of the symphony (Stuttgart, 1990).

28. See my article "An Unfinished Symphony by Mendelssohn," *Music & Letters* 61 (1980): 293–309.

29. By 1831, however, Mendelssohn evidently could no longer apprehend the "misty mood of Scotland" and set his preliminary work aside, presumably taking it up again only in 1841. See his letter of 29 March 1831 in Sutermeister, *Reisebriefe*, 214.

30. See the composer's letter of 30 July 1829 in Hensel, *Familie* 1:268. On the sketches for the symphony, see Seaton, "A Draft for the Exposition of the First Movement of Mendelssohn's 'Scotch' Symphony."

31. The tetrachord, A–G–F–E, is already heard in the bass line at the opening of the symphony (mm. 2–4).

32. The fugato is characterized by the use of the tritone. On Mendelssohn's other uses of fugal writing to depict struggle, see my "*Me voilà perruqué:* Mendelssohn's Six Preludes and Fugues Op. 35 Reconsidered," in *Mendelssohn Studies*, 191ff.

33. W. A. Lampadius, *The Life of Felix Mendelssohn-Bartholdy*, trans. William Leonard Gage (Boston, n.d.), 270.

34. Ibid., 269.

35. Leipzig, 1843.

36. *AmZ* 45 (1843): col. 342. Signed "A.K." See also Robert Schumann's review (*Neue Zeitschrift für Musik* 18 [1843], 155–56), though Schumann had the remarkable misapprehension that the A Minor Symphony was inspired by Mendelssohn's visit to Italy.

37. See further my "Mendelssohn's Ossianic Manner, with a New Source: *On Lena's Gloomy Heath*," in *Mendelssohn and Schumann: Essays on Their Music and Its Context*, ed. Jon W. Finson and R. Larry Todd (Durham, NC, 1984), 137–60.

38. An earlier Ossianic opera, Méhul's *Uthal* (1806), had employed this scoring as well.

39. From Schumann's celebrated review of Berlioz's *Symphonie fantastique*, in *NZfM* (31 July 1835); trans. in Robert Schumann, *On Music and Musicians*, ed. Konrad Wolff, trans. Paul Rosenfeld (Berkeley and Los Angeles, 1983), 165.

40. For a detailed study of these three works, see my *Mendelssohn: "The Hebrides" and Other Overtures* (Cambridge, 1993).

41. Frederick Niecks, *Programme Music in the Last Four Centuries: A Contribution to the History of Musical Expression* (London, 1907), 164.

42. Eduard Devrient, *My Recollections of Felix Mendelssohn-Bartholdy and His Letters to Me*, trans. Natalia Macfarren (London, 1869), 22–23.

43. August Wilhelm Schlegel, *Shakespeares dramatische Werke*, 9 vols. (Berlin, 1797–1810; rpt., 1825).

44. Letter of 15 February 1833, in Mendelssohn, *Briefe an deutsche Verleger*, ed. Rudolf Elvers (Berlin, 1968), 25–26.

45. Marx, *Erinnerungen aus meinem Leben* 2:232.

46. Tovey, *Essays in Musical Analysis*, 410.

47. "Über Mendelssohn's Musik zum 'Sommernachstraum,'" *NZfM* 40 (1854): 233–37.

48. See my "Of Sea Gulls and Counterpoint: The Early Versions of Mendelssohn's *Hebrides Overture,*" *19th-Century Music* 2 (1979): 197–213.

49. Benedict, *Sketch of the Life and Works of the Late Felix Mendelssohn Bartholdy* (London, 1850), 20; *Gesammelte Schriften über Musik und Musiker von Robert Schumann*, ed. F. Gustav Jansen, 4th ed. (Leipzig, 1891), 1:181n.; Henry F. Chorley, *Music and Manners in France and Germany* (London, 1844), 1:276.

50. See his letter of 7 April 1834 to Fanny Hensel, in Mendelssohn, *Briefe aus den Jahren 1833 bis 1847* (Leipzig, 1863), 36ff.

51. *AmZ* 35 (1833): col. 214.

52. See Schumann's review of January 1836 in *NZfM*, rpt. in *Robert Schumanns Schriften über Musik und Musiker*, 5th ed. (Leipzig, 1914), 1:142, where the *mésalliance* anecdote appears in a footnote; also Mendelssohn's letter of 30 January 1836 to his sister, Fanny, in *Briefe aus den Jahren 1833–1847*, ed. Paul Mendelssohn-Bartholdy (Leipzig, 1878), 74.

53. Published in a musical almanach in 1840 and then posthumously as the Duet Op. 77, No. 3. See further Mendelssohn, *Briefe an deutsche Verleger*, ed. Elvers (Berlin, 1968), pp. 349–52.

Selected Bibliography

Abraham, Gerald. "The Scores of Mendelssohn's 'Hebrides.'" *Monthly Musical Record* 78 (1948): 172–76.

Cooper, J. Michael. "'Aber eben dieser Zweifel': A New Look at Mendelssohn's 'Italian' Symphony." *19th-Century Music* 15 (1992): 169–87.

Filosa, A. J. "The Early Symphonies and Chamber Music of Felix Mendelssohn Bartholdy." Ph.D. dissertation, Yale University, 1970.

Finscher, Ludwig. "'Zwischen absoluter und Programmusik': Zur Interpretation der deutschen romantischen Symphonie." In *Über Symphonien*, ed. Christoph-Hellmut Mahling, 103–15. Tutzig, 1979.

Friedländer, Max. "Ein Brief Felix Mendelssohns." *Vierteljahrsschrift für Musikwissenschaft* 5 (1889): 483–89.

[Grove, George?]. "Mendelssohn's Unpublished Symphonies." *Monthly Musical Record* 1 (1871): 159–60.

Hensel, Sebastian. *Die Familie Mendelssohn 1729 bis 1847*. 7th ed. Berlin, 1911.

Heuss, Alfred. "Das 'Dresdner Amen' im ersten Satz von Mendelssohns Reformations Sinfonie." *Signale für die musikalische Welt* 62 (1904): 281, 305.

Kinsky, Georg. "Was Mendelssohn Indebted to Weber?" *Musical Quarterly* 19 (1933): 178–86.

Konold, Wulf. "Opus 11 und Opus 107: Analytische Bemerkungen zu zwei unbekannten Sinfonien Felix Mendelssohn Bartholdys." In *Musik Konzepte* 14/15: *Felix Mendelssohn Bartholdy,* ed. Heinz-Klaus Metzger and Rainer Riehn, 8–28. Munich, 1980.

————. "Die zwei Fassungen der 'Italienischen Symphonie' von Felix Mendelssohn Bartholdy." In *Bericht über den Internationalen Musikwissenschaftlichen Kongress Bayreuth 1981,* ed. Christoph-Hellmut Mahling and Sigrid Wiesmann, 410–15. Kassel, 1984.

————. *Felix Mendelssohn Bartholdy: Symphonie Nr. 4 A-Dur Op. 90, "Die Italienische."* Munich, 1987.

————. "Mendelssohn's Jugendsymphonien." *Archiv für Musikwissenschaft* 46 (1989): 1–41, 155–83.

Mintz, Donald. "*Melusine: A* Mendelssohn Draft." *Musical Quarterly* 43 (1957): 480–99.

————. "The Sketches and Drafts of Three of Felix Mendelssohn's Major Works." Ph.D. dissertation, Cornell University, 1960.

Oechsle, Siegfried. *Symphonik nach Beethoven: Studien zu Schubert, Schumann, Mendelssohn und Gade.* Kassel, 1992.

Seaton, Douglass. "A Draft for the Exposition of the First Movement of Mendelssohn's 'Scotch' Symphony." *Journal of the American Musicological Society* 30 (1977): 129–35.

Silber-Ballan, Judith. "Mendelssohn and the 'Reformation' Symphony: A Critical and Historical Study." Ph.D. dissertation, Yale University, 1987.

————. "Mendelssohn and His 'Reformation' Symphony." *Journal of the American Musicological Society* 40 (1987): 310–36.

Todd, R. Larry. "Of Sea Gulls and Counterpoint: The Early Versions of Mendelssohn's *Hebrides* Overture." *19th-Century Music* 2 (1979): 197–213.

————. "An Unfinished Symphony by Mendelssohn." *Music & Letters* 61 (1980): 293–309.

————. "Mendelssohn's Ossianic Manner, with a New Source: *On Lena's Gloomy Heath.*" In *Mendelssohn and Schumann: Essays on Their Music and Its Context,* ed. Jon W. Finson and R. Larry Todd, 137–60. Durham, NC, 1984.

————. *Mendelssohn: "The Hebrides" and Other Overtures.* Cambridge, 1993.

Tovey, Donald. *Essays in Musical Analysis.* London, 1935–37. Reprint in 1 volume, 1981.

Walker, Ernest. "Mendelssohn's 'Die einsame Insel.'" *Music & Letters* 26 (1945): 148–50.

Witte, Martin. "Zur Programmgebundheit der Sinfonien Mendelssohns." In *Das Problem Mendelssohn,* ed. Carl Dahlhaus, 119–27. Regensburg, 1974.

Wolff, Hellmuth Christian. "Zur Erstausgabe von Mendelssohns Jugendsinfonien." *Deutsches Jahrbuch der Musikwissenschaft* 12 (1967): 96–115.

CHAPTER FIVE

Berlioz

D. Kern Holoman

That Hector Berlioz became a symphonist at all shows at once the stubborn independence of his thinking and his consistent readiness to embrace progressive ideas from multiple traditions and cultures. His own culture favored the lyric stage above all else, with religious music and military music ranking next in the taste and experience of his countrymen. Among his French contemporaries—Fromental Halévy (1799–1862), Adolphe Adam (1803–56), and Ambroise Thomas (1811–96) are the closest to Berlioz in age—there was not a single major symphonist. At the Conservatoire the curriculum assumed, rightly, that virtually all its graduates would earn their principal livelihood either on the opera stage or in the pit. The young Berlioz was himself primarily formed by the repertoire of Gluck and Spontini, neither of them a symphonist—nor was his principal teacher, Jean-François Le Sueur, who composed operas and sacred oratorios. It is thus hardly surprising that Berlioz's major youthful works were in those genres: some *scènes dramatiques*, the oratorio *Le Passage de la Mer rouge* (c. 1823–24) a solemn Mass (1824, recently recovered), and an ambitious opera, *Les Francs-Juges* (1826).[1]

The Beethoven symphonies as offered from 1828 by the new Société des Concerts du Conservatoire fundamentally and radically changed his creative course.[2] But if his entire symphonic accomplishment is in one way or another concerned with Beethovenism—and there were scarcely any other symphonies in his repertoire—it is also true that from the beginning Berlioz was less concerned with purity of the symphonic genre as he inherited it than with the symphony as a forum for experiment and progress toward his own ideals as a composer of dramatic music. The symphony as a genre was immeasurably freer in this respect than opera, so constrained in Paris by house conventions and professional and personal relationships of which he had little part.

By dramatic music Berlioz meant, of course, music that expressed the innermost essence of life as he understood it from his own experiences. He believed unquestioningly in music's ability to convey a depth of feeling richer and truer than was possible with any other art form.[3] Virtually all his symphonic music is evocative of intense emotional states; often it is programmatic, that is to say, molded by his imagination of a particular tableau or vignette. Sometimes it is overtly pictorial, as in the guillotine chop or arrival of the Beloved in the *Fantastique*. Occasionally it appears to reflect a line-by-line response to a chosen text, as in the Love Scene and other passages from *Roméo et Juliette*.

These responses he would fit into what he took to be more or less conventional formal designs, based on the four movement types of the Beethoven models. Yet in Beethoven he also found precedent for the kinds of Romantic freedoms that dominated the thoughts of his contemporaries in literature and painting. His particular palette was that of words, feelings, and orchestral sound. To more than a little degree, it was the search for the right mix of these elements, and not the integrity of genre itself, that occupied his intellect.

Berlioz used the word *symphony* to describe four works: the *Symphonie fantastique* (1830), *Harold en Italie* (1834), *Roméo et Juliette* (1839), and the *Grande Symphonie funèbre et triomphale* (1840)—all of them from the period of his first maturity (Ill. 5.1).[4] But the last of these is an occasional work that falls more comfortably into the family grouping that includes the Requiem (1837), Te Deum (1849), and the patriotic cantatas (e.g., *Le Cinq Mai*, 1835; *Hymne à la France*, 1844; *L'Impériale*, 1854).[5] *La Damnation de Faust* of 1846, which Berlioz calls a *légende dramatique* instead of a *symphonie*, nevertheless represents the natural outcome of the symphonic arguments that had occupied him from the *Fantastique* to *Roméo et Juliette*. In turn the symphonic discoveries of *Roméo et Juliette* and *Faust* inform the manner of the great works that followed—*L'Enfance du Christ* (1854), *Les Troyens* (1858), and *Béatrice et Bénédict* (1862)—at every turn.

Berlioz was not especially pleased by the rapid and almost universal adoption during his lifetime of the term "program music" to suggest an alternative to "absolute" and by extension proper music, and he had much to say about the limits of musical imitation and dramatic intent.[6] He does not appear to have been especially fond of the dilettantish programs of Liszt and his followers, and it is well that he did not live to ponder the implications of the Mahler-and-Strauss brand of programmatic explanation. In the 1950s the American scholar Jacques Barzun, uncomfortable with the suggestions of a qualitative distinction between "pure" music and the undeniably different music of Berlioz, promoted the notion that Berlioz's music must not presuppose "a knowledge of some story or series of events which it follows or illustrates," and that "the master's music was no more and no less tied than any other composer's to

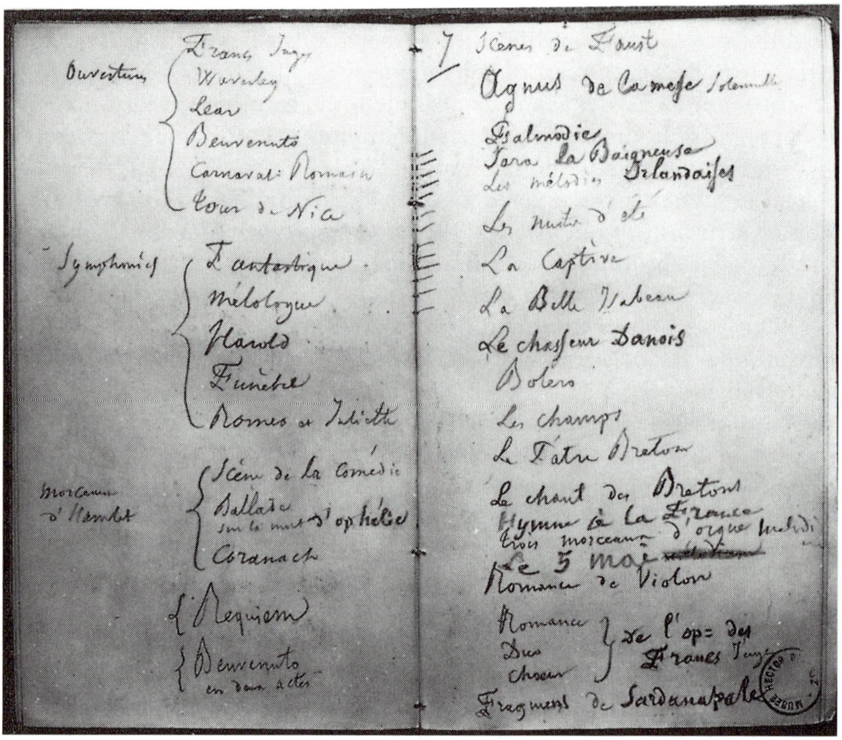

ILLUSTRATION 5.1. Autograph inventory of works, found in a pocket notebook of 1845. Musée Berlioz, La Côte-St.-André.

something outside itself."[7] He admits that "keeping out so-called extraneous ideas or perceptions while composing, hearing, or analyzing music is impossible and unnecessary," but cannot help implying that fastidious listeners ought to try to do otherwise. And he states flatly that distributing the program of the *Fantastique* "goes against the composer's wishes." Today we may well want to assign that sort of attitude to the midcentury modernist/abstractionist creed that so feared sentiment in musical thinking, notably any suggestion of picture music—the creed that many now believe ended up driving paying listeners from the concert hall.

However that may be, the identity of the *Symphonie fantastique* is inextricably linked to its printed program, just as each of the works that follow embraced a new solution to the issues that the program was first meant to address. To quibble over what and what not to hear in the Berlioz symphonies misses the point entirely, since he so consistently invites his listeners to swim in the sea of associative pleasures that music alone can provide.

Symphonie fantastique (1830)

It has long been traditional in Berlioz study—especially with the *Fantastique*—to attempt tracing the roots of his creative world to other composers and repertoires, the better to counter the old complaints about the quality of his discipline and craft.[8] (Fétis on the *Fantastique*: "What a good thing it isn't music.") Precedents and models for many details of the Berlioz style—or styles—are indeed to be found, not just in Beethoven, Rossini, and Weber but in the thoroughly French tradition of Gossec and Méhul. He was well, if unusually, schooled: one no longer takes seriously the charges of a defective "technique," and now that we know virtually everything he composed, and the contexts in which his work emerged, a view of Berlioz as a prevailingly rational artist, and a rather orderly one at that, seems firmly established.

But, in truth, finding precedents for the details does little to locate the true aesthetic of his symphonies in any mainstream, French or Viennese; rather they seem a watershed that helped define Romanticism's approach to symphonic thinking and to form post-Romanticism. It is thus thoroughly fitting to come full circle and wonder anew at the very originality of it all. In the case of the *Fantastique*, a first symphony rivaled only by Brahms's and Mahler's in overturning the symphonic norms, this has much to do with the lavish new orchestral sounds uncovered by its composer. Berlioz's keen sense of orchestral possibility was built on the high virtuosity of the Paris players. The orchestra pit of the Paris Opéra, at its best, was a garden of delights, and at the Conservatoire these same instrumentalists had formed their Société des Concerts to investigate the modern symphonic repertoire. At the beginning, at least, the Société des Concerts was all about orchestral progress: for instance, its very first concert on 9 March 1828 included a demonstration of the new piston-valved horn by the great Meifred.

From the first bars of the first movement, then, the *Fantastique* has to do with an extraordinary new attitude toward orchestral deployment, one that carries on through the pair of harps at the beginning of the second movement, the echo dialogue of English horn and offstage oboe in the "Scène aux champs," the splendid brass band work in the "Marche au supplice," and virtually the whole of the finale. The string writing (note especially the nine-part divisi in the first movement, mm. 410ff., the ten parts at the start of the finale, and later in the movement the *col legno* with wind trills and bass pizzicati, mm. 444ff.) represents a quantum leap forward in technique from anything he had so far composed. His interest in the battery, where he was fond of stationing himself, was well ahead of its time: not just the thunder music produced by the four timpanists (movt. 3, mm. 177ff.), but also the studied use of sticks (*baguettes d'éponge, baguettes de bois, baguettes de bois recouvert en peau*; see, e.g., movt. 5, mm. 69ff.) and the grand bass drum rolls for two players at the end of the finale (mm.

Example 5.1. Berlioz, *Symphonie fantastique*
a. movt. 3, mm. 87–92

b. movt. 5, mm. 6–9

485ff.). Later, in *Harold en Italie* and afterward, he would expand his repertoire of percussive effects to include the "Italian" sparkle of cymbals, triangle, and tambourines, not to mention the antique cymbals he had first seen in Pompeii.

And the orchestrational subtleties of the *Fantastique* go well beyond technicalities of scoring and the simple novelty of sonic effects. In his association of register with gender—the soulful masculine cello strophe of the "Scène aux champs" dissolving into paroxysm with answer by the soprano-specific *idée fixe*, for example, or the grotesque masculine laughter and shrill feminine giggles of the Witches' Sabbath (Ex. 5.1)—he finds one of his most reliable methods of evoking the characterizations necessary for dramatic symphonic discourse. (Note here, too, the liberating effect on orchestral texture of the many rhythmic values through which he darts and which he combines and permutes unlike in any precedent music he could have known.) Such association of orchestral register and timbre with male and female voice parts is what goes on to identify Harold, the Abruzzi mountaineer, the Prince of Verona, Romeo, Juliet, Queen Mab, and a host of others.

The other conceptual turning point represented by the *Fantastique* was of course the narrative program and the *idée fixe* that goes with it (Ex. 5.2)—the *idée fixe* heard complete as the theme of the first movement and then alluded to by transformed citation in each subsequent move-

EXAMPLE 5.2. Berlioz, *Symphonie fantastique*, the beginning of *idée fixe*

ment. Berlioz wrote out the program in longhand in April 1830, during the flush of inspiration that in his case often amounted to deep emotional distress ("Une idée fixe me tue," he wrote in February.)[9] Ultimately the program underwent a great deal of revision, as occasion and the composer's growing understanding of what he had composed seemed to dictate.[10] On the whole, however, these changes are insignificant, and the basic events remain the same in each redaction: the "Reveries and Passions" of the artist as he longs for his beloved; "A Ball," where he recognizes her in a crowded salon (a kind of scenario to which he returns in the "Fête chez Capulet" in *Roméo et Juliette*); a "Scene in the Country," with dreams of the beloved in pastoral surroundings; and the two movements where his thoughts become hallucinations, the "March to the Scaffold" and "Dream of the Witches' Sabbath." What intrigued Berlioz's contemporaries most about his treatment of the *idée fixe* was the manner of its transformation, notably in the finale's "Mockery of the Beloved" passage. This was a central model for Liszt's thematic treatment in the *Faust* Symphony, and few symphonic composers after Berlioz and Liszt were entirely free of its spell.

Both the program and the *idée fixe*, as well as a good deal of the rest of the musical content of the *Fantastique*, are rich with autobiographical allusion. As everybody knew, Berlioz himself was the "young musician, troubled by that spiritual sickness which a famous writer [Chateaubriand] has called *le vague des passions*" and wracked with hallucinations (and in real life a tendency to nosebleeds and quinsy). His passion had been unleashed by the appearance of the Irish actress Harriet Smithson as Ophelia and Juliet in 1827, at precisely the moment in his life when both his romantic sensibilities and his sexuality demanded release.[11] Miss Smithson, not surprisingly, declined his advances; by the time the *Fantastique* was composed a fresh romantic interest had taken her place, and by the first performance on 5 December 1830, to all appearances, she had become no more than a chapter from what Berlioz liked to think of as the novel of his life.[12]

Other autobiographical allusions come in the form of material drawn from other contexts into the new symphony. The first of these is the long introduction in the first movement: three strophes of a melody Berlioz says comes from his childhood, conceived to fit a text of the eighteenth-century moralist Florian (mm. 3ff.). Not just any text: for *Estelle*, the source, was linked in the composer's mind with the object of his first adolescent fantasy, Estelle of the pink slippers.[13] The *idée fixe* had already appeared as the theme of *Herminie*, Berlioz's Prix de Rome cantata of 1828, though there without the heart palpitations added for the *Fantastique* (mm. 78ff., violins II and low strings). It seems clear that a preliminary version of the "Marche au supplice" had figured in *Les Francs-Juges*, Berlioz's opera of 1826 that had just recently been revised but not performed.[14] And we now know that the principal theme of the third movement, the Scene in the Countryside, was borrowed as well: from the 1824 *Messe solennelle*, recovered in 1992 (Ex. 5.3). What is remarkable about these primarily melodic borrowings, here and throughout Berlioz's works,[15] is the facility with which he adapts the material to its new surrounding. While a common dramatic situation often links source and reuse (or reuses), the resulting passage inevitably sounds specific to its new surrounding—often as though determined by it.

EXAMPLE 5.3.
Berlioz, *Messe solennelle,* movt. 3 (Gratias), mm. 29–32

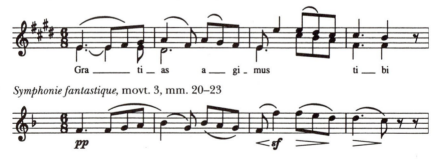

Symphonie fantastique, movt. 3, mm. 20–23

Formal analysis of the *Fantastique* begins of necessity with reference to traditional sonata practice, as did Schumann's essay in the *Neue Zeitschrift für Musik* based on his reading of Liszt's piano transcription.[16] Little is traditional about the structures, however: certainly not the three sonata-like movements, with their thoroughly unconventional proportions—proportions made even more exotic in the first and last movements by long introductions (Ex. 5.4). In fact Berlioz betrays more than a hint of callowness toward sonata practice, as for example in his meandering, episodic developments: consider the development of the first movement, where the string of patterns and effects seems all but to abandon the treatment of the second theme (mm. 180–228). Motivic development

EXAMPLE 5.4. Berlioz, *Symphonie fantastique*
movt. 1: *Rêveries, Passions*

		Devel.			
Introduction		Exposition	Recapitulation		
		Th. I Th. II	Th. I	Th. II	Coda
Time		4:28 5:46	6:47	8:02	11:30
		5:59			
M. no.		64/72 150	239	311	503
		166			

movt. 5: *Songe d'une nuit de sabbat*

Introduction	Exposition		Development	Recap.	
	Th. I	Th. II			Coda
Time	2:48	5:06	6:06	7:38	8:40
M. no.	127	241	305	407	480

in the Beethovenian sense was never his primary aim, and in later works intermovement thematic reference and solid global control of structure and pacing across multiple movements result in a strength of formal design that compensates for a certain naïveté about—or simple disinterest in—what the Viennese had really been up to. Berlioz is at his most natural in prevailingly strophic procedures, where his fertility of invention can be expressed by means of varied resettings and ongoing transformation of given material. In the "Scène aux champs," despite its formidable length the conceptual high point of the *Fantastique*, strophic design interacting with programmatic episodes evokes the mix of pastoral tranquillity and internal upheaval described by the printed narrative.

Harmonically Berlioz now finds himself on solid footing, with little hint of the stases that had troubled him in *Les Francs-Juges.* The key scheme of the movements (C major–A major–F major–G minor–C major) is compellingly Romantic, with the progression from movement to movement exceptionally strong: indeed, movements 3–5 need playing without pause, so that the thunder of the executioner's procession can replace the faded thunder of the countryside, and so the motion from the G-major "Hurrahs" at the end of the "Marche au supplice" to the stunning diminished-seventh chord on A♯ at the beginning of movement 5 can be absorbed to proper effect. The *Fantastique* also dwells strongly on the ♭6-inflected cadences and the interplay of ♭6 and ♮6 that go on to become Berliozian trademarks (Ex. 5.5).[17]

EXAMPLE 5.5. Berlioz, *Symphonie fantastique*, movt. 1
a. mm. 17–18

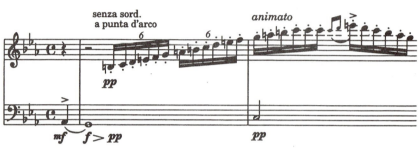

b. mm. 87–94

Given both the novelty and the extreme technical difficulty of the *Fantastique*, its live birth was relatively uncomplicated: an abandoned attempt to read it at the end of May 1830, then a full performance, respectfully received, on 5 December 1830. This came on the heels of Berlioz's winning the Prix de Rome and only a few days before his departure for Italy. One critical dividend of the premiere was the dawn of Berlioz's intimacy with Liszt, who swept backstage to cultivate a friendship, leaving with the idea for a solo piano transcription. In Italy, it appears, Berlioz's first major compositional effort was to revise the second and third movements. This project was well underway when news reached him that he had been jilted, back in Paris, by his fiancée, the young piano virtuosa Camille Moke; and in planning for the murder-suicide that seemed in the offing, he left marginalia instructing the conductor Habeneck in Paris to tidy up the revisions—though later ended up doing the work himself.[18] The autograph score thus contains the 1831–32 reading, with little evidence of the original text and almost none of the original movements 2–3. From this text Liszt completed and published his solo version and Schumann wrote his influential review. With a few further details polished, Berlioz finally allowed the *Fantastique* to be published in full score in 1845.

Proof that his inner emotional state and the subject matter of his work are inextricably tangled is that even before the crisis of the broken engagement subsided, Berlioz began to formulate a sequel to the *Fantastique*, a second part of his *Episode de la vie d'un artiste*. Composing this *mélologue* was largely a matter of writing the text for the six orations, since all the music was recycled from former work.[19] The sequel was ready in time to be featured with the second performance of the *Fantastique*, on 9 December 1832, a few weeks after the composer's return from Rome. Harriet Smithson was induced to come to the concert, and she recognized her portrait: a true courtship began, concluding in their wedding the following October at the British embassy. The *mélologue* came just as Parisian Romanticism achieved full flower, and in that context the 1832 concerts and one in 1835 served their purpose well. Retitled *Lélio*, it was played once more in Berlioz's lifetime, in Weimar in February 1855 as part of Berlioz Week, a festival organized by Liszt. The *Fantastique* was played behind a scrim; the actor in front of the curtain appeared to sleep through the hallucination, then awoke at the beginning of the sequel.[20]

Harold en Italie (1834)

Harold en Italie is the central artifact of Berlioz's Prix de Rome sojourn, though in many ways Italy lies at the core of a good half of everything he wrote, from *La Captive* (Subiaco, February 1832) to both *Les Troyens* and *Béatrice et Bénédict* at the end of his career. When Paganini came to commission a dramatic concerto for his Stradivarius viola, Berlioz's first idea was to reframe his *Intrata di Rob-Roy MacGregor*, one of the obligatory *envois* from Rome, which had failed in its premiere at the Société des Concerts on 14 April 1833.[21] With its titular allusion to Walter Scott's novel and an *allegro* with melodic material perhaps developed from Robert Burns's "Scots wha' hae wi' Wallace bled," the overture seemed ripe for reuse as *Les Derniers Instants de Marie Stuart*, two movements for viola solo, orchestra, and chorus. But then, Berlioz writes,[22] another movement came to him, and another, and meanwhile his imagination had grown more persuasively occupied by fond memories of Italy—not so much Rome as the rustic Abruzzi brigands and *pifferari*—than by Scottish lore. What resulted was a four-movement symphony with viola solo, cast as a panorama of vignettes overseen by the Romantic hero Harold, whose name was borrowed from Lord Byron's *Childe Harold*.[23] *Harold en Italie*'s hero, of course, is Berlioz himself: he had already described the vistas, pilgrim's march, and mountaineer's serenade in a string of articles that began in 1832 (later absorbed into his *Voyage musical en Allemagne et en Italie*, 1844, one of the primary sources for the *Mémoires*, 1870).[24] The text that became chapters 37–40 of the *Mémoires* amounts to a level of precompositional activity that strongly parallels the *Fantastique*'s program.

At first glance *Harold en Italie* seems the least progressive of Berlioz's symphonies, to be numbered among the relatively few conservative works of the fertile decade from 1830 that saw the breathtaking advances of the Requiem, *Cellini*, and the *Nuits d'été* as well as the third and fourth symphonies. The four-movement scheme—with *adagio* and *allegro* in sonata form, a slow march, scherzo, and finale with thematic recall of the previous movements—feel almost routinely Beethovenian. But with *Harold* Berlioz makes his next great aesthetic strides: in the domains of rhythm and the use of performance space.

The viola soloist—Harold—is instructed to stand well apart from the rest of the orchestra, in a splendid instance of the Romantic paradigm. The violist's motive as presented in the opening *adagio*, almost an *idée fixe*, is a tender but also rather brooding phrase in two halves (Ex. 5.6a), square and simple enough that it tends to fit effortlessly into the diverse contexts of the movements that follow (movt. 2, mm. 64–88; movt. 3, mm. 65–95 and 167–90; movt. 4, mm. 80–96). Much of the *adagio*, including the great canon with ornamental surges up and back through the orchestra (mm. 73–84) was adopted from the comparable position in *Rob-Roy*, though the woodwind canon is new with *Harold* (Ex. 5.6b). (Compare the decorative filigree, at which Berlioz was becoming increasingly expert, with the *Fantastique*, movt. 3, mm. 67ff., and *Roméo et Juliette*, movt. 3, mm. 367ff.) The fugal opening, measures 1–13, is newly composed; possibly this passage served as a model for the beginning of Mendelssohn's *Elijah*, in D minor and along similar melodic lines.[25]

The unusual visual and acoustic effect of the violist's placement represents a step beyond the offstage oboe in the *Fantastique* (and its conspicuous absence at the end of the movement) in Berlioz's continuing investigation of performance space as compositional opportunity. A high spot of spatial control in *Harold* is the center section of the Pilgrim's March, the *canto religioso* exchanged in long note values between winds and strings (from back to front of the orchestra) as the viola's two-octave arpeggiations *sul ponticello* move in sixteenths and contrabass pizzicati continue the march rhythms in quarters and eighths (representing motion from side to side; mm. 169–248). Here Berlioz has engaged musical space in virtually all its defining parameters. Yet another spatial component is in play near the very end of the work, with an offstage reminiscence of the Pilgrim's March from three solo strings with the viola soloist, still onstage, completing the quartet. From these passages it is a natural step to the apocalyptic, in-the-round style of the Requiem on the one hand, and, on the other, such delicacies as the offstage angel chorus-with-closing-door of *L'Enfance du Christ*.

The rough model for the Pilgrim's March is the funeral cortège from the *Eroica*, a movement that incited rapturous prose from Berlioz's pen owing to the poignancy of its dissolution[26]; the rhythmic gesture is that of the Allegretto of Beethoven's Seventh. As in Beethoven, the march passes by in a crescendo/decrescendo, and the chanting of the monks

EXAMPLE 5.6. Berlioz, *Harold en Italie*, movt. 1
a. mm. 38–45

b. m. 73

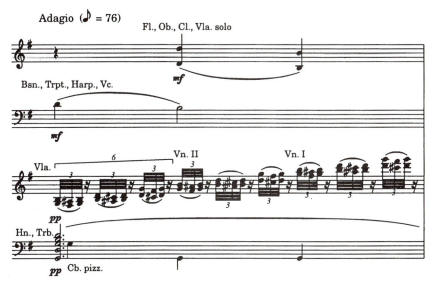

and monastery bell are roughly equivalent to Beethoven's tattoos and fan-fares. Particular to Berlioz is the manipulation of the march melody to conclude each phrase at a higher pitch level (Ex. 5.7).

Berlioz surely found the source of his conspicuous new rhythmic vitality—most apparent, perhaps, in the Roman Carnival scene of *Benvenuto Cellini,* which comes just after *Harold*—in the naïve yet riotous musical behavior of the peasant bands he encountered in the streets of Rome and in his sojourns in the Abruzzi.[27] The rhythmic fabric of *Harold* reaches one of its peaks in the three-way *réunion des thèmes* of the Abruzzi serenade, movement 3 (Ex. 5.8), a passage of which the composer was proud enough to cite it in his *Grand traité d'instrumentation et d'orchestration modernes* of 1843. Another comes in the roaring inebriation that ends the fourth movement, "Orgie de brigands" (mm. 518–end). In fact, the finale has only one truly thematic subject, the result of careful sketching in what may

EXAMPLE 5.7. Berlioz, *Harold en Italie*, movt. 2

have been the initial working out of ideas for the Paganini project.[28] If the Brigand's Orgy veers uncomfortably close, tactically, to the digressive style of the early sonata movements, that is at least in part a function of the phantasmagoria being sought by the composer. At issue is the catalogue of *souvenirs*, in the style of Beethoven's Ninth, swept away in Bacchic revelry. (The suggestion, from the viola's silence, is that the narrator abandons his watch to join in the excitement.) The sudden rise to a major-mode peroration (m. 449), completing the overall key scheme G minor/major–E major (flavored with C major)–C major–G minor/major, begins the process of closure, with the offstage reminiscence, drunken semicollapse, and momentum regained in a charge to the final bars. In these surroundings elegance of form would have amounted to a contradiction of purpose.

Harold en Italie was composed during a relatively brief period of domestic bliss, the only one that he was ever to enjoy: the first months of his marriage to Harriet Smithson. The ripening of his spirit is palpable: *Harold* is by turns exuberant and introspective, but always it has an inner warmth and perhaps even bespeaks hints of rare self-satisfaction. The experience of composing it, and the fond memories it evoked, were a major springboard to the glories of *Cellini*. Little matter that Paganini declined to play it: Chrétien Urhan, who did play it in 1834, was also a virtuoso, and his temperament was rather more suited to the role. Little matter, either,

EXAMPLE 5.8. *Harold en Italie*, movt. 3, mm. 166–69

that the fastidious Narcisse Girard proved incapable of conducting *Harold*'s rhythmic and metric ploys, for that failure is precisely what prompted Berlioz's decision to become a true *chef d'orchestre* and in due course to develop a comprehensive theory of the conductor's role in symphonic performance.[29] (The score of *Harold* is peppered with instructions to the conductor: see movt. 1, m. 435; 2, mm. 16, 131; 3, mm. 116ff.; 4, mm. 46, 514, 530, 562). Both circumstances—that Paganini did not play *Harold*, and that Berlioz determined thenceforth to conduct his own works himself—set the stage for his symphonic masterpiece, *Roméo et Juliette*.

Roméo et Juliette (1839)

Paganini at last heard *Harold* when he attended Berlioz's concert of 16 December 1838. Afterward, overcome by what he had heard, he came to the stage to lavish praise on the composer and join the chorus of admirers proclaiming a new successor to Beethoven; the next day he sent Berlioz a bank draft for twenty thousand francs, an altogether royal *gratification* meant not merely to congratulate but also to atone.[30] For Berlioz the best use of the gift was obvious: to support his daily expenses (and pay back old debts) while he undertook a major new symphonic work that was unlikely to recoup its production expenses. Within a few weeks of Paganini's gift—24 January 1839, Berlioz tells us—he had begun *Roméo et Juliette*.[31]

There is much to suggest that in fact the idea for a *Romeo and Juliet* symphony had begun to take shape in his mind shortly after Harriet Smithson's appearances with the English Shakespeare company in 1827. ("I shall marry that woman and write my greatest symphony on the play.")[32] Emile Deschamps, the librettist for *Roméo et Juliette*, says that Berlioz had approached him to do the text shortly after the Shakespeareans had made their mark.[33] Moreover, Berlioz's excitement at discovering that the Prix de Rome cantata text for 1829 was *La Mort de Cléopâtre* may have stemmed at least in part from the fact that he had already considered the parallel scene of Juliet sealed in the Capulets' vault. The pizzicato rhythmic motive—the throbbing heartbeats—from Cleopatra's aria "Grand Pharaons, nobles Lagides" are mirrored at Romeo's invocation in the tomb scene;[34] one melodic gesture from the aria appears in the symphony early on (Ex. 5.9). At the head of the autograph score of this movement from *Cléopâtre*, Juliet's chilling "What if, when I am laid into the tomb?"—said to have been delivered by Miss Smithson with electrifying terror—appears as an epigraph.[35]

EXAMPLE 5.9.
Berlioz, *Cléopâtre*, movt. 3, mm. 16–19

Berlioz, *Roméo et Juliette*, movt. 1, mm. 115–21

Certainly a *Romeo and Juliet* project was on his mind in Italy. With Mendelssohn, riding in the countryside, he mentioned the possibility of a scherzo for Queen Mab, later fearing his friend would rob the idea. (Mendelssohn's response, doubtless, was the *Midsummer Night's Dream* scherzo.) His review of Bellini's *I Capuletti ed i Montecchi*, which he saw in Florence in February 1831, makes clear that he himself had been considering how he might set his favorite episodes:

> To begin with, the dazzling ball at the Capulets', where amid a whirling cloud of beauties the young Montague first sets eyes on 'sweetest Juliet,' whose constant love will bring her to the

grave; then those furious pitched battles in the streets of Verona, with the 'fiery Tybalt' presiding like the personification of anger and revenge, the glorious night scene on Juliet's balcony, where the lovers murmur the music of tender love, as sweet and pure as the watchful moon smiling down upon them; the dashing Mercutio and his sharp-tongued, fantastical humor; the cackling nurse; the stately hermit, even in his cell caught up in the tragic conflict of love and hate, and striving to resolve it; and then the catastrophe, extremes of joy and despair drained to the dregs in the same instant, passion's heat chilled in the rigor of death; and, at the last, the solemn oath sworn by the warring houses, too late, on the bodies of their children, to abjure the feud which shed so much blood, so many tears. My eyes streamed to think of it.[36]

In short, the genesis of *Roméo et Juliette* is representative of what had become Berlioz's typical compositional process: attraction to a theme dear to his heart, long pondering of the central vignettes and episodes, and waiting to spring to work until he was certain his capabilities were sufficient to the task.

He wrote with assurance and conviction—incorporating here and there, as was his custom, useful phrases from previously composed ephemera—and was done with the bulk of the work in thirty weeks.[37] Nor was he able to contain his conception of a symphonic *Romeo and Juliet* into four or five movements with choral finale, as was almost surely his original intent: the cortège of strewn flowers was too poignant to pass over, the tomb scene too central, the song "Premiers transports" too personal. At length there were seven movements:[38]

Introduction; Prologue; Strophes; Scherzetto
Roméo seul–Grande Fête chez Capulet
Scène d'amour
La Reine Mab
Convoi funèbre de Juliette
Roméo au tombeau des Capulets
Final

An interval was envisaged between "La Reine Mab" and the "Convoi funèbre," in part to distinguish between the amorous and tragic halves of the story, in part to allow the full chorus egress onto the stage.

Berlioz knew *Romeo and Juliet* as filtered through David Garrick's performing version and John and Charles Kemble's subsequent adaptations, in the French of Le Tourneur (1778) and François Guizot (1821); Emile Deschamps had also begun a full translation. The vital questions of what Shakespeare Berlioz saw and, more significantly, what texts he read have now been answered, and though the lineage is complex, we are now able to construct his conception of *Romeo and Juliet* as the combining of the powerful memories of 1827 with a gradually increasing knowledge of the differences among the texts.[39] It is the Garrick tradition, for example, that drops the prologues and the character of Rosaline, rewrites the Queen Mab speech, introduces the sung funeral dirge, and allows the lovers their last embrace in the Capulet's tomb. Shakespeare's low comedy and every hint of bawdiness are systematically removed. Berlioz began *Roméo et Juliette* with the swordplay because that is what he had seen in Paris, and for the same reason Rosaline does not figure in the story at all.

From the beginning the most delicately poised component of *Roméo et Juliette* was its narrative strategy of chanted recitatives sung by a small prologue chorus. The Coryphée was a familiar figure on the French stage, anyway, and Berlioz had concluded some years before that recitative offered a better and possibly less obtrusive device than the kind of printed story used for the *Fantastique*.[40] But radical strategies are dangerous ones, and Berlioz left the first performances doubting, as did one of the reviewers, that he had found the proper role for the prologues and their chorus.[41] The complete performance in Vienna in January 1846 gave him an opportunity to review the matter, with the result that he removed a second, post-intermission prologue and incorporated thematic foreshadowings into the first (Ill. 5.2). (At the same time, cuts were made in the *Mab* and the finale.) With that a cogent and attractive formal organization had been perfected.

Tonally *Roméo et Juliette* is framed by the B minor of the rival families at the beginning and toward the end, rising to an apotheosis B-major finish; at the center it is anchored by the F major–A major–F major of the "Fête chez Capulet," "Scène d'amour," and "Mab." Orchestrationally it is concerned with the interplay of instruments and voices (and instruments taking the roles of voices), and with the progress, modeled on Beetho-

ILLUSTRATION 5.2. Sketch for the orchestral interlude in the prologue to *Roméo et Juliette*, mm. 37–62 (found on the verso surface of a collette over p. 63 of the autograph, **F-Pc** ms. 1165.

ven's Ninth, from orchestral to choral dominance through carefully rea-soned transitions.[42] Note how gradually the vocal force is revealed, from the soloists and recitative chorus at the beginning, to the offstage men in the "Scène d'amour," the full Capulet chorus in the "Convoi funèbre," then all three united in the finale. The orchestra's retreat begins in mm. 62–67 of the "Convoi funèbre," where it relinquishes the fugue to the chorus.

Another key to the formal strength of *Roméo et Juliette* is a thematic cyclicism fashioned at several structural levels. At issue in the choral recitative is simple foreshadowing by the orchestra of material to come (of the Ball music: at mm. 36ff.; "Ah! quelle nuit, quel festin!": m. 56; Romeo alone: m. 69; love music, m. 91; funeral cortège: mm. 321 and 331).[43] In the "Fête chez Capulet" the melody of Romeo alone from the opening *adagio* becomes the overlain component of the *réunion des thèmes*, following the precedents in the *Fantastique* finale and *Harold* serenade.[44] Here, too, there is a continuance of the foreshadowing technique, as the tambourines and timpani beginning at measure 76 suggest the "bruit lointain de bal et de concert." With the *réunion des thèmes*, reminiscence begins to control the thematic interleaving. The transition from the Ball Scene to the Balcony Scene, then, is accomplished as the young men pass-ing by sleepily recall the delights, and the principal theme, of the *fête*. That Romeo and Juliet's delirious embrace in the Tomb Scene cites the earlier love theme is strongly sensed; less obvious is that the moment of Juliet's awakening uses the neighbor-note motive associated with her character in the love scene (Ex. 5.10a). The introductory fugal skirmish is immediately transformed by augmentation into the voice of the Prince of Verona; its recapitulation as the quarreling families interrupt Friar Lawrence's narrative is a bold indication that closure is at hand (Ex. 5.10b).

In a striking essay, Ian Kemp has demonstrated that a great deal of the three most imaginative movements of *Roméo et Juliette*—the "Scène d'amour," "Mab," and the Tomb Scene—may develop from the com-poser's line-by-line reactions to his source text.[45] It may be, then, that the

EXAMPLE 5.10a. Berlioz, *Roméo et Juliette*
movt. 3, mm. 127–29

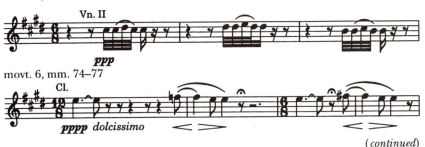

movt. 6, mm. 74–77

(*continued*)

EXAMPLE 5.10b.
movt. 1, mm. 1–2

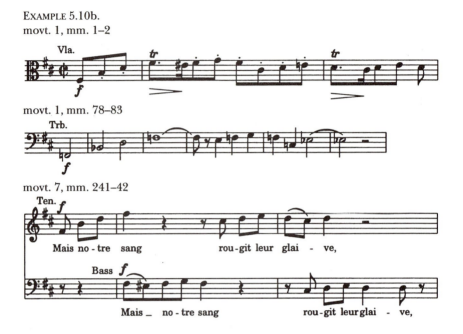

movt. 1, mm. 78–83

movt. 7, mm. 241–42

adagio consists not merely of Romeo and Juliet episodes, made rondo-like as they entwine in the recurrences of the love theme, but that the sections of Shakespeare's balcony scene are directly reflected in Berlioz's love music, with Romeo evoked by violas and cellos, Juliette by woodwinds:

> Section 1, mm. 125–79. Romeo in the garden, Juliet unaware of his presence. "But soft . . . She speaks, yet she says nothing." "Oh Romeo, Romeo." A–c♯–A / A–C.
>
> Section 2, mm. 181–242. Juliet: "What man art thou?"; they converse. C–A–f♯. (Transition, mm. 243–45).
>
> Section 3, mm. 246–73. Juliet's monologue: "Thou know'st the mask of night is on my face." f♯–A.
>
> Section 4, mm. 274–end. Exchange of vows and good nights: "Lady by yonder blessed moon I vow," etc. Rondo-like structure built around A-major statements of the full love theme. Nurse calls from within (mm. 332ff.?). Coda (mm. 372ff.): "Good night, good night!" "Parting is such sweet sorrow . . ."

As the lovers keep delaying the moment of their separation, the movement extends itself ever further, dominated by ever more climactic iterations of the love theme.

A close reading of the French Mab scene, as given in the tenor scherzetto at the beginning, helps explain the curiously end-heavy organization of "La Reine Mab" as well. Mab inspects her chariot and coachman (mm. 1–69), then sallies forth on her ride, the scherzo proper. At the trio

(mm. 354ff.) she gallops into a page's brain, the lad dreaming a soft serenade as he sleeps beneath a castle tower. The short reprise of the scherzo
(mm. 431ff.) takes Mab and her music into a new episode: through the
neck of a sleeping soldier (mm. 475ff.), dreaming of battle (mm. 544ff.)
with drums (mm. 556ff.); he wakes and swears (mm. 603ff.) then goes
back to sleep and starts to snore (mm. 631ff., four bassoons on a low B♭
and horn). Meanwhile Mab has undertaken her last mission, to dress and
deliver a young girl to a ball: hence the coda's citation (mm. 615ff.) of the
"Ballet des ombres" of 1829—a dance piece with the added glitter of antique cymbals, whose primary motive of descending fifths is foreshadowed
in the Mab theme itself. Day breaks (mm. 720ff.) and Mab disappears into
thin air.

No doubt whatever surrounds the proposition that the Tomb Scene
is essentially line-for-line narrative. Berlioz implies as much in his petu-
lant note at the bottom of the page of score ("Le public n'a point d'imagination . . ."[46]). With the Garrick dénouement at hand, the incidents are
clear:

action/dialogue		*measure number*
R.	*arrives at the tomb*	1
R.	Oh my love, my wife	48
	(Shakespeare 5.3.91ff.)	
R.	*drinks poison, kisses her, sinks*	68
J.	Where am I? (Garrick)	74
R.	She speaks, she lives;	90
	. . . Her senses are unsettled	
J.	Support me!	147
R.	Oh I cannot . . . Cruel poison	158
J.	Thou rav'st—lean on my breast	170
	. . . A moment stay [*she faints*]	
J.	I will kiss thy lips	
	Oh happy dagger! . . . let me die	193

With a summary pizzicato cadence of cellos, the orchestra's role as
primary teller of the tale is finished. In overall effect the choral finale is
not Beethovenian at all, but Meyerbeerian: an operatic closing tableau toward which the crescendo of vocal forces had been building all along. It is
the occasion for a compositional *mise au point:* setting the balance (Père
Laurence juxtaposing the contralto and tenor and the start; the recapitulation of the fugue; the return of the prologue chorus), completing the
frame, and achieving the apotheosis close.

By the time of *Roméo et Juliette*, Berlioz had settled comfortably into
the highly personal melodic idiom of telescoping, asymmetric lyricism

EXAMPLE 5.11. Berlioz, *Roméo et Juliette*, movt. 2, mm. 1–10

that is perhaps the chief hallmark of his mature lyric practice (Ex. 5.11). The meanders and ambiguities of this unaccompanied violin line succeed well in epitomizing Romeo's unfulfilled desire. Wagner, who was present for one of the first performances, surely gained from this passage the germ of *Tristan*'s opening bars (and at length the composers traded published copies of *Roméo* and *Tristan*, with fulsome dedications).[47] A similar meandering pervades the fugue subject of the "Convoi funèbre," rich with soulful ebb and flow, an almost giddy search for meaning by stunned mourners strewing rose petals because there is little more to be done. Berlioz seems to have shed whatever obligation he may have felt to Viennese periodicity. This much, and a great deal more about *Roméo et Juliette*'s theory and purpose, seems clear from the "Strophes," where Berlioz composes out his dedication: to first love, higher than all poetry, or perhaps that poetry itself—

> Dont Shakespeare lui seul eut le secret suprême
> Et qu'il remporta dans le ciel!

The first performances (24 November, 1 and 15 December 1839; Ill. 5.3) were the most successful of all his premieres, with strong sales and excellent critical and public reception. And while the complete work was not especially portable, *Roméo et Juliette* lent itself to excerpting: the "Strophes" for the *partie vocale* of many concerts; the "Fête chez Capulet," "Scène d'amour," and "Queen Mab" scherzo for orchestral showpieces, and the finale where an extravaganza was in order.[48] The three symphonic excerpts achieved a strong foothold in the Paris repertoire, where—like the three shorter excerpts from *La Damnation de Faust*—they remained as long as the orchestral societies thrived. The full score and parts were published in 1847, with a second edition in 1857. In 1858 the Swiss publisher Rieter-Biedermann offered a bilingual vocal score, one of the most beautiful of all the Berlioz publications.

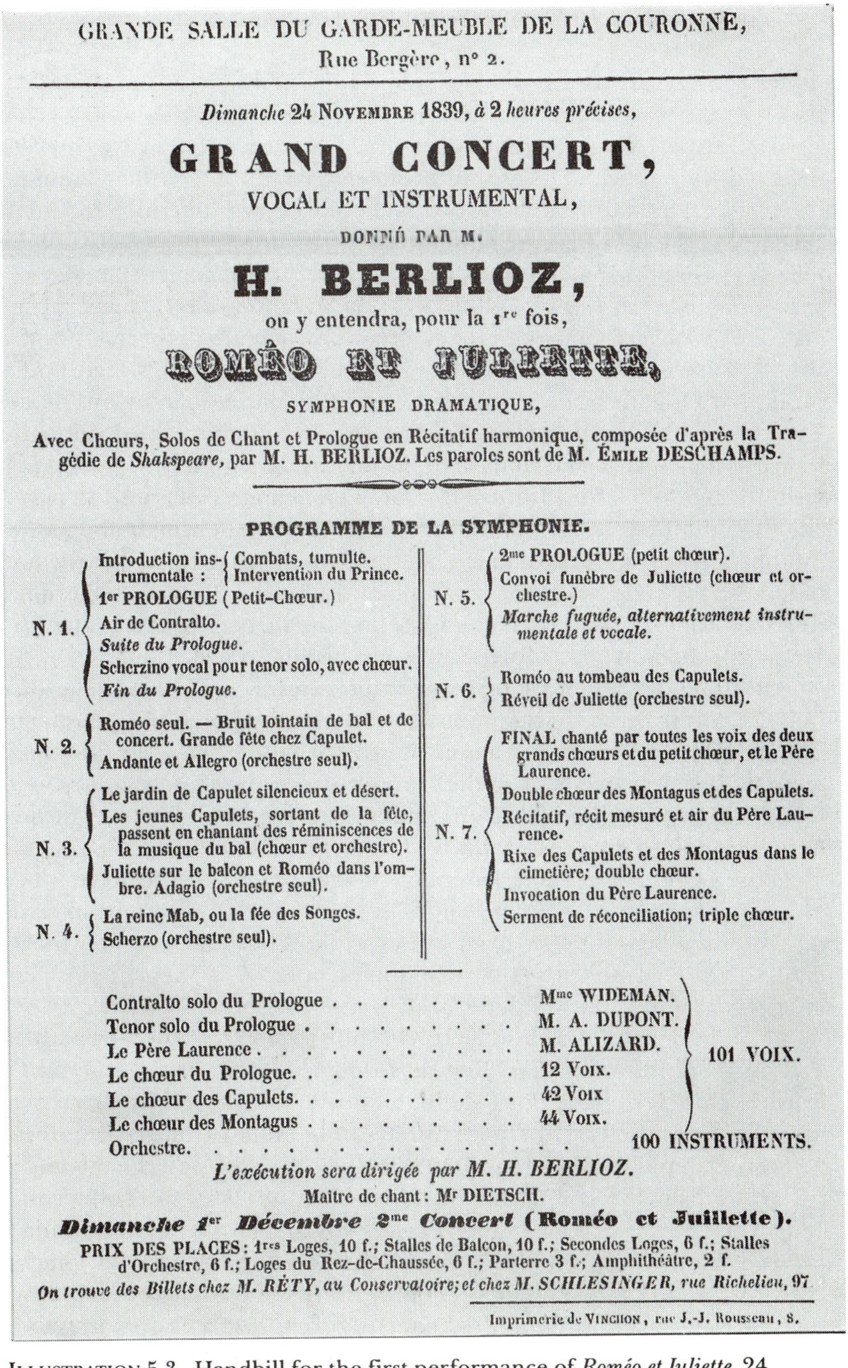

GRANDE SALLE DU GARDE-MEUBLE DE LA COURONNE,
Rue Bergère, n° 2.

Dimanche 24 Novembre 1839, à 2 heures précises,

GRAND CONCERT,

VOCAL ET INSTRUMENTAL,

DONNÉ PAR M.

H. BERLIOZ,

on y entendra, pour la 1re fois,

ROMÉO ET JULIETTE,

SYMPHONIE DRAMATIQUE,

Avec Chœurs, Solos de Chant et Prologue en Récitatif harmonique, composée d'après la Tragédie de *Shakspeare*, par M. H. BERLIOZ. Les paroles sont de M. ÉMILE DESCHAMPS.

PROGRAMME DE LA SYMPHONIE.

N. 1.
- Introduction instrumentale : Combats, tumulte. Intervention du Prince.
- 1er PROLOGUE (Petit-Chœur.)
- Air de Contralto.
- *Suite du Prologue.*
- Scherzino vocal pour tenor solo, avec chœur.
- *Fin du Prologue.*

N. 2.
- Roméo seul. — Bruit lointain de bal et de concert. Grande fête chez Capulet.
- Andante et Allegro (orchestre seul).

N. 3.
- Le jardin de Capulet silencieux et désert.
- Les jeunes Capulets, sortant de la fête, passent en chantant des réminiscences de la musique du bal (chœur et orchestre).
- Juliette sur le balcon et Roméo dans l'ombre. Adagio (orchestre seul).

N. 4.
- La reine Mab, ou la fée des Songes.
- Scherzo (orchestre seul).

N. 5.
- 2me PROLOGUE (petit chœur).
- Convoi funèbre de Juliette (chœur et orchestre.)
- *Marche fuguée, alternativement instrumentale et vocale.*

N. 6.
- Roméo au tombeau des Capulets.
- Réveil de Juliette (orchestre seul).

N. 7.
- FINAL chanté par toutes les voix des deux grands chœurs et du petit chœur, et le Père Laurence.
- Double chœur des Montagus et des Capulets.
- Récitatif, récit mesuré et air du Père Laurence.
- Rixe des Capulets et des Montagus dans le cimetière; double chœur.
- Invocation du Père Laurence.
- Serment de réconciliation; triple chœur.

Contralto solo du Prologue	Mme WIDEMAN.	
Tenor solo du Prologue	M. A. DUPONT.	
Le Père Laurence	M. ALIZARD.	101 VOIX.
Le chœur du Prologue.	12 Voix.	
Le chœur des Capulets.	42 Voix	
Le chœur des Montagus	44 Voix.	
Orchestre.	100 INSTRUMENTS.	

L'exécution sera dirigée par M. H. BERLIOZ.

Maître de chant : Mr DIETSCH.

Dimanche 1er Décembre 2me Concert (Roméo et Juillette).

PRIX DES PLACES : 1res Loges, 10 f.; Stalles de Balcon, 10 f.; Secondes Loges, 6 f.; Stalles d'Orchestre, 6 f.; Loges du Rez-de-Chaussée, 6 f.; Parterre 3 f.; Amphithéâtre, 2 f.

On trouve des Billets chez M. RÉTY, au Conservatoire; et chez M. SCHLESINGER, rue Richelieu, 97

Imprimerie de VINCHON, rue J.-J. Rousseau, 8.

ILLUSTRATION 5.3. Handbill for the first performance of *Roméo et Juliette*, 24 November 1839. Collection of Richard Macnutt.

Symphonie funèbre et triomphale (1840)

Furthest from the Beethovenian symphonic tradition is the *Symphonie funèbre et triomphale* in three movements, for military band with optional chorus in the finale. Nevertheless, Berlioz's title leaves no question as to his view of the work's genre, and it constitutes one outgrowth of the ruminations on a Napoleonic military symphony that had preoccupied him since 1832.[49] In some respects it thus caps the Revolutionary tradition (represented most familiarly in Gossec's miniature "Marche lugubre" and of course the "Marseillaise"), much as *Les Troyens* was the last of the great *tragédies lyriques*.[50]

The *Symphonie funèbre* was composed for the tenth anniversary of the July 1830 Revolution, the three-day insurrection that had placed Louis-Philippe d'Orléans at the head of a constitutional monarchy in France. (For two of those three days, Berlioz was locked into the Institut de France as a Prix de Rome contestant, while just across the river the Louvre was under siege.) The 1840 celebration was meant to impress the populace with the decade of relative prosperity that had ensued, and Louis-Philippe's government was always glad to emphasize the place of the arts in domestic tranquillity. Thus it had financed for the Place de la Bastille a noble monument by the architect Joseph-Louis Duc, beneath which the remains of the warriors of July 1830 would be laid to rest.

Berlioz was commissioned to compose music for the cortège that took the coffins from their temporary crypt at the church of St.-Germain l'Auxerrois to the new mausoleum. During the entombment he envisaged an introspective movement in the manner of a funeral oration, followed by a full-blown apotheosis for the moment when the spectators turned their attention to the great column rising heavenward.

The commission came late enough that he was forced to produce even more quickly than usual, and it is likely that all three movements were drawn, at least in part, from earlier work. We know the center movement to have come from the abandoned opera *Les Francs-Juges*;[51] the outer movements may well have been begun for the *Fête musicale funèbre* Berlioz considered for a time in 1835. Though no one could have gathered much of the work at its first performance, with the funeral march heard in Doppler effect along the boulevards and the second two movements compromised by the noise of retreating military units, the government proclaimed itself well satisfied with the new work and the interest it had aroused in the community of artists. Wagner, who probably came along with the professional musicians of Paris to hear the dress rehearsal, was transfixed: "This symphony will exalt the hearts of men so long as there is a nation called France."[52] Berlioz himself was fond of the Apotheosis, and went on to program it frequently. Text and a chorus to sing it were added for a Brussels concert in September 1842; later a new text was composed to celebrate the triumph of French industry for the Paris Industrial Exhibition of 1843.

What is important about the *Symphonie funèbre et triomphale* is the breadth of its scale. Solemn tempi and slow harmonic rhythm underpin a dazzling phrase treatment (Ex. 5.12) and wonderfully contemplative interplay of major and minor modes (see, for example, mm. 48–54ff. of movt. 1). Berlioz came to have his doubts about music for the outdoors,[53] but the omnipresent tattoo of the field drums is always shattering of impact, and the crescendo of fanfares into the Apotheosis (movt. 3, mm.

EXAMPLE 5.12. Berlioz, *Symphonie funèbre et triomphale*, movt. 1, mm. 4–20

1–17) succeeds admirably in the open air. At issue, again, is the use of musical space, and the work is among those Berlioz numbers in the catalogue of "architectural" music he had composed.

The *Symphonie funèbre* has stayed outside the major repertoire largely owing to its instrumentation, but also because French *pompe funèbre* seems out of place in the modern concert hall. It is nonetheless central to the Berlioz oeuvre, having sealed his authority among the bureaucrats as a figure of national significance. Nobility of gesture, too, helps define the Berlioz style.

A Word on *Faust*

The ultimate result of Berlioz's quest for a dramatic symphony was of course *La Damnation de Faust* (1846). That it was his greatest financial failure is ultimately no more than a biographical detail: but for *Les Troyens*, to which it inexorably led, *Faust* is his most perfect composition.

Genre was no longer a point of confusion with *Faust*, though the one-man public concert Berlioz had done so much to foster was already on the wane. The mix of media is one of the work's great strengths, allowing him to follow up the full range of his interests—in characterization, balletic music, aria, and grand choral tableau—within a loose plot and following a libretto he was free to change to suit his purposes. His control of substance, form, and force is now altogether idiomatic, almost tidy. The networking of thematic linkages essayed in *Roméo et Juliette* is now even more pervasive: consider the foreshadowings in the opening orchestral scene, on the *plaines d'Hongrie*, of the "Marche hongroise" and two different motives from the "Ronde des paysans" (mm. 90ff.), also how the "Air de Méphistophélès," "Chœur de gnomes et de sylphes," and "Ballet de sylphes" (scene 7) all grow from the same basic melody. The panoramic and architectural device of *Harold* and the Requiem is harnessed anew with the Chorus of Students and Soldiers (scene 8) and the terrifying Ride to the Abyss and plunge into Pandemonium (scenes 13–19). *Faust* had begun from the notion of revisiting the *Huit Scènes de Faust* of 1828–29; it expanded during Berlioz's peregrinations to become his memoir of the 1845–46 foray into Austro-Hungary, Bohemia, Poland, and Germany.[54]

As an evening-long concert, longer than *Roméo et Juliette* by nearly an hour, it is much more than Berlioz's Fifth Symphony. *Faust* is the summary of all he had learned about the symphonic style at home and abroad. Like Beethoven's Ninth, it has a valedictory quality, the suggestion that a career's curiosity has been satisfied. The rest of Berlioz's life would be devoted to other kinds of compositions.

The Overtures

Strictly speaking, there are five concert overtures, three early (*Waverley*, c. 1826; *Le Roi Lear*, 1831; and *Rob-Roy*, considered above) and two late (*Le Carnaval romain*, 1843; and *Le Corsaire*, 1844). Along with these we usually count the opera overtures, as Berlioz did (see Ill. 5.1): *Les Francs-Juges* (1826, probably revised c. 1829), *Benvenuto Cellini* (1838), and *Béatrice et Bénédict* (1862)—also because they are often coupled with the concert overtures on commercial recordings. In fact, the number of single-movement concert works is considerably larger, including, for example, the *Grande Fantaisie sur La Tempête* (1830), the *Marche funèbre pour la dernière scène d'Hamlet* (1844), and the *Marche de Rákóczy* (1846). For more than two decades, from 1832, Berlioz organized and eventually conducted many dozens of concerts of his own music, and in Paris especially that demanded fresh one-movement works with each new season: newly composed material, but often also excerpts from his larger works, songs newly orchestrated, and the occasional arrangement of works by other composers (Léopold de Meyer's *Marche marocaine*, 1845, for example, and

Schubert's "Erlkönig," 1860; Weber's *L'Invitation à la valse*, an audience favorite at the Berlioz concerts, had been orchestrated for ballet music in the 1841 Paris production of *Der Freischütz*). In this corpus, too, we find Berlioz contemplating, often ravishingly, some of the same symphonic propositions that are at issue in the multimovement works, though with the concision and constraints the one-movement repertoire tended to imply.

Berlioz's teacher Le Sueur had promoted the *Francs-Juges* and *Waverley* overtures, unsuccessfully, as early as February 1828.[55] He was right to see exceptional promise in both: the young composer's strong melodic gifts, his natural sense of orchestral color and texture, and his growing interest in the commingling of symphonic and narrative discourse. The booming brass figure in *Les Francs-Juges*, for example, seems that of a threatening, perhaps villainous presence—that of Olmerick, it turns out, the opera's chief vigilante—and the long treble duo in close harmony at the center of the work, probably drawn from a scene in the opera, is underpinned with "rough and violent" outbursts from the strings in what Berlioz called a "dual character," certainly somehow programmatic (Ex. 5.13).[56] In the case of *Le Roi Lear*, Berlioz himself tells us that the timpani flourishes from measure 66 allude to Lear's entry into his council chamber, drawn from the composer's own experience of the French king's entry at Mass; he encourages us to hear the king's madness during the storm (mm. 342ff.) and does not oppose our hearing the second theme in the oboe solo as that of Cordelia (m. 151; Ex. 5.14).[57] The early

EXAMPLE 5.13. Berlioz, *Ouverture des Francs-Juges*, mm. 194–205

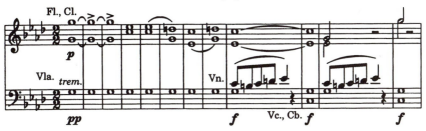

EXAMPLE 5.14. Berlioz, *Le Roi Lear*, mm. 151–59

overtures have shortcomings that suggest maturity still in the offing, but they demonstrate the coalescing of a movement type—*adagio,* sonata-like *allegro* with recapitulation of the *adagio* theme and drive to peroration—to be found in both later overtures. It took the Mediterranean experience, however, to brighten Berlioz's outlook and loosen him up.

The earliest manifestation of that experience among the overtures is in that for *Benvenuto Cellini,* where the formal type and the Italian brio first commingle. With *Le Carnaval romain* and *Le Corsaire* we arrive in the domain of major work by a composer in his prime. The *allegro* of *Le Carnaval romain* comes, of course, from the carnival scene of *Benvenuto Cellini,* rebarred in ⁶⁄₈ but otherwise virtually note-for-note for some two hundred measures; and the *adagio* with the celebrated solo for English horn comes from the opening love duo, "O Teresa, vous que j'aime plus que ma vie." The new setting of old material, however, is thoroughly of its era, with an A-major saltarello introduction brushed aside for the solo in C, then an eyebrow-raising lift from C major into E major and fall back to A for a third strophe with canon and the Italianate filigree so strongly reminiscent of the similar strophe in *Harold* (Ex. 5.15; cf. Ex. 5.6b). In the

EXAMPLE 5.15. Berlioz, *Le Carnaval romain,* mm. 53–54

peroration the interplay of saltarello, canon, and advanced metric device leads to a brassy close with sustained salute on the last chord—another device of which Berlioz was fond.

The rhythmic idiom of *Le Corsaire* is more than a little akin to the other Italy-inspired works as well, notably in the metric ambiguity of the opening figure, so like that of the *Benvenuto Cellini* overture. Begun during Berlioz's curative sojourn in Nice in 1844 (hence its original title *La Tour de Nice*), *Le Corsaire* was meant to investigate the speed, spatial vastness, and uncertainties of life at sea—though otherwise the Byronic (and Fenimore Cooper-esque) allusions seem minimal. The focus is on contrapuntal treatment of the *allegro* theme in inversion and canon, Neapolitan inflections, and toward the end splashes of harmonic daring that by then were not so much shocking to new listeners as sources of instant delight.

Even during Berlioz's lifetime complete performances of his symphonies, other than the *Fantastique,* were rare, and after his death they faded from the repertoire of the major orchestras for the rest of the century. But by that time the *Fantastique* had already shaped the symphonic thinking of Liszt and his followers, notably Mahler; and the Berlioz sound lingered strongly with the Russian nationalists and Tchaikovsky—as did personal memories of the fading master, by the time of his last visit to Russia in 1867 a full-fledged legend.[58] Through Rimsky-Korsakov, Berliozian ideals reached directly into Stravinsky's conceptual world, however dismissive he eventually cared to be about them.[59] The 1855 edition of the orchestration treatise with the appended essay on conducting (*L'Art du chef d'orchestre*), having been translated into the major European languages, served both greater and lesser music students as a sourcebook for generations. One might well conclude that until the Berlioz renaissance of the late 1950s and 1960s the grand post–Romantic symphony orchestra itself, with its virtuoso *chef,* its specially built venues, and its vibrant repertoire, was his chief legacy.

Notes

1. Documentation of the dates of composition and known sources for cited works may be found in Holoman, *Catalogue of the Works of Hector Berlioz,* New Berlioz Edition (hereafter abbreviated as NBE), vol. 25 (Kassel, 1987). On the recovered Mass of 1824, see Hugh Macdonald, "Berlioz's *Messe solennelle,*" *19th-Century Music* 16 (1993): 267–85; consult also the miniature score, ed. Macdonald (Kassel, 1993), the vocal score, ed. Eike Wernhard (Kassel, 1994), and the recording by John Eliot Gardiner with the Monteverdi Choir and Orchestre Revolutionnaire et Romantique, Philips 442 (1994), recorded at Westminster Cathedral, London, 12 October 1993.

2. Programs are given in Antoine Elwart, *Histoire de la Société des Concert du Conservatoire . . .* (Paris, 1860), and E.-M.-E. Deldevez, *La Société des Concerts, 1860 à 1885* (Paris, 1887). My forthcoming study of the Société des Concerts includes all programs from founding until dissolution, accessible on the Internet. I treat the matter of Berlioz's own collection of performance parts in "Orchestral Material from the Library of the Société des Concerts," *19th-Century Music* 7 (1983): 106–18.

3. And, for a time, in the superiority of symphony to opera. On giving the central movements of *Roméo et Juliette* to the orchestra: "instrumental language . . . is richer, more varied, less precise, and by its very indefiniteness incomparably more powerful" than opera ("Observations" at the head of the published score).

4. Additionally Berlioz sketched *Le Retour de l'armée d'Italie. Simphonie militaire en 2 parties* in his sketchbook of 1832–36, and in the *Mémoires* recounts an incident of c. 1852 in which he conceived of a symphony in A minor in his sleep, then forgot it. See nos. 62 and Works Contemplated but Not Composed XV in Holoman, *Catalogue.* On the sketchbook, see Holoman, "The Berlioz Sketchbook Recovered," *19th-Century Music* 7 (1984): 282–317 and *separatum* facsimile.

5. On a projected *Fête musicale funèbre* of 1835, see no. 72 of Holoman, *Catalogue.* No. 110 is the *Chant des chemins de fer* for the inauguration of the Paris-Brussels railway in 1846, the composition of which Berlioz regarded as a service to his country as well.

6. While the published score of the *Fantastique* calls distributing the program "indispensable," by 1855 he was prepared to sanction programs printed with the movement titles alone, since "the symphony offers, the composer hopes, enough musical interest in itself quite apart from all dramatic intention." He treats challenges to the concept of a printed program in a footnote added to the versions published in the late 1830s (NBE 16:170). See also the feuilleton "De l'imitation musicale," *Revue et Gazette musicale* (1, 8 January 1837): rpt. in *Hector Berlioz: Cauchemars et passions,* ed. Gérard Condé (Paris, 1981), 98–109.

7. Barzun, "The Meaning of Meaning in Music: Berlioz Once More," *Musical Quarterly* 66 (1980): 1–20; citations from pp. 2–3. Barzun's reference to a close and admiring student of Berlioz's œuvre, who introduced an address by saying that Berlioz only composed music that was *about* something, is to the present author. Barzun laid down the gauntlet in chapter 7, "Program Music and the Unicorn," of his majestic *Berlioz and the Romantic Century* (New York, 1950; 3d ed. 1969). Consider, too: "Berlioz did not for a moment suppose [*Roméo et Juliette*] to be a piece of story-telling. Those who have heard in the Love scene Juliet's Nurse knocking on the door must take the responsibility, no less than the credit, for such an interpretation. They will get no backing from Berlioz nor from his knowledgeable listeners" ("Romeo and Juliet in Music," 1953/1962, in *Critical Questions* [Chicago, 1982], 153). Cf. Ian Kemp's contrary view in the article cited in n. 42. And: "Berlioz believed . . . the thing called program music was a contradiction in terms" (introduction to *Berlioz: The Art of Music and Other Essays,* trans. and ed. Elizabeth Csicsery-Rónay [Bloomington, Ind., 1994]). David Cairns treats the "muddled, contentious question or non-question of Programme Music" in his *Berlioz, 1803–1832: The Making of an Artist* (London, 1989), 334–37.

8. Julian Rushton cites some of the more notorious assaults on Berlioz in chapter epigraphs to his *The Musical Language of Berlioz* (Cambridge, 1983).

9. Berlioz, *Correspondance générale* (herafter abbreviated as *CG*), vol. 1, ed. Pierre Citron (Paris, 1972), no. 153.

10. See NBE 16, ed. Nicholas Temperley (Kassel, 1972), pp. 168–70; also Temperley, "The *Symphonie fantastique* and Its Program," *Musical Quarterly* 57 (1971): 593–608.

11. On Harriet Smithson and her effect on the Romantics, see notably Peter Raby, *Fair Ophelia: Harriet Smithson Berlioz* (Cambridge, 1982).

12. The long citation from the first of Hugo's *Feuilles d'automne* that appears on the title page of the *Fantastique* autograph, added in 1831 or 1832, treats the image of one's life as an open book: "And though yet at the age when the future still smiles, / My heart's book of hours is already full." The same citation appeared in the printed program for the 1832 concerts of the *Fantastique* and its sequel, and

concluded Joseph d'Ortigue's biographical sketch of Berlioz that appeared in the *Revue de Paris* of 23 December. See Holoman, *Berlioz* (Cambridge, MA, 1989), 137–39.

13. See *Mémoires*, chapter 3, and the concluding "Travels in Dauphiné." The song was "Je vais donc quitter pour jamais / mon doux pays, ma douce amie," no. 6 in Holoman, *Catalogue*.

14. See Hugh Macdonald, "A Berlioz Controversy and Its Aftermath," *ADAM* 331–33 (1969): 38–43; also relevant facsimiles in NBE 16:183–84.

15. See Hugh Macdonald, "Berlioz's Self-Borrowings," *Proceedings of the Royal Musical Association* 92 (1965–66): 29–33; rpt. in *The Garland Library of the History of Western Music*, vol. 9 (New York 1985), 79–96.

16. Schumann's analysis, "Sinfonie von H. Berlioz," appeared in the *Neue Zeitschrift für Musik* 3 (1835): 1–2, 33–35, 37–38, 41–44, 45–46, and 49–51; rpt. in Schumann's *Gesammelte Schriften*, 5th ed. (Leipzig, 1914), 1:69–90. Edward T. Cone translates it in his Norton Critical Score of the *Fantastique* (New York, 1971).

17. See a more comprehensive example in Holoman, *Berlioz*, 105, following Edward T. Cone (Norton Critical Score, 277).

18. See Holoman, *The Creative Process in the Autograph Musical Documents of Hector Berlioz, c. 1818–1840* (Ann Arbor, MI, 1980), 262–82, esp. p. 265 and pp. 278–79.

19. No. 1, "Le Pêcheur," had been composed "four or five years earlier"; no. 2, the "Choeur d'ombres," came from *Cléopâtre* (no. 36 in Holoman, *Catalogue*); no. 3, the "Scène de brigands," was probably the same as the "Chanson des pirates" (cat. no. 34); nos. 4 and 5, the "Chant de bonheur" and "La Harpe aéolienne," come from *La Mort d'Orphée"* (cat. no. 25); no. 6 was the *Ouverture de La Tempête* (cat. no. 52).

20. Peter Bloom's impressive series of articles on the *Mélologue / Lélio* is cited in Holoman, *Catalogue*, no. 55, and in Bloom's own edition of the work, NBE 7 (1992).

21. The Academy referred to the failure at the next Prix de Rome distribution ceremony: "L'auteur a été jugé par le public, et il ne nous est plus permis de prononcer" (*Séance publique annuelle*, 12 October 1833).

22. *CG* 2, ed. Frédéric Robert (1975), no. 384.

23. Byronian subject matter inspired, as well, Berlioz's overture *Le Corsaire*, Liszt's *Tasso*, Tchaikovsky's *Manfred* Symphony, and dozens of other works of the nineteenth century. See John Warrack, "Byron," *New Grove Dictionary of Music and Musicians*, 6th ed., ed. Stanley Sadie (London, 1980), 2:552–53.

24. See "Sources of the Memoirs," in *The Memoirs of Hector Berlioz*, trans. and ed. David Cairns (London, 1990), 537–39. Full citations of these articles appear in Holoman, *Catalogue*, Prose Works, C: Feuilletons.

25. Mendelssohn is not known to have been at a live performance of *Harold*, but the work can scarcely have been unknown to him and would have spoken to him powerfully in any event, since the main experience he and Berlioz shared was their time together in Italy; see *Mémoires*, chapter 33 and "Travels in Germany I," letter 4.

26. "The shreds of lugubrious melody, alone, naked, broken, crushed," and the wind instruments "shouting a cry, a last farewell of the warriors to their companion at arms" (*A Travers Chants*, 42–43).

27. *Mémoires*, chapters 37–38.

28. See Holoman, "Sketchbook Recovered," 293–96.

29. *Mémoires*, chapter 45.

30. The *Mémoires*, chapter 49, describes Paganini as kneeling at Berlioz's feet and kissing his hand. Paganini's letter to Berlioz of the next day, published in facsimile in the press, began "Beethoven spento non c'era che Berlioz che potesse farlo rivivere."

31. The note in Berlioz's hand at the end of the autograph score, **F-Pc** ms. 1165, reads: "Cette Symphonie commencée le 24 Janvier 1839 a été terminée le 8 Septembre de la même année, et exécutée pour la 1re fois au Conservatoire sous la direction de l'auteur le 24 Novembre suivant."

32. Cited, with disclaimer, in *Mémoires*, chapter 18. The English critic, probably Charles Gruneisen, told the story in the *Illustrated London News*, 12 February 1848, after Jules Janin's version in his review of the premiere, *Journal des Débats*, 29 November 1839.

33. Preface to *Macbeth et Roméo et Juliette, tragédies de Shakespeare, traduites en vers français . . .* by Emile Deschamps (Paris, 1844), rpt. in Deschamps, *Œuvres complètes* (Paris, 1874), vol. 6.

34. The entire aria was reused for the *Le Retour à la vie*; see n. 19.

35. **F-Pc** ms. 1505, fol. 23^r.

36. *Revue européene*, 15 March 1832, p. 48; trans. from my edition of the work, NBE 18:viii–ix.

37. The principal motive of "Le Ballet des ombres" (cat. no. 37) appears in "La Reine Mab," mm. 615–59; passages from *Sardanapale* (cat. no. 50) appear in movt. 2, mm. 81–86ff. and 129–32ff.

38. Despite the attempt of Charles Malherbe and Felix Weingartner to numerate their "critical" edition otherwise ("Old" Berlioz Edition, vol. 3, 1901), every contemporaneous source agrees on the seven-movement structure.

39. That he added the note that appears at beginning of the Tomb Scene (movt. 6) to the published score ("Le public n'a point d'imagination . . ." and thus the scene should be suppressed unless the audience is extremely familiar with "le cinquième acte de la tragédie de Shakespeare avec le dénouement de Garrick") is proof of this proposition. This idea seems to date from 1845–46.

40. A footnote added to the program of the *Fantastique* sometime during the 1830s reads: "If the few lines of this program had been the sort that could have been recited or sung between each of the movements of the symphony, as the chorus of ancient tragedy did, their meaning would not have been misunderstood" (see NBE 16:167–68).

41. Stephen Heller, "A Robert Schumann, à Leipzig," *Revue et gazette musicale* (1839): 546–49, 560–62.

42. I follow the reasoning of Ian Kemp, "*Romeo and Juliet* and *Roméo et Juliette*," in *Berlioz Studies*, ed. Peter Bloom (Cambridge, 1992), 37–79; see p. 48.

43. From a deleted passage, we gather that the passage at m. 278ff., notably the descending scale in the low strings, is to be associated with Tybalt's banishment from the ball. See Kemp, 53, 63.

44. Note also the complex *réunion des thèmes* set up at the beginning of the Roman Carnival scene in *Benvenuto Cellini* (no. 8, mm. 28ff.: "Vous voyez, j'espère . . .").

45. Kemp, "Romeo and Juliet."

46. Movt. 6; see NBE 18:253.

47. Wagner's presentation copy, sent 21 January 1860 before the Wagner concerts in Paris on 25 January and 1 and 8 February, is inscribed: "Au grand et cher auteur de / Roméo et Juliette / l'auteur reconnaissant de / Tristan et Isolde."

48. A list of complete and excerpted performances appears in Holoman, *Catalogue*, 202.

49. See Holoman, *Catalogue*, no. 62; and Holoman, "Sketchbook Recovered," 290–92.

50. On the Revolutionary tradition, see the extraordinary work of Constant Pierre (1855–1918), notably *Musique exécutée aux fêtes nationales de la Révolution française* (Paris, 1893–94), *Musique des fêtes et cérémonies de la Révolution française* (Paris, 1899), and *Les Hymnes et chansons de la Révolution française* (Paris, 1904).

51. A facsimile of the fragment that proves this proposition is given by Macdonald in NBE 19:100.

52. Dresden *Abendzeitung*, 14–17 June 1841, rpt. in *Richard Wagner's Prose Works*, ed. William Ashton Ellis (London, 1899), 8:136.

53. "Open-air music is a chimera," for example, in the feuilleton of 27 July 1846 in the *Journal des Débats*, cited by Macdonald in NBE 19:x. This concerned a performance of the work by 1800 in the Paris Hippodrome.

54. A map of Berlioz's journey of 1845–46 appears in Holoman, *Berlioz*, 326.

55. Le Sueur to Boucher, 11 February 1828, given by Tiersot in *Lettres de musiciens écrites en français du XVe au XXe siècle*, vol. 2 (Turin, 1924), 535–36.

56. The libretto of *Les Francs-Juges* appears in Holoman, *Autograph Musical Documents*, 291–325.

57. Berlioz does not correct the king of Hanover's following "it all: the King's entry into his council, the storm on the heath, the terrible scene in the prison, and Cordelia's lament" (*Mémoires*, chapter 59); he tells the anecdote about the drum fanfare in a letter to the king's chamberlain, Baron Donop, of 2 October 1858, *CG* vol. 5 (ed. Hugh Macdonald and François Lesure, 1988), no. 2320.

58. See Rimsky-Korsakov, *My Musical Life*, trans. Judah A. Joffe (rev. ed. New York, 1942), 82–83; Stasov, *Selected Essays on Music*, trans. Florence Jonas (London, 1968), 161–69; and the Stravinsky anecdote cited in n. 59.

59. Stravinsky is a partisan of the old argument that Berlioz wrote flawed bass lines: "Berlioz's reputation as an orchestrator has always seemed highly suspect to me. I was brought up on his music; it was played in the St. Petersburg of my student years as much as it has ever been played anywhere in the world. . . . He was a great innovator, of course, and he had the perfect imagination of each new instrument he used, as well as the knowledge of its technique. But the music he had to instrumentate was often poorly constructed harmonically. No orchestral skill can hide the fact that Berlioz's basses are sometimes uncertain and the inner harmonic voices unclear." Stravinsky and Robert Craft, *Conversations with Igor Stravinsky* (Berkeley and Los Angeles, 1958; rpt. 1980), 29.

Selected Bibliography

Berlioz, Hector. *La Damnation de Faust.* Ed. Julian Rushton. New Berlioz Edition, vol. 8a–b. Kassel, 1979, 1986.

———. *Grand traité d'instrumentation et d'orchestration modernes.* Paris, 1843. 2d ed., with *L'Art du Chef d'orchestre.* Paris, 1855. Reprint. Westmead, Farnborough, Hantshire, 1970.

———. *Harold en Italie.* Ed. Paul Banks. New Berlioz Edition, vol. 17. Kassel. Forthcoming.

———. *Lélio, ou Le Retour à la vie.* Ed. Peter Bloom. New Berlioz Edition, vol. 7. Kassel, 1992.

———. *Mémoires.* Paris, 1870. Ed. Pierre Citron. Paris, 1991. Trans. and ed. David Cairns. London, 1990.

———. *Overtures.* Ed. Diana Bickley. New Berlioz Edition, vol. 20. Kassel. Forthcoming.

———. *Roméo et Juliette.* Ed. D. Kern Holoman. New Berlioz Edition, vol. 18. Kassel, 1990.

———. *Symphonie fantastique.* Ed. Nicholas Temperley. New Berlioz Edition, vol. 16. Kassel, 1972. See also Edward T. Cone, ed., below.

———. *Symphonie funèbre et triomphale.* Ed. Hugh Macdonald. New Berlioz Edition, vol. 19. Kassel, 1967.

Bockholdt, Rudolf. *Berlioz-Studien.* Münchner Veröffentlichungen zur Musikgeschichte, vol. 29. Tutzing, 1979.

Cairns. David. *Berlioz, 1803–1832: The Making of an Artist.* Vol. 1 of 2 projected. London, 1989.

———. "Reflections on the *Symphonie fantastique* of 1830." In *Music in Paris in the Eighteen-Thirties / La Musique à Paris dans les années mil huit cent trente,* ed. Peter Bloom, 81–96. Stuyvesant, NY, 1987.

Cone, Edward T., ed. *Berlioz: Fantastic Symphony.* Norton Critical Scores. New York, 1971.

———. "Inside the Saint's Head." *Musical Newsletter* 1 (1971): 3–12, 16–20; 2 (1972): 19–22. Rpt. in *The Garland Library of the History of Western Music* 9:1–19. New York, 1985.

Dömling, Wolfgang. *Hector Berlioz: Die symphonisch-dramatischen Werke.* Stuttgart, 1979.

———. *Hector Berlioz: Symphonie fantastique.* Meisterwerke der Musik, vol. 19. Munich, 1985.

Holoman, D. Kern. *Berlioz.* Cambridge, MA, 1989.

———. *Catalogue of the Works of Hector Berlioz.* New Berlioz Edition, vol. 25. Kassel, 1987.

———. *The Creative Process in the Autograph Musical Documents of Hector Berlioz, c. 1818–1840.* 2d ed. Ann Arbor, MI, 1980.

Kemp, Ian. "*Romeo and Juliet* and *Roméo et Juliette.*" In *Berlioz Studies,* ed. Peter Bloom, 37–79. Cambridge, 1992.

Liszt, Franz. "Berlioz und seine Harold-Symphonie," *Neue Zeitschrift für Musik* 43 (1855): 25–32, 37–46, 49–55, 77–84, 89–97. Rpt. in *Gesammelte Schriften,* vol. 4 (Leipzig, 1882), 1–102.

Macdonald, Hugh. *Berlioz.* The Master Musicians. London, 1982.

———. *Berlioz Orchestral Music.* BBC Music Guide. London, 1969.

———. "Berlioz's Self-Borrowings." *Proceedings of the Royal Musical Association* 92 (1965–66): 29–33. Rpt. in *The Garland Library of the History of Western Music* 9:79–96. New York, 1985.

Primmer, Brian. *The Berlioz Style*. London, 1973.

Rushton, Julian. "The Genesis of Berlioz's 'La Damnation de Faust.'" *Music and Letters* 56 (1975): 129–46.

———. *The Musical Language of Berlioz*. Cambridge, 1983.

———. *Berlioz: Roméo et Juliette*. Cambridge Music Handbooks. Cambridge, 1994.

Temperley, Nicholas, "The *Symphonie fantastique* and its Program." *Musical Quarterly* 57 (1971): 593–608.

Recordings of Berlioz Works on Original Instruments

Les Francs-Juges Overture. In *Early Romantic Overtures*. London Classical Players, cond. Roger Norrington. EMI compact disc CDC 7 49889 2, 1990.

Symphonie fantastique. London Classical Players, cond. Roger Norrington. EMI compact disc CDC 7 49541 2, 1989.

Symphonie fantastique. Orchestre Revolutionnaire et Romantique, cond. John Eliot Gardiner. Philips compact disc 434 402-2, 1993. Also Philips video disc 440 070 254-1, 1993.

CHAPTER SIX

Liszt

Kenneth Hamilton

Your orchestral works represent . . . your personal art in a monumental form; and in that they are so new, so incomparable to anything else, criticism will take a long time to find out what to make of them.

— RICHARD WAGNER TO FRANZ LISZT, JULY 1856[1]

Wagner's remarks, written immediately after receiving the scores of the first six symphonic poems—*Les Préludes, Tasso, Orpheus, Mazeppa, Prometheus,* and *Festklänge*—foretold with more than Delphic precision the perplexities that still tend to reign when Liszt's symphonic works are mentioned. Wagner himself must take some of the responsibility for this. His essay "On Franz Liszt's Symphonic Poems" (1857) shrouds its wisdom in the master's usual obfuscatory prose and can scarcely have contributed greatly to the understanding of musicians faced with some of the most perplexing music of the era. The four years following Wagner's article saw the publication of six more symphonic poems (*Hungaria, Héroïde funèbre, Ce qu'on entend sur la montagne, Die Ideale, Hunnenschlacht,* and *Hamlet*), the *Dante* and *Faust* Symphonies, and the magnificent *Two Episodes from Lenau's "Faust."* By 1862 Liszt felt able to write, with uncharacteristic immodesty, "After having, as far as I could, solved the greater part of the *symphonic* problem set me in Germany, I mean now to undertake the *oratorio* problem."[2] He was not to return to the symphonic poem for nearly twenty years, when *From the Cradle to the Grave* formed an austere and aptly titled addendum to his mature achievements.

Liszt had not originally intended that orchestral music should loom quite so large in the output of his Weimar years. Although he had sketched a *Revolutionary* Symphony as early as 1830 (with material that later went into *Héroïde funèbre*) and had conceived "symphonic compositions" based on Dante and Faust in 1839,[3] his initial plans for Weimar had been to establish himself as an opera composer—the conventional route to success for the ambitious artist. He arrived there in 1848, the world's most acclaimed piano virtuoso, and proceeded to work on the Italian opera *Sardanapale* (after Byron), abandoned three years later after copious sketches and the usual wrangling over the libretto. The reasons for Liszt's change of course are not entirely clear, but among them were certainly dissatisfaction with even the final state of the *Sardanapale* libretto, a growing awareness of the uncertainties of operatic production, and increasing involvement with the operas of Wagner, whose *Lohengrin* Liszt premiered in Weimar in 1850. It would be a gross distortion, however, to think of Liszt as an opera composer manqué taking refuge in symphonic composition. Throughout the 1840s, long before a note of *Sardanapale* was penned, he was sketching music that would later be used in his orchestral works. The shelving of his operatic plans merely allowed him to concentrate his energies on a solution to the "symphonic problem" as he perceived it.

Quite simply, Liszt felt that orchestral music in Germany was in a rut. Too many composers contented themselves with churning out pallid sonata forms modeled after prescriptions such as those given by the theorist A. B. Marx or Liszt's own teacher Carl Czerny, in his *School of Practical Composition* of 1848. These forms were "too often changed by quite respectable people into *formulae*,"[4] and German music was wallowing, he thought, in a slough of mediocrity from which he was compelled to rescue it. In France the cause of true art could easily be left in the capable hands of Berlioz, whose music Liszt put on a par with Wagner's—and there was, for him, no higher praise—but in Germany the mantle of Beethoven had still to be taken on. Beethoven's works raised "the *great* question, which is the axis of criticism and of musical thought—namely, how far is traditional or recognized form a necessary determinant for the organism of thought?"[5]

From this point of view, Liszt divided Beethoven's work into two styles, not the customary three: "the first, that in which traditional and recognized form contains and governs the thoughts of the master, and the second, that in which the thought stretches, breaks, recreates and fashions the form and style according to its needs and inspirations."[6] In following the latter path with his own works, Liszt sought the alliance of literature and the visual arts. Music would be revitalized by the inspiring force of some sister work of art: a play, poem, or painting. Forms would then be fashioned according to the subject matter to be expressed, and as a result would never descend into routine. Such music would be programmatic only in a general sense and not slavishly follow an external narrative down to minute details, for in the last analysis the quality and coherence of the music would stand or fall by itself. Liszt was unequivocal: "In the end it comes principally to this—*what* the ideas are, and *how* they are carried out and worked up—and that always leads us back to *feeling* and *invention*."[7]

It seems necessary to stress this last point, for discussion of the merits or limitations of Liszt's theory of program music often tends to obscure rather than illuminate the works themselves. Like Wagner, whose ideas on music drama show such striking parallels with his own conception of dramatic orchestral music, Liszt did not follow any theory consistently. To examine an almost totally programmatic work by Liszt we need look no further than a melodrama such as *Der traurige Mönch*, which follows a text with virtually onomatopoetic exactitude—though even here elements of recapitulation show that Liszt is trying to shape an artistic whole. The idea of programmatic orchestral music was hardly new, and Liszt was familiar with examples by Beethoven, Berlioz, Mendelssohn, and Spohr, not to mention such minor works as Berwald's *Erinnerungen an der norwegischen Alpen* (performed in Vienna in 1842), which he could well have known. Nor did his search for new forms preclude adapting the tried and trusted sonata to his purposes. As Richard Kaplan, among others, has pointed out, several of the first group of symphonic poems—*Tasso, Les Préludes, Orpheus*, and *Prometheus*—as well as the first movement of the *Faust* Symphony are in sonata form.[8] To this list we can add *Festklänge*. In general, the later group of symphonic poems and the *Dante* Symphony show a more radical approach to form.

This is perhaps the place to point out that in considering the development of Liszt's orchestral works, the only reliable chronology is that of publication. Although *Ce qu'on entend sur la montagne*, for example, is often described as having been composed 1848–49, this refers only to the initial version of the piece, which went through three reworkings before appearing in print in 1857 in the version usually heard and discussed today. The revisions altered both the structure and much of the content of the piece. The same is true for other works, and it is obvious from Liszt's letters that he was in the habit of making substantial changes even after he had received the proofs of a piece. Liszt regarded this constant search for improvements as a characteristic of the true artist; how his copyists and sorely tried publisher regarded this can only be imagined.

The designation "symphonic poem" itself did not appear until April 1854, when *Tasso* was performed at a Weimar concert under that rubric. Previously Liszt had referred to his orchestral works simply as concert overtures, although *Ce qu'on entend* also sported the lofty appellation *Méditation Symphonie*. It has long been known, too, that *Les Préludes* had an earlier life as the overture to a choral setting of Joseph Autran's *Les quatre élémens*. The overture was initially composed between 1845 and 1849, based on themes from the choruses. In the same period Liszt jotted down the title *Les Préludes*—that of a poem from Lamartine's *Nouvelles méditations poétiques*—in the N.5 sketchbook, presumably with the intention of putting it to some musical use later. The adaptation of the overture into what we now know as the symphonic poem *Les Préludes* took place between 1853–54, and when the piece was published in 1856 it did indeed carry a deceptive claim to be "d'après Lamartine," along with a preface so vacuous as to fit almost any piece of music. Liszt obviously felt that a post facto association with Lamartine's *Les Préludes* would give the audience a crutch to lean on when hearing the piece for the first time, but it tells us nothing useful about the music, which was conceived in other circumstances.[9]

Mazeppa, too, is an amalgam of music from independent sources, the first half originating in a piano study only later given the title "Mazeppa," and the second half a reworking of the *Arbeiterchor* of 1848. Liszt had certainly been considering Mazeppa as a musical subject for a long time even before the piano study was relabeled (we find the name jotted down in the N.6 sketchbook, 1829–32), and there can be no doubt of the revised music's brilliance in portraying Mazeppa's nightmarish ride. But we must not lose sight of the fact that much of it had initially no programmatic association at all.

Admittedly, *Les Préludes* and *Mazeppa* are extreme cases. The other symphonic poems, and the two symphonies, are mostly what they claim to be. *Festklänge*, for example, is simply a festival overture written in anticipatory celebration of Liszt's cruelly thwarted marriage to the Princess Wittgenstein. It carries and requires neither program nor explanatory preface. *Hamlet* also has no preface, and is most often broadly described as a general character study of the brooding prince, lacking specific programmatic references. This is not so. In fact, *Hamlet* is the most programmatic of all Liszt's symphonic poems, evoking crucial scenes from the play in detail. This was pointed out by Liszt's first biographer, Lina Ramann, and then promptly ignored by subsequent scholars or dismissed as an example of overcreative analysis.[10] We can see from Ramann's *Lisztiana*, however, that she had this interpretation of *Hamlet* from Liszt himself.[11] It must have been a perverse whim on his part to attach an irrelevant preface to *Les Préludes*, then deliver *Hamlet* naked into the world (though in fact there is one footnote, to the effect that the central section represents Ophelia).

Programmatic or not, *Les Préludes* was Liszt's most popular orchestral work during his lifetime, a position it has maintained to this day. The other symphonic poems and symphonies made their way slowly and were generally regarded as pieces of revolutionary novelty, standard-bearers of the avant-garde. Yet Liszt's claim to be the successor of Beethoven was no empty boast, for the Music of the Future had many roots in the music of the past. His treatment of sonata form was heavily influenced by the works of Beethoven that loomed largest in his musical background: the piano sonatas, the symphonies, and the concert overtures. Before he arrived in Weimar Liszt had already prepared piano transcriptions of the Fifth, Sixth, and Seventh symphonies and the overtures to *Coriolan* and *Egmont;* by the mid-1860s he had transcribed Beethoven's entire symphonic corpus.

He was also active as a conductor of Beethoven's works from 1840 onward. It is not a surprise, then, to find the key sequence of *Les Préludes* modeled on that of Beethoven's "Waldstein" Sonata—a first group in C major, cantabile second subject in E major, and, after a development with more than a little of Mendelssohn's *Hebrides* Overture in it (and a touch of Berlioz), a recapitulation in which the second subject turns to the tonic via A major. Even the transformation, so typically Lisztian, of the second subject into a rumbustious march parallels the similar transformation of the "Ode to Joy" theme in the last movement of the Ninth Symphony. Liszt was discerning in his reminiscences of Beethoven, and his adaptation of wonderful moments from Beethoven's works generally results in equally splendid effects in their newfound home. The hushed expectancy of mankind gazing up at the stars from the "Ode to Joy," for example, reappears toward the end of the magnificent *Héroïde funèbre* (Ex. 6.1).

The implacable chromatic ground bass in the peroration of the first movement of the *Dante* Symphony (mm. 604–25) undoubtedly has an elder brother in the coda of the first movement of the Ninth. We may also, when we hear the gradual development from tenebrous rumblings to grandiose unison theme that opens *Ce qu'on entend sur la montagne*, feel we've heard that song before—at the beginning of the Ninth—even though Liszt's harmonies roam further afield than Beethoven's. The expanded tonal structure—a massive three-key exposition going from Eb to the mediant F# and finally coming to rest on the conventional dominant Bb at measure 208—is an expansion of a scheme adumbrated by Beethoven in Liszt's old warhorse the "Emperor" Concerto and further worked out in Schubert's last piano sonata.[12] We may even see in the second group of *Die Ideale*—a beautifully languid theme going through the keys of D, B, and E (mm. 198–264) but never quite settling in any of them—a successor of the sequential second subject in Beethoven's *Coriolan* Overture. When we also consider that Liszt's fondness for repeating a slow introduction at the center of a movement was probably inspired by the "Pathétique" Sonata, we may reasonably ask why his music was considered by Wagner and others as "so new, so incomparable to anything else."

Wagner himself gave a partial answer in "On Franz Liszt's Symphonic Poems." Beethoven's *Leonora* Overture No. 3, he believed, is weakened by the appearance of a conventional recapitulation in the tonic after the dramatic development section. Surely the piece would be better if the recapitulation were omitted altogether and Beethoven had proceeded straightaway to the triumphal coda. This would have created a new form more suited to Beethoven's expressive intents in the overture—the type of programmatic form that, according to Wagner, Liszt had the daring and imagination to develop for his symphonic poems. We need not agree with Wagner's analysis of the deficiencies of *Leonora* No. 3 to realize that he has hit upon one of the more striking features of Liszt's symphonic music: a formal ingenuity that often demands that it be heard against the

EXAMPLE 6.1.

a. Beethoven, arr. Liszt, Symphony No. 9 in D Minor Op. 125, movt. 4, mm. 106–13

(*continued*)

EXAMPLE 6.1. (*continued*)
b. Liszt, *Heroïde funèbre*, mm. 271–79

music: a formal ingenuity that often demands that it be heard against the background of conventional sonata form for its full effect.

Tasso is a fine example. After the slow opening, culled from a fragment of what will be the principal theme, a violent *allegro energico* begins. This seems as if it ought to lead to the exposition of the main sonata allegro theme and, to be sure, at measure 33 a pedal G appears to prepare for the entry of an agitated theme in C minor. The music works itself up into a fury—and suddenly comes to rest on a *fff* interrupted cadence; this brings back the slow music from the beginning and again leaves us baffled on a dominant pedal. When the main theme finally appears, at measure 63, it turns out to be a long, lyrical melody, *adagio mesto*. Expectations of a tempestuous C-minor *allegro* have been deliberately set up and thwarted, an inspired parallel to the frustrations of the poet Tasso's life.

The music before measure 63 is therefore all introduction, itself in an ABA' form, with a Berliozian change of tempo between sections. The A part of the introduction recurs, varied, before the central minuet section, and the BA' music returns before the final *trionfo*, which simultaneously recapitulates the minuet and the *adagio mesto* in the tonic C major and provides a jubilant coda to the work. It should be noted how close this is to Wagner's *Leonora* prescription of passing over the conventional recapitulation and going straight to the coda. The *adagio mesto*, which otherwise behaves as any good exposition should and moves to the contrasting key area of E major, is never recapitulated in its original form, but only as a transformed *allegro maestoso e pomposo* crown to the coda. If we add to this treatment of the exposition and recapitulation the fact that the normal development section is replaced by a minuet in F♯—a tritone from the tonic—and that the entire work is ostentatiously derived from the *adagio mesto* tune, the perplexity of contemporary critics becomes a little easier to understand.

Even today, the construction of a work like *Festklänge* obviously puzzles many writers. In fact, it is in another of Liszt's ingenious sonata-form variants, again with a dual-tempo introduction presenting the significant motives in various "wrong" keys. The main *allegro* in C major begins at measure 62, wending its jubilant way to measure 111, where it lands with aplomb on an emphatic chord of B major. We now might assume a second group in the median key of E (the contrasting key area in *Prometheus, Tasso, Orpheus, Les Préludes,* and *Faust*), but Liszt takes a surprise cutoff, via an augmented-sixth harmony on B, to emerge in G minor, which turns to the major with a nonchalantly lyrical melody at measure 139. A second group in the dominant appears positively antiquated in this "Music of the Future" and is especially surprising when heralded by an obvious preparation of the mediant key. Liszt seems to be about to make amends by bringing on a polonaise in B♭ at measure 158, but within a few bars it, too, arrives in the dominant, reaching a witty climax (mm. 199ff.) with a variant of the augmented-sixth harmony that deflected the music to G in the first place.

EXAMPLE 6.2. Liszt, *Hamlet*, mm. 1–4

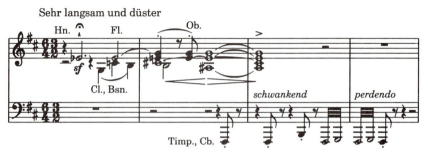

The tonal game played by Liszt in *Festklänge* has no programmatic inspiration. Only the appearance of a polonaise as part of the second group, in honor of Princess Wittgenstein's Polish birth, hints at the work's personal meaning for the composer. *Hamlet*, on the other hand, is a different matter. The opening theme was intended as a setting of "To be or not to be," the rhythm of which it fits perfectly (Ex. 6.2). (The direction *schwankend* obviously refers to Hamlet's notorious, and eventually fatal, vacillation.) The course of the famous soliloquy is paralleled closely by the following music, but Liszt then jumps back in the play for the apparition of the ghost (mm. 50ff.: *schaurig*), which eventually stirs Hamlet into action portrayed by this noble theme (Ex. 6.3).

The characteristic flattened leading tone and accompanying harmony, preventing a firm perfect cadence in B minor, is the musical parallel of the irresolution that afflicts Hamlet, even at his most energetic. The action is brought to a sudden halt by the arrival of Ophelia (mm. 161ff.), whose solicitude is answered by a passage marked *ironisch* and composed of fragments of Hamlet's motives. ("Get thee to a nunnery" is surely intended.) This episode—the center of the work—is followed by an *allegro molto* that transforms a languid section from the introduction into an anguished portrayal of the act 3, scene 4, meeting between Hamlet and Gertrude. At the climax slashing chords represent the killing of Polonius behind the arras ("The rat! The rat!" said Liszt to Lina Ramann during a performance of *Hamlet* in its two-piano version—a reference to Hamlet's "How now? A rat! Dead for a ducat, dead," rather than to a perfidious member of the audience.) The exigencies of musical form require Liszt to kill Polonius a second time before a repeat of the work's opening "To be or not to be?" leads to a short, intense funeral march. The question has been answered in the negative, and the music sinks into oblivion. Close parallels between the symphonic poem and the play do not result in a rambling, formless piece of music. The work is constructed in an arch form—with the scene between Hamlet and Ophelia as its keystone—and with the whole underpinned by a pervasive use of thematic transforma-

EXAMPLE 6.3. Liszt, *Hamlet*, mm. 106–14

tion and by the varied repeat of significant sections. It is certainly one of Liszt's greatest achievements.

The constant thematic transformation found in *Hamlet* usually looms large in any discussion of the symphonies and symphonic poems. Liszt himself was rightly proud of his versatility, but he can hardly be said, as some have suggested, to have invented the technique. We have already commented on the "Lisztian" transformation of the "Ode to Joy" theme into a Turkish march in the last movement of Beethoven's Ninth, and the continual transformations of the "Lebewohl" figure in the first movement of the *Les Adieux* Sonata are equally impressive. Liszt made no secret of the importance of Schubert's *Wanderer* Fantasy for the thematic working of his mature music, but most influential of all was Berlioz. The debased distortion of the *idée fixe* during the last movement of the *Symphonie fantastique* was surely the inspiration for the thematic parody in the "Mephistopheles" movement of the *Faust* Symphony. In fact, the opening of that movement is so close to the opening of the Witches' Sabbath that we might talk in terms of a conscious tribute, if we are charitable, or brazen theft if we are not. The manner in which the *idée fixe* functions as a dramatis persona in the *Symphonie fantastique* foreshadows Liszt's equally dramatic use of thematic return and metamorphosis.

In the *Faust* Symphony we experience the vicissitudes of the themes of the "Faust" movement as those of Faust himself. When the Faust themes return suddenly to darken the face of the "Gretchen" movement, the impact is virtually operatic: a familiar character has suddenly reappeared onstage. Liszt repeats the effect in the last movement, where the vision of Gretchen (mm. 417–30) is serenely immune to Mephistopheles's tricks. The stroke of genius is that the reminiscence here is twofold, recalling dramatically the entrance of Faust in the second movement while simultaneously mirroring the return of the slow, stark, keyless introduction at the center of the "Faust" movement. Both passages begin with a unison A♭, but the later A♭ is sustained high in the strings as the woodwinds intone the Gretchen theme below in a harbinger of eventual redemption.

This striving for wordless music drama conditions Liszt's use of preexistent themes for symbolic purposes. What better means of underlining the futility and sheer waste of war than by a hollow quote of "Aux armes, citoyens!" from the "Marseillaise" in *Héroïde funèbre?* (This was a particularly sensitive issue for Liszt, who had been criticized for keeping well away while his compatriots died during the 1848 Hungarian revolution.) The triumph of Christianity over paganism is represented by the gradual assertion of the plainchant "Crux fidelis" in *Hunnenschlacht*, the procession of penitents in *Die nächtliche Zug* by "Pange lingua."

These references speak directly to the keen listener; other associations are intelligible only to a reader of the score, and sometimes not even then. The main thematic material of "Inferno" from the *Dante* Symphony is formed by setting directly several passages from the poem itself, all quoted in the score. But the reference of the only new theme to appear in the "Mephistopheles" movement of the *Faust* Symphony is thoroughly obscure. This theme (first heard at mm. 47–52) appears in Liszt's early *Malédiction* Concerto with the description "pride," an apt association in the context of the symphony but one that Liszt has nowhere indicated in the score. The origin of the languid melody that forms the basis of *Tasso* is no secret. Liszt tells us in the preface to the score that he had heard a gondolier sing the first lines of Tasso's *Gerusalemme liberata* to this Italian folk tune: "The Venetian melody breathes so gnawing a melancholy, so irremediable a sadness, that a mere reproduction of it seems sufficient to reveal the secret of Tasso's sad emotions." Liszt loved this type of melody, and Italianate cantilena was an essential part of his musical style, though frequently arrayed in quite un-Italian chromatic harmony. Of the two original themes quoted in Example 6.4, from *Les Préludes* and *Héroïde funèbre*, the first would hardly be out of place in Rossini's *La donna del lago*, while the second transcends particular associations in its transfigured beauty.

EXAMPLE 6.4.
a. Liszt, *Les Préludes*, mm. 70–73

b. Liszt, *Heroïde funèbre*, mm. 152–56

It is a measure of Liszt's genius that he was able to weld a cosmopolitan range of influences—ranging from Italianate melodic writing to Germanic developmental procedures, with Hungarian gypsy music and French grand opera thrown in for good measure—into a distinctive personal style. His model in this was undoubtedly Meyerbeer, whose music, often disgracefully underrated today, shows a similar stylistic eclecticism. Liszt admired Meyerbeer's operas, even in the face of the self-serving attacks of Wagner and the pious moralizing of Schumann. The exultant *andante maestoso* of *Les Préludes* (mm. 35ff.) is not so far removed from the world of *Les Huguenots* (the climax of the "Blessing of the Daggers" scene in act 4 offers the most obvious parallel) and, on a more intimate scale, the unusual viola accompaniment to Gretchen's theme in the second movement of the *Faust* Symphony could only have been suggested by the viola obbligato to Raoul's famous "Plus blanche que la blanche Hermine" in act 1—another eulogy of girlish innocence. Some find the all-embracing amalgam that constitutes Liszt's musical style off-putting. Liszt could well in reply have adapted the celebrated remark of Terence—"I am a musician: nothing musical is alien to me." Certainly there can be few things in Liszt quite as jarring (for those susceptible) as the constant flux be-

EXAMPLE 6.5. Liszt, *Dante Symphony*
a. "Inferno," mm. 287–90

(*continued*)

EXAMPLE 6.5. (*continued*)
b. "Gretchen," mm. 15–19

tween "old" and "new, improved" Wagner in the Paris version of *Tann-häuser*. Like Wagner, Liszt exercised rigorous self-control in adapting his style to the dramatic subject of a work. It is no accident that Francesca da Rimini should be depicted in the first movement of the *Dante* Symphony by a suave Italian theme harmonized in thirds, while Gretchen should emerge as a girl of quite different, almost Mozartian stamp (Ex. 6.5).

Liszt was only too well aware of critical objections to his music during his lifetime, and by the end had come to expect the hail of vituperation with which certain quarters of the press would greet a new piece, along with the obligatory comments about sticking to piano playing. Ironically some of the most persistent criticism was directed against the main technique Liszt used to render his music more intelligible to the public—repetition of sections, occasionally exactly, but mostly with variations in key or orchestration. As the most successful concert artist of the nineteenth century, Liszt was always concerned with the effectiveness of his music before an inexperienced audience, in all likelihood hearing the piece for the first time. In a review of some of Schumann's larger piano works, which also made use of large-scale repetition, he commented: "It is mistaken to regard repetition as poverty. From the point of view of the audience it is indispensable to the understanding of the idea; from the point of view of art it is virtually identical to the demands of clarity, order, and effect."[13]

The Classical masters appeared to be of the same opinion, if we take their repeat marks literally: consider the scherzo of Beethoven's Seventh in its almost interminable authentic form. Liszt's mistake was apparently to try to make his repetitions more varied than those of his predecessors. But Liszt had no hesitation in cutting his own music for individual performances, and several of the symphonic poems have possible cuts marked in the score. Some of these cuts are certainly worth considering for live performance, though they are by no means the only possible ones. The cut marked in *Prometheus* omits the recapitulation of the first subject entirely and produces a different, but equally interesting form, analogous to Chopin's second and third piano sonatas, in which the recapitulation begins with the second subject. The cut of ten measures (371–81) in the reprise of the slow introduction at the center of the *Faust* Symphony first movement, which several conductors follow (though it is not indicated in the score), probably derives from the practice of Liszt himself.[14]

But before wielding the blue pencil too readily, we should consider the second part of Liszt's comment on repetition: that it is necessary for clarity, order, and effect. The gargantuan sonata structure of *Ce qu'on entend sur la montagne* is articulated by means of large-scale repetition: two repeated blocks (mm. 309–408 and 520–99) stand like pillars to mark the beginning and end of the development section. These units not only contain some of the finest music in the whole work—music that can well bear restatement—but also perform an essential function in rendering the construction of such a monumental work comprehensible to the listener.

Indeed, the problem of intelligibility is all the more pressing in the light of Liszt's gift for complex chromatic harmony. The opening of *Hamlet*, quoted in Example 6.2, is typical of Liszt's most involved style; the limpid harmonies of the opening of *Orpheus*, though superficially simpler, are among of the most sophisticated creations of his art (Ex. 6.6).

Liszt initially sounds a mysterious unaccompanied G on the horns—the dominant of the tonic key of C. Instead of a dominant harmony, however, a second-inversion chord of E♭ unrolls on the harp. A pause. The G is sounded again, the bass falls to A, and we hear a dominant seventh chord—but that of the key of D. After another pause, the third repeat of the G takes us back from the threshold of D to the first-inversion dominant seventh of F. This actually resolves to a root position chord of F, but the resolution is only partial, for the melody note G now produces a mildly dissonant seventh above the bass. The seventh should eventually resolve to an F, and so it does, after a melisma, except by this time (m. 18) the bass has fallen to D to imitate the figure in the treble, and the consequent chord is simply the inversion of another dissonant seventh: D–A–C–F. This chord falls onto a first-inversion G-major harmony in the next measure, and we are all set for a long-awaited cadence in the tonic. The tonic certainly arrives at measure 20, but in a weak second inversion. The bass line only briefly touches on C before it plants itself firmly on B♭ to start the process all over again, this time leading to a definite perfect cadence in G major. This wonderfully subtle mastery of harmony is altogether ex-

EXAMPLE 6.6. Liszt, *Orpheus,* mm. 1–26

(*continued*)

quisite, the expected resolutions gently deflected by a supple chromaticism that never leads to excess; it deftly captures the chaste lines of the visual art of the ancient world from which Liszt claimed to have taken his inspiration. The remainder of *Orpheus* is on a similarly exalted level: for ten minutes one can almost believe that the magical powers attributed to Orpheus's music in myth might not be so exaggerated after all.

If *Orpheus* represents Liszt's music at its most restrained, the *Dante* Symphony demonstrates his powers of tone painting on an epic scale. The term "tone painting" is particularly appropriate here, in that the composer at one time cherished the idea of linking his music to a diorama of scenes from Dante's *Divine Comedy*, to be projected before the audience during performances. Had this plan come to fruition, we might be able to call Liszt the first film composer, but his vision was at least partially fulfilled in that many later film composers used not only the illustrative techniques developed in Liszt's orchestral music but even large chunks of the symphonies and symphonic poems themselves to pad out their scores.

When we hear Prometheus's titanic sufferings accompanying a storm-tossed ship in *Captain Blood*, we realize that Liszt bequeathed to Hollywood more than a legendary life. But Liszt's inheritors have so overused certain effects from his works that some highly original passages now either teeter on the brink of cliché or fall headlong over it. This is especially true of the tempestuous chromatic writing in "Inferno" of the *Dante* Symphony. If we are able to ignore associations built up in our own century, "Inferno" can hardly fail to make a vivid impact.

Liszt's tour of "Inferno" is in three parts: a tempestuous exposition portraying the torments of hell, a central interlude depicting the doomed love affair of Francesca da Rimini, and a recapitulation in which the music of the first part returns in varied form. The slow introduction bellows out the inscription above the gates of hell, including the famous "Lasciate ogni speranza, voi ch'entrate" (Abandon all hope, ye who enter here) with which Dante's God greets the children of perdition. The rhythmically articulated descending chromatic scale, immediately following, goes on to take a lead role in the *allegro frenetico*. This *allegro*, though highly chromatic, is firmly grounded in the key of D minor. There is no second-subject key area in the normal sense, but the transformation of the descending chromatic scale into a variety of more diatonic patterns, beginning at measure 163, supplies an inspired analogy. The return of the "Lasciate" theme concludes the exposition, its wandering bass landing on B♭ in measure 266 to produce a gloriously unexpected chord of B♭ major, and this awesome consonance seems even more terrifying as a symbol of ineluctable damnation than anything that has gone before. Liszt's transition to the central section makes magical use of instrumental color—in particular harp glissandi—to give the effect of a dramatic scene change. Indeed, his skill in producing a kaleidoscope of orchestral color reaches its zenith in the *Dante* Symphony, typified by the gradual raising of the orchestral tessitura from the subterranean brass choruses of "Inferno" to the Magnificat that gives us a glimpse of paradise, its ethereal harmonies resonating high in the orchestra.

The tonal journey follows the same path from a Stygian D minor in "Inferno," obsessed with unstable tritonal harmonies, through the B minor of "Purgatorio," to the modally inflected B major of the Magnificat. There are, of course, contrasts within the movements, the most striking being Francesca da Rimini's *andante amoroso* in F♯ major, which reminds us of the fleeting pleasures of carnal sin that appear to demand an eternity's retribution in hell. The opening of "Purgatorio" achieves part of its force from the memory of the end of "Inferno," the D minor softening to D major as Dante and Virgil climb up from hell to see the brightness of the stars. The gentle lilt of the strings illustrates Dante's metaphor of a bark undulating on the waves, from which the travelers see dawn appear in the east. Liszt's music here is of an almost divine beauty that compensates the listener abundantly for the all-too-realistic tedium of purgatory's fugue.

Perhaps only those who have endured the fugue are worthy of the incandescent Magnificat that brings this fascinating work to its mystic close.

In the orchestral score Liszt appended a second, *fortissimo* ending to the *Dante* Symphony of markedly inferior quality. A footnote to the piano solo transcription of the work, by Liszt's pupil August Stradal, informs us that in later life Liszt considered the quiet ending to be the more suitable conclusion. A similar alternative exists for the *Faust* Symphony, which was originally conceived without the choral finale usually performed today. Liszt admitted that the choral finale was a "stumbling block" at the first Weimar performance and that many of his friends, including Wagner, had urged him to omit it in favor of the purely orchestral ending that also appears in the score.[15] The rather grandiloquent setting of the "Chorus Mysticus" from the second part of Goethe's *Faust* is perhaps a mistake, marring the conclusion of one of Liszt's greatest works. The orchestral ending substitutes a fine peroration based on the most assertive of Faust's themes.

This theme, a setting of the words "Im Anfang war die Tat" from the opening monologue of the first part of Goethe's *Faust*, is initially found in the second subject group of the first movement—a masterly portrait of Faust, his frustrations and ambition. As in *Tasso*, the introduction is in three sections (slow–fast–slow), with the fast section vigorously taking up the opening motive of augmented triads in what seems to be the start of an *allegro* exposition. This comes to a brutal halt in a passage of violent *fff* chords (mm. 61–64), foreshadowing Liszt's equally rhetorical method of shortening the recapitulation (mm. 442–46). When the true *allegro* exposition begins in C minor (mm. 71ff.), its first subject is an entirely new theme, although as it continues it incorporates motivic elements from the introduction. The development section will later reiterate this theme in a false recapitulation in C♯ minor, all the more convincing because it is the relative minor of the second subject key of E. This deceptive repeat is stopped in its tracks by the return of the slow introduction, which bisects the development and consequently the whole movement—a necessary point of reference in a structure so large. As the slow introduction is virtually keyless, it does nothing to resolve the tonal flux of the development, which at first carries on unhindered until measure 400, when a dramatic diminished-seventh chord makes way for the augmented-triad motive from the slow introduction yet again. This time the whole-tone implications of its melodic structure are brought to the fore in a visionary passage that eventually ushers in the recapitulation via E major. Liszt, with the cunning of a practiced confidence man, has successfully created the impression that we are somehow going back to the second subject key in an arch form. Instead he plunges into C minor (mm. 415–22) in an inspired parallel to the entry of the exposition from an implied E minor at the end of the introduction (mm. 66–71). We have not heard the last of E major even now, for the second subject group emerges in that key (mm. 451ff.) again. A suave enharmonic modulation takes us firmly back to C major.

"Gretchen" prepares different tonal surprises. If the "Faust" movement seems occasionally to get stuck in the second subject key, then "Gretchen" has an addiction to the tonic itself. After a lengthy statement of the main theme (see Ex. 6.5b) in A♭ major, Liszt initiates a move toward A major that never quite reaches its goal but ends up in a short passage illustrating "he loves me—he loves me not" (mm. 51–56). The main theme returns in the tonic and again begins a move away, this time to the threshold of E (mm. 72ff.). Once more the music is deflected back to the tonic, in which key the second theme unfolds in a leisurely fashion (mm. 83ff.). The recapitulation follows the same tonal course with few variations. It is this tonal stasis that accounts for the tremendous impression made by the entry of Faust's music in C minor at the center of the movement (mm. 111ff.), as well as contributing to the success of Liszt's delicate portrait of Gretchen.

Liszt is often described as an "episodic" composer, and the judgment is easy to understand when we consider how vivid are the contrasts his music presents. But so many of the most startling effects in the *Faust* Symphony and other works are meticulously prepared and executed on such a large scale that only a facile analysis could describe them as anything but symphonic in the genuine sense. That the *Faust* Symphony is conceived on the largest scale of all is shown by "Mephistopheles," simultaneously a varied recapitulation of the "Faust" movement and a resolution of the drama. "Mephistopheles" represents the zenith of Liszt's art of thematic transformation and demonstrates that he was among the greatest of variation composers, though he rarely wrote a standard variation set. Few artists, having produced a movement of the length and complexity as the first movement of *Faust*, would then undertake the composition, for the finale, of yet another on the same blueprint. It is a measure of his genius that throughout "Mephistopheles" he is able to form something new, retaining the structure of "Faust" yet never giving the impression that his creativity has been exhausted. This constant striving for the original and novel inspires all his orchestral music, even when he is obviously standing on the shoulders of the giants of the past. True to his convictions, Liszt never sank into the apathy of routine, and as his music takes an ever firmer place in the orchestral repertoire we too may echo the verdict of the angels in Goethe's *Faust*: "He who ever strives, him alone can we save."

Notes

1. *Correspondence of Wagner and Liszt*, trans. and ed. Francis Hueffer (London, 1888), 2:152 (letter 217, 12 July 1856).

2. *Letters of Franz Liszt*, ed. La Mara, trans. Constance Bache (London, 1894), 2:33 (letter 9, to Dr. Franz Brendel, 8 November 1862).

3. Liszt, *Journal des Zÿi*, in *Mémoires par Daniel Stern*, ed. Daniel Ollivier (Paris, 1927), 180. Also quoted in Sharon Winklhofer, "Liszt, Marie d'Agoult, and the 'Dante' Sonata," *19th-Century Music* 1 (1977): 27.

4. La Mara, *Letters of Liszt* 1:273 (letter 154, to Louis Köhler, 9 July 1856).

5. Ibid. 1:151–52 (letter 91, to Wilhelm von Lenz, 2 December 1852).

6. Ibid.

7. Ibid 1:271 (letter 154, to Louis Köhler, 9 July 1856).

8. Richard Kaplan, "Sonata Form in the Orchestral Works of Liszt: The Revolutionary Reconsidered," *19th-Century Music* 8 (1984): 142–52.

9. A fine study of the *Les Préludes* affair is Andrew Bonner, "Liszt's *Les Préludes* and *Les Quatres Elémens: A Reinvestigation,"* *19th-Century Music* 10 (1986): 95–107.

10. Lina Ramann, *Franz Liszt als Künstler und Mensch*, vol. 2 (Leipzig, 1894), 292–99.

11. Lina Ramann, *Lisztiana*, ed. Arthur Seidl (Mainz, 1983), 258. The program for Hamlet proposed by Edward Murphy in "A Detailed Programme for Liszt's 'Hamlet,'" *Journal of the American Liszt Society* 29 (January–June 1991): 47–60, seems to have no source other than the author's own overly fertile imagination.

12. A perceptive discussion of both the Beethoven and the Schubert works is found in Charles Rosen, *Sonata Forms*, rev. ed. (New York, 1988), 249–61.

13. *Gesammelte Schriften von Franz Liszt*, ed. Lina Ramann (Leipzig, 1881), 1:103.

14. See László Somfai, "Die musikalischen Gestaltwandlungen der *Faust-Symphonie* von Liszt," *Studia Musicologica Academiae Scientiarum Hungaricae* 2 (1962): 119.

15. La Mara, *Letters of Liszt* 2:31 (letter 8, to Dr. Franz Brendel, 29 August 1862). Admiration for the choral ending is nowadays, however, widespread.

Selected Bibliography

Bonner, Andrew. "Liszt's *Les Préludes* and *Les Quatres Elémens:* A Reinvestigation." *19th-Century Music* 10 (1986): 95–107.

Kaplan, Richard. "Sonata Form in the Orchestral Works of Liszt: The Revolutionary Reconsidered." *19th-Century Music* 7 (1984): 142–52.

Koch, Lájos. *Franz Liszt: ein bibliographischer Versuch.* Budapest, 1936.

Mueller, Rena. "Liszt's 'Tasso' Sketchbook: Studies in Sources and Revisions." Ph.D. dissertation, New York University, 1986.

Saffle, Michael. *Franz Liszt: A Guide to Research.* New York, 1991.

Somfai, László. "Die musikalischen Gestaltwandlungen der *Faust-Symphonie* von Liszt." *Studia Musicologica Academiae Scientiarum Hungaricae* 2 (1962): 87–137.

Suttoni, Charles. "Liszt Correspondence in Print: An Expanded, Annotated Bibliography." *Journal of the American Liszt Society* 25 (1989).

Wagner, Richard. "On Franz Liszt's Symphonic Poems." In *Richard Wagner's Prose Works*, trans. William Ashton Ellis, vol. 3, 236–54. London, 1894.

Walker, Alan. *Franz Liszt.* Vol. 1: *The Virtuoso Years, 1811–1847.* Rev. ed., London, 1989. Vol. 2: *The Weimar Years, 1848–1861.* London, 1989. Vol. 3: *The Final Years, 1861–1886.* London and New York, 1996.

Watson, Derek. *Liszt.* Rev. ed. London, 1990.

Williamson, John. "The Revision of Liszt's 'Prometheus.'" *Music and Letters* 47 (1986): 381–90.

CHAPTER SEVEN

The French Symphony
David, Gounod, and Bizet to Saint-Saëns, Franck, and Their Followers

Ralph P. Locke

The landscape of French music, as observers have long noted, often resembles a wide and pleasant plateau rather than, as at times in Germany and Italy, an uneven vista of a few sun-speckled mountains looming over dark valleys of mediocrity. From the seventeenth century to the middle of the twentieth, French music in any given period has usually reveled in a prevailing "contemporary 'classical' idiom" (as Martin Cooper put it), a style that reflects a relatively consistent approach to certain favored genres and that is widely shared among a number of the country's skilled craftsmen and the occasional craftswoman.[1] In the mid-nineteenth century, to be specific, there was no single French figure equivalent in authority and influence to Beethoven or Rossini, Wagner or Verdi; instead, a generally accepted stylistic synthesis reigned in the works of a number of reliable, "middle-of-the-road" composers such as D.-F.-E. Auber and Charles Gounod. Similarly, at the turn of the twentieth century, there was no French equivalent of Puccini or Richard Strauss, but rather a cluster of composers—Camille Saint-Saëns, Gabriel Fauré, Jules Massenet—whose works, despite their many profound differences, share certain basic stylistic traits and compositional preoccupations. Berlioz and Debussy, the figures who for many music lovers today embody French music from around 1850 and 1900, respectively, were in some ways marginal, or at least highly controversial, in their time. The exceptions prove the rule.

As Cooper's book reveals, though, this integrative tendency toward a single accepted French style has often been counterbalanced, or enriched, by a splintering tendency, manifested in the various cliques and articulate spokesmen vying publicly, passionately, for the authority of determining what shape that new "classical" style should take, what aesthetic guidelines should predominate. The French people's love of argument and manifesto has tended to produce prominent composer-writers (Rameau, Grétry, Berlioz, Debussy, and, in more recent days, Messiaen and Boulez) promoting musical principles and works dear to them, as well as bands of propagandists pressing for French acceptance or rejection of the ideas of reformers from foreign lands, such as Gluck, Wagner, Stockhausen, or John Cage.

During the years under study here, an ever-increasing number of composers turned eagerly to symphonic production, and many of the resulting works share significant features.[2] Most notably, toward the end of the century, certain compositional techniques associated with late Beethoven, Liszt, and Wagner (including cyclical themes and a highly chromatic harmonic vocabulary) became deeply rooted through the work and teaching of César Franck and Vincent d'Indy.[3] But other trends, if less widely trumpeted, were no less important. Throughout the century, pedagogues and critics urged students to carry onward the great Austro-German "symphonic tradition" embodied in the works of Haydn, Mozart, early Beethoven, Mendelssohn, and Schumann. Berlioz and Liszt (during his Paris years and after) urged the development of "program music" as the logical and necessary next step in symphonic development. And some, such as Camille Saint-Saëns, positioned themselves precariously between two or more of these rival camps. The net result is a number of important symphonies (and symphonic poems, which we must largely leave in silence here) by a dozen or more talented figures, including Félicien David, Ernest Reyer, Gounod, Georges Bizet, Saint-Saëns, Franck, Edouard Lalo, Ernest Chausson, Paul Dukas, Albéric Magnard, d'Indy, and Debussy. The best of these works are richly characterful and dramatic, as one might expect from a nation that prized opera above all other musical genres, but, as recent performances and recordings have amply confirmed, they also manifest a coherence and a persuasive power that refuse to fade.

Reestablishing the Symphony in France

In the late eighteenth century, France had been a land of symphonies. Native products, such as the symphonies and *symphonies concertantes* of François Gossec and Simon Leduc, as well as works of Haydn and the Mannheim composers, could be heard at several important concert series and were put on sale by the many prominent music publishers of Paris. The Revolution of 1789 put the brakes on much of this activity, which had been patronized to a large extent by the aristocracy.[4] But symphonies kept being written into the early nineteenth century. The best of the lot, with the possible exception of the first of Etienne Méhul's four remarkable symphonies (G Minor, 1809), is Luigi Cherubini's Symphony in C Major (1815), written on commission for the Royal Philharmonic Society of London (as would be several other major symphonies by Continental composers, including Beethoven's Ninth and Saint-Saëns's Third). Cherubini was born and trained in Italy but resided in France beginning in the late 1780s; by the time of his symphony (which he later reworked as his Second String Quartet, with a different slow movement), he had written a number of important French operas and had begun holding a series of influential posts in official French musical life, ultimately including the directorship of the Conservatoire. That his only symphony was composed for London reflects the absence of a major concert series in Paris. One such series, focusing on the symphonies of Haydn, had been tried for a time at a glass-ceilinged hall in the rue de Cléry; and during the Bourbon Restoration (1814–30) the Conservatoire mounted occasional student concerts under the skilled leadership of the violinist-conductor François-Antoine Habeneck.

It was Habeneck who, in the 1820s, finally planted the symphony concert firmly again, and now lastingly, in French soil. His Société des Concerts du Conservatoire was astonishingly democratic, the players receiving equal shares of the profits, in marked departure from the extreme disparities that characterized the government-directed wage structures in the pit orchestras of the Opéra and other theaters. Habeneck's explicit mission was to bring the symphonies of the masters, notably Haydn, Mozart, and Mendelssohn, but especially Beethoven, to resonant life, and he spared no effort. (He rehearsed the Ninth for several seasons before he felt the performance worthy enough to be heard publicly.) Wagner and other visitors to Paris admired the results: precise, coherent, somewhat brisk readings that put orchestras in Germany to shame.[5]

But Habeneck had little wish to promote French symphonies. Perhaps he felt that the series should provide a counterweight to the Opéra, where he was conductor and where the latest Parisian composers, whether native-born or adopted, had their ballets and grand operas performed regularly: Auber, Rossini (resident in Paris since 1823), Hérold, Meyerbeer, Halévy, Adam, Donizetti (during an extended working visit around 1840). One Frenchman did get several of his four symphonies heard at Habeneck's and other concerts in the 1820s and 1830s: Georges Onslow (1784–1853; his family was English, but he grew up in France). Berlioz, seeking to make his career in Paris's musical life, was delighted in 1829 to meet Onslow and to be praised by him for the recently published *Huit Scènes de Faust*; for Berlioz, Onslow was no less than "the person who, now that Beethoven has died, holds the scepter of instrumental music."[6] German orchestras picked up Onslow's symphonies for a time, but posterity everywhere decided differently, burying his music in obscurity, perhaps because its energy and charm do not outweigh the sometime amateurishness of its phrase-to-phrase coherence.[7]

Far better in this respect is the Symphony in D Major of Juan Crisóstomo Arriaga (1806–26), a nineteen-year-old student at the Conservatoire who had moved to Paris three or four years earlier from his native Spain and was quickly gaining recognition. His early death from tuberculosis was recognized as a great loss by such traditionalists as the critic François-Joseph Fétis. The composer probably never heard his symphony performed, and it remained unpublished for more than a century.[8] Two symphonies (1813, 1814) written by Ferdinand Hérold (1791–1833) in his early twenties, after completing his Conservatoire studies with Méhul, are also more than competent, but Hérold, like so many other Parisian composers, devoted his efforts thereafter to the stage, enriching the orchestral repertoire only with his overtures, notably that to *Zampa* (1831).[9]

The Midcentury Descriptive Symphony: Félicien David

The only French composers to have made a lasting mark in the 1830s and 1840s with symphonies or symphony-derived works were Berlioz (see chap. 5) and a composer whom Berlioz hailed as a standard-bearer of the newer programmatic approach to symphonic composition: Félicien David (1810–76). They both did it largely on their own, copying parts by hand, renting a hall, hiring players, placing advertisements in the newspapers, and urging friendly journalists to mention their work in the chatty feuilletons that kept the culture addicts of the day up to date. They often lost money on such ventures, but they did get heard, and occasionally a work made a splash.

The biggest splash of 1844, indeed perhaps the most influential French symphonic work of the middle decades of the century, was David's *Le Désert*. Laid out a bit like Berlioz's *Roméo et Juliette* and likewise inspired in part by the *Pastoral* and Ninth of Beethoven, this musical tale of a caravan moving through an unnamed Arabian desert includes purely instrumental numbers (Ex. 7.1 shows part of the "Marche de la caravane," with its zurna-like oboe descant) and pieces with male chorus and tenor solo, but adds to all this a connecting spoken text in free, unrhymed verse, sometimes declaimed over long-held notes in the low strings that are meant to reflect the vast desolation of the desert sands (Ex. 7.2). David proudly dubbed the resulting new musico-literary genre *ode-symphonie* (symphonic ode).[10] Equally novel was David's use in *Le Désert* of several Arab tunes that he had collected while traveling in the Middle East. *Le Désert* was performed numerous times in Paris in 1844–45 and, within months, David himself undertook to conduct it on tour, in Lyon and Marseille, Berlin (including a performance at the Prussian royal court at Potsdam), Leipzig, and Vienna.

EXAMPLE 7.1. David, *Le Désert*, no. 2: Marche de la caravane, mm. 20–27, oboe descant above the march tune in muted strings

EXAMPLE 7.2. David, *Le Désert*, no. 1, mm. 24–29: spoken narration over long notes in the low strings and a lyrical entry for French horn, all clearly depicting the text: "In the desert all is still, and yet—oh, the mystery of it!—in that silent calm the pensive and lonely soul hears melodious sounds."

David was particularly eager to show off another of his symphonies, a purely instrumental one in E♭ major (the key of Beethoven's *Eroica*), in Germany, which he and others considered the "land of the symphony."[11] But it was *Le Désert* that made the greatest impression there and everywhere, most of all for its several movements based on authentic Arab tunes, including a muezzin call.[12] Performances were mounted and editions published in many countries—including Italy and America—with the text translated into the local language, as was often done also for operas when exported.

David, after returning to Paris, continued to mine the vein of the *ode-symphonie* in a work retelling the discovery of the New World, *Christophe Colomb* (1847): its concluding section allowed him to write yet more exotic dances and songs ("Danse des sauvages" and a lullaby entitled "La Mère indienne"). This work, too, created a stir in France and elsewhere, though few were aware of its specific relationship to David's experiences, fifteen years earlier, in the utopian socialist community of Saint-Simonians. (Two of the movements are retexted versions of choruses that he wrote for the movement, and Columbus, leading Europe to the New World, is an allegorized version of the Saint-Simonian leader Barthélemy-Prosper Enfantin.)[13]

Blends of symphony and oratorio continued to be composed in France in subsequent years, notably Ernest Reyer's *Le Sélam* (1846), a work transparently modeled on *Le Désert* and more polished if less tuneful, and, much later, César Franck's *Psyché* (1887–88).[14] David's introduction of spoken declamation into the symphony (itself inspired perhaps by Berlioz's *Le Retour à la vie* [*Lélio*] and experiments in "melodrama" by Jean-Jacques Rousseau and other earlier composers) produced only a few sturdy progeny (e.g., Franck's *La Rédemption* [1871–74]) but woke with new vigor in the twentieth century in such varied works as Schoenberg's *Gurrelieder,* Debussy's *Le Martyre de Saint-Sébastien,* Prokofiev's *Peter and the Wolf,* Aaron Copland's *A Lincoln Portrait,* Leonard Bernstein's *Kaddish* Symphony, Joseph Schwantner's *New Morning for the World,* and various oratorio-like works by Honegger and Stravinsky.

Negotiations within the Tradition: Gounod, Bizet, Early Saint-Saëns

Around the middle of the century, a handful of symphonies were produced in what we might call the Parisian manner: engaging, colorful, characterful, though the question of national "style" is greatly complicated by the fact that the works are in many ways modeled, like symphonies from the same period in Germany and elsewhere, on by-then classic Austro-Germanic examples of the genre by Haydn, Mozart, Beethoven, or Mendelssohn.

(Schubert's symphonies were little known.[15]) The composers of these midcentury works—most notably Gounod, Bizet, and the young Saint-Saëns—are better known today for their work in such other genres as opera, church music, or concerto. Some symphonies were written as student exercises: a young composer—little different from Arriaga and Hérold earlier in the century—would attempt a symphony much as he or she wrote school fugues, string quartets, or—for the Prix de Rome competition—cantatas and pieces for chorus and orchestra. In contrast, some symphonies testify to a composer's yearning, in the middle or end of his or her career, to compose music that can at once give pleasure and be taken seriously (two goals not easily reconciled at the time) and can do so without the prop of plot, poetic verses, or sacred message.

The latter, "midlife" scenario fits the case of Charles Gounod (1818–93), who suddenly produced two symphonies in 1855, at age thirty-eight. He was of course one of the age's most fluent melodists for the stage: his *Faust* (1859) would quickly become one of the most beloved operas in the international repertory. But he felt in his heart that, though opera was the only way in which a composer could have "regular and systematic" contact with an audience, religious and symphonic music formed the "highest sphere" of music.[16] He knew the works of his German predecessors in many genres, as can be seen, for example, in his strikingly Schubertian songs for voice and piano. He wrote the two symphonies to "console myself" (as he put it) over the failure of his opera *La Nonne sanglante*.[17] Both are works of remarkable tightness and cogency, though occasionally bland in melody and too obviously modeled, at various spots, on Haydn, Mozart, and—in the case of the second, in the key of E♭ major (again)—Beethoven's *Eroica* and perhaps Mendelssohn.[18] They were played to much critical and public acclaim at concerts led by Jules Pasdeloup and were often repeated, entire or as movement-long "fragments," over the next ten years.[19] The words of the composer Adolphe Adam about the First (in D major) remind us of the nationalistic aura that could be attached to a French composer's embracing the genre: "It would be a happiness and a glory for France to be able to offer a music so sensible, so pure, and so inspired, in opposition to the divagations of what is called the modern German school."[20]

No doubt some composers, like Gounod, were better than others at turning such a tradition-laden exercise into real music. Jeffrey Cooper briefly discusses a number of midcentury French composers who wrote symphonies, whetting one's appetite to hear the works (to the extent that they survive) in performance: Adolphe Blanc, Théodore Gouvy, Louise Farrenc, Louis James Alfred Lefébure-Wély, Georges Mathias, Henri Reber, Scipion Rousselot, Célestien Tingry.[21] Most interesting of all, perhaps, are two "special cases": a Symphony for Piano Solo (1857) by Charles-Valentin Alkan (nearly as impressive as his Concerto for Piano Solo [i.e., without orchestra, 1857]), and the symphony *La Nuit des tropiques* (1859) of Louis Moreau Gottschalk, a work that might better be described as a pair of symphonic poems or mood pieces, drenched in exotic stylistic conventions of the day, especially—in the last movement—Caribbean musical idioms.[22] Gottschalk, it should be added, is not usually thought of as French, for he was born in New Orleans. Still, he was primarily French-speaking and received the bulk of his musical training in Paris, where he was based from 1842 to 1853 (ages thirteen to twenty-four). Indeed, the symphony was probably completed on French territory, namely, on the Caribbean islands of Guadeloupe and Martinique.[23]

Among all the midcentury French symphonies, the single most astonishing was written by seventeen-year-old Georges Bizet (1838–75). This Symphony in C Major (1855) was possibly a school effort (its origins are unclear), and it certainly takes off from identifiable models, notably the First Symphony of Gounod, who was one of Bizet's teachers and who remained the irascible younger composer's devoted supporter.[24] Nonetheless, it shows a master's hand. Particularly striking are the sinuous oboe tune (Ex. 7.3), which Winton Dean sees as one of Bizet's many debts

EXAMPLE 7.3. Bizet, Symphony in C Major, movt. 2, Oriental-style oboe solo, mm. 9–15

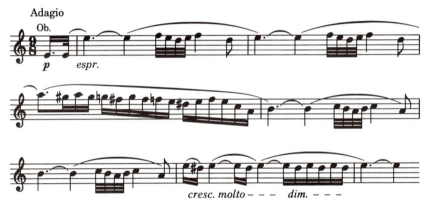

(there are several obvious ones in *Les Pêcheurs de perles*) to the orientalism of Félicien David, the raised or Lydian fourth degree in the trio section of the third movement (French rustic in effect, though allied in spirit to similar devices in Chopin's mazurkas), and the effervescent finale.[25] The symphony was suppressed by the composer—perhaps because he feared that its similarities to Gounod's would raise eyebrows—and for decades after his death lay in manuscript, unexamined, until discovered at the Conservatoire Library in 1933. Two years later, and eighty years after Bizet composed it, the Symphony in C Major received its first performance and was published by Universal Edition (in a version that greatly altered the timpani part). Quickly the work ensconced itself in the orchestral repertoire; George Balanchine even made it into a delightful ballet.[26]

Bizet, it should be added, struggled over one other symphony four years later and finally destroyed it. He also composed an *ode-symphonie,* entitled *Vasco de Gama* (1859–60). A multimovement symphonic poem in C major entitled *Roma* (1860–68, rev. 1871) and the programmatic overture *Patrie* (1873) are occasionally performed but lack conviction, a criticism that perhaps also could apply to—and explain—Bizet's several attempts around the same time to compose grand opera (e.g., *Ivan IV*) in the vein of Giacomo Meyerbeer and his own father-in-law, Fromental Halévy.[27] Lighter orchestral works, notably the *Petite Suite* (1871, based on five pieces from his *Jeux d'enfants* for piano four-hands) and the two suites drawn from incidental music for Alphonse Daudet's play *L'Arlésienne* (1872) recapture better the alert agility of his magical Symphony No. 1.

Of all the French composers active at midcentury, Camille Saint-Saëns (1835–1921) had the most natural gifts for extended instrumental composition: already by age thirty-five he had composed four symphonies—two numbered, two unnumbered—and five concertos. (The much-loved Third Symphony, a later work, will be discussed below.) These various compositions gained for him the label of "symphonist"—a curse, he complained, that slowed his parallel career in the opera world. (It took him twenty years to get *Samson et Dalila* accepted for performance at the Paris Opéra.) That label was attached to him early. Saint-Saëns's remarkably accomplished First Symphony Op. 2 (in, yet again, the Beethovenian key of E♭) was written in 1853, when he was only eighteen. It was first performed anonymously, yet both Gounod and Berlioz instantly proclaimed its virtues. (The orchestra was the short-lived Société Sainte-Cécile, whose conductor, François Seghers, in order to increase the work's chances of being accepted, had submitted it as "a symphony by an unknown author, which had been sent to him from Germany.")[28] Berlioz surely enjoyed the delicate, procession-like tread of the second movement, so reminiscent of *Harold en Italie;* he may also have taken the crescendo buildup to the simple but grand opening theme of the last movement (complete with saxhorns and a quartet of harps) as an homage to the concluding *allegro non troppo e pomposo* of his own *Symphonie funèbre et triomphale,* though Saint-Saëns soon goes a different way, turning the theme into a subject for an accomplished fugue-cum-development.[29]

Saint-Saëns had special affection for his Symphony No. 2 in A Minor Op. 55 (1859), a piece written for a more modest orchestra than the First, and one that seems poised between being a true symphony and what, a bit later, would be called a suite by Tchaikovsky or *scènes* by Massenet.[30] The conventions of the symphonic genre are immediately flouted in the striking neo-Baroque fugal opening movement, notable especially in that, unlike the equivalent movement in Louis Spohr's consciously antiquarian *Historical* Symphony, it is based on a quite up-to-date, indeed consciously experimental theme, consisting of a downward string of thirds, beginning on the fifth degree and extending nearly two octaves (thus containing within it, in succession, the notes of the tonic chord, the subdominant,

EXAMPLE 7.4. Saint Saëns, Symphony No. 2 in A Minor Op. 55, movt. 1, string-of-thirds fugal theme, mm. 66–69

and finally the dominant seventh minus its root: Ex. 7.4).[31] The middle two movements are in a more standard midcentury symphonic style, the *adagio* in particular resembling what might be called a Schumannesque intermezzo (e.g., the Romanze of Schumann's Fourth Symphony), but with a more personal, touchingly chromatic episode for winds near the end. The finale is a lively tarantella clearly inspired by the finale of Mendelssohn's "Italian" Symphony but also by the sonata-rondo finales of Haydn's "London" symphonies.[32] The Haydn influence is most overt at the spot where the composer hints teasingly that the main theme is about to return for the last time. Unlike in Haydn, though, the theme does not immediately arrive; instead Saint-Saëns, thinking perhaps of the ghostly reappearance of the scherzo in the finale of Beethoven's Fifth, brings back the chromatic episode from the second movement, before the finale theme bustles the work to its cheerful end.[33]

The two early and unnumbered Saint-Saëns symphonies (in A and F, the latter titled *Urbs Roma*) were written at, respectively, ages fifteen (i.e., before the First) and twenty-one (i.e., after the Second); both were suppressed by the composer but survive and are occasionally performed. They show much imagination, though the various influences—Haydn, Mozart's "Jupiter," Beethoven, Mendelssohn, Schumann, leavened with a bit of the opéra-comique style of Auber—seem less well digested. Finding the strength of personality that would command and channel his native energy, ease, grace, and early-won store of stylistic awareness would remain Saint-Saëns's lifelong challenge.

Performance Opportunities and the Dawn of Wagner

A more practical problem also loomed for Saint-Saëns and like-minded midcentury French composers: how to get their symphonies and other serious extended works performed. Concert overtures and single movements from symphonies were more easily accepted by the philharmonic societies that dominated those years: the Société des Concerts du Conservatoire, the Société de Sainte-Cécile, and Jules Pasdeloup's Société des

Jeunes Artistes. But even short orchestral works had competition from opera overtures: in the years 1828–71 there were some three dozen Paris performances of the overture to Méhul's *Le Jeune Henri* and four dozen of *Guillaume Tell*.[34] The warm welcome given Gounod's symphonies was atypical: Saint-Saëns's remarkable Second Symphony was performed only unwillingly by Pasdeloup and remained unpublished for eighteen years (1878).

By the 1860s the situation had grown desperate. The Société des Concerts under Habeneck's various successors (Narcisse Girard, Théophile Tilmant, Georges Hainl) remained unsympathetic to living French composers. The Société Sainte-Cécile, which had welcomed the symphonies of Gouvy, disbanded in 1855; and concerts put on by a single composer—Berlioz's usual recourse—remained exhausting and financially as perilous as ever. In 1861 Pasdeloup renamed his series the Concerts Populaires de Musique Classique and reoriented it toward larger audiences paying cheap prices—for admission to a four-thousand-seat amphitheater of abysmal acoustic. Such efforts, admirable from many points of view, went hand in hand with a narrower and more consistently foreign repertoire: of the 280 performances of symphonies (an impressive number) at the Concerts Populaires in the years 1861–70, all but three involved the old Austro-Germans or more recent German-oriented composers (Niels Gade, Anton Rubinstein).[35]

One fabulously exciting composer, though, was regularly performed by Pasdeloup: Wagner. His works, though as German in character as those of Beethoven or Schumann, were to usher in a new era in French symphonic composition. Wagner himself failed to connect with the Parisian public, much less with the influential critics Fétis and Berlioz, when in 1859–61 he oversaw the Paris *Tannhäuser* and presented several promotional concerts of his music. But increasingly over the next few decades, overtures and orchestral excerpts from his operas were performed to an appreciative reception, especially after the founding of two new orchestral series, led by, respectively, Edouard Colonne (beginning in 1875) and Charles Lamoureux (from 1881). Lamoureux's concert performances of *Tristan* excerpts, beginning in 1889, were particularly acclaimed.[36] Thus, though many of Wagner's most important operas did not reach the Paris stage until the very end of the century, certain crucial features of his music were gradually absorbed by music lovers at symphonic concerts.

French composers, of course, could go further, poring fascinatedly over Wagner's published scores and making pilgrimage to Munich or Bayreuth. In addition, Wagner's libretti and prose writings were promptly published in French translation and discussed in the press, with the result that various of his theories helped set the agenda for critics of music and opera. (Some agreed with Wagner's views; others found them inconsistent or entirely mistaken.) Wagner's writings, including his myth-laden libretti, also influenced the writings of political and, increasingly, literary figures, including the poets Charles Baudelaire (an early admirer) and Stéphane Mallarmé. The *Revue wagnérienne*, published at somewhat erratic intervals during the years 1885–88, quickly became a mouthpiece for the symbolist movement, hailing Mallarmé as "symphonist and Wagnerian poet," because of his evocative, sometimes obscurely metaphorical verses.[37]

A very different response to Wagner's nationalism, and to the humiliating course of the Franco-Prussian War, was the founding in 1871 of the Société Nationale de Musique, whose aim was to let the works of French composers, especially instrumental works, be heard in concerts in Paris and the provinces. Over the next few decades, Franck, d'Indy, Saint-Saëns, Duparc, Holmès, Fauré, the young Debussy, and many others collaborated in and took inspiration from the Société, though Saint-Saëns eventually withdrew from it, protesting its inclusion of non-French works.[38] In 1894 d'Indy and others also formed a music school, the Schola Cantorum, which by 1900 directly challenged the hegemony of the Conservatoire and extended for several decades the influence of various Franckist (or, more specifically, d'Indyist) attitudes and compositional practices.[39]

That much of this activity was stimulated by Wagner's achievement does not necessarily mean that Wagner's musical style, procedures, and dramaturgical conceptions exerted a dominant influence on French opera and orchestral music. On that question opinions still vary. The writings of the day do little to clarify the matter, for lazy or ignorant critics invoked the "Wagnerian" epithet in confusing ways, often as a means of praising or blaming (depending on their viewpoint) a composer who offered an opera or program symphony based on a folk tale or national epic, who broke down conventional formal divisions (between aria and recitative, or between the movements of an instrumental work), who boldly enriched his or her harmonic language with chromaticism or dissonance (e.g., Bizet, in *Carmen*), or who made expanded use of the orchestra, especially of the brass.[40]

Still, various of these features, whether one takes them for proof of Wagnerism or not, can be seen in nearly all the symphonies written in the last decades of the nineteenth century, most strikingly in those composed by the disciples of Franck and d'Indy, such as the first three (1889, 1892, 1895) of Albéric Magnard's four symphonies, the first two of Guy Ropartz's five (1894, 1900), and several major orchestral works by Augusta Holmès, including the program symphony *Lutèce* (Lutetia, i.e., France; 1878) and the symphonic poems *Irlande* and *Pologne* (both 1882).[41] (Holmès, though born in France, was devoted to the independence of her parents' native Ireland and other oppressed or occupied nations.) For present purposes, though, we will focus in the next two sections on works of more major composers, beginning with the four best-known symphonies from the second half of the nineteenth century, then moving to two that are equally distinguished but less often heard. All but one of these six works were composed in the six-year period 1885–90, evidence of a concerted response to music from Germany but also of a productive rivalry among French composers at the time. The sixth, by Dukas, came a bit later, in 1896.

Saint-Saëns's Third, the Franck, the Chausson, and d'Indy's "Mountain" Symphony

The "big four"—the Franck D Minor, the Saint-Saëns Third, the Chausson B♭, and d'Indy's *Symphonie sur un chant montagnard français* (Symphony on a French mountaineer's song, with piano obbligato)—have one particularly striking feature in common: dramatic recurrence of melodic material in subsequent movements. Franck and his students made something of a religion out of this procedure, which became known as cyclicism, but clear and interesting examples can also be found in such non-Franckist composers as Saint-Saëns. The latter's Symphony No. 3 in C Minor Op. 78 (1884–85, the "Organ" Symphony), derives many of its themes, by some form of melodic or rhythmic alteration, from one or the other of two motives in the work's restless opening theme (Ex. 7.5). Saint-Saëns most likely based his approach not on Wagner's leitmotiv system (as d'Indy, enlisting Saint-Saëns to the Franckian cause, was later to imply in his *Course of Musical Composition*)[42] but rather on Lisztian principles of "thematic transformation." (Saint-Saëns modeled his symphonic poems on those of Liszt, and dedicated the Third Symphony to his memory.)[43] Indeed, cyclicism has its roots much further back than Liszt and Wagner: in Berlioz and Schumann and, before them, in Schubert and Beethoven.[44]

Each of these four symphonies creates a sonic world of its own and moves at its own distinctive pace. The Saint-Saëns is based on the conventional four movements, but with significant structural alterations, apart from the thematic links just noted. The first movement, according to a

EXAMPLE 7.5. Saint-Saëns, Symphony No. 3 in C Minor Op. 78, movt. 1, mm. 12–14

note written by Saint-Saëns for the London premiere, is interrupted "in its developments"; that is, the recapitulation is foreshortened and joined by a linking passage to the slow movement. "The composer," the note continues, "has thus sought to shun in a certain measure the interminable repetitions which are more and more disappearing from instrumental music [these days]."[45] The slow movement, in D♭ major, is one of Saint-Saëns's most affecting. Equally admirable is the scherzo (in which an obbligato piano briefly appears); the melody of its trio, stated in the trombones, almost exactly echoes the opening pitches of the slow movement, though these are now harmonized in an astonishingly different manner (the opening note, A♭, is now the tonic instead of the dominant). Another slow interlude, this time rather improvisatory in spirit (like some of the links in Mendelssohn's concertos), leads to an extended finale built on yet further variants of the main tune of the first movement, but now in a triumphant major mode (Ex. 7.6). At its high point the movement makes fine rhetorical use of the organ, which had also appeared, more as soulful doubling than as an independent presence, in the slow movement.[46]

EXAMPLE 7.6. Saint-Saëns, Symphony No. 3 in C Minor Op. 78, transformation of Ex. 7.5 in what is effectively movt. 4 (i.e., the latter half of what the score shows as movt. 2), mm. 195–99

The narrative strand of "victory through struggle" that Saint-Saëns reenacts in the Third Symphony was of course common to many of the most enterprising symphonies of the nineteenth century, from Beethoven's Fifth to Brahms's First—though the latter was so far unknown to many in France. But few were so systematic about building spiritual uplift into the symphony as César Franck: his Symphony in D Minor (1885–86) enacts the minor-to-major process within the first movement, repeats it in the second (in B♭-minor-to-major), and concludes with a major-mode finale that eventually brings back the opening of the second movement, now in D minor (the key of the first movement), with the sole aim, it seems, of vanquishing both theme and key by, finally, restating the main theme of the first movement, now in the brassy assertiveness of D major.

As with the Saint-Saëns Third, there are many other links between thematic kernels in the piece;[47] the value of such connections is undercut, though, by the fact that certain of the tunes themselves are either nagging in quality (often pivoting obsessively around a single pitch, especially the third or fifth degree) or else somewhat platitudinous (as at the beginning

EXAMPLE 7.7. Franck, Symphony in D Minor, movt. 1, mm. 129–36: metrically square, melodically static in second-key material

of the finale) or both (as in the F-major theme at m. 129 of the first movement; see Ex. 7.7). Equally exasperating is the constant modulation by sequence, often by chains of major or minor thirds, a remnant, no doubt, of Franck's methodical habits of improvisation at the organ. This and other attributes of Franck's style—such as his rigid adherence to four-bar phrases—have sometimes been attributed to his not having been born and trained in France: his family was Belgian, of German origin. The tyranny of the square phrase, though, was a widespread phenomenon, and two of the composers who did the most to challenge it, in different ways, were foreign: Wagner and Brahms.[48] Nonetheless, Franck's second movement is by common consent a perfect gem: he was rightly proud of how the main section and the faster trio (essentially slow movement and scherzo) then combine with perfect ease (Ex. 7.8).[49]

EXAMPLE 7.8. Franck, Symphony in D Minor, movt. 2, mm. 184–87, showing the combination of contrasting themes: slow movement (English horn) and scherzo (violins)

Chausson's Symphony in B♭ (1889–90) has often been described as something of a clone of the Franck, yet it is quite un-Franckian in its welcome flexibility of phrase structure. The themes throughout are clear cut and memorable, being mostly pentatonic or modal (e.g., Dorian in movt. 3 at rehearsal letter D). What we will call the symphony's introduction blends solemn warnings redolent of the *Ring* cycle (Ex. 7.9) with yearning phrases similar to those in the analogous spot in Tchaikovsky's *Romeo and Juliet*, and the theme of the second-key area is harmonized with numerous half-diminished chords right out of *Tristan*. Still, the music sounds totally confident and, oddly, never unoriginal: the development section refreshingly transforms the head motive of the primary-key material, giving it the scherzo-like rhythm and character of the transitional theme first heard at rehearsal letter D, and leads back into the recapitulation by means of a more agitated version of the introduction, set against fragments of various themes from the body of the movement (rehearsal letter K).

EXAMPLE 7.9. Chausson, Symphony in B♭, movt. 1, mm. 1–5. Note the tonally disorienting tonic minor chord in m. 3. (Piano reduction from Chausson's own version for piano four hands)

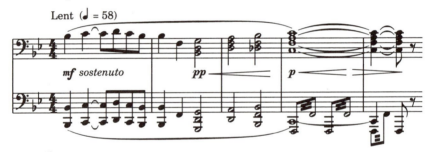

The second movement caused Chausson months of grief, but the resulting music is among his finest, its chromaticism as ripely sincere as the best Grieg, its flow of thought intuitive, rather than, as in the Franck, systematic.[50] The last movement is less convincing. One memorable moment in the development section is the return of bits of the first movement (the scherzo-ish transformation noted above) at rehearsal letter E, in alternation with third-movement material.[51] In contrast, the successive recasting of the third movement's own second theme into various new moods (static-pastoral at rehearsal letter H and, in the recapitulation, triumphant-affirmative at letter M) suggests late nights at the writing desk. The movement concludes with a sudden return of the introduction, first given out as a solemn brass chorale (letter O), then as an effective, rather Lisztian (or perhaps *Götterdämmerung*ian) peroration; refreshingly, though, the final measures are gentle and regretful, rather than stentorian.[52]

D'Indy's "Mountain" Symphony with piano obbligato (1886) announces its regionalism up front: the folk tune in question comes from

EXAMPLE 7.10. D'Indy, *Symphonie sur un chant montagnard français*, movt. 1: the modally and metrically irregular folk tune, mm. 11–18

his beloved Ardèche province, where the family's estate was located (though he himself was raised in Paris): hence the French sobriquet *Symphonie cévenole*, after the Cévennes Mountains. The tune—or, rather, d'Indy's artful reworking of it at the beginning of the symphony—oscillates enchantingly between two modes (Ionian and Aeolian: see Ex. 7.10), lending an outdoor freshness that affords relief from the Franckian sequences and the sometimes turgid orchestration, as does the glinting brightness of the busy yet well-integrated (not soloistic) piano part. D'Indy, the most active proselytizer among Franck's disciples, later insisted in lectures and widely circulated writings that he and Franck had picked up the Beethovenian thread that the Germans themselves had dropped.[53] (He offered particularly harsh and ignorant evaluations of the symphonies of Brahms and Mahler, but also of Tchaikovsky, whom he considered an unimaginative imitator of German tradition.[54]) D'Indy was a right-wing nationalist and outspoken anti-Semite, always ready to mount the speaker's platform, in his music as in his writings; yet his most reliable musical inclinations were probably for milder and more "picturesque" music. Another of his best works is "regional": the symphonic triptych *Jour d'été à la montagne*.

Continuing the Classic-Romantic Tradition, and Recovering It: Lalo and Dukas

In contrast to the four symphonies just discussed, two other late nineteenth-century symphonies set themselves somewhat apart, relating more directly to Classical and early Romantic traditions. It is perhaps for this reason that they have been somewhat neglected until recent decades. Edouard Lalo's Symphony in G Minor (1885–86, first performed by and dedicated to Lamoureux, 1887) predates by a short time the four symphonies just discussed. As the longtime violist in the Armingaud

Quartet, Lalo had mastered the German chamber music repertoire from Haydn to Schumann; unlike most of his contemporaries in France, he even gradually learned to admire the music of Brahms, which he at first found colorless and insufficiently tuneful.[55] Certain stylistic debts to Schumann—whom he called "the great poet, powerful and inspired"[56]—are particularly apparent in the first movement of the symphony (as also in that of his stirring Cello Concerto): the vigorous syncopations, for one, and an earnest effort at deriving connective material from rhythmic scraps of the themes. Indeed, the occasional similarities to Brahms or Bruckner that some have noticed (as in Ex. 7.11, which seems at first a minor-mode version of the opening of Brahms's Second Piano Concerto) may perhaps be traced to a common source in Schumann and other first-generation German Romantics.

EXAMPLE 7.11. The "master phrase" from Lalo, Symphony in G Minor, movt. 1, mm. 1–3

The airy scherzo that follows derives ultimately from an early symphony that Lalo dismembered after "the great potentate" Pasdeloup (Lalo recalled) declared it detestable. The middle section of the movement had particularly baffled Pasdeloup: this section departed so boldly from the "classical" style of the scherzo proper that it made the dismissive conductor break out laughing.[57] The passage still seems vividly dramatic, almost Berliozian, beginning as it does with a solemn, partly modal (Aeolian) tune played by the winds in *pianissimo* unison, then a dotted tune of similar archaic hue in unison strings (marked *sans aucune nuance*, i.e., maintaining a strictly level *pianissimo*), after which the two tunes conjoin to powerful effect in the strings (Ex. 7.12).[58] The slow movement contains several very persuasive moments ripe with late-Romantic (one is tempted to say proto-Mahlerian) appoggiaturas. The finale is a sonata-rondo, in quite traditional keys, whose main theme is a dance in $\frac{12}{8}$ meter, something of a gloss on (again) the saltarello finale of Mendelssohn's "Italian" Symphony.

The Brahmsian theme noted earlier (Ex. 7.11)—in a letter Lalo called it the *phrase maîtresse*—is announced by the strings at the very outset of the introduction to the first movement and recurs vigorously in the brass in the development section and in the coda of that movement, now in the tonic major. The scoring of the theme is heavy here: two each of trumpets and cornets, four horns, three trombones, and tuba. Lalo then quickly redirects the music toward G minor to close the movement, as if rejecting an easy optimism. We may be more than usually entitled to

EXAMPLE 7.12. Lalo, Symphony in G Minor, movt. 2, contrasting middle section, mm. 114–21, showing the combination of two themes (here in the strings)

evoke, with some caution, moods and philosophical attitudes when discussing this symphony. Lalo himself said, "[the theme] predominates in the first movement, and I bring it back in the other movements whenever my *musico*-poetic and -dramatic intentions . . . seemed to me to require its appearance." (His emphasis in the term "*musico*-poetic" was aimed at discouraging literary readings that were too fantastically explicit.[59]) At the end of the slow movement, the motto, now in the low brass and bassoons, brings ill omens, and it begins and ends the finale as well, casting yet further shadows over a dance movement that, owing to the prevailing minor mode, seems nervous and edgy. The symphony's ending is enormously effective: it recalls the close of the first movement but then reworks it with more definitive sternness.

Ten years later Paul Dukas offered a Symphony in C Major (1895–96) that parallels the Lalo in that it follows certain structural traditions quite strictly: the first movements of both works are more or less straightforward examples of textbook sonata form; Lalo even chooses the relative major for his secondary key area. (Dukas "arpeggiates" downward: C major, A minor, F major.) But Dukas composed only three movements, omitting a scherzo, and in quiet defiance of both Schumann and the Berlioz/Liszt/Wagner tradition he makes no use of cyclical motives—though the opening tune of the finale may be seen as a more resolute version of the closing theme of the first movement. The result is one of the best French symphonies ever written, a worthy companion to the Bizet, the Franck, and the Saint-Saëns Third.

Whereas with Lalo one has the sense of a composer actively working in a still-living tradition, a work meant to continue the achievements of the recent past, the Dukas seems somehow different: a work that by dint of serious study recaptures some of the thought processes, though not the "sound" (harmonic vocabulary, orchestral textures), of the Classical and early Romantic masters.[60] Unlike the Franck disciples and other post–Wagnerians (notably Bruckner), who kept their music in a nearly constant state of modulatory flux, Dukas recaptures, as in the second (A-minor) theme of the first movement, Haydn's and Beethoven's knack of playing with the listener's expectations, offering balanced pairs of phrases whose second, consequent, members do not end quite as expected, thus propelling the music onward. Example 7.13 gives the first phrase, with its appealingly colored harmonies. If Lalo seems neoclassical in a Brahmsian way, continuing a tradition in which he has grown up, Dukas seems to be looking back more self-consciously, finding strength in the compositional logic typical of music from what to someone of his generation must have seemed a quite distant era. In this he may be seen as a close predecessor to Stravinsky and Prokofiev, in their respective neoclassical phases, and to his own pupil Maurice Ravel.

EXAMPLE 7.13. Dukas, Symphony in C Major, movt. 1, second-key material, in the strings, mm. 63–66

Old and New Impulses at the Turn of the Century: d'Indy versus Debussy

Ravel composed no symphonies. Debussy, as we shall see, both did and did not. D'Indy, who never shied away from making public statements in both music and prose, wrote two symphonies after the "Mountain."[61] The *Sinfonia brevis "De bello gallico"* (1916–18) is a programmatic work, describing and heroizing the French military effort against the Germans: the mobilization for the Battle of the Marne, the barracks songs of the soldiers, and so on.[62] It is thus a particularly concrete example of the "message" symphony, a category that arguably includes the Franck D Minor and numerous other symphonies by members of the Franck circle (e.g., Ropartz's Second).[63] D'Indy's Second Symphony, in B♭ Op. 57 (1902–3), can likewise be counted a "message symphony"; although d'Indy did not reveal any specific message (through published program or subtitle), pupils of d'Indy offered impressive-sounding explications of its portrayal of spiritual and philosophical struggle.[64] Heard today, the symphony proves a fascinating effort, more uneven than many of the works discussed earlier in this chapter, but as great as the best of them in the many stretches where d'Indy hits and holds his stride.

The first movement relies on a textbook version of sonata form (though satisfyingly so), a point to which d'Indy drew attention in his discussion of the symphony.[65] There are the inevitable Franckist patches of queasy modulatory machinations, and some puzzling, abrupt shifts in orchestral texture and rhythmic activity. Another Franckist trait is the movement's—indeed the whole symphony's—dependence on two motto motives heard at the outset of the slow introduction (Ex. 7.14a–b; d'Indy described them as being, to some extent, "antagonistic" to each other). The first is rhythmically rather lame but acquires visionary force when, toward the end of the development section, it is stated, over static yet unsettled harmonies, by piccolo trumpet and then trombone.

EXAMPLE 7.14. D'Indy, Symphony No. 2 in B♭ Op. 57, movt. 1, mm. 1–4: the two contrasting motives, one anguished, the other soaring upward (doubt vs. religious enlightenment?)

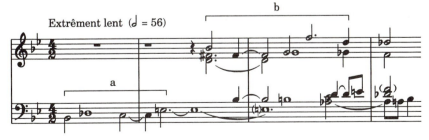

The second movement begins with a few artful measures of quasi-improvisation on this same first motto. The movement proper then sets forth a wondrously passionate slow melody of flexible phrase length (stated in the English horn, clarinets, first horn, and violas), based on the symphony's second motto. After a climactic sequential passage, the movement's contrasting theme appears: an intriguing dotted-rhythm march with a heavily modal flavor (alternating bars of Lydian and Dorian; rehearsal number 36). Some of the most beautiful passages in the remainder of the movement again involve solo statements—this time in various wind instruments—over static harmonies: one for flute over gently pulsating violins is a free paraphrase of the movement's main theme, but (as d'Indy himself noted) stated up a whole step, while the accompaniment remains in the tonic.

The third movement was described by d'Indy as an intermezzo with two trios. The initial statement of the theme sounds rather archaic, owing to its Phrygian lowered second degree, its pleasingly ambiguous metric profile (written entirely in $\frac{2}{4}$ but sometimes sounding as if the downbeat is an upbeat), and its being stated softly and in the melancholy tones of a solo viola. The two main later statements are metrically reconfigured (first a giguelike $\frac{3}{8}$, then a rambunctious $\frac{2}{8}$), such that the strong beats now fall on different notes of the theme than before.[66] The last movement reworks the motto themes yet again, separately and together, in episodes of sharply contrasting character: these include a fugue (marked "solemn"), whose high point is a glowing entry by (again) the high trumpet; a jaunty tune in triplets and $\frac{5}{4}$ meter; and a grand, triumphant peroration, as persuasive as any in Mahler or Strauss, in which various themes are now altered to fit the major-mode context.[67]

By the time of the premiere of the Second Symphony (1904), d'Indy was clearly recognized as a conservative. (Seven years later, Fauré, Florent Schmitt, and Charles Koechlin took the step of founding an alternative to the Société Nationale, the Société Musicale Indépendante, which did much to promote the music of Ravel and other young composers.) Yet he was by no means an isolated curmudgeon: on the contrary, numerous composers adhered, to a greater or lesser extent, to his principled compositional stance, resulting in a continuing stream of symphonies of recognizably traditional build. Increasingly they incorporated, as d'Indy's works did not, up-to-date developments in harmony and orchestral texture.[68]

Debussy, the chief inventor of many of those new techniques, abandoned the writing of symphonies—and indeed any activity that smacked of academicism and good behavior—early on. His one symphony was planned in 1880, when he was eighteen years old and living in Italy and Russia as part of the retinue of Madame Nadezhda von Meck, Tchaikovsky's patroness.

Only a concluding (?) *allegro* survives, in Debussy's own version for piano four hands. Apparently, like the various *duos symphoniques* for two pianists (some at one piano, others at two) of Lefébure-Wély, Cécile Chaminade, and others, it was never orchestrated; perhaps, like most of those, it was never intended to be.[69] The music is quite un-Debussyan, being little more than a collage of then-fashionable styles of "serious" music: a Brahmsian opening, with the melody in syncopated parallel thirds (the whole movement is rather clogged with these thirds), a slow theme in rising sequences that seems closely modeled on the equivalent passage in Schumann's Piano Quartet in E♭ Op. 47, a rather forced effort at development of these themes (launched by a fanfarelike triplet motive over tremolos and again relying on sequences), a brief recapitulation, and an extensive major-mode coda transforming earlier materials into a banal heroic march that swings, pseudo-passionately, in (effectively, though not so notated) $\frac{12}{8}$ meter, inspired perhaps by one of Liszt's symphonic poems or the final trio from Gounod's *Faust*.[70] Only one distinctive moment stands out: a brief passage of elegantly purling, harmonically static arabesque in C (Ex. 7.15) and, later, E♭ major. The somewhat confusing title page mentions two other movements: Andante and Air de ballet; it is not known whether he ever wrote these.

EXAMPLE 7.15. Debussy, *allegro* from unfinished symphony in B minor, mm. 43–44

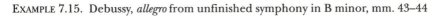

The words "Air de ballet" may seize our attention, because ballet music was traditionally regarded as almost the polar opposite of true symphonic music. Indeed, some of Debussy's most striking orchestral music throughout his career (as well as much of his piano music) was to be based on dance, notably the middle movement of the *Nocturnes* ("Fêtes," 1899), all three movements of the *Images pour orchestre* ("Gigues," "Ibéria," "Rondes de printemps"; 1906–9), and of course several scores written to be danced. In these he was continuing a separate strand of orchestral music in France that had been developing side by side with the purely symphonic for many decades: equally artful and often entrancing pieces relatively free of ambitious pretensions, concerned primarily with delighting the listener and evoking places, colors, and the movement of human bodies. These antecedents included the symphonic poems of Saint-Saëns (a particularly entrancing one—*Le Rouet d'Omphale*—reflects the busy motion of a spinning wheel),[71] Augusta Holmès, and others; the sets of orchestral *scènes* by Massenet;[72] individual pieces such as Chabrier's *España*

and *Scherzo-valse*, extended multimovement works such as Franck's afore-mentioned *Psyché*, for chorus and orchestra (recounting the legend of Psyche and Eros); and suites drawn from ballets or incidental music to plays, such as the courtly dances that Delibes wrote for Victor Hugo's *Le Roi s'amuse*, Bizet's previously mentioned music for the play *L'Arlésienne*, and Fauré's exquisite *Masques et bergamasques*.

Pieces from this other, nonsymphonic tradition tend to mingle structural clarity, historical allusiveness (often through archaic harmonies, balanced phrase structure, and pastiches of outmoded dance types such as the sarabande), vivacious and varied rhythms, and intriguing displays of orchestral timbre. These "nonsymphonies," as we might call them, were to serve as an important stylistic source (and perhaps form a more relevant context than the French symphonies we have been studying) for certain urbane strands of music written in the first half of the twentieth century: for Debussy's color-drenched *La Mer* (1903–5), a work that comes as close as anything in Debussy's oeuvre to being a symphony, which is to say not very close;[73] for Ravel's *Rapsodie espagnole*, *Alborada del gracioso*, *Boléro*, *Le Tombeau de Couperin*, *Daphnis et Chloé*, and *Ma mère l'oye;* and for Busoni's *Turandot* Suite, Stravinsky's neoclassical works (including the ballets *Apollo* and *Agon* and the two orchestral symphonies), and music of such varied composers as Alfredo Casella, Albert Roussel, Ottorino Respighi, Francis Poulenc, Darius Milhaud, William Walton, and Aaron Copland.

For that matter, it might even be argued that this much-loved body of light orchestral music by Saint-Saëns, Chabrier, and others formed an essential part of the motivating context for the symphonies that have been the focus of the present chapter. Although the aim of creating what we might call "the great French symphony" may sometimes have been "megalomaniacal" (as Ropartz was later to assess it),[74] it may also be seen as a courageous effort on various composers' part to free themselves—by way of the Beethovenian symphonic tradition and the Liszt/Wagner grand gesture—from the seductive charms of their country's somewhat limited and lightweight musical traditions.

At the same time, and in a more positive vein, those native traditions may have helped give the French symphonies something that sets them apart from those of other countries. The appealing spontaneity of the Chausson (and the two shimmering harps), the plangent English horn solo that opens the second movement of the Franck, the clarity and self-confidence of the first movement of the Dukas, the methodical playfulness with which Saint-Saëns prestidigitates certain themes in the "Organ" Symphony, the eloquent trumpet and woodwind solos in the d'Indy Second, not to speak of the exoticism in David's *Le Désert* and in the slow movement of the Bizet—all these show the healthy mark of French culture. The repertoire of French symphonies amounts to a treasure house still waiting to be explored.

Notes

I wish to thank the following for helpful suggestions: Jöel-Marie Fauquet, Annegret Fauser, Brian Hart, James Parakilas, Philip Sims, Jürgen Thym, and Keith Waters.

1. Martin Cooper, *French Music from the Death of Berlioz to the Death of Fauré,* (London, 1951), 153.

2. Danièle Pistone gives a valuable overview of nineteenth-century French symphonies, tabulating twenty or so from 1800 to 1830 (or more, if one counts the Arriaga, four symphonies rather than two for Méhul, plus the *symphonies concertantes* by numerous composers working, though not all born, in France), twenty-eight from 1830 to 1880 (not counting the four by Berlioz, five pieces by Louise Bertin [see n. 21], or seven symphonies of David and Gouvy mentioned only in the footnotes), and nineteen from 1880 to 1900 (but she omits the Holmès symphony and the unpublished d'Indy symphonies noted below). See Pistone, *La Symphonie dans l'Europe du xix*e *siècle: Histoire et langage* (Paris, 1977), 78–95. The figures for 1830–80 might be further augmented to include various idiosyncratic works discussed below.

3. A lengthy, well-informed study of all the disciples, their interrelationships, and their works is Laurence Davies, *César Franck and His Circle* (Boston, 1970). Many of Davies's evaluations (which sometimes swing to extremes) are summarized in "The Symphony in France," a chapter in his *Paths to Modern Music: Aspects of Music from Wagner to the Present Day* (New York, 1971), 139–52.

4. On the changing social and economic conditions of music making in Paris, see Ralph P. Locke, "Paris: Centre of Intellectual Ferment," in *Music and Society: The Early Romantic Era, Between Revolutions, 1789–1848,* ed. Alexander Ringer (Englewood Cliffs, NJ, 1991), 32–83. The *Music and Society* series is published in the United Kingdom under the title *Man and Music.*

5. Jeffrey Cooper, *The Rise of Instrumental Music and Concert Series in Paris, 1828–1871* (Ann Arbor, MI, 1983), 21–37.

6. Hector Berlioz to Albert Du Boys, 24 April 1829, in *Correspondance générale,* ed. Pierre Citron (Paris, 1972–), 1:249–50.

7. Boris Schwarz, "The Symphonies of Georges Onslow," in *La Musique et le rite sacré et profane: Actes du XIII*e *Congrès de la Société Internationale de Musicologie,* vol. 2, ed. Marc Honegger and Paul Prévost (Strasbourg, 1986), 623–36.

8. Eric Frederick Jensen, *Walls of Circumstance: Studies in Nineteenth-Century Music* (Metuchen, NJ, 1992), 1–7; *New Grove Dictionary of Music,* s.v. "Arriaga" (by Dennis Libby).

9. The recent publication of symphonies by Hérold and Onslow is reviewed by Peter A. Bloom in *Music Library Association Notes* 40 (1984): 632–33.

10. On the coordination of speech, song, and orchestral music in French program symphonies and the like, see Angelus Seipt, "Vokale und symphonische Sprachebene in der französischen Programmsymphonik des 19. Jahrhunderts," in *Die Sprache der Musik: Festschrift Klaus Wolfgang Niemöller zum 60. Geburtstag,* ed. Jobst Peter Fricke (Regensburg, 1989), 513–26.

11. David's views are reflected in an article by his friend and manager Sylvain Saint-Etienne, "Sur l'anniversaire du 8 décembre," *La France musicale* 9, no. 3 (18 January 1846): 21–22. A few other purely instrumental symphonies and chamber works by David were received coolly (Cooper, *Rise,* 179); others remain unper-

formed and unpublished. The recent publication and recording of the Brass Nonet in C Minor (1841)—a kind of symphony for reduced forces—reveals a composer who, had he received the right encouragement and coaching, might have produced a substantial body of engaging, colorful, characterful symphonies in the Parisian manner. See Chris Larkin, "Félicien David's *Nonetto en ut mineur: A New Discovery and New Light on the Early Use of Valved Instruments in France,*" *Historic Brass Society Journal* 5 (1993): 192–202, and Ralph P. Locke, "Breezes from the Orient, Airs from the Parisian Salon: Félicien David Now on Disc," *Journal of the American Liszt Society* 33 (January–June 1993): 44–49.

12. Dorothy Veinus Hagan, *Félicien David, 1810–1876: A Composer and a Cause* (Syracuse, NY, 1985), 67–86. See also Jonathan Bellman, ed., *Exotic Styles in Western Music* (Boston, forthcoming).

13. Ralph P. Locke, *Music, Musicians, and the Saint-Simonians* (Chicago, 1986), 136, 214–15, 254–55, 271, and Hagan, *David,* 103–23. Further details, including original and revised layers of the spoken narration, are given by Annegret Fauser, "Félicien Davids *Christophe Colomb:* eine saint-simonistische Parabel?" in *Die Entdeckung Amerikas auf der Opernbühne,* ed. Malena Kuss and Jürgen Maehder (Frankfurt, forthcoming).

14. Other midcentury descriptive (or "poetic") symphonies, with solo voices and chorus, were composed by Emile Douay—who also wrote one (lost?) instrumental symphony, it seems—and by Louis Lacombe (Cooper, *Rise,* 179–80, 190–91). Details in Robert Laudon, *Sources of the Wagnerian Synthesis: A Study of the Franco-German Tradition in 19th-Century Opera* (Munich, 1979). Pistone also mentions symphonies with vocal components by Cécile Chaminade (*Les Amazones,* 1888) and Benjamin Godard (1878, 1886); see her *Symphonie dans l'Europe,* 94–95.

15. For an overview of works from *le pays de la symphonie,* see Frank E. Kirby, "The Germanic Symphony in the Nineteenth Century," *Journal of Musicological Research* 14 (1994): 193–221.

16. Charles Gounod, *Autobiographical Reminiscences,* trans. W. Hely Hutchinson (London, 1896), 136.

17. Ibid., 151.

18. See Gervase Hughes, "Gounod's Symphonies," in his *Sidelights on a Century of Music: 1825–1924* (London, 1969), 9–13; also contemporary reviews in J.-G. Prod'homme and A. Dandelot, *Gounod (1818–1893): Sa vie et ses oeuvres,* 2 vols. (Paris, 1911), 1:161–64.

19. Jeffrey Cooper has traced eleven complete performances of one or the other symphony in the years 1855–64, ten of them at Pasdeloup's concerts (*Rise,* 45, 125).

20. Quoted in Prod'homme and Dandelot, *Gounod* 1:161.

21. Cooper, *Rise,* 33, 41, 45, 169–206. Bea Friedland, *Louise Farrenc, 1804–1875: Composer, Performer, Scholar* (Ann Arbor, MI, 1980), 155–72. In addition, five chamber symphonies by Louise Bertin remain unpublished.

22. The first movement is in E♭ major, the second is basically in B♭ (opening in G minor) but ends, with little concern for convention, in C. The first movement seems modeled in part on Mediterranean night scenes in Berlioz and David ("Roméo seul" and the "Scène d'amour" from *Roméo et Juliette,* the "Hymne à la nuit" from *Le Désert*). The title of the symphony is identical to that of the second part of David's *Christophe Colomb.*

23. John G. Doyle, *Louis Moreau Gottschalk 1829–1869: A Biographical Study and Catalogue of Works* (Detroit, 1982), 261, 306. Gottschalk's Symphony No. 2, '*A Montevideo* (1868), is distinctly less "symphonic," being a one-movement free fantasy on national tunes of Uruguay and the United States.

24. Lesley B. Wright, "Gounod and Bizet: A Case of Musical Paternity," *Journal of Musicological Research* 13 (1993): 31–48. Rey Longyear observes similarities between the slow movement of the Bizet and two movements from Beethoven's quartets Op. 18; see his *Nineteenth-Century Romanticism in Music*, 3d ed. (Englewood Cliffs, NJ, 1988), 184. Further on the history and style of the Bizet, see Howard Shanet, "Bizet's Suppressed Symphony," *Musical Quarterly* 44 (1958): 461–76.

25. Some editions (e.g., Choudens) remove the Lydian quality by adding flats to the Bs in the second half of the trio.

26. "Symphony in C" (1948).

27. Winton Dean, *Bizet*, 3d ed. (London, 1975), 166–70.

28. Saint-Saëns's *Musical Memories*, as cited in Daniel Fallon, "The Symphonies and Symphonic Poems of Camille Saint-Saëns (Ph.D. dissertation, Yale University, 1973), 85. On the compositional history of Saint-Saëns's symphonies, see Sabina Teller Ratner, *Camille Saint-Saëns: An Annotated Thematic Catalogue of His Complete Works*, 2 vols. (Oxford, 1995–). The entries also include excerpts from Saint-Saëns's unpublished letters giving detailed instructions on how to perform the works.

29. In 1896 Saint-Saëns recalled, with a mixture of modesty and irony, that the work was full of "reminiscences of Mendelssohn, Schumann, Félicien David and also *Faust*[,] which was not composed until much later" (cited in Fallon, *Symphonies*, 119).

30. Indeed, there is an orchestral Suite in D from 1863; Pistone and others label this a symphony (*Symphonie dans l'Europe*, 84; cf. Fallon, *Symphonies*, 196–99).

31. In all fairness, Spohr's symphony is less a simple "style copy" than writers have generally assumed: see Klaus Hortschansky, "Musikalische Geschichte und Gegenwart zur Sprache gebracht: zu Louis Spohrs 6. Sinfonie G-Dur op. 116," in Fricke, *Die Sprache der Musik* (see n. 10), 251–82.

32. Fallon, *Symphonies*, 187, 192.

33. Fallon finds more subtle references to the first movement and scherzo as well, "hidden in the mirth of the movement" (*Symphonies*, 192).

34. Cooper, *Rise*, 126–27.

35. Ibid., 50.

36. The concert life in Paris in the late nineteenth century is well treated in Julien Tiersot, *Un demi-siècle de la musique française, 1870–1919*, 2d ed. (Paris, 1924); Annegret Fauser, *Der Orchestergesang in Frankreich zwischen 1870 und 1920* (Laaber, 1994), 140–65; and (with a more personal and ideological slant) Michel Faure, *Musique et Société, du Second Empire aux années vingt: Autour de Saint-Saëns, Fauré, Debussy et Ravel* (Paris, 1985), 19–40.

37. Théodore de Wyzewa, in *Revue wagnérienne*, June 1886, cited in Gerald D. Turbow, "Art and Politics: Wagnerism in France," in *Wagnerism in European Culture and Politics*, ed. David C. Large and William Weber (Ithaca, NY, 1984), 134–66 (quotation: p. 162).

38. Performance of French works on the Colonne concerts and certain other series was greatly stimulated when, in 1897 (or perhaps earlier), the Ministry of

Education and Fine Arts began stipulating that, in exchange for the yearly government subsidy, these concert series must program a set number of minutes of previously unperformed music by living French composers. By 1904 the requirement had become formalized as comprising three hours of new French music, including at least four works that were each a half hour or more in length (Fauser, *Orchestergesang*, 147–52, 184–91).

39. The Schola also became, in part for patriotic and religious reasons, a center for the revival and study of early music, notably sixteenth-century church music and the works of Rameau. See Fiamma Nicolidi, "Nationalistische Aspekte im Mythos von der 'alten Musik' in Italien und Frankreich," in *Nationaler Stil und Europäische Dimension in der Musik der Jahrhundertwende*, ed. Helga de la Motte-Haber (Darmstadt, 1991), 102–21.

40. One 1884 critic complained that Ernest Chausson's symphonic poem *Viviane* was "more concerned to put certain procedures of Wagner's to work than about serving us a dish of his own making" (cited in Jean Gallois, *Ernest Chausson: L'Homme et son oeuvre* [Paris, 1967], 135n).

41. Fauré also made several failed attempts at writing a symphony, notably in 1884.

42. More precisely, d'Indy does not so much derive "cyclical themes" from leitmotivs as universalize them into a single aesthetic principle, thus blurring the distinction between them: "The *cyclical theme*, in the symphonic domain, and the *guiding motive* (Leitmotiv), in the dramatic realm, are in the end one and the same thing. . . . This adaption of a single theme to infinitely variable expressive shapes remains the fertile principle of any truly *composed* work." (Vincent d'Indy, *Cours de composition musicale*, [Paris, 1900–1950], vol. 2, pt. 1, 385.)

43. Liszt acknowledged the dedication by letter before he died in 1883. See Fallon, *Symphonies*, 375.

44. Wildly overstated yet intriguing is Michel Faure's assertion that cyclicism is rooted not just in compositional impulses but in the spirit of the time: it is, he claims, the musical equivalent of the government's increasing economic protectionism and French society's growing xenophobia (*Musique et Société*, 293–94).

45. In Fallon, *Symphonies*, 370 and 459–71 (appendix 4, which is the complete program note). Some writers, misled by this statement, have claimed that it is the middle or "development" section of the first movement that is truncated. The foreshortened recapitulation and the *attacca* connection to the slow movement echo analogous procedures in Schumann's Fourth Symphony.

46. D'Indy lays these variations out nicely in *Cours*, vol., 2, pt. 1, 382–83, and pt. 2, 166–70.

47. Again, d'Indy explores the possibilities in *Cours*, vol. 2, pt. 2, 160–66.

48. Guy Ropartz and others rightly noted that the piece holds together better when not played too slowly (Norman Demuth, *César Franck* [New York, 1949], 86–88).

49. Franck's comment is cited in Léon Vallas, *César Franck*, trans. Hubert Foss (New York, 1951), 213. He was also proud of setting up a conflict of tonalities throughout the piece: D and F are established in the two respective statements of the exposition of movt. 1, related keys to both are explored in the "double development" section, and D finally triumphs over F at the end of that movement and of course at the symphony's end (see d'Indy, *Cours*, vol. 2, pt. 2, 161).

50. Compare, for example, the three statements of the primary material, at m. 1 and at rehearsal letters B and F: the differences in atmosphere and orchestration are quite substantial; more striking still (precisely for Chausson's naturalness in achieving it) is the compression of the theme in the two later statements.

51. Previous writers argue for family resemblances between various of the themes in movts. 1 and 3, yet none, to my knowledge, notes the literal return of the scherzo material: see various views summarized in Ralph Scott Grover, *Ernest Chausson: The Man and His Music* (Lewisburg, PA, 1980), 131, as well as Davies, *Franck*, 191. Gallois simply calls it a new transformation of the main theme in *Ernest Chausson*, 140.

52. A comparison of two different printed full scores (E. Baudoux, and the International Music Publishers 1947 reprint of a revised version of the same) and the composer's own piano-vocal score (E. Baudoux) reveals discrepancies and outright errors in tempo indications and metronome marks, and occasionally in pitches as well.

53. D'Indy focuses on his (as he saw it, Beethovenian) manipulations of the folk tune in *Cours*, vol. 2, pt. 2, 170–74.

54. Ibid., 158.

55. Edouard Lalo, *Correspondance*, ed. Joël-Marie Fauquet (Paris, 1989), 13–14, 77, 123–24 ("boring"—1878), 128 (asks that the publisher Simrock send him any new Brahms pieces—1879), 136–37, 162, 289 ("in the old form[s], but without being a pastiche of Beethoven"—1888).

56. Ibid., 123.

57. Ibid., 302. Before reusing the scherzo in the G Minor Symphony, he inserted it into his opera *Fiesque*, based on Schiller's *Fiesko*; that work, however, remained unperformed.

58. For the function of the scherzo's music in *Fiesque*, see Hugh Macdonald, "A Fiasco Remembered: *Fiesque* Dismembered," in *Slavonic and Western Music: Essays for Gerald Abraham*, ed. Malcolm Hamrick Brown and Roland John Wiley (Ann Arbor, MI, 1985), 163–85.

59. Lalo, *Correspondance*, 169–70. The letter, to the critic Adolphe Jullien, opens with a kind of minimanifesto against Jullien's statement in his review of the symphony that there must be a "poetic or dramatic intention [to this theme] about which it would be good to be informed." See also pp. 284–85, 295.

60. Performances would gain from following the metronome marks in the errata sheet that Dukas carefully appended to copies of the score nearly thirty years later (1924).

61. Two earlier symphonies remain unpublished.

62. Davies calls it an "embarrassing failure" (*Franck*, 301), but the Theodor Guschlbauer recording reveals it to be quite effective. Certain details (e.g., the explicit evocation of men on the march and the parody of German music) cause one to wonder if it had some influence on other pieces that invoke war or military exercises, such as the Nielsen Fifth, Prokofiev's *Alexander Nevsky*, the Shostakovich Seventh, or Respighi's *Pines of Rome*. On its program, see Brian Jack Hart, "The Symphony in Theory and Practice in France, 1900–1914," (Ph.D. dissertation, Indiana University, 1994), 100.

63. Ibid., 206–11.

64. Ibid., 100–101, 156–58, 211–24. In so doing, the Franckist critics were carrying on a hermeneutic tradition that went back to early Beethoven criticism (see Robin Wallace, *Beethoven's Critics: Aesthetic Dilemmas and Resolutions during the Composer's Lifetime* [Cambridge, 1986]).

65. More precisely, the second key area is in the dominant, the recapitulation begins in the tonic, and the second theme returns in an unexpected key (G♭ major) but works its way back to the tonic. See d'Indy, *Cours*, vol. 2, pt. 2, 175–76 (all references to d'Indy's analysis below are from these pages).

66. Davies, otherwise lukewarm on the Second, praises d'Indy's "extraordinary control of rhythmic accentuation," especially his "astute handling" of meter: "over and over the music passes smoothly and imperceptibly from four to five—sometimes even to seven—beats in the bar. . . . He is perhaps the supreme exponent of [metric fluency and] suppleness in the orchestral field" (*Franck*, 301).

67. Further on the use of motives in this symphony (including some inversion), see D'Indy, *Cours*, vol. 2, pt. 2, 175–76. Some of d'Indy's most important points are summarized, with fuller musical examples, in Longyear, *Nineteenth-Century Romanticism in Music*, 3d ed. (Englewood Cliffs, NJ, 1988), 277–78.

68. These include symphonies (post–1900) by Magnard, Ropartz, Silvio Lazzari, Maurice Emmanuel, Albert Roussel, Florent Schmitt, Charles Tournemire, Arthur Honegger, and, much later in the century, Henri Dutilleux; there are of course also many "symphonies" for organ (e.g., by Henri Vierne and Charles-Marie Widor). Certain other French symphonies, in contrast, depart heavily from traditional models (e.g., Charles Koechlin's several symphonies, and Olivier Messiaen's *Turangalîla*) or else affect a firmly joshing attitude toward those models (e.g., the early chamber symphonies of Darius Milhaud).

69. The manuscript turned up in Russia in 1925; the score was published in 1933. Some scholars consider the surviving *allegro* the first movement of a four-, not three-movement symphony.

70. Debussy knew more of the music of his predecessors than some might suspect; for example, he had recently prepared the published two-piano arrangement of the Saint-Saëns Second Symphony.

71. Possible antecedents here include Schubert's song "Gretchen am Spinnrade" but also the "Fileuse" dance from the last act of Delibes's ballet *Coppélia*.

72. The various sets are devoted to Alsace, to Hungary, to various "fairy scenes," and so on.

73. Hart, after careful review of the evidence, terms *La Mer* a "symphonic suite" ("Symphony," 342–47, 358–78).

74. Guy Ropartz, "Les Oeuvres symphoniques de Paul Dukas," *Revue musicale* 166 (May 1936), cited in Georges Favre, *Paul Dukas: Sa vie, son œuvre* (Paris, 1948), 53–54.

Selected Bibliography

GENERAL

Bloom, Peter, ed. *Music in Paris in the Eighteen-Thirties*. Stuyvesant, NY, 1987.
Brody, Elaine. *Paris: The Musical Kaleidoscope, 1870–1925*. New York, 1987.

Cooper, Jeffrey. *The Rise of Instrumental Music and Concert Series in Paris, 1828–1871.* Ann Arbor, MI, 1983.

Cooper, Martin. *French Music from the Death of Berlioz to the Death of Fauré.* London, 1951.

Davies, Laurence. *César Franck and His Circle.* Boston, 1970.

Davies, Laurence. "The Symphony in France." In *Paths to Modern Music: Aspects of Music from Wagner to the Present Day,* 139–42. New York, 1971.

Hart, Brian Jack. "The Symphony in Theory and Practice in France, 1900–1914." Ph.D. dissertation, Indiana University, 1994.

Locke, Ralph P. "Paris: Centre of Intellectual Ferment." In *Music and Society: The Early Romantic Era, Between Revolutions, 1789–1848,* ed. Alexander Ringer, 32–83. Englewood Cliffs, NJ, 1991. The *Music and Society* series is published in the United Kingdom under the title *Man and Music.*

Nef, Karl. *Geschichte der Sinfonie und Suite.* Leipzig, 1921.

Pistone, Danièle. *La Symphonie dans l'Europe du xixᵉ siècle: Histoire et langage.* Paris, 1977.

Shattuck, Roger. *The Banquet Years: Origins of the Avant-Garde in France, 1885 to World War I.* Rev. ed. New York, 1968.

Wright, Gordon. *France in Modern Times: From the Enlightenment to the Present.* 3d ed. New York, 1981.

BIZET

Dean, Winton. *Bizet.* 3d ed. London, 1975.

Shanet, Howard. "Bizet's Suppressed Symphony." *Musical Quarterly* 44 (1958): 461–76.

CHAUSSON

Barricelli, Jean-Pierre, and Leo Weinstein. *Ernest Chausson: The Composer's Life and Works.* Norman, OK, 1951.

DAVID

Hagan, Dorothy. *Félicien David (1810–76): A Composer and a Cause.* Syracuse, NY, 1986.

DEBUSSY

Lockspeiser, Edward. *Debussy: His Life and Mind.* 2 vols. London, 1962–65.

DUKAS

Ropartz, Guy. "Les Oeuvres symphoniques de Paul Dukas." *Revue musicale* 166 (1936): 61–68.

FRANCK

Vallas, Léon. *César Franck.* Trans. Hubert Foss. New York, 1951.

GOUNOD

Prod'homme, J. G., and A. Dandelot. *Gounod (1818–1893): Sa vie et ses œuvres.* 2 vols. Paris, 1911.

D'INDY

Paul, Charles B. "Rameau, d'Indy, and French Nationalism." *Musical Quarterly* 58 (1972): 46–56.
Vallas, Léon. *Vincent d'Indy.* 2 vols. Paris, 1946–50.

LALO

Lalo, Edouard. *Correspondance.* Ed. Joël-Marie Fauquet. Paris, 1989.
Macdonald, Hugh. "Lalo, Edouard." In *New Grove Dictionary of Music and Musicians.* London, 1980.

SAINT-SAËNS

Fallon, Daniel. "The Symphonies and Symphonic Poems of Camille Saint-Saëns." Ph.D. dissertation, Yale University, 1973.
Harding, James. *Saint-Saëns and His Circle.* London, 1965.

CHAPTER EIGHT

Bruckner

J. Stephen Parkany

Anton Bruckner searched, in the eleven symphonies that dominate his output, to resolve the conflicting demands of public expectation and personal yearning: to link conservative sonata forms with deeper signs of his cultural, religious, and nationalist heritage—simply stated, to establish his identity as a great visionary of the late Romantic symphony. Yet he never made a living from his composition at any stage of his prominent career as organist and, later, university lecturer in counterpoint. He composed as a true amateur: on nights, weekends, and holidays, rarely consulting colleagues, nor even striving particularly, until his last years, for performances.[1]

Nor did he ever clearly explain why, at midcareer, he turned to focus his attention on the symphony. Before his late thirties Bruckner had composed no orchestral music at all, except in conjunction with a few large choral scores. But from forty, and especially following his decisive move to Vienna at forty-four, he wrote little else. He made the transition quickly, one of very few prominent composers to have absorbed principles of form and orchestration largely from textbooks, or at least to have admitted so doing. Aside from one token royalty of fifty gulden for his Third Symphony, paid by a supportive publisher to underscore the circumstance,[2] Bruckner never earned a schilling from his symphonies. (The sacred music, by contrast, was generally commissioned.)

He seldom shared his thoughts about his current projects and then only with a few cronies and trusted students, occasionally with a prominent conductor or critic. Thus the evidence for Bruckner's astonishing creative transformation lies in sporadic programs and scenarios, in isolated but revelatory comments he made over the years about his technique and aesthetics, and in his various responses to the changed Germanic political culture. The enduring paradox of the Bruckner symphonies is that they are exceptionally private musings on a grandly public scale: chamber music, one might say, where the chambers were the great cathedrals and concert halls of the era. His is a strong, singularly idiomatic voice of late Romanticism.

Within a firmly conservative overall paradigm, the symphonies differ greatly in harmonic fabric, rhythm, texture, and degree of daring. Consistent to all of them is the dynamic of ongoing evolution and development: there is little strict repetition, but rather a kaleidoscope of basic motives undergoing ceaseless change and transformation. Conventional formal schemes, linear developing variation, and powerful intertextual signals are synthesized to project the individual personality of each gargantuan musical child.[3] One senses the family resemblance—the large scale, the limited orchestral palette, the reliance on the orchestral choirs—but cannot settle on a single symphonic persona, as Bruckner delights in altering the outward character from one work to the next. Thus the electric First Symphony is followed by the referential "Annulled," then the lyrical Second; the Fourth (*Romantic*) is followed by the "academic" Fifth.

Bruckner's scenarios draw on Romantic stereotypes, as in the vaguely heroic program for the Fourth and the grander, disquietingly imperialist scenario for the Eighth. The archetype is Wagnerian: an intensification of waves that build from motivic seeds to swell with every evolutionary phrase into overwhelming peaks.[4] These essentially melodic waves can be expressive, even intimate; yet for Bruckner intimacy can be grand, as in the love themes and funeral elegies of great *adagios*, or the sweeping first-movement opening themes that always define the character and motivic identity of overall work. (It is on these opening themes and *adagios* that this study primarily focuses.) Ultimately Bruckner reconceives the symphony as dynamic instrument of a pan-Germanic triumph through struggle.[5]

EXAMPLE 8.1. Bruckner, Fourth Symphony, movt. 1, mm. 1–9

Take, as a case in point, the opening of Symphony No. 4 (*Romantic,* the composer's own subtitle), composed in 1874 and revisited in 1878 and 1880 (Ex. 8.1). The program is telling:

Medieval city—Dawn—From the city towers issue morning waking-calls—The gates open—The knights spring forth on proud steeds into the open air; the magic of the forest surrounds them—Forest murmurings—Birdsong—And thus the Romantic image unfolds.[6]

The tonic E♭ triad, *ppp* in tremolo strings, is attacked imperceptibly: the symphony does not so much begin as simply appear. (The conductor Otto-Werner Mueller dubbed this a "fermata of silence—followed by a fermata of silence in E♭.")[7] The Romantic call of the Waldhorn unfolds, "stepping up distinctly" (*immer deutlich hervortretend*), its first C♭ resplendent with modern sensibility. The simple directness of utterance hides a complex tonal organization. The extreme economy of melodic and rhythmic motive in fact unleashes far-reaching transformations: the sonata form unfolds from the portentous opening to the splendid conclusion, when the horn call blazes in a final tutti affirmation.

All Bruckner symphonies start with such premelodic ideas that evolve into full symphonic dress. The underpinning is always a soft, nonthematic backdrop in the strings, tailored to match the design of the theme. Gathering inertia leads to an apotheosis of the principal tonality, and often of the original motive as well. Bruckner absorbed this attitude toward organic unity from Richter, via his teacher, Otto Kitzler. He raised it to an explicit, if flexible, formal scheme, and an utterly Romantic one at that, exploiting the primal idea of change as the basic currency of forward motion.

Even after successfully joining the great Viennese culture, Bruckner composed as a nervous outsider, an artist of perennial insecurities, hardly acknowledging his own ideals. The result was his flawed public posture, the urban calumny of Bruckner as country interloper and inarticulate, simpleton "God's child."[8] Today his ideals seem further compromised by the events of this century. Hitler, another Upper Austrian, often professed his admiration for Bruckner and made secular shrines in the Nazi years out of the monasteries of St. Florian and Kremsmünster.[9] Party spokesmen fervently extolled him as *gottgläubig* (believing in God). But not *katholisch* or *Christliche*: creative religion stuck in the craw of Hitler and the Nazis. The music of Bruckner, Wagner, and the other "Aryan" composers was useful primarily as fanfare—backdrop music for ceremony and occasion.[10] The naïve grandiosity of this mild individual, who enjoyed his collegial relationships with both Jews and Protestants, became distorted into superpatriotism.

In fact, Bruckner represented much older, central traditions: frank assimilation of the Lutheran chorale heritage, North German polyphony, the Beethovenian symphony, and Wagnerian drama. Now it is for these things that we listen to Bruckner, as well as for the unfettered idealism that so often seems the mark of authentic greatness.

Bruckner's symphonies arrange themselves into four groups, though a chronological approach is compromised by the many mid-course corrections he made along the way. The three early symphonies from Linz, 1862–69, are a student symphony of 1863 and its companion Overture in G Minor, the Symphony No. 1 (1865–66), and the "Nullified" Symphony in D Minor (1869), composed during Bruckner's first vacation after his move to Vienna in 1868. The mammoth Symphonies Nos. 2–4 are from Vienna, 1871–74, each later undergoing agonizing revision. Symphonies Nos. 5–7, Vienna, 1875–84, are more controlled overall and were left unrevised. Symphonies Nos. 8 and 9, grandiose works for the large Wagnerian orchestra, come from Vienna, 1884–96. Both place the scherzo before the *adagio*, following Beethoven's Ninth.

Linz: The Early Symphonies (1862–69)

Bruckner's seven-year "Sechter studies" (1854–61) made him the equal of the redoubtable contrapuntist, though his own lines have a lyrical sensibility not to be found in the work of his teacher. More crucial to his sudden emergence as symphonist were brief, purposeful "graduate" studies: in the standard formal schemes with Otto Kitzler (1861–63), and later in Lisztian and Wagnerian tonal procedures with Ignaz Dorn (1863–65).[11] The concert Overture in G Minor, 1862–63, was Bruckner's first sonata-form movement for orchestra, following models by Schumann, Mendelssohn, and Weber ("who could then be heard in Linz," as Kurth put it). Square and baldfaced, the overture is hardly prepossessing, though Kurth gives ample attention to "its subtly concealed motivic connections and inner transitions, . . . an isolated foretaste of [Bruckner's] later . . . developmental principle."[12] Kitzler, for his part, dismissed—forty years later—the "Student" Symphony, sometimes called No. -1 (F Minor, 1863), as "not particularly original,"[13] and an effort in 1864 to win a performance from Franz Lachner, directory of the Munich Conservatory, was to no avail. Nevertheless, both overture and symphony show Bruckner's dawning obsession with orchestral music and his ambition to achieve an autonomous voice. The latter is Bruckner's only work to feature repeat signs after the exposition.

After the seven years of study with Sechter and over a year with Kitzler, Bruckner jubilantly released himself, in 1863, from formal study, a "chained dog free of his chains."[14] Still seeing himself primarily as a composer of sacred music, his first post–Kitzler effort was the impressive Mass in D Minor (1864). Two other choral masses dominate his remaining Linz years: the E-Minor Mass (1866), a sustained and highly original evocation of Renaissance practice, and the more Wagnerian Mass in F Minor (1868). These three masses are among the few Romantic landmarks in the genre.

All the same, Bruckner's studies with Kitzler had confirmed his symphonic impulses. In 1865–66 Bruckner composed what he called the First Symphony of his "free" maturity: Symphony No. 1 in C Minor (rev. 1890–91). With new confidence in his progressive inclinations, he brought the piano draft with him when he returned to Munich to attend the premiere of *Tristan und Isolde* (May 1865). Typically reticent to show his work to Wagner himself, Bruckner did interest a few other leading musicians there, notably *Tristan*'s conductor, Hans von Bülow. Playing through the first movement, von Bülow was much taken with a trombone passage (probably mm. 94ff. at the end of the exposition): "This is dramatic!"—to which Bruckner rejoined, "Ah! That's just it!"[15] Gingerly, he had begun to make himself known.

Bruckner's pet name for the First was *das kecke Beserl:* Upper-Austrian idiom for "saucy fellow" or "fresh kid," doubtless indicating both his characteristic diffidence and a certain degree of pride as well.[16] The somber, energetic C-minor march at the start is, by the standards of the era, somewhat mystifying, since few symphonies had ever begun that way. (Later ones certainly would: Mahler's Sixth; more abstractly, Bruckner's own Eighth and Ninth.) But the opening sets in motion a centrifugal expansion. Even as the first phrase concludes, the bass sinks away in an extended deceptive cadence, aiming far ahead. And the first climax is a transformation of the march theme into three submotives, each in its own rhythm (Ex. 8.2a) At such points once senses a brash neophyte working hard for attention; indeed, though he extends such rhythmic combinations later in the work and at times in subsequent symphonies, they are never again quite so complex.

The diaphanous, cantabile second theme is a concealed mutation of the contour of the first. Thus the continuous, frankly crude drive of the opening wave does not pause until after the stunning trombone entrance at measure 94 (Ex. 8.2b), with its sudden expansion of the orchestral frame and unconcealed allusion to the "Pilgrim's Chorus" from *Tannhäuser.* This is less a quotation than a powerful emblem of the composer's artistic indebtedness to the man he thought of as *Meister aller Meisters.* It stands out quite beyond the sonata, too, in that the outburst never recurs. The coda of the movement focuses on a dark C minor, but at the same time opens a few windows on the C-major coda of the finale by hinting at the culminatory brass chorales.

Bruckner's fervid partisan Helm wrote of the second movement that "a deeper, more important *adagio* had not been written since Beethoven." Certainly the agonized *adagio* theme is extraordinary, continually recasting itself through one nightmarish phrase after another over twenty unbroken measures—no resting point comes until the cadence at m. 20. In response to Hans Richter's 1891 remark that Bruckner "must have been very much in love to write this *adagio*," the composer readily agreed: "So I was indeed, the whole time!"[17]

EXAMPLE 8.2. Bruckner, First Symphony, movt. 1
a. mm. 10–11

b.

Wagner, *Tannhäuser* ("Pilgrims Chorus")

Bruckner, First Symphony, movt. 1, mm. 94–97

In what made for a backhanded compliment, the ferocious scherzo and its wistful trio were the only parts of the First to win unanimous praise in Bruckner's own time. The movement experiments in its coda by making a direct, simple link, Beethoven-fashion, to the finale, such that the finale is Bruckner's last symphonic outer movement to begin *fortissimo*. This amused him in later years: "This *kecke Beserl* says right away, without much nonsense, 'Here I am!'" (Ex. 8.3). With earthy satisfaction, he goes on: "There I didn't skin any cats [i.e., didn't fuss] and composed the way I

EXAMPLE 8.3. Bruckner, First Symphony, movt. 4, mm. 1–2

wanted to."[18] Most Bruckner finales are more freely built than the corresponding first movements, this one remarkably so. It gradually reaches
the major, but not all at once, as in the other minor-key symphonies. The
process here is drawn out in steps, so that C minor is more effectively dis-
pelled. Each gesture toward C major brings the brass choir forward more
and more, in massed chorale-like density.

For all its brilliant structure, the First is too busy, too conventional to
exemplify the mature Bruckner, at least in foreground content. Until the
final chorale, it does not catch the majesty that pervades the subsequent
symphonies. Yet the actual kinship of the First with its successors is close
and fundamental: in its chromatic Wagnerian counterpoint, fine developing variation, bold and concentrated developmental processes, and confident tone. So what the otherwise un-Brucknerian Adorno once called the
"astonishingly explicit First"[19] is a decisive emergence. In it Bruckner successfully defines his distinctive approach to organic formal process.

In his first year after moving to Vienna Bruckner finished, or perhaps composed in its entirety, what became known as the *Nullte* ("Annulled" or "Nullified") Symphony in D Minor, often called Symphony
No. 0. Probably he wrote the bulk of it back in Linz in the summer of
1869, during his first holiday from the Vienna Conservatory.[20] Like the
First, it is a labored search for a more public style, evoking on the one
hand Renaissance and Baroque choral textures and on the other the now-
idiomatic "Bruckner sound" of majestic harmonic rhythm and anti-
phonies of the orchestral families in four-part choirs—the architecture,
one might say, of the Ringstrasse, with which it is roughly contemporaneous. However steady its advance over the First, the "Annulled" is uneven.
It cannot sustain its three tonalities through to the very end, for one thing:
the symbolic gesture of the turn to the major mode at the end of the piece
is insufficiently prepared by the finale, which fails to absorb the advanced
language of the opening. And of the opening static D minor Dessoff asked,
"So then, where's the first theme?"[21] Thereafter Bruckner took particular
care to make his initial thematic motives clear from the start.

Nevertheless, the "Annulled" displays the characteristic profile of
the later symphonies for the first time, a kind of vanguard pointing the
way to the great works that followed. Many of its features—diatonic clarity
disguised by complex polyphony, more simply phrased melody—represent Bruckner's most advanced thinking of the 1860s.

The rest of Bruckner's symphonic career largely clarifies the formal
and textural processes of the First and "Annulled." Yet Bruckner suppressed them both. As soon as there was a greater D-minor symphony (the
Third), confronting Beethoven's Ninth in more sophisticated fashion and
even earning Wagner's blessing, he felt free to abandon, to annul, the earlier effort. He returned to the First, a generation after writing it, to effect
a large-scale revision that says more about the new era than about the
worth of the original.

Vienna, 1871–74: Symphonies Nos. 2–4

After the "annulment" came two particularly busy years when Bruckner was too unsettled for any large-scale composition, the longest fallow patch in his career. Reports of another nervous breakdown in these years do not specify the cause—perhaps a new romantic infatuation, his exhausting duties at the Conservatory alongside his private counterpoint studio, or the indifferent response of Bruckner to Vienna and of the Viennese to his early symphonies. The Second Symphony in C Minor (1871–72, revised 1875–76 and 1877) marks his recovery and the dawn of a new self-confidence. He had made a name for himself as a superb counterpoint lecturer by upholding Sechter's forbidding "Fundamentals" in a more humane, better illustrated, even folksy fashion.[22] He had also taken Dessoff's condescending attitude toward the First—dismissed, also, by the Vienna

EXAMPLE 8.4.

a. Bruckner, First Symphony, movt. 1, mm. 2–4

b. Bruckner, Second Symphony, movt. 1, mm. 3–6

c. Bruckner, Second Symphony, movt. 4, mm. 1–3

d. Bruckner, Second Symphony, movt. 1, mm. 20–21

Philharmonic for "wildness and daring"—to heart. Now he effectively replaced it with another, clearer Symphony in C Minor. This, too, was scorned by the Philharmonic as "nonsense" and "unplayable," but was nevertheless praised by Liszt.[23]

Both symphonies start with the same diatonic yet harsh A♭ appoggiatura (Ex. 8.4a,b). Here it resolves directly, not just to G but on to a balancing F♯ lower appoggiatura and a lyrical repeat of the same crisis in the very next phrase two measures later. (He digests the A♭/F♯ motive in a kind of parody at the beginning of the finale; Ex. 8.4c.) At length a stable cadence in C is reached in mm. 25–26. This is introduced by the signature "Bruckner rhythm," here alternating duplets and triplets in a stentorian trumpet signal (Ex. 8.4d). The long opening theme still seems quite regular compared to that of the First Symphony, which makes no tonic cadence at all until the recapitulation. In this case there is a premature C-major climax (mm. 40–45), easily deflected to C minor and then E♭ major for the second group. The movement follows a gentle but insistent course, as in the unison codetta theme and simple answers beginning at measure 97. But final climaxes tend toward the cacophonous at the wood-wind-and-brass triplets versus string duplets that conclude the movement (mm. 554–65), not gently.[24]

The sustained, boundless lyricism of the work is foiled only by the *adagio* (*Feierlich, etwas bewegt*), featuring Bruckner's first use of the Classical double-variation form he later adopted for the last three symphonies. Its first theme is a contrapuntal composite of the string and wind lines, while the cellos and violas dominate a dense texture from within. The solemn chorale of the second theme (Ex. 8.5) is enhanced rather than parodied by its measured pizzicato, with majestic rejoinders in each phrase from a solo horn.

EXAMPLE 8.5. Bruckner, Second Symphony, movt. 2, mm. 34–37

EXAMPLE 8.6. Bruckner, Third Symphony, movt. 1
a. m. 1

b. mm. 5–12

The "Wagner" Symphony, No. 3 in D Minor (composed 1872–73, rev. 1874, 1876–77, and 1889) signals its dedicatee in the opening solo trumpet call (Ex. 8.6), clearly drawn from its ostinato backdrop. Wagner accepted the dedication of the 1873 version, among the longest symphonies ever composed, after Bruckner imposed it on him, playing him the score at the first Bayreuth Festival in 1876. More sycophantic than its length are the numerous Wagnerian allusions, though Bruckner excised most of these from the 1889 score. (Generally, here, I refer to this 1889 final version, the basis for both the Haas and Nowak editions.)

The ubiquitous D-minor ostinato layers support each new phrase, until the climaxes of measures 31 and 87. The slowly cascading triadic violin figures do not stand on their own, but rather support the more explicit theme of the calm yet tragic trumpet melody, which avoids monotony by quickly generating its own contrapuntal and textural layers. These sustain the motivic flow that carries through the first movement into the symphony as a whole: note, for example, how the first theme is renewed in the gentle, similar second theme and the main incantation of the scherzo. The trumpet call, of course, comes from a long D-minor tradition, especially the Viennese precedents of *Don Giovanni* and Beethoven's Ninth.

Intertextual reference, already habitual to Bruckner, now becomes part of the general development plan. In the first movement, a trumpet-dominated chorale, so marked, occurs in the approach to the cadence of the exposition (mm. 199–205). Soon, too, there is a calm Stabat Mater cadence in a majestic, other-worldly VI–V–IV (mm. 247–54). Chorale references are even more prominent elsewhere in the symphony: the *misterioso* third theme of the second movement (mm. 73–76), for instance, and the majestic second theme of the finale (Ex. 8.7).

EXAMPLE 8.7. Bruckner, Third Symphony, movt. 4, mm. 69–72

Hanslick's notorious notice of the Third after its hapless premiere (under the composer, with the Vienna Philharmonic)—"Beethoven's Ninth meets Wagner's *Walküre*, and is trampled under her hooves"—was not far from wrong.[25] Yet Hanslick undervalues Bruckner's technical and spiritual self-identity: both structure and organic process have reached their most assured level yet. The work survived, moreover, its many substantial, though generally intelligent, revisions and abridgements—most of which were effected, despite tales to the contrary, with Bruckner's own involvement.

By evoking the emphatic E♭ horns of Beethoven's *Eroica* and Weber's *Freischütz* in his *Romantic* Symphony, No. 4 in E♭ (1874, rev. 1878–80, 1886), Bruckner asserted kinship with the preceding generations and their concerns. He also adhered to the elemental E♭ horn call in his very last alteration to the score in 1886, when he made the motive stand out at the end of the finale (mm. 533–541).[26]

As the Fourth is the first Bruckner symphony to be based on a major triad, the brass chorale episodes are thus correspondingly luminous. Central to the first movement is the expanded chorale that culminates the development (mm. 305ff.). The block triads are panconsonant, avoiding seventh chords and incurring dissonance only through suspension. The majestic pace and texture of this passage are complemented by the energizing, robust obbligato for violas. Equally evocative uses of the horns dominate the entire symphony, including the dark C-minor second-movement march—surely indebted to Schubert's Trio Op. 100—and the famous hunt scherzo (Ex. 8.8).

Some of this amounts to eloquent fantasy. A more fundamental identity occurs each time the opening horn call returns in the tonic (see Ex. 8.1): when the solo horn at the start becomes two horns in octaves, at the start of the recapitulation (mm. 365ff.), and finally at the end of the movement, with all four horns in unison (mm. 557–73). This constitutes development on its most basic level: a triple unfolding of the motive.

EXAMPLE 8.8. Bruckner, Fourth Symphony
a. Schubert Piano Trio Op. 100 compared with movt. 2, mm. 1–5

b. movt. 3, mm. 3–10

Note, too, the prominent C♭ in m. 7 (Ex. 8.1). Often in Bruckner, important modulations turn on such details of Romantic chromaticism: in the transition at measure 75, for example, when a dramatic shift F–D♭ hangs on the pivotal F in the horn. Extensions of this kind of chromaticism dominate the finale, where it is prominent both in the derivative opening and the titanic unison theme (Ex. 8.9a,b). The extended, tragic coda is based on the opening of the finale, now with a simultaneous woodwind inversion (Ex. 8.9c). This was Bruckner's first magnificent final chorale, and in it we find the outcome of the initial C♭: a slow, thrilling Phrygian cadence, F♭ to the long-prepared E♭.

EXAMPLE 8.9. Bruckner Fourth Symphony, movt. 4
a. mm. 3–10

Vienna, 1875–84: Symphonies Nos. 5–7

Bruckner began the Symphony No. 5 in B♭ Major (1875–76) in early 1875, not long after finishing his first draft of the Fourth. The new work departs from the Fourth in avoidance of stock Romantic and Wagnerian allusions, exploiting orthodox contrapuntal texture far more explicitly than heretofore. There are striking links between the Fifth and the simultaneous advance in Bruckner's career. In May 1875 his efforts to gain a higher professional standing bore fruit when the University of Vienna at last approved his long-running application to lecture part-time in harmony and fugue, adjunct to his Conservatory post. The university overruled fervent but largely picayune resistance from its own adjunct professor Eduard Hanslick, already Bruckner's anti-Wagnerian enemy.[27] To mollify Hanslick's pride of position, Bruckner was officially unpaid to start. This was quietly corrected before long, as praise grew for both the substance and style of his lectures. The era saw over time not only an increasing acceptance in Vienna of Bruckner's Wagnerian party but also the increasing stature of pan-Germanic ultranationalist views, emanating in large measure from Bruckner's own rural Upper Austria.[28]

In repeated applications to the university, Bruckner had stressed that "the true, highest science never forsakes art, but always supports it."[29] In his inaugural lecture he proclaimed music to be a scientific discipline (*Musikwissenschaft*). He suggested that "our spiritual life [has] moved ahead so far," making "colossal progress in two centuries," that in all the atoms of music, "in their inner organism, full edifice of the art was at last reorganized." He then went on to introduce the basic principles of harmony and fugue, showing how composers used them to develop a distinctive art.[30]

Thus the ascetic contrapuntal strategy of the Fifth, including the climactic fugue in the finale, invokes the notion that the contrapuntal tradition—so basic to his work as organist and now university teacher—lies at the core of the symphony and indeed of Western counterpoint. Among the new features for Bruckner, if not for others, were the slow introduction, the "ground bass" motive, and the ongoing rhythmic ostinato. The half-octave descent-and-return motive (Ex. 8.10), diatonic but for one E♮, bisects the B♭ scale neatly. This motive generates from the four-part counterpoint (mm. 3ff.) and goes on to serve as the core of a developing variation.

EXAMPLE 8.10. Bruckner, Fifth Symphony, movt. 1, mm. 1–2

The slow introduction returns to prepare the finale, in perhaps plainer fashion than is customary for Bruckner. And in a large intermovement linkage, a single D-minor motive, clearly derived from the first movement, starts both the *adagio* and scherzo (Ex. 8.11). Finally, the tonic cadence of the finale (mm. 460ff.) encompasses all principal themes of both outer movements. Brucknerians like to see, too, invocations of Renaissance head-motive technique, though for all his knowledge of a cappella music, he expressed no interest in reviving it.

In short, the Fifth shares the values of the lectures: a deeper, holistic level of counterpoint than even his own melody had theretofore suggested, less decoration (less Schubert, less Wagner), and above all greater clarity of texture: fewer tremolos, briefer ostinatos, less opposition of the

EXAMPLE 8.11. Bruckner, Fifth Symphony
a. movt. 2, mm. 1–4

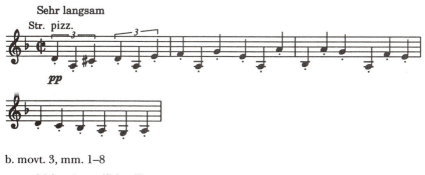

b. movt. 3, mm. 1–8

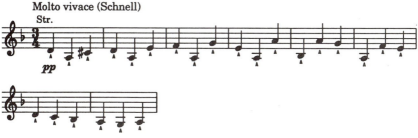

orchestral choirs. And the brisk, strict harmonic rhythm gives it a new and sober authority.

The Symphony No. 6 in A Major (1879–81) is the Ugly Duckling among its fellows: relatively short (at just under an hour), conventional of form, and with the usual hazy opening tremolos supplanted by a telegraphic ostinato (Ex. 8.12a). All Bruckner openings make a kind of counterpoint of tremolo and ostinato. Here the lively hemiola rhythm generates an unusual and consistent technical language for the symphony as a whole. The Phrygian cast of the first theme, a balancing of major and minor triads against minor seconds and sevenths, sets the tone: ersatz modes rich in major triads but not governed by them. The themes are linked even more than is usual for Bruckner. Thus the little fanfare (Ex. 8.12b) echoes a bit of the first theme, leading to a second group (Ex. 8.12c) that is less a new theme than an extension of the first. Around this, a lyrical brass texture maintains an eloquent aura, which quietly culminates in the first-movement coda, with its background trumpet line, sustained for over fifty luminous measures to the cadence (mm. 317–69).

Such lyricism pervades the symphony, whether or not derived directly from the start. The *adagio* begins with a broad-bowed (*lang gezogen*)

EXAMPLE 8.12. Bruckner, Sixth Symphony
a. mm. 3–6

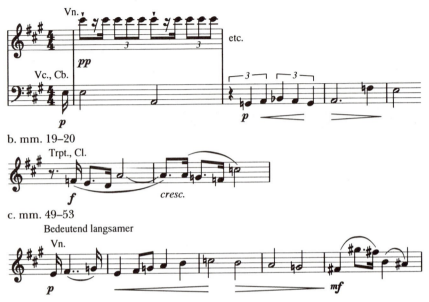

b. mm. 19–20

c. mm. 49–53

phrase for all strings (Ex. 8.13) in spacious, gently chromatic counterpoint. Whether any of the romance is linked plausibly to an old flame, or
even in one case to Bruckner's recently deceased mother, matters less
than the lyrical dignity itself. Kurth waxed eloquent about Bruckner's
contrapuntal resources at the start of the finale, observing again the per-

EXAMPLE 8.13. Bruckner, Sixth Symphony, movt. 2, mm. 1–4

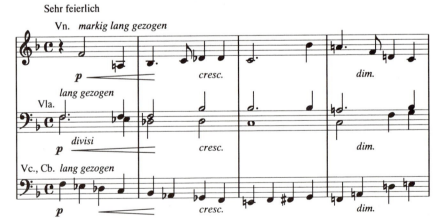

EXAMPLE 8.14. Bruckner, Sixth Symphony, movt. 4, mm. 3–6

vasiveness of dynamic formal process: an unlikely yet clear counterpoint between the "nonthematic theme" in the violins and the bass pizzicato, and even the tiny imitation in the second clarinet (Ex. 8.14).

The Seventh Symphony in E Major (1881–83), composed when he was sixty, was the first real symphonic success of Bruckner's life. (The re-fashioned Third and Fourth would soon match it, as would, later, the Eighth.) Its themes are laid out in sweeping fashion, broadly elegant and easily extended phrases that join together almost without pause. For instance, the first theme of the first movement, a single chromatic modulation, reaches its first preliminary climax on the dominant, measure 38 (Ex. 8.15). This broad, lyrical sweep manages to transform themes into a

EXAMPLE 8.15. Bruckner, Seventh Symphony, movt. 1, mm. 25–40

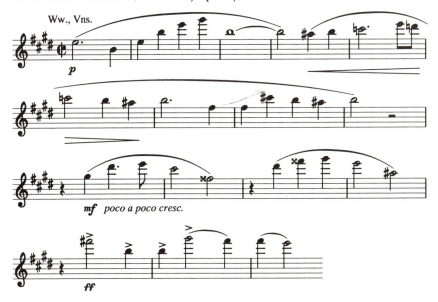

seamless melodic instrument, not so much modulating as peeling away layers. Yet the sonata form itself is relatively conservative.

Acclaim for the Seventh arose in large part from the second movement, an impressive lament for Wagner. Bruckner loved to recount how he wrote the climactic passage for four Wagner tubas over a standard contrabass tuba just after learning of Wagner's sudden death on 13 February 1883.[31] But this tale requires some poetic license: Bruckner had drafted most of the Seventh, including the *adagio*, the year before. The double-variation form, A-B-A'-B'-A", alludes simultaneously to Beethoven's Third, Fifth, Seventh, and Ninth, Schubert's Ninth, and Bruckner's own Second.

The start of the *adagio* (Ex. 8.16) presents the famous opposition of two intertextual motives. The first of these (mm. 1–3) clearly derives from the Wälsung motive in Siegfried's Funeral Music (*Götterdämmerung*, act 3)—"not color, but soul," Kurth said—and obviously links Siegfried and Wagner. The second motive (mm. 4–5), three rising pitches, is an equally personal allusion, to the "in Te, Domine, speravi / Non confundar in

EXAMPLE 8.16. Bruckner, Seventh Symphony, movt. 2, mm. 1–6

aeternum" in the coda of Bruckner's own Te Deum (1881–84). Here, too, the associative meaning is clear: release from the initial gloom. If this allusion seems tenuous, consisting as it does of no more than a *do-re-mi*, common meter, and a simple anacrusis and downbeat, there is proof in the compositional process. For the Te Deum was not finished until 1884, after the symphony was done, and it is the symphony's version, from measure 23 of the *adagio*, that is adapted for the long intensification of "Non confundar in aeternum." Haas's transcription of the 1881 Te Deum drafts shows beyond a doubt that the issue is more than one of simple quotation.

The *adagio* culminates twice, in a towering public climax (m. 177), then a more private one (mm. 185–93; Ex. 8.17). The first reinterprets the B in C♯ minor as leading tone of C, allowing a full group of trumpets, horns, and timpani to shine brilliantly in C major. But the climax fades, leaving the Wagner tubas alone. The C (as B♯) finally pushes clearly to the actual tonic C♯, for the first time in the movement. Bruckner may well have inserted this postclimactic passage in immediate response to Wagner's death, confirming the entire *adagio* as a *Trauermusik* for Wagner.

EXAMPLE 8.17. Bruckner, Seventh Symphony, movt. 2, mm. 185–88

But the Seventh appealed to a broader public than the Wagner partisans alone. Among private testimonials Bruckner most prized was the telegram sent by Johann Strauss Jr.—more famous than Bruckner, Brahms, and Wagner put together—just after the first Viennese performance: "I'm quite overwhelmed.—It was one of the greatest experiences of my life."[32] And Strauss was not alone, as the Seventh went on to garner support from one end of the Germanic world to the other. It is only symphony to have been printed directly from the autograph (**A-Wn** Mus. Hs. 19,479), and one of three—with the Fifth and Sixth, shortly before—that he never felt needed revision.

Vienna, 1884–96: Symphonies Nos. 8–9

Symphony No. 8 in C Minor (1884–90) has a heroic scenario, signaled not just in its strongly nationalist allusions centrally placed in all four movements, but in how they firmly orient the tonal structure of the whole toward a finale of near epic struggle and eventual triumph. Bruckner was devastated when Hermann Levi, who had conducted the triumphant premiere of the Seventh in Munich in 1884, demurred from leading a performance of the Eighth as it stood in 1887. Brucknerians reacted with more than a hint of anti-Semitism. But so elaborate, prolonged, and indeed confusing is the first version—of the finale in particular—that Levi's coolness, which was hardly an outright rejection, seems quite responsible. In any case, the correspondence on this matter was, however strained, far too tactful to give any evidence of racial slurs.

Accordingly, Bruckner, who had avoided revisions since the difficult births of the earlier Vienna symphonies, now began to rewrite the work. Each revision for the 1890 final version focuses on the overall tonal drama while trying to preserve the essential motivic shaping. Thus the much tighter revised first movement avoids the premature triumph that bedevils the 1887 version. The soft, sepulchral minor-key march—"Death's

EXAMPLE 8.18. Bruckner, Eighth Symphony, movt. 1, mm. 410–13

clock" (*Totenuhr*), he called it—is a new strategy for Bruckner (Ex. 8.18).[33] Like the first movement of Beethoven's Fifth, the "Marche au supplice" of the *Fantastique,* and the "Mephistofeles" movement of Liszt's *Faust* Symphony, all march-infused movements Bruckner had studied closely, this ending defers any triumph to the eventual finale.[34]

Elsewhere there is a strong dose of tragic Wagnerianism: in the opening theme, the plagal cadence of the scherzo, and the thickly shifting textures of the *adagio.* All this amounts to a blatantly nationalistic text, a program in all but name. More than the paradigmatic Beethoven's Fifth, where the issue is a simpler triumph over fate, the Eighth seethes with the grandiose militaristic dreams then surrounding the concept of pan-Germanic nationhood.

Bruckner had moved on immediately to his Ninth Symphony in D Minor (1887–96, unfinished) before hearing of Levi's negative reaction to the Eighth. From the outset it strikes a deeper, more tragic tone than any of the others in its broader motivic-rhythmic profile and the tonal bluntness of its opening motive. Moreover, Bruckner managed to preserve this distinctive character through all the years of delay during which his primary attention was focused on the comprehensive revision of the Eighth and his rewriting of the early symphonies. Sketching of the Ninth was already well advanced in 1887, but he did not allow himself to return to it full time before 1891. Even then, he was preoccupied by other works, particularly the Psalm 150 (1892, closely recalling the 1884 Te Deum) and *Helgoland* (1893–94), a work of bombastic nationalist doggerel. Retiring in 1895 to devote full time to the symphony, Bruckner was at length too ill to complete it: three movements were finished by November 1894, with more than one hundred pages of powerful sketches for the immense finale left behind at his death on 4 September 1896 (after a year of suffering from severe pneumonia). At the premiere of the Ninth in 1903, in Löwe's heavily doctored score, the existence of a fourth movement was left unmentioned.

The Ninth deploys D minor in an almost blatantly monumental fashion, with expanded late-Romantic orchestral textures and striking

EXAMPLE 8.19. Bruckner, Ninth Symphony, movt. 1, mm. 19–26

harmonic climaxes far remote from the tonic but easily managed through the virtuoso counterpoint of which Bruckner was by then the continent's unrivaled master. The solemn first movement treads, even more slowly than the composer ever had before, over a soft unison D tremolo. From measure 19 its spreads portentously outward to E♭ and D♭, then C♭, with a C♭-major fanfare soon overlaid in the eight horns (Ex. 8.19). Less a modulation than a broad pause to intensify the unison peak of the first theme on the tonic D (mm. 63–75), this first harmonic side trip will be recalled unconventionally in the codetta of the exposition on D (mm. 167ff.), then C♭ (mm. 183ff.). One characteristic reflection is the elegantly simple harmonization of the second theme (mm. 97ff.), using not a I–V–I in A major but a haunting I–III–I. The III–I inverts the ♭vi to the tonic harmony of the first theme.

The side trip at measure 19 also predicts the bracing openings of both the scherzo and the *adagio,* as well as the E-major tonality of the *adagio.* The start of the scherzo, on an augmented-sixth variant on C♯, includes the oboe sustaining a *pp* C♯ for three dozen bars before the D brutally resolves this nonfunctional leading tone. The magnificent opening of the *adagio,* too, is unsettling, as one expects some key other than the tonic (Ex. 8.20a). The chorale gesture on D (mm. 5–6) and its magnificent resolution to E, toward which the Paganiniesque opening B had aimed after all, play doubly against ordinary formal schemes.

This *adagio,* like those of the Seventh and Eighth, uses a complex double-variation scheme, rendered tonally unstable by the beginning. To compensate for it the movement is made to cohere through recurring elements. The loudest, certainly, are the much-protracted tutti chords of the dominant ninth (mm. 17–28, 121–28, 167–72, and 199–202), capped by a strident eleventh (mm. 203–06). And then there are the personal, perhaps career-summarizing, allusions. The cadence at measures 29–40 (Ex. 8.20b) is adapted from the Miserere of the Gloria in the D-Minor Mass, Bruckner's first post–Kitzler composition (1864). The dignified second theme, measures 45–76 (Ex. 8.20c), is marked "Farewell to Life." Wagner tubas make their now-symbolic appearance in measures 225–26.

EXAMPLE 8.20. Bruckner, Ninth Symphony, movt. 3
a. mm. 1–7

b. mm. 29–32

c. mm. 45–46

Finally, there are allusions in the woodwinds and horns to the two preceding symphonies: to the Eighth Symphony at measures 231–34, and to the opening of the Seventh at measures 223–25, 229–30, and 237–43.

The Case of the Finale

The still-current myth that Bruckner had left no more than scarcely coherent sketches for a finale can be traced back to the period just after his death. It was difficult for the Viennese to acknowledge that a good many pages had been lifted from the manuscript soon after Bruckner's death by his disciples, including both Franz Schalk and Ferdinand Löwe. The only available edition of the sketches and drafts was an obsessive yet careless and incomplete effort of the Viennese librarian Alfred Orel,[35] made available in a 1934 publication of the first three movements with the finale in an intimidating appendix. It was a back-to-back performance of this version alongside the aging Löwe's still-prominent score that launched the first critical edition of Bruckner's works. But in Orel's edition the coda, so essential for a Bruckner symphony, did not exist at all, and but for a few sections, the finale remained unorchestrated. Even though Orel finally disowned his work, the Brucknerians shied away from updating the edition. Conductors have preferred to give the first three movements alone.

In recent years, critical study of the sketches, notably by Marianna Sonntag and John A. Phillips,[36] has shown that Bruckner established the continuity of the movement with counts of phrase lengths and cues to the sketches scrawled in pencil additions to the ink draft. Not only is the movement almost completely drafted, but there are coherent sketches and an overall plan for the coda. Meanwhile, a viable performing reconstruction of the finale by Nicola Samale and Giuseppe Mazzuca, based on the full autograph material at the Vienna Municipal Library, was recorded by Teldec in 1988; this replaced other, less well advised attempts of the CD industry to complete the movement based on the Orel edition alone. John Phillips's 1994 revised critical edition, in collaboration with Samale and Mazzuca, presents a thoroughly viable solution.

The sketches, in an ever-deteriorating hand, show both continuity sketching and dozens of repeated attempts to mold particular modulations and problematic phrases. Early on we see a grandiose chorale, then a still larger culminatory fugue. The movement opens with a chromatic motive over a G pedal in off-tonic timpani, much like that of the Eighth. A fuller sketch, 8 June 1895, has sequential extension of the motive blossom into a majestic chorale, still within the exposition. In a later stage the expected return of the tonic D after an extended excursion is achieved by a ponderous fugal restatement. Later in the genesis, the bare early statement of the subject is replaced by a more continuous exposition in short score and its recapitulation.

The longest sketch, that leading to the reprise of the theme, involves a transition to the familiar opening of the 1884 Te Deum. The obvious, poetic explanation is that Bruckner proposed this ending *in extremis*, though the sketches suggest it to be something more than a last-minute solution. Orel, nevertheless, was but the first of many to reject this possibility, on the grounds that the two works were separated by ten years and that there was no plausible connection between the D minor of the symphony and the C major of the Te Deum. Yet the Te Deum displays textural and tonal strategies and motivic language quite as broad as the Ninth, and just as compelling.[37] And the tonal connection, in view of the D–E links between the first movement and *adagio* (with its strong feints toward C), is less forced that it might seem. On the whole it does not appear that Bruckner meant to abandon the notion.

Circumstantial evidence points to greater advance on the finale than is generally acknowledged. Franz Bayer, the choral conductor of Steyr, visited Bruckner in spring 1896, and on returning home the local paper reported: "The concluding movement of the Ninth Symphony he has probably completely sketched out, but, as he himself expressed to Herr Bayer, he no longer hoped to be able to complete his working-out."[38] Bruckner's doctor, Richard Heller, reported that he spoke of "wanting to introduce the Allelujah of the second movement" in the coda.[39] The

Auer biographies seem to describe the now lost coda of the Ninth as having at least four themes "piled on top of one another, as in the finale of the Eighth." It is with a feasible and authoritative use of this counterpoint that Phillips's score concludes. In any event, we need accept neither Orel's disingenuous evasion of a true conclusion nor the solution of performers since, to cut short the Ninth after the elegiac *adagio*. Instead it makes sense, for a composer as concerned as Bruckner was with matters of eschatology, to encourage a wider crop of finale-including solutions.

A Note on the Critical Editions

Bruckner himself was partly to blame for the editorial questions that have plagued the symphonies since his lifetime. So eager had he suddenly grown for further successes, after the premiere of the Seventh in 1884–85, that to gain new publications and performances he let himself be pressed into wholesale cutting of several symphonies and into allowing other hands to set about rescoring his work. Most of his own cuts were gross slashings of large-scale thematic returns, thereby often ruining well-calculated proportions. The rescorings were grosser still, converting Bruckner's chamber textures into raucous, striding passages dominated by the brass band. Bruckner acquiesced to most of these, but it is telling that at the same time he carefully preserved his original autograph scores intact.

The ringleaders of the purge, which in fact succeeded in winning easier acceptance for the symphonies after Bruckner's death, were his most avid disciples, the brothers Josef and Franz Schalk and Ferdinand Löwe. All three had become prominent conductors in Austrian Wagnerian circles.[40] The Bruckner Critical Edition responded to Löwe's continued promulgation of his own edition of the posthumous work. And the disputes were encouraged by rival publishers: Schalk's Universal Edition (Vienna), which still keeps the altered Schalk-Löwe scores on its backlist, and Breitkopf and Härtel (Leipzig), who produced Robert Haas's First Critical Edition.

The divergent editorial practices of the Haas and Nowak editions have to do with differing attitudes toward Bruckner's nationalism during and after the Nazi years, and with Haas's dismissal after World War II for his Nazi party connections. Both Robert Haas and his successor, Leopold Nowak, headed the Music Division of the Austrian National Library. They oversaw most of the Bruckner manuscripts, which the composer had willed to the library. The First Critical Edition (Haas), and the postwar Second, largely under Nowak, were thus "authentic" editions. Nowak's revisions were, by his own admission, little more than proofreading of Haas. Still, it was Nowak and his successor, Günter Brosche, who presented the "Student" and "Annulled" Symphonies and the earlier versions of the first symphonies.

The largest controversies surround brief passages in the Second and Fourth Symphonies and substantive disputes about the Eighth. Nowak felt constrained to accept Bruckner's wholesale amputation of sizable sections of the *adagio* and finale of the Eighth. Though believing the cuts harmed the work, he imagined that "nothing can be done about it," since the changes were in Bruckner's own hand. On the whole, Haas was the more sensitive editor, and gifted with better musical judgment.

Notes

I dedicate this chapter to my wife, June Melchior, sine qua non. Valued helpers included Dr. Barbara Halpern and Ms. Diane Judd, the Music Department faculty and staff of Amherst College, Smith College, the University of California, Berkeley, and Victoria University of Wellington. Still others, though far from all, are named in the notes below.

1. Early Vienna confidants were the brothers Alois and especially Rudolph Weinwurm, fellow choral conductors; Rudolph took a post at the Vienna Conservatory about the same time as Bruckner. Later disciples included the teenage Mahler and Wolf and especially (though not always to Bruckner's benefit) the conductor-composers Ferdinand Löwe and Franz and Joseph Schalk.

2. Theodore Rättig, who had just published the work. Rättig then took a substantial loss when Mahler objected to Franz Schalk's later alterations and successfully insisted that they be redone. See Paul Banks, "Vienna: Absolutism and Nostalgia," in *The Late Romantic Era*, ed. Jim Samson (London, 1991), 85–86.

3. The childless bachelor Bruckner often claimed his symphonies as his children, especially in later years. See August Göllerich and Max Auer, *Anton Bruckner: Ein Lebens- und Schaffensbild* (hereafter Göllerich–Auer), 4 vols. in 9 (Regensburg, 1922–37), vol. 4, part 2, 184, referring to the Eighth Symphony.

4. The most significant critical treatment of Bruckner's evolutionary formal process, despite such flaws as the use of outmoded editions, remains the immense *Bruckner* of the Austro-Swiss theorist Ernst Kurth (2 vols., Berlin, 1925). See also my "Kurth's *Bruckner* and the Vocabulary of Symphonic Formal Process" (Ph.D. dissertation, University of California, Berkeley, 1989), adapted in part as "Kurth's *Bruckner* and the Adagio of the Seventh Symphony," *19th-Century Music* 11 (1988): 262–80 (esp. p. 267). A recent and useful English-language summary and introduction is *Ernst Kurth As Theorist and Analyst*, ed. and trans. Lee A. Rothfarb (Philadelphia, 1991); see especially "The Symphonic Wave," 151–207.

5. While ever a dutiful subject of the Hapsburg Franz Josef, Bruckner also paid homage to Franz Josef's Hohenzollern cousin Kaiser Wilhelm in Berlin, dedicating the revised score of the Eighth Symphony (1890), his longest and most self-consciously imperialist work, to Kaiser Wilhelm; the Seventh had been dedicated to Franz Josef. It is uncertain whether in his last years Bruckner felt a greater allegiance to the Austrian Kaiser (his final landlord: at the end of his life Bruckner was honored with a small house in the Imperial Gardens) or to the pan-Germanic ideal he and others would have seen centered in Berlin.

6. Göllerich–Auer, vol. 4, part 1, 188.

7. Otto-Werner Mueller, in a conducting seminar at the Yale School of Music, 1976.

8. Göllerich–Auer, vol. 3, part 2, 232.

9. See Bryan Gilliam, "The Annexation of Anton Bruckner: Nazi Revisionism and the Politics of Misappropriation," *Musical Quarterly* 78 (1994): 584–604, with appendix, "Joseph Goebbels's Bruckner Address in Regensburg (6 June 1937)," trans. John Michael Cooper, 605–09.

10. One paper from the 1994 Bruckner Reception Conference (in *Perspectives on Anton Bruckner*, ed. Paul Hawkshaw and Timothy Jackson, forthcoming) recounts one official party fanfare trumpeting the opening motive of the Bruckner Third.

11. See Elisabeth Maier, "Ignaz Dorns Charakteristiche Sinfonie 'Labyrinth-Bilder'," In *Bruckner-Symposion: Bruckner und die Musik der Romantik*, report of the International Bruckner Festival, 1987 (Linz, 1989), 69–78.

12. Kurth, *Bruckner*, vol. 2, 1152.

13. Kitzler, *Musikalische Erinnerungen* (Brünn/Brno, 1904), passim.

14. Göllerich–Auer, vol. 4, part 1, 143–44.

15. Göllerich–Auer, vol. 3, part 1, 316.

16. Göllerich–Auer, vol. 3, part 1, 345; vol. 4, part 2, 678–79; and vol. 4, part 3, 206 give a variety of citations for Bruckner's use of *kecke Beserl*. The last, from Bruckner's sympathetic partisan Theodor Helm, indicates that he used the term affectionately.

17. Göllerich–Auer, vol. 3, part 1, passim, recounts Bruckner's lengthy courtship of the devout butcher's daughter Josefine Lang, her eventual rejection (regarding Bruckner as old, awkward, and "always idiotically dressed"), and his pathetic despondency. Bruckner's janitor brother Ignaz recalled, "Tony got ugly about it." Bruckner suffered a serious nervous breakdown soon afterward.

18. Auer, *Anton Bruckner: Seine Leben und Werk* (popularization of Göllerich–Auer; Zurich, 1936), 186.

19. Adorno, review of a Frankfurt Museum Concert conducted by Clemens Krauss, *Die Musik*, May 1926, rpt. in Adorno, *Musikalische Schriften IV*, vol. 19 of *Gesammelte Schriften*, ed. Rolf Tiedemann and Klaus Schultz (Frankfurt, 1984), 72.

20. For years the date of the "Annulled" Symphony was the only major problem of chronology in Bruckner studies. For various reasons but with little real evidence, scholars (especially Leopold Nowak) claimed an earlier date for the work, usually 1865. In 1983, however, Paul Hawkshaw's fresh examination of sketches and draft reaffirmed my sense, shared by others, that 1869 is the only workable date for the "Annulled." See Hawkshaw, "The Date of Bruckner's 'Nullified' Symphony in D Minor," *19th-Century Music* 6 (1983): 252–63.

21. Göllerich–Auer, vol. 4, part 2, 197.

22. Simon Sechter, *Die Grunsätze der musikalischen Komposition* (Leipzig, 1853–54). On Bruckner's use of the Sechter see Göllerich–Auer, vol. 3, part 1, 306ff., 315–17. Also see Friedrich Eckstein, *Erinnerungen an Anton Bruckner* (Vienna, 1923), and Karl Hruby, *Meine Erinnerungen an Anton Bruckner* (Vienna, 1901).

23. Cooke, "Bruckner," in *The New Grove Late Romantic Masters* (London, 1985), 15. The "Second Critical Edition" of the Symphony No. 2 and its previous versions have only recently appeared, edited by the avid American amateur

William Carragan. Carragan was also consultant for a recording that compares the different versions (Bruckner-Orchester Linz, cond. Kurt Eichhorn, Camerata 2-30 CM 195/96). The cuts for the final 1877 version still seem judicious.

24. Last-movement parodies of the first follow a tradition dear to Bruckner, especially from Beethoven, Berlioz, and Liszt. See August Halm, *Die Symphonie Anton Bruckners* (Munich, 1913; rev. ed., 1923; rpt., 1975), 147–70; also see Halm's cogent treatment of the first-movement opening motive, 79–81.

25. Göllerich–Auer, vol. 4, part 2, 227.

26. Bruckner clarified the motive at the behest of Anton Seidl, who had become the conductor of the New York Symphony. This final revision of the Fourth is in the Special Collections department of the Columbia University Library.

27. On 4 May 1874 Hanslick belittled Bruckner's first university application for his lack of a doctorate, cited precedent that "composition study" was out of place at the university, and claimed that faculty pension rights must have been Bruckner's principal object. Göllerich–Auer, vol. 4, part 1, 292–94.

28. One ultranationalist leader in Parliament in the 1870s and 1880s was August Göllerich, father of Bruckner's student and biographer.

29. Letter to the faculty "Professorial Collegium," 10 May 1874; Göllerich–Auer, vol. 4, part 1, 296–97.

30. Bruckner's lecture was officially delivered 24 April 1876; a draft was read 25 November 1875, when he was also finishing his draft of the Fifth Symphony (Göllerich–Auer, vol. 4, part 1, 374–76). Bruckner's colorful examples, all Germanic, were from Bach, Handel, Mozart, Beethoven, Schubert, and Wagner. For instance: "That's the way it is with Leporello! We recognize him, even if he is wearing Don Giovanni's cloak" (Göllerich–Auer, vol. 4, part 1, 31).

31. Bruckner told the tale in such terms years later (23 January 1894) to his partisan Theodor Helm and Helm's son. Göllerich–Auer, vol. 4, part 2, 80–81.

32. Göllerich–Auer, vol. 4, part 2, 431.

33. Göllerich–Auer, vol. 4, part 2, 451.

34. Göllerich–Auer, vol. 4, part 2, 306ff.

35. Alfred Orel, critical edition of Bruckner, Symphony No. 9 (Leipzig, 1934); compositional material for all movements, including sketches and drafts for the finale, are excerpted and described at numbing length.

36. Mariana Sonntag, *The Compositional Process of Anton Bruckner: A Study of the Sketches and Drafts of the Ninth Symphony*. Ph.D. dissertation, University of Chicago, 1987. See also Sonntag, "A New Perspective on Anton Bruckner's Composition of the Ninth Symphony," *Bruckner-Jahrbuch 1989/90* (Linz, 1989), 77–113. John Phillips, revised critical edition of Bruckner, Symphony No. 9 (Vienna, 1994).

37. Carl Dahlhaus, in *Nineteenth Century Music* (Berkeley and Los Angeles, 1989), 188–90), offers a rare close motivic analysis of the Te Deum.

38. *Styrer Zeitung*, 10 May 1896. This foreboding came well before Bruckner's final pneumonia set in.

39. Max Auer identified this as a passage in the trio of the Eighth Symphony (movt. 2), which in turn invokes the Te Deum.

40. Thomas Leibnitz, of the Music Division of the Austrian Library, documents Bruckner's relationship with his editors in *Die Brüder Schalk und Anton Bruckner* (Tutzing, 1988).

Selected Bibliography

CRITICAL EDITIONS

Bruckner, Anton. *Sämtliche Werke* ["First Critical Edition of the Original Versions"]. Ed. Alfred Orel (1930), Robert Haas (from 1930). 12 vols. Vienna, 1930–49. (Final versions only.)
——. *Gesamtausgabe* ["Second, Revised Complete Edition"]. Ed. Leopold Nowak (1951–92), Gander Brisk (1992–). Vienna, 1951– . (Includes many first and intermediate versions, final versions, and first publications of the "Student" and "Annulled" Symphonies and the Overture in G Minor.)
——. Symphony No. 4. Rev. ed. Vienna, [1880].
——. Symphony No. 7. Eulenburg Miniature Scores. Foreword by H. F. Redlich. London, 1958.

BOOKS AND ARTICLES

Auer, Max. "Anton Bruckners letzter behandelnder Arzt." In *In Memoriam Anton Bruckner*, ed. Karl Kobald, 21–35. Zurich, 1924.
——. *Anton Bruckner: Sein Leben und Werk.* Adapted from August Göllerich and Max Auer, *Anton Bruckner: Ein Lebens- und Schaffensbild* (Regensburg, 1922–37). Zurich, 1932.
——. *Bruckner.* Zurich, 1923.
Bruckner, Anton. *Gesammelte Briefe: Neue Folge.* Ed. Max Auer. Regensburg, 1924.
——. *Vorlesungen über Harmonieleher uns Kontrapunkt an der Universität Wien.* Ed. Ernst Schwanzara. Vienna, 1950.
Carragan, William. Liner Notes for Bruckner, Symphony No. 2, comprising selected movements from the 1871, 1872, and 1877 editions, all ed. Carragan. Bruckner-Orchester Linz, Kurt Eichhorn, conductor. Camerata 2-30 CM 195/96 [1992].
Cooke, Deryck. "Bruckner." *The New Grove Late Romantic Masters*, 1–73. London, 1985. Slightly revised, by Hans Hubert Schönzeler, from the article in *The New Grove Dictionary of Music and Musicians*, 6th ed., ed. Stanley Sadie. London, 1980.
Dahlhaus, Carl. "Bruckner und die Programmmemusik: Zum Finale der Achten Symphonie." In *Anton Bruckner: Studien zur Werk und Wirkung*, ed. Christoph-Helmut Mahling, 7–32. Tutzing, 1988.
——. "Ist Bruckners Harmonik formbildend?" *Bruckner-Jahrbuch* 1982/83 (Linz, 1984): 19–26.
——. *Nineteenth-Century Music.* Trans. J. B. Robinson. Berkeley and Los Angeles, 1990. Originally pub. as *Die Musik des 19.Jahrhunderts* (Wiesbaden, 1980).
——. *The Idea of Absolute Music.* Trans. Roger Lustig. Originally published as *Die Idea der absoluten Musik* (Kassel, 1978).
Futwängler, Wilhem. "Anton Bruckner." In *Ton und Wort* (Wiesbaden, 1982), 102–38.
Federhofer, Hellmut. "Heinrich Schenkers Bruckner-Verständnis." *Archiv für Musikwissenschaft* 39 (1982): 198–217.
Floros, Constantin. *Brahms und Bruckner: Studien zur musikalischen Exegetic.* Wiesbaden, 1980.

Gilliam, Bryan. "The Annexation of Anton Bruckner: Nazi Revisionism and the Politics of Appropriation." *Musical Quarterly* 78 (1994): 584–604. With appendix: "Joseph Goebbel's Bruckner Address in Regensburg (6 June 1937)," trans. John Michael Cooper, 605–9.

Göllerich, August, with Max Auer. *Anton Bruckner: Ein Lebens- und Schaffensbild.* 4 vols. in 9. Regensburg, 1922–37.

Grasberger, Franz. "Schubert and Bruckner." In *Schubert-Kongress Wien 1978*, ed. Otto Brusatti, 215–18. Graz, 1979.

Haas, Robert Anton Bruckner. Potsdam, 1934.

Halm, August. *Die Symphonie Anton Bruckners.* Munich, 1913. Rev. ed. 1923. Reprint. 1984.

Hawkshaw, Paul. "The Manuscript Sources for Anton Bruckner's Linz Works: A Study of His Working Methods from 1856 to 1868." Ph.D. dissertation, Columbia University, 1984.

———. "The Date of Bruckner's 'Nullified' Symphony in D Minor." *19th-Century Music* 6 (1983): 252–63.

———, and Timothy L. Jackson, eds. *Perspectives on Anton Bruckner.* Selected from Perspectives on Anton Bruckner: An International Symposium, New London, CT, 1994. Forthcoming.

Hruby, Carl. *Meine Erinnerungen an Anton Bruckner.* Vienna, 1901.

Jackson, Timothy L. "Bruckner's Metrical Numbers." *19th-Century Music* 13 (1983): 101–31.

Kurth, Ernst. *Bruckner.* 2 vols. Berlin, 1925. Reprint. Hildesheim, 1971. Extensive excerpts, including "The Symphonic Wave," ed. and trans. Lee A. Rothfarb, in *Ernst Kurth: Selected Writings*, 151–207. Cambridge, 1991.

Leibnitz, Thomas. *Die Brüder Schalk und Anton Bruckner.* Tutzing, 1988.

Nowak, Leopold. *Anton Bruckner: Musik und Leben.* Linz, 1973.

Orel, Alfred. *Anton Bruckner: Das Werk, Der Künstler, Die Zeit.* Vienna, 1925.

Parkany, Stephen. "Bruckner and the Vocabulary of Symphonic Formal Process." Ph.D. dissertation, University of California, Berkeley, 1989.

———. "Kurth's Bruckner and the Adagio of the Seventh Symphony." *19th-Century Music* 11 (1988): 262–81.

———. "The *'kecke Beserl'* and Bruckner's Symphonic Tradition." In *Atti del XIV. Congresso dells Società Internazionale di Musicologia* (Bologna, 1987), 3:811–14.

Redlich, H. F. *Bruckner and Mahler.* Rev. ed. London, 1963.

Röder, Thomas. "Auf dem Weg zur Bruckner Symphonie: Untersuchungen zu den ersten beiden Fassungen von Anton Bruckners Dritter Symphonie." Ph.D. dissertation, University of Wiesbaden, 1987.

Röthig, Claudia Catharina. *Studien zur Systematik des Schaffens von Anton Bruckner auf der Grundlage zeitgenössicher Berichte und autographer Entwürfe.* Göttingen, 1978.

Sechter, Simon. *Die Grundsätze der musikalischen Komposition.* Leipzig, 1853–55.

Sonntag, Mariana. *The Compositional Process of Anton Bruckner: A Study of the Sketches and Drafts of the Ninth Symphony.* Ph.D. dissertation, University of Chicago, 1987.

Steinbeck, Wolfram. "Schema als Form bei Anton Bruckner: Zum Adagio der VII. Symphonie." In *Analysen: Festschrift für Hans Heinrich Eggebrecht*, ed. Werner Breig, Reinhold Brinkmann, and Elmar Buddle, 304–23. Stuttgart, 1984.

Wagner, Manfred. "Bruckner in Wien." In *Anton Bruckner in Wien: Eine kritische Studie zu seiner Persönlichkeit*, ed. Franz Grasberger, 9–74. Graz, 1980.

———. *Bruckner: Monographie.* Mainz, 1983.

CHAPTER NINE

Brahms

David Brodbeck

"Now, where is Johannes?" asked Robert Schumann, in a letter to Joseph Joachim of January 1854. "Is he not yet allowing timpani and drums to resound? He should always recall the beginnings of Beethoven's symphonies; he should seek to make something similar. The beginning is the main thing; once one has begun, the end comes as if by itself."[1]

This pronouncement must have come easily to Schumann. His First Symphony, after all, begins with a clear recollection, not of Beethoven, to be sure, but of nothing less formidable than Schubert's "Great" C Major; and his sketching of the composition, advancing as if by itself, was completed in a matter of four days. But Brahms could not have hoped to duplicate such a feat. If the challenge that Schumann had laid down in his letter to Joachim had been a private matter, not so were the claims made in his famous essay "Neue Bahnen," published in the *Neue Zeitschrift für Musik* a few months earlier.[2] In those well-known lines Schumann introduced the twenty-year-old composer as a musical Messiah, who already had made remarkable strides in the realms of lieder and piano and chamber music but would some day "lower his magic wand where the massed might of choir and orchestra can lend its strength" and so present "still more wonderful glimpses into the mysteries of the spirit world"—who would someday write, Schumann seemed to be saying, a worthy successor to Beethoven's Ninth. This charge became an obsession to Brahms, and one with which he grappled long and hard, from two ill-fated attempts in the 1850s, through a protracted struggle to bring forth the First Symphony (1876), to the Olympian achievement of the Fourth (1885).

To judge from the opening *maestoso* of the Piano Concerto in D Minor Op. 15, which can be traced back to material that dates from the spring of 1854, the young Brahms did not at first back away from Schumann's challenge. With timpani resounding, the concerto begins with a reinterpretation of the first pages of Beethoven's Ninth—although in

Brahms's hands the dramatic and suspenseful process of the model unfolds breathlessly in only a few bars' time. Whereas Beethoven gradually (and inexorably) develops from tonally ambiguous fifths a well-formed theme that arpeggiates the tonic, and only then, in a varied repetition, leads unexpectedly to an arpeggiation of B♭, Brahms, in a sudden dramatic burst, lets loose at once with his plunge through the submediant.

Although this allusion evinces Brahms's high ambitions for the piece, his ideas originally took shape, not in a concerto or any other orchestral dress, but in a Sonata for Two Pianos, the first three movements of which were finished by early April 1854. From the start, however, Brahms probably had in mind to compose a symphony, and by July he had even orchestrated the first movement.[3] But considering the probable role played in the conception of the work by Beethoven's Ninth, it is not surprising that Brahms progressed slowly, if at all, on the finale. Thus no mention was made of any last movement when on 30 January 1855 the young composer finally mustered the courage to announce the piece to Schumann: "By the way, I spent all last summer trying to write a symphony; the first movement was even orchestrated, and the second and third composed. (In D minor ⁶₄ slow)."[4] Borrowing gestures from Beethoven's tragic opening movement was one thing, but emulating his choral finale—and, as Christopher Reynolds has argued, Brahms might well have intended to do just that—was something else again. The Beethovenian model—with its great length and complex form, its thematic recollections, recitatives, and choral setting of the "Ode to Joy"—was in every respect daunting.[5]

Yet only a few days after reporting to Schumann, Brahms saw a way out of his dilemma. He dreamed that he had used two parts of his "hapless symphony," as he described the piece to Clara Schumann on 7 February 1855, in a piano concerto, consisting of "the first movement and scherzo with a finale, terribly difficult and grand." Thus was the symphony abandoned and its first movement, indeed, eventually revised as the opening *maestoso* of the First Piano Concerto.[6]

The Serenades

The later years of the decade were to be more productive. Working alternately in Hamburg and the small court of Lippe-Detmold, where he served as piano teacher, choral conductor, and pianist, Brahms undertook a different kind of "technical preparation," studying the vast repertoire of Classical chamber and orchestral music. The initial outcome of this study may be seen in the two Serenades, in D major (Op. 11), and A major (Op. 16).

The A-Major Serenade, scored for double woodwinds, two horns, and a string section consisting of only violas, cellos, and basses, was the less problematic of the pair and forever held a special place in the composer's heart. Most writers have suggested that Brahms omitted violins from his orchestra after the example of Méhul's Ossianic opera *Uthal* (1806). A more convincing explanation of the unusual band—indeed, an explanation that may even account for Brahms's very decision to compose the work—is suggested by Clara Schumann's response to Mozart's Serenade, K. 361/370a, retold in a letter to Brahms of 8 November 1858:

> Recently I heard for the first time a Mozart Serenade (B♭ major) for 13 wind instruments, during which it became completely clear to me how this [serenade] was specifically imagined for these 13 instruments while yours [the D Major Serenade] requires a full orchestra throughout. . . . What struck me in particular in the Mozart was a great monotony of sound—I generally don't like to hear several movements of only wind instruments, in which case the oboe especially, often so wonderfully moving otherwise, becomes completely exhausting.[7]

It seems probable that Brahms took Clara's negative remarks about K. 361 as a challenge, so to speak, to write a lengthy wind-dominated serenade of his own (likewise in thirteen parts), in which the monotony of tone color that comes too easily to the genre might be circumvented. After all, as Tovey noted, the composer's omission of violins seems calculated "to throw the wind into high relief," while the presence of the lower strings means that the winds are at the same time "relieved from the burden of supplying their own background."[8]

The opening *allegro moderato*, which Frau Schumann received in early December 1858, illustrates Brahms's approach to the problem. The winds dominate the texture, with the clarinets and bassoons, soon to be joined by the flutes, initiating a beautiful ascending opening period (mm. 1–8). The violas and cellos are reserved for a counterstatement of the main theme (mm. 9ff.), but even then the woodwinds do not give way, as the first flute and clarinet combine in a more active, descending counterpoint. Brahms makes do with a single statement in the recapitulation (mm. 217ff.); once more the bassoons initiate the main theme, but this time the clarinets are replaced by the violas, which offer a heterophonic accompaniment in gentle triplets.

Work on the piece continued well into the following year. In September 1859 Brahms sent Clara the beautiful *adagio non troppo* and the *quasi menuetto*, together, once more, with the first movement, if not also the finale; and the entire five-movement cycle was in her hands by November. The centerpiece of the work, both literally and expressively, is the extraordinary *adagio*, in the tonic minor, with its modulating ostinato bass, melancholic principal theme, intricate counterpoint, and central episode in the distant key of A♭ major.

Sandwiched around the composition of the A-Major Serenade was work on a more stubborn cousin, the Serenade in D Major. In its first incarnation, dating from the summer of 1858, the piece consisted of four movements only and was scored for a chamber ensemble of winds and strings. Although there was talk from the start that the piece should be converted into a symphony, at the end of the year Brahms actually made the work seem less symphonic by adding two scherzi. Nevertheless, at some point this new forty-minute, six-movement version of the piece had acquired a dress such that when, in early 1859, plans for its premiere were being made, Brahms actually considered including it, together with the equally massive D-Minor Concerto, on his Hamburg Philharmonic concert of 25 March. In the end, however, the Serenade was given in a separate soirée in Hamburg on the twenty-eighth, in which Joachim led a "small orchestra" that Brahms had engaged for the occasion.[9] All in all, the composer was satisfied with the two Hamburg performances, and in a report to his student Laura von Meysenburg he exuded real pride over both members of his major-minor pair: "I am quite pleased with my first orchestral attempts, and I hope with confidence that they will gain friendly listeners in Detmold as well."[10]

If "Neue Bahnen" forms an indispensable part of the context in which to understand the aborted D-Minor Symphony, then the D-Major Serenade must be read in conjunction with a kind of rejoinder to Schumann's essay by Franz Brendel. On 10 June 1859 the *Neue Zeitschrift* led with Brendel's inaugural address to the first Tonkünstlerversammlung of what later became the Allgemeiner Deutscher Musikverein. Here Brendel proposed replacing the expression "Music of the Future" with "New German School," which he held was led by Wagner, Liszt, and Berlioz, and which represented, in a kind of synthesis of historical periods, the "entire post–Beethoven development."[11] Brahms, who knew at first hand the problem of following in the steps of Beethoven, and who had by then come to very different terms with the Baroque and Classical past, responded angrily. In August 1859 he reported to Joachim that "his fingers often itched to start a fight, to write something anti-Liszt." Significantly, it was the recent orchestral works of the Weimar master—the *Dante* Symphony and newly published symphonic poems—that Brahms singled out for scorn, likening them to so many contagions in a spreading "plague." And for that reason it is scarcely surprising that his contemporaneous First Serenade—which opens with a virtual quotation of Haydn's "London" Symphony and continues with references to a large number of other "healthy" models—plays like something "anti-Liszt."[12]

In view of this context—considering both Brahms's struggle (and desire) to compose a symphony and his horror at the evident advance of Liszt's new orchestral paradigms—it is understandable that he finally reworked the piece once more. On 8 December 1859 he asked Joachim to return the score and to include with it some music paper in a large format. "I need the paper," he wrote, with a certain sense of resignation, "in order finally to turn the First Serenade into a symphony. The work is a kind of mongrel, I see, nothing is right. I had such beautiful, great ideas for my first symphony, and now!"[13] Brahms was less candid to Karl Bargheer, the first violinist in the Detmold orchestra, who interrupted him one day at work. As Max Kalbeck related the story:

> Bargheer surprised him . . . at noon. Everything in his room, piano, bed, table and chair, was covered with leaves of full score [*Partiturbogen*], which Brahms, who was accustomed to rising very early, had filled with writing in the morning. "I am setting the Serenade for orchestra," he said; "it will be much better." When Bargheer asked him whether then it would be a symphony, Brahms expressed his opinion that "If one wants to write symphonies after Beethoven, then they will have to look very different!"[14]

Notwithstanding this disavowal, the orchestral score that Brahms produced originally was headed "Sinfonie-Serenade"; and it was this designation that Joachim used when he recorded his great happiness upon receiving the work at Christmas 1859 and again two months later, when requesting both score and parts for a forthcoming rehearsal of the new version. Yet when Brahms complied with this request he expressed his final view of the work in no uncertain terms: "Here come the score and parts to the D-Major *Serenade*, if I may."[15]

Although the two Serenades can be linked on the basis of genre and time of origin, they do not stand in the relation to one another that characterizes many other such couplings by Brahms. As is well known, the composer frequently came forth with pairs of "serious" and "cheerful" realizations of a genre: the Piano Quartets in G minor Op. 25 and A major Op. 26 (pub. 1863), the C-Minor and A-Minor String Quartets Op. 51 (1873), the *Academic Festival* and *Tragic* Overtures Opp. 80 and 81 (1880), the two late Sonatas for Clarinet and Piano Op. 120 (1895), and so forth. Brahms acknowledged this habit in regard to his symphonic œuvre when, in comments of 1890 to Viktor Koessler concerning the possibility of adding a couple of new works to a catalogue that already numbered four, he said that he had "already done enough with the two pairs of serious and cheerful symphonies."[16] What he did not (and had no reason to) acknowledge was an earlier pair that had preceded the first two published symphonies: when we link the "cheerful" (erstwhile) D-Major "Sinfonie-Serenade," not to the Serenade in A Major, but to the "serious" (aborted) D-Minor Symphony, we can appreciate Brahms's continuous struggle with the genre throughout the 1850s. That struggle continued into the next decade, and once again Brahms began to follow his "serious" muse.

The First Symphony

It remains a mystery when Brahms set to work on the First Symphony. Evidently the first person to lay eyes on the music was the composer's friend Albert Dietrich, with whom Brahms spent a holiday in June 1862. In his memoirs Dietrich recalled that "in Münster am Stein Brahms . . . showed me the first movement of his C Minor Symphony, which however appeared only later and considerably revised." Elsewhere, addressing Kalbeck's question of whether Brahms had composed the movement during that summer, Dietrich gave critical evidence regarding both the comparatively early date of the piece and the nature of the composer's subsequent revisions: "The first movement of the C-Minor Symphony was already finished in Münster am Stein, though it lacked the slow introduction." But as for when this opening *allegro* might actually have been written, Dietrich was unable to provide any clues whatsoever.[17]

For his part, Kalbeck conjectured that the first movement, a dramatic essay whose tonality and "fateful" rhythmic motive come straight from Beethoven's Fifth, had originated much earlier, in the emotionally troubled year of 1855. Just as Schumann's suicide attempt in February 1854 and Brahms's first live experience of Beethoven's Ninth in the following month had, in his view, given rise to the ill-fated Symphony in D Minor, so he reasoned that the composer's hopeless love for Clara Schumann (which was in full bloom by early 1855) and his initial experience at that very time of Robert Schumann's incidental music to Byron's *Manfred* (whose protagonist is driven to guilt and despair over an incestuous love) form the soil in which the first movement of the C-Minor Symphony "began . . . to germinate" (*begann . . . zu keimen*). Indeed, encouraged by a thematic similarity between the second themes of the *Manfred* Overture and Brahms's symphonic *allegro*, Kalbeck even suggested that the later work could be understood autobiographically as "the depiction of the relations between Johannes, Robert, and Clara."[18]

In accordance with this reading, the biographer thus identified the main theme as a picture of Brahms himself (Ex. 9.1a). In fact, this shape is typical not only of Brahms but of Schumann, to whom, as Reynolds has noted, the later composer frequently paid tribute just by means of echoing this pattern.[19] And in this case Brahms recalls not only this "Schumann cipher" but also one of the earlier composer's own ciphers for his wife—both of which are taken from Schumann's last published symphony, the Fourth (Ex. 9.1b). But whereas Schumann, fittingly, had linked the two ideas in a kind of musical marriage, Brahms never allows them to be joined. On the contrary, in his *allegro* it is not the "Schumann cipher" but a foreboding chromatic line (C–C♯–D)—what Kalbeck termed the *Schicksalsmotiv*—that is bound into the music representing Clara Schumann (see Ex. 9.1a). Thus the emotional flavor of the

EXAMPLE 9.1.

a. Brahms, First Symphony, movt. 1, mm. 42–46

b. Schumann, Fourth Symphony, movt. 1, m. 29

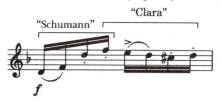

movement, wherein both the chromatic line and Clara motive figure prominently, is enhanced by the recognition that the dashing theme that seems a portrait of the composer draws its lines from material that recalls Clara's late spouse.[20]

Now, Kalbeck did not argue that Brahms actually wrote any music for the symphony in 1855; he held only that the work's "germ" (which I take to mean something like "source of inspiration") dated from that year. Indeed, a more immediate stimulus to the actual composition of the work might date from a few years later and involve, not autobiographical considerations, but the continuing ideological skirmish of the day concerning the historical roles played by Beethoven and Schumann and the merits of the *Zukunftsmusik*. This struggle came to a head in the spring of 1860, which saw not only the premature publication in May of Brahms and Joachim's ill-fated "Manifesto" against Brendel's *Neue Zeitschrift*, with its policy of favoring music of the New German School, but also the commemoration of the fiftieth anniversary of Schumann's birth on 7–8 June in a festival organized in Zwickau by none other than Brendel himself. Although Brendel had dutifully appealed for the participation of all who had "personally stood near to the immortal Master," Brahms, Joachim, and Clara would have nothing to do with the affair, traveling instead to the Lower Rhine Music Festival in Düsseldorf ("this national meeting of praiseworthy musicians," as Joachim described it), and leaving Brendel an opening to continue the recent war of words in his subsequent report on the "Erinnerungsfeier":

If something of a shadow was cast on the otherwise unclouded festival, it was the observation that some of Schumann's special friends and admirers had not come, although I am permitted to make this reproach only with caution, since I cannot know whether other private engagements had been involved. Yet there is now a little circle of Schumann's admirers that seems to want to take his cult as its private possession. . . . The unquestionable one-sidedness this implies, which is intensifying to the point of becoming pathological, is immediately apparent, and no impartial person will agree with this faction if it maintains that the spaces in the artistic temple are so limited that there is room only for itself and Schumann.[21]

In this heavy atmosphere, both Clara and Joachim encouraged Brahms to work. Especially suggestive is Clara's letter of 21 June 1860: "I hope very much that you are . . . working quietly in your little ground-floor room. People like you take in nature's charms everywhere and thereby create nourishment for their spirit. . . . A fine stormy sky can in this way pass into a symphony—who knows what already happened!?"[22] To be sure, we shall never know with certainty what by that date had "already happened" in the genesis of the First Symphony. But if the seeds of Brahms's *allegro* had been sown amid the traumatic events of the mid-1850s, the blossoming might well have occurred during the troubled time surrounding the "Manifesto" and the Schumann festival. For by alluding to Schumann's last published symphony, by identifying even with the late composer's persona, Brahms stakes his claim to precisely what Brendel would have denied him—to be the privileged executor of Schumann's musical estate.

Brahms showed the completed *allegro* to Dietrich, as we have seen, in June 1862, at which time he shared the music also with Clara, who immediately sent word of the symphony to Joachim. But when Joachim pressed the composer for information regarding the new piece, he was put off by the laconic response: "after 'Symphony by J. B.' you may place a '?'"[23] And though Brahms received a number of other inquiries about the unfinished orchestral work over the next decade—a highly productive period that saw the completion of a steady stream of impressive choral-orchestral works but no symphony—his responses (such as they were) tell us next to nothing.

But what really was there for Brahms to report on? Except for an early version of the famous "alphorn theme" of the finale (mm. 30ff.), there is simply no trace from the 1860s of more than the opening *allegro*.[24] And when the next decade began, the prospect of ever completing a work that would be worthy of Beethoven must have seemed remote. As Brahms put it in a well-known remark to Hermann Levi that probably dates from the early 1870s: "I will never compose a symphony! You have no idea how it feels to one of us when he continually hears behind him such a giant."[25]

Yet a breakthrough in the stalled compositional process—stimulated, oddly enough, by a giant from the more remote past—was close at hand. In the summer of 1874 Brahms began serious work on the finale and evidently grew satisfied enough with his progress that he permitted himself to mention the piece to his eager publisher Fritz Simrock when the two met in July in Switzerland.[26] As I have argued elsewhere, this last movement, notorious from the start for its echo of Beethoven's setting of Schiller's "Ode to Joy," evidently owes even more to Brahms's study of a rather different choral-orchestral movement: the ostinato chorus "Ach, Herr! lehre uns bedenken," from J. S. Bach's funeral cantata *Gottes Zeit ist die allerbeste Zeit* BWV 106, thc *Actus tragicus*. Indeed, the *Freudenthema* is not echoed until the third bar of Brahms's melody and comes to dominate the tune only in its second half; the famous head motive—already anticipated in the opening bars of the slow introduction, where it outlines the rhetorical figure *saltus duriusculus*, a traditional mourning topos— seems to be related instead to the distinctive ground bass from Bach's chorus (Ex. 9.2). Lying at the heart of the movement, one of Brahms's most complex and stunning forms, is an extensive thematic process whereby this funereal "Bachian" head motive and the descending tetrachord that had originally accompanied it both eventually lose their separate identities and are transformed, at the climax of the movement, into

EXAMPLE 9.2.
a. J. S. Bach, Cantata No. 106, movt. 2, mm. 48–50, 58–60

b. Beethoven, Ninth Symphony, movt. 4, mm. 124–27

(*continued*)

c. Brahms, First Symphony, movt. 4, mm. 1–2, 12–14

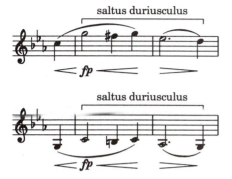

d. Brahms, First Symphony, movt. 4, mm. 62–78

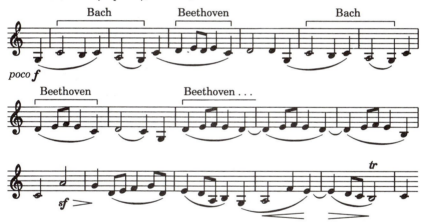

the alphorn theme (Ex. 9.3). This powerful return of music representing the timeless and transcendental realm of nature is decisive: it effectively displaces from any further significant role in the work the motive that had been derived from Beethoven's Ninth, and with that it symbolizes Brahms's inability, in the end, to embrace the joyful, optimistic worldview that Beethoven's theme so clearly represented.[27]

It is impossible to know how much of this was accomplished (or even envisaged) in 1874; all material traces of Brahms's effort from this time have disappeared. In any case, much remained to be done when the composer returned to Vienna in the fall, and in the following summer, passed

EXAMPLE 9.3. Brahms, First Symphony, movt. 4
a. mm. 1–5

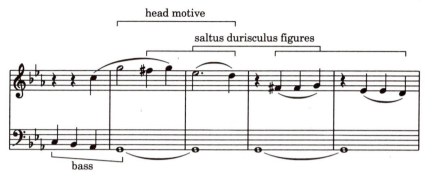

b. mm. 28–31

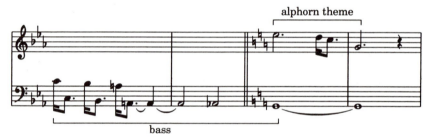

c. mm. 118–19

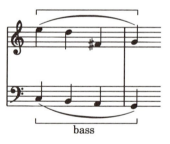

d. mm. 285–88

in Ziegelhausen bei Heidelberg, he quipped to his friend Franz Wüllner that he had chosen to work on a variety of "highly useless things" in order to avoid having "to look a symphony straight in the face."[28] By the next year, however, Brahms was hard at work again on the piece. Perhaps he was stimulated by the impending Bayreuth premiere of that other long-awaited magnum opus, Wagner's *Ring* cycle; in any event, during a summer holiday spent in 1876 at remote Saßnitz, a Baltic Sea resort on the isle of Rügen, the last movement was finally completed.

At last the end was in sight. With the turbulent opening *allegro* in C minor joined in place now by a victorious finale in C major—with the outlines of the plot archetype of Beethoven's Fifth Symphony thereby firmly established—the suitable character and dimensions of the two middle movements could be envisaged. Brahms, working by turns in Hamburg and Lichtenthal, quickly completed a lyrical *poco adagio* in E and, in place of a true scherzo, an intermezzo-like *allegretto grazioso* in A♭. The inscription appearing at the end of the autograph scarcely conveys all the sweat that went into the making of the whole; it reads simply: "J. Brahms Lichtenthal Sept. 76."

Yet even now the composer was not satisfied. In October, after launching plans for the premiere—to be given, not in the glare of publicity in Vienna, but in provincial Karlsruhe—Brahms worked the symphony over some more, revising both middle movements.[29] Moreover, it was not until the following spring, after a period of several prepublication performances on the Continent and in England, that the second movement took on its definitive form. With that the symphony could finally be sent off to the publisher, and in late October 1877 Simrock issued both the full score and the composer's own four-hand arrangement.

Given its length, complexity, and serious demeanor, the symphony was bound to meet with a mixed reception. Even the composer's closest fiends initially were moved more to respect than to love. In October 1876 Clara Schumann noted in her diary that she had not truly been stirred by the long-awaited new piece, regretting above all its lack of "melodic warmth." Two months later, after witnessing a rehearsal in Vienna, Theodor Billroth admitted to Eduard Hanslick his antipathy toward the "Faustian" first movement, with its "long-winded" rhythm, harmonies of "unpleasant effrontery," and general mood of "irritating *Sehnsucht*."[30]

It is not surprising, then, that with the critics and much of the public, too, the success of the symphony was only limited. The reaction in Vienna, where Brahms introduced the work on 17 December 1876, nicely illustrates the point.[31] Although the composer was warmly welcomed to the podium and called back many times at the end, the overall reception was noticeably muted. Several reviewers reminded their readers of Schumann's "Neue Bahnen," and—encouraged by the main theme of the finale—most insisted on measuring the symphony against a Beethovenian yardstick. Some actually charged Brahms with epigonism, while others judged the work too introverted for the Viennese taste, not "popular" enough in tone, inaccessible to all but the connoisseur. Even Hanslick himself, in an overwhelmingly positive review that left no mistaking his own conviction that his friend had come off well against the Beethovenian standard, complained that Brahms "seems to favor too one-sidedly the great and the serious, the difficult and the complex, and at the expense of sensuous beauty. We would often give the finest contrapuntal device (and they lie bedded away in the symphony by the dozen) for a moment of warm, heart-quickening sunshine."[32]

So it went, in more or less the same terms, wherever the symphony was performed during its first few seasons. And if no one really doubted that Brahms had emerged as the leading symphonist of his day, the standing of his work in comparison to those of Schumann, not to speak of Beethoven, would for some time remain a matter of contention—and one that, as we shall see, was given a pointed focus in the fall of 1877, with the rechristening of the work by Hans von Bülow as "The Tenth Symphony."[33]

The Second Symphony

Brahms wasted little time in creating for the "serious" C-Minor Symphony a "cheerful" companion. By the time the one had appeared in print, a new symphony in D major, a product of the composer's summer holidays of 1877 in Pörtschach and Lichtenthal, was nearly ready to be sent to the engraver. To Billroth there was nothing "Faustian" about this piece; it was all "blue skies, rippling streams, sunshine, and cool green shadows." In his own notices Brahms adopted his usual ironic mode of discourse; thus on the same day he warned Simrock that the symphony was so "melancholic" as to require "black borders" and informed his Leipzig friend Elisabeth von Herzogenberg that she could gain a clear idea of the piece by going to her piano and, "with feet alternating on the two pedals, "strik[ing] the chord of F minor for a good while, alternating treble and bass, *ff* and *pp*."[34] In truth, we might imagine that the Second Symphony was calculated to meet the objections raised to the First—though, to be sure, Brahms made no artistic compromises. Clara Schumann probably sensed all this when the composer played her parts of it at the piano; in a diary entry of 3 October 1877 she not only registered her own delight with the new work but correctly predicted that with this symphony Brahms would "have a more successful effect with the public than with the first, however much this one also delights the musician with its geniality and wonderful workmanship."[35]

Both sides in this dialogue are *echt wienerisch*. It is fitting, therefore, that the Imperial City was first to hear the work. In November 1877 Brahms read his four-hand arrangement with Billroth and then collaborated with his friend Ignaz Brüll in a private performance before friends in the piano salon of Friedrich Ehrbar; several weeks later, on 30 December, Hans Richter introduced the symphony to the public in a concert of the Philharmonic. The Viennese immediately embraced the new work; the delightful third movement was encored, and the composer was called repeatedly to the stage. Ludwig Speidel even dubbed the piece the "Wiener Sinfonie," noting in his review how Brahms had reflected "the fresh healthy life which is only to be found in beautiful Vienna."[36]

Indeed, the opening paragraphs sound for all the world like the slow introduction to a waltz by Johann Strauss: the Romantic nature symbolism of quiet horns and dolce woodwinds, the leisurely tempo and triple meter, the gentle murmuring in the lower strings, then a similar stirring in the violins, gradually descending and becoming softer, the hushed close on the dominant seventh—it all makes for the beginning of a tale from the Wienerwald. And Brahms continues the illusion for a moment longer beginning at measure 44, where the first violins introduce a beautiful lilting tune that betokens the waltz cycle proper. Before long, however, this theme yields to clearly transitional material, and with that we begin to understand the first part of the movement, not as a slow introduction, but as the first group in a sonata form.[37]

If the genre evoked at the outset is associated with Johann Strauss, the structural conceit recalls a work by an earlier Viennese master: the first thirty-two bars of Schubert's String Quintet in C likewise "pretend" to be a slow introduction (and one with a similar long-range I–II–V progression). It is not Brahms's deceptive beginning, however, but his beautiful second group, with its famous echo of the "Wiegenlied" Op. 49, No. 4, that alludes most directly to this quintet. Consider the tonal plan of his three-key exposition; the two keys of the second group are not in parallel modes, as in the first movement of the C Minor Symphony (♭III–♭iii) or, later, the analogous movements of the Third (III–iii) and Fourth symphonies (v–V). Instead, in line with Schubert's typical practice, the second group unfolds two third-related keys (iii–V). The initial sudden move (again, "Schubertian") from D major to F♯ minor, at measure 82, proves unsustainable, as the tune soon heads back to the tonic, with a half close on A at measure 89; then at measure 102, following a beautiful prolongation of V and an attenuated cadence in the mediant key, the process is begun anew, leading finally to V/V at measure 118 and the dominant itself ten bars later. Schubert had anticipated this remarkable process in the first movement of his quintet (mm. 60–98), with its twice-unfolded tonal scheme of E♭ to C to G; and Brahms's virtual duplication of Schubert's texture—theme in the inner string parts, surrounded by a pizzicato bass line and arpeggiated chords in the violins—clinches the relationship.[38]

What is most significant to consider, however, is Brahms's rather different, tighter treatment of the unorthodox strategy of reestablishing the tonic in the middle of the second group; whereas Schubert had made good on the implications of the half close in C minor with an obvious I–IV–V cadence in the home key, Brahms withholds the tonic in root position. (Harmony on D does enter at m. 98, but it is approached contra-puntally and soon transformed into the German-sixth chord of F♯ minor.) By the same token, Brahms has no part of Schubert's early anticipation of the dominant key, at the end of the first statement of the tune; reserving the tonal goal until the end of the double period avoids what must have been an uncongenial, seemingly anticlimactic effect in the Schubertian model. At the end of the exposition, however, Brahms renews the allu-sion, concluding, as had Schubert, with the second theme transformed to serve as closing material (mm. 156ff.).

Brahms's choice of model is telling. The quintet is unusually dark for an essay in C major; it conveys, to borrow the apt descriptions of John Reed, "[a] sense of cosmic nostalgia, [a] yearning for a lost paradise . . . [an] unconcerned regard for easeful death."[39] By the same token, all is not sunny in the first movement of Brahms's D-major pastorale. As Vin-cenz Lachner disapprovingly noted in a letter to the composer of August 1879, the "idyllically serene atmosphere" of the opening is disturbed by the entry in measure 32 of the "rumbling kettledrum" and "gloomy, lugubrious tones of the trombones and tuba."[40] Brahms's response to this criticism, in which he likened the symphony to the motet *Warum* Op. 74, No. 1—a somber companion product from the summer of 1877 whose text begins "Why is light given to those who toil and life to the broken-hearted?"—was unusually frank and telling:

> I would have to confess that I am, by the by, a severely melan-cholic person, that black wings are constantly flapping above us, and that in my output—perhaps not entirely by chance—the symphony is followed by a little essay about the great "Why." If you don't know the (motet) I will send it to you. It casts the required shadow on the serene symphony and per-haps accounts for those timpani and trombones.

Surprised, perhaps, by his intimacy, Brahms hastened to add: "All this, and especially that passage [with timpani and trombones], is not to be taken so very seriously and tragically!" Yet, as Reinhold Brinkmann has ar-gued, the letter reads genuinely enough as a "confession," and one that points to a measure of truth underlying the apparently jesting descrip-tions quoted earlier regarding the character of the work.[41] Moreover, in a number of subsequent appearances, the trombones—often, as in the pas-sage singled out by Lachner, sounding a diminished-seventh chord—seem to carry their traditional associations with either terror or gloom. In short, these remarks imply that Brahms's idyll is not as untroubled as most past criticism has assumed.

Ambiguity and restlessness inhabit the work from the very outset, which, for all the sheer beauty of its nature symbolism, conflates models of dramatically opposing styles (Ex. 9.4). On the one hand, Brahms re-hearses several leading features of Beethoven's Piano Sonata Op. 28

EXAMPLE 9.4.

a. Brahms, Second Symphony, movt. 1, mm. 1–5

b. Beethoven, "Pastorale" Sonata, movt. 1, mm. 1–6

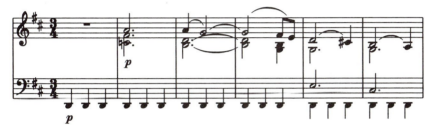

c. Beethoven, *Eroica* Symphony, movt. 1, mm. 1–6

("Pastoral"); on the other—and what seems more surprising in view of the heroic style it invokes—the opening theme in the horns closely resembles the main theme of the *Eroica* Symphony. But unlike Beethoven in either the sonata (with its reiterated tonic bass note) or symphony (with its famous opening chords), Brahms invests the first notes of his piece with real thematic significance, which is felt throughout the opening movement and across the entire work as well. Lachner was unable to contain his enthusiasm for this "organic" approach to form:

> Who else could write such a symphony! From a few roots you form the subject, which is built into a unified whole, as nature produces an organic creation.
>
> What haven't you formed from the first three notes of the bass! It is unbelievable how this single measure has been realized, in both broad expansion and tight contraction.

Lachner (like many subsequent commentators) focused solely on the neighbor-note figure of measure 1 (D–C♯–D), not also the ensuing lower fourth (A) or, for that matter, the horn theme beginning in the second bar, for which this bass provides support. Actually, much of the interest (and ambiguity) of the movement stems from the rhythmic, harmonic, and textural interaction between the two lines (see Ex. 9.4a). Which is the "main theme"? And where does the rhythmic stress fall? Surely it is difficult not to hear the bass line as proceeding from a downbeat in measure 1 (on the tonic) to an upbeat in measure 2 (on the dominant); yet the horn theme, when it comes, adds weight to the second measure, giving it the quality of a downbeat. In any case, the two lines, now joined in a tonic $^6_4$ chord, seem headed together toward a full close in measure 5, and the horn, to be sure, descends to the expected D; but the bass leaps upward to F♯, evading the cadence and initiating a sequence of its opening four-note idea. Meanwhile, the woodwinds take over the tune, apparently beginning in an accented measure, but offering an archetypal anacrustic figure (rising scalewise from dominant to tonic).

Only in measure 44, with the introduction of the "waltz theme," is anything like a structural downbeat on the tonic achieved. But clarity is soon given up again.[42] In the transition (mm. 59ff.), for example, the four-note motive and horn theme are rhythmically altered, here being presented successively, there, in various new combinations. Still another combination of the two is offered on the heels of the "Schubertian" second group, where, beginning in measure 127, Brahms celebrates the clear arrival at last in the dominant key with the familiar neighbor-note idea, now set to a propulsive rhythmic figure borrowed, again, from the first movement of the *Eroica* Symphony (mm. 65ff.) and supported in the bass with a detached, accented version of the horn theme. Then, in a celebrated passage marked by not only a displaced bar line but also a treacherous syncopation that far exceeds any such writing in the *Eroica* (mm. 135–52), the music gives up any semblance of rhythmic and metric certainty.

This complex discourse continues in the development. The section begins, to be sure, with a quiet recollection of the "idyllic" opening bars; but this quickly gives way to a forceful fugato based on the rising motive from measures 6–7. Measure 224 marks the simultaneous return of the neighbor-note idea and the choir of trombones, which ominously summons the figure in several overlapping, dissonant presentations in hemiola rhythm. Tension is maintained as the music builds to a climax beginning in measure 246, where the horn theme (itself now briefly in $^3_2$) and neighbor-note figure (in $^6_8$) are soon set off against a new bass in $^3_4$. And yet the real climax is still to come, at measure 282, whose terrifying rising third (derived from the horn theme) is sent hurtling through the entire orchestra, in a huge expansion of an idea borrowed from the *Eroica* (mm. 359–62).

In measure 290–92 the development concludes—or, rather, begins to yield imperceptibly to the recapitulation—when, in the most telling of all the recollections of Beethoven's Third Symphony, the triadic horn theme recurs "prematurely" in the tonic against a quiet string tremolo (which here offers one more variation of the four-note motive). Beethoven, of course, had settled matters almost immediately by means of a forceful "double return" of main theme and tonic key. Brahms, by contrast, prolongs and revels in the ambiguous moment. A strong cadential progression is begun (I–vii^7/V–ii), supporting a sequence of the "waltz theme" and building in intensity; yet this culminates, not in the expected full close, but in a sudden moment of quiet, anxious stillness (m. 298). There, shrouded by an expressive half-diminished seventh chord and plaintive descending line in the upper woodwinds (both borrowed from the minor mode), the gloomy trombone choir intones an augmented, harmonized version of the original bass line. Only in measure 302, as the ii^7 harmony yields to the tonic $^6_4$, does the horn theme return, albeit now in the oboe—the horns themselves continue to explore the hemiola— and coupled with the "waltz theme" sounding in the violas.

The recapitulation, then, offers no structural downbeat—and neither, at first, does the coda, which grows out of an elided deceptive cadence at measure 447 (on $^6_5$) and then, over a prolonged dominant, offers a beautiful cadenza for solo horn. Developing the stepwise motive from measure 4 that had promised but never delivered a tonic cadence, this expressive passage leads, finally, to full closure in measure 477 and a version of the opening material in which, for the first time, the bass motive and horn theme are locked in a single downbeat-oriented phrase.

To Lachner, this "transfiguration" provides a "peaceful dénouement" to all the struggles that had proceeded it; he was perplexed, accordingly, by Brahms's decision to throw a shadow over things by ending inconclusively with a plagal cadence—and one colored, at that, by the minor mode and sounding a dissonance against the dominant pedal point (mm. 516–20). Brahms justified this striking mixture of G-minor harmony and pedal point on A on both sensual and rational grounds. Not only, he wrote, did it produce "a delightfully beautiful sound" (*ein wollüstig-schöner Klang*), but it came about "as logically as possible."

But Lachner's belief that the purpose of the passage beginning at measure 477 was to provide final resolution was mistaken. Matters begin to unravel straightaway, albeit "logically," as the composer would have it. Measure 485 initiates a variation of the preceding eight bars, with the melody now incorporating expressive chromatic ornaments and the bass evidently destined to repeat as a ground. The expected cadence is interrupted in measure 493, however; the music gets stuck on the minor subdominant, which is arpeggiated downward in hemiola rhythm while the neighbor-note figure gradually becomes disentangled from the foregoing tune. Then follows a new ostinato (m. 497), founded on open harmony and offering the scherzolike material from measures 66ff. that had been omitted from the recapitulation. The repetition of the upper voice begins after eight bars; that of the bass, remarkably, after only seven—with the difference being made up by a virtual quotation, in the flute and oboe, of the ending of Brahms's song "Es liebt sich so lieblich im Lenze" Op. 71, No. 1, a setting of an ironic pastoral text by Heine that seems particularly well suited here.[43] During the second statement of the ostinato, then, as the pizzicato violins and viola push the neighbor-note figure to the off-beat, the outer voices are out of phase by one bar. At measure 513 the neighbor-note figure, now restored to both the tonic and its original four-note shape but remaining quiet and off the beat until the end, is coupled for the last time with the horn theme, bringing about the peculiar close that offended Lachner's sensibilities. Even at the end, Brahms provides no answer to the great "Why."

The beginning of the second movement (*adagio non troppo*, B major) broods on the same question; here, as Walter Frisch has observed, the "themes remain fragmentary, avoiding closure and mutating instead into new ideas; every cadence is sidestepped; harmonic areas, including the tonic and dominant, are implied but never established; and the metrical framework evades the authority of the bar line."[44] And so it goes throughout this elusive movement, which combines elements of A-B-A and sonata form. To be sure, the *dolce* second theme (mm. 33–44) provides a ray of sunlight; but this graceful melody peters out soon enough, never to return. The development is marked by two recurrences of the lugubrious neighbor-note figure for trombone and tuba (mm. 55–56, 60–61), each set over diminished-seventh harmony and coupled with a drifting chromatic motive; the recapitulation embraces an anguished secondary development in lieu of the second theme (mm. 87ff.); and the brief coda, based on the inscrutable opening idea, dies away to the muffled beat of the timpani (mm. 97ff.).

For the third movement (*allegretto grazioso*, G major), Brahms again eschews a true scherzo in favor of something more delicate, this time beginning, so to speak, "im Ländler Tempo," with the woodwinds, offering a free inversion of the four-note motive from the first movement, supported by a pizzicato bass line. Schubert can be heard in the graceful tri-partite opening period (mm. 1–32), whose final phrase is beautifully shaded by harmonies borrowed from the parallel minor. Twice, in varied form, this music recurs. The opening idea is treated to a pair of "Schubertian" reharmonizations beginning at measure 107 (only to become ensnared in a stark ostinato beginning at m. 114); then, at measure 194, the first phrase returns in the distant key of F♯ major, which magically yields to the second phrase (and the tonic key) in measure 207. Interspersed, in a manner that recalls the scherzi of Schumann's symphonies, are two "trios," each played *presto ma non assai* (but set in contrasting meters of $\frac{2}{4}$ and $\frac{3}{8}$) and evoking, not Viennese *Gemütlichkeit*, but Mendelssohn's characteristic "elfin style."

The finale (*allegro con spirito,* D major) begins *sotto voce* in the unison strings but soon develops into one of Brahms's most unbuttoned and richly scored essays. The familiar neighbor-note figure from the opening *allegro* surfaces everywhere in this sonata-rondo: as head motive of the first group, accompaniment to the big *largamente* second theme (mm. 78ff.), and progenitor of the whirling eighth notes that mark the closing group (mm. 114ff.). In the development, however, the neighbor-note figure has to share prominence with its partner in the primary group, the theme built on falling fourths that had first appeared in mm. 9–17. The one is heard quietly, in the tonic and then on the dominant of F♯ minor (mm. 155, 170); the other enters with a sudden explosion (m. 184). The trombones and tuba, having been silent since the end of the *adagio*, make their raucous return at the peak of the ensuing climax (m. 202), but then, just as suddenly, an unexpected new mood emerges. The head motive, transformed into something *tranquillo*, passes through several keys (mm. 206ff.), leading, in measure 234, to a mysterious recollection of the falling fourths, out of which the main theme eventually emerges. It is an extraordinary, even chilling moment, recalling the occasionally overcast skies of the first movement. As Tovey put it: "The original key is reached in darkness, and the cold unison of the first theme meets us like the grey daylight on a western cloud-bank opposite the sunrise."[45] But these would be the last clouds in the work. The recapitulation is straightforward, and the coda, focusing on the second group in the way that the development had focused on the first, builds to a brilliant close.

The Overtures

Like the First Symphony, the Second was subjected to a test period in performance. Most of these trial runs, occurring during the winter and spring of 1878, were led by Brahms himself; on one occasion each, Joachim and Wüllner took the baton. These, however, led to nothing like the significant revision that had been made in the *andante* of the First Symphony (which now, in its final published form, was making the rounds, too). Simrock worked on the score, parts, and four-hand piano arrangement during the summer and released the piece at the end of August.

Several weeks later, during the last week of September, Brahms was a guest of honor at the celebration of the fiftieth anniversary of the Hamburg Philharmonic, which included, in addition to a festive banquet and group excursion up the Elbe, three orchestral concerts. Forming the symphonic bill on these occasions were Haydn's Symphony No. 83 in G Minor ("La Poule"), Beethoven's *Eroica,* the C-Major Symphony of Schumann, and, in its first performance in his hometown, Brahms's recent Symphony No. 2. As if this symbolic train of masters were not enough, the status that the sudden appearance of two impressive symphonies had brought Brahms as Germany's leading composer of "absolute music" was formally conferred during the following March, when the University of Breslau awarded him an honorary Doctorate of Philosophy. The diploma read: "vir illustrissimus . . . artis musicae severioris in Germania nunc princeps."

These public acknowledgments, in both word and deed, that Brahms was "Beethoven's heir" were more than Wagner could stand. In July 1879 the older composer, who must have been seething for some time on account of von Bülow's heralding of "the Tenth," vented his anger in the essay "Über das Dichten und Komponieren," writing acidly about the "street singer" and "Jewish czardas player" who happened also to be a "sterling symphonist disguised in a Numero Zehn." Though this composer might have been crowned the "serious Prince of Music" (*ernster Musikprinz*), Wagner punned on the Latin of Brahms's diploma, the face behind his mask—Brahms had been sporting a beard since the previous summer—was perfectly ordinary, which made it all the more unfortunate that "many people [in powerful positions] are actually deceived by the mask, and Hamburg festival banquets and Breslau diplomas perchance come forth as a result."[46]

Wagner continued to dig at Brahms in "Über das Opern-Dichten und Komponiren im Besonderen," which appeared in September 1879.[47] Then, two months later, in "Über die Anwendung der Musik auf das Drama," he mounted a full-scale attack against the "symphony composi-tions" of Brahms and other composers of the "Romantic-Classical school" by way of validating his own crucial role in history. No longer, to be sure, did he link the birth of music drama directly to the late works of Beethoven; "programmatic instrumental music" now was given its due as a necessary intermediate stage. But Wagner held fast to his position that it was only he, not the younger composer, who had truly understood Beethoven's mission and carried out his assignment:

> If we take another glance at the "classical" instrumental com-position of our most recent times, which has been completely untouched by the aforementioned gestational process [lead-ing to the music drama] [*von dem bezeichneten Gebärungsprozesse unberührt gebliebene "klassisch" Instrumental-Composition*], then we will find that this "classical survivor" [*"klassisch Geblieben"*; i.e., Brahms] is an idle pretense, and beside our great Classical masters has planted us a highly unpleasant hybrid of "wanting to" and "being unable to" [*von Gernwollen und Nichtkönnen*; i.e., the First Symphony]. . . . The way of our symphonies and the like was and is nowadays *weltschmerzlich* and catastrophic; we are somber and grim, then again dashing and daring; we yearn

for the confusion of the dreams of youth; demonic obstacles disturb us; we brood, even rage; and then finally, to *Weltshmerz,* the tooth is pulled out [*wird . . . dem Weltschmerz der Zahn aus-gerissen*]; now we laugh and humorously show the gaping gum of the world [*Weltzahnlücke*], competent, sturdy, upright, Hungarian or Scottish—unfortunately for others, boring.[48]

Having made his complicated pun equating the painful process of pulling a tooth (*Zahn*) and the succession of ideas in Brahms's *Numero Zehn,* Wagner underscored his point in a less opaque style:

> We cannot believe that instrumental music has been assured of a thriving future by the creations of its latest masters. First and foremost, however, we could be doing ourselves some harm by unthinkingly assigning these works to the Beethovenian legacy because we should actually come to realize the completely un-Beethovenian things about them. And that ought not to be too difficult, considering how unlike Beethoven they are in spirit, despite the Beethovenian themes that we still come across.

Later, Wagner returned to the metaphorical toothache, mocking its supposed remedy:

> But those [composers of the "Romantic-Classical" school] transferred their chamber into the concert hall. What had before been fixed up as quintets and the like was now served up as symphonies. Paltry "melody-chaff" [*Melodien-Häcksel*], comparable to a mixture of hay and old tea, of which no one knows what he is sipping, but dispensed under the label "Genuine" [*Ächt*] for the alleged imbibing of *Weltschmerz.*

Here, adumbrating an important new theme in music criticism, Wagner faulted Brahms for treating the symphony, not as a grand genre directed toward the masses, but as a kind of misplaced chamber music that presumably could only be appreciated intellectually by the educated elite. And though Wagner could not have known it, Billroth had already shown Brahms that he held the despised latter view when he made the following comments only a few days before the Viennese premiere of the very piece that Wagner had found so irritating:

> I wished I could hear the [C-Minor] symphony all by myself, in the dark, and began to understand King Ludwig's private concerts [*Sonderabenden*]. All the silly, everyday people who surround you in the concert hall and of whom in the best case [only] fifty have enough intellect and artistic feeling to grasp the essence of such a work at the first hearing—not to speak of understanding; all that upsets me in advance. I hope, however, that the musical masses here have enough musical instinct to

understand that something great is happening there in the orchestra.[49]

In Billroth's Vienna, as we shall see, the "sociology" of Brahms's symphonies would soon become a politically charged topic.

Meanwhile, during the summer of 1880 Brahms responded in his
own way to the Breslau honor (and to Wagner's recent jibes) by composing the "cheerful" (and un-Beethovenian) *Academic Festival* Overture Op.
80—a far cry from chamber music. Actually, the piece begins very quietly
in the First Symphony's C minor, though the presence of bass drum and
cymbals serves as the tongue in cheek that might have been expected of
Brahms under the circumstances. This material eventually gives way to a
highly original sonata form in C major, fleshed out with a variety of borrowed tunes—"a merry potpourri of students songs à la Suppé" was how
Brahms described the work to Kalbeck, in a reference to the overture to
Franz von Suppé's operetta *Flotte Bursche*. But Malcolm MacDonald is
surely correct in hearing echoes, too, of Wagner's *Meistersinger* overture
(in the same key of C major), above all in the coda, which offers a truly
Wagnerian apotheosis of "Gaudeamus igitur," complete with broad unison theme, full wind chorus, loud percussion, and rushing strings.[50] For
what work of Wagner's is more fit for a Brahmsian parody here than this
one, with its emphasis on preserving "the sacred German art"? No doubt
Brahms would have taken additional satisfaction in knowing that, whereas
Wagner had combined his themes in solemn (if, to Brahms, simple-
minded) counterpoint, he, the "serious Prince of Music," had artfully woven student songs (the work of the Apprentices) into a sophisticated essay
in sonata form.

Even more sophisticated is the "dark" Beethovenian companion
piece, the *Tragic* Overture Op. 81, which Brahms completed during the
same summer.[51] This work begins abruptly and ambiguously with widely
spaced hammered chords of first-inversion D minor followed by an open
fifth on A. If the two hammer strokes recall the opening of Beethoven's
Coriolan Overture (by way of the *Eroica* Symphony), the tonal ambiguity
they introduce (open fifths on A supporting the falling fourth A–E in the
upper voice) derives from the tragic first movement of the Ninth Symphony, which, after some doubt, likewise turns out to be in D minor.
Whereas Beethoven, typically, builds tension by means of motivic repetition, Brahms, after his own fashion, launches immediately into a tonally
uncertain melody in the unison strings, *sotto voce*. Less predictably, the finale of the Ninth is recalled, too, in the manner in which Brahms enriches his basic sonata form with a variety of overlapping formal types; as
James Webster has noted, sonata-without-development, sonata-rondo,
A-B-A, and ritornello principles can all be seen at work here.[52] The piece
makes a worthy successor to Beethoven's *Coriolan* and Schumann's *Manfred* overtures; of Wagner's *Eine Faust-Ouvertüre*, the only other significant
example in a slender tradition, there is hardly a trace.

The Third Symphony

Wagner's last barbed comments about Brahms appeared in the "Open Letter to Friedrich Schön," published in the *Bayreuther Blätter* in July 1882:

> But as the Gospel has faded since the cross of the Redeemer has been hawked like merchandise on every street corner, so has the genius of German music grown silent ever since it has been hauled around the world-mart by the métier, and pseudo-professional gutter-witlessness celebrates its progress.[53]

Scarcely hidden in this assessment is the pointed contrast Wagner draws between his own "sacred festival drama," *Parsifal*, which was to be given its premiere a few weeks later in the Festspielhaus in Bayreuth (and was never, according to Wagner's directive, to be performed elsewhere) and Brahms's "profane" orchestral works, which were then being championed by von Bülow in far-flung touring concerts with his Meiningen Orchestra (the happy reception of which, Wagner bitterly continued, only went to show that the taste of the public had become so debased that posterity would choose to preserve nine symphonies by Brahms but at most only two by Beethoven). Since Brahms had himself composed only two symphonies by this time, he must have kept Wagner's remarks in mind when during the following summer he finally set down his Third. Even more, as we shall see, he must have been thinking of Wagner's music.

This story begins during the first week of May 1883, when Leipzig played host to the twentieth Tonkünstlerversammlung of the Allgemeiner Deutscher Musikverein. The opening of the jubilee was marked in the *Neue Zeitschrift für Musik* with a reverential greeting by its publisher, C. F. Kahnt, of the society's honorary president: "Welcome, thou most admirable master Franz Liszt, who, though deeply mourning for having recently lost Pollux and having now like Castor to pass through life's course alone, yet with thy presence honors this festivity and with thine appearance places upon it a golden crown!"[54] Liszt's deceased twin brother was of course Wagner, who had died during the previous winter. The festival, predictably enough, reflected the tone set in Kahnt's salute: throughout the proceedings the late master of *Zukunftsmusik* was commemorated; the living one, celebrated.

Yet the presence of Brahms's work was by no means inconsiderable. Sharing a billing with a number of pieces by Wagner and Liszt were the Violin Concerto Op. 77 and the "Gesang der Parzen" Op. 89. Brahms, with little taste for the Musikverein and its activities, declined to attend these concerts; he remained in Vienna instead, where on 7 May he celebrated his fiftieth birthday in the convivial company of his friends Hanslick, Billroth, and Arthur Faber. But from afar Brahms must have savored the ironic juxtapositions of his music with art of the New German School. This he ensured by means of a delightful deceit. By prevailing upon

Hanslick to publish a false report of his imminent (and perhaps startling) departure for Leipzig, Brahms could look forward to enjoying an irony of his own making: "It is not always necessary to be completely truthful—in regard to the change!" he wrote to his friend, "But I have a strong hidden reason to read in print the world-historic occasion of my departure—and to have it read!"[55]

To account for this journalistic dissimulation we must recall certain events from the troubled spring of 1860, which saw the appearance of Brahms's unfortunate "Manifesto" against the New German School and the celebration a few weeks later of Schumann's fiftieth birthday at the Zwickau festival that had been organized by Brendel and the Weimarites. As we have seen, Brahms shunned Brendel's festival and instead attended the more "praiseworthy" gathering of musicians in Düsseldorf. Brendel, in turn, read Brahms's failure to appear as a sign that the young composer and his circle refused to recognize that the New Germans might have any rightful claim to Schumann's patrimony and was seeking instead to seize "his cult as its private possession." And shortly thereafter, as if to confirm the accusation, Brahms hatched the dramatic opening *allegro* to his First Symphony, with its telling echoes not only of Beethoven's Fifth but also of Schumann's Fourth.

Twenty-three years (and two symphonies) later, on the occasion of his own fiftieth birthday, Brahms seems to have contrived a rehearsal of all those events, although not without adding some delicious twists. Having this time been invited to another event dominated by the New Germans, he peevishly raised expectations that he would take part only to snub the affair entirely. Yet the composer did head north—not for Leipzig, but Cologne, where in the middle of May he finally celebrated his golden jubilee in public, as he had marked Schumann's a quarter century earlier, at the Lower Rhine Music Festival, with performances of the Second Symphony and Second Piano Concerto Op. 83. The Rhineland struck a resonant chord, and within a week's time the composer, whose plans for the forthcoming summer remained open when he departed Vienna, had settled into rooms in Wiesbaden, where in the months that followed he crafted his Third Symphony.[56]

To Kalbeck, the act of composing this great work within sight of the Rhine seemed momentous. The river, steeped in nationalistic lore, as also in memories of the composer's Romantic youth, provided the fifty-year-old Brahms a natural setting in which to take stock of himself and his place in history, even to compose a "justification for his artistic existence."[57] The symphony does make one significant, if indirect, allusion to the Rhine: Brahms took both the prevailing hemiola rhythm and the main theme of the first movement from the opening *allegro* of Schumann's "Rhenish" Symphony (whose composer, in turn, had drawn this material from the slow movement of his own "Spring" Symphony). But echoes of Wagner and Liszt, the composers to whom Brahms had recently been joined in the Leipzig concerts, resound quite as distinctly. Taken together, these references speak directly to the question of his musical *Anschauung* at age fifty; through them we can begin to take the measure of the "artistic" justification that Kalbeck sensed underlay the whole.

Brahms's allusions to the "Rhenish" Symphony must be heard against the background of the *Eroica*. Schumann, who produced his work shortly after taking up his duties in Düsseldorf, in Beethoven's Rhenish homeland, had himself followed the master's lead in a variety of ways, by duplicating the use of triple meter and key of three flats, and by likewise beginning with a theme that sets out triadically. At the same time, the development sections of both works in question unfold in large sequences and include important episodes in the tonic minor. Yet Schumann's symphony breathes a different air from Beethoven's—a circumstance perhaps easiest to see in his duplication of Beethoven's celebrated early entry of the horns just before the recapitulation. The strategy that in Beethoven's hands produces a moment's powerful and decisive drama (mm. 390ff.) instigates in Schumann's work a leisurely episode (mm. 368ff.).

How apposite, therefore, that Kalbeck should have seen the Rhine River flowing through Brahms's Third, and that Hans Richter should have dubbed the work a second *Eroica*. For Brahms seems not only to have recognized Schumann's use of Beethoven's Third as a model for the "Rhenish" but also to have sought to reconcile the two in the first movement of his own Third Symphony (*allegro con brio*, F major). Elided to the work's famous motto (F–A♭–F), which Brahms introduces in an ambiguous opening that amounts to a characteristic enrichment of the brusque introductory chords of the *Eroica*, is a quotation (transposed into F major) of the theme presented toward the end of the first movement of the "Rhenish" (Ex. 9.5).[58]

Which is not to say that Beethoven and Schumann shared equally in the formulation of the work. Again the treatment of the "early horn

EXAMPLE 9.5.
a. Brahms, Third Symphony, movt. 1, mm. 1–4

(*continued*)

EXAMPLE 9.5. (*continued*)
b. Schumann, "Rhenish" Symphony, movt. 1, mm. 449–51

entry" addresses the issue of aesthetic orientation. In stages, through instrumentation, key, and thematic material, Brahms gradually evokes the "Rhenish" (and, in turn, the *Eroica*). The process begins toward the end of the development (mm. 101ff.), where, following an extended *agitato* treatment of the second subject that pushes from C♯ minor to a half cadence in G minor, Brahms suddenly clears the air with an unexpected turn upward by half step to E♭ major, in which key, significantly, the solo horn sings the motto. Then, a few measures later, still in E♭, the bassoons and low strings present the movement's main theme—that is, the theme taken from Schumann (mm. 112ff.). With these references in place Brahms "corrected" Schumann's "misreading" of the premature entry by linking his development and recapitulation with two overlapping statements of the motto (mm. 120–24), thereby restoring to the moment something of its original high drama.

As Brahms would have known, Beethoven evidently derived the opening gesture of the *Eroica* from Haydn's String Quartet in E♭ Op. 71, No. 3, expanding on the earlier composer's strategy of setting a piece into motion with an isolated, forceful statement of the tonic chord by doubling the number of presentations. Brahms's own subsequent expansion involved interpolating a neighboring vii⁷/V harmony between the two tonic chords, thus creating the striking progression that appears at the beginning of Schubert's String Quintet in C. Of special interest here is Schubert's use of the progression in a passage that deceives us into thinking we are hearing a slow introduction instead of the primary theme of the *allegro*. Taking the opposite approach in his Third Symphony, Brahms uses this chord progression in a brief passage that seems at first to have all the earmarks of genuine "primary" material—here are not sharp, dry chords (as in Beethoven), but richly scored and fully sustained harmonies (as in Schubert)—only to elide in measure 3 to what turns out to be the "real" main theme (albeit one that, owing to its arpeggiated triadic descent, embodies elements of a cadential idea).

As Beethoven had borrowed his striking opening from a Haydn string quartet, so had Schubert modeled his unusual chord progression on the slow introduction of Haydn's Symphony No. 97 (mm. 1–4)—where, significantly, it is begun by a single brusque opening chord but soon develops into something resembling a closing gesture. Haydn subsequently made good on the implications of this opening by using the material as the closing theme of his *vivace* (mm. 97ff.). In the same way Brahms's main theme likewise appears eventually in its natural habitat, recurring not only at the end of the first movement (where it is not quite fully closed melodically and metrically), but in the last pages of the finale (where closure is complete). Concluding this "history"—and thereby virtually exhausting the thematic possibilities—Brahms used Haydn's closing theme, together with the secondary theme of the *Eroica* (mm. 83–91) as a model for his transitional theme (mm. 15ff.).[59]

Brahms's treatment of this bridge offers the first clue that at least a few strands in this dense web of allusions to "Classic Romantic" masters had been reserved for Wagner.[60] Here the modulation from the tonic to the second key is brought about by means of a real sequence: the model (mm. 15–22) moves from F to Db; the sequence (mm. 23–30) sets out in Db and thus comes around to the mediant, A. Since this eminently Wagnerian use of real sequence as an expositional expedient is rarely encountered in Brahms's oeuvre, its unfolding here registers something of a surprise, especially as this follows on the heels of the theme derived from Schumann. Yet Brahms makes this sudden and unexpected orientation toward Wagner unmistakable in the conclusion of this section (mm. 31–35), wherein the general reference yields to a specific one: these bars resonate with the "harmonies and melodic phrase" of a passage in the Venusberg music from *Tannhäuser*.[61]

This Wagnerian context for the transition suggests, in turn, an explanation for the unusually strong arrival in A major well before the appearance of the secondary theme (mm. 31 and 35, respectively). If the final four bars of the transition are an invitation to delve into Wagnerian waters, then the ensuing idyllic secondary theme (mm. 35–42) may be read as Brahms's reply. This only increases the significance of the drone bass underpinning the new melody: it is not merely an easy means of evoking a pastoral atmosphere, but a pointed one by which Brahms demonstrated the continuing viability, even in the post–Wagnerian world, of diatonic harmony, made sumptuous here by the many beautiful dissonant clashes that the tune creates against the pedal point (and by the characteristically supple phrase rhythm of the passage). In other words, by juxtaposing chromatic and diatonic treatments of the same key, Brahms was able to demonstrate all the more effectively the rich possibilities remaining to be explored within the confines of traditional tonality.

This rejection of the Wagnerian style helps to explain why, of all the Wagner operas, Brahms chose to echo *Tannhäuser*, whose famous vocal contest debates the issue of the true nature of love. After all, he could scarcely have failed to see how the opera's contest between two minnesingers of the thirteenth century paralleled the real-life struggle over aesthetic matters waged in the music of late nineteenth-century Germany's two greatest composers. But despite Wagner's invectives, Brahms clearly respected his "adversary," and the whole passage seems calculated to offer a tribute to the style of a composer whom he generally admired, coupled with an assured demonstration of a more congenial alternative.[62]

More startling is the evident influence on the symphony of that other leading light of the New German School, Liszt—the real target of the "Manifesto" of 1860. The Lisztian influence may be perceived in a feature of the Third that is truly extraordinary: the dispersal of the elements of a sonata form across the course of a four-movement cycle.[63] In undertaking this conflation Brahms took up the challenge of the symphony in distinctly Lisztian terms, essaying a *Gesamtform* best known from the older composer's Piano Concerto in E♭. Here, however, Brahms offers no homage, gentle correction, or respectful airing of artistic differences, but rather a blistering critique of his model.[64]

Liszt's concerto demonstrates the principle, not of "Mehrsätzigkeit in der Einsätzigkeit" (which he realized most purely in the great Piano Sonata in B Minor), but of its less familiar correlate: each of its four movements can be reduced into one or another element of textbook sonata form. Thus the opening *allegro maestoso*, in the tonic, offers a "masculine" primary theme group; the *quasi adagio*, in the submediant, presents a "feminine" contrasting theme; the *allegretto vivace* stands as a scherzo but culminates in a grand retransition that restates the primary material; and the finale brings about the rest of the "recapitulation," focusing on a marchlike transformation of the secondary material, but embracing other themes as well.

In his own way, Brahms achieves a similar continuity across the entire span of his work. Not only does the second movement (*andante*, C major) incorporate the motto into the closing bars of its folklike opening theme (mm. 21–23), but so too is this idea recalled in the finale (*allegro*, F minor). Although the third movement is not motivically united with the others, it forms a natural pairing with the preceding *andante* by virtue of its leisurely tempo (*poco allegretto*), Romanze character, and key (C minor). (Brahms is at his farthest remove here from the traditional minuet or scherzo; indeed, the beautiful main theme, presented initially in the tenor register of the cellos and then, in the reprise, by the solo horn, quotes the opening of the slow movement of Schumann's Fourth Symphony.) Taken together, these two intermezzi (both in the dominant) stand as a kind of a long-range secondary group in the middle of the symphony.

Brahms's handling of both thematic material and the crucial pitch conflict between the notes A (the third of the tonic harmony) and A♭ (the middle note of the motto), joined at the very outset of the work, likewise reveals the underpinnings of a large-scale sonata form. The inscrutable secondary theme of the *andante* (mm. 41–50) is omitted from the recapitulation of that movement, only to return in the finale, the "recapitulation" of the entire piece, where it serves as a mysterious interlude in the first group (mm. 19–29), forms the triumphant peak of the development (mm. 149–70), and, gently transfigured into a chorale along with the head motive of the main theme and the familiar motto, plays a central role in the coda (mm. 280–97). This last passage, in turn, prepares the way for the autumnal return of the main theme of the opening *allegro*, wherein the A/A♭ conflict finally is straightened out, as the minor mode yields unequivocally to the major.

This celebrated reappearance of the opening theme at the end of the symphony at once clinches the Lisztian background of the work and clarifies a profound difference in the composers' attitude and approach. When we recognize that the marchlike finale of Liszt's concerto is based on the beautiful theme of his slow movement, we may be amused or offended—but not edified. In contrast stand the final pages of the Third Symphony, whose effect is dependent on everything that has transpired in the work. The return there of the opening theme brings resolution at last to the many issues that Brahms had earlier left unresolved. This return, as Walter Frisch has cogently put it, "constitutes one of Brahms's most persuasive thematic transformations because it seems genuinely to embody all the thematic, harmonic, metrical, and formal processes that have spanned the symphony since the theme's initial appearance."[65]

In an important study, Margaret Notley has reminded us of a paradox that existed in Vienna in the years following Wagner's death, when, in Kalbeck's words, "music got mixed up with politics."[66] The liberal establishment—whose members, including men such as Hanslick, Billroth, and Kalbeck himself, came from the educated German and Jewish-German middle and upper middle classes—championed the ostensibly "conservative" music of Brahms, valuing above all its rational and logical basis; quite naturally, the focus of musical life for this group fell on chamber music. The antiliberal (and increasingly anti-Semitic) alliance—which eventually gained power in the year of Brahms's death with the mayoral election of Karl Lueger—tended, by contrast, to take up the cause, not only of the late Bayreuth master, but of Anton Bruckner, whose monumental symphonies, all but ignored previously, came to be valued for the powerful and direct emotional impact they could have upon the larger masses.

Among the first musical events of the day to be made into a cause célèbre was the premiere of the Third Symphony, which was led by Hans Richter with the Vienna Philharmonic on 2 December 1883 and marked by a carefully staged demonstration by the partisans of Wagner and Bruckner. This opposition came to very little, however, and the new symphony secured for the composer one of his greatest Viennese triumphs, receiving generally favorable reviews from all sides of the political spectrum. Indeed, for all its allusions to the "Classic-Romantic" tradition, the Third might even be described, without too much exaggeration, as the work of a "Wagnerian symphonist": Brahms's treatment of the three-note motto—as opening idea, accompaniment, transitional gesture, lyrical melody, and so on—seems well in keeping with the new "monumental" generic norms, while the appearance in the finale of various "characteristic styles"—*misterioso*, heroic, chorale—could only have encouraged quasi-programmatic interpretations.⁶⁷ But Brahms's next orchestral composition would be a very different kind of work, and coming in the midst of Bruckner's belated rise to fame on the strength of his Symphony No. 7 in E Major (which included Wagnerian echoes of its own and was played widely throughout the German Empire in 1884–85), it stands as a pointed manifesto of the traditional musical values he espoused.

The Fourth Symphony

As the First Symphony had been quickly joined by the Second, so the Third soon gained a sibling of its own. Working in Mürzzuschlag during the summers of 1884 and 1885, Brahms gave birth to his most austere and personal orchestral work, the Symphony in E Minor. Although the composer returned here to the darker mode in which he had begun his first symphonic essay, this time he blazed a new path. The First Symphony, following the archetype established by Beethoven's Fifth and Ninth, progresses from a dramatic minor-key opening to a joyous major-key finale. The Fourth Symphony, by contrast, knows no precedent; it begins like an elegy and culminates in a grave passacaglia that marks the work as a tragedy through and through.

The subject of Brahms's unusual finale alludes to the ciacona bass in the final chorus of Bach's Cantata *Nach dir, Herr, verlanget mich,* BWV 150 (Ex. 9.6). Already in January 1882 the composer had told von Bülow his opinion that Bach's ascending stepwise bass would, if suitably modified with some chromaticism, make a good point of departure for a *Sinfoniesatz.*⁶⁸ Yet Brahms might well have been mulling over this idea since 1874; as I have argued elsewhere, his study of the same cantata very likely had stimulated his use in the finale of the First Symphony of both an ostinato bass and significant allusions to a structurally similar movement from Bach's Cantata No. 106.⁶⁹ But if Brahms's immediate challenge at that earlier time had been to envisage a triumphant finale that would resolve the implications of his turbulent opening *allegro,* he had now—and

Example 9.6.

a. Brahms, Fourth Symphony, movt. 4, mm. 1–8

b. J. S. Bach, Cantata No. 150, movt. 7, mm. 1–5

with no real symphonic examples lying before him—to imagine a sequence of three movements that would lead inexorably to the tragic conclusion he had in mind.

The composer was understandably apprehensive about how such a symphony would be received, and when he began to circulate it, in September 1885, he warned his friends that in Mürzzuschlag the cherries never ripen.[70] At the beginning of the month the full score of the first movement went to Elisabeth von Herzogenberg (who subsequently played it for Clara Schumann). Some five weeks later, after Brahms had returned to Vienna from Mürzzuschlag and performed the whole work through at the piano with Ignaz Brüll in the company of Billroth, Hanslick, Kalbeck, Richter, and other intimates, Elisabeth was sent the two-piano score as well. Meanwhile plans had been made for a rehearsal with the Meiningen Orchestra, which von Bülow had eagerly placed at Brahms's disposal. This reading went well; performances with the Hoforchester were scheduled for 25 October and 1 November, and the work was taken immediately on a hectic tour of Germany and Holland. By the end of the season upward of twenty additional performances had been given, not only by Brahms and von Bülow with the Meiningen players, but also by Joachim in Berlin and Richter in both Vienna and London. Simrock issued the two-piano edition in May 1886; the full score appeared that October.

Although nowadays the symphony is admired for its rigorous tonal and motivic logic, that attribute counted for something less during the composer's lifetime. In his review of the Viennese premiere, for example, Theodor Helm, who had become one of Bruckner's champions in the press, judged the piece to be "music for musicians," adding that "the public missed 'die Melodie.'" Yet, as Helm readily acknowledged—and as can be seen easily in Brahms's imaginative treatment of his opening theme of descending thirds and ascending sixths—the work is "a masterpiece . . . of invention."[71] Not only does the theme grow from a single interval (Ex. 9.7a), but the resulting chain of thirds figures prominently throughout the first movement, serving as the accompaniment to the second theme (mm. 57–73) and later as a new extension of an important rhythmic motive (mm. 190–92 and 208–10), and recurs to great effect in both the scherzo and finale. At the same time, the two triads that can be formed from the first four notes of the chain (E minor and C major) represent the principal keys in the overall tonal plan. Both outer movements are in the tonic minor, while the *andante moderato* (in the tonic major but including a number of Phrygian inflections) is strongly inclined toward the flat submediant, in which key the scherzo makes its boisterous entry.

Working from the opposite direction, the passacaglia synthesizes a number of ideas introduced earlier. For one thing, the subject itself resonates with bits and pieces of previous material, such as the closing phrase of the first movement's main theme (mm. 15–19), the clarinet's

EXAMPLE 9.7. Brahms, Fourth Symphony, movt. 1
a. mm. 1–4

b. mm. 19–22

wistful tune in mm. 107–8 of the second movement, and the unusual disjunct succession of tutti chords occurring toward the end of the scherzo (mm. 317–26). Moreover, the striking French-sixth chord of its original harmonization (m. 7) rests on a "Phrygian" F♮ that harkens back to the tonal language of the second movement. Even the overriding formal principle can be understood as a realization of earlier implications. The first movement includes several variations of the main theme; the principal subject of the *andante* is artfully varied upon its return in the reprise (compare mm. 5ff. and 64ff.); and the second theme of the scherzo not only is immediately restated with variation in the exposition, but in the recapitulation's counterstatement is treated to real thematic transformation (compare mm. 63ff. and 258ff.). In view of these manifold relationships it is perhaps not surprising—though still no less remarkable—that toward the end of the work Brahms effects a genuine cross-pollination: by combining the descending third chain and ascending passacaglia subject in the last two variations (mm. 233–36 and 241–45), he demonstrates how, after all, the symphony's two dissimilar thematic germs can really be understood as one.

All this is challenging enough, and matters are scarcely helped by the work's unusually pungent harmonic language, with its frequent use of augmented and diminished thirds and fourths and cross-relations of various sorts. Thus the symphony drew puzzled first reactions from even the composer's most faithful admirers. After Brahms and Brüll had concluded their reading of the first movement, for instance, Hanslick described the experience as resembling a thrashing "by two terribly clever men"; and the following day a skeptical Kalbeck urged the composer to scrap the scherzo and offer the passacaglia as an independent composition. Even Elisabeth von Herzogenberg, a most perceptive and sympathetic critic, was initially disturbed by what she considered to be Brahms's preoccupation with *Augenmusik*:

> It seems to me as though this work were designed too much for the eye of the microscope, as though all the beauties were not laid bare for every simple admirer, and as though it were a tiny world for the wise and learned, only a small part of which might be had by the common people who walk in darkness. I've discovered a number of passages at first only with my eyes and must confess that I would have understood them only with my "mind's ears" [*mit den Ohren meines Verstandes*], not with the senses or feeling, if my eyes had not come to my aid.[72]

The subject here was the first movement (*allegro non troppo*), where every note seems to bear some thematic or structural significance. The elegiac main theme, as we have seen, grows out of a single interval, the third, which is sounded in two chains, first descending and then ascending (mm. 1–8).[73] These yield to an expressive turning figure (mm. 9–14), featuring octave leaps taken from mm. 4–5 and set over a rising chromatic bass, and finally to a full close in the tonic (mm. 15–18). Next comes, not anything suggesting as yet a sonata-form transition, but a varied renewal of the entire opening process, with "superimposed echoes" of the third-chain in running eighth notes set over a staggered chain beginning on a different note from before (Ex. 9.7b). Only with the reappearance of the turning figure (m. 27) does the variation begin to break loose of the tonic and lead, finally, to a passionate transitional theme (mm. 45–53). Heralded by an important fanfare-like prolongation of V/v (mm. 53–57), the ensuing second theme, in B minor, is itself played twice, first by the cellos and then, slightly varied, the violins (mm. 57ff.). After developing seamlessly through a wealth of thematic ideas, at turns mysterious and triumphant, the second group concludes, now in the major dominant, with a wistful final reference to the main theme (mm. 137–44) that leads back to what appears to be a repeat of the exposition.

This "repeat" soon begins to swerve from its former course, however, and gives way to the development, which offers three variations on the main theme (mm. 157ff., in G minor; mm. 169ff., in B♭ minor; and mm. 219ff., in G♯ minor). The episode in B♭ minor is particularly noteworthy on account of its "microscopic" detail; here Brahms not only combines a two-voice canon on a forceful variation of the first phrase (with the descending third filled in and the ascending sixth displaced by an expressive appoggiatura), a two-voice inversion canon based on the turning figure from measure 9, and a firmly articulated ascending scale, but then repeats the whole rich combination in triple counterpoint.

In stark contrast to this passage of *Augenmusik* stands the retransition and beginning of the recapitulation, which have a immediate "physical" effect, albeit not of the kind normally associated with the events surrounding the "double return" of tonic key and main theme. The development gradually winds down (mm. 227ff.), with an ever-decreasing dynamic level and written-out ritard, and as the turning figure is passed back and forth among the woodwinds and strings, it is transformed before our eyes into the familiar chain of descending thirds, outlining not V⁷ (which is never really sounded) but ii⁷, out of which the main theme naturally emerges at measure 246. The comparable passage in the Second Symphony, as we have seen, is marked by a similar ii⁷ harmony and slackening tempo that gently gives way to the restated main theme. But the Fourth is far more radical: the written-out ritard is extended into the first phrase of the main theme itself, which now stretches out over three times its original length and includes a new emphasis on C-major harmony. It is an extraordinary moment of virtual stillness, whose mystery is only heightened by the quiet murmuring that lies underneath in the strings and harkens back to the most plaintive episode of the development (mm. 192–202).

The lack of a "syntactic climax" at the outset of the reprise might of course be explained in terms of tragedy; there can be no resolution so early, and the decisive catastrophe must be withheld until the very end. Momentum builds after measure 369, where, toward the conclusion of an otherwise regular recapitulation, the fanfare figure initiates a vehement "secondary development" that culminates in a "statistical apotheosis" of the main theme in the coda (mm. 394ff.). Surely the grip of tragic fate is suggested here by Brahms's strict and unrelenting canonic treatment of his subject, and the point is driven home by the plagal cadence that is drummed out at the end.

The famous opening melody of the *andante moderato*, sounded first by the horns but soon doubled by most of the other winds, alludes to the related opening gestures of Schubert's "Great" C-Major Symphony and Schumann's "Spring" Symphony Op. 38 (Ex. 9.8). Like Schubert, Brahms begins with a stepwise melody extending a third in both directions

EXAMPLE 9.8.

a. Brahms, Fourth Symphony, movt. 2, mm. 1, 5

(*continued*)

b. Schubert, "Great" C-Major Symphony, movt. 1, m. 1

c. Schumann, "Spring" Symphony, movt. 1, mm. 1–2, 39–41

around a central tone; like Schumann, he subsequently enriches the harmonic possibilities by transposing the theme by a major third. But in his own fashion, Brahms employs this stepwise motive as the linchpin in a remarkable long-range formal process.

Despite its lack of accompaniment and focus on the pitch E, Brahms's theme is initially perceived in Schubert's key of C major (albeit starting on Schumann's mediant). The entry of the clarinets in measure 4 opens up a new harmonic vista, however, and the unexpected dyad they introduce, E–G♯, becomes the springboard for a sonata-like movement in E major. The principal theme grows out of the same stepwise motive, transposed upward into the new key but harmonized with a healthy dose of the notes D♮ and C♮ that had been prominent in its original incarnation. As a result, the introductory horn call now assumes in the memory a strange tinge of C major overlaid with the Phrygian mode. And having thus created the implication that the first note of the stepwise motive might just as well be tonic (or root) as mediant (or third), Brahms soon provides three linked realizations: in the transitional theme at measure 30, which begins firmly in the established tonic key but starts from E instead of G♯; the V/V of measures 36–40, which is prolonged by means of stepwise thirds encircling the chord root; and the gorgeous secondary theme in B major for the cellos (mm. 41ff.); which combines features of both.

Each reading of the stepwise motive is given its due in the modified reprise, but neither is capable of sustaining itself. When the principal theme returns in measure 64, it is shorn at first of the disturbing "modal" notes in the accompaniment, yet it rests uneasily on $^6_4$ harmony and soon yields to developmental treatment of the Phrygian motive. This in turn quickly builds to a climactic outburst on the stepwise figure that earlier had prolonged V/V but that now culminates on the significant chord of C major (mm. 84ff.). Nevertheless, the secondary theme emerges on course in measure 88, and in a lushly scored passage for eight-part strings projects the alternative reading of the stepwise motive in the tonic key. When Brahms subsequently adds a vigorous syncopated counterstatement in the upper reaches of the orchestra, we might imagine that a genuine confirming apotheosis is at hand (mm. 98ff.). All momentum is suddenly lost, however, and we find ourselves instead in the midst of a mysterious episode in which diminished-seventh harmony supports quiet, misremembered fragments from the first group (mm. 106–10).[74] Nor are matters clarified in the ensuing coda (mm. 113ff.). Closure is signaled by the forceful return of the horn call, beginning on E as in the introduction but now harmonized after the manner of the transition with an E-major triad. None of the Phrygian inflections is suppressed, however, and before long the C major that had been originally implied is made explicit in the accompaniment, too. The movement concludes, not with any traditional tonal resolution, but with a resigned arpeggiation of the Neapolitan chord (II in the Phrygian mode) that yields directly to a final E-major harmony.

Nothing about the final bars of the *andante* betrays the exuberant character that marks the ensuing *allegro giocoso* (C major). Yet the pairing may be explained in part by reference to a striking passage that drew Brahms's notice in Carl von Winterfeld's *Johannes Gabrielli und sein Zeitalter* (1831): "In the face of the bright, cheerful Ionian the gloomy Phrygian must utterly melt away." Indeed, the brilliant "Ionian" opening of the third movement surely does do much to dispel what Malcolm MacDonald has called the "magnificent miasma" of the *andante*.[75] But Brahms also gives evidence of his acquaintance with Schubert's lesser-known symphonies, which he had recently edited for Breitkopf & Härtel's newly launched Gesamtausgabe. In the sketched Symphony in E Major, D. 729 (which Brahms examined but declined to publish), he would have found a precedent for including a C-major scherzo in a symphony whose keynote is E; and from the scherzo of Schubert's own *Tragische* Symphony in C Minor, D. 417, he might well have taken the idea of employing double counterpoint between the outer voices of his opening subject (compare mm. 5–8 and 39–42 in D. 417 with mm. 1–5 and 35–38 in the *allegro giocoso*).[76]

Although Brahms's movement is a scherzo in character (the only real example in his symphonic oeuvre), it unfolds as a lively sonata form. The jesting quality is owing in part to the movement's instrumentation: piccolo, contrabassoon, and triangle complement the composer's standard orchestra. A more subtle contributor to this character are Brahms's many plays upon expected formal procedures. Nothing seems amiss when the first six bars of the principal theme return in the tonic to initiate the development (mm. 89–94), nor does the lively development itself seem out of the ordinary. And though suspicions are raised by the fleeting appearance at measure 181 of a pastoral "trio" in D♭ (*poco meno presto*), the ensuing V pedal seems to point in an obvious enough direction. The real surprise comes in measure 199, when the recapitulation explodes with the *third* limb of the principal theme, a mock-military outburst that begins on ♭III.

In the exposition, by contrast, Brahms is reluctant to give up the tonic. To be sure, the transition appears to establish the orthodox second key by way of V/V (m. 44), but the full cadence on C that follows six bars later (supporting the descending third chain) sounds more like a tonicization of the home dominant than a firming up of the second key. Indeed, the insouciant secondary theme (mm. 52ff.) is most likely heard in the tonic. The latter stages of the symmetrical recapitulation thus lie heavily on the subdominant, and the coda understandably begins with a lengthy compensatory pedal on V. Yet surprises are in store during a last rehearsal of the opening group. The first limb is "recapitulated" in F major (at m. 311); the third, for the only time in the movement, in C major (at m. 337). A final statement of the opening idea in the tonic brings to a close one of Brahms's most ebullient movements.

This triumph is short-lived: a recrudescence of the tragic mood occurs at the very outset of the finale (*allegro energico e passionato*), which begins at one blow, with the subject harmonized with forbidding chords by the wind band (with trombones and timpani). What follows is a masterly set of thirty variations and coda in the Baroque tradition of the valedictory ostinato. Like the chaconne finale of J. S. Bach's Partita in D Minor for Solo Violin, BWV 1004, for example, the *allegro energico* is in a minor key and slow triple time with a stressed second beat; both its bass line and principal theme are freely varied; the variations are often grouped in pairs; and it includes a contrasting section in the parallel major key followed by a decisive reappearance of the opening idea and texture. To be sure, similar features are found in a number of other Baroque works with which Brahms was familiar, and significant resemblances to post–Baroque examples might be cited as allusions as well.[77] Yet the "wonderful and incomprehensible" D-Minor Chaconne, to quote Brahms's description of the piece when he sent Clara Schumann his transcription of it for piano left hand in 1877, must at least be recognized as a crucial source of inspiration and a rod by which Brahms could measure his own achievement. As he confessed to his friend, "Should I imagine that I had written this piece [the Chaconne], been able to conceive it, I know for certain the enormous excitement and violent emotions would have made me mad."[78] With emotions in check, Brahms found himself adequate to this task some eight years later, in the movement that must be judged the apotheosis of his considerable variation technique.

According to Kalbeck, the composer justified his use of variation form in a symphonic finale by citing the precedent of Beethoven's *Eroica*

Symphony.[79] Like his predecessor, Brahms not only concludes with a set of variations on a subject that eventually finds its rightful home in the bass, but provides the movement with the outlines of a dramatic structure. In spite of that, Brahms is far stricter in his regard for the imperatives of variation form; he gets along without Beethoven's introduction, partial variations and extensions, frequent changes in key, and fugal episodes, and every variation save the last adheres to the eight-bar phrase-length of the subject. Several do depart from the original cadential pattern, however, and as a result of these syntactic changes we cannot help but recognize a functional differentiation of parts relating in some way to sonata form.[80]

The "primary group" comprises two equal subgroups. In the first (consisting of the original statement and Vars. 1–3), the subject appears in the upper or a middle voice; in the second (Vars. 4–7) Brahms removes the subject to the bass and introduces a surging countermelody in the violins that includes two references to the third chain (mm. 38–40 and 62–64) on its way to a sharp rhythmic climax and forceful hemiola cadence in the tonic. The next four variations (consisting of two pairs) act as the "transition"; here the music seems to open up tonally, notwithstanding the lack of any modulation—first by means of an alteration in the ending of the subject (Vars. 8–9), then by the harmonic vagaries of a chain of dominant seventh chords (Var. 10), and finally by a prolonged half cadence (Var. 11). The "exposition" concludes with an unusually affective "secondary group" of four double-length variations (resulting from a change from $\frac{3}{4}$ to $\frac{3}{2}$ meter). Now the subject serves merely as scaffolding for melodic ornamentation by the solo woodwinds. In response to what Tovey described as "the most pathetic flute passage since Gluck's wonderful Adagio in the Elysian scene of Orfeo" (Var. 12), the oboe and clarinet enter with a quiet dialogue in E major that recalls Schumann's setting in the song "Süsser Freund" of the words "Do you know now the tears I am crying? Should you not see them, my beloved?" (Var. 13).[81] The major mode is maintained in the next two variations, as the subject returns to the bass and the trombones strike a funereal tone (Vars. 14–15). Grief seems to sap all remaining energy, and before the implied cadence can be completed the section expires on a quiet inscrutable harmony.

Showing a strategy that is common to each of the other three movements, the "development" begins with a reprise of the subject in its original setting (Var. 16). The disruption comes even earlier than before, however; in the fourth bar the strings take up a fierce minor-key variant of the cadential figure that the trombones had left uncompleted and initiate a lengthy passage full of motivic manipulation and tonal digressions (Vars. 17–22). The "retransition" concludes on a strongly articulated dominant chord (Var. 23) and yields dutifully to the "recapitulation" of the first three variations (Vars. 24–26). The pathetic "secondary group" would seem to bear no repeating and is replaced by more graceful strains that emphasize G major (Vars. 27 and 28), whose sweet parallel thirds pave the way for the celebrated synthesis of descending third chain and ascending passacaglia subject, sounding somewhat tentative at first but then thundering in canon between the basses and violins (Vars. 29 and 30).

The canon is maintained through a four-bar extension of the final variation, steadily building tension through a steady crescendo and ritardando until the outset of the lengthy coda (*più allegro*). Now the harmonized subject bursts out once more in the wind band (mm. 253–60), but it is accompanied this time by violent rushing strings and truncated to resemble the comical anticipation of itself that had taken place in measures 317–25 of the scherzo. Twice more Brahms refers ironically to the previous movement. First, a remarkable series of chromatic modulations leads to a distorted recollection of the oddly scored harmonies that had appeared at the beginning of the scherzo's development (mm. 97–106), against which the ominous trombones play a compressed version of the truncated subject (mm. 273–78). Then, in the manner of Brahms's treatment of the main theme of the scherzo, the compressed truncated subject is sounded repeatedly against itself in inversion (mm. 289–301). The terror of these final pages is palpable, as we seem caught up in "a veritable orgy of destruction, a frightful counterpart to the paroxysm of joy at the end of the last symphony of Beethoven."[82]

Although Brahms later made notations for at least one more symphonic essay, by 1890 he had decided that he had done enough already in his "two pairs of serious and cheerful symphonies." During the remaining years of the composer's life, the two major-key works, retaining the public favor with which they had generally been greeted, claimed the lion's share of concert performances. But the minor-key works must inevitably stand out in any biographical or historical account. After all, it was in the First Symphony that Brahms, realizing in an individual and powerful way the plot archetype associated with Beethoven's Fifth and Ninth symphonies, capped his long and strenuous effort to write a work worthy of comparison with those sterling examples. And it was in the Fourth Symphony that he achieved something greater still. No longer do the giant's footsteps hover in the background; here Brahms turned the Beethovenian plot archetype on its head, writing an end-accented symphony that "looked very different" indeed from those of the earlier master. As represented so strikingly in the antithesis to Beethoven's choral finale that occurs at the end of his tragic chaconne, Brahms thus met Schumann's great expectations on the most uncompromising terms imaginable.

Notes

1. *Robert Schumanns Briefe: Neue Folge,* ed. F. Gustav Jansen (Leipzig, 1904), 390. Unless otherwise noted, all translations are mine.

2. *Neue Zeitschrift für Musik* 20 (28 October 1853): 185–86.

3. The relation between the first movements of the sonata and concerto is reported by Brahms's friend Albert Dietrich; see his *Erinnerungen an Johannes Brahms in Briefen besonders aus seiner Jugendzeit* (Leipzig, 1898), 45, repub. as *Erinnerungen an Johannes Brahms in Briefen aus seiner Jugendzeit* (Leipzig, 1989), 151. On Brahms's orchestration, see *Johannes Brahms Briefwechsel* (hereafter *Briefwechsel*), 19 vols. to date (consisting of 16 orig. vols., rev. ed. [Berlin, 1912–22; rpt. Tutzing, 1974] and a *Neue Folge* consisting of 3 vols. to date [Tutzing, 1992–]), vols. 5–6: *Johannes Brahms im Briefwechsel mit Joseph Joachim*, ed. Andreas Moser, 2 vols. (vol. 1: 3d ed., 1921; vol. 2: 2d ed., 1912), 5, 55–56; and *Briefwechsel*, vol. 4: *Johannes Brahms im Briefwechsel mit J. O. Grimm*, ed. Richard Barth (1912), 13. My view that the sonata was conceived as a symphony is elaborated in chapter 1 of my forthcoming Cambridge Music Handbook, *Brahms: Symphony No. 1* (Cambridge, 1996).

4. *Clara Schumann–Johannes Brahms: Briefe aus den Jahren 1853–1896*, ed. Berthold Litzmann, 2 vols. (Leipzig, 1927), 1:69.

5. See Christopher Reynolds, "A Choral Symphony by Brahms?" *19th-Century Music* 9 (1985): 3–25.

6. *Schumann-Brahms Briefe* 1:76. Work on the concerto movement dates principally from the fall of 1856. The symphony's scherzo, on the other hand, was revived only much later, in the funeral march of the German Requiem; see Dietrich, *Erinnerungen an Johannes Brahms*, 45 (new ed., p. 151). Reynolds speculates on the eventual fate of other parts of the abandoned symphony in "A Choral Symphony by Brahms?" 14–18.

7. Berthold Litzmann, *Clara Schumann: Ein Künstlerleben nach Tagebüchern und Briefen*, 3 vols. (Leipzig, 1902–8), 3:43.

8. Donald Francis Tovey, *Essays in Musical Analysis*, vol. 1: *Symphonies* (London, 1948), 133.

9. The genesis of this work can be pieced together from Brahms's correspondence with Joachim, Julius Otto Grimm, and Clara Schumann; see *Briefwechsel* 4:77, 5:215, 228–30, and Litzmann, *Clara Schumann* 3:43, 47–48. On the preparations for the Hamburg performance, see *Briefwechsel* 5:198–99, 235; it is clear from the context that these two undated letters, entered as nos. 142 and 170 in the third edition of the correspondence, belong together and date from February 1859.

10. Quoted in Styra Avins, *Johannes Brahms: Life and Letters* (Oxford, in press); see also Florence May, *The Life of Brahms*, 2 vols. (London, 1905), 1:234, where Frl. von Meysenbug is identified simply as the lady-in-waiting on Princess Friederike of Lippe-Detmold.

11. *Neue Zeitschrift für Musik* 50 (1859), 272.

12. *Briefwechsel* 5:248–49, 258–59. For a compendium of Brahms's allusions, see James Webster, "Schubert's Sonata Form and Brahms's First Maturity (II)," *19th-Century Music* 3 (1979): 59–60, and the references cited there.

13. *Briefwechsel* 5:226–27. It is clear from the context that this letter (no. 163 in the 3d ed.) should follow no. 185 and thus dates from December 1859, not, as suggested by Moser, December 1858.

14. Max Kalbeck, *Johannes Brahms*, rev. ed., 4 vols. in 8 (Berlin, 1915–21; rpt., Tutzing, 1976), 1:339. Brahms's last remark is corrected in accordance with Bargheer's "Erinnerungen an Johannes Brahms in Detmold 1857–1865" (unpublished typescript preserved in the Lippische Landesbibliothek, Detmold), from which Kalbeck derived his account.

15. *Briefwechsel* 5:261. The emphasis on the word "Serenade," which is not included in the published edition, is found in the original letter, preserved in Hamburg, Staats- und Universitätsbibliothek Carl von Ossietzky.

16. Kalbeck, *Brahms* 4:216.

17. Dietrich, *Erinnerungen an Brahms*, 42 (new ed., p. 141); and "Fragebogen für Herrn Hofkapellmeister Albert Dietrich," ed. Max Kalbeck, transcribed in Musikantiquariat Hans Schneider, *Katalog 100: Johannes Brahms: Leben und Werk, seine Freunde und seine Zeit* (Tutzing, 1964), 15–16 (emphasis added and inaccurate transcription of "D-moll" in place of "C-moll" corrected).

18. Kalbeck, *Brahms* 1:233, 3:93. Clara herself noted the same thematic similarity; see Ernst Rudorff, "Johannes Brahms: Erinnerungen und Betrachtungen," *Schweizerische Musikzeitung* 97 (1957): 83.

19. See Reynolds, "A Choral Symphony by Brahms?" 7–8, 21.

20. For a full discussion of this autobiographical subtext, see Brodbeck, *Brahms: Symphony No. 1*, chapter 3.

21. *Neue Zeitschrift für Musik* 52 (25 May 1860): 200; *Briefwechsel* 5:267; *Neue Zeitschrift für Musik* 52 (15 June 1860): 224.

22. *Schumann-Brahms Briefe* 1:312.

23. In her letter to Joachim of 1 July 1862, Clara quoted the opening bars of the *allegro*: "Johannes recently sent me—imagine what a surprise—a symphonic first movement. . . . The movement is full of wonderful beauties; the motives are treated with a masterly skill, as indeed is becoming more and more typical with him" (Litzmann, *Clara Schumann* 3:123). For the subsequent exchange of letters between Joachim and Brahms, see *Briefwechsel* 5:320, 321.

24. *Pace* Tovey, who believed that the composer "kept the first three movements with him for ten years before attacking the finale" (Tovey, *Essays in Musical Analysis* 1:84).

25. Quoted in Kalbeck, *Brahms* 1:165.

26. Kalbeck, *Brahms* 3:89–90; *Briefwechsel*, vols. 9–10: *Johannes Brahms: Briefe an P. J. Simrock und Fritz Simrock*, ed. Max Kalbeck, 2 vols. (1917), 9:181, 187.

27. For an analysis of the finale in these terms, see Brodbeck, *Brahms: Symphony No. 1*, chapter 5; a related discussion is found in Reinhold Brinkmann, *Late Idyll: The Second Symphony of Johannes Brahms*, trans. Peter Palmer (Cambridge, MA, 1995), 33–44.

28. *Briefwechsel*, vol. 15: *Johannes Brahms im Briefwechsel mit Franz Wüllner*, ed. Ernst Wolff (1922), 59.

29. The preparations for the first performance can be followed in *Briefwechsel*, vol. 16: *Johannes Brahms im Briefwechsel mit Otto Dessoff*, ed. Carl Krebs (1922), 142–48.

30. Litzmann, *Clara Schumann* 3:340; *Billroth und Brahms im Briefwechsel*, ed. Otto Gottlieb-Billroth (Berlin and Vienna, 1935), 228, no. 1.

31. See Ingrid Fuchs, "Zeitgenössische Aufführungen der ersten Symphonie von Johannes Brahms in Wien: Studien zur Wiener Brahms-Rezeption," in *Brahms-Kongress Wien 1983: Kongressbericht*, ed. Susanne Antonicek and Otto Biba (Tutzing, 1988), 167–86.

32. Eduard Hanslick, *Music Criticisms 1846–99*, trans. and ed. Henry Pleasants (Baltimore, 1950), 127–28.

33. See the open letter to Bartholf Senff of 27 October–4 November 1877, in Hans von Bülow, *Ausgewählte Schriften, 1850–1896* (Leipzig, 1896), 369–72. For an

excellent introduction to the *Rezeptionsgeschichte* of Brahms's symphonies, see Walter Frisch, *Brahms: The Four Symphonies* (New York, in press), chapter 7; I address the early reception of the First in *Brahms: Symphony No. 1*, chapter 6.

34. Letter to Brahms of 14 November 1877, in *Billroth und Brahms*, p. 251; letters to Simrock and Elisabeth von Herzogenberg of 22 November 1877, in *Briefwechsel* 10:56 and *Briefwechsel*, vols. 1–2: *Johannes Brahms im Briefwechsel mit Heinrich und Elisabet von Herzogenberg*, ed. Max Kalbeck (4th edn., 1921), 1:32.

35. Litzmann, *Clara Schumann* 3:364–65. A reviewer of the first English performance noted that "whereas the first symphony was purely abstract, or, as the German would say, 'absolute,' music, written by its composer for himself and for fame, in the D major there are more abundant signs that Brahms wishes to conciliate the favor of the public." Quoted in *Dwight's Music Journal*, 26 October 1878, 325.

36. *Fremden-Blatt*, 3 January 1878, 5; quoted in Angelika Horstmann, *Untersuchungen zur Brahms-Rezeption der Jahre 1860–1880* (Hamburg, 1986), 331.

37. Brahms later plays on this deception. Since the whole of mm. 1–43 is included in the repetition of the exposition, we are not fooled again into thinking that the "waltz" beginning at m. 44 is the "main theme." Yet in the first measures of the recapitulation (mm. 302–49), which offer a substantially rewritten version of the exposition, we are once more confounded: this time the ideas from mm. 1ff. and 44ff. are combined, thus synthesizing the two earlier possibilities.

38. In typical fashion Brahms derived his arpeggiated accompanimental figure here from what the violins had played in the preceding transition (cf. mm. 67ff.). In the recapitulation the accompanimental figure is different because the material preceding the second group is different, but still the same principle obtains (compare mm. 323ff. and 350ff.).

39. John Reed, *Schubert: The Final Years* (London, 1972), 241.

40. This and several subsequent passages quoted below from a remarkable exchange of letters between Brahms and Lachner are taken from Reinhold Brinkmann, "Die 'heitre Sinfonie' und der 'schwer melancholische Mensch': Johannes Brahms antwortet Vincenz Lachner," *Archiv für Musikwissenschaft* 46 (1989): 294–306; my translations are adapted from Brinkmann, *Late Idyll*, 126–29.

41. Brinkmann, "Die 'heitre Sinfonie' und der 'schwer melancholische Mensch'," 302–06; and Brinkmann, *Late Idyll*, 162–75.

42. For a sensitive discussion of these matters, see David Epstein, *Beyond Orpheus* (Cambridge, MA, 1979), 162–75.

43. In his personal copy of the first edition Brahms inscribed this passage with the text of the song; for a facsimile, see *Johannes Brahms: Sinfonie Nr. 2 D-Dur, op. 73*, ed. Constantin Floros (Mainz, 1984), 206.

44. Walter Frisch, *Brahms and the Principle of Developing Variation* (Berkeley and Los Angeles, 1984), 123.

45. Tovey, *Essays in Musical Analysis* 1:106.

46. Richard Wagner, *Gesammelte Schriften und Dichtungen*, 3d ed., 10 vols. (Leipzig, 1887–88), 10:137–51; see pp. 148, 150.

47. Ibid. 10:152–75.

48. Ibid. 10:176–93. The following passages are drawn from pp. 181–83.

49. *Billroth und Brahms*, 225–26.

50. Kalbeck, *Brahms* 3:252, n. 1; Malcolm MacDonald, *Brahms* (New York, 1990), 272.

51. "The overtures are a pair," Brahms explained to Wüllner when announcing a forthcoming performance of the two in Breslau in a letter of November 1880; "the one cries, the other laughs." *Briefwechsel* 15:94.

52. James Webster, "Brahms's *Tragic* Overture: The Form of Tragedy," in *Brahms: Biographical, Documentary, and Analytical Studies,* ed. Robert Pascall (Cambridge, 1983), 99–124.

53. Wagner, *Gesammelte Schriften und Dichtungen* 10:292.

54. [C. F. Kahnt], "Zur zwanzigsten Tonkünstlerversammlung des Allgemeinen Deutschen Musikvereins in Leipzig," *Neue Zeitschrift für Musik* 79 (1883): 209.

55. Quoted in Kalbeck, *Brahms* 3:380. Hanslick's untruthful report appeared on 3 May 1883 in the *Neue Freie Presse:* "Johannes Brahms will depart at the end of this week for the music festivals in Leipzig and Cologne."

56. There is no credible basis for Kalbeck's belief that the beginning of the symphony stemmed from an earlier time. The only documentary evidence that he could adduce in support of this position was Brahms's typically ironic reference to the symphony, in a letter of 15 September 1883 to his publisher Fritz Simrock, as some "Notenblätter aus Jugendzeit" (*Briefwechsel,* vols. 11–12: *Johannes Brahms: Briefe an Fritz Simrock,* ed. Max Kalbeck, 2 vols. [1919], 11:28–29; Kalbeck, *Brahms* 3:387, n. 1). But surely the biographer was misled here by a wholly typical display of Brahms's self-deprecating wit. For a different point of view, however, see Robert Pascall, "The Publication of Brahms's Third Symphony: A Crisis in Dissemination," in *Brahms Studies: Analytical and Historical Perspectives,* ed. George S. Bozarth 283–84 (Oxford, 1990).

57. Kalbeck, *Brahms* 3:379–80.

58. On the ambiguous quality of the opening bars, see Epstein, "Brahms and the Mechanisms of Motion," in *Brahms Studies: Analytical and Historical Perspectives,* 194. The similarity with the "Rhenish" was noted already in Theodor Helm's report on the premiere in *Musikalisches Wochenblatt* 14 (1883): 654. The widespread tradition of assigning not only musical but biographical significance to the three-note motto stems from Kalbeck alone, who improbably held that the pitches stand for the composer's putative *Wahlspruch* "Frei aber froh" (Free but happy); see *Brahms* 1:98, 2:445, 3:386; and cf. Michael Musgrave, "*Frei aber Froh*: A Reconsideration," *19th-Century Music* 3 (1980): 251–58.

59. The allusions to Haydn and Beethoven in the transition were brought to my attention in Raymond Knapp's "Allusive Webs, Generic Resonance, and the Synthesis of Traditions in Brahms's Symphonies" (paper delivered at the Annual Meeting of the American Musicological Society, Oakland, CA, November 1990). On the subtle differences between the endings of the first and last movements, see Robert Bailey, "Musical Language and Structure in the Third Symphony," in *Brahms Studies: Analytical and Historical Perspectives,* 415–16.

60. Michael Musgrave has suggested that the importance that Brahms places on the work's motto—his treatment of the notes F–A♭–F as a leitmotiv, so to speak—might imply that the Third was meant in part as an homage to Wagner; see Michael Musgrave, *The Music of Brahms* [London, 1985], 221–22. But the role of the motto in this regard should not, I think, be overstated; after all, Brahms had previously deployed such cells in his first two symphonies (C–C♯–D and D–C♯–D–A, respectively).

61. J. A. Fuller-Maitland, *Brahms* (1911, rpt. Port Washington, NY, 1972), 149. For an earlier observation of this reference, see Hugo Riemann, *Johannes Brahms:*

Erläuterung seiner bedeutendsten Werke (Frankfurt am Main, [n.d.]), 101. For a more recent one, see Bailey, "Musical Language and Structure in the Third Symphony," 405–7.

62. Elsewhere I have discussed a similar occurrence in the second movement of the symphony; see my "Brahms, the Third Symphony, and the New German School," in *Brahms and His World*, ed. Walter Frisch (Princeton, 1990), 70–72. Bailey, "Musical Language and Structure in the Third Symphony," 405–09, suggests that the melody with which Brahms initiates the coda of the *andante* (mm. 108–10) evokes a passage from the "Immolation Scene" at the end of *Götterdämmerung;* as Ivor Keys has noted (*Johannes Brahms* [London, 1989], 186), this theme soon grows into the work's "great erotic moment." For a provocative recent analysis of the symphony, see Susan McClary, "Narrative Agendas in 'Absolute' Music: Identity and Difference in Brahms's Third Symphony," in *Musicology and Difference: Gender and Sexuality in Music Scholarship*, ed. Ruth A. Solie (Berkeley and Los Angeles, 1993), 326–44.

63. For an excellent account of Brahms's intriguing form (but without reference to any model that the composer may have had in mind), see Frisch, *Brahms and the Principle of Developing Variation*, 129–42. See also Bailey, "Musical Language and Structure in the Third Symphony," 410–13.

64. The E♭ Concerto was one of the works performed in the Leipzig concerts that Brahms had stood up; for Elisabeth von Herzogenberg's caustic report to Brahms on this performance, see my "Brahms, the Third Symphony, and the New German School," 75.

65. Frisch, *Brahms and the Principle of Developing Variation*, 242.

66. Margaret Notley, "Brahms as Liberal: Genre, Style, and Politics in Late-19th-Century Vienna," *19th-Century Music* 17 (1994): 107–123; Kalbeck, *Brahms* 3:402.

67. See Carl Dahlhaus, *Nineteenth-Century Music*, trans. J. Bradford Robinson (Berkeley and Los Angeles, 1989), 269–71; and A. Peter Brown, "Brahms' Third Symphony and the New German School," *Journal of Musicology* 2 (1983): 451–52. Even Clara Schumann and especially Joseph Joachim responded to the work in unusually poetic, even programmatic terms; see *Schumann-Brahms Briefe* 2:273–74 and *Briefwechsel* 6:212. But as Dahlhaus notes, the pastoral secondary theme of the first movement, which develops artfully (and economically) out of its opening measure, still illustrates a compositional approach that, outside of Brahms's hand, would normally be associated with chamber music.

68. Siegfried Ochs, *Geschehenes, Gesehenes* (Leipzig, 1922), 199–200; for a sensitive discussion of this matter (with reference to still other possible models), see Raymond Knapp, "The Finale of Brahms's Fourth Symphony: The Tale of the Subject," *19th-Century Music* 13 (1989): 3–17.

69. See Brodbeck, *Brahms: Symphony No. 1*, 67–68.

70. Letters to von Bülow (quoted in Kalbeck, *Brahms* 3:447) and Elisabeth von Herzogenberg (*Briefwechsel* 2:74). In his letter to von Bülow, Brahms described the imposing new work as "ein paar Entr'actes"; soon thereafter, evidently referring to the scherzo and finale, he teased Kalbeck by making reference to his latest polka and waltz. The early acquaintance of Brahms's circle with the work may be followed in Kalbeck, *Brahms* 3:446–56; *Briefwechsel* 2:73–106; and *Schumann-Brahms Briefe* 2:292–98.

71. Helm's review appeared in the 19 January 1886 issue of the *Deutsche Zeitung*. Hugo Wolf, writing in the 24 January 1886 issue of the *Wiener Salonblatt*, was less fair-minded, sneering at Brahms's dubious ability "to make something out of nothing"; see *The Music Criticisms of Hugo Wolf*, trans. Henry Pleasants (New York, 1978), 184–87. The same attitude was demonstrated by the Viennese wit who reportedly sang the opening theme to the words "Es fiel ihm wieder mal nichts ein!"; see Siegfried Kross, "Brahms the Symphonist," in *Brahms: Biographical, Documentary, and Analytical Studies*, 141.

72. *Briefwechsel* 2:86. This passage comes from a letter that Elisabeth had written on 8 September 1885 but did not post; instead she enclosed it with another from 31 September [*sic*] in which, with the passing of some time, she was able to form a clearer impression and so evaluate the movement rather more positively. Kalbeck, on the other hand, retained some skepticism; Richard Heuberger recounted "a strange conversation" concerning the work that took place in January 1887 in which the biographer stated that Brahms, "despite his significance, is no master of the foremost rank, since execution prevails over power of invention. There is a lack of the great, noble popularity, that appealing to the common people, which, for example, distinguished Beethoven. 'Symphonies must really be understandable to the common people. Brahms's symphonies will never become that.'" Richard Heuberger, *Erinnerungen an Johannes Brahms: Tagebuchnotizen aus den Jahren 1875 bis 1897*, rev. ed., ed. Kurt Hofmann (Tutzing, 1976), 156.

73. Models for this theme have been sought in Handel's *Messiah*, Beethoven's "Hammerklavier" Sonata, and Mozart's G-Minor Symphony; it is difficult to make a strong case for allusion, however, since the pattern in question forms an important feature in Brahms's style. For a convenient résumé (with an argument that Brahms generally used descending thirds as a emblem for death), see Kenneth Hull, "Brahms the Allusive: Extra-Compositional Reference in the Instrumental Music of Johannes Brahms" (Ph.D. dissertation, Princeton University, 1989), pp. 117–53. The Fourth is unique among Brahms's symphonies in beginning without benefit of a slow introduction (First Symphony) or motto (Second and Third symphonies). The autograph does show, however, that after completing the full score Brahms at first added but finally struck out a four-bar introduction; this unfolds the progression IV⁷–I and thus would have been related to, among other salient ideas, both the transformed version of the main theme occurring at the outset of the recapitulation and the plagal-like cadence with which the movement ends. See Louis Litterick, "Brahms the Indecisive," in *Brahms 2: Biographical, Documentary and Analytical Studies*, ed. Michael Musgrave (Cambridge, 1987), 223–35.

74. Here, as Kenneth Hull has noted, Brahms makes an ironic allusion to the B theme from the second movement of Beethoven's Symphony in C Minor, the very piece that established the heroic plot archetype from which Brahms was daring to deviate. Indeed, just as Beethoven's theme foreshadows the main subject of the triumphant finale, so does Brahms's theme, with its stepwise ascent through a diminished fifth, anticipate the passacaglia subject of his finale. See Hull, "Brahms the Allusive," 97–117.

75. MacDonald, *Brahms*, 316.

76. These relationships have been noted in Brian Newbould, *Schubert and the Symphony: A New Perspective* ([n.p.], 1992), 105–06, 171n.

77. Knapp ("Tale of the Subject," 6–11) argues for a dense web of allusions to works including Buxtehude's Chaconne in E Minor, François Couperin's Passacaille in B Minor, Beethoven's Thirty-Two Variations in C Minor, and even the *andante* of Schubert's "Unfinished" Symphony.

78. *Schumann-Brahms Briefe* 2:111.

79. Kalbeck, *Brahms* 3:454.

80. See also Hull, "Brahms the Allusive," 165–73, and Robert Pascall, "Genre and the Finale of Brahms's Fourth Symphony," *Music Analysis* 8 (1989): 233–45.

81. Tovey, *Essays in Musical Analysis* 1:122. For an intriguing discussion of Brahms's "ironic allusion" to "Süsser Freund," see Hull, "Brahms the Allusive," 199–226.

82. Felix Weingartner, "The Symphony since Beethoven," in *Weingartner on Music and Conducting* (1926; rpt., New York, 1969), 276.

Selected Bibliography

Bailey, Robert. "Musical Language and Structure in the Third Symphony." In *Brahms Studies: Analytical and Historical Perspectives*, ed. George S. Bozarth, 405–21. Oxford, 1990.

Brahms, Johannes. *Sinfonie Nr. 1*. Ed. Giselher Schubert. Mainz, 1981.

———. *Sinfonie Nr. 2*. Ed. Constantin Floros. Mainz, 1984.

———. *Sinfonie Nr. 3*. Ed. Christian Martin Schmidt. Mainz, 1981.

———. *Sinfonie Nr. 4*. Ed. Christian Martin Schmidt. Mainz, 1980.

Brinkmann, Reinhold. "Die 'heitre Sinfonie' und der 'schwer melancholische Mensch': Johannes Brahms antwortet Vincenz Lachner." *Archiv für Musikwissenschaft* 46 (1989): 294–306.

———. *Johannes Brahms, Die Zweite Symphonie: Späte Idyll*. Munich, 1990. Revised and translated as *Late Idyll: The Second Symphony of Johannes Brahms*. Trans. Peter Palmer. Cambridge, MA, 1995.

Brodbeck, David. *Brahms: Symphony No. 1*. Cambridge, 1996.

———. "Brahms, the Third Symphony, and the New German School." In *Brahms and His World*, ed. Walter Frisch, 65–80. Princeton, NJ, 1990.

Brown, A. Peter. "Brahms' Third Symphony and the New German School." *Journal of Musicology* 2 (1983): 434–52.

Clara Schumann–Johannes Brahms: Briefe aus den Jahren 1853–1896. Ed. Berthold Litzmann. 2 vols. Leipzig, 1927. Translated as *Letters of Clara Schumann and Johannes Brahms, 1853–1896*. 2 vols. 1927. Reprint. New York, 1971.

Dunsby, Jonathan. *Structural Ambiguity in Brahms: Analytical Approaches to Four Works*. Ann Arbor, MI, 1981.

Epstein, David. "Brahms and the Mechanisms of Motion: The Composition of Performance." In *Brahms Studies: Analytical and Historical Perspectives*, ed. George S. Bozarth, 191–226. Oxford, 1990.

Fink, Robert. "Desire, Repression & Brahms's First Symphony," *repercussions* 2 (1993): 75–103.

Frisch, Walter. *Brahms and the Principle of Developing Variation*. Berkeley and Los Angeles, 1984.

———. *Brahms: The Four Symphonies*. New York, in 1996.

Fuchs, Ingrid. "Zeitgenössische Aufführungen der Ersten Symphonie op. 68 von Johannes Brahms in Wien: Studien zur Wiener Brahms-Rezeption." In *Brahms-Kongreß Wien*, ed. Susanne Antonicek and Otto Biba, 167–86. Tutzing, 1988.

Haas, Frithjof. "Die Erstfassung des langsamen Satzes der ersten Sinfonie von Johannes Brahms." *Die Musikforschung* 36 (1983): 200–11.

Horstmann, Angelika. *Untersuchungen zur Brahms-Rezeption der Jahre 1860–1880.* Hamburg, 1986.

Hull, Kenneth. "Brahms the Allusive: Extra-Compositional Reference in the Instrumental Works of Johannes Brahms." Ph.D. dissertation, Princeton University, 1989.

Johannes Brahms Briefwechsel. 19 vols. to date. 16 orig. vols. Rev. ed. Berlin, 1912–22. Reprint. Tutzing, 1974. *Neue Folge.* 3 vols. to date. Tutzing, 1992– .

Kalbeck, Max. *Johannes Brahms.* Rev. ed. 4 vols. in 8. Berlin, 1915–21. Reprint. Tutzing, 1976.

Knapp, Raymond. "Brahms and the Problem of the Symphony: Romantic Image, Generic Conception, and Compositional Challenge." Ph.D. dissertation, Duke University, 1987. Rev. ed. in press.

———. "Brahms's Revisions Revisited." *Musical Times* 129 (1988): 584–88.

———. "The Finale of Brahms's Fourth Symphony: The Tale of the Subject." *19th-Century Music* 13 (1989): 3–17.

Kross, Siegfried. "Brahms the Symphonist." In *Brahms: Biographical, Documentary and Analytical Studies*, ed. Robert Pascall, 125–45. Cambridge, 1983.

Litterick, Louise. "Brahms the Indecisive." In *Brahms 2: Biographical, Documentary and Analytical Studies*, ed. Michael Musgrave, 223–35. Cambridge, 1987.

Litzmann, Berthold. *Clara Schumann: Ein Künstlerleben nach Tagebüchern und Briefen.* 3 vols. Leipzig, 1902–8.

MacDonald, Malcolm. *Brahms.* New York, 1990.

McClary, Susan. "Narrative Agendas in 'Absolute' Music: Identity and Difference in Brahms's Third Symphony." In *Musicology and Difference: Gender and Sexuality in Music Scholarship*, ed. Ruth A. Solie, 326–44. Berkeley and Los Angeles, 1993.

McCorkle, Margit L. "The Role of Trial Performances for Brahms's Orchestral and Large Choral Works: Sources and Circumstances." In *Brahms Studies: Analytical and Historical Perspectives*, ed. George S. Bozarth, 295–328. Oxford, 1990.

Musgrave, Michael. "Brahms's First Symphony: Thematic Coherence and Its Secret Origin." *Music Analysis* 2 (1983): 117–33.

———. "Die Erste Symphonie von Johannes Brahms: Stilistische und strukturelle Synthese." In *Probleme der Symphonischen Tradition im 19. Jahrhundert*, ed. Siegfried Kross and Marie Luise Maintz, 537–44. Tutzing, 1990.

———. "*Frei aber Froh*: A Reconsideration." *19th-Century Music* 3 (1980): 251–58.

———. *The Music of Brahms.* London, 1985.

Newman, S. T. M. "The Slow Movement of Brahms's First Symphony: A Reconstruction of the Version First Performed Prior to Publication." *Music Review* 9 (1948): 4–12.

Notley, Margaret. "Brahms As Liberal: Genre, Style, and Politics in Late Nineteenth-Century Vienna." *19th-Century Music* 17 (1994): 107–23.

Osmond-Smith, David. "The Retreat from Dynamism: A Study of Brahms's Fourth Symphony." In *Brahms: Biographical, Documentary, and Analytical Studies*, ed. Robert Pascall, 147–65. Cambridge, 1983.

Pascall, Robert. "Genre and the Finale of Brahms's Fourth Symphony." *Music Analysis* 8 (1989): 233–45.

———. "The Publication of Brahms's Third Symphony: A Crisis in Dissemination." In *Brahms Studies: Analytical and Historical Perspectives*, ed. George S. Bozarth, 283–94. Oxford, 1990.

———. *Brahms's First Symphony Andante: The Initial Performing Version: Commentary and Realisation*. Papers in Musicology, No. 2. Department of Music, University of Nottingham, 1992.

Reynolds, Christopher. "A Choral Symphony by Brahms?" *19th-Century Music* 9 (1985): 3–25.

Schachter, Carl. "The First Movement of Brahms's Second Symphony: The First Theme and its Consequences." *Music Analysis* 2 (1983): 55–68.

Steinbeck, Wolfram. "Liedthematik und symphonischer Prozess: Zum ersten Satz der 2. Symphonie." In *Brahms-Analysen*, ed. Friedhelm Krummacher and Wolfram Steinbeck, 166–82. Basel, 1984.

Tovey, Donald Francis. *Essays in Musical Analysis*. Vol. 1. *Symphonies*. London, 1948.

Wagner, Richard. *Gesammelte Schriften und Dichtungen*. 3d. ed. 10 vols. Leipzig, 1887–88.

Webster, James. "Brahms's *Tragic* Overture: The Form of Tragedy." In *Brahms: Biographical, Documentary, and Analytical Studies*, ed. Robert Pascall, 99–124. Cambridge, 1983.

CHAPTER TEN

Dvořák

Michael Beckerman

At first blush the fact that Antonín Dvořák wrote nine symphonies might mark him as a typical nineteenth-century symphonist—even an epigone of the famous nine. Yet Dvořák himself never counted that high. When the *New World* Symphony was completed he wrote "Symphony No. 8" on the autograph. When it was published it received the designation "Symphony No. 5," and for some years it was known as "Symphony No. 7." Today it is called, correctly, Symphony No. 9. This peculiar history is revealing about Dvořák's career as a symphonist: he presumed his first symphony to be gone for good, and never saw the publication of the next two. We must also note that unlike most of his great contemporaries he wrote dozens of orchestral works that are not symphonies, many of which are programmatic in nature (see Table 10.2). Thus to tell the story of Dvořák's symphonies means to explore some of the central artistic, personal, and political issues with which he was concerned.

Unless otherwise noted the Burghauser numbering of works will be used, since it alone preserves the appropriate chronology:

TABLE 10.1   Dvořák's Symphonies

First Efforts		
Symphony No. 1, *Bells of Zlonice*	B. 9	1865
Symphony No. 2 in B♭ Major Op. 4	B. 12	1865
Three Youthful Symphonies		
Symphony No. 3 in E♭ Major Op. 10	B. 34	1873
Symphony No. 4 in D Minor Op. 13	B. 41	1874
Symphony No. 5 in F Major Op. 76	B. 54	1875
Four Later Symphonies		
Symphony No. 6 in D Major Op. 60	B. 112	1880
Symphony No. 7 in D Minor Op. 70	B. 141	1885
Symphony No. 8 in G Major Op. 88	B. 163	1889
Symphony No. 9 in E Minor Op. 95	B. 178	1893
(From the New World)		

Dvořák As Thinker and Composer

In his memoirs Karel Sázavský recalled a journey he took with Antonín Dvořák in 1896:

> We, along with Dvořák, had reached the Pavlovsky Mountains. "What is that?—I never noticed it before. What a curious thing!" I told him all I knew about the hills, about where you go to climb them. I mentioned the legend—but the Master no longer seemed to be listening. Knowing his way, I was sure that he was turning something over in his mind and that in a little while he would come out with something original—the result of his cogitations. I was just beginning to think I had been mistaken, but in a little while the Master began: "I always envied Wagner that he could write. Where would I be today if I could write! And I can't speak, either.—But listen," and he raised his voice under the stress of some strong emotion: "if I could speak I should call our nation here and I should climb up that hill and from there I should tell them something, and tell it to them straight. But I can't speak." And then he relapsed once more into silence and for a long time gazed out from the carriage at the Pavlovsky Mountains.[1]

So much for the simplicity often attributed to his intellect. In the pantheon of nineteenth-century music no composer has been easier to misunderstand than Dvořák. Configured as a kind of Slavic Brahms, his stature as a composer of absolute music was advertised and later positively enforced by his supporters. Yet any perception that Dvořák's work, and his symphonic work in particular, conforms to an approach stressing "absolute" over "program" music is erroneous. In fact, his evolution was toward an ever more programmatic approach. Though Dvořák lived and composed until 1904, his last orchestral work without a program was the Eighth Symphony, written in 1889, and according to an English critic who interviewed him at the time of the London premiere, there was a story in there, too. In the last fourteen years of his life he wrote only the hybrid *New World* Symphony, operas, and tone poems.

    In addition to creating an "absolute Dvořák," historians have also tended to elevate his lyrical side. Ideas of potent conflict in Dvořák's music, or problematic musical approaches, are suppressed in favor of the Music Lover's Dvořák: a carefree Slavic creature of *dumky* and *furiants*. Yet when we look at his music and see the drama of the last five symphonies, two of which are in minor keys and one of which—the Fifth—is constantly undermining its own stability, we might find Sázavský's account of Dvořák's needing to speak out a compelling and truthful one.

    There have been many attempts to write about Dvořák's music, and several serious books that deal with his symphonies (see the Selected Bibliography). Only one of them tries to deal explicitly with the issue of meaning: Antonín Sychra's *Estetika Dvořákovy symfonické tvorby* (The aesthetic of Dvořák's symphonic works; Prague, 1959). Sychra exhaustively delineates the associations of each work, whether musical (i.e., with Brahms, Czech chorales, folk songs) or extramusical (literary or personal). Too often discussions of music involve mere description or reduction: Dvořák was under the impression that he was trying to communicate something, and this essay speculates about some of the things he may have been trying to say.

First Efforts

Dvořák's first two symphonies form a kind of pair: both were written in 1865, and neither was published during the composer's lifetime. The final page of the autograph score of the First notes: "Composed 14 February–24 March 1865." It is believed that Dvořák entered this work in a competition in Germany. Apparently he told this to his composition class, indicating that he never heard another word about the award. When his pupils asked him how he felt about that he is said to have replied, "Hmm, what did I do? I sat down and wrote another." And even though he entered it in a catalogue of "works that I have torn up and burned," the manuscript was found and purchased at a secondhand bookshop in Leipzig in 1882. Thus the First Symphony is the only one of Dvořák's early symphonic compositions that did not receive subsequent—and sometimes quite extensive—revision.

It begins strikingly (Ex. 10.1). In this early work we see the composer indulging in a variety of types of modeling. It is in C minor and, like Beethoven's work in the same key, has the key pattern C minor–A♭ major–C minor–C major. Yet the primary model for this music is clearly Wagner, under whose spell the symphony was written: it externalizes Wagnerian energy and harmony.[2]

EXAMPLE 10.1. Dvořák, First Symphony movt. 1, mm. 1–6

Conventional wisdom has it that the nickname *The Bells of Zlonice* is not an explicit reference but rather a loose reminiscence of the composer's early years there. But I believe that the beginning of the symphony could well be meant to suggest the bells of the title, and the striking opening with its forceful brass, may be a reflection of his youthful striving.

Several writers, including most notably Sychra, have pointed to close connections between this symphony and the twelve *Silhouettes* for piano, and there may well be linkages with several other youthful works, such as the song collection *Cypresses*.

The Second Symphony was composed in 1865 but completely revised in 1888 in conjunction with its first performance. If, perhaps, it reveals the inexperience of youth, it also shows extraordinary technical ability: musicians, like mathematicians, demonstrate their gifts at an early age. Dvořák's Second Symphony is a remarkable work, sounding in places more like Janáček than Beethoven or Wagner. Though it does not always remind us of his later music, the individuality and depth of this music is striking indeed. The composer himself admired the work enough to revise it twenty years after its composition. Those interested in the Second Symphony need only look at the editorial commentary to the complete edition to see the enormous number of revisions undertaken by the composer between the composition in 1865 and the time the score was submitted for publication, unsuccessfully, to Simrock in 1887.[3]

Three Youthful Symphonies, 1873–75

Dvořák's next three symphonies were critical for his future. The Third and Fourth were submitted to the commission responsible for awarding the state prize for poor and talented artists. They certainly impressed the judges—Johann von Herbeck (director of the Imperial Opera) and the critic Eduard Hanslick—and Dvořák was awarded a young artist's grant. This marked the beginning of his successful association with the Viennese musical establishment, and especially with Brahms. These works also significantly mark the incorporation of "Czechness" into his compositional repertory.

Over seven years separate the Third Symphony from its predecessors, and by then we find a composer with a far greater sense of structural control. Though it sounds little like the music for which the composer came to be primarily known, this is a marvelous symphony, combining real craft with youthful experimentation, unabashedly Wagnerian as it recalls moments from *Tannhäuser, Siegfried,* and *Das Rheingold,* and permeated with fascinating and unpredictable musical details. It is the composer's only three-movement symphony. The compelling opening, with its majestic turn and hints of great power in the descending bass line, provides several different gestures for the development. The stepwise descent of the second theme forms a lyrical counterbalance (Ex. 10.2a–b).

The second movement is an *adagio* in C♯ minor marked "Tempo di marcia." It is actually two movements in one, since the middle section in D♭ is as long as a conventional *adagio*. It is safe to say that most minor-key

EXAMPLE 10.2. Dvořák, Third Symphony, movt. 1
a. mm. 1–8

b. mm. 77–80

marches in the nineteenth century are one way or another funereal; thus identifying the slow movement in the Third Symphony is appropriate when we understand that Dvořák probably wrote more funeral marches than any other composer of the century, with conspicuous entries in such works as *The Wood Dove, Rusalka, A Hero's Life, Poetic Tone Pictures* and *The Specter's Bride.* Not only do these all feature the conventional dotted funeral rhythm, but they usually have wrenching chromatic descents as a metaphor for death. When we add a funeral march to the E♭ key of the symphony, it becomes quite likely that Beethoven's *Eroica* is lurking, somewhere behind the scene, as a model. And in turn the movement is a prototype for the funereal *largo* from the *New World,* with the key succession reversed.

The finale takes both the gravity of the *Meistersinger* Prelude and the dancing finale of Beethoven's Seventh as starting points. Its opening features the gambit of beginning the theme in the tonic with a surprise restatement a tone lower.

Composing the Third Symphony was a real struggle for Dvořák. Among the crosshatched notes in the autograph, the first, though difficult to decipher, is quite revealing:

> I wrote this symphony in the year 1872 and a year later I (orchestrated?) it . . . I immediately . . . burned . . . the work. . . . I did not like it . . . I have used it in one of the *Legends*. A pity![4]

The Fourth Symphony was composed between the end of 1873 and the beginning of the following year. Its original form is difficult to determine, but the scherzo may have been first composed as a separate work. There were several revisions before a planned but unrealized performance by the Philharmonic Society in London in 1888.[5] One might argue that here Dvořák spent a good deal of creative energy trying to recompose *Ma vlast* and *Tannhäuser*. The latter was his favorite opera: not only are there dozens of references to it scattered throughout compositions from the early symphonies to *A Hero's Life*, but we even have the composer on record telling Seidl about his favorite Wagnerian opera.[6] Two of the most astute commentators on Dvořák's style, Otakar Šourek and John Clapham, sometimes fall into the trap of treating the composer's interest in Wagner as if it were a disease from which he only gradually recovered. But disease or not, he assuredly never recovered from it. Rather, he placed his Wagnerian mask alongside other acquired styles that he adapted for personal, artistic, and commercial reasons. The Fourth Symphony may be said to mark the beginning of Dvořák's use of a conscious "Czech" style, which would have been understood as such by his own audience and by audiences abroad.[7]

Dvořák's dialogues with Smetana are also endless, particularly in the programmatic works and the operas. A single example will suffice to show his preoccupation with the issue of national music as Smetana saw it: the place where political history and music converge in the story of the Hussites. Though much of Europe considered them destructive marauders from the East, the Czechs have always regarded the Hussites as the epitome of national heroism. Their musical rallying cry "Ye Who Are God's Warriors" (Ex. 10.3)—a kind of Czech "Ein' feste Burg"—appears prominently in Smetana's work, most conspicuously at the conclusion of *Libuše* and the last two tone poems from *Má vlast*. Dvořák quotes the full melody only once, in his *Hussite* Overture, but references to it recur throughout his compositions, particularly his symphonies; in the Fourth the reference comes in the scherzo (Ex. 10.4). This same melody reappears in a set of programmatic pieces for piano four hands titled *Z Šumavy* (From the Šumava Mountains). The title of the movement in question is "In Stormy Times," a formulation that certainly recalls the Hussite days, and particularly the line from *Libuše* that precedes the appearance of the Hussite hymn: "Storms swirl all around, yet only they stand firm."

EXAMPLE 10.3.   "Ye Who Are God's Warriors"

Kdož jste bo - ží bo - jov - ní - ci   a zá - ko - na je - ho,

pros-tež od Bo - ha po - mo - ci   a dou - fej - te v ně - ho,

že ko - nec - ně s nim vždy - cky zví - tě - zí - te.

EXAMPLE 10.4.   Dvořák, Fourth Symphony, movt. 3, mm. 22–28

Ob., Cl., Bsn.

Note, too, a device in the Fourth Symphony that becomes one of Dvořák's favorite ways of creating a cyclical whole: a reminiscence of opening bars of the first movement at the end of the scherzo. Thematic recollections are common throughout his work: consider, for example, the Suite for Piano in A Major and both serenades. In the Fifth Symphony there is a recollection of the opening fanfare hidden in the trumpets at the very end. The *New World* Symphony, of course, is full of thematic reminiscences.

The Fifth Symphony, in F, was completed in 1875, though because almost no sketches survive we know very little about its genesis. It was somewhat revised before publication in 1888, when, to appear to offer a "new" work by Dvořák, Simrock gave it the opus number 76 and called it the "Third" (after the "First"—actually the Sixth—and the "Second," now known as the Seventh). Šourek suggests that the F Major Symphony originally suffered from its numbering, since compared to the symphonies in D major and D minor "it could not be looked upon as but a step back."[8]

This is not entirely true, for the Fifth Symphony is in some ways a microcosm of Dvořák's symphonic output, and one of his most interesting works. It is often described as "pastoral," as the key and atmosphere of the opening would lead us to believe, and on the surface the Fifth appears disarmingly lyrical, even quaint (Ex. 10.5a). Yet just beneath that surface is a roiling sea of dramatic gesture and deception. The opening progresses to a kind of climax, and it is at this point that the true character of the symphony becomes evident. For instead of a bold reprise of the main theme, or the reinforcement of the tonic key, we find the whole undermined by a chromatic descent (Ex. 10.5b). If this were the only such

EXAMPLE 10.5. Dvořák, Fifth Symphony, movt. 1
a. mm. 1–5

b. mm. 45–48

gesture in the symphony, it might be considered an insignificant anomaly, but tonal surprise is the norm throughout. The slow movement is in A minor, hardly a key for a pastoral symphony, and the scherzo begins with much deception (Ex. 10.6a). When the main material arrives at last, with its first note held out like a dancer's leap, the scherzo proves to be one of the composer's finest inspirations, and one of his most overwhelmingly joyous (10.6b).

With another daring stroke Dvořák begins the finale in the key of A minor, where it remains for over fifty measures. Even when it finally reaches F major, the sense of stability is undermined by another chromatic descent (Ex. 10.7). In the final bars there is the thematic reminiscence cited above.

In the interlude between the composition of his Fifth and Sixth Symphonies, 1875–80, Dvořák became recognized as one of the leading young composers in Europe. He continued to cultivate his Slavic persona with such works as the enormously successful Slavonic Dances and the explicitly national Czech Suite. Also completed during this time were the lesser-known Slavonic Rhapsodies. Perhaps the most ambitious work of this period, and the most artistically successful, is the Symphonic Variations, given the opus number 78 by Simrock despite its having been com-

EXAMPLE 10.6. Dvořák, Fifth Symphony, movt. 3
a. mm. 1–6

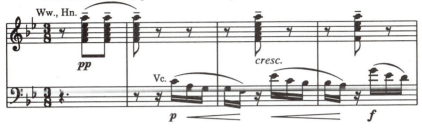

b. mm. 17–25

EXAMPLE 10.7. Dvořák, Fifth Symphony, movt. 4, mm. 55–56

posed after the Fifth Symphony. Even though the work is not explicitly
identified as "Czech," its short theme uses a Lydian inflection at the very
beginning, leaving no doubt as to the intentions of the composer. He
seems to have wished to find a less introspective version of Brahms's
Haydn Variations, exploring issues of structure and pacing that would be
critical for the success of his later symphonies.

Symphony No. 6 in D Major Op. 60

One of Dvořák's more important artistic relationships was with Hans Richter, conductor (at the time) of the Vienna Philharmonic. Richter had successfully performed Dvořák's Third Slavonic Rhapsody in 1879, and in a letter to Simrock the composer described a "delightful evening" spent with the conductor during which "I had to promise Richter a symphony for the next season."[9] It was finished in late 1880, but a range of problems (including perhaps anti-Czech intrigues in the Vienna orchestra) made it impossible to have the premiere there; the first performance was in Prague in 1881. The Sixth is perhaps the most conventional of Dvořák's symphonies—a kind of dues-paying to the Viennese symphonic tradition—but also one of his most powerful artistic statements. And it is his most substantial essay in "absolute" symphonic compositions, the least likely of his later symphonies to have a program lurking behind.

The first bars of any composition mediate between the sounds of ordinary life and the special world of a particular piece; they function as a scrim through which the entire composition begins to be experienced. The pulsing introductory gesture of the D-Major Symphony has a noble lineage, recalling Mozart's Symphony No. 40, Beethoven's *Eroica*, and Schubert's "Unfinished" (Ex. 10.8a). Like Beethoven's opening, what seems to be an entirely triadic theme of almost military character (enhanced by trumpets at the restatement) becomes "problematized" at the end of the phrase by a move to E minor (Ex. 10.8b). Sychra believed that this theme may have been based on a Czech folksong, "Ja mám koně"(I have a horse). This may or may not be the case: there are dozens of folk songs, Czech and otherwise, on which this melody might (or might not) be based. In this way it is a bit like the theme from Smetana's *Vltava* (The Moldau)—liberated, it is thought, from a Swedish operetta—which has a

EXAMPLE 10.8. Dvořák, Sixth Symphony, movt. 1
a. mm. 1–4

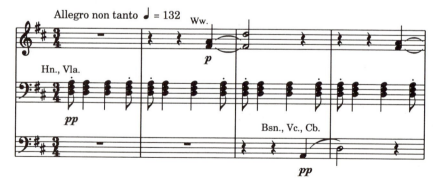

b. mm. 6–9

counterpart in virtually every European country. The beauty of such themes is their very simplicity.

The handling of the development and the coda reflects Beethoven's model. The transition back to the main theme is quite strikingly modeled on the development in Beethoven's Fifth Symphony, with its groups of three chords ascending stepwise (Ex. 10.8c). The jovial and expansive coda culminates in an unexpected and powerful syncopation in the brass

c. mm. 310–15

(mm. 499ff.) that both anticipates the *furiant* rhythms of the scherzo and recalls the first pitches of the Hussite chorale. This is followed by a martial, Handelian version of the opening theme, which had been carefully omitted from the recapitulation. Among the particular joys of this symphony, in fact, are the codas of the outer movements, which seem to combine martial and religious sentiment in good measure, along with just the right amount of technical display.

The second movement is a monothematic *adagio* rich in orchestral color, while the scherzo is a glorious bacchanale offset by the pastoral trio. After the jagged and unbalanced scherzo, the finale revives the festive and military atmosphere of the opening. The conclusion features whirling fugal textures that culminate in a chorale statement of the main idea (Ex. 10.9). This is comedy in the Shakespearean sense, the antithesis of the work that would follow.

EXAMPLE 10.9. Dvořák, Sixth Symphony, movt. 4, mm. 453–55

Symphony No. 7 in D Minor Op. 70

In 1935 Tovey wrote that Dvořák's D-Minor Symphony could stand "along with the C-Major Symphony of Schubert and the four symphonies of Brahms, as among the greatest and purest examples in this art form since Beethoven. There should be no difficulty at this time of day in recognizing its greatness."[10] Yet despite its real power, it has never enjoyed better than third place among the composer's symphonies, after its two followers. Without diminishing in any way the symphonies in G major and E minor, we must recognize that by many measures the Seventh Symphony is his most ambitious and personal. The cast of characters who contributed to the emotional climate from which the work sprang includes Simrock, Brahms, the London audiences, and a train full of ardent Czech nationalists. For musical compositions do not just happen spontaneously but are the result of a particular decision, and in this case we know a great deal about why Dvořák meant to write a work so different in tone from its predecessor.

Dvořák was undergoing a profound self-examination. When, after the success of his D-Major Symphony in London, he received an invitation from the Philharmonic Society to compose and conduct another, he remarked that the new work "must be capable of stirring the world." In 1885 he wrote to Simrock that it "must be something really worthwhile, for I don't want Brahms's words to me, 'I imagine your next symphony will be quite different from this one' [the D-Major] to go unfulfilled." Meanwhile he had written on the manuscript score: "This main theme occurred to me during the arrival of the ceremonial train from Pest at the National Station in 1884."[11] This train brought 442 Czech and Hungarian patriots for a special event at the National Theater, and their presence in the capital was viewed as a provocative gesture, a symbolic demand for nationhood.

It is of course impossible to explain fully the connection between Dvořák's musical imagination and his patriotic sense, but in light of all the factors listed above it seems clear that he decided on at least two things for the Seventh: that he would write a dramatic symphony, and that he would populate it with nationalist symbols. Most potent of these was the embedding of the Hussite melody in the heart of his main theme as an ominous symbol of national struggle, enhanced by the diminished chord at the end of the phrase (Ex. 10.10). Whatever else is true for the symphony, it is somehow concerned with struggle; all the musical metaphors for battle are there, including the darkened military key, the accumulation of short- and long-term dissonance, the quasi-military fanfares. The power of this music, of course, is that we do not really need to know much about the nature of the struggle to configure it as such, and to adapt it to our own terms.

EXAMPLE 10.10. Dvořák, Seventh Symphony, movt. 1, mm. 1–6

The second movement is a quasi-pastoral chorale, continually interrupted by a series of deeply moving recitative queries that recollect the instability and passion of the first movement (Ex. 10.11a–b). Three of the

EXAMPLE 10.11. Dvořák, Seventh Symphony, movt. 2
a. mm. 1–4

b. mm. 18–21

c. mm. 32–33

four movements in the traditional symphony have what might be considered a normal range of formal shapes. Not so for slow movements, which can take almost any form without being thought anomalous. This *poco adagio* is filled with brilliant incidental detail, rich outpourings of texture that elude conventional formal molds, appearing and slipping away—as in the passage for horn and winds beginning at measure 32 (Ex. 10.11c).

The scherzo is one of Dvořák's great achievements, pitting a staccato descending subject against a legato countersubject in sequential opposition (Ex. 10.12a). No movement tries harder to accentuate the *furiant* hemiola rhythm, such that depending on the placement and dynamics the same material can seem either delicately elfin or brutal. It has even been suggested that the battle between the two themes is a staged brawl between a *furiant* and a waltz, that is, between the Czech and Viennese impulses in the composer's artistic personality.[12] The tension is relieved (but

EXAMPLE 10.12. Dvořák, Seventh Symphony, movt. 3
a. mm. 1–8

(*continued*)

b. mm. 167–71

also, of course, ultimately heightened) by a pastoral trio, which, incidentally, is given further shape by an unstable middle section of its own. The transition from the trio back to the scherzo contains a superb but vicious negation of the pastoral (Ex. 10.12b).

The finale is a most mysterious movement in terms of affect and intent. It hinges on the amount of tension accumulated by an arching octave leap followed by a semitone descent to the Lydian fourth (Ex. 10.13a). This motive in several forms, including a ghostly variant like something out of the final movement of Berlioz's *Symphonie fantastique*, permeates the entire movement on many levels. It is relieved only by the second subject, undoubtedly a kind of homage to Brahms. The culmination of the work, and the final resolution, occurs only at the very end, when the opening theme becomes a chorale and the C♯ is finally allowed to slip down to C♮ (Ex. 10.13b).

EXAMPLE 10.13. Dvořák, Seventh Symphony, movt. 4
a. mm. 1–4

b. mm. 426–29

Symphony No. 8 in G Major Op. 88

Except for the *New World*, the Symphony in G Major is Dvořák's best-known symphony, though it is a peculiar work wherein departures from the norm constitute the true essence of the music. In program notes for the first performance the composer maintained that he had tried to put his thoughts in a manner different from "the regular and ordinarily used forms."[13] This sounds suspiciously like a statement he made several years later about the *New World*: "The second movement is an Adagio. But it is different from the classic works in this form."[14] In the case of the *New World* he went on to divulge the reason: a program we will consider below. In that case, then, the particularities of the formal treatment are to be taken as effects created by the gravitational pull of the program. While Dvořák divulged no such program for his G Major Symphony, we do have the following from a review in the *Musical Times* of the first English performance of Dvořák's Symphony No. 8: "The *Adagio* is exceedingly original in character and treatment. There is a story connected with it, which, however, the composer keeps to himself, and his audience would gladly know, since it is impossible not to feel that the music tries hard to speak intelligibly of events outside itself."[15]

There are several possible explanations why he did not proffer a program for the G-Major Symphony. First, and least likely, it may not have one. More probably there is a program that he was simply reticent about revealing. One has the impression that what we know about the extramusical associations of Dvořák's works is more a matter of happenstance than anything else. In the case of the *New World* it was the onslaught of the American press that caused him, almost inadvertently, to give away the secrets in the composer's workshop—or some of them. Many writers share our English critic's nagging sense that the Eighth is *about* something and his consequent frustration at not being able to pin it down. But this is not necessarily a drawback. What is true for this work is essentially true for much, perhaps most, other music: we know it's about *something*, but we don't know what.

The form of the first movement is puzzling. Overall it is cast in G major, but a chorale in a modally tinted G minor introduces each of the three main units of the form as a kind of "motto" (Ex. 10.14a). The "main" theme, a bird song played by the flute, is thus somewhat unsettling, for though it is pastoral in tone it has neither the power it would have had as an opening gesture nor the effect of a contrasting subject within a ternary setting. Rather it is ephemeral, seeming more a matter of color than of theme (Ex. 10.14b), and together the two themes form a kind of Czech yin and yang.

The appearance of the motto before the development dulls the sonata by giving the movement a rondo-like feel and weakening the long-range tension. Yet the injection of the minor motto darkens the move-

ment in an affective sense, and if one consequence of this choice is to in-
hibit the sense of a symmetrical and inevitable unfolding of ideas, another is the extraordinary variety of opportunities so provided. Some of
the developmental episodes in the woodwinds are among the finest orchestral writing of the century (Ex. 10.14c).

EXAMPLE 10.14. Dvořák, Eighth Symphony, movt. 1
a. mm. 1–6

The second movement recalls two passages from Dvořák's piano cycle *Poetic Tone Pictures*, written about the same time as the symphony: the
opening gesture reminds us of "The Old Castle," while the C-major middle section resembles the "Serenade," though here rendered with an almost satirical twist. The third movement, *allegretto grazioso*, once again features the juxtaposition of a brooding G-minor waltz and a bright G-major
trio. The gorgeous middle section appears to be a recollection of a fragment from the opera *The Stubborn Lovers*, and the G-minor waltz may be
tied to the charming little piano piece "Grandfather Dances with Grand-
mother," from *Two Pearls*.

The finale recalls the triadic material of the opening movement, as well as its stately character, and proceeds as a series of free variations. The Czech character of the piece is reinforced by opening fanfares that quite clearly contain the notes of the Hussite chorale "Ye Who Are God's Warriors," used so often by Dvořák to evoke the Czech past—fitting indeed for a work that was dedicated to the Czech Academy (Ex. 10.15).

EXAMPLE 10.15. Dvořák, Eighth Symphony, movt. 4, mm. 1–6

Three Overtures Opp. 91, 92, and 93

No works embody more clearly Dvořák's turn to program music than the three overtures written between the completion of the Eighth and Ninth Symphonies. They originally comprised a single large cycle, perhaps intending to rival Smetana's *Ma vlast*. Several years after their composition the composer decided to split them up into three opus numbers, and thus three individual works. Here is his explanation as it appears in a letter to Simrock:

> Originally the overtures had one title only: Nature, Life and Love. But as each overture is a work of its own, I want to change the names as follows: Overture F major, "In Nature" Op. 91, Overture A major, "Carnival" Op. 92, Overture F♯ minor, "Othello" or "Tragic" or even "Eroica"? Or should I leave it just "Overtures"? But still it is to a certain extent program music.[16]

Even as he completed the *New World,* with its compelling mixture of spirituals, Wagner, Czech song, and Native American imagery, he was struggling with other programmatic issues, and also with matters of cyclicity and connection. Taken together, the overtures reveal three significant components of Dvořák's worldview. *In Nature's Realm* seeks to stake its claim in the pantheon of musical pastorals, the style so critically important to Dvořák as he plotted his course through *Rusalka* and the *New World.* *Carnival* is clearly intended to epitomize the national impulse, while *Othello* is a tortured and problematic work, inscrutable, brutal, and complex. That *Othello* and to a certain extent *In Nature's Realm* have been suppressed from the repertoire in favor of the rollicking *Carnival* seems merely a function of our fondness of oversimplifying Dvořák's work.

Symphony No. 9, *From the New World*

In the century since its composition, the *New World* Symphony has received enormous and uninterrupted attention, particularly in the United States. For this reason we shall focus on only two of the many approaches that have been taken to the work: explaining its programmatic sources and exploring its reception. Dvořák was brought to the United States in 1892, for the princely sum of fifteen thousand dollars, to head the National Conservatory in New York City. The energetic and visionary Jeanette Thurber, the founder-benefactor of that institution, made it clear that she wanted him to adopt American idioms in his compositions—in other words, to do for American music that which he had supposedly already done for Czech music. All the evidence suggests that Dvořák, wearing an American mask, composed his symphony as a kind of object lesson for American composers.

It is, at least in part, a program symphony, based on images derived from Longfellow's *Song of Hiawatha*. The middle two movements are definitely based on Longfellow's poem ("It is in reality," said Dvořák of the *adagio*, "a study or a sketch for a longer work, either a cantata or an opera which I propose writing, and which will be based upon Longfellow's 'Hiawatha'"), and some critics have gone beyond this to argue that the entire work is a grand "Hiawatha Symphony."[17] Aside from the scherzo, which seems to have been an attempt to suggest Indian music, the thematic material for the symphony probably came from the songs that Henry Thacker Burleigh, an African-American singer and composer, sang for Dvořák shortly after his arrival in the United States.[18] These several contexts make it clear that the *New World* is a transitional work for its composer, at once his last symphony and his first mature symphonic poem.

It is important to stress at the outset that the *New World* was written almost entirely in New York City before Dvořák had a chance to travel to the wide open spaces of the midwest. Thus, like Borodin's *Steppes of Central Asia* or Copland's *Appalachian Spring*, it is an urban fantasy of imagined open spaces.

The slow introduction may be based on sketch material intended for the composer's setting of "America," which later became the variation movement of the E♭ Quintet for Strings Op. 97. The following allegro molto with its range, scope, and rhythmic character, is meant to suggest something dynamic and bustling. Dvořák claimed to have used two "Americanisms": the "Scotch snap," a strong sharp accent on the first short beat of a measure (Ex. 10.16; at least two scholars believe this to be a versification of the word "Hiawatha"—thus a "hero" motive), and the pentatonic scale. Commentators have long been fond of pointing out that such devices exist amply in Czech folk music and that it would therefore be silly to consider them American. It is truer, however, to say that what is in fact the quite distinctive sound of the American works results from his

EXAMPLE 10.16. Dvořák, Ninth Symphony, movt. 1, mm. 24–27

careful accentuation, isolation, and enhancement of tendencies that had been present in his music from the beginning. E. H. Gombrich reminds us that it is too simple to believe that painters paint what they see: it is more that they see what they paint. What Dvořák did in the *New World* was to harness materials he had already assimilated, a formidable arsenal of styles, to create his musical vision of the United States. Both the motto and the ongoing thematic reminiscences were ways of knitting the literary pictures together into a seemingly "natural" logic.

The musical images of the *largo* were inspired, according to Dvořák, by the section in *The Song of Hiawatha* titled "The Wooing." The language, that of range and space surely meant to evoke the American landscape, is strong on drones and parallel intervals. The opening may well be related to the verses describing the homeward journey of Hiawatha and Minnehaha: "Pleasant was the journey homeward." The C♯-minor interlude—one of the differences from traditional form to which Dvořák alluded in his *New York Herald* interview—may be related to the sickness of Minnehaha, and the passage that follows is surely that of her forest funeral. The C♯-minor transition was meant to represent a "gradual awakening of animal life in the prairie," he said to Henry Krehbiel of the *Daily Tribune*.[19]

In his *Herald* interview Dvořák said that the scherzo represented the place in *Hiawatha* "where the Indians dance," that is, the section following the wooing, titled "Hiawatha's Wedding Feast." Three main events take place at the wedding: a dance, a love song, and a story. The E-minor opening, certainly suggesting the Dance of Pau-Puk-Keewis, gives way to a lyrical passage in E major, a kind of pseudo-trio and another formal anomaly (Ex. 10.17). This is undoubtedly based on the love song of Chibiabos, "Onaway, awake beloved," a passage the composer set once again while trying to complete his "Hiawatha" opera. The C-major trio, with its

EXAMPLE 10.17. Dvořák, Ninth Symphony, movt. 3, mm. 68–71

mysterious trills, probably recalls the story of Iagoo, in which a group of arrogant Indians are changed into birds.

Dvořák only claimed that these two movements were based on *The Song of Hiawatha*, and there is no historical evidence connecting either of the outer movements with the poem. We might explain the lack of connection between the poem and the first movement by suggesting that the composer did not begin to read *Hiawatha* until after the composition of the movement was well underway. But it is difficult to believe that he cast the poem aside after basing both inner movements on it. For this reason there may be a connection between the finale and the chapter "The Hunting of Pau-Puk-Keewis," which begins, "Full of wrath was Hiawatha." A tenuous argument, to be sure, but we must remember with our anonymous English critic that this music seems constantly to reach beyond itself to communicate in tangibilities.

Dvořák's admonition in May 1893 to James Creelman of the *Herald*—one of the fathers of "Yellow Journalism"—that the future of American music should be based on "Negro melodies"[20] created a firestorm in the press. For months before the premiere the papers debated the question of indigenous material, and whether national music could be said to exist at all. The premiere, on 15 December 1893, refocused the debate in dozens more articles in all the major newspapers and music periodicals. Such luminaries as Philip Hale, Henry Krehbiel, and James Huneker crossed swords over whether or not the *New World* was truly American. "All that it is necessary to admit," wrote Krehbiel, "is the one thing for which he has compelled recognition—that there are musical elements in America that lend themselves to beautiful treatment in the higher forms of the art."[21] The acidic Huneker countered: "Dvořák's is an American symphony: is it? Themes from negro melodies; composed by a Bohemian; conducted by a Hungarian and played by Germans in a hall built by a Scotchman. About one third of the audience were Americans and so were the critics. All the rest of it was anything but American— and that is just as it can be."[22]

The composer's last words on the matter, according to his American-born secretary Kovařík, took it all in stride: "So I am an American composer, am I? I was, I am, and I remain a Czech composer. I have only showed them the path they might take—how they should work. But I'm through with that! From this day forward I will write the way I wrote before!"[23]

The *New World* symphony became an instant classic. It was natural to assume that more symphonies would follow from Dvořák's pen. Yet, though he lived another eleven years, he wrote no more works in that genre. Indeed, after completing the cello concerto and two string quartets in 1895, all his music was explicitly programmatic, and there were no more multimovement instrumental works at all.

Dvořák had contemplated a cycle of overtures as early as 1891. On his return from the United States he began a collection of symphonic poems based on the ghoulish legends of the Czech poet K. J. Erben. Of this massive plan only four were finished: *The Wood Dove, The Golden Spinning Wheel, The Noon Witch,* and *The Water Goblin.* These contain Dvořák's most explicit references to the connection between musical events and extra-musical sources. In several cases, he wrote the text over the score, and in a series of letters, particularly to Robert Hirschfeld, articulated the details of the relationship between music and text.[24]

It seems fitting that Dvořák's final orchestral work in 1897 returns to the inscrutability of his earlier programmaticism. Titled *A Hero's Life,* this single-movement work is clearly related to the composer's personal experiences: "Naturally I was thinking more of a champion of the spirit, an artist, and I believe I depicted the hero accurately in the first theme. This theme is full of energy, resolution and power (*molto vivace*)."[25] Like so many hero works of the period, this one contains the death of the hero (another funeral march) and a kind of resurrection or apotheosis. The issue was still the question of linking musical affect with images from outside the world of absolute music. And like Richard Strauss he found the solution in opera, writing in 1904:

> In the last five years I have written nothing but operas. I wanted to devote all my powers, as long as God gives me the health, to the creation of opera. Not, however, out of any vain desire for glory, but because I consider opera the most suitable form for the nation. This music is listened to by the broad masses, whereas when I compose a symphony I might have to wait years for it to be performed. . . . [My publishers] look upon me as a composer of symphonies, and yet I proved to them long years ago that my main bias is toward dramatic creation.[26]

In opera the relationship between music and text, and between music and affect, is acknowledged, conventional, and a trifle simpler. With this discovery he had left the strange and unresolved arena of symphonic music behind.

TABLE 10.2
Dvořák's Orchestral Works

(Titles are given with opus numbers where available. The "B" numbers
correspond to the chronological listing in Jarmil Burghauser's thematic
catalogue.)

Symphony No. 1	B. 9	1865
Symphony No. 2 in B♭ Major Op. 4	B. 12	1865
Tragic Overture Op. 1	B. 16	1870
Symphony No. 3 in E♭ Major Op. 10	B. 34	1873
Symphony No. 4 in D Minor Op. 13	B. 41	1874
Symphonic Poem	B. 44	1874
(Rhapsody No. 1 in A Minor) Op. 14		
Nocturne in B Major Op. 40	B. 47	1882–83
Serenade in E Major Op. 22	B. 52	1875
Symphony No. 5 in F Major Op. 76	B. 54	1875
Symphonic Variations Op. 78	B. 70	1877
Serenade for Wind Instruments Op. 44	B. 77	1878
Slavonic Dances Op. 46	B. 83	1878
Slavonic Rhapsodies Op. 45, Nos. 1–3	B. 86	1878
Slavnosti pochod Op. 54	B. 88	1878?
Czech Suite Op. 39	B. 93	1879
Overture to *Vanda* Op. 25	B. 97	1879
Prague Waltzes	B. 99	1879
Polonaise in E♭	B. 100	1879
Symphony No. 6 in D Major Op. 60	B. 112	1880
Polka, "For the Prague Students" Op. 53a	B. 114	1880
Legends Op. 59	B. 122	1881
Scherzo Capriccioso Op. 66	B. 131	1883
Hussite Overture Op. 67	B. 132	1883
Symphony No. 7 in D Minor Op. 70	B. 141	1885
Slavonic Dances Op. 72	B. 147	1887
Symphony No. 8 in G Major Op. 88	B. 163	1889
In Nature's Realm Op. 91	B. 168	1891
Carnaval Op. 92	B. 169	1891
Othello Op. 93	B. 174	1892
Symphony No. 9 in E Minor Op. 95	B. 178	1893
(*From the New World*)		
Suite in A Major Op. 98b	B. 190	1895
The Water Goblin Op. 107	B. 195	1896
The Noon Witch Op. 108	B. 196	1896
The Golden Spinning Wheel Op. 109	B. 197	1896
The Wild Dove Op. 110	B. 198	1896
A Hero's Life Op. 111	B. 199	1897

Notes

1. The Pavlovské vrchy ("Pavlovsky range") is a low ridge of limestone hills in southern Moravia. They are barren and rocky and thus quite unusual in the Czech lands. A series of legends is associated with the varied rock shapes.

2. Dvořák's passion for Wagner is easy to document, in both his words and his compositions. The most important early contact with Wagner came on 8 February 1863, when the composer appeared in person to conduct a program of his own works, some completely unknown in Prague. The program consisted of *A Faust Overture*, Entry of the Mastersingers and Pogner's Address; the *Meistersinger* and *Tristan* preludes, Siegmund's Love Song, and the overture to *Tannhäuser*. Dvořák writes: "I had just heard *Die Meistersinger*, and not long before Richard Wagner himself had been in Prague. I was perfectly crazy about him, and recollect following him as he walked along the streets to get a chance now and again of seeing the great little man's face."

3. *Complete Edition of Dvořák's Works*, ser. 3, vol. 2: *Symphony in B♭ Major* (Prague, 1959), xiii–xvi.

4. *Complete Edition of Dvořák's Works*.

5. For a discussion of the genesis of this work, see Frantisk Bartos's introduction and commentary to the Fourth Symphony in the Supraphon edition. (Prague, 1981).

6. In his memoirs, Jan Josef Kovařík recalled the following: "One day the Master asserted that the best of Wagner's operas was 'Tannhäuser'—with this Seidl did not agree, and it gave rise to a long debate, which did not finish that day." Only fragments of Kovařík's recollections have been published, although many passages appear in Otakar Šourek's *Dvořák: Letters and Reminiscences* (Prague, 1954).

7. I have tried to deal with the issue of Dvořák's "Czech" style in "The Master's Little Joke: Dvořák and the Mask of Nation," in *Dvořák and His World* (Princeton, 1993), 134–54.

8. Otakar Šourek, *The Orchestral Works of Antonín Dvořák* (Prague, 1957), 79.

9. Letter to Simrock, 20 November 1879, in Dvořák, *Korespondence a dokumenty* (Correspondence and documents), ed. Milan Kuna, 3 vols. (Prague, 1987–89), 1:185.

10. Donald Francis Tovey, *Essays in Musical Analysis*, vol. 2 (London, 1956), 94.

11. Letter to Antonín Rus, 22 December 1884, *Korespondence* 1:460; letter to Simrock, February 1885, ibid. 2:23; cited in the Complete Edition, ser. 3, vol. 7, 226.

12. This was suggested in an unpublished paper by Garry Zeigler (Washington University, 1991).

13. From Knittl's introduction to the program of the thirteenth popular concert of the Umělecká Beseda in Prague; Šourek, *Život a dílo Antonína Dvořáka* (The life and work of Antonín Dvořák), 3d ed. (Prague, 1954–57), 2:32.

14. From an unsigned interview-article in the *New York Herald*, 15 December 1893.

15. *Musical Times*, 1 May 1890, 279.

16. Letter to Simrock, 4 November 1893, *Korespondence* 3:219.

17. See James Hepokoski, "Culture Clash," *Musical Times* 124 (1993): 685–88; and especially Robert Winter's lengthy discussion in his CD-ROM disc *Antonín Dvořák: Symphony No. 9, "From the New World."* "It is in reality": *New York Herald*, 15 December 1893.

18. We know, from several sources, that Burleigh sang "spirituals" for Dvořák, although we do not know precisely when. There is no doubt that the third main theme of the first movement is based on "Swing Low, Sweet Chariot." It is my belief that the *largo* is similarly based on "Steal Away," and the finale is related to the song "Don't Be Weary Traveler," all of which can be found in Harry Burleigh's published arrangements of spirituals. See *The Spirituals of Harry Thacker Burleigh* (Miami, 1984).

19. Henry Krehbiel, "Dr. Dvořák's American Symphony," *New York Daily Tribune*, 15 December 1893.

20. From 21 May, with the publication of "Real Value of Negro Melodies" in the *New York Herald*, there were at least ten different articles about this matter. See my "On the Real Value of Yellow Journalism: James Creelman and Antonín Dvořák," *Musical Quarterly* (1993): 749–68.

21. In the *New York Daily Tribune*, 17 December 1893.

22. James Huneker, "The Second Philharmonic Concert: Dvořák's New Symphony," *Musical Courier*, 20 December 1893.

23. From an undated communication titled "Poznamky ku vaš stati 'Américka tvorba Antonína Dvořáka'" (notes for your study "The American works of Antonín Dvořák"), 2.

24. In an unpublished paper, Paul Bertagnolli argues that almost all the quotations from Tannhäuser suggest that Wagner himself may be the hero. Further, see John Clapham, "Dvořák's Unknown Letters on his Symphonic Poems," *Music and Letters* 66 (1975): 277–87.

25. Ibid., 286.

26. Interview in *Die Reichswehr*, Vienna, 1 March 1904.

Selected Bibliography

Abraham, Gerald. *100 Years of Music.* Chicago, 1964.

Bernstein, Leonard. *The Infinite Variety of Music.* New York, 1966.

Beckerman, Michael. *Dvořák and His World.* Princeton, NJ, 1993.

Clapham, John. *Dvořák.* New York, 1979.

———. *Antonín Dvořák: Musician and Craftsman.* London, 1966.

Döge, Klaus. *Dvořák.* Mainz, 1991.

Dvořák, Antonín. *Korespondence a dokumenty* (Correspondence and documents). Ed. Milan Kuna. 3 vols. Prague, 1987, 1988, 1989.

Layton, Robert. *Dvořák's Symphonies and Concertos.* Seattle, 1978.

Robertson, Alec. *Dvořák.* London, 1964.

Šourek, Otakar. *Antonín Dvořák: Letters and Reminiscences.* Prague, 1954.

———. *The Orchestral Works of Antonín Dvořák.* Prague, 195?.

———. *Život a dílo Antonína Dvořáka* (The life and work of Antonín Dvořák). 4 vols. 3d ed. Prague, 1954–57.

Sychra, Antonín. *Estetika Dvořákovy symfonické tvorby* (The aesthetic of Dvořák's symphonic works). Prague, 1959. Published in German as *Antonín Dvořák: Zur Ästhetik seines sinfonischen Schaffens.* Leipzig, 1973.

Tibbetts, John C. *Dvořák in America.* Portland, OR, 1993.

Tovey, Donald Francis. *Essays in Musical Analysis.* Vol 2. London, 1946.

Winter, Robert. *Antonín Dvořák: Symphony No. 9, "From the New World."* Voyager CD-ROM, 1994.

CHAPTER ELEVEN

Tchaikovsky

Joseph C. Kraus

When visitors enter the large living and work room of Pyotr Ilyich Tchaikovsky, carefully preserved at the Tchaikovsky State House–Museum in Klin, their attention is drawn to two large portraits that dominate the walls filled with photographs of family and friends. On one wall there stands directly in the center a large picture of Tchaikovsky's father, Ilya Petrovich; opposite in the same relative position is as large a portrait of Anton Rubinstein, under whom Tchaikovsky studied composition at the St. Petersburg Conservatory.[1] The dichotomy presented by these two figures—one the composer's birth father, the other his "musical" father—offers us an apt metaphor embodying the essence of Tchaikovsky's symphonism, and its basic problem: a conflict between personal, lyrical expression (represented by his father, a boundlessly warm and personable individual) and loyalty to the demands of the Germanic symphonic tradition (espoused by Rubinstein, the champion of Beethoven, Schumann, and Mendelssohn in Russia).

For Tchaikovsky, the concept of symphony as an abstract, impersonal genre was simply an impossibility. In a famous letter to Sergei Taneyev written in defense of his Fourth, he describes the symphony as "the most lyrical of all musical forms," an expression of the soul's emotions "for which there are no words."[2] In this sense the symphony differed from the symphonic poem only in that it lacked a specific literary reference, its expression instead involving a series of deeply felt emotions (Schumann's *Seelenszustände*).[3] Tchaikovsky's gift for creating deeply affective musical material, particularly with respect to melody, can be traced to his early musical formation, when, as a young child, he was exposed to the arias of Bellini and Donizetti, as well as the complete score of Mozart's *Don Giovanni*. A steady diet of Italian and French opera in the 1860s solidified his sense of the musically dramatic, as well as the musically elegant. On the other hand, his training at the St. Petersburg Conservatory in the early 1860s under the theorist Nicholas Zaremba and pianist/composer Anton Rubinstein (both staunchly conservative Germanophiles) instilled in the young Pyotr Ilyich a sense of duty to the tenets of strict counterpoint and "organic" form, the latter of which presented him with substantial difficulties. In discussing his orchestral works up to the Second Symphony, the noted critic Herman Laroche summarized the problem: "This lack of wholeness, this method of composing big musical works from heterogeneous parts not in harmony with each other has until recently constituted the most serious and profound ailment in Mr. Tchaikovsky's music. It appears that he was able to cope with all other technical difficulties, but mastery of form persistently eluded him."[4]

Later, in 1878, Tchaikovsky admitted to a "lack of organic continuity in the sequence of the separate episodes" and predicted that his works would never be "models of form," since this strength was not a natural part of his "musical organism."[5] With respect to Tchaikovsky's symphonic first movements, two basic weaknesses in the sonata-form construction may be cited. First, the composer consistently fashions the first theme group as a small ternary form, in order to obviate the need for an organically conceived transition to the second group; following statement–contrast–dramatic restatement of theme 1, a brief link (sometimes as short as four measures) leads directly to the second half of the exposition.[6] Second, in an attempt to conceive an "organic" continuation of the material, Tchaikovsky often resorts to rather pedantic contrapuntal writing within his development sections, perhaps using Schumann as a model.[7]

The difficulty with a fully organic conception in Tchaikovsky's symphonies may also be traced to his method of inventing musical material. Unlike most of his contemporaries, Tchaikovsky often turned to established stereotypes when fashioning a musical theme. This conventional material—whether a march, waltz, or polonaise from Western sources, or a Russian song or dance tune—was often static and did not easily submit to continuous development. In particular, the inner repetitions characteristic of much folk music render any further development all but impossible; only some type of variation of the whole tune is practicable. Likewise, the expansive, lyrical melodies that originate from Western operatic stereotypes resist any sort of continuous development. Paradoxically, Tchaikovsky's reliance on conventional material resonates more closely with the compositional spirit of the late eighteenth century, when composers valued what could be done with the material (*ars*) more highly than the originality of the material itself (*ingenium*).[8] Hence, we encounter in the symphonies of Tchaikovsky a complex of conflicts among the Romantic need for self-expression, the confinement of Classical forms, and the composer's somewhat anachronistic approach to musical invention. The playing out of these conflicts, with its attendant successes as well as failures, embraces the essence of his symphonism.

The Early Symphonies

Although the First Symphony Op. 13 was completed in 1866, its compositional roots extend back for several years, to Tchaikovsky's days as a student in St. Petersburg. It was during this time that we encounter the only prior attempt to compose a major orchestral work—*The Storm*, an overture completed in the summer of 1864. Not only did Tchaikovsky borrow thematic material from this piece for the First Symphony (the second theme of *The Storm* serving as the main material for the slow movement of the First), but he also established a basic working principle that he would use in the First Symphony and throughout his career: though he originally conceived of the overture as a programmatic symphonic poem based on Ostrovsky's play of 1860, he later modified the program so the movement would conform to the sonata-form schema. This hybridization of symphonic poem and abstract symphony became typical of Tchaikovsky's approach and is readily apparent in the First Symphony. Its vaguely extramusical title, *Winter Daydreams*, suggests a mild programmaticism modeled on Beethoven's *Pastoral* Symphony or on one of Mendelssohn's "landscape" essays. In fact, while Tchaikovsky was working on the symphony in the summer of 1866, he would entertain relatives and friends by playing through Mendelssohn's "Italian" Symphony at the keyboard. The opening of Symphony No. 1 (Ex. 11.1) does display a delicacy of texture not unlike the beginning of the *Hebrides* Overture, with its shimmering string tremolandos providing the barest of backgrounds for a repetitive opening motive in solo woodwinds.

The opening thematic material itself, however, is not Mendelssohnian; rather, it bespeaks influence from another quarter—the Russian folk music that Tchaikovsky first experienced as a child in Votkinsk in the Urals. In Ex. 11.1, note the characteristic emphasis on the "plagal" perfect fourth between scale steps 1 and 4 (marked by brackets); musically, this "plagal cell" may emphasize 4 as upper neighbor to 3 (mm. 6–7) or may feature a direct leap between 1 and 4, with a gap-filling motion by step in the opposite direction (mm. 9–10). Tchaikovsky's treatment of this folklike material is also typical, particularly with respect to manipulation of the phrase rhythm (bar groupings), as shown by the numbers printed between the staves.[9]

Notice that in the first phrase (mm. 5–8) the idea has been regularized to a "Western" length of four bars by the extension of the final tone in measure 8. Immediately, however, the composer begins to play with the

EXAMPLE 11.1. Tchaikovsky, Symphony No. 1 ("Winter Daydreams"), movt. 1, mm. 5–73

(*continued*)

49 - 57
similar to
40 - 48

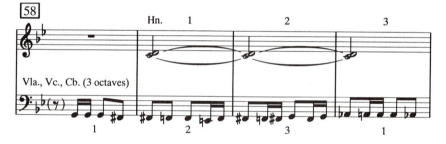

Hn.

Vla., Vc., Cb. (3 octaves)

f#°7- - - - - - - - - - - - - - - - - -> Fdom.7

Vn.

(etc.)

Bb

phrase length by repeating the plagal cell from measure 11 in measure 12, thus expanding the second phrase to five bars.[10] An expansion also occurs in the next unit of six bars, as time is given for the string tremolos to shift up an octave in measures 17–18. When the first theme is treated in sequence in measures 29–37, the original four-bar unit is now compressed to three bars, as shown; even the G minor $^6_4$ at measure 37 is "clipped short" to continue the three-bar groups. (Note also the inverted German sixth, a Tchaikovskian harmonic stereotype, in measure 36; the brief reference to this sonority—which may also be interpreted enharmonically as a dominant seventh of the previous Neapolitan chord—prepares for its more dramatic use later, as it ushers in the restatement of the opening theme, *fortissimo*.)

The accompanying motive introduced at measure 40 illustrates Tchaikovsky's penchant for adding decorative counterpoint to the main thematic material, and also provides another example of his compositional play with phrase rhythm: measures 40–49 (presenting the accompanimental motive) divide into 4 + 3 + 3. While the three-bar units continue in the lower strings in measures 58–63, Tchaikovsky adds to the texture horn dyads that also articulate three-bar groups—though one measure later than the lower strings. This "hypermetrical dissonance" is rectified at measure 67 by the inclusion of a fourth bar in the lower stratum. The expansion of the previous normative three-bar unit also provides a harmonic turning point, the f♯°7 of measures 64–66 being transformed into F7 to prepare for the next principal statement of the theme in B♭ major in measure 68. The violins' presentation of the theme presents three-bar units, as first suggested by the sequence beginning in measure 29, and in direct opposition to the opening woodwind phrases.

The compositional play between three- and four-bar units, as well as the general flexibility of the phrase rhythm heard in this example, constitutes one of the important ways in which Tchaikovsky "plays" with conventional material in his symphonic compositions. Moreover, this play is not unlike the musical wit found in the works of such Classical composers as Haydn and Mozart.[11] In this respect, at least, Tchaikovsky may be considered a "Classical" composer in the Mozart tradition, an attribution that no doubt would have pleased him greatly, considering his veneration of the Viennese composer.[12]

The remainder of the first movement of the symphony is equally superb. The second theme group, in the dominant, was completely rewritten in 1874 for the published version of the work. Though the original has a closer motivic connection to the first theme (whose rhythm now appears as an accompanying bass line), the later version is more melodious and memorable; interestingly enough, both versions emphasize three-bar groups, the norm eventually established for the folklike first theme. Tchaikovsky calls on a wide variety of contrapuntal procedures in the development section, superimposing fragments derived from theme 1 and the suffix of theme 2 (which had not been changed in the 1874 revision). A flexible phrase rhythm prevents the large-scale sequences from becoming too predictable, thus avoiding a stodgy, learned effect. Since the beginning of the 1866 coda made use of the original second subject, this passage was revised in the final version by retaining the original bass (the accompanimental motive from Ex. 11.1) and substituting the new theme 2 in the upper voices, adjusting certain intervals to fit its new surroundings. The accompanimental motive in the bass also closes the movement, its successive fragmentation into silence providing a fitting counterweight to the gradual building of the texture witnessed at the beginning of the movement.

The two inner movements of the First Symphony met with the approval of Tchaikovsky's former teachers, Rubinstein and Zaremba, and were first performed together at a concert sponsored by the Russian Musical Society in St. Petersburg on 23 February 1867. The programmatic title "Land of Mists, Land of Gloom" for movement 2 should not be taken too seriously, for the first portion of the lyrical main theme had already appeared in the second theme group of *The Storm*, composed two years earlier. The continuation of the theme (in solo oboe) is more Russian in nature, abounding in the plagal cells and inner repetition already seen in the folklike opening of the first movement. The scherzo also borrows from preexistent material, this time the third movement of the aborted Piano Sonata in C♯ Minor from 1865. In addition to transposing the piece downward to C minor (iv of the main tonality, G minor), Tchaikovsky added a four-bar introduction that contains displaced bar-line effects and hemiola, two of the principal types of metrical dissonance featured in the scherzo proper. Although the lightness of this scherzo reminds some commentators of Mendelssohn, the extensive use of displaced hemiola (1–2–3 | 1–2–3) in section A and shifted bar lines in section B calls to mind Schumann's *Carnaval*, a piece undoubtedly played many times by Anton Rubinstein, Tchaikovsky's mentor.[13] A waltz in E♭ newly composed for the symphony functions as the trio. Its melody in string octaves, given harmonic support by the woodwinds, establishes a combination often used in Tchaikovsky's waltzes for orchestra. The stereotypical emphasis on tonic and dominant in the first part is relieved by a tonicization of the mediant (G minor) via its own supertonic seventh and dominant; the sixteen-bar prolongation of the A half-diminished $^6_5$ in mm. 150–65 recalls Tchaikovsky's fondness for the ii$^6_5$ in his exercises at the Conservatory.

With the finale of Op. 13 we encounter the first example of what Preston Stedman labels the "Russian festive finale."[14] The folk song "Raspashu li ya mlada, mladeshenka" serves as the seed for the entire movement. In the slow introduction it is stated numerous times in G minor against a constantly changing accompaniment of descending and ascending lines, a technique pioneered by Glinka in his *Kamarinskaya* scherzo for orchestra of 1848. A transition to the main *allegro maestoso* is accomplished through an increase in tempo (m. 47), with a restatement of the folk song in tonic major. As the tempo accelerates further, Tchaikovsky isolates the D–E–D upper-neighbor pattern emphasized in the folk tune, using it as a motivic link to the first theme of the sonata form, which features the same upper neighbor pattern, as a motivic parallelism (D–[B–G]–E–D, mm. 66–67, 68–69); the descending fourth from D to A in measures 71 and 73 is also easily traceable to the opening two measures of the folk tune.

The smooth evolution from slow introduction to fast first theme has clear precedents in Schubert (the "Great") and Schumann (the "Spring"). Theme 2 (in the unconventional key of B minor) brings back the folk song, in a rigorous setting. After this fine beginning, the movement bogs down in the development section, due to the heavy-handed and painfully regular fugato on the folk song in measures 181–200. Tchaikovsky attempts to provide some relief by an emphasis of five-bar units in the following fugato on theme 1 and its suffix (see particularly mm. 213ff.), but the expansion of the four-bar prototype by a diminution of the second half of the unit is rather contrived. Indeed, the incorporation of the folk tune into the "Germanic" sonata form is not completely successful, with form and content somewhat at odds with one another. The flexibility of technique found in the first movement is perhaps Tchaikovsky's signal achievement in the First Symphony.

Symphony No. 2 in C Minor (1872) is Tchaikovsky's finest essay in nationalism, written at a time when the influence of the *Kuchka* (in the person of Mily Balakirev) was at its strongest.[15] Sketched during a pleasant summer spent with relatives and friends in the Russian countryside, the *Little Russian* (so named because of its use of folk tunes from the Ukraine—"Little Russia") received immediate praise, particularly for its final movement, a set of variations on the song "Zhuravel" (The crane).[16] A folk song also dominates the opening movement: "Vniz po matushke po Volge" (Down along Mother Volga) is presented in its original form, with all of its implied metrical irregularities, in the slow introduction, and is subjected to several different harmonizations and textures, in the style of Glinka. Although the first and second themes of the original *allegro commodo* exude an intensely serious emotionalism not connected with folk music, Tchaikovsky ties these materials to the slow introduction in several subtle ways. For example, themes 1 and 2 share the scale-degree pattern ♯1–2–5, an allusion to the "Russian" perfect fourth between 5 and 2 emphasized in the first measure of the folk melody.[17] Moreover, the choice of A♭ major (VI) for the second theme reflects the repeated use of A♭ (as upper neighbor to G) in the final unit of the opening folk song. "Mother Volga" returns literally to close the exposition, is treated contrapuntally in the development, ushers in the recapitulation, and fades into the distance to round off the coda—in short, this folk song is in every way an integral part of the first movement.[18]

Unfortunately, this is not the case in Tchaikovsky's later revision, dating from 1879. Responding to criticism that the opening movement was too long, lacking economy of form and material, the composer fashioned an entirely new first theme with a short, concise motive dutifully modeled after Beethoven. The original theme 1 was adapted to become the new theme 2, with the addition of a string obbligato. The resulting contrast between motivic and lyrical themes for areas 1 and 2 of the exposition produced formal clarity, but the delicate relationship between introduction and exposition discussed above was completely obliterated. Furthermore, the composer eliminated the statements of the folk tune at the end of the exposition and the beginning of the recapitulation, further damaging the knit of the first version.

The loss of the original theme 2, with its harmonic restlessness, is keenly felt, particularly because it contains several beautiful illustrations of Tchaikovsky's use of chromatic harmony. One such passage is provided in harmonic reduction in Ex. 11.2. A brief development of the initial statement in A♭, this music contains passing references to several chromatic third-related keys, C major (III) at measures 134–36, and B major (enharmonic ♭III) at measures 136–37. The most interesting and characteristic aspect, however, is the bass line, which descends chromatically through two octaves to give overall direction to the excerpt. Note the extensive use of contrary motion in measures 138–42, with several voice exchanges (marked by crisscross lines); this typical Tchaikovskian device prolongs b♯°7, respelled as a°7 at measure 139. The enharmonic reinterpretation is suggestive, for if the b♯ °⁶₅ in the previous measure is similarly respelled (see the lower system of the example), we can recognize its function as a common-tone diminished seventh chord embellishing the structural dominant.[19] Tchaikovsky creatively employs two different nineteenth-century harmonic stereotypes to shape this passage, each on a different level of structure: V–(ct°7)–V explains the basic plan, while chromaticism in contrary motion (a favorite of Schubert, among others)[20] enlivens the musical surface at the rapid-fire speed so characteristic of his chromatic patches.[21]

In addition to borrowing from external sources, Tchaikovsky borrows from himself in the second movement of the symphony. The wedding march from act 3 of his rejected opera *Undine* (1869) supplies the refrain for an unpretentious seven-part rondo form in E♭ major. The understatement of the march stereotype (accomplished by delicate combinations of woodwinds and solo timpani) can be explained by the theme's original association with a water spirit; though "simple and attractive,"[22] its square phrase rhythm does not suggest any "play" with received military conventions. This is not the case with the middle (C) section, based on another Ukrainian tune, "My Spinning Wheel."[23] After initial statements in C minor (with characteristic fourth leaps), a nine-bar extension in measures 89–97 expresses the voice leading pattern A♭⁵ – +⁵ – ⁶ – +⁶,

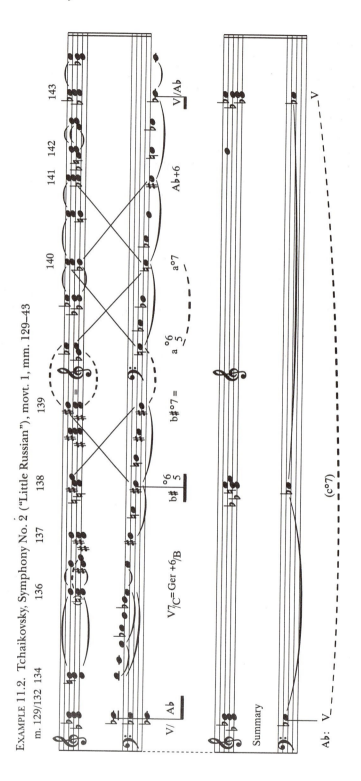

EXAMPLE 11.2. Tchaikovsky, Symphony No. 2 ("Little Russian"), movt. 1, mm. 129–43

postponing the arrival of the dominant (G) and building tension toward a climactic return of the folk tune. This stretching of the phrase rhythm imparts a heightened dramatic meaning to the tune upon its return, and again demonstrates Tchaikovsky's manipulation of bar groupings to alter the signification of conventional material.

Such compositional play comes to center stage in the scherzo, where the composer regularly combines $\frac{3}{8}$ bars into groupings of three and six, fashioning a regular triple (rather than duple) hypermeter. In the second reprise of the binary structure Tchaikovsky adds fragmentary woodwind commentary in decorative counterpoint, producing a rapid yet delicate interplay between winds and strings reminiscent of the "Queen Mab" Scherzo of Berlioz.[24] In measures 91–96 he even manages to "nest" hemiolas at two different metrical levels: the six-bar phrase divides 2 + 2 + 2 (instead of the now-expected 3 + 3), and each two-bar unit divides into 2 + 2 + 2 eighth notes, contradicting the $\frac{3}{8}$ time signature. The following trio in $\frac{2}{8}$ continues the emphasis on threes and sixes, as a "rustic" woodwind choir announces regular six-bar phrases. The contrast with the preceding scherzo calls to mind the second movement of Beethoven's Ninth Symphony, a work that Tchaikovsky had come to know well during his student days at the St. Petersburg Conservatory.[25]

With the C-major finale of the Second we witness Tchaikovsky's most substantial accomplishment in nationalism. The variations on "The Crane" that comprise the first theme of the sonata form serve as homage to Glinka's *Kamarinskaya*, which Tchaikovsky considered to be a watershed in the development of a Russian symphonic style.[26] Even the repeated cadential phrase at the end of the theme group smacks of Glinka, its bass (C–B♭–A♭–G♭) conjuring up the whole-tone sorcery from certain passages of *Ruslan*. The strange syncopation of theme 2 (in A♭, using the same key relationship as in the original first movement) is soon overcome by further variations on the folk song. The development embraces a curious pastiche of both themes; its seemingly rhapsodic chromatic sequences are actually structured by chains of major thirds (for the treatment of theme 2 in mm. 349–57, D–G♭–B♭) and minor thirds (for the entire development: D♭ (325) – B♭ (357) – G (V, 421 and 477). The spontaneity of the thematic and tonal treatment indicates a Tchaikovsky unfettered by the expectations of the Germanic tradition in this, his most "Russian" symphony.

If the Second Symphony represents Tchaikovsky in his most nationalistic moments, the Third Symphony Op. 29 shows the composer at his most self-consciously Germanic. Written quickly in the summer of 1875, it is the first major work to follow the B♭-Minor Piano Concerto. After Nikolai Rubinstein's vicious attack on the concerto for its awkward piano writing and formal weaknesses in the famous "Christmas Eve incident" of 1874,[27] it is plausible that Tchaikovsky was determined to move forward with respect to "organic" writing in his newest symphony, especially in the first movement. A carefully fashioned evolution may be traced from the funeral march of the slow introduction (with its characteristic descending diminished fourth in the motive F–C♯–D–E–F) through a gradual change of tempo to the *allegro brillante* at measure 80, which, after the initial triadic shape, also features descending fourth and fifth leaps, followed by step motion in the opposite direction.[28] The first four notes of theme 2 in solo oboe, measure 143 (F♯–D–C♯–B, descending), constitute an exact inversion of the first four pitches of theme 1 (D–F♯–G–A, ascending); although theme 2 is more lyrical, its accompaniment continues the military rhythms of the first theme—again promoting continuity. The closing material at measure 198 brings the military convention back to the forefront, "diatonicizing" the falling diminished fourth from the introduction, now a perfect fourth.

All of these procedures smack of Schumann's calculated attempts at such organicism in his First, Second, and Fourth symphonies.[29] Despite the best of intentions, the themes themselves here are so commonplace that the connections between them are of little consequence. This is particularly apparent in the development section, when Tchaikovsky's contrapuntal manipulations of their fragments—often undifferentiated strings of quarter- or eighth-note values—resemble classroom exercises. The colorful chains of major and minor thirds from the finale of the Second give way here to traditional movements through the circle of descending fifths in predictable eight-measure units (e.g., mm. 230–37: G♯–C♯, F♯–B). Although the three-key scheme of the exposition is adroitly handled in the recapitulation (the original D–b–A becoming D–e–D), and the Schumannesque coda (*più mosso*) gallops to a conclusion, one is left wishing for more than mere technique, for "more matter and less art."

With the charming *alla tedesca* (the "extra" movement) Tchaikovsky is again in his own element—an orchestral waltz with leanings toward the Austrian Ländler, despite the German title. Its attractiveness is enhanced by several plays on conventions. First, the opening phrase (mm. 3–6) begins with a chord progression that usually signifies "ending": ii–V–I in B♭ major.[30] Moreover, by beginning on the second beat of the $\frac{3}{4}$ measure and regularly articulating pairs of quarters, Tchaikovsky indulges in a displaced hemiola pattern that pokes fun at simple triple meter. After a contrast, he plays further with the hemiola, providing bass reinforcement at measure 70, compressing a sequential unit from two measures (mm. 74–75 and 76–77) to one (78), and inserting two extra measures (mm. 79–80). The opening phrase then returns to fulfill its proper function as a cadence. Although the delicate woodwind chords in triplets in the trio may remind some of a Mendelssohn scherzo, the long stretches of displaced bar lines articulated by these chords invoke Schumann's rhythmic experiments.

The central *andante* movement forms the expressive core of the Third Symphony. Its main theme, in D minor, presents an interesting combination of lyrical operatic style with Russian folk song: measures 1–4 clearly indicate the former, measures 5–8 effect a transition (by introducing triplets and inner repetition of the perfect fourth leap), and measures 9–16 indicate the latter, with many references to plagal melodic cells in triplet rhythm. The contrasting idea, in B♭ major, begins simply enough, but builds to a tremendous climax at measures 50–51 that reiterates G–A♭–G (5–6–5 in the local area of C minor); a similar neighbor pattern (B♭–A, 6–5 in D minor) served as an expressive source in the opening phrase. Although this movement offers a model example of a Classical form—the "slow-movement sonata form" without development section—Tchaikovsky does not sacrifice invention for the sake of formal clarity.

The scoring of the fourth-movement scherzo prompted praise from Balakirev, scorn from Cesar Cui.[31] Written as a perpetuum mobile, its constant sixteenth-note passages (strangely reminiscent of Chopin's "Revolutionary" Etude) are split between first violins and solo woodwinds, using a technique common to Berlioz's overtures. Traces of Glinka may be found in several brief whole-tone passages, as well as in the trio (a march borrowed from Tchaikovsky's Cantata for Peter the Great, 1872), where changing harmonies over a stubborn bass pedal point recall several variations of *Kamarinskaya*.[32] The "studied" approach of the first movement returns in the finale of the symphony, an orchestral polonaise in *tempo di polacca* (the source of the symphony's inappropriate nickname, "Polish"). To the strict seven-part rondo structure Tchaikovsky adds another academic fugal section, producing the form A–B–A–C–fugue–A–B–A. Though formally taut, there is little play on the polonaise convention to produce musical interest, and the specter of Schumann may again be felt in the unnecessary woodwind-string doublings within the main theme. The finest work in the Third Symphony can be heard in its internal movements, where the composer is free from his perceived responsibility to Germanic principles of form and thematic process.

The Later Symphonies

Though work on the Fourth Symphony began less than two years after the completion of the Third, the interim proved to be pivotal for Tchaikovsky, both personally and professionally. In January of 1876 he first heard Bizet's *Carmen*, which affected him deeply, according to his brother Modest. A later letter reveals that Tchaikovsky was captivated by the score's simple grace and charm, and by the plot's emphasis on "destiny, *fatum*"— a concept with which he was becoming more and more preoccupied.[33] The year 1876 also saw Tchaikovsky at Bayreuth for the first complete production of Wagner's *Ring* cycle, which (despite his general disapproval) was to have an influence on his next two orchestral works, *Francesca da*

Rimini and the Fourth Symphony. In 1877 Tchaikovsky suffered the severest emotional crisis of his life when he attempted marriage with Antonina Milyukova, a former Conservatory student who professed her love for him in several letters in early May 1877. Soon after this—and perhaps because of it—Tchaikovsky embraced a suggestion from friends that he compose an opera based on Pushkin's *Eugene Onegin*. He could not help but see the parallel between Tatyana (who professes her love for Onegin in a letter) and Antonina, and he may have interpreted the coincidence as "fateful." From a more practical standpoint, he also viewed the marriage as a way to protect his reputation from the threat of rumors about his homosexuality.[34] The disastrous failure of this union caused him to leave his teaching post at the Moscow Conservatory to become a free agent, with the financial support of his new friend and confidant Madame Nadezhda von Meck.

Although it is convenient to interpret the plot of the Fourth Symphony as an autobiographical account of Tchaikovsky's emotional crisis, the chronology of its inception shows that most of the sketches for the work were completed by early May 1877, before the marriage and its subsequent failure. Rather, it is the more general concept of Fate, with which Tchaikovsky so strongly identified in the case of *Carmen*, that serves as the extramusical basis of the work—Fate as it shapes the destinies of all humankind, not just his own specific destiny.[35] In Fate the composer had found an expressive concept of ample scope for the extended symphonic sonata-form movements; indeed, the irresistable progress of destiny meshes well, in his hands, with the conflict and eventual tonic resolution typical of sonata form. It was Fate, then, that allowed Tchaikovsky to reconcile his need for personal expression with the Germanic structures he had found so problematic in the earlier symphonies.

The opening horn motto of the first movement clearly announces an entirely new phase in Tchaikovsky's symphonism (Ex. 11.3). If we are to believe his private explanation to Madame von Meck (the secret dedicatee of the work), the motto represents Fate itself, and functions as "the seed of the whole symphony."[36] A new compositional maturity can be heard in the horn call's multiple suggestions: while it presents a conventional polonaise rhythm, it also invokes the fateful horn signal from the scherzo of Beethoven's Fifth (movt. 3, mm. 19ff.). The allusion to Siegfried's horn call in measures 3–4 commingles with the Russian plagal cell in measure 4, here used to expand the phrase, thus delaying the climactic c^2 in measure 5. Recalling the spear leitmotiv from the *Ring*, the scalar descent in the low brass in measures 5–6 again extends the phrase, heightening the impact of the bass E in the following bar. The tonal disruption of the first harmonic interval (E/A♭) in measure 7 imparts new menace to the horn fanfare, while the repeated A♭s against constantly changing harmonies (the startling enharmonic E major at mm. 11 and 12, b^{o7} at m. 13, and D♭$^{+6}$ at m. 17) suggest Verdi's dramatic shifts. Though

EXAMPLE 11.3. Tchaikovsky, Symphony No. 4, movt. 1, mm. 1–27

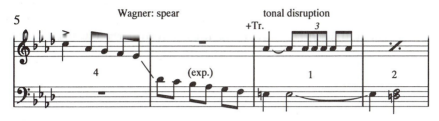

one might question the uncommon spelling of the major sonority in mm. 11 and 12, it is actually the correct one, as mm. 17–20 demonstrate. Shown by arrows on the example, the B♮ is a neighbor-note displacement of C, the E♮ (m. 19) a displacement of F. The gradual resolution of both displacement tones in these bars produces in measure 20 the first clear tonic chord, this harmonic metamorphosis signaling the acceptance of Fate, which forms the next stage in Tchaikovsky's program. The stretching of the material from measure 3 in measures 21–22 again speaks of transformation, with the D♭–C emphasis of measures 23–26 forming the final motivic link to the exposition's first theme, where resignation before Fate is complete. The subtleties of signification, phrase rhythm, and harmony heard in this introduction are as individual a stamp on symphonic writing as one is likely to encounter.

The tonal plan of the first movement is also unique, using a concept last heard in the "freer" development section of the Second Symphony finale—the chain of minor thirds. The three-key exposition (first tried in a more traditional way in the opening movement of the Third) articulates F minor for the first theme (resignation before Fate), A♭ minor—rather than major—for the second theme (the escape into the world of "daydreams"), and C♭/B major for the third theme (the appearance of happiness). The vast enlargement of the exposition over previous first movements allows Tchaikovsky to exercise his considerable melodic gifts more completely and reduces the importance of the development section. The latter, ushered in by the resurgence of the Fate motto and dominated by the *valse triste* syncopations of the first theme, is barely longer than the single theme group on which it is based. Several statements of the motto literally interrupt the development to force a recapitulation of themes 1 and 2 in D minor;[37] the same modulation from the exposition may then reinstate the tonic F major for theme 3. This "vision of happiness" is overturned by the final statement of the motto, which accomplishes the change to minor mode for the coda. In this movement the coda is more than mere extension: after the unorthodox and drastically brief recapitulation of theme 1 in the "wrong" key, the return of this theme in the tonic key in the coda is an absolute necessity, imparting to this final section an added weight that is lacking in the previous symphonies.

Although the slow movement of the Fourth is usually credited with providing lyrical contrast, its technique should not be taken for granted. The main theme in solo oboe intones the tetrachord D♭–C–B♭–A, which connects with the D♭–C upper-neighbor pattern still ringing in the listener's ears from the coda of the previous movement; however, the status of D♭ has changed from unstable upper neighbor to stable third degree of B♭ minor. The folklike fragment in F that forms the basis for the middle section is also shaped by a descending tetrachord, F–E–D–C. By far the most striking passage of the movement occurs in the second strain of the

A section (e.g., mm. 42–49), where the coloristic chordal retrogression A♭–G♭, A♭–e♭ (V–IV, V–ii in D♭) might very well embody the nostalgia that Tchaikovsky describes in his program for Nadezhda von Meck. The novel string pizzicatos of the scherzo (of which the composer was justly proud) are based on the same F–E–D–C tetrachord heard in the central section of the slow movement.

After the great strides in symphonic construction of the first movement, the last movement is bound to disappoint listeners who expect a similar type of architecture. Turning again to variations on a preexistent folk theme, as he did in the last movement of the Second, Tchaikovsky offers a "festive finale" that actually moves a step backward from Symphony No. 2. Instead of using the folk tune ("Vo polye beryozinka stoyala," On the bank a little birch stood) as the primary thematic material, he relegates it to the B sections of a quasi-rondo form (A–B–A–B–A) and "Westernizes" its six-beat phrases by adding two beats of rest;[38] the variations also lack the textural and harmonic range of those based on "The Crane." The extreme sectionalization of the movement, with little (if any) relation between the brilliant style and march conventions of the principal theme and the folk song that follows, identifies with a typically "Russian" episodic treatment of form. While this is perfectly valid in and of itself, it suffers by comparison with the more integrated structure of the first movement. There seems to be little musical motivation for the intrusion of the Fate motto after the second B section, suggesting that this move indeed depends on a program for its justification: "the festive merriment of the people," which is interrupted by "irrepressible *fate*."[39] The innovation of the Fourth Symphony lies not in its finale, but in the high level of synthesis achieved in the opening movement.

By the time of the composition of the Fifth Symphony in the summer of 1888, Tchaikovsky had overcome his personal crisis, establishing his own residence and embarking on a successful international career as composer and conductor. Given the example of the Fourth Symphony, it has been all too easy to interpret the Fifth as another "Fate" symphony, especially since Tchaikovsky sketched a brief literary program for the first movement that again centers on the idea of resignation before Fate or Providence. Recent scholarship has shown, however, that this textual program dates from early in the compositional process (around April of 1888), when he was simply exploring possibilities; a letter written to the Grand Duke Konstantin Konstantinovich at the beginning of June, during the actual drafting of the work, indicates that Tchaikovsky had dropped the idea of a specific program.[40] Nonetheless, the motto that opens the work (and recurs in every movement, in the manner of the programmatic *Manfred* Symphony of 1885) does resonate with the concept of Fate established in the Fourth, and its transformation from lament in E minor to triumphal march in E major in the finale suggests at least a mild programmaticism of the kind seen in the "strife to victory" plot of Beethoven's Fifth.

One of the most interesting features of Tchaikovsky's Fifth Symphony is a purely musical one—its ingenious tonal plan, shown in Ex. 11.4. (White noteheads indicate major keys, black noteheads minor; statements of the motto [M] are also noted.) The symphony's "tonal plot" involves a conflict between E (the main tonic) and D, first presented in the exposition of movement 1; the conflicting key of D major assumes full prominence

EXAMPLE 11.4. Tchaikovsky, Symphony No. 5, tonal plan

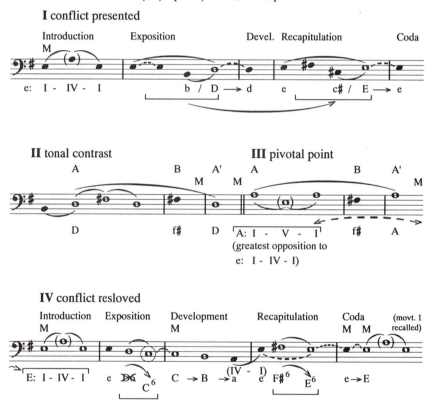

as the principal tonic in the second movement. Although the idea of a polarity between two keys, and its subsequent resolution in favor of the tonic, is a Classical principle, the juxtaposition of keys related by second (rather than third or fifth) is an innovation, and the function of D in the overall scheme is an interesting one. As shown in Ex. 11.4, the overall progression of key areas is E–D–A–E; the A major of the valse can be viewed as a large-scale subdominant, and the D major of the preceding slow movement as IV/IV. The plan I–IV/IV–IV–I emphasizes plagal motions, with the subdominant replacing the dominant on a high structural level. The importance of plagal relationships—a Russian harmonic stereotype—is prepared in the opening movement by repetitions of the progression I–IV–I in both the refrain and first theme group; in addition, the development section of the finale concludes not with the dominant but with the subdominant, articulating a large I–IV–I for exposition, development, and recapitulation. Tchaikovsky further integrates the tonal plan by using F♯ minor for the middle sections of both the second and third movements: as upper third to D and lower third to A, F♯ links these two movements together.

The resolution of the conflict between E and D in favor of the tonic is reinforced by several details of the last movement indicated in Ex. 11.4. The shifting of D down by whole step to C in the exposition weakens the former and introduces the latter as the key for the motto at the beginning of the development. The replacement of the step relation E–D by the third relation E–C is appropriate, since C is lower third to E and upper third to A, the key of the previous movement. Just as the slow movement and the waltz were knit together by a common third relation, so are the waltz and the finale. Whether conscious or not, the tonal architecture of the Fifth Symphony shows a unique blending of the Classical concept of tonal polarity with the cyclic principle of the nineteenth century.[41]

The interplay of motivic ideas in the Fifth, in relation to the expression of emotional states, shows a new subtlety as well. A summary of thematic material is given in Ex. 11.5. Though based on march conventions, both the motto and theme 1 of the first movement manage to overcome their conventional underpinnings through "cross-fertilization" by Russian plagal melodic cells (underscoring scale degree 4 as upper neighbor to 3) and the plagal progression I–IV–I. Pitted against these shapes are the descending fifth leap and ascending sixth of theme 2; the latter reverses the falling sixth from measures 5–6 of the motto, just as theme 2 reverses the darker mood of the opening and brings the exposition to an emotional climax. The positive sentiment associated with the second theme group is brought to full fruition in the next movement's famous horn solo (p. 319); note that after circling around the tonic, this theme also outlines 1–4–3, as in theme 1 of the first movement, but its new major-mode context suggests transformation. The agitation of movement 2's middle section in F♯ minor features the more "negative" descending sixth from the motto; though the motto seems to interrupt the B section at measure 99, Tchaikovsky's choice of an A dominant $^4_2$ at this point actually leads the music back to D major for the return of the horn solo—a subtlety not encountered in the "motto interruptions" of the Fourth Symphony.

In the valse the "negative" falling sixth from the motto also undergoes a transformation, when it is now heard at the beginning of the "positive" principal theme in A major; in fact, the $c♯^2$–e^1 of movement 3 directly contradicts the c^2–e^1 sixth sounded at the conclusion of the motto (movt.

EXAMPLE 11.5. Tchaikovsky, Symphony No. 5, thematic material

(*continued*)

II. Andante cantabile

Moderato con anima

III. Valse

Allegro moderato

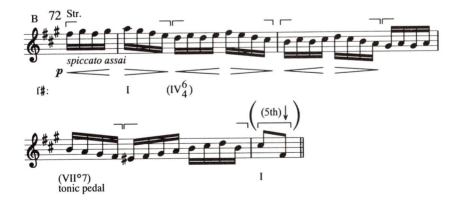

(*continued*)

EXAMPLE 11.5. (*continued*)

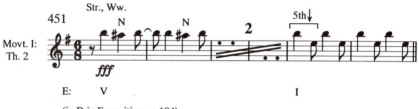

(in D in Exposition, m.194)

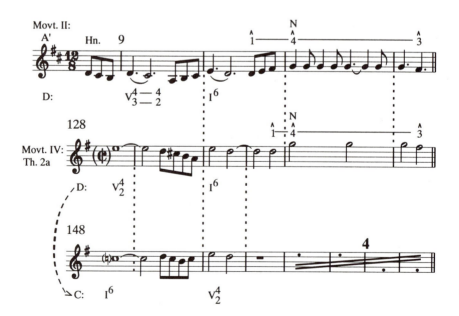

1, mm. 27–30). The polyrhythms of the decorative perpetuum mobile in the central B section (suggesting bars of $\frac{2}{4}$) force a reappraisal of F# minor: though this key is associated with agitation in the previous movement, it now accompanies music that plays lightheartedly with the normal attributes of the perpetuum mobile convention. The motto, now a mere suffix to the structural cadence that closes the movement, has lost its original sixth descent, and is associated for the first time with a major triad, preparing for its more complete transformation at the beginning of the finale. The main theme of the last movement (p. 320) inverts the upper neighbor pattern from movement 1 and recalls a moment of jubilation from the first movement, as shown. Theme 2a, in D major, revisits the 1–4–3 pattern in D from the horn solo of the second movement, but as the tonality shifts downward to C (signaling the demise of D), the 1–4–3 outline is eliminated, paralleling the removal of D as a threat to E in the tonal plan (see Ex. 11.5). The quotation of theme 1 from the first movement in E major (without its original syncopation) provides a final corroboration of the evolution of both tonal plan and "strife to victory" plot in the symphony. It is in this work that Western technique and personal expression are joined together to produce a thoroughly convincing symphonic essay.

The genesis of Symphony No. 6 in B Minor may be traced to May 1891, when Tchaikovsky was returning to Europe after a highly successful American tour. During the sea voyage he sketched a plan for a programmatic symphony entitled *Life!*: "First movement—all impulse, confidence, thirst for activity. Must be short. (Finale *death*—result of collapse.) Second movement love; third disappointment; fourth ends with a dying away (also short)."[42] His first attempt at realizing his intentions was the unfinished Symphony in E♭ Major, sketched in the autumn of 1892 but eventually reworked as the Third Piano Concerto Op. 75, the Andante and Finale Op. 79, and the Scherzo-fantasie Op. 72, No. 10. In February 1893 he again took up the idea of a program symphony, but by this time the program had become more subjective and specifically autobiographical, according to a letter written by the composer to the dedicatee of the symphony, his beloved nephew Vladimir "Bob" Davidov.[43] Tchaikovsky never actually divulged the program, which led to later speculation ranging from portrayals of homosexual despair to a prediction of his own death from cholera (which occurred eight days after the first performance). While these idiosyncratic positions are highly questionable, Tchaikovsky's fear of death (well documented in his correspondence) likely played a role in his conception of the outer movements, and the struggle to overcome that fear can be easily felt in movement 1.[44] The striking *adagio lamentoso* that concludes the work surely carries through the intent of the original program of 1891, with its broadly conceived decrescendo, "dying away" in its final measures. The "Pathetic" Symphony (a title conceived after the fact by

Modest) is indeed about "Life," since life inevitably must confront its own mortality.

Directness of expression and economy of form reach their highest synthesis in the first movement. The opening bassoon solo effectively sets the tone, yet also prepares for the opening motive of the first theme group. The construction of theme 1's antecedent phrase (mm. 20–23, dividing 1 + 1 + 2, a + a' + b) revisits a basic Classical stereotype, but its opening rhythmic gesture evokes Romantic feeling; folk song is also signified (though indirectly) by the varied repetition of the fragmentary first measure and by its narrow range. Though Tchaikovsky follows his well-established habit of casting the first theme group as a small ternary form, a steady textural and dynamic crescendo produces continuity; further, the restatement of the opening idea is in D♯ minor and F♯ minor, rather than the original B minor. Instead of a more conventional rhythmic drive to theme 2, the composer lets the agitated sixteenths from the original idea fade away, reforming themselves into longer note values whose pitches (D–B–A, cellos) clearly prefigure the second theme; the effect of a transition that fades into silence (yet truly prepares what is to come) is a unique solution to a symphonic problem that had plagued the composer from his earliest essays in sonata form.[45]

The motivic nature of the first theme makes it an effective source for contrapuntal manipulation during the brief development section, which includes a solemn chant quotation from the Russian Requiem liturgy in low brass (certainly an indication that the secret program of the work involves the concept of death). The recapitulation again startles the listener by introducing a new and highly dramatic motive for brass between theme 1 and a greatly reduced theme 2; the brief coda later transforms this menacing motive into a calmly resigned one in B major, which also refers to the opening pitch cell of theme 2 (in inversion). The unity achieved in this passage, however, sounds completely natural and unforced, as opposed to early attempts (for example, in the first movement of the Third Symphony).

In the inner movements of Symphony No. 6 Tchaikovsky offers his most innovative plays on the conventions of the waltz and the march. For the famous *allegro con grazia* he cleverly subtracts one beat from every other measure of a waltz to produce $\frac{5}{4}$ meter; in the central section, the use of a D pedal point under shifting harmonies, as well as a strongly repetitive rhythmic figure, recalls folk techniques, now successfully wed to the "higher" world of the ballet. Movement 3 begins as a scherzo in $\frac{12}{8}$, with the march topic (in $\frac{4}{4}$) only gradually emerging in the B sections of its A-B-A-B form. Either idea by itself might have been considered insufficient, but their combination here certainly brings to mind the spirit (if not the letter) of the Classical *Witz*. There is also play in Tchaikovsky's phrasing of the march, where a four-bar prototype is expanded into six by motivic repetition (e.g., mm. 71–76, 81–86, and 91–96).

In the highly original final movement, form gives way to expressive function as the traditional finale conventions are discarded, surely for programmatic reasons. The conflict between the finality of death and humanity's will to live is perfectly reflected in the last movement's primary materials: theme 1, with its parallel dissonant $^4_3$ chords in B minor evoking death's sting (perhaps a reference to the parallel dissonant seventh chords in the first phrase of the Bach chorale "Es ist genug"); and theme 2, with its simple, hymnlike four-bar phrases in D major rising to higher and higher registers. It is interesting that both ideas initially outline perfect-fourth descents (f♯²–c♯² versus d²–a¹), but the latter balances this descending scale by a rise to a² (e.g., mm. 43–45). After a resurgence of the opening, theme 2 also returns, now in B minor, its rising contours removed, and even its descending steps adjusted intervallically to conform to those of theme 1 (B–A–G–F♯, mm. 148–49). This descending Phrygian tetrachord is perfectly expressive of human mortality.

Though the audience at the first performance of the Sixth was perplexed by this finale, listeners at the second hearing—a memorial concert held less than two weeks after the composer's death—grasped its message all too well, jumping to the conclusion that Tchaikovsky had foretold his own death. Other fanciful notions (particularly his supposed suicide and his image as a "tragic soul tormented by his homosexuality") were soon to follow.[46] This is indeed unfortunate, for it has negatively affected critical reception of Tchaikovsky's works, most notably the symphonies, and often clouded our understanding of these compositions. We need to put aside the myths surrounding Tchaikovsky the man and acknowledge Tchaikovsky the symphonic composer—an individual who succeeded in resolving the conflicts between his need for emotional self-expression, his Germanic training, and his Russian roots. Surely, in his last years (which by all accounts were happy and fulfilling ones) Tchaikovsky could look up from his work in the living room at Klin and view the large portraits of both Anton Rubinstein and Ilya Petrovich Tchaikovsky with deep satisfaction.

Notes

1. See, for example, the illustration in John Warrack, *Tchaikovsky* (New York, 1973), 186–87.

2. Letter to Sergei Taneyev dated 27 March/8 April 1878, quoted in David Brown, *Tchaikovsky: A Biographical and Critical Study*, vol. 2: *The Crisis Years (1874–1878)* (London, 1982), 163.

3. See Anthony Newcomb, "Once More 'Between Absolute and Program Music': Schumann's Second Symphony," *19th-Century Music* 7 (1984): 233–34.

4. Herman A. Laroche, "A New Russian Symphony," *Moscow Bulletin*, 7 February 1873, no. 33; trans. and ed. Stuart Campbell, in *Russians on Russian Music, 1830–1880: An Anthology* (Cambridge, 1994), 266. Laroche felt at this time that

the Second Symphony represented a great step forward in solving the problem—an opinion he later repudiated.

5. Letter to Nadezhda von Meck, August 1878, quoted in Brown, *Tchaikovsky* 2:238.

6. Brown provides many useful illustrations of this tendency in *Tchaikovsky;* see, for example, 1:266, ex. 64, where he relates the ternary construction of the first theme group of the Second Symphony (movt. 1) to a similar structure found in the first movement of Beethoven's *Eroica* Symphony.

7. The worst offender here is perhaps the first movement of Symphony No. 3, though similar problems may be found in the opening movement of the Fifth Symphony, for example.

8. See Carl Dahlhaus, "Issues in Composition," in *Between Romanticism and Modernism*, trans. Mary Whittall (Berkeley and Los Angeles, 1980), 40.

9. These groupings of measures are also referred to as hypermeasures: just as beats group into measures, measures group into hypermeasures. For a clear explanation of this topic, see William Rothstein, *Phrase Rhythm in Tonal Music* (New York, 1989).

10. This reiteration of the perfect fourth is also characteristic of the internal construction of Russian folk melodies; see, for example, Warrack, *Tchaikovsky*, 69.

11. For a thought-provoking treatment of this subject, see V. Kofi Agawu, *Playing with Signs: A Semiotic Interpretation of Classical Music* (Princeton, NJ, 1991).

12. See, for example, his letter to Nadezhda von Meck dated 16/28 March 1878, in *"To my best friend": Correspondence between Tchaikovsky and Nadezhda von Meck*, trans. Galina von Meck, ed. Edward Garden and Nigel Gotteri (Oxford, 1993), 219–22.

13. For an exploration of Schumann's rhythmic influence on Tchaikovsky, see my "Analysis and Influence: A Comparison of Rhythmic Structures in the Instrumental Music of Schumann and Tchaikovsky," in *Tchaikovsky: The Centenary Conference* (Metuchen, NJ, forthcoming).

14. Preston Stedman, *The Symphony*, 2d ed. (Englewood Cliffs, NJ, 1992), 161.

15. Recall Balakirev's involvement in the composition of *Romeo and Juliet* in 1869, and in Tchaikovsky's *Fifty Russian Folk Songs* arranged for piano duet, from the same year.

16. Tchaikovsky wrote to Modest that when he played the finale on the piano at the Rimsky-Korsakov's, "the whole company all but tore me to pieces in their enthusiasm." Letter of 13/25 February 1873, quoted in Edward Garden, *Tchaikovsky* (London, 1973), 42. See also Laroche's praise for the finale, in *Russians on Russian Music*, 257–58.

17. The melody also contains the plagal cell 4–1–2–3, already encountered in movts. 1 and 2 of the First Symphony.

18. Garden sees a parallel between this scheme and the formal plan of Balakirev's tone poem *1000 Years*; see *Tchaikovsky*, 41.

19. The a^{o7} at m. 140 is further transformed (by means of chromatic voice exchange) into an inverted augmented sixth chord at m. 141, and connects through semitone voice leading to the structural dominant at m. 143.

20. See, for example, "Der Wegweiser" from Schubert's *Die Winterreise*, analyzed in Aldwell and Schachter, *Harmony and Voice Leading*, 2d ed. (San Diego, 1989), 540–41; or the G-Major String Quartet D. 887, movt. 1.

21. Henry Zajaczkowski discusses Tchaikovsky's harmonic idiom in chapter 3 of *Tchaikovsky's Musical Style* (Ann Arbor, MI, 1987). Though he covers contrary motion on pp. 64–67, his examples are limited to single voice exchanges, and he neglects to explore the broader contexts for such progressions, as I have done in Ex. 11.2.

22. Warrack, *Tchaikovsky*, 70.

23. Tchaikovsky had already harmonized this tune in *Fifty Russian Folksongs*, as No. 6.

24. Tchaikovsky heard Berlioz's *Romeo and Juliet* when the aged French composer visited Russia for the second time in 1867 (Warrack, *Tchaikovsky*, 70). David Brown also cites the scherzo of Borodin's First Symphony as a model for Tchaikovsky's movement (*Tchaikovsky* 1:258–59).

25. He is known to have played the Ninth Symphony (as well as works by Schumann and Glinka) in piano duet arrangements with fellow student Herman Laroche. See Alexander Poznansky, *Tchaikovsky: The Quest for the Inner Man* (New York, 1991), 64.

26. Brown, *Tchaikovsky* 1:265, 267.

27. Herbert Weinstock, *Tchaikovsky* (New York, 1943), 105–06.

28. David Brown demonstrates some aspects of this evolution in *Tchaikovsky* 2:43, ex. 105.

29. In pointing out the Schumann connection, commentators often cite a relationship between Schumann's Third and Tchaikovsky's Third, since both have five movements; Tchaikovsky surely knew of this precedent, since Schumann's Symphony No. 3 was one of his favorites. See Alexandra Orlova, *Tchaikovsky: A Self-Portrait*, trans. R. M. Davison (Oxford, 1990), 83.

30. Agawu discusses this type of rhetorical play in *Playing with Signs*, 56–62.

31. Garden, *Tchaikovsky*, 64–65.

32. See David Brown, *Mikhail Glinka: A Biographical and Critical Study* (London, 1974), 273.

33. Brown, *Tchaikovsky* 2:58–60.

34. Ibid.

35. This principle is essential for a bona fide understanding of the work. For example, Susan McClary's homosexual interpretation (*Feminine Endings* [Minneapolis, 1991], 69–79) may indeed describe a possible experience for some present-day listeners, but it has little bearing on the composer's original conception.

36. See *To My Best Friend*, 183–87, for the complete text of this often quoted letter, dated 17 February/1 March 1878.

37. Compare this function for the motto to the more modest insertions of the folk tune to start development and recapitulation in the Symphony No. 2, movt. 1.

38. Balakirev retains the original phrase lengths in his *Overture on Three Russian Themes*.

39. See Brown, *Tchaikovsky* 2:176.

40. See Donald Seibert, "The Tchaikovsky Fifth: A Symphony without a Program," *Music Review* 51 (1990): 36–45.

41. See my "Tonal Plan and Narrative Plot in Tchaikovsky's Symphony No. 5 in E Minor," *Music Theory Spectrum* 13 (1991): 21–47.

42. N. V. Tumanina, *Chaikovskii: Velikii master (1878–1893)* (Moscow, 1968), 404; quoted in Poznansky, *Tchaikovsky*, 558.

43. Poznansky, *Tchaikovsky*, 558.

44. Brown and others interpret the Sixth as another "Fate" symphony (*Tchaikovsky* 4:450), while Poznansky sees a "conflict between platonic passion and the desires of the flesh" that Tchaikovsky felt for his nephew Bob (*Tchaikovsky*, 559).

45. In the original sketch of this passage Tchaikovsky actually overlapped the transition and second theme; only later did he separate them by rests and add further ascending arpeggiation to the string line.

46. For a complete discussion of the controversy surrounding Tchaikovsky's death, see Brown, *Tchaikovsky* 4:478–85, and Poznansky, *Tchaikovsky*, chapter 30, especially pp. 605–8. Brown accepts Alexandra Orlova's contention that the composer was forced by a court of honor to commit suicide to avoid a homosexual scandal; Poznansky, citing a lack of any hard evidence for such a claim, labels it as a myth transmitted only by persons outside of Tchaikovsky's immediate circle of family and friends.

Selected Bibliography

Brown, David. *Tchaikovsky: A Biographical and Critical Study.* 4 vols. New York, 1978–91.

Cooper, Martin. "The Symphonies." In *The Music of Tchaikovsky,* ed. Gerald Abraham. New York, 1946.

Jackson, Timothy L. "Aspects of Sexuality and Structure in the Later Symphonies of Tchaikovsky." *Music Analysis* 14 (1995): 3–25.

Keldysh, Yuri. "Tchaikovsky's Symphonism and the Evolution of Symphonic Thinking in the Nineteenth Century." *Sovetskaya Muzyka* 1990/12:92–101.

Kholopov, Yuri. "On the System of Musical Forms in the Symphonies of Tchaikovsky." *Sovetskaya Muzyka* 1990/6:38–45.

Kraus, Joseph C. "Tonal Plan and Narrative Plot in Tchaikovsky's Symphony No. 5 in E Minor." *Music Theory Spectrum* (1991): 21–47.

Poznansky, Alexander. *Tchaikovsky: The Quest for the Inner Man.* New York, 1991.

Pribegina, Galina A. "Tchaikovsky's Sixth Symphony (Based on the Manuscript Materials)." In *Iz istorii russkoi i sovetskoi muzyki* (From the history of Russian and Soviet music), vol. 2, ed. Aleksei Kandinskii and Juliya Rozanova. Moscow, 1976.

Seibert, Donald C. "The Tchaikovsky Fifth: A Symphony without a Program." *Music Review* 51 (1990): 36–45.

Tchaikovsky, Modest I. *Zhizn P. I. Chaikovskogo* (The life of P. I. Tchaikovsky). 3 vols. Moscow, 1900–1902. Abridged and trans. Rosa Newmarch in *The Life and Letters of Peter Ilich Tchaikovsky by Modeste Tchaikovsky.* London, 1906.

Tchaikovsky, Pyotr I. *Polnoye sobraniye sochineny: literaturnye proizvidenia i perepiska* (Complete edition: Literary works and correspondence). 17 vols. Moscow, 1953–81.

Vaidman, Polina E. *The Creative Archive of P. I. Tchaikovsky.* Moscow, 1988.

Warrack, John. *Tchaikovsky Symphonies and Concertos.* 2d ed. London, 1974.

Zajaczkowski, Henry. "The Symphonies of Tchaikovsky." Bachelor's thesis, University of Sheffield, England, 1978.

CHAPTER TWELVE

Elgar

James Hepokoski

In the complex discourse network in which the modern European symphony was involved in the decades around 1900 there were no neutral materials. Within any new work, every musical gesture, every combination of timbres, every traditional or unusual structure, every programmatic or aesthetic intention inevitably evoked resonances and comparisons with a now reified, culturally politicized, and largely Germanic canon. By this time the liberal-humanist institution of art music (the cultural apparatus constructing, surrounding, and serving the concept of "Great Music") had crystallized into its characteristic substructures and, arguably, was at the crest of its power and prestige. New symphonic offerings to that institution's local outlets served as commentaries both on its validity and on the values of the circles that sustained it economically and intellectually. Taking seriously such broader, more overtly contextual terms renders any nonproblematized, reductionist overview of any individual piece potentially misleading. This is the central problem that current commentators face in confronting the musical works of this period.

Edward Elgar's two symphonies are a case in point.[1] Completed in 1908 and 1911 (just before the New Music challenges in England began to bite down in earnest),[2] they may be regarded both as the equals of any other European symphonies of the period in quality of construction and richness of content and as two of the last major compositions written before the liberal-humanist consensus began to fall apart. Here it will be possible only to suggest some of the central issues of musical-generic process and structure in the two symphonies. My aim is not to present pocketable "solutions" to these works but rather to encourage a new kind of conversation about them.[3]

As is the case with any formalized public discourse, the two Elgar symphonies are concerned with many things simultaneously. They offer multiple layers of coexisting, contrasting topics that are neither hierarchically arranged nor ultimately resolved. These differing layers are accessible at virtually every moment of music, and this feature renders each musical event multivalent. For our purposes we may identify five topical threads:

1. Elgar's two symphonies thematize the institution of the symphony itself. Like many works of this period, they grapple with the problem of "symphony-ness" in modern times. Thus the composer sought to align their rhetoric with that of the canon of culturally accepted masterpieces and thereby to establish their own position within it. Among the most evident strategies toward this end are the devices of allusion, reference, and the appeal to precedent: Elgar pointedly called attention to "the repertory" by evoking specific works, procedures, or passages of Beethoven, Schumann, Wagner, Brahms, and others. This practice of frequent near-quotation or passing allusion—"intertextuality"—was an essential feature of his expressive world. Among other things, it sought to affirm that world's continued legitimacy in an age of increasingly sharp class and cultural challenge.

2. With regard to large-scale architecture, Elgar made use of several families of "structural deformation."[4] The standard sonata-deformation procedures, which may be found in many nineteenth-century canonic works, were methods of overriding selected defaults of normative pre- and post-*Formenlehre* practice to produce shapes that can no longer profitably be categorized as mere "sonatas." In short, to understand the broad rhetoric of these symphonies is to recognize the expressive potential of the sonata-deformation procedures that Elgar adopted. I shall emphasize three in the discussion below: the introduction-coda frame, the off-tonic sonata, and the nonresolving recapitulation.

3. As nearly every commentator has noted, in 1908 Elgar was concerned with producing the first widely acclaimed, successful English symphony. This helps to account for the self-conscious monumentality of both symphonies. (Their modern, fully "let-out" quality far exceeds in size, scope, and expressive range the symphonies of the Royal College of Music composers, Parry and Stanford.[5]) More than that, though, it suggests that these symphonies are concerned with the political triumph of the performance event itself, the institutional legitimization of a certain cultural stratum of English music, or its coming of age in a discourse network that was emphatically Germanic. The celebrated blessing in 1908 of the First Symphony by no less a personage than its German dedicatee and conductor Hans Richter was of more than anecdotal interest: this was the validation for which Elgar and his English audiences had long yearned.[6]

4. A key feature of Elgar's works is their participation in an apparently elaborate, gamelike code of private meaning. Through sketch evi-

dence and on the basis of the composer's letters and remarks it is clear that numerous individual musical gestures commemorated, symbolized, or recalled personal events, acquaintances (as in the *Enigma*'s "friends pictured within"), specific places, or privately relevant literary allusions. Assembling such tantalizing references and using them as a basis for interpretive speculation has been a favorite sport of Elgarians over the years. At times the references seem to be intimately revealing: the fragmentary evidence suggesting that the Second Symphony, like the Violin Concerto that precedes it, might be (again, among other things) an otherwise unutterable declaration of his love for Alice Stuart-Wortley (whom he called "Windflower") is particularly persuasive.[7]

5. More broadly, the two Elgar symphonies survey the composer's general world vision. That vision ranges widely, from the expansive or boisterous to the desperately conflicted and, further, to the fully interior, intimate, and private. But it is touched throughout by a melancholy awareness of the dreamlike quality and transitoriness of things: ghosts of unsustainability, regret, and loss of innocence lurk everywhere. In this valedictory world the magnificent, *fortissimo* moments of attainment and affirmation seem simultaneously to be melting away, and Elgar often shores up such moments with rises and underswells in unexpected places, as if he were trying to sustain an illusion forever slipping away from his grasp. In such an environment of dissolution, diminuendos and simple descending sequences can take on enormous expressive significance.

First Symphony

Written during a period in which he was championing the concept of "absolute music,"[8] Elgar's First Symphony merits examination from a variety of angles, but none of them will get very far without a knowledge of the work's "main plot," its governing structural and tonal plan. In brief, it is this: a stable framing tonality, A♭ major—suggesting, we may suppose, something like initial wholeness or identity—is made first to encounter (or to initiate) an elaborate chromatic process that swirls negatively around a tonality representing complete otherness, D minor. Then, by degrees through the four movements, A♭ major tries to step "from outside" into that otherness to subdue it and ultimately to absorb it back into itself. The attempt is made but fails in the first movement; the second, third, and fourth movements are played out largely on territory claimable by the forces of D minor: their principal tonics are F♯ minor, D major, and D minor again, although the last movement's sonata deformation is absorbed triumphantly into the A♭ frame near its end. The First Symphony gives us the familiar *per aspera ad astra* musical plot, well known to Elgar's time from Beethoven's Fifth Symphony, Liszt's *Tasso*, Strauss's *Death and*

Transfiguration, and a host of other works. Here, however, it is here given a subtle, double-key twist.

The first movement may be described as a "failed" D-minor sonata set into an A♭ introduction-coda frame. As such, the "sonata" or "inner" portion is in dialogue with the rare sonata-deformation family of the off-tonic sonata, those that are unfolded entirely, or nearly so, in a sonata-governing key that is not the overriding tonic of the movement. Normally, some sort of absorbing gesture into the "true tonic" is made toward the end of such a movement.[9] In this procedure the establishing of the "true tonic" is crucial. Elgar described the A♭ introduction, *andante: nobilmente e semplice,* with its characteristic melody and striding, "English" bass (Ex. 12.1), as "intended to be simple &, in intention, noble & elevating . . . the sort of ideal *call* (in the sense of persuasion, not coercion or

EXAMPLE 12.1. Elgar, Symphony No. 1, movt. 1, mm. 3–9

command) & something above everyday and sordid things."[10] Even when we first encounter it, though, it already seems weighted down in its four flats, instrumental doubling, solemn pace, and referential allusions to the canon. In its hymnic spaciousness and general function the theme seems to recall the introduction-coda frame of the overture to *Tannhäuser,* which (apart from the issue of key) probably served as one of the models for this movement. Yet the Ideal Call seems more specifically to allude to the opening of *Parsifal,* both in its "A♭-ness" and in the pitches from its sixth to its twelfth note.

Filled with arduous tensions, the first movement's inset *allegro* "sonata" is too complex to confront adequately here, but we may note that its exposition moves from a D-minor, but tonally restless, first theme

(Ex. 12.2) through a highly personalized transition into a multivoiced "second theme" in the orthodox III, F major (rehearsal no. 12; its first-violin strand is shown in Ex. 12.3). It then reinvigorates the D-minor tensions of the first theme (in a partially obscured allusion to an expositional repeat that in fact never occurs) and leads to a brief final zone of exposition, centered around a strained, desperately clouded A minor (v, rehearsal no. 17, led by half-diminished seventh, Amfortas-like brass cries, *tutta forza*) that shatters into near-wreckage at the close (*allargando*, then *poco rit.*)

EXAMPLE 12.2. Elgar, Symphony No. 1, movt. 1, 3 mm. after rehearsal no. 5

EXAMPLE 12.3. Elgar, Symphony No. 1, movt. 1, rehearsal no. 12

The struggle is pursued further in the developmental space, although that zone begins quietly with the intrusion of the "external" Ideal Call on C at rehearsal number 18. The recapitulatory space (rehearsal no. 32) reinstates the D-minor first theme, but this time Elgar adjusts the transition to produce the second theme not on the expected D major, but rather on the framing tonality, A♭ (rehearsal no. 38). This potentially redemptive A♭ "from outside" soon decays, however, and the music swerves toward a "lost" F minor for its final zone (rehearsal no. 44). Manifestly *in extremis*, this F minor is immediately subjected to the same sort of wreckage heard earlier at the exposition's close. (The deformation type alluded to here is that of the nonresolving recapitulation, which inevitably signals a sonata in tonal crisis or "sonata failure.")[11] In the coda (rehearsal no. 48, recalling the onset of the developmental space) Elgar invokes the

Ideal Call, now bruised after the loss of the first battle, to peek out in its own A♭, to survey the damage among the ruins, and to prepare for another day.

In the second movement the final section of the five-part, F♯-minor scherzo (with a B♭ trio visited twice) subjects its principal motives to radical deceleration. When the initial sixteenth-note figure (Ex. 12.4a) is sufficiently braked, it becomes the start of the third movement, the D-major *adagio* (Ex. 12.4b; notice, though, the nuanced, half-step deviation from the pattern in Ex. 12.4b, m. 7, and compare it with Ex. 12.4a, m. 4).[12] This is the heart of the symphony, a meditation comparable only to such things as the cavatina from Beethoven's Op. 130 Quartet or the *adagietto* from Mahler's Fifth Symphony. From the standpoint of the D-minor "inner" narrative its D-major tonality would suggest a redemptive endpoint for the work. But just as the D minor is only a subordinate tonic, so this D major, introduced as the cool submediant shadow of F♯ minor, represents only a partial solution to the tonal problem set out in the first movement.[13] In long-range terms the crucial event that occurs here is the inlaying of variants of the Ideal Call theme into the tonally mobile parts of this sonatina (sonata without development). Allusions to the Ideal Call are heard, for example, in the middle voices of the broadly spanned second theme (Ex. 12.5).

While the second theme articulates the standard V (A major) in the exposition, in the otherwise orthodox recapitulatory space (beginning at rehearsal no. 100) it returns in the "wrong" key of C♯ major (rehearsal no. 102, enharmonically more relatable, it would seem, to the A♭ "outer" sphere). Thus Elgar suggests a potential second encounter with a nonresolving recapitulation. Within a few bars, however, the second theme is transformed into a "new theme" that snugly secures D major and is an even more recognizable variant of the Ideal Call. Here the "failed" second theme casts off its cloak to reveal its essence, *molto espressivo e sostenuto* (Ex. 12.6). This celebrated passage, which Elgar associated (apparently in 1908) with the words from the end of *Hamlet*—"The rest is silence"—is the centerpoint of the work.[14] Since this was the passage that he had first sketched—in 1904, in fact, three or four years prior to his sustained work on the piece—we may suppose that he designed much of symphony to lead into it.

The finale unmasks the contingent nature of the preceding D major by shifting back to D minor in its *lento* introduction, by reinstating some of the "struggle" music from the first movement's developmental space (no. 24), by introducing a new theme of external threat (Ex. 12.7)—in fact, it is a negative variant of the Ideal Call (note especially the version in Ex. 12.5)[15]—that will also become the tonally shifting "quasi-military" closing theme of the exposition, and by reinvoking the vulnerable Ideal Call theme (*con sord.*, "last desk only") on two different pitch levels, B♭ and a tentative, unstable A♭. The D-minor *allegro* itself is shaped according to the model of the sonata type so often favored by Brahms in his finales, in

EXAMPLE 12.4. Elgar, Symphony No. 1
a. movt. 2, mm. 5–10

b. movt. 3, mm. 1–12

EXAMPLE 12.5. Elgar, Symphony No. 1, movt. 3, rehearsal no. 96

which a nonrepeated exposition is immediately followed by the onset of the recapitulatory space (here, rehearsal no. 120, also feigning an expositional repeat) that leads into an extensive development and may rejoin the recapitulatory space some time later, as it does here, essentially where it left off from it.[16]

The whole movement, whose second theme (beginning on B♭ at rehearsal no. 114) evokes the parallel section of Brahms's Third Symphony, is a rough-and-tumble, neo-Lisztian battle between the forces of light and dark. At issue is whether and how the three-tiered exposition, [d] / [B♭–(F)] / [unstable d, Ex. 12.7, sequenced through various levels and ultimately dissolving],[17] will be resolved in the recapitulatory space. In fact, the tonally mobile second and third themes are not resolved at all: the Brahmsian second theme returns (rehearsal no. 137) down a major third, [G♭–(C♯)], and the third (rehearsal no. 141) stresses F minor, although it does pass, sequentially, through A♭ (5 mm. after rehearsal no.

EXAMPLE 12.6. Elgar, Symphony No. 1, movt. 3, rehearsal no. 104

Molto espressivo e sostenuto

EXAMPLE 12.7. Elgar, Symphony No. 1, movt. 4, mm. 6–9

141). Once again, more menacingly, we face the problems of the off-tonic sonata and the nonresolving recapitulation. But at this point, again as if "from outside," the Ideal Call, now as deus ex machina, breaks through to "quash" (Elgar's word) the disorder and to absorb the sonata process into its own A♭ *grandioso* identity (rehearsal no. 146).

"There is no programme [to it]," wrote Elgar about a month before its premiere, "beyond a wide experience of human life with a great charity (love) and a *massive* hope for the future."[18] Not victory, then, in the Beethovenian-Lisztian sense, but only hope: this is more modest—and tinged with Elgarian doubt. The sheer stress and trembling of the A♭ "resolution" can leave us with lingering questions about how affirmative this symphony actually is.

Second Symphony

No such extreme tonal plan guides the more orthodox, but no less powerful, Second Symphony of three years later. Instead, this symphony offers riches of an altogether different kind. Here one is faced with a perhaps even more labyrinthine network of thematic interrelationships and motivic cross references among the movements. Moreover, as we know from research into the work's genesis, the thematic material is enticingly suggestive in connotation and encourages multiple interpretations. Singling out two of these, Christopher Kent has concluded that "the symphony was designed to be seen outwardly as the 'loyal tribute' of a subject to his deceased monarch [Edward VII, to whose memory Elgar dedicated the work]; inwardly as the chivalrous adoration of a beautiful woman [Alice Stuart-Wortley] by a sensitive artist."[19]

Further complicating the task of interpreting the work, Elgar headed the published score with the first two lines of an eight-stanza poem of Shelley, "Rarely, rarely, comest thou, / Spirit of Delight!" and suggested in a letter to his publishers that it was the whole poem, an extended song to the experience of loss, that was relevant to "the mood of the Symphony . . . but the music does not illustrate the whole of the poem, neither does the poem entirely elucidate the music."[20] Among the poem's key lines: "Many a weary night and day / 'Tis since thou are fled away. / How shall ever one like me / Win thee back again?" Who or what is this "thou," this "Spirit of Delight," now all but lost in ashen disillusion? Not just one thing, we may suppose, but many. Some of the likeliest candidates, none of which excludes the others, are the innocence, faith, and purity of the "clean" world of youth; the only partially sublimated erotic fantasy of his love for Alice Stuart-Wortley; the once-healthy tradition of the genre of the symphony and the culture for which it had bracingly stood; the exuberant, unproblematic joy that music had brought to the composer in his "'learning' days," before its enchantments had been subjected to the processes of rationalization and marketplace competition.[21]

While each of these could be pursued at length, we should also observe that other layers of meaning coexist with them. The Second also has an encyclopedic quality, as though Elgar had been determined to summarize the history of the symphonic experience itself through both structure and allusions to the canon—and yet to fashion the whole into a work suffused with valediction and farewell to a time of institutional confidence now passing away and no longer unproblematically accessible. Thus the E♭ tonic inescapably summons up the tradition of the *Eroica*, which includes Schumann's "Rhenish," Bruckner's Fourth, and the "modern" recomposition of the *Eroica*, Strauss's *Ein Heldenleben*. The C-minor, ritualistically ennobled Funeral March (movement 2) strengthens the *Eroica* reference—and alludes in passing, perhaps, to the parallel movement in Bruckner.[23] But in its moments of apotheosis (rehearsal nos. 76–77, 85–86) it also self-consciously recalls Siegfried's Funeral March. The dazzling rondo-scherzo (a recomposition of ideas from the "ghost" episode in the first movement's developmental space) more than once conjures up *Till Eulenspiegel*. The echo of Brahms, especially the First and Third Symphonies, resurfaces throughout the work. And so on.

Elgar reinforced this institutional aspect of the Second—its celebration of the institution of art music—in many ingenious ways. We might notice, for instance, the persistent presence and growth of a family of related rhythmic (long-short) and intervallic motives dominating much of the first movement and fully unfurled, one might argue, only in the finale—apparently as the *telos* or goal of the entire symphony. Although some members of the motive family are planted in the opening "Spirit of Delight" motto theme itself, we first encounter the basic idea emphatically in the work's ninth measure, rehearsal number 1 (Ex. 12.8a, first and second violins), where its obsessive long-short alternations have the effect of the launching the symphony proper—a noble prow knifing its way through the symphonic waters. Within five measures the idea is reshaped into an even bolder, characteristically Elgarian melodic contour (Ex. 12.8b). At rehearsal number 5 (Ex. 12.9, which Elgar dubbed the

EXAMPLE 12.8. Elgar, Symphony No. 2, movt. 1
a. mm. 9–10

b. mm. 13–14

EXAMPLE 12.9. Elgar, Symphony No. 2, movt. 1, rehearsal no. 5

"Careggi Allegro," recalling the site of its original conception in Tuscany) it is recast into the shape that most clearly foreshadows its fuller realization in the finale. Here in the first movement these forward-plunging variants often serve as something of a conveyor belt, speeding us to and from the stations of the movement's main thematic events. Nominally continuations or transitions, these forms of the idea represent the principle of forward motion itself. It is their backwater that pools to form the *dolce e delicato* second theme proper (rehearsal no. 11, beginning on a veiled or "shy" G minor that tentatively edges its way upward toward the "correct" B♭ [rehearsal no. 12], then lapses back to G only to settle down a fifth, on C [rehearsal no. 13] in order to work through more "transitional," chromatic excursions), and it is their accumulative power that gathers mass to thunder out the decisive closing themes (for example, rehearsal no. 20, a *maestoso* variant of the second theme, now in B♭).

The second movement (Funeral March) subtly varies a number of motivic offshoots from the first: compare the *più mosso, sostenuto* section at rehearsal number 73 and six measures after rehearsal number 82, for instance, to Example 12.8b.[24]

It is in the subsequent scherzo, though, that the rhythmically energized, long-short repetitions more audibly resurface to replay their forward-driving role: Example 12.10 shows the first of its scherzo appearances, *sonoramente* at rehearsal number 93. But it is in the finale's sturdy

EXAMPLE 12.10. Elgar, Symphony No. 2, movt. 3, rehearsal no. 93

second theme (rehearsal no. 139) where the idea seems finally to come into its own. Here it plants its feet, then strides forth fully revealed—with swaggering confidence and a proud contrapuntal "academicism"—rising upward and swinging back and forth between the initial, tonic statement and its dominant-level, slightly altered answer (Ex. 12.11). In the exposition it articulates the subdominant, A♭; the closing theme, at rehearsal number 142, establishes the dominant, B♭. Significantly, in the recapitulatory space, it is this second theme that definitively secures the E♭ resolution at rehearsal number 160; the resolution is confirmed by the return of the closing theme in E♭ at rehearsal number 163.[25]

So much might seem a traditional exercise in motive tracking, but in this case the point behind it may be a master key to the whole. For when Elgar first sketched the Example 12.11 theme in 1903—along with the finale's main theme and the nine-measure passage beginning five measures after rehearsal number 155, it may be counted among his first ideas for the symphony—he labeled it "Hans himself!" This referred, of course, to the venerable Hans Richter, who for the English was the embodiment of the institutional concert and who was also an ardent and loyal champion of Elgar.[26] Simply put, in 1909–11 Elgar seems to have planned the first three movements of the Second Symphony to lead to a finale that had been substantially preconceived as a symphonic movement that, at least in part, was to be a tribute to Richter. Considering the growth within the motivic family suggested in Examples 8–11, one might argue that within this stratum of meaning all roads lead to Hans. Now in fact it was Elgar, not the recently retired Richter, who on 24 May 1911 conducted the Second's premiere (Richter had conducted that of the First)—but this matters little. To Elgar, Richter doubtless personified the quintessential con-

EXAMPLE 12.11. Elgar, Symphony No. 2, movt. 4, rehearsal no. 139

ductor. Consequently, the "Hans himself!" *telos* in the Second Symphony need not be exclusively linked to only a single person. More broadly, the Second Symphony drives toward and finally achieves the "resolving," arm-swinging image of itself being conducted on the podium in the institutional ceremony of the public concert.

Elgar's Second Symphony thus seeks to accomplish something extraordinary: in addition to its several other private and public meanings, it manages to comment on, and then to illustrate, the act of its own performance. By extension, one of its "purely musical" programs is that of the act of bringing canonic artworks to life in the concert ceremony. This must be why it is so concerned to absorb, exemplify, and bid farewell to a grand tradition that was then ebbing inexorably away under a welter of new cultural, aesthetic, and political challenges. "Rarely, rarely comest thou, / Spirit of Delight!" Those who take the time to investigate Elgar's Second thoughtfully will find it to be nothing less than the *summa* of the modern institutional symphony.

Notes

1. At the end of his life, in the early 1930s, Elgar began a Third Symphony but never completed it. See the discussion in Jerrold Northrop Moore, *Edward Elgar: A Creative Life* (Oxford, 1984), 795–96, 799–800, 803–21; Robert Anderson, *Elgar in Manuscript* (Portland, OR, 1990), 175–85; and Christopher Kent, "Elgar's Third Symphony: The Sketches Reconsidered," *Musical Times* 123 (1982): 532–37.

2. Nothing happens overnight, of course, but a useful English event to keep in mind is the premiere of Schoenberg's Five Pieces for Orchestra by Sir Henry Wood and the Queen's Hall Orchestra on 3 September 1912.

3. The principal sources of information on the works' compositional and performance histories are Moore, *Edward Elgar*, 507–50, 594–611, the most comprehensive general account of the composing these two symphonies; Michael Kennedy, *Portrait of Elgar*, 2d ed. (London, 1982), 213–51; Anderson, *Elgar in Manuscript*, 97–112; and Christopher Kent, "A View of Elgar's Methods of Composition through the Sketches of the Symphony No. 2 in E♭ (op. 63)," *Proceedings of the Royal Musical Association* 103 (1976–77): 41–60.

Special attention should also be drawn to the forewords, commentaries, discussions and reproductions of sketches, and citations of variants and corrections in the beginnings of the scores of the two symphonies as published in the Elgar Complete Edition (Novello): No. 1 (1981) with remarks by Jerrold Northrop Moore and Christopher Kent, and No. 2 (1984) with remarks by Moore and Robert Anderson. One might also mention the efficient prefaces by Diana McVeagh in the recent Eulenburg Editions of the two symphonies, nos. 8005 and 8006 (London, 1985).

4. The terminology of this paragraph is my own. The issue of exploring, defining, and categorizing structural deformations is enormously complex. I have laid out some of its elements and problems more fully, particularly with regard to the concept of "sonata deformation," in the following: "Structure and Program in

Macbeth: A Proposed Reading of Strauss's First Symphonic Poem," in *Richard Strauss and His World*, ed. Bryan Gilliam (Princeton, NJ, 1992), 67–89; "Fiery-Pulsed Libertine or Domestic Hero? *Don Juan* Reinvestigated," in *Richard Strauss: New Perspectives on the Composer and His Work*, ed. Bryan Gilliam (Durham, NC, 1992), 135–76; *Sibelius: Symphony No. 5* (Cambridge, 1993), 4–7, 19–30, 94–95.

5. Elgar's opinions regarding the constricted qualities of his symphonic predecessors in England were made public in March 1905 in the first of his Peyton Lectures at the University of Birmingham. See "The Inaugural Lecture" and the subsequent November 1905 lecture "English Composers" in Elgar, *A Future for English Music and Other Lectures*, ed. Percy M. Young (London, 1968), 22–65, 75–95.

6. In 1939 W. H. Reed, a violinist in the London Symphony and a member of Elgar's circle, recounted a story that doubtless had widespread private resonance in 1908 and 1909 (*Elgar* [London, 1939], 79). According to Reed, on 6 December 1908 Richter preceded his rehearsals with the London Symphony—in anticipation of the First Symphony's London premiere (the actual first performance had taken place in Manchester on 3 December)—with the words, "Gentlemen . . . let us now rehearse the greatest symphony of modern times, written by the greatest modern composer . . . *and not only in this country*." Reed goes on to report that Richter, "almost with the sound of tears in his voice," had said of the third movement, "Ah! this is a *real* Adagio—such an Adagio as Beethove' would 'ave writ'." Cf. also Richard Strauss's much-noted earlier praise of Elgar in 1902 as a "Meister," "the first English progressivist," after a German performance of *The Dream of Gerontius* (Moore, *Edward Elgar*, 368–69).

7. The known references in the symphonies are provided in most of the recent Elgar literature: see especially Moore, *Edward Elgar*, and the introductory material provided in the Novello critical edition. On Alice Stuart-Wortley and the Second Symphony see also Kent, "A View of Elgar's Methods of Composition," as well as Kennedy, *Portrait of Elgar*, 160–61, and Jerrold Northrop Moore, ed., *Edward Elgar: The Windflower Letters* (Oxford, 1989).

8. See, e.g., his widely discussed Birmingham lecture in November 1905 on Brahms's Symphony No. 3, along with the responses that it provoked, in Elgar, *A Future for English Music*, 96–110.

9. Two of its most prominent predecessors are (possibly) the first movement of Schumann's Piano Fantasy in C Major and (more certainly) the finale of Mahler's First Symphony. For the first movement of the much-analyzed Fantasy I would propose the viability of an alternative, albeit unorthodox, reading. Its effect is to submit the various standard hearings—all of which confront an unusually designed movement presumably guided only by the forces of a governing C tonality—to a *Gestalt* shift comparable to that illustrated by the famous rabbit-duck optical illusion. (In that illusion, of course, neither image, rabbit or duck, has exclusive rights to "correctness.")

In this reading of the extraordinarily subtle Schumann piece, much of whose "logic," once perceived, could be seen to foreshadow that of the initial movement of Elgar's First Symphony, the impulsive, introductory C-major *Klang* is channeled into an E♭ (off-tonic) sonata deformation that begins in m. 29 (with the same theme, briefly touched upon). The second theme appears on two tonal plateaus, D minor (m. 42) and, with a greater sense of arrival, F major (m. 62, effectively a still-anticipatory V/V of E♭). The developmental space begins as a non sequitur in m. 82; the C-major introductory frame soon tears further into the "sonata" fabric at m. 97—a common feature of the deformation with introduction-coda frame—and leads to the partially episodic, partially developmental *Legendenton* section. (On deformations incorporating partially developmental spaces, see, e.g., my *Sibelius: Symphony No. 5*, 6–7.) The E♭ recapitulatory space—the crucial, determining feature of this alternative reading—begins with a return to the E♭ first theme in m. 225, and the second theme eventually finds its way to the E♭ tonic (m. 254, thus "resolving" the off-tonic sonata deformation). The coda's task (m. 274) is to reinstate the primary framing identity of C—that of the giver, so to speak, not that of the E♭ sonata-deformation gift.

In the Mahler finale, an F-minor sonata deformation (second theme, D♭ major) is played out through the end of the recapitulatory space, which shifts dramatically (through the "breakthrough," or *Durchbruch*, principle) to the symphony's D-major tonic. We may also note in passing that the default slow movement within a four-movement symphony or sonata—when it, too, is in some sort of sonata structure—may be regarded, in a larger sense, as an off-tonic sonata, but one that in the tradition does not seek resolution within the movement itself.

10. To Ernest Newman, who was preparing the first set of program notes, 4 November 1908 (Moore, *Edward Elgar*, 520).

11. Perhaps needless to say, the concept of sonata "failure" here is not intended as a criticism; rather it is a way of describing a crucial element of what appears to be the expressive or narrative intentions of the composer—of the musical "story" that is unfolded in, around, and through the sonata. Some precedents: Beethoven's *Egmont* Overture, Glinka's Overture to *Russlan and Ludmilla*, Tchaikovsky's *Romeo and Juliet*, and Strauss's *Macbeth*. See Hepokoski, *Sibelius: Symphony No. 5*, 94–95 (n. 17).

12. For the second and third movements' origins in a projected string quartet from late 1907 see Anderson, *Elgar in Manuscript*, 97–101.

13. At this point, the onset of the *adagio*, Elgar was surely evoking—or recreating—the effect of the famous G major/E♭ major shift into the beginning of "Nimrod" in the *Enigma Variations*.

14. In 1908 Elgar returned to his 1904 sketch, mentioned in the text above, and penned those words on it. The sketch is reproduced in facsimile as part of the introductory remarks by Moore and Kent in the Elgar Complete Edition version of the symphony published by Novello (n. 3 above). See also Anderson, *Elgar in Manuscript*, 97.

15. About a month before the premiere Elgar told Ernest Newman that he had not realized the connection between this theme and the opening motto theme. In addition, in 1934 Elgar referred to an essential feature of this symphony as the dismissing or quashing, obviously in the fourth movement, of the "quasi-military" or "coarser themes." For both points, see Moore, *Edward Elgar*, 538–39.

16. It may also rejoin the recapitulation, of course, at other points as well, including its opening. This sonata procedure has been much noted and discussed (under other designations) in the literature. One of the first articles to deal with it was Robert Pascall, "Some Special Uses of Sonata Form by Brahms," *Soundings* 4 (1974): 58–63.

17. The prominent D minor throughout the third (and final) expositional zone also suggests a separate deformation procedure: that of the tonic expositional close (which may also be found, for example, in the first movements of Mahler's

Fourth and Eighth Symphonies). Here the simultaneous return of the introductory theme (Ex. 12.7) also suggests features of a larger recycling or rotation.

18. To Walford Davies, 13 November 1908, in Moore, *Edward Elgar*, 540.

19. Kent, "A View of Elgar's Methods of Composition," 42. In the initial years of its reception it was commonly assumed that the symphony's funeral march referred to the death of Edward VII. (The king died on 6 May 1910; Elgar formally drafted the second movement in November and December 1910 and revised and scored it in late January and early February 1911; the symphony's premiere took place on 24 May 1911.) Elgar scholarship, however, has established that some of the principal ideas for the movement probably preceded the king's death: in an unpublished typescript Dora Penny recalled Elgar playing for her on 11 April 1910 (immediately upon his return from what seems to have been a significant visit to Alice Stuart-Wortley and her family at Tintagel) a version of the slow movement for the projected Second Symphony. This featured—in Moore's paraphrase of Penny's words—"a long, treading $\frac{4}{4}$, the sound of a funeral march." Moreover, Elgar seems to have decided to dedicate the work to Edward VII even before the latter's death, "so that dear kind man will have my best music." (Moore, *Edward Elgar*, 573–74, 597–98, 604–6; see also the probable connection of a passage of the funeral march [rehearsal nos. 74–76, also associated with a never-written second *Cockaigne* Overture, subtitled "The City of Dreadful Night"] with the death of Elgar's close friend, Alfred Rodewald, who had died in 1903, in Kennedy, *Portrait of Elgar*, 160 and 246, and Kent, "A View of Elgar's Methods of Composition," 50–51.) Nonetheless the occasion of the 1911 premiere, coupled with the dedication, certainly invited the more "public" interpretation, which we may accept as a de facto layer (but not the only layer) of the work's meaning.

20. Letter of 13 April 1911 to Alfred Littleton (of Novello), in Moore, *Edward Elgar*, 599.

21. As in Elgar's telling letter to Edward Speyer and his wife at Christmas 1909, recalling his life "when a boy, when the world of music was opening & one learnt fresh *great* works every week—Haydn, Mozart, and Beethoven. Nothing in later life can be even a shadow of those 'learning' days: now, when one knows all the music and all the mechanism of composition, the old mysterious glamour is gone & the feeling of *entering*—shy, but welcomed—into the world of the immortals . . . is a holy feeling & a sensation never to come again, unless our passage into the next world shall be a greater & fuller experience of the same warm, loving & *growing* trust—this I doubt" (Moore, *Edward Elgar*, 560).

22. In the C-minor slow-movement march of Bruckner's Fourth Symphony, for example, the added oboe counterpoint to the midmovement reprise of the main theme could (possibly) be a model for a similar, more extended effect in the Elgar (Bruckner, 1878–80 version, rehearsal letter G, mm. 129ff.; Elgar, reheasal no. 79, which the composer envisaged as "the feminine voice [that] *laments* over the broad manly 1st theme"; quotation rpt. in Moore, *Edward Elgar*, 606.) More generally, it may be argued that Elgar's funeral march is not very distant in spirit from certain slow movements in Bruckner: not only that of the Fourth Symphony but also—and especially—that of the Seventh.

23. Similarly, it is clear that the funeral march's second theme (rehearsal no. 71) alludes to that of the first.

24. Apparently bothered by its subdominant tonality, Tovey referred to Ex. 12.11 as a "transition theme" and deferred the label of "second group" to what I

have designated as the closing theme (*Essays in Musical Analysis, Symphonies and Other Orchestral Works* [Oxford, 1989], 303). Kent, "A View of Elgar's Compositional Methods," 57, agreed with Tovey, calling it a "second theme" that "serves as the basis of the transition passage"; on the other hand, Moore, *Edward Elgar*, 609, hears it—properly, in my view—as the "second subject." One should not belabor the issue of "correct" *Formenlehre* designations in this repertory, of course, and quibbles about them are generally devoid of much meaning. Still, three-tiered expositions, with each tier marked by an emphatic theme, are by no means unknown in Elgar, and the many precedents in Schubert, Brahms, and Bruckner are too well known to need citation here. The crucial feature, as mentioned in the text above, is that this second theme secures the tonic in the recapitulatory space.

25. The sketch is discussed and reproduced as part of Anderson's and Moore's introduction to the Novello critical edition of the symphony; see also Anderson, *Elgar in Manuscript*, 108. The 1903 dating is from Kent, "A View of Elgar's Compositional Methods," 57. Anderson, *Elgar in Manuscript*, 107, appears to suggest that the date might be as late as 1905. The various "Second Symphony" finale themes from this early period seem to have been originally planned as the finale for a First Symphony, in E♭, to be dedicated to Richter. It was the A♭ Symphony of 1908, of course, that Elgar finally dedicated to Richter.

26. Jerrold Northrop Moore, *Edward Elgar: A Creative Life*, 795–96, 799–800, 803–21; Robert Anderson, *Elgar in Manuscript*, 175–85. Moore, *Edward Elgar*, 507–50, 594–611, provides the most comprehensive general account of the composing of these two symphonies; Michael Kennedy, *Portrait of Elgar*, 2d ed. (London, 1982), 213–51; Anderson, *Elgar in Manuscript*, 97–112; Christopher Kent, "A View of Elgar's Methods of Composition," 41–60.

Selected Bibliography

Anderson, Robert. *Elgar*. New York, 1993.

———. *Elgar in Manuscript*. Portland, OR, 1990.

———, and Jerrold Northrop Moore. "Foreword" and [Robert Anderson], "Commentary," to Elgar, Symphony No. 2, v–xxxvii. Elgar Complete Edition. Borough Green, Sevenoaks, Kent, 1994.

Kennedy, Michael. *Portrait of Elgar*. 2d ed. London, 1982.

Kent, Christopher. "A View of Elgar's Methods of Composition through the Sketches of the Symphony No. 2 in E♭ (op. 63)." *Proceedings of the Royal Musical Association* 103 (1776): 41–60.

———. "Elgar's Third Symphony: The Sketches Reconsidered." *Musical Times* 123 (1982): 532–37.

Moore, Jerrold Northrop. *Edward Elgar: A Creative Life*. Oxford, 1984.

———, and Christopher Kent. "Foreword" and "Commentary" to Elgar, Symphony No. 1, v–viii. Elgar Complete Edition. Borough Green, Sevenoaks, Kent, 1981.

Tovey, Donald Francis. *Essays in Musical Analysis: Symphonies and Other Orchestral Works*. Oxford, 1989.

CHAPTER THIRTEEN

Richard Strauss

Bryan Gilliam

By the time of *Der Rosenkavalier* (1910) most of Strauss's tone poems were as much a part of any orchestral season as the Beethoven symphonies, and their popularity has remained undiminished. The same cannot be said of the works of other tone poets: Max von Schillings, Siegmund von Haussegger, Friedrich Klose, Felix Weingartner, or Alexander Ritter—composers whose shortcomings point sharply to Strauss's strengths. For at their best his tone poems exhibit an orchestral brilliance, a sure-footed sense of timing, and—most important—a command of musical form at one with its programmatic material, where narrative and structural strategies seem to coalesce.

The last two decades of the nineteenth century represent Strauss's most intense period of symphonic composition. Thereafter he became increasingly preoccupied with opera. The fact that he considered himself primarily an opera composer for most of his adult life might surprise a number of American concertgoers who are by and large introduced to Strauss's music by way of his symphonic works. In fact the composer of *Don Juan* (1888) and *Till Eulenspiegel* (1895) exceeded even Wagner in operatic output; but unlike Wagner—and many other opera composers, for that matter—Strauss's early roots were not to be found in music for the theater, but rather with purely instrumental composition. Early on, in the 1870s and early 1880s, he composed works in a Classic-Romantic idiom that surely pleased his conservative father. Later, after his conversion to the aesthetics of Wagner and Liszt in 1885, he produced his tone poems from *Macbeth* (1888) through *Ein Heldenleben* (1898) and, thereafter, the *Symphonia domestica* (1903) and *Eine Alpensinfonie* (1915).

Early Strauss; *Aus Italien*

Strauss was a precocious musical talent: he began piano lessons at age four, composed his first works at age six, took up the violin at eight, and at eleven began studying formal composition. Behind this formal study lay an imposing musical influence, that of his father, Franz Strauss, one of the finest horn players in Europe. The arch-conservative Franz raised the young Strauss on the classics: Haydn, Mozart, Beethoven, Schubert, and a certain amount of Mendelssohn, Schumann, and Spohr.[1] And as late as the early 1880s he would go over his son's compositions, making numerous comments and criticisms. In Munich Franz Strauss conducted an amateur orchestra called the Wilde Gung'l, an ensemble that helped introduce Richard to the world of symphonic composition. Young Strauss played violin in the Wilde Gung'l, and his earliest orchestral pieces were written for the group; here he learned the craft of orchestration on a very practical level, his father guiding the way. Strauss composed marches, concert overtures, and other works during these years, and in late spring or early summer 1880, at the age of sixteen, he wrote his First Symphony in D Minor.

Franz Strauss helped copy out the score and parts, and the symphony premiered in the Odeonsaal under Hermann Levi in 1881. It was well received, one critic, for instance, praising its "competence in the treatment of form as well as remarkable skill in orchestration. . . . The work cannot lay any claim to true originality, but it demonstrates throughout a fertile musical imagination, to which composition comes easily."[2] The D-Minor Symphony is strongly indebted to early nineteenth-century German musical Romanticism, that of Schumann, Weber, and especially Mendelssohn.

By 1882 Strauss had completed a Second Symphony in F Minor, his first work to gain real international attention. While searching Europe for promising young talent, Theodore Thomas made contact with Strauss, who proudly showed him the new score. Thomas was enthusiastic and, on the spot, promised a performance (1884) with the New York Philharmonic Society. This turned out to be the world premiere.

The Symphony in F Minor, despite a formal clarity—one might say a rigidity—reminiscent of the earlier D-Minor Symphony, represents a significant advance over its predecessor in harmonic richness, orchestration, and counterpoint. Strauss may well have been overly seduced by his emerging contrapuntal skills, which Brahms criticized after hearing a performance in Meiningen. Beyond his well-known response, "ganz hübsch, junger Mann," Brahms advised: "Your symphony contains too much playing about with themes. This piling up of many themes based on a triad, which differ from one another only in rhythm, has no value."[3] Strauss recalled that Brahms's criticism "always clearly remained in my mind," implying that he meant to pay heed to the older master. But the technique—

for better or worse—remained a substantive part of his compositional style.

One of the signal events in Strauss's life resulted from his move to Meiningen as Hans von Bülow's conducting assistant. Strauss was in the midst of what he called his "Brahmsschwärmerei" ("Brahms kick"), largely galvanized by the influence of von Bülow, who in his later years had become one Brahms's most ardent supporters. Strauss's "Wandrers Sturmlied" (Wanderer's storm song, 1885) and *Burleske* (1886) are strongly indebted to Brahms.[4] But soon after his arrival in Meiningen, he met Alexander Ritter, who quickly became one of the most influential musical figure in Strauss's early adult musical life.

Ritter, a composer and violinist in the Meiningen orchestra, introduced Strauss to the works and writings of Wagner, the symphonic poems of Liszt, the philosophy of Schopenhauer, and the aesthetics of Hausegger. At length he led Strauss to reject Hanslick and Brahms: "[He] proved to me that the road led from the 'musical expressionist' Beethoven . . . via Liszt who, with Wagner, had realized correctly that Beethoven had expanded the sonata form to its utmost limits . . . and that in Beethoven's successors and especially Brahms, sonata form had become an empty shell, in which Hanslick's high-sounding phrases, the invention of which required little imagination and personal aptitude for form, could easily be accommodated."[5] Strauss's credo—"New ideas must search for new forms"—seemed embodied in Liszt's symphonic poems, where "the poetic element was really the formative element."[6] *Aus Italien*, he said, was his "first hesitant attempt" in that direction.

Strauss left Meiningen in 1886, having accepted a conducting post at the Munich Court Opera, but before taking it up on 1 August he spent most of his spring touring Italy. In a letter to his mother of 11 May 1886 he offers a report of the various sites, but more interesting than the narrative is his running musical commentary in the left-hand margin of the document—"tonal impressions" in C major, A major, G major, and C minor.[7] The marginalia ultimately saw their way into *Aus Italien* (1886), which consists of movements in G major, C major, A major, and G major, respectively. On 23 June Strauss—back in Munich—wrote von Bülow that he had sketched out a symphonic fantasy in Italy and was nearly finished with the first movement. It would be his "first step toward independence," dedicated to von Bülow.[8]

Aus Italien is the only symphonic work where Strauss himself published an explicit program.[9] The first movement ("Auf der Campagna": *andante*) suggests the atmosphere experienced by the composer as he viewed the sun-bathed Roman Campagna from the Villa d'Este at Tivoli. He called it a prelude, and this introductory movement—the closest to Liszt in overall construction—is based on three fundamental themes. The second movement ("In Roms Ruinen": *allegro con brio*) suggests "fantastic images of vanished glory, feelings of melancholy and grief amid the brilliant sunshine of the present." But the listener will have a difficult time finding much grief or melancholy in this cheerful movement cast in sonata form. Of all the movements it shows the clearest affinity to Brahms, not only in its sonata structure but in the metrical displacements, phraseology, and woodwind doublings as well.

The third movement ("Am Strande von Sorrent": *andantino*) is Strauss's first serious attempt at musical pictorialism, even though he confessed to von Bülow that, before Rome, he "never really believed in inspiration through the beauty of Nature."[10] Strauss goes to some length to describe the images he sought to depict: the rustling of wind in the leaves, bird songs, sea murmurs, and the like. This movement serves as an early example of Strauss's unique ability to conjure up vivid sonic pictures primarily through orchestrational craft. The lyrical A-minor middle section of this tripartite movement represents—according to the composer—a "solitary song" of the sea, "contrasted with the sensations experienced by the human listener, which are expressed in the melodic elements of the movement. The interplay in the separation and partial union of these contrasts constitutes the spiritual content of this mood picture."

The fourth and most controversial movement, "Neapolisches Volksleben" (*allegro*), was said by Strauss to be based on "a well-known Neapolitan folk song, and in addition a tarantella which [he] heard in Sorrento is used in the coda." The well-known Neapolitan folk song was no less than the popular song "Funiculi, funicula," composed in 1880 by Luigi Denza to celebrate the construction of the funicular on Mount Vesuvius.[11] In the finale Strauss intended to illustrate the bustle of Naples in a "hilarious jumble of themes." And it certainly is an amusing hodgepodge, especially in the development section, where motives generated from "Funiculi, funicula" interact in a setting more appropriate to *Elektra*. One suspects Strauss knew the *Roman Carnival* Overture, for he called this last movement "pretty wild and more so than Berlioz."[12] He conducted the premiere on 2 March 1887 in Munich and was delighted by the controversy it occasioned.

The First Cycle of Tone Poems: *Macbeth, Don Juan, Tod und Verklärung*

On 24 August 1888, the year *Macbeth* was finished, Strauss wrote von Bülow that since the F-Minor Symphony he had found himself trapped in a steadily escalating antithesis between poetic content and formal structure. The inherited forms seemed passé, even arbitrary; they were "random patterns that mean nothing either to the composer or the listener." He began to think it "a legitimate artistic method to create a correspondingly new form for every new subject."[13] He would try to resolve this tension in *Macbeth*, for if *Aus Italien* had been a hesitant step toward program music, *Macbeth*—though for several reasons it did not receive its premiere until after *Don Juan* and *Tod und Verklärung*—was his first full-fledged *Tondichtung*. In composing it Strauss felt that he had "set out upon a completely new path."[14]

It was not without detours, for the work went through more changes than any of his other tone poems. Most commentary on the *Macbeth* revisions, which has taken Strauss's own remarks at face value, focuses on the altered ending—the cutting of the so-called "triumphant march of Macduff"—and on the revisions of orchestration that came after the premiere on 13 October 1890;[15] the revised version was first performed on 29 February 1892. (Both were conducted by the composer.) Recent research, however, demonstrates that the *Macbeth* revisions were far more extensive than previously believed. Strauss's structural reworking, especially in parts of the development and recapitulation, shows just how seriously he was struggling with the conflicting demands of narrative and form.[16]

For *Macbeth*, which Strauss thought his "most independent and purposeful work," was based neither on moods nor impressions but on a specific piece of literature—his only symphonic work to evolve from a play. Yet it is his most ambiguous tone poem in terms of the specifics of the narrative. There is little agreement, for that matter, on the precise relationship between the play and the score. Some writers reject the idea that the music was generated by a detailed program at all. The sole extramusical text that appears in the printed score is the labeling of the "Macbeth" and "Lady Macbeth" themes (mm. 6ff. and 64ff., respectively). Of these two captions, only "Lady Macbeth" includes a quotation from the play ("Hie thee hither . . . ," act 1, scene 5; see Ex. 13.1).

EXAMPLE 13.1. Richard Strauss, *Macbeth*
a. mm. 6–9

b. mm. 64–66

Hie thee hither, that I may pour my spirits in thine ear, and
chastise with the valour of my tongue, all that impedes thee from
the golden round, which fate and metaphysical aid doth seem
Lady Macbeth. to have thee crown'd withal.

The most convincing analysis of *Macbeth* is that of James Hepokoski, who—in going back to the earliest programmatic commentary (Heinrich Reimann, 1892)—explored the concept of "structural deformations," where structural paradigm and narrative strategy coexist in complex relationships.[17] Hepokoski recognizes a modified sonata form and hypothesizes narrative meanings for the structural modifications.

"Completely new path" or no, *Macbeth* has failed to find a firm place in the concert repertoire. Those sympathetic to the work stress that it was neither performed nor published for some two years after its completion. By then *Macbeth* had to compete with *Don Juan* and *Tod und Verklärung*, both of which achieved quick fame. But *Macbeth* is more than a victim of circumstance. For one thing it lacks the cogency and convincing pacing so evident in the two subsequent works. And despite the revisions, where Strauss sought to restrain the inner voices—largely through modifying the orchestration—the better to highlight the principle themes, *Macbeth* still falls short of *Don Juan* and *Tod und Verklärung* in sonic clarity.

Dahlhaus ignores *Macbeth* when he describes *Don Juan* as the "dawning of 'musical modernism,'" but his omission is understandable, for *Don Juan* received the earlier premiere (November 1889, Weimar); it also displays Strauss's modernity in sharper relief.[18] *Don Juan*'s provocative subject matter, brilliant orchestration, sharply etched and evocative themes, novel structure, and tight pacing created a sensation at the time and earned Strauss his stature as a symphonic composer of international note. In *Don Juan* he found his voice as a tone poet, and in so doing distanced himself from the Wagner-Liszt notion of music as inherently sacred.

His attempt in *Don Juan* to "desacralize" music shows an element of his artistic personality that remained constant to the end. The paradox is that while Strauss was immersed in Wagner's musical style and technique, his basic philosophy of art could have been no more different: in fact he used Wagner's "sacred apparatus," even his "sacred language," to demythologize the philosophy that gave us that very language. *Don Juan* is flagrantly pictorial, funny, and altogether secular. Its libertine hero simply thumbs his nose at the world.

The Don races forward "always toward new victories"—and not the triumphs of battle, but those of the bedroom. But the three excerpts from Nicolas Lenau's verse play that appear in the score merely describe Don Juan and his worldview, without narrative specifics. Nonetheless, to judge from both the music and the composer's comments, the work goes well beyond the Lenau fragments: Don Juan has various love affairs, attends a masked ball, and takes part in a deadly duel. The relation of structure to narrative is not as clear as with *Macbeth*. Some commentators recognize a modified sonata form not unlike that of *Macbeth*, others call it a rondo, and some find a synthesis of the two.[19]

Cosima Wagner, an admirer until then, sensed Strauss's new aesthetic direction as he played and discussed *Don Juan* with her in Weimar in February 1890. She was sharply critical, thinking that Strauss had seriously erred in his choice of subject matter. Self-proclaimed custodian of her late husband's ideals, she was offended by both the blatantly erotic passages—the skyrocketing opening, for example, an explicitly erotic profile of the potent Don—and the concrete narrative. She urged him not to become preoccupied with surface elements and evocative themes, but rather to seek "eternal motives" that could be perceived at various levels and in various manifestations.[20] Strauss's reply was polite, even deferential: "I think I have understood [you] correctly, and I look forward to producing evidence next time we meet, in the form of my third symphonic work [*Tod und Verklärung*], . . . that I have perhaps already made a significant advance, even in the choice of subject."[21]

The subject matter of his third symphonic work may indeed have been loftier, but otherwise it is doubtful that Cosima's advice fell on sympathetic ears.[22] *Tod und Verklärung*, the most metaphysical of his tone poems, is based not on a preexisting literary source but on the composer's own conception: a dying artist, obsessed by an artistic Ideal, transfigured at death to recognize his Ideal in eternity. As with *Don Juan*, an extramusical prefatory text (by Ritter) was published with the score.[23] Ritter's poem, which postdates the composition, is criticized as being too detailed and largely extraneous to Strauss's expressive aims. But the importance of Ritter to Strauss should not be underestimated; Ernst Krause even suggests that the so-called theme of the "Ideal" was borrowed from Ritter's symphonic waltz *Olafs Hochzeitsreigen* (Olaf's wedding dance).[24]

In a letter of 1895 to Friedrich von Hausegger, Strauss treats his program at length: A man lies asleep on his deathbed. He awakens racked with great pain, which subsides as he reflects on his past life: childhood and the passions of youth. "While the pain resumes, the fruit of his path through life appears to him. The idea, the Ideal which he has tried to realize, to represent in his art, but which he has been unable to perfect, because it was not for any human being to perfect it. The hour of death approaches, the soul leaves the body, in order to find perfected in the most glorious form in the eternal cosmos that which he could not fulfill on earth."

Tod und Verklärung was finished in November 1889, while Strauss was Kapellmeister in Weimar; seven months later he conducted the premiere, in Eisenach. To ask why a healthy composer in his twenties might write a work about death is to misconstrue Strauss's basic compositional attitude. It was not a compulsion to express innermost autobiographical feelings that drove him on, but rather his fascination with certain images, characters, and situations. In *Tod und Verklärung* the death is less at issue than the transfiguration—a concept that weaves its way through much of Strauss's music, from the tone poems of the nineteenth century to the operas of the twentieth.

The musical subdivisions of *Tod und Verklärung* are fairly clear, although their relationship to modified sonata form is somewhat fuzzier. It begins with a quiet, syncopated introduction ("breathing heavily and irregularly") followed by an agitated exposition ("he is racked by terrible pain"). The developmental area is episodic: dreams of childhood, youthful passions, followed by what Strauss considered the main theme of the work—that of the artistic Ideal. The restatement of that theme in the extended C-major coda is what Strauss called the "point of culmination."[25] This musical apotheosis is one of the most exquisite moments in all of Strauss's tone poems; even his arch-conservative father was genuinely moved. Eduard Hanslick declared that *Tod und Verklärung* "exemplifies a composer moving in the direction of music drama,"[26] though he could not have been aware that Strauss was already composing his first opera, *Guntram.*

Tod und Verklärung ends the feverish tone poem activity of the late 1880s; Strauss would not compose another major symphonic work for six years. During this hiatus he was preoccupied with his first opera, a three-act Wagnerian epigone entitled *Guntram.* From the outset Ritter encouraged Strauss to write his own libretto, but such work did not come easily: begun in 1887, it occupied the young composer for some five more years. The story is a curious mixture of *Tannhäuser* and *Parsifal,* the music also abundantly informed by Wagnerism. Act 3, Strauss admitted, was "hyper-*Tristan*-ish."

Here the minnesinger Guntram renounces love, but after rejecting counsel from his fraternal order he embarks on a solitary journey, leaving both friends and his beloved Freihild. The contrast with *Tannhäuser* is instructive, for whereas Tannhäuser travels to Rome for penance, Guntram—who was originally to make a pilgrimage to the Holy Land—sets off on his own path.[27] Ritter, a devout Catholic, was horrified and urged Strauss to change the ending; his refusal to do so seriously affected their friendship.

The Weimar premiere, 1894, received a lukewarm response, and the first performance in Munich, in 1895, was an outright failure. Future performances of *Guntram* were canceled, despite initial promises to the contrary, and for the first time Strauss had to deal head on with strong conservative elements in the Bavarian capital. Having just been appointed court conductor at the Munich Opera, he was considerably dismayed by the negative reaction by the musicians, the vehemence of the press, and what he took to be the duplicity of the Munich Opera management.

The failure of *Guntram* was central to Strauss's artistic development. It rekindled a dormant love-hate relationship with the city of his birth that endured to the end. But Strauss learned much from this setback: he recognized that he was no librettist, saw the dangers of the Wagnerian shadow (and even by the end of composing the opera had been distancing himself from Bayreuth), realized the harshness of Munich's philistinism, and—consciously or not—discovered that he needed to explore further the problem of narrative in a purely symphonic medium.

The Second Cycle of Tone Poems:
Till Eulenspiegel, Also sprach Zarathustra, Don Quixote, Ein Heldenleben

Three of the four works that make up the second cycle are significantly longer that those of the first: *Ein Heldenleben* is nearly three times the length of *Don Juan*. The size of Strauss's orchestra increases as well, and his orchestrational technique bespeaks an increasing preoccupation with the graphic depiction of extramusical elements. Yet the second cycle begins like the first, when Strauss returns to a literary theme after the personal, metaphysical *Tod und Verklärung*. And, like the first cycle, the second ends with a nonliterary work—*Ein Heldenleben*, perhaps the culmination of the nineteenth-century tone poem.

One further characteristic unites both cycles, namely, Strauss's focus on male characters: Macbeth, Don Juan, Till Eulenspiegel, Don Quixote. With *Salome* (1905), the first mature opera, his preoccupation turns to the female psyche: Elektra, the Marschallin, Ariadne, the Dyer's Wife, Arabella, Daphne. Neither of Strauss's twentieth-century tone poems, the *Symphonia domestica* and *Eine Alpensinfonie*, is concerned primarily with a male protagonist.

Shortly after the *Guntram* premiere, Strauss decided to compose another stage work—a light, satirical opera to poke fun at provincial narrow-mindedness. The one-act *Till Eulenspiegel bei den Schildbürgern* (1894) never got beyond an incomplete text draft. In mythical Schilda, a medieval town populated by empty-headed philistines, the hapless burgers initially sentence Till Eulenspiegel to death, then ultimately make him their mayor.[28]

Why Strauss scrapped the opera for a tone poem remains a mystery. The details of the later, quite different scenario can be gleaned from the extensive programmatic notes (complete with measure numbers) written by the composer into Wilhelm Mauke's copy of the score.[29] "Bar 1: Once upon a time there was a knavish fool / Bar 7: —named Till Eulenspiegel. / 5 bars before 3: He was a wicked goblin / 6 bars before 6: —up to new tricks." And so on. Till hops on horseback to ride through the market, disguises himself as a minister and then mocks religion, flirts with women, poses as an academician engaging in double-talk with his philistine audience, and by the end of the work finds himself on trial and sentenced to death by hanging.[30]

Till Eulenspiegel, unlike the earlier tone poems, lacks the designation *Tondichtung* in the subtitle. Instead the title suggests a specific form: *Till Eulenspiegel's Merry Pranks, after the Old Rogue's Tale, set in Rondeau Form for Large Orchestra.* Richard Specht suggests that the first prank may well be the use of the term "rondeau" in the subtitle,[31] for the only real connection with the old French *forme fixe* is the composer's choice of spelling. Strauss later wrote of "an expansion of rondo form through poetic content" and cited the last movement of Beethoven's Eighth Symphony as a model.[32] Given the episodic nature of the work as well as the libertine qualities of its protagonist, a rondo treatment seems entirely appropriate.[33] But, as in *Don Juan,* it is hardly conventional: the sense of rondo is achieved mostly by the return of Till's two themes to articulate his various adventures. In fact, *Till Eulenspiegel* might just as easily be seen as a kind of ritornello structure.

Completed in May 1895, *Till Eulenspiegel* was premiered with great success six months later under Franz Wüllner in Cologne. It is Strauss's most compact tone poem, and his most often performed. Despite the humor and satire, all handled with remarkable lightheartedness, *Till Eulenspiegel* is scored for a larger ensemble than any of the previous works. Strauss had learned much about orchestral details and nuance during the six years since *Tod und Verklärung,* evinced by his brilliant the use of the ratchet when Till rides through the market, the piercing D clarinet when he whistles in the face of death, and the like. (Many of these sound effects found their way into the later operas.) Indeed, after completing *Till Eulenspiegel,* Strauss once again toyed with the idea of composing an opera, this time in five acts, on the same theme, perhaps with the idea of pouring scorn on the Munich that had just rejected *Guntram.* Ultimately, however, he turned his attention to *Also sprach Zarathustra.* A new stage work would not emerge until 1901, when Strauss—still smarting from the *Guntram* debacle—composed *Feuersnot.* Not surprisingly, it contains many of the elements of *Till Eulenspiegel bei den Schildbürgern,* most importantly the protagonist Kunrad, a magician who casts a spell on the narrow-minded citizens of medieval Munich.

Also sprach Zarathustra manifests the composer's preoccupation, toward the mid-1890s, with the work of Nietzsche. If his letters to Ritter are to be believed, Strauss read mostly Schopenhauer while composing *Guntram* and began to read Nietzsche only toward the end of that period. Ritter, of course, blamed Strauss's "blasphemous" ending to *Guntram* on the influence of Max Stirner and, more especially, of Nietzsche. He may have been right about this, the composer's protests notwithstanding.[34]

What Strauss derived from Nietzsche and how much of it directly informed his tone poem is a question that has been posed countless times since the premiere of *Also sprach Zarathustra* in November 1896. One thing is certain: Nietzsche helped validate Strauss's agnosticism, which in any event predated his engagement with the philosopher's work and remained consistent to his death.[35] Part of his antagonism toward organized religion, particularly Christianity, was rooted in the belief that ancient Greece served as an important model for modern Germany—a conviction held by many German artists and intellectuals at the time, among them Nietzsche. Strauss's lifelong belief in the individual, who has the power to change the world around him and control his destiny without thought given to a doubtful hereafter, is thoroughly consistent with Nietzschian thought.

Straussian agnosticism was optimistic, affirmative, and seemingly unclouded by many of the darker aspects of Nietzsche's writings. Mahler, for one, was fascinated with this murkier, more metaphysical side. In quoting from "The Drunken Song of Midnight" in his Third Symphony (also 1896), Mahler focuses on humankind's desire for eternity, on the fundamental conflict between finite Man and infinite Nature—a tension that would be revisited at greater length in *Das Lied von der Erde*, 1909.

Strauss originally subtitled his tone poem "Symphonic Optimism in Fin-de-siècle Form, Dedicated to the Twentieth Century."[36] Later he substituted "Freely after Nietzsche," a description that aptly suggests his liberal treatment of the book's prologue and four sections. Each section contains between sixteen and twenty-two speeches of Zarathustra, and of these some eighty subsections, Strauss chose eight: "Of the Backworldsmen," "Of Great Yearning," "Of Joys and Passions," "Funeral Song," "Of Science," "The Convalescent," "The Dance Song," and "The Night Wanderer's Song." If there is some narrative, paratextual thread connecting these, the letters and sketches offer little or no clues. Quite possibly the composer chose those sections of Nietzsche's work that most appealed to his imagination, that seemed the most promising for musical treatment. Nearly half of the selections refer to either dance or song.

The overall theme of *Also sprach Zarathustra* concerns the conflict between Nature (C major) and Mankind (B major). "Musically speaking," according to Strauss "[this is] the conflict between the two most distant tonalities (the [minor] second!)."[37] Yet Strauss portrays Mankind not in search of eternity, but rather struggling to transcend religious superstition. Above a fair sketch for the opening fanfare, which begins with the fundamental tones C–G–C, the composer wrote: "The sun rises. The individual enters the world or the world enters the individual."[38] He labels the quiet theme immediately following the introduction (cellos, basses) as "pious fear." The ensuing A♭-major "Von den Hinterweltern"—despite the beauty of the divided strings, its melodic sweep, and magnificent upward sequential momentum—offers a parody of religion. Ironic quotations from the Mass ("Credo in unum deum") and later the Magnificat reinforce Strauss's distance from, not identification with, his material.[39] Differences in tempo notwithstanding, the themes associated with "Von den Hinterweltern" and with Till Eulenspiegel's mocking religion share a certain flavor, especially in terms of the parallel thirds and the divided-viola scoring (Ex. 13.2).[40]

EXAMPLE 13.2.

a. Strauss, *Also sprach Zarathustra*, 17 mm. after rehearsal no. 1

b. Strauss, *Till Eulenspiegel*, 8 mm. before rehearsal no. 13

The premiere of *Also sprach Zarathustra* took place in Frankfurt on 27 November 1896, with the composer conducting. He stipulated that neither the selected lines from Nietzsche's prologue—though published in the full score—nor any sort of "concert guide" be printed in the program, a directive inconsistent with the premieres of earlier programmatic works. The evening was a great success; by now a Strauss premiere had become an international event. The young Béla Bartók called it a "bolt of lightning" that lifted him out of artistic stagnation. The bombastic opening fanfare—though since trivialized and commodified by various branches of popular culture—is Strauss's best-known passage, even if the listener may never have heard the name of its composer.

The earliest idea for *Don Quixote* occurred to Strauss within months of the *Zarathustra* premiere, but he did not begin composing it in earnest until spring of the following year. By then he was, in fact, simultaneously considering another tone poem, *Held und Welt* (ultimately *Ein Heldenleben*), for which *Don Quixote* would serve as the comic other side of the coin.[41] The tragicomic *Don Quixote* returns us to the satirical world of *Till Eulenspiegel*, and like it *Don Quixote* is not given the designation *Tondichtung* in its subtitle. Once again Strauss's full title, the longest of all, suggests not so much genre as formal procedure: *Don Quixote (Introduction, Theme and Variations, Finale): Fantastic Variations on a Theme of Knightly Character for Large Orchestra*. Nor is the question of genre all that simple, for the work—which features a solo cello with solo viola and orchestra[42]—represents a conglomeration of generic and formal models: tone poem, theme and variations, and concerto.[43] Why, for the first time, did Strauss choose a theme and variations? Are they, in fact, real variations?

The broad layout of *Don Quixote* consists of an introduction, ten variations, and an extended coda of sorts. These serve to evoke the main characters (prologue), ten episodes from the legend, and the death of the Don (epilogue). Once again Strauss chooses a mere handful of incidents from a large literary work. In the tradition of *Don Juan* and *Till Eulenspiegel*, *Don Quixote* unfolds episodically. But these episodes are more self-contained: as each discrete "chapter" unfolds, so does a new variation. The theme and variations seem to incorporate the rondo principal as well, along the lines of the two precedent works. The themes themselves are rarely varied—rather, their timbral, harmonic, and rhythmic contexts are—in musical description of the antihero and his hapless sidekick Sancho Panza as they plot their famous course: (1) the Don's adventure with the windmills, (2) his battle with the sheep, (3) the conversation between knight and squire, (4) the adventure with the procession of penitents, (5) Don Quixote's nocturnal vigil over his armor, (6) his meeting with the peasant girl, (7) the ride through the air, (8) the trip on the enchanted boat, (9) the battle with two priests on their mules, and (10) Don Quixote's combat with the knight of the shining moon. In the epilogue the Don returns home, where he dies a peaceful death.

With *Don Quixote* Strauss reaches a new level in his command of the orchestra, notably in his ability to create seemingly concrete sonic images through novel instrumental combinations and juxtapositions: the bleating sheep (winds and brass), the use of wind machine for the *Luftfahrt*, or the wet snap pizzicatos that evoke the waterlogged antiheros, who have just fallen out of the "enchanted" boat. Yet *Don Quixote* also reaches the limits of musical onomatopoeia. Ernest Newman, an early champion of Strauss, believed that its realism had exceeded the boundaries of program music as a narrative musical genre. Rudolf Louis expanded upon this issue in *Die deutsche Musik der Gegenwart:*

> No musician before now has ever advanced nearly so far in the art of letting the listener *see*, as it were, with his ears. This is the source of Strauss's unique and personal strength, that he has developed the ideal, elevated gestures of the tonal language of Liszt into a gestural language of great specificity that undertakes quite seriously not only to interpret the events of an external musical plot in tone (by revealing the music that is latent in them) but to *draw* them until they are recognizable to the inner eye.[44]

Don Quixote fell short of warranting the designation "masterpiece," Louis thought, because the "deictic" Strauss sought to compete with Cervantes rather than to interpret him.

The work premiered under Franz Wüllner in Cologne on 8 March 1898, with the German cellist Friedrich Grützmacher as soloist. Strauss did not attend, hearing it for the first time when he conducted the Frankfurt performance ten days later. It was well received, though inspired perhaps more curiosity from the audience than sympathy. Critics were divided, but few disagreed that Strauss's next logical step should be the stage and not the concert hall. The reviews suggested a growing aesthetic conflict in Strauss's music between industry and inspiration, between Strauss the artisan and Strauss the artist. His detractors denied neither his command of thematic material nor his brilliance as an orchestrator; his flaw, they thought, was his habit of relying more on technical ability than artistic instinct. We have come full circle back to Cosima Wagner's misgivings about *Don Juan*.

Ein Heldenleben remains the most controversial of Strauss's tone poems. Critics derided it, most of all for the egotism implied by what appeared to be the composer's heroic self-portrayal. But closer scrutiny of *Heldenleben*'s genesis—which is intimately bound to that of *Don Quixote*—reveals the superficial nature of such critique. For one thing, any view of *Ein Heldenleben* that does not take *Don Quixote* into account fails from the outset. In a letter to the conductor Gustav Kogel, for example, Strauss writes that "*Don Quixote* and *Heldenleben* are conceived so much as immediate pendants that, in particular, *Don Q.* is only fully and entirely comprehensible at the side of *Heldenleben*."[45] Throughout his conducting career Strauss was fond of pairing the two works.

Sketches indicate in fact that the earliest musical ideas for *Heldenleben* may have emerged while Strauss was working on the Dulcinea love theme of *Don Quixote*, sometime during the spring of 1897.[46] Written above a preliminary sketch for the opening of the later work is a curious annotation concerning the end, an "Adagio / longing for peace after the struggle with the world, / refuge in solitude: the Idyll." The parallel with *Don Quixote* is obvious, for after struggles and misadventures the Don, like the hero, renounces the world and returns home. Cervantes and his Don offered copious material to characterize an antihero; to characterize his hero it was natural enough for Strauss to look within himself, to his internal and external struggles, and of course his love for his wife, Pauline.[47] But the six sections of the work—the hero, the hero's adversaries, his life's companion, his deeds of war, his works of peace, and his retirement from the world—are not so much autobiographical as simply informed by the world he knew the best. And he was scarcely ready, in 1898, to retire.

Some writers see the overall form as consisting of six continuous sections, but the general contours of sonata form seem a better summary of the compositional plan: expository material (the hero, his adversaries, his beloved), developmental material (struggle), and recapitulation (the decision to turn his back on war and seek solace in domestic love). The focus on domestic love is vital to *Heldenleben* and to Strauss's creative output in general;[48] Hepokoski recognizes the centrality of this theme as far back as *Don Juan*. The woman behind his preoccupation was of course the composer's wife, Pauline de Ahna. She inspired most of the early lieder, Freihild in *Guntram*, *Don Juan*, the wife in *Symphonia domestica*, the Dyer's Wife in *Die Frau ohne Schatten*, and Christine in *Intermezzo*; in *Ein Heldenleben* her presence is to be sensed first at the violin solos, then in the ensuing love-making scene in G♭ major.

The massive *Ein Heldenleben* marks not only the end of the second cycle but in some respects the culmination of nineteenth-century symphonic poems. This sense is heightened toward the end by the dizzying recollection of themes from previous tone poems (as well as operas and lieder) in seemingly effortless juxtapositions and simultaneities.[49] His choice of quotations—mostly love themes—is noteworthy, for virtually all of them are directly or indirectly related to his "Heldensgefährtin," Pauline. The Frankfurt premiere, Strauss conducting, took place as the century was drawing to its close in 1899. By then he had left Munich for his new post at the Berlin Court Opera.

After *Ein Heldenleben*: Strauss in the Twentieth Century

Strauss was happy to leave Munich for Berlin in 1898, and the geographic move coincided with a major turning point in his creative life: now he would dedicate himself to composing opera. The satirical *Feuersnot* (1901) was the first step, but it was *Salome* (1905) that established him as an opera composer of true stature. Berlin, bustling capital of the German empire, offered an ideal atmosphere for writing operas. From *Feuersnot* to *Capriccio* (1941), Strauss was able to complete a new opera every two to five years.

During the twentieth century Strauss also made at least seven forays into the realm of symphonic music, five of which failed to result in complete works.[50] The other two—the *Symphonia domestica* and *Eine Alpensinfonie*—were overshadowed by the operas. Strauss first drew up his plan for a domestic symphony on 25 May 1902, while vacationing in Sandown, Isle of Wight. A pre-sketch scenario ("Ideas for a Family Scherzo, with Double Fugue, on 3 Themes") offers a rough outline—partly in verse—for a work originally entitled *Mein Heim: Ein sinfonisches Selbst- und Familienporträt* (My home: A symphonic self- and family portrait):

> Mein Weib, mein Kind, meine Musik
> Natur und Sonne, die sind mein Glück.
> Ein wenig Gleichmut und viel Humor
> Drin thut mir's der Teufel selbst nicht vor!
>
> [My wife, my child, my music
> Nature and sun, they are my joy
> A little calm and much humor
> There even the devil himself can teach me nothing!]

F major 1st theme: Papa returns from his trip, tired

B major 2nd theme: Mama

D major 3rd theme: Bubi, a mixture, however a greater similarity to
  Papa

The three take a walk outdoors. Evening time, cozy family table.

Mama brings Bubi to bed. Papa works. Papa and Mama *seul: scène
  d'amour.*

Le Matin: Bubi cries, joyful awakening.

And then a little quarreling and arguing (Mama begins, but Papa
  ·ends it),

Reconciliation and cheerful ending.[51]

The final score follows the scenario fairly closely.[52]

Strauss always called the work a symphony or symphonic poem,
never a tone poem, and the four sections correspond to the traditional
symphonic movements: introduction (presentation of the major characters and their themes), *scherzando* (the child at play, his parents' happiness), cradle song and *adagio* (the child is put to bed, thereafter the parents' nocturnal *scène d'amour*), and finale: double fugue (a new day begins
with the quarreling suggested in the scenario, and a happy reconciliation). Especially important is the tritonal relationship between the music
for the husband and that of the wife, and their main themes are inversions of each other; the child's tonality falls in between (Ex. 13.3).

EXAMPLE 13.3. Richard Strauss, *Sinfonia domestica*
a. The Husband, mm. 1–5

b. The Wife, rehearsal no. 3

c. The Son, 10 mm. after rehearsal no. 15

The *Symphonia domestica*, which lasts some three-quarters of an hour,
premiered in Carnegie Hall, Strauss conducting, on 21 March 1904. It inspired controversy from the first, perhaps even more than *Heldenleben:* to
suggest oneself as a hero had seemed distasteful enough, and now at issue
was the banal, everyday world of family life. Strauss insisted that no pro-

gram notes be published, and on various occasions tried to distance himself from the extramusical details. To Romain Rolland he declared that "the program is nothing but a pretext for the purely musical expression and development of my emotions, and not a simple *musical description* of concrete everyday facts."[53] But here he was clearly placating Rolland, who was bewildered by a program that he felt diminished an otherwise beautiful work. To others he boasted that his ability to differentiate musically between a knife and a fork was the "highest triumph of musical technique."[54]

Moreover, both the scenario and the sketches clearly gainsay his explanation to Rolland, showing a purposeful and modern celebration of the everyday, where Strauss tried to "reveal the profundity inherent in the mundane."[55] "What could be more serious than married life?" he asked. "Marriage is the most profound event in life, and the spiritual joy of such a union is heightened by the arrival of a child. [Married] life naturally has its humor, which I also injected into this work in order to enliven it."[56] The *Symphonia domestica* is, in its idealized picture of domestic love, a natural and logical extension of the matters at issue in *Ein Heldenleben*. Literal autobiography would hardly have been so attractive, since at the time Strauss and his wife were separated and even contemplating divorce.

Strauss's last major symphonic work, *Eine Alpensinfonie*, is often glossed over, thought by some to be the nadir of his symphonic work. The years separating *Domestica* and *Eine Alpensinfonie* were those of the best-known operas: *Salome, Elektra, Der Rosenkavalier, Ariadne auf Naxos*, and acts 1 and 2 of *Die Frau ohne Schatten*. Why then did he suddenly return to the symphonic medium? The facile answer is, of course, that while the composer was waiting impatiently for act 3 of *Die Frau* from Hugo von Hofmannsthal, he turned to it for lack of any other significant project.

But the initial ideas for *Eine Alpensinfonie* come from well before: just after the turn of the century, in an extension of Strauss's preoccupation with Nietzsche in the 1890s. The earliest sketches can be traced to 1902, and they are fairly extensive. Nine years later, Mahler's death reawakened his interest in the project: "The death of this aspiring, idealistic, energetic artist," he wrote in his diary, "[is] a grave loss. . . . Mahler, the Jew, could achieve elevation in Christianity. As an old man the hero Wagner returned to it under the influence of Schopenhauer. It is quite clear to me that the German nation will achieve new creative energy [*Tatkraft*] only by liberating itself from Christianity. . . . I shall call my alpine symphony: *Der Antichrist*, since it represents: moral purification through one's own strength, liberation through work, worship of eternal, magnificent nature."[57] This original title—*Der Antichrist*—was surely inspired by Nietzsche's essay of the same name, published in 1896, the year of *Also sprach Zarathustra* and Mahler's Third.

But Strauss did not choose Nietzsche's essay as a paratext, turning instead to the alpine landscape—perhaps the most grandiose natural image known to him—that surrounded his home in Garmisch. Early on, he summered in these mountains, first at Marquartstein and then in Garmisch, devoting most of his time to composition. He was hardly alone, for fascination with the mountains has firm roots in the German Romantic literature.[58]

As in *Also sprach Zarathustra*, Strauss goes beyond envy of eternal nature to celebrate the natural surroundings themselves. The ascent and descent from an alpine mountain serve as a metaphor for that celebration. Both works begin at sunrise; in the score Strauss specifies twenty-two tableaux for this twenty-four-hour alpine journey.[59] In fact, *Eine Alpensinfonie* is outwardly unphilosophical. Unlike the deep post–Romantic complexity of Mahler's Third, Strauss quite simply proclaims—with startling beauty—the glories of the sensual, natural world. He delights in expressing the alpine landscape in concrete detail. Mahler declared that he had captured all nature in his Third Symphony, but Strauss seems to try to better the boast. *Eine Alpensinfonie* is unprecedented in his symphonic output both in duration (fifty minutes) and size (over 140 performers with the offstage horns, trumpets, and trombones). Mahler was criticized for his use of cowbells, but such sound effects seem benign next to Strauss's wind and thunder machines.

He conducted the premiere in Berlin on 28 October 1915, with Germany in the midst of World War I. Critical reaction was mixed: some dismissed it as mere musical description, while others called it "cinema music" (*Kinomusik*). Skeptics were confounded by the modernistic treatment of a traditionally German Romantic icon. Specht, meanwhile, lauded the "fundamentally non-German" (*undeutsch*) conception.[60] The *Alpensinfonie* has enjoyed a startling renaissance over the past decade or so, a rediscovery that serves to underscore the remarkable Strauss revival in general.[61]

By the time of the *Alpensinfonie* Strauss had established himself as Germany's foremost opera composer, yet finally the twentieth-century move from tone poem to opera was not a major shift in compositional approach. That *Till Eulenspiegel* began as an opera and became a tone poem illustrates the close relationship between the genres. Both suggest the composer's predilection for translating situations, images, and words into music, whether the venue was to be the concert hall or the opera house. Strauss's path toward opera began with his tone poems, which offered him the opportunity to explore and to refine the language of musical illustration. Only after fully exploiting the possibilities of this genre did he begin to focus successfully on opera.

Strauss's choice of subject matter can seem inconsistent or idiosyncratic: the everyday *Symphonia domestica* and the decadent *Salome* are, after all, adjacent works. But the underlying themes—whether a chapter from Cervantes or a view of the Alps from his Garmisch backyard—fascinated him personally; they were subjects that catalyzed his musical imagination and challenged his intellect. He was a literary composer only insofar as he used the extramusical idea as a catalyst; he was not outwardly a philosophical or especially reflective tone poet. In rejecting the abstract, Strauss composed tone poems of brilliant directness that have consistently delighted audiences over the decades and will surely continue so to do.

Notes

1. Strauss, "Reminiscences of My Father," in *Recollections and Reflections*, ed. Willi Schuh, trans. L. J. Lawrence (London, 1953), 127.

2. Willi Schuh, *Richard Strauss: A Chronicle of the Early Years, 1864–1898*, trans. Mary Whittall (Cambridge, 1982), 52.

3. Ernst Krause, *Richard Strauss: The Man and His Work*, trans. John Coombs (Boston, 1969), 154.

4. R. Larry Todd explores this "Brahmsschwärmerei" c. 1885 in "Strauss before Liszt and Wagner: Some Observations," in *Richard Strauss: New Perspectives on the Composer and His Work*, ed. Bryan Gilliam (Durham, NC, 1992), 3–40.

5. Strauss, "Recollections of My Youth and Years of Apprenticeship," in *Recollections and Reflections*, 138–39.

6. Ibid., 138.

7. Richard Strauss, *Briefe an die Eltern*, ed. Willi Schuh (Zurich, 1954), 98.

8. *Hans von Bülow–Richard Strauss Correspondence*, ed. Willi Schuh and Franz Trenner, trans. Anthony Gishford (London, 1953), 51.

9. Strauss provided this unique programmatic guide in 1889 for the *Allgemeine Musikzeitung*. It is reproduced, in English translation, in Schuh, *Chronicle*, 139.

10. *Bülow–Strauss Correspondence*, 34.

11. Strauss was not alone in believing this tune to be an old Neapolitan folk song. Rimsky-Korsakov also created a musical setting, and the tune remained popular for decades.

12. *Bülow–Strauss Correspondence*, 51.

13. Ibid., 82–83.

14. Schuh, *Chronicle*, 142.

15. Shortly after its completion in 1888, von Bülow criticized the score, observing that it would be impossible for a tone poem based on Shakespeare's *Macbeth* to end with the triumph of Macduff.

16. Indeed, sketches indicate that Strauss had run into problems as early as the beginning of the development section. Here the sketching breaks off, and Strauss began a new work: the Violin Sonata in E♭. It represents Strauss's last assay into the field of absolute music until his so-called "Indian Summer" period of the 1940s. See Scott Warfield's Ph.D. dissertation, "The Genesis of Richard Strauss's *Macbeth*" (University of North Carolina, 1995).

17. James Hepokoski, "Richard Strauss's *Macbeth*," in *Richard Strauss and His World*, ed. Bryan Gilliam (Princeton, NJ, 1992), 67–89.

18. Carl Dahlhaus, *Nineteenth-Century Music*, trans. J. Bradford Robinson (Berkeley and Los Angeles, 1989), 330.

19. The most comprehensive recent study of *Don Juan* is Hepokoski's "Fiery-Pulsed Libertine or Domestic Hero? Don Juan Reconsidered," in *Richard Strauss: New Perspectives*, 135–76. In the second section of his article Hepokoski summarizes the various structural interpretations and ultimately offers one of his own, namely, that the work exploits both structures, but they are not synthesized. The work begins as a rondo (with the various episodes and Don Juan's recurring theme) and at the moment of greatest tension, when the protagonist experiences his moment of collapse (the *Durchbruch*), it becomes a sonata form.

20. *Cosima Wagner–Richard Strauss: Ein Briefwechsel*, ed. Franz Trenner (Tutzing, 1978), 32. Cosima was likely echoing her late husband ("On Franz Liszt's Symphonic Poems" [1857]), where he stresses the importance of the "musical thread" (*musikalische Fade*) over the "scenic motive" (*szenisches Motiv*).

21. The fact that he called *Tod und Verklärung* his third tone poem underscores how Strauss considered *Aus Italien* a "first step" rather than a tone poem in its own right.

22. Later on Strauss would maintain that the mind that created *Tristan* was "as cool as marble," a suggestion that says more about himself than about Wagner.

23. There are actually two versions of Ritter's poem: the one copied by Strauss onto the autograph and the revision as given in the published score.

24. Krause, *Richard Strauss*, 236.

25. From an unpublished memorandum quoted in the exhibition catalog *Richard Strauss Ausstellung zum 100. Geburtstag*, ed. Franz Grasberger and Franz Hadamowsky (Vienna, 1964), 127, henceforth cited as *Strauss-Ausstellung* catalog. We know that Strauss considered this the most important theme from a musical context as well. Whenever *Tod und Verklärung* was quoted musically (*Ein Heldenleben*, *Krämerspiegel*, Four Last Songs) the composer usually chose this theme.

26. Roland Tenschert, *Richard Strauss und Wien* (Vienna, 1949), 15.

27. Guntram's rejection of the Holy Land may well be related to the fact that Strauss was immersed in Schopenhauer and, especially, Nietzsche at the time. Nietzsche would resurface as the catalyst for Strauss's *Also sprach Zarathustra*.

28. See Kurt Wilhelm, "Die geplante Volksoper *Till Eulenspiegel*," in *Richard Strauss Jahrbuch 1954* (Bonn, 1953), 102–9. Till describes himself to the citizens of Schilda: "The scourge of the Philistines, the slave of liberty, reviler of folly, adorer of nature." Wilhelm's article is abridged in English trans. in Schuh, *Chronicle*, 503–08.

29. Strauss did so for Mauke's use in putting together a guide to *Till Eulenspiegel*. See Mauke's *Till Eulenspiegels lustige Streiche*, Der Musikführer no. 103 (Stuttgart, 1896).

30. Strauss's notes for Mauke may be found, in English trans., in Schuh, *Chronicle*, 398.

31. Richard Specht, *Richard Strauss und sein Werk* (Leipzig, 1921), 1:221.

32. *Strauss-Ausstellung* catalog, 127.

33. In his discussion of *Don Juan*, Alfred Lorenz recognizes rondo, with its episodes and returning rondo theme, as a structural metaphor for sexual libertinism. See Lorenz, "Neue Formerkenntnisse, angewandt auf Richard Straussens 'Don Juan,'" *Archiv für Musikforschung* 1 (1936): 452–66. Lorenz is discussed in depth in Hepokoski's "*Don Juan* Reinvestigated," 144–45.

34. It has been suggested that, early on, Strauss denied reading Nietzsche in order not to irritate his father.

35. Just ten months before his death, Strauss declared: "I shall never be converted and I will remain true to my old religion of the classics until my life's end!" Schuh, *Chronicle*, 294.

36. "Symphonischer Optimismus in fin-de-siècle-Form, dem 20. Jahrhundert gewidmet." See Arthur Seidl, *Moderner Geist in der Deutschen Tonkunst* (Berlin, 1900), 91.

37. *Strauss-Ausstellung* catalog, 127. Theoretically speaking, the two most distant keys of the diatonic scale are separated by a tritone, not a minor second. Strauss would explore the augmented fourth duality in *Symphonia domestica*. Nonetheless, contrasts of a minor second were important to suggest opposite realms: for example the brash, young Octavian (E major) versus the older, wiser Marschallin (E♭ major); and, in *Ariadne*, the banal, everyday behind-the-scenes prologue (C major) versus the sublime ending of the opera (D♭ major).

38. See Garmisch sketchbook, Tr. 3, fol. 16. In preliminary sketches the C–G–C figure is described as "[the] universe, always immovable, fixed, unchangeable." See Tr. 2, fol. 38ᵛ.

39. Strauss again turns to a static, diatonic A♭ major in *Salome* at the moment when John the Baptist first mentions Christ (rehearsal no. 132): "He is in a boat on the Sea of Galilee." In a letter to Stefan Zweig, Strauss once remarked: "Perhaps you are not aware how passionate an anti-Christ I am. . . . I tried to compose the good Jochanaan more or less as a clown." *A Confidential Matter: The Letters of Richard Strauss and Stefan Zweig, 1931–1935*, ed. Schuh, trans. Max Knight (Berkeley and Los Angeles, 1977), 90.

40. The most extensive use of the viola in an ironic or mocking way is, of course, the depiction of Sancho Panza in *Don Quixote*.

41. In a diary entry of 16 April 1897, Strauss writes: "Symphonic poem *Hero and World* begins to take shape; as a satyr play to accompany it—*Don Quichote*. Franz Alexander [Strauss] progresses well, as does his dear mother." (The son, Franz, was born on 12 April 1897.) See Schuh, "Der Sohn im Wort und in der Musik des Vaters," *Festschrift Dr. Franz Strauss* (Tutzing, 1967), 104.

42. Strauss's experience with writing for solo cello dates back to age seventeen, when he wrote the Sonata in F Major Op. 6 for the cellist Hans Wihan. Two years later he wrote a Romanza for Cello and Orchestra (WoO 75), also for Wihan.

43. The closest model may well be Berlioz's *Harold in Italy*.

44. Rudolf Louis's remarks about Strauss's tone poems appear in English translation in Gilliam, *Richard Strauss and His World*, 305–10.

45. Schuh, *Chronicle*, 461.

46. I am indebted to John Michael Cooper for bringing this information to my attention: see Cooper, "The Hero Transformed: the Relationship between *Don Quixote* and *Ein Heldenleben* Reconsidered" *Richard Strauss-Blätter* 30 (1993): 3–21.

47. It is not well known, perhaps due to Schuh's misreading of Strauss's sketch annotations, that the hero's adversaries were as much internal as external. In a sketchbook he writes: "Ultimately he arises in order to confront the inner enemies (doubt, disgust) and external enemies." See Garmisch sketchbook, Tr. 5, fol. 20ᵛ.

48. Strauss's son, Franz, was born just four days before Strauss's first documented mention of *Heldenleben* on 16 April 1897 (see note 41). He saw wife and son for the first time on the fifteenth.

49. The fact that he did not quote *Aus Italien* serves as further evidence that he did not consider it a tone poem in its own right.

50. In 1899 Strauss briefly toyed with the idea of a tone poem to be called *Frühling;* early the next year he sketched out a scenario for a symphonic work called *Künstlertragödie*. Later on, shortly after completing *Salome,* he envisaged a symphonic work (*Vier Frauengestalten der National Gallery*) that would be based on four female portraits in the London National Gallery: Paul Veronese's *Sleeping Girl,* William Hogarth's *The Shrimp Girl,* Joshua Reynold's *Heads of Angels,* and George Romney's portrait of Lady Hamilton. During the mid-1920s, he planned a work entitled *Trigon: Sinfonia zu 3 Themen.* The fifth of these unrealized projects (*Die Donau,* 1941–42) got the farthest; some 411 measures of *Particell* survive.

51. Schuh, "Der Sohn im Wort," 106. This plan was jotted down on the inside back cover sheet of a Garmisch sketchbook (Tr. 8). It was subsequently removed.

52. Indeed, Strauss's next detailed portrayal of his family life would be *Intermezzo* (1921), an *opera domestica* based on his wife's mistaken belief that he was having an affair. Ironically, Strauss received Pauline's letter of accusation one day after he had sketched out the 25 May *Symphonia domestica* scenario.

53. Letter to Rolland (5 July 1905) in *Richard Strauss and Romain Rolland: Correspondence, Diary, and Essays,* ed. Rollo Myers (Berkeley and Los Angeles, 1968), 29.

54. Krause, *Richard Strauss,* 221–22.

55. Leon Botstein, "The Enigmas of Strauss: A Revisionist View," in *Richard Strauss and His World,* 22.

56. Hermann Unger, *Lebendige Musik in zwei Jahrtausenden* (Cologne, 1940), 305.

57. Richard-Strauss-Archiv, Garmisch: *Tagebuch* 1911. Cited, in part, in Herta Blaukopf, "Rivalität und Freundschaft," in *Gustav Mahler–Richard Strauss: Briefwechsel,* ed. Herta Blaukopf (Munich, 1980), 210–11.

58. We recall that Zarathustra left his home for the mountains and after ten years descended. Later on one thinks of such works as Thomas Mann's *Magic Mountain.* Moreover, around the time of *Eine Alpensinfonie* and shortly thereafter, a veritable mountain cult had grown up in German popular culture. Siegfried Kracauer discusses at length the genre of *Bergfilme* in the 1920s in *From Caligari to Hitler: A Psychological History of German Film* (Princeton, NJ, 1947), 110–12.

59. Night, Sunrise, The Ascent, Entry in the Forest, Wandering by the Brook, By the Waterfall, Apparition, On the Flowering Meadows, On the Pastures, Through Thicket and Briar to Wrong Paths, On the Glacier, Dangerous Moment, On the Summit, The Vision, Mists Arrive, The Sun Gradually Darkens, Elegy, Calm before the Storm, Tempest and Storm—Descent, Sunset, Echo, and Night.

60. Specht, *Richard Strauss und sein Werk,* 348.

61. During the 1960s and early 1970s one could find one or two recordings in record catalogs; today there are over a dozen different interpretations. The past decade has witnessed numerous Strauss festivals and recording projects. The years 1989 and 1990 saw international Strauss conferences in Leipzig and Durham, North Carolina, respectively. In August 1992 Bard College held a two-week Strauss festival, which involved lectures, panel discussions, and eleven concerts.

Selected Bibliography

CORRESPONDENCE

Hans von Bülow–Richard Strauss Correspondence. Ed. Willi Schuh and Franz Trenner. Trans. Anthony Gishford. London, 1953.

Gustav Mahler–Richard Strauss: Correspondence, 1888–1911. Ed. Herta Blaukopf. Trans. Edmund Jephcott. Chicago, 1984.

Richard Strauss: Briefe an die Eltern, 1882–1906. Ed. Willi Schuh. Zurich, 1954.

Richard Strauss and Romain Rolland: Correspondence, Diary, and Essays. Ed. Rollo Myers. Berkeley and Los Angeles, 1968.

OTHER SOURCES

Armstrong, Thomas. *Strauss's Tone Poems.* Oxford, 1931.

Brecher, Gustav. *Richard Strauss: Eine monographische Skizze.* Leipzig, [1900].

Del Mar, Norman. *Richard Strauss: A Critical Commentary on His Life and Works.* 3 vols. London, 1962–72.

Erhardt, Otto. *Richard Strauss: Leben, Wirken, Schaffen.* Freiburg, 1953.

Finck, Henry. *Richard Strauss: The Man and His Works.* Boston, 1917.

Gilliam, Bryan. "Strauss's Preliminary Opera Sketches: Thematic Fragments and Symphonic Continuity," *19th-Century Music* 9 (1986): 176–88.

———, ed. *Richard Strauss and His World.* Princeton, N.J., 1992.

———, ed. *Richard Strauss: New Perspectives on the Composer and His Work.* Durham, NC, 1992.

Jefferson, Alan. *Richard Strauss.* London, 1973.

Kennedy, Michael. *Richard Strauss.* The Master Musicians. 2d ed. London, 1988.

———. *Strauss Tone Poems.* BBC Music Guides. London, 1984.

Klauwell, Otto. *Geschichte der Programmusik von ihren Anfangen bis zur Gegenwart.* Leipzig, 1910.

Krause, Ernst. *Richard Strauss: The Man and His Works.* Trans. John Coombs. Boston, 1969.

Murphy, Edward. "Tonal Organization in Five Strauss Tone Poems," *Music Review* 44 (1983): 223–33.

Muschler, Reinhold. *Richard Strauss.* Hildesheim, 1924.

Newman, Ernest. *Richard Strauss.* Living Masters of Music. London, 1908.

Schrenk, Walter. *Richard Strauss und die neue Musik.* Berlin, 1924.

Schuh, Willi. *Richard Strauss: A Chronicle of the Early Years, 1864–1898.* Trans. Mary Whitall. Cambridge, 1982.

Seidl, Arthur. *Straussiana: Aufsätze zur Richard Strauss-Frage aus drei Jahrzehnten.* Regensburg, [1913].

Specht, Richard. *Richard Strauss und sein Werk.* 2 vols. Leipzig, 1921.

Steinitzer, Max. *Richard Strauss.* Berlin and Leipzig, 1911.

Strauss, Richard. *Recollections and Reflections.* Ed. Willi Schuh. Trans. L. J. Lawrence. London, 1953.

Tenschert, Roland. "Die Tonsymbolik bei Richard Strauss," *Die Musik* 26 (1933–34): 646–52.

———. *Dreimal Sieben Variationen über das Thema Richard Strauss.* Vienna, 1944.

Trenner, Franz. *Richard Strauss: Dokumente seines Lebens und Schaffens.* Munich, 1954.

————, ed. *Die Skizzenbücher von Richard Strauss*. Veröffentlichungen der Richard-Strauss-Gesellschaft, Munich. Tutzing, 1977.

————, ed. *Richard Strauss Werkverzeichnis*. Veröffentlichungen der Richard-Strauss-Gesellschaft, Munich. Munich, 1993.

Wachten, Edmund. "Das Formproblem in den sinfonischen Dichtungen von Richard Strauss." Ph.D. dissertation, University of Berlin, 1933.

Waltershausen, Hermann W. von. *Richard Strauss: Ein Versuch*. Munich, 1921.

Williamson, John. "The Straussian Tone Poem As Drama." In *Strauss: Also sprach Zarathustra*. Cambridge Music Handbooks. Cambridge, 1993.

CHAPTER FOURTEEN

Mahler: Symphonies 1–4

Stephen E. Hefling

Gustav Mahler's symphonic works constitute both a culmination and a transition at a crucial moment in Western music: he is both the last in the long tradition of Austro-Germanic symphonists and a harbinger of the New Viennese School of Schoenberg and his followers. A world-class opera conductor, Mahler nevertheless concentrated his creative efforts on lieder and, especially, the symphony. His concept of that genre was vast indeed; as he explained to his friend and confidante Natalie Bauer-Lechner during the composition of the Third, "'Symphony' means to me: to build a world with all the resources of the available techniques. The continually new and changing content determines its own form. In this sense, I must always first learn again to create my means of expression anew, even if I am completely in command of the technique, which, I believe, I can now maintain of myself."[1]

Yet he also insisted that such progressive music "does not deserve the name symphony" unless it maintains organic musical coherence. He said of his Fourth Symphony, "Such a work must have something cosmic about it, must be as inexhaustible as life and the world, if it is not to soil its name. And its organism must be *one*, which may not be dissolved by anything unorganic, any patches and binding."[2] Moreover, Mahler frequently acknowledged the strong influence of personal experience on his symphonic worlds; midway through the composition of the Second Symphony he observed:

> My two symphonies treat exhaustively my entire life; it is experience and suffering that I have written down with my life-blood. Truth and poetry in music; and if someone understands how to read well, my life must in fact appear transparent to him in them. So strongly are creation and experience interwoven for me that, if henceforth my life should flow calmly like a

stream through a meadow—I think I would no longer be able to create anything proper.[3]

To unite such cosmic scope, structural cogency, and wide-reaching worldview was Mahler's lifelong artistic quest. Consciously and critically he sought to fuse the compelling musico-dramatic logic of Beethovenian formal command with the psychological intensity of utterance developed by Wagner (whose work he idolized), as well as the lyrical immediacy of Schubert. And almost as influential were the philosophers, poets, and novelists Mahler read time and again: Schopenhauer, Kant, Goethe, Fechner, Rückert, Lipiner, Jean Paul, Dostoevsky, and many others affected him deeply. It is certain that his efforts to make music "treat exhaustively of my entire life" were decisive for both form and content of his first four symphonies, which Mahler himself viewed as a self-contained tetralogy.[4] Yet a perplexing aspect of his oeuvre remains that while he (correctly) denied composing program music in any simplistic way, he nevertheless drafted and discussed programmatic outlines for each of his first four symphonies—then denied these programs any interpretive validity.[5]

Understood in context, Mahler's programmatic utterances can provide metaphorical hints of what he sought to manifest musically; but grasping that context requires familiarity with the complex view of art and the world in which Mahler and his associates were steeped from their student days. Schopenhauer, Wagner, and early Nietzsche were their guiding lights—writers whose work is closely interrelated, and whose thought was absorbed and crystallized by the young poet-philosopher Siegfried Lipiner, Mahler's intimate friend and mentor for over two decades.[6] As we shall see, Lipiner's derivative notion of art as redemption is most immediately apparent in Mahler's Second Symphony, the *Resurrection*; it is also the key to understanding why Mahler could consider that works so disparate as his first four symphonies constitute a tetralogy. But first a brief sketch of the background is in order (with the caveat that brevity necessitates glossing over many subtleties).

Kant, the critical idealist, claimed that we know only the phenomenon, never the *Ding-an-sich* (the thing-in-itself, or in its essence). But Schopenhauer denies this. First, emphasizing his view that all knowledge is conditioned by the subject, he declares that even such notions as space, time, and causality exist only in and for our understanding, and are therefore subjective in nature.[7] Then he boldly posits that *will* is the thing-in-itself, and is directly manifest to us: "it is the one thing known to us immediately, and not given to us merely in the representation, as all else is."[8] By will Schopenhauer understands not only the "in-itselfness" of our individual being, as immediately present in body and consciousness, but also every blind force of nature: "It is the innermost essence, the kernel, of every particular thing, and also of the whole."[9]

As manifest in human beings, the will is in many respects akin to Freud's later notion of the unconscious id, as Thomas Mann and others have observed.[10] And like Freud, who would insist that the ego does not fully control unconscious instinct, Schopenhauer declares that our intellect is merely the servant of the will's desires. He is, then, a determinist, and a pessimistic one: life is an endlessly egocentric cycle in which we are driven by the desires of the will, which are at best only partially satisfied; ennui or restlessness invariably ensues, and the cycle repeats itself. Schopenhauer referred to this as the wheel of Ixion:[11] according to Greek mythology, Zeus punished Ixion's attempt to seduce Hera by binding him to a fiery wheel that rolls perpetually through the sky. The suffering inherent in this vicious circle can be reduced only by recognizing the deceptive egoism of the *principium individuationis* (the principle of individuation) and suppressing the individual will. Schopenhauer suggests two ways in which this might occur. One is the effect of grace, as in Christian or Buddhist religion.[12] The other is the temporary stilling of the will that occurs through dispassionate aesthetic contemplation of art; at such moments, according to Schopenhauer, the beholder temporarily becomes "*pure* will-less, painless, timeless *subject of knowledge*."[13]

And music, in Schopenhauer's view, is the highest of arts. This is because music operates without concepts: whereas painting or sculpture (in the nineteenth century, anyway) had to make use of images, and poetry required the conceptualization of words, music was a direct and immediate manifestation of the will, without mediating concepts. In Schopenhauer's words, "music never expresses the phenomenon, but only the inner nature. . . . It gives the innermost kernel preceding all form, or the heart of things. . . . We could just as well call the world embodied music as embodied will."[14] Whenever words (including sung texts) or images are linked with music, they remain mere analogies of its deeper meaning: "music never expresses the phenomenon, but only the inner nature."[15] On this position, of course, true music could not be program music in the ordinary sense, because stories are conceptualizations and expressions of phenomena.

Schopenhauer's philosophy deeply influenced both the poetry and the music of *Tristan und Isolde* (Mahler's favorite work of musical theater), and Wagner's "Beethoven" essay of 1870 is largely Schopenhauer rehearsed from Wagner's musical viewpoint. For present purposes we should note that, drawing on Schopenhauer's separation of will and representation, Wagner emphasizes the psychological distinction between inward-facing and outward-facing consciousness. Music comes from man's inner life, and is in fact a product of the same mental process as dreaming. But just as the dream of deepest sleep (which is completely removed from outward-looking consciousness) translates itself into a lighter "allegoric dream" that is perceived just before waking, so too, according to

Wagner, the composer approaches the notions of waking consciousness to present a record of his inner vision. Thereby music takes on outward form, especially rhythmic form, to reach forth toward the consciousness of the present without abandoning its direct connection to the timeless universal will.[16] In his later essay "Religion and Art" (1880, written during the composition of *Parsifal*), Wagner claims that the inner life of the will which is music points directly toward his idiosyncratic notion of Christianity. And the role of the artist becomes even more important than hitherto: he is the "poet-priest," purveyor of truth, and mediator of the "crushingly sublime."[17]

In the early 1870s young Friedrich Nietzsche was very much under the spell of Wagner, to whom he dedicated his first major work, *The Birth of Tragedy from the Spirit of Music* (1872). Here Schopenhauer's duality of will and *principium individuationis* is transposed into the tension and interaction between Dionysian and Apollonian energies. Metaphorically, the two polarities may be likened to intoxication (Dionysus) versus dreaming (Apollo), or orgiastic passion as opposed to harmonious restraint. The Apollonian world is that of fair illusion and the plastic arts. The Dionysian realm, however, is rapture and ecstasy such as that aroused by the potent coming of spring; it is union of man and nature; and it is also music, the immediate language of the will. "Transform Beethoven's 'Hymn to Joy' into a painting," Nietzsche writes; "let your imagination conceive the multitudes bowing to the dust, awestruck—then you will approach the Dionysian."[18]

Dionysian ecstasy tears aside the veil of illusion, shattering the *principium individuationis:* thereby nature celebrates an aesthetic event—for in Nietzsche's view, "it is only as an aesthetic phenomenon that existence and the world are eternally justified."[19] And it is the titanic, tragic artist-hero who defiantly reveals Dionysian wisdom through sacrilege and hubris; just such a hero was Aeschylus's Prometheus, who, believing that man and the gods were mutually dependent, challenged divine supremacy and seized fire for humankind. Prometheus's punishment was severe, yet worth enduring: "The splendid 'ability' of the great genius for which even eternal suffering is a slight price, the stern pride of the artist—that is the content and soul of Aeschylus's poem."[20]

According to Nietzsche, the power that delivered Prometheus from the torturing vultures and transformed the myth into a vehicle of Dionysian wisdom was "the Heracleian power of music"; attaining its highest manifestation in tragedy, music invests myth with new and more profound significance. Nietzsche expands on this as follows:

> It is only through the spirit of music that we can understand the joy involved in the annihilation of the individual. For it is only in particular examples of such annihilation that we see clearly the eternal phenomenon of Dionysian art, which gives expression to the will in its omnipotence, as it were, behind

the *principium individuationis*, the eternal life beyond all phenomena, and despite all annihilation . . . the hero, the highest
manifestation of the will, is negated for our pleasure, because
he is only phenomenon, and because the eternal life of the will
is not affected by his annihilation . . . music is the immediate
idea of this life.[21]

For Nietzsche "all that comes into being must be ready for a sorrowful end"; the "maddening sting of these pains" pierces us just at the moment when, in Dionysian ecstasy, we anticipate the indestructibility and
eternity of infinite primordial joy. The "metaphysical comfort" of art is
only momentary.[22]

When Mahler first came to know Siegfried Lipiner, the young poet
had already published *Prometheus Unbound* (1876), a work that co-opts
nearly all the major motives of Wagner's "Beethoven" and Nietzsche's
Birth of Tragedy—the revelation of inner essence through allegorical
dream, the necessity of active sin and hubris, the redemption of the hero
through annihilation, the role of the poet-apostle, man's Dionysian ecstasy
and subjugation of the individual will, the tragic character of suffering,
and so forth. Yet (prior to *Parsifal*) it also manifests an unusual Christian
slant: a quotation from 1 Corinthians (15:36) is the motto of the work—
"What you sow shall not come to life unless it has died first"—and it is
Christ who appears to Prometheus at his moment of deepest despair, offering salvation for humanity if they agree to accept suffering for the sake
of their redemption in place of the nothingness that has resulted from
their senseless struggles.[23]

Two years after the poem was published, Lipiner summarized his
view of Promethean striving and suffering in a lecture, "On the Elements
of a Renewal of Religious Ideas in the Present," which also discusses the
role of art in that renewal. Here Lipiner asserts that the artist already
dwells in a world above reality, which is a religious facet of his being,
whether he acknowledges it or not. His specifically artistic function is to
manifest this special vision in a generally accessible manner.[24] Art is a symbolic abbreviation of life—and this leads man to the lofty realization that
the world itself is a work of art. In such moments of insight the spirit is
filled with the holiest religious agitation.[25] Echoing Nietzsche, Lipiner
claims for the tragic hero the status of man, mediator, and god all at
once.[26] Tragedy, he says, is religion, and in tragic art man becomes religious; through its power of release from transitory human nature, man
feels his resurrection as a deity. In tragedy

we suffer to the extreme, then, only bleeding, man wrests himself from his transitory self, and in [tragedy] the joy of all joys
rushes through us, for in this bleeding tearing-oneself-away we
feel the omnipotence and magnificence of the higher self, our
own godliness. . . . Here the truest son of Prometheus, proud
and daring, as never before, may praise the divinity, for he

himself is become this divinity. Here and only here are death and time overcome, here and only here are the sting of pain and victory of hell torn away. . . . The giant Pain is here—and only here—properly finished; it overcomes the giant I.[27]

Not coincidentally, these last lines, like the motto of Lipiner's *Prometheus*, unquestionably call to mind Mahler's concluding verses in the Second Symphony for anyone familiar with it:

> O believe, my heart, O believe:
> Yours is . . . what you longed for!
> Yours, what you loved,
> What you struggled for. . . .
> O Pain! You all-penetrating one!
> From you I have broken away!
> O Death! You all-conquering one!
> Now you are conquered!
> With wings which I have won for myself in fervent striving of Love
> I will soar . . .
> I will die in order to live!

For redemption was indeed the issue that preoccupied Mahler throughout the gestation of his first two symphonies; it had become the "Alpha and Omega of his life and art"[28] by the time he completed the Second, which he regarded as the "true, loftier solution" to the struggle that inspired his First.[29] (Yet here we anticipate somewhat: although the solution he espoused was broadly familiar to him from his student days, Mahler had no specific conception of either text or music for his *Resurrection* chorus until 1894, six years after the work was begun.)

That, in brief, is the complex philosophical background that informs each of Mahler's first four symphonies. And it suggests why Mahler withdrew his programmatic commentaries, fearing they would be misunderstood: given the nature of music, a program could offer only "a few milestones and signposts for the journey—or, shall we say, a star map in order to comprehend the night sky with all its luminous worlds."[30] Mahler's worldview was too complex to condense into a concert-book sketch; the listener who sought to tick off specific pictures and plots in his music would miss the point. But bearing all this in mind, the programs can be used as metaphorical hints of meaning.

The First Symphony (*Titan,* 1885?–1888)

"Only when I experience do I 'compose'," Mahler once wrote, "and only when I compose do I experience!"[31] The experience leading to the composition of his First Symphony, appropriately dubbed "Mahler's *Werther*" by Bruno Walter,[32] was a series of passionate yet unsuccessful love affairs, two of which are especially noteworthy. In Kassel during the winter of 1884–85 Mahler composed the *Lieder eines fahrenden Gesellen* (Songs of a wayfarer) for his beloved, the soprano Johanna Richter. Then three years later in Leipzig, enchanted by Marion von Weber (wife of the famous composer's grandson), he completed the First Symphony at white-hot speed, substantially incorporating two of the *Gesellen-Lieder* into the new symphonic work. It also included an entire movement—the "Blumine" *andante*, later removed—that was a token of love for Marion.[33] Mahler denied none of this, yet stressed that it was only the impulse for the work: "I would like to see it emphasized that the symphony begins at a point beyond the *love-affair*, that lies at the basis of it, in that it dates from earlier in the creative artist's emotional life. But the outer experience was the *occasion* [*Anlaß*] for the work, not its content."[34]

Four programmatic outlines of varying length survive for the First Symphony. These may be conflated and paraphrased as follows:

> For the 1893–94 performances Mahler entitled the work "'Titan,' a Tone Poem in Symphony Form," in two parts: he evidently had in mind a powerful, somewhat naive young hero, his life and suffering, and his struggle and defeat by fate. Part I, "From the Days of Youth," begins with the first movement, "Spring Without End." The slow introduction represents the awakening of nature after a long winter's sleep; the long-held A harmonics suggest the sunlight of the summer day shimmering and glimmering through the branches. In the course of the movement, Nature, as though revealing herself making music, grasps us with her radiance, and also with her uncanny mysticism. The hero and we are swept forward by Dionysian jubilation, as yet completely unbroken and untroubled. At the close of the movement, where the timpani have the theme, the hero bursts out laughing and runs away. Originally there followed the "Blumine" Andante, a sentimental, rapturous love episode, jokingly also called the hero's "youthful asininity" by Mahler. In the scherzo, "In Full Sail," the young man comports himself in a more powerfully masculine, robust, fit-for-life manner; Mahler also likened it to a bridal procession expressing boundless joy and delight.
>
> Part II, "Commedia humana" ("The Human Comedy"), begins "Aground," when the hero has "found a hair in his soup." Extrinsically, one could picture the proceedings as follows: A funeral procession passes by the hero, and he is seized by the complete misery and abject sorrow of the world, with all its lacerating contrasts and ghastly irony. The external inspiration came from a children's fairy-tale illustration, "The Hunter's Funeral

Procession," in which animals of the forest in farcical postures accompany the coffin of the deceased hunter to the grave. The "Bruder Martin" funeral march should be imagined as though played torpidly by a miserable provincial band (just the way they play at funerals). In the midst of this we hear the coarseness and banality of the world in the sounds of an intermingling Bohemian amateur ensemble; the irony is especially sharp after the interlude when the funeral band returns from the burial, striking up the customary "merry tune" (which here cuts through to the marrow). Immediately follows "Dall' Inferno" ("Out of Hell"), like the sudden, terrifying scream of a heart wounded to the quick: the hero is abandoned to the most fearful struggle with all the sorrow of the world. Again and again when he seems to have raised himself above destiny and to have become master of it, he is hit on the head by Fate, as is the motive of victory with him. Only in death does he achieve the victory, having conquered himself and his lost illusions (which are evoked by the return of themes from previous movements, as though the sun suddenly emerged after a stormy night). He rises anew and triumphs because he has succeeded in creating his own inner world, which neither life nor death can take away from him. Then follows the magnificent victory chorale![35]

It is, then, a symphony concerned with the inner life of a hero. Beethoven's *Eroica* and Berlioz's *Fantastique,* two of Mahler's favorite works, which both contain phantasmal funeral marches, are clear precedents. And as in the *Fantastique,* this Titanic hero is a projection of the composer himself, as confirmed by Mahler's quotations from his autobiographical *Lieder eines fahrenden Gesellen.* The drama begins with the awakening of nature in spring and the hero's untroubled Dionysian rapture; he succumbs to erotic enchantment and dances "in full sail" ("Blumine" and the scherzo; see also below). But Nietzsche's "maddening sting of pain" arrives just when primordial joy seems limitless: the love episode, this "youthful asininity" as Mahler called it *post facto,* turns sour. (In Schopenhauer's view, the sexual manifestation of the *principium individuationis* typically begets suffering.) The veil of fair illusion is torn aside, and all that has come into being must be ready for a sorrowful end: the hero envisages his funeral procession as like that of a fairy-tale woodcut, in which he is mocked by the animal inhabitants of nature; more than tragic in the Nietzschean sense, this moment is bitterly ironic, based as it is on the minor-mode "learned" treatment of "Bruder Martin" (= "Frère Jacques"). Emerging from this nocturnal terror with a scream, the hero struggles with titanic persistence to wrest himself from his transitory being. He "arises anew and triumphs because he has succeeded in creating his own inner world"—the inner world of tragic art that denies the *principium individuationis.* He has conquered himself and can endure the memory and temptations of his past illusion; lasting jubilation breaks out. The hero has accepted the necessity of suffering for redemption and is reborn as an artist who preserves and expounds the legacy of myth through music, which overcomes the world of appearances.

The First Symphony was originally cast in two large parts (*Abteilungen*) of three and two movements respectively. It opens with a remarkable variant on traditional first-movement sonata procedure with slow introduction: the "awakening of nature," marked "slow, dragging, like a sound of nature" (*Wie ein Naturlaut*) in the score, commences with pedal point As sustained in all registers (A–a^4); harmonics in all the string sections evoke "the shimmering and glimmering of the air."[36] The first melodic interval is a thrice-heard perfect fourth (here A–E): this is the basic kernel for much of the motivic material throughout the work. Sounds of distant hunting parties (first in the clarinets, then in offstage trumpets) and the call of a cuckoo gradually establish the sustained As as a dominant pedal; and this subtle yet wide-reaching dominant tension will be maintained for the greater part of the movement's exposition. While precedents for such "nature music" extend at least back to Beethoven's *Pastoral*, and include Weber's *Der Freischütz*, Berlioz's *Fantastique*, and lieder by Schubert and Schumann, it seems likely that Wagner's "Forest Murmurs" in *Siegfried* and Mahler's own "Waldmärchen" movement in *Das klagende Lied* (1880) are the most immediate influences. Stylized *Naturlaut* passages of various sorts feature prominently in many of Mahler's later works as well. Indeed, the awesome beauty and power of nature were fundamental to the conception of his music: from 1893 on he chose to compose only during summer months, secluded in a small "composing hut" by a lake or in the woods of the Austrian countryside (Ill. 14.1).

A slightly menacing transition (with chromatic inflections in divided cellos and basses, four mm. after rehearsal no. 3ff.) ushers in the lied material that will infuse the entire first-movement exposition, which comprises a reshuffling of the first three strophes from Mahler's own "Wayfarer" song "Ging' heut' morgens uber's Feld." The opening lines of the text (Mahler's own) provide a good metaphor for the inner feeling conveyed in this music:

> I went out this morning over the field,
> Dew still hung on the grass,
> And the zesty finch said to me:
> "Hey, there! Right?
> Good morning! Hey, right? You!
> Isn't it a beautiful world?
> Beautiful world?
> Zink, zink!
> How the world pleases me!

No sooner has the tonic (D major) arrived with the opening phrase of the song than Mahler begins establishing the dominant (rehearsal no. 5ff.);

ILLUSTRATION 14.1. Steinbach am Attersee, where Mahler completed his Second Symphony (summers of 1893 and 1894) and composed all of his Third (1895–96). Mahler's composing hut—his *Häuschen*—is beside the tree near the shore at the right of the photograph; in the background are the imposing Höllengebirge. Bruno Walter writes of his visit here in 1896: "When, on our way to his house, my glance fell upon the Höllengebirge, whose forbidding rocky walls formed the background of an otherwise charming landscape, Mahler said: 'No need to look there any more—that's all been used up and set to music by me.'" (Walter, *Gustav Mahler*, trans. Galston, p. 14). Photograph courtesy of the Internationale Gustav Mahler Gesellschaft, Vienna.

the "new" key area, already prominent in the introduction, is projected through secondary dominant (nine mm. after rehearsal no. 6ff.) and cadentially confirmed more than thirty bars after it was introduced (seven mm. after rehearsal no. 7). But no contrasting thematic material appears here: Mahler continues to spin forth smooth, symmetrical phrases from "Ging heut' morgens." Schubert, especially the "Unfinished," was probably his inspiration for an exposition based entirely on lied-like material, but Mahler's "monothematic" treatment of sonata procedure is rooted in Haydn and Mozart (e.g., the "Haffner" Symphony, K. 385). And the lack of contrast seems fitting for the "Dionysian jubilation, as yet entirely unbroken and untroubled," that Mahler sought to project here.

As in each of Mahler's first three symphonies, the development section of the First emphasizes musical drama more than motivic working-out. (Beethoven had managed both; Mahler would achieve a better balance beginning with his Fourth.) In Brucknerian fashion he allows the momentum of the exposition's closing section to dissipate almost to a standstill before the double bar, then proceeds into the new section at a reflective pace. The "awakening nature" of the introduction returns and reverses the tonal direction of the exposition: the dominant now gives way to a generous passage of tonic (rehearsal no. 15ff.; even a conservative theorist such as Koch would allow this, but it is effective here precisely because the exposition had been so dominant-focused). In the course of this Mahler exploits the tonal tension between line and chord, a Wagnerian procedure he would deploy frequently: the passage from rehearsal numbers 13 through 14ff. and after is vertically based on F but presses horizontally toward A (minor). The chromatic material from the earlier introduction recurs here, and the cellos and horns introduce plaintive material, partially derived from the lied, that will prove decisive for the movement's outcome (Ex. 14.1).

EXAMPLE 14.1. Mahler, First Symphony, movt. 1
a. mm. 185ff. (4 mm. before rehearsal no. 14ff.)

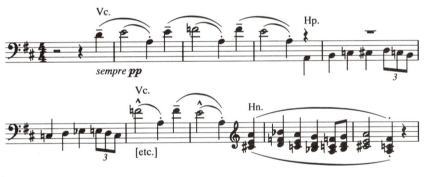

b. m. 358 (rehearsal no. 26ff.)

"Ging heut' morgens" returns with D major, and the lied phrases are reshuffled, ornamented, and modulated (D–A–Db–Ab–C–F) with no loss of cheerful vigor.[37] But matters become more serious with the modal shift to F minor (eight mm. after rehearsal no. 21): the music soon fixates on fragments from the material shown in Example 14.1; linear and vertical polarities again conflict (F minor/Db major, four mm. before rehearsal no. 23ff.), and there ensues a thirty-bar struggle for tonal and motivic clarification that prefigures the much longer conflict manifest in the symphony's finale. (Here again, Wagner's influence seems apparent.) Then comes the "breakthrough," the unexpected, characteristically Mahlerian change of scene that fascinates many commentators: from nowhere a *for-tissimo* D chord, with hunting calls in winds and brass, precipitates the tonal and thematic recapitulation. Both the nature of the song material it-self and its use in the development invite a shortened reprise; it acceler-ates seamlessly and ebulliently into a brief coda, which resembles the close of the exposition.[38]

At the 1889 Budapest premiere the "Blumine" *andante* was the sym-phony's second movement. In revising the work for the Hamburg and Weimar performances of 1893–94, Mahler first deleted "Blumine" from his autograph score, then reinstated it. After that season he never played it again, and he did not include it in the published score of 1897—yet nei-ther did he destroy the manuscripts.[39] The movement is a simple, modi-fied ternary serenade in C major, lightly scored, with prominent solo trumpet; in key, texture, and thematic style it was clearly designed to stand apart from the rest of the symphony. Repetitive and slightly saccha-rine, "Blumine" may well have caused Mahler to wince in later years ("youthful asininity"); but as noted, he inscribed a copy of it to Marion von Weber in 1888, and unquestionably it had a place in the overall scheme of the work, as the remaining thematic allusions in both the scherzo and finale attest.

The scherzo stems from the folksy Austrian *Ländler* tradition Mahler knew from Schubert's piano music and Bruckner's symphonies;[40] but here the dance takes on extraordinary *Schwung* and boldness. Several mo-tives recall "Hans und Grethe," Mahler's early song about sweethearts at a May dance, and there are also references to "Blumine," as shown in Ex-ample 14.2. The second of these launches a long episode in C♯ (rehearsal no. 8), marked "Wild": its raucous counterpoint, straining contours, and biting orchestration show Mahler able to muster as much musical rawness as his most important contemporary, Richard Strauss. The trio ("In slow waltz time" in the autograph) stops just short of overplaying its suave, flat-tering charm; echoes of the first section, plus the brusque return to it, suggest the symphonic hero is happier in the lusty scherzo *Ländler*.

Musical irony and grotesquerie were not altogether novel in the late 1880s; the great lieder cycles of Schubert and Schumann were standard fare, and the Berlioz *Fantastique*, if not universally revered (especially in Vienna), was certainly known. But the pungent combination Mahler of-fered his early listeners in the slow movement of the First Symphony left nearly all of them utterly nonplussed;[41] precedents notwithstanding, no one had done anything quite so bizarre—and Mahler himself never again wrote music quite so blatantly parodistic. Formally, the movement is like a ternary funeral march with trio; the A section includes the minor-mode canon on "Bruder Martin" plus the "Bohemian amateurs" lampoon (and also the "merry tune" in the closing A section). The contrasts are indeed "lacerating," not least because the material itself is musically "low-born"—the first of many times Mahler would challenge the tradition of art music through interpolation of banality. The "trio" provides repose, but this is

EXAMPLE 14.2. Mahler, First Symphony
a. "Blumine" movement, mm. 5–6

Andante allegretto

b. movt. 2, (scherzo), mm. 18–20 (4 mm. after rehearsal no. 2)

Kräftig bewegt, doch nicht zu schnell

c. movt. 2, mm. 68–71 (rehearsal no. 8ff.)

Wild

less than reassuring for listeners who know "Die zwei blauen Augen" (The two blue eyes), Mahler's *Wayfarer* song on which it is based:

> I went out in the silent night
> In the silent night, over the dark heath.
> No one bid me farewell,
> Farewell, farewell, farewell!
> My companions were love and sorrow!
>
> By the road stands a linden tree,
> There for the first time I rested in sleep
> Under the linden tree!
> It snowed its blossoms over me,
> Then I knew not what life does
> Everything, everything was good again!
> Ah, everything good again!
> Everything! Everything! Love, and sorrow,
> And world, and dream!

Mahler's discussion with Natalie Bauer-Lechner about the extraordinary orchestral effects in this slow movement offers us a striking glimpse of how he approached this facet of his art overall:

I told Mahler what an unbelievable sound-impression the First, and particularly the "Bruder Martin" movement, made upon me each time. "And so it must," Mahler responded. "That lies in the manner in which I use the instruments, which, in the first movement, are entirely hidden behind a shining sea of tone—just as a glowing body is invisible behind the brightness that emanates from it. In the third movement the instruments are again disguised in another way, and proceed as though in a strange transformation: everything must sound dull and muted, like shadows that pass by us. That each entrance in the canon should appear clearly, surprising in its sound color—drawing attention to itself somewhat—caused me a lot of headaches in the instrumentation, until I finally brought it to expression just as it today has that rare, disorienting, uncanny effect on you. And in fact I believe how I achieved this has not yet occurred to anyone else. When I want to bring forth a soft, restrained tone, I don't let it be played by an instrument that can easily deliver it, but assign it to an instrument that can produce it only by straining and forcing, and often even over-straining and overstepping, its natural limitations. So the basses and bassoon often have to squeal in the highest notes, and the flutes puff deep below. . . .

While in the first and third movements the orchestra steps back behind its own subject-matter, in the second and fourth, on the other hand, I was at pains to have it be recognized most brilliantly.[42]

Indeed. Mahler's "terrifying scream" at the onset of the last movement was so brilliantly powerful at the premiere that one fashionable lady convulsively dropped everything she was holding.[43] To underscore the struggles and ultimate victory in this drama, Mahler has mixed aspects of rondo and sonata procedures, as shown in Table 14.1, which also identifies the most prominent connections with previous portions of the symphony. The overall tonal scheme is "progressive"—F minor to D major, "Dall' Inferno al Paradiso" (D major being associated with the untroubled jubilation of the first movement).[44] This plus the abrupt modulations and highly episodic nature of the material would seem to belie traditional sonata procedure; yet sonata influence seems apparent in the developmental passages, the partial recapitulation in F minor, and the symmetry of the first and final C sections, which function like codetta and coda.[45]

A crucial moment for the ultimate victory in the finale is the tonal breakthrough of the "victory chorale" from C up to D between rehearsal numbers 33 and 34 (see Ex. 14.3). The basic procedure is Wagnerian ("expressive" tonality), but the particulars vexed Mahler considerably, and he was quite proud of the "freest and most daring modulation" he finally adopted: "my D chord had to sound as though it had fallen from

TABLE 14.1
Mahler, First Symphony, movt. 4, outline of formal procedure

6	8	9+5	16	21	22	26	28	30+4	33-1
Int.	A1A2A3		B	Trans.	A	C	A	Int.	C
			[~"Blumine"]	[~ 1st mvt. int.]	[developed]	(Chorale, *p*)	(dev.)		(Chorale, *fff*)
V/f→f - - - -			/Db- - - - - - -/g			C	c	V/c- - - //	

34	38	39	40-5	45	46	49	51-1	52	54ff
C	Trans.		B	(A1)A1	A3	Trans.		C→	Coda
(chorale extended)	[~1st mvt. int.; ~"Blumine"]			[= 1st mvt. climax]					(C ext.)
D! - - - - - - - - /C; ^{F}/V ped. - - - - f (4/Db) ~~~~~~~~~^{V}/$_D$ → **D**									

heaven, as though it came from another world."[46] Richard Strauss thought this passage should bring the work quickly to conclusion, but Mahler viewed it as an illusory redemption:[47] the Dionysian hero had to accept more battering and personal annihilation, the overcoming of the *principium individuationis*, before lasting victory could obtain. And it finally does so in a triumphant apotheosis rivaling the best such moments in Beethoven.

EXAMPLE 14.3. Mahler, First Symphony, movt. 4, mm. 369–74 (1 bar before rehearsal no. 33ff.)

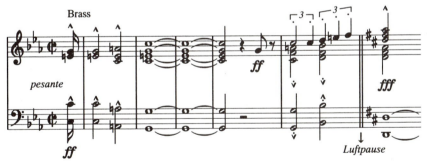

The Second Symphony (*Resurrection,* 1888–94)

Characteristically for Mahler, the jubilant victory of the First could not long satisfy him. Indeed, in January 1888, before the symphony was finished and while its creator was still in the throes of his passionate but illicit affair with Marion von Weber, Mahler began sketching the C-minor opening of the Second Symphony and was terrified by one of the uncanny visions that occasionally gripped him while composing. "He saw himself lying dead on a bier under wreaths and flowers (which were in his room from the performance of the *Pintos*), until Frau von Weber quickly took all flowers away from him."[48] Mahler subsequently titled this movement "Todtenfeier" (Funeral rites)—doubtless an allusion to his vision of the bier, but almost certainly also to Adam Mickiewicz's epic poem *Dziady*, which Siegfried Lipiner had just brought out in German translation—entitled *Todtenfeier*—the previous year. Part 4 of *Todtenfeier (Dziady)* is an elaboration on the *Werther* theme: the hero Gustav, in love with Maria, takes his own life after she marries someone else. Thereupon he is condemned as a wandering soul to hover in the vicinity of his beloved until she departs from earth and becomes an angel; thus Gustav has become, in Lipiner's words, a Werther *sub specie aeternitatis* (from the point of view of eternity). For Lipiner, Gustav's suicide represents nothing less than "*the Fall of Man* and its punishment"—and in his (and Mahler's) view, such Promethean defiance leads toward self-transcendence and salvation.[49] As Mahler later said of the "Todtenfeier" movement, "it is the hero of my D-major symphony whom I am bearing to the grave."[50]

As he had in the First Symphony, Mahler again turned to the *Lieder eines fahrenden Gesellen* for motivic material, this time to the suicidal third song, "Ich hab' ein glühend Messer" (I have a burning knife)—for Mahler's wayfarer, like Mickiewicz's Gustav, is utterly obsessed by the haunting image of his beloved. As Examples 14.4 and 14.5 show, the song provides the substance not only for the symphonic movement's main

EXAMPLE 14.4.
a. Mahler, Second Symphony, movt. 2 ("Todtenfeier"), analytical sketch of opening theme

b. Mahler, *Lieder eines fahrenden Gesellen*, No. 3, analytical sketch of opening (transposed)

theme but also for its shattering climax, just before the recapitulation: this is the moment when, psychologically, the hero recalls his suicide and his ensuing realization that his life was not actually ended by the dagger. The sounding of the *Dies irae* shortly before (eight mm. before rehearsal no. 17) provides an unmistakable hint of what is at hand. Throughout the sketching process Mahler shaped the movement around its cataclysmic denouement, which is dramatically compelling precisely because it does not obliterate but rather reawakens the hero's inner consciousness. Recapitulation, and therefore broad symphonic sonata procedure, are appropriate to such a drama, and that is the formal scheme in which Mahler convincingly cast it. Exposition and reprise, equal in length, flank an immense bipartite development: this consists of two great waves of energy, the second more powerful than the first, that swell toward the high point. Structurally, the overall scheme of the development hinges on the expressive semitonal conflict between E and E♭: this issue is already present in the exposition's lyrical second theme (rehearsal nos. 3–4), which begins serenely in E major and shifts within bars to an acrid close in E♭ minor.[51] Several passages of the development (rehearsal no. 12ff., five mm. after rehearsal no. 16ff., one m. before rehearsal no. 18ff.) seem to verge on losing control: Mahler presses tonal coherence to the limit by (in Schenkerian

EXAMPLE 14.5.

a. Mahler, Second Symphony, climax of movt. 1, mm. 324–29 (one bar before rehearsal no. 20ff.), analytical sketch

b. Mahler, *Lieder eines fahrenden Gesellen*, No. 3, mm. 66–68 (transposed), analytical sketch

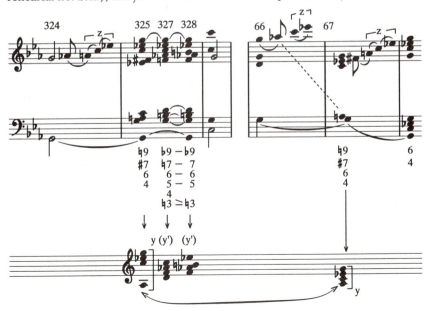

terms) all but swamping the middleground continuity with agitated fore-ground dissonance—a technique he will deploy with increasing sophisti-cation in later works as well.

Although completed only months after his First Symphony, Mahler's "Todtenfeier" movement considerably surpasses the First in both formal cogency and dramatic intensity. The inspiration of the Werther figure *sub specie aeternitatis* presented remarkable opportunities for music's inward-facing flow of feeling; but it also presented a major obstacle: how to con-tinue a symphonic world that begins in suicide. Mahler managed to sketch the opening of the A♭ *andante* much as he would eventually use it in the completed work, but then he was stumped; moreover, his changes of position from Leipzig to Budapest and then to Hamburg, plus the deaths of his parents and one of his sisters, greatly disrupted Mahler's ex-istence, and he composed very little between 1889 and 1892.[52]

The breakthrough from the "Budapest stagnation," as Mahler called it,[53] came in February 1892 with the composition of the Wunderhorn song "Das himmlische Leben," which would ultimately become the finale of the Fourth Symphony.[54] Here in a child's vision of heaven was an an-swer to the despair of "Todtenfeier"—it is a reversal of the Fall and a re-turn to Eden, in which delicious food is everywhere, the music is incom-parable, and martyrs dance. But musically this strophic lied would hardly balance the vast C-minor sonata movement Mahler had written.[55] Never-theless, the text of "Das himmlische Leben" continued to enchant him: "What roguishness intertwined with the deepest mysticism is hidden in it! It is everything turned on its head, and causality has absolutely no validity. It's as though you suddenly saw the far side of the moon!"[56] A childlike mixture of symbolic levels is characteristic of the poem as a whole—this is no Dantean paradise of clear hierarchical order. On the surface every-thing seems blissfully nonsensical; as one digs deeper in the imagery, which is laced with many scriptural allusions, it becomes more deeply complex. Although today we now know these *Wunderhorn* verses were the work of a single learned writer,[57] Mahler probably considered them to be folk poetry: "One certainly doesn't suspect everything that lies hidden in this thing, which seems so unpretentious at first glance."[58] But no fewer than five other movements in Mahler's Third and Fourth symphonies are closely related to it; indeed, the entire Fourth was "composed into" "Das himmlische Leben," where, in Mahler's words, "the child, although in a chrysalis state, already belongs to this higher world, [and] clarifies what it means."[59] Such was also the final fate of Goethe's Faust, whose soul had been received as a child, in chrysalis state, into the celestial choir of youths:

> Gerettet ist das edle Glied
> Der Geisterwelt vom Bösen:
> *Wer immer strebend sich bemüth,*
> *Den können wir erlösen.*[60]

> Now saved is the noble member
> Of the world of spirits, from evil:
> *Whoever striving never ceases,*
> *Him are we able to save.*

Mahler would not dare to set these famous lines until 1906, in his Eighth Symphony; yet it seems clear that, from a different perspective, he envisaged a similar ending for his symphonic hero as early as 1892.

During the summer of 1893 Mahler composed more *Wunderhorn* songs—"Des Antonius von Padua Fischpredigt" (St. Anthony of Padua's sermon to the fishes), "Urlicht" (Primal light), and "Rheinlegendchen" (Little Rhine legend)—in both piano and orchestral settings. But before even scoring the satirical "Fischpredigt" for orchestra, he transformed it into a scherzo for the symphony that lay unfinished; echoing Schopenhauer, Mahler observed that "one can express so much more with music than the words literally say. The text actually comprises only a hint of the deeper content to be drawn out of it."[61] He also completed the *andante* he had begun in Leipzig. But ideas for the finale were not yet forthcoming, and he was not yet planning to include "Urlicht" in the symphony.

The "lightning bolt" of inspiration Mahler received at Hans von Bülow's funeral service ("Todtenfeier") in March 1894 is well known: Klopstock's "Auferstehen" (Resurrection) hymn, which was sung by the boys' choir of the Michaeliskirche, would become the text for the Second Symphony's choral finale. But only part of it, for this was to be no orthodox Christian resurrection: the text Mahler himself added to two stanzas of Klopstock makes clear that the Dionysian jubilation of this finale celebrates the Faustian heroic striving for self-transcendence of the impassioned individual. The "inner experiences" Mahler described in his programs and marked in the autograph score—the initial "scream of death," the quaking of the earth on the day of the Last Judgment (opening, two mm. before rehearsal no. 14., etc.), the marching forth of peasants and kings (rehearsal no. 15) and the Great Roll Call (see Ill. 14.2) and the bird of death (rehearsal nos. 29–31)—are all fairly transparent.[62] "And now comes nothing of what all expected; no divine judgment, no blessed and no damned; no good, no evil ones, no judge! . . . softly and simply swells forth: 'Arise, yes, arise,' . . . to which the words themselves are sufficient commentary."[63] The source for this universalist notion of salvation was probably the philosopher Gustav Theodor Fechner (Lipiner's teacher), who declared that "there is no heaven and no hell in the usual sense of the Christian, the Jew, the heathen, into which the soul may enter . . . after it has passed through the great transition, death, it unfolds itself according to the unalterable law of nature upon earth . . . quietly approaching and entering into a higher existence."[64]

As the words Mahler set for the chorus dissolve previous expectations, so too its entrance dispels the implications of form in the

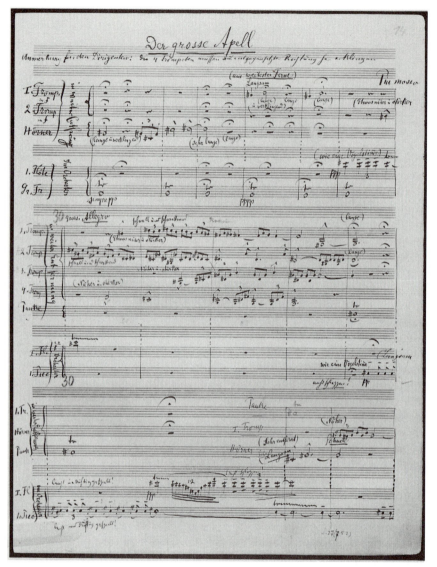

ILLUSTRATION 14.2. Mahler, Second Symphony ("Resurrection"), finale: "Der grosse Ap[p]ell" (The Great Roll Call, mm. 448ff.), autograph manuscript. Of this passage Mahler said: "As though from the other world—the great roll call sounds again. Finally only the far-distant sounding voice of the Bird of Death from the last grave is heard, and at last it, too, dies away.—And now comes nothing of what all expected; no divine judgment, no blessed and no damned; no good, no evil ones, no judge! Everything has ceased to be. And softly and simply swells forth: 'Arise, yes, arise'" (*NBL2*, 40 [*NBLE*, 44]). Photograph courtesy of the Pierpont Morgan Library, New York, Kaplan Deposit.

TABLE 14.2
Second Symphony, finale, outline of formal procedure.

	2	4	7	10	14	26+8	29	31ff
Int.		A	B	A'	'Development'	'Recap.' (Int.)	*	Chorus...
b♭/C → C		f	b♭	D♭→C	(mainly f/F)	b/c♯→ D♭		G♭ (→ E♭)

(* = "The Great Roll Call")

movement up to that point (Table 14.2). Although a central tonality has not been clearly established, thematically it would seem as though a modified sonata-rondo were in progress. Following the Great Roll Call, Mahler allows the unfolding of the text to direct the musical flow; the seven strophes are articulated by interspersed orchestral interludes, and also through alternation of chorus and soloists. Nearly all of the motivic material in this joyous conclusion has been introduced earlier in the movement; the overall tonal progression is from G♭ to E♭ major, whereby the grim associations of E♭ minor in the "Todtenfeier" movement are completely transformed.

The obvious precedent for this finale, as Mahler himself was nervously aware, is Beethoven's Ninth:[65] the opening "scream of terror," the references to previous movements (especially the "Todtenfeier" climax—rehearsal no. 14ff., and five mm. after rehearsal no. 19ff.), the instrumental recitative passage only later texted (rehearsal no. 7ff.), the big orchestral march section, the minor-to-major modal transformation resolving the business of the first movement, and of course the interruption and subsequent integration of the voices—all owe their inspiration to Beethoven's apotheosis of Elysian joy. But Beethoven had infused both unity and developmental drive into his finale through masterly expansion of classical variation technique; once fully underway, the entire movement becomes a gigantic set of variations on the folklike "Freude" melody. Mahler had not yet developed the technique to attempt such a structure, which would in any case have been too obviously derivative. He drew instead on his growing capacity to blend contrasting musical episodes into a psychologically compelling sequence that presses toward resolution through climax. Such a procedure, which owes as much to Wagner as to symphonic tradition, was Mahler's modus operandi in *Das klagende Lied* (1880), and also in the finale of the First Symphony, to which this "Resurrection" chorus was to be the "loftier solution"; one need only briefly compare the two movements to realize how far the composer has advanced.

Mahler introduces his vast resurrection fresco with "Urlicht," a simple *Wunderhorn* song for alto solo: "For it I need the voice and unpretentious expression of a child," Mahler said, "just as I imagine . . . that the soul is in heaven, where, in a chrysalis-like state it must begin everything anew as a child."[66] As already noted, such was Faust's ultimate fate, and also that of Mahler's child in "Das himmlische Leben," the song that ended his creative stagnation after "Todtenfeier." While the linkage "Urlicht" provides is convincing, the sequence of movements preceding it is rather disjointed, largely because both the *andante* and scherzo were written before Mahler had any notion of how the symphony would conclude. This bothered him for some time; programmatically, he rationalized the inner movements as interludes from the life of the departed hero—the *andante* a love episode, the scherzo a distorted reflection of his disoriented despair, as though one were watching couples dancing but could not hear the music that moved them. Mahler considered switching the two, then abandoned that idea and demanded in the score a pause "of at least five minutes" following the first movement (a pause rarely observed in performance today).[67]

The Third Symphony (1895–96)

Surviving sketches for the Second Symphony indicate that Mahler was already thinking about a new work as early as 1893, and on arriving at his summer quarters in 1895 he set to work at once.[68] The earliest drafts of movement titles for the new symphony outline a vast work in six or seven movements, culminating in the child's vision of Heaven, "Das himmlische Leben," which he now called "Was mir das Kind erzählt" (What the child tells me).[69] Whereas the writing of the Second Symphony had been a tortuous six-year affair, this new work poured forth quickly. All but the first movement had reached the orchestral draft stage by summer's end, at which point Mahler summed up the work for his longtime friend Fritz Löhr:

> My new symphony will last about 1½ hours—it's all in *grand* symphonic form.
>
> The emphasis of my *personal* emotional life (that is, what the things say to *me*) corresponds to the particular conceptual content. [Movements] II–V *incl.*[usive] are supposed to express the *successive stages* of being, which accordingly I shall express thus
>
>   II. W[hat] t[he] *flowers* t[ell] m[e]
>   III. W. t. *animals* t. m.
>   IV. W. t. *night* t. m. (Man)
>   V. W. t. *morning bells* t. m. (the *angels*)
>   —these last two numbers with *text* and singing.

VI. W. love *tells* m. is a summary of my feelings in respect to *all being,* which does not transpire without *deeply painful* digressions, which, however, gradually resolve into a *blessed trust:* "die *fröliche* Wissenschaft." As conclusion, d[as] h[immlische] L[eben] (VII), to which I have given the definitive title:

"*What the child tells me*"

No. I, *Summer marches in,* is supposed to suggest the humorous-subjective content. Summer is conceived as a *victor*—amidst all that *grows and blooms, crawls and flies, thinks and desires,* and, finally, *what we have intuition of.* (Angels—bells—transcendental).—

Over and above all, *eternal love* moves within us—as rays come together in a focal point. Now do you understand?[70]

During the course of the Third Symphony's gestation, the order of movements and their titles underwent a baffling number of changes. But the central theme of the work never wavered: it was to convey the inner essence of being, evolving from raw nature to the realm of divinity. This reflects not only the influence of Schopenhauer's concept of will, but also Fechner's teaching that the entire cosmos is an inwardly alive spiritual hierarchy extending from atoms up to God, who "is at once the base and the summit."[71] When Mahler resumed work on the first movement in the summer of 1896, he knew he was writing from new and different perspectives; as he told Bauer-Lechner,

The highest questions of humanity, which I posed and sought to answer in the Second: Why do we live? and: Will we also exist beyond this life?—here these can no longer concern me. For what must all of that signify in the totality of things, where *everything* lives and *must* live and *will live*? Can a spirit that ponders the eternal creative thought of the godhead in a symphony such as this, die? No, one gains trust: everything is eternally and intransitorily well born; as Christ teaches, "In my Father's house are many dwellings"; and here human sorrow and misery no longer has a place. The most sublime cheerfulness reigns, an eternally beaming day—for gods of course, not for men, for whom it is the dreadful Unknown, a thing never to be held fast.[72]

As the first movement grew to enormous proportions—in alarm Mahler realized that it would last half an hour or longer—the composer made a major structural alteration: "Das himmlische Leben," the song that had set Mahler thinking about the Third as early as 1893, would be transferred to a new Fourth Symphony. As a result, the numerous

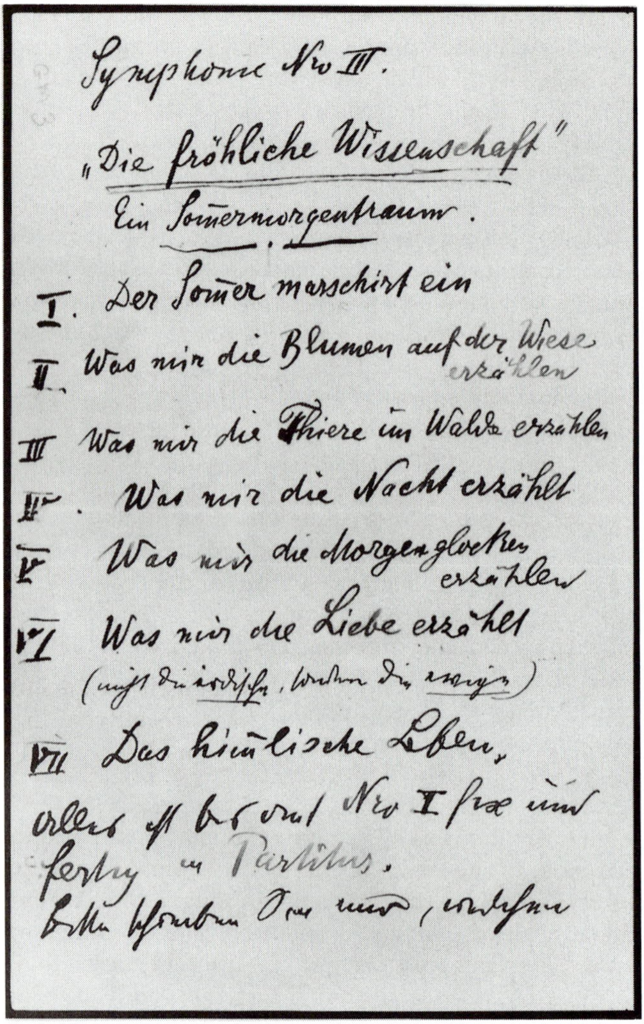
Symphonie No III.
„Die fröhliche Wissenschaft"
Ein Sommermorgentraum.
I. Der Sommer marschirt ein
II. Was mir die Blumen auf der Wiese erzählen
III Was mir die Thiere im Walde erzählen
IV. Was mir die Nacht erzählt
V Was mir die Morgenglocken erzählen
VI Was mir die Liebe erzählt
(nicht die irdische, sondern die ewige)
VII Das himmlische Leben.

ILLUSTRATION 14.3. Mahler, autograph letter from August 1895 to his friend Hermann Behn listing the programmatic titles for the Third Symphony: "Symphony No. III. / 'The Joyous Science' / A summer morning's dream. / I. Summer marches in / II. What the flowers in the meadow tell me / III. What the animals in the forest tell me / IV. What the night tells me / V. What the morning bells tell me / VI. What love tells me (not *earthly*, but *eternal*) / VII. Heavenly life [ultimately transferred to the Fourth Symphony]." Photograph courtesy of the Pierpont Morgan Library, New York, Mary Flagler Cary Collection, MFC M214.B419(1).

thematic allusions to "heavenly life" he had already woven into several movements of the Third would no longer culminate in its finale: instead, this work would conclude with the impressive *adagio* entitled "What love tells me." Here Mahler believed that "everything is resolved into peace

and being; the Ixion wheel of appearance is finally brought to a standstill"[73]—an allusion to Schopenhauer's doctrine of overcoming the will's
relentless cyclic quest for satisfaction.

The Third is the most loosely organized of Mahler's symphonies
(sprawling, some would say), and also the most overtly programmatic. As
the underlying evolutionary scheme would suggest, the range of musical
language across the span of the work is wide indeed, from the airy delicacy of the minuet ("What the flowers tell me") to the sardonic squawking
of the scherzo ("What the animals tell me") to passages like the first
movement's introduction, which, according to Mahler himself, "is hardly
music any longer, but almost just sounds of nature [*Naturlaut*]."[74] He
knew that such writing drew musical discourse away from traditional order toward chaos, and he feared the results; yet he also felt irresistibly
swept ahead by the work.[75] The overall result of such freedom and diver-
sity, as Adorno observes, is that the Third "thumbs its nose at the thought
of order and yet is so crammed with material and so rigorously composed
that it never slackens."[76]

In composing the "Todtenfeier" movement of the Second Symphony, Mahler had worked hard to forge intensely expressive individual
episodes into a dramatically compelling sonata-procedure movement. But
in the first movement of the Third Symphony, as Adorno succinctly puts
it, "the sonata pattern is really no more than a husk over the intrinsic, unfettered course of the form. In it Mahler takes greater risks than he ever
did again"; form has become "the objectification of chaos."[77] The course
of this "Panic abundance" may be sketched in broad outline as follows,
drawing upon Mahler's own discussions, programmatic inscriptions
(those from the autograph full score are in small capitals), and performance indications.[78] The movement is structured on the third-related
tonal centers of D (major/minor) and F (chiefly major): the slow introductory material (rehearsal nos. 1–19) centers on D minor (with transition toward F via D♭, C, and A minor [rehearsal nos. 18–23]), while summer's march, when fully under way, focuses on F (rehearsal nos. 23–26ff.).
Just before rehearsal number 27 this material shifts rather quickly to D
major, which functions as a secondary key area for the remainder of the
exposition (through twelve mm. after rehearsal no. 28). The recapitulation commences with the opening introductory material again centered
on D (rehearsal nos. 55–62); the march returns (rehearsal no. 62), again
focuses on F (rehearsal no. 64), and rationalizes the remainder of the
reprise to that tonality.

Of the movement's introduction Mahler noted:

> It is eerie, how from the soulless, rigid material, life gradually
> breaks forth—I could almost have called it "What the rocky
> mountains tell me.". . . Over the introduction . . . hangs again
> that mood of brooding summer noon heat, in which not a
> breath stirs itself, all life is halted, the sun-drenched air glim-

mers and shimmers. In the midst of it wails youth, enchained life, struggling for deliverance from the abyss of still rigid-lifeless Nature.[79]

Mahler labeled the bold opening horn flourish "DER WECKRUF!" ("REVEILLE!"). This is immediately followed (three mm. before rehearsal no. 1 ff.) by an adumbration of the fourth movement, Nietzsche's "O Man, take heed," later to be sung by the alto soloist. The music marked "Schwer und dumpf" (ponderous and muffled) at rehearsal number 2 ff., which returns at rehearsal number 13, is very likely what Mahler had in mind when he spoke of soulless, rigid, sun-drenched nature, while the moans of enchained life seem first to emerge at rehearsal number 3. "PAN SCHLÄFT" ("PAN SLEEPS") is marked over the *pianissimo* music at rehearsal number 11 (which recurs at rehearsal no. 18), while the chipper fanfare at rehearsal number 12 is dubbed "DER HEROLD!" ("THE HERALD!").

With the march music of the exposition, enchained life "achieves breakthrough and victory."[80] The transition to this is gradual, but once underway the music "tumbles forth frantically."[81] While it is possible to isolate discrete motives during this ceaseless ebullient tramp, not even the shift to D major brings genuine contrast; rather, the new key further heightens and brightens the march, which reaches its high point just at exposition's close. But there the cadence is shockingly undercut by a lunge of a third to Bb[6] (twelve mm. after rehearsal no. 28) together with a relapse to the realm of the introduction (rehearsal nos. 29–35): this launches the development.

Yet what ensues is not really a goal-oriented "working-out" development in the Viennese tradition; rather, it resembles five sizable episodes that reshuffle previous material and then yield the stage. The first of these is the return of the introduction just noted (centered on D minor), while the second (rehearsal nos. 35–43) rehearses introductory and march materials in a more lyrical vein than hitherto (D to F, then up to Gb). "DAS GESINDEL!" ("THE MOB!") at rehearsal number 43 is a march-*cum*-polka run amok, with shrieking wind band and bloated offbeats (chiefly in Bb, then Eb, minor). As this subsides somewhat, the initial "REVEILLE" idea is launched by the trombones in C (rehearsal no. 49), accompanied by other march motives in the winds: "DIE SCHLACHT BEGINNT!" ("THE BATTLE BEGINS!"). This precipitates Nature at strife with herself in "DER SÜDSTURM! VORWÄRTS STÜRMEN!" ("THE SOUTHERN GALE! STORM FORWARD!"; rehearsal no. 51). As Mahler described it, "In a march tempo that sweeps everything aside it roars ever closer and closer, louder and louder, swelling up like an avalanche, until the entire uproar and all the exultation burst forth over you."[82]

The storm shifts from Db to Gb (a semitone above the F-major tonic) and subsides. Then follows the most audacious moment of this bold movement: a perfunctory snare drum roll summons attention, the horns sound "REVEILLE" in F without warning—and the reprise is at hand. This portion of the movement is artfully condensed and varied, yet satisfies as a full symphonic recapitulation: just this "objectification of chaos" provides Mahler's longest single movement with overall cogency it could not have achieved otherwise.

As in the First Symphony, Mahler decided to divide the Third into two large parts (*Abteilungen*): (1) the first movement, and (2) the remaining five, which he designed to be "as multifaceted as the world itself."[83] The first of these, the "flower" and "animal" pieces, are relatively short, "humorous" (in Mahler's sense of the word), and formally fairly straightforward—a minuet with two trio sections (A-B-A-B-A), and a modified rondo (A-B-A-C-A-B-C-A). Both are delightful character pieces, almost like landscapes in sound.[84] Mahler spoke of the minuet as "the most carefree thing I have ever written—as carefree as only flowers can be. Everything wavers and sways in the air, with greatest lightness and nimbleness, as flowers in the wind gently lull themselves on supple stems. . . . As you can well imagine, it doesn't remain in the realm of innocent flower cheerfulness, but suddenly becomes serious and severe. It sweeps over the meadow like a storm wind and shakes the leaves and blossoms, which groan and moan on their stems as though begging for deliverance into a higher realm."[85]

The principal material (A) of "What the animals tell me" is based on Mahler's *Wunderhorn* song "Ablösung im Sommer" (Changing the guard in summer), which concerns a nightingale replacing a dead cuckoo as the lead singer in the forest. Mahler described the scherzo that grew from this scion as "the most scurrilous and yet the most tragic that ever was—as only music can mystically lead us from the one to the other in a single turn. This piece is truly as though all of Nature made a face and stuck out her tongue. Yet there is such a ghastly Panic humor in it that shock overcomes one more than laughter."[86] The C section in this rondo-esque scheme is the famous lyrical posthorn episode (rehearsal nos. 14, 27; marked "DER POSTILLON" in the autograph)—"scandalously audacious" and "kitsch" according to Adorno, but "utterly bewitching in its nostalgic simplicity and tender, innocent beauty" in de La Grange's view.[87] Mahler initially planned that the tune be played by a flügelhorn, whose sound he had loved since childhood, and he subsequently revealed that in composing this spot he had in mind a poem by Lenau entitled "Der Postillon," which begins "Gentle was that night in May."[88] From these hints it would seem he intended to evoke a stratum of nocturnal calm transcending the din of the forest's animals. Neither appearance of the posthorn silences the beasts for long, but just before the movement's close they are brusquely interrupted by an awesome trembling (rehearsal no. 31), reminiscent of the climactic disruptions preceding the first movement's development and coda. According to Mahler, "once again falls the rigid shadow of lifeless Nature, of still uncrystallized, unorganic matter. But here this suggests a relapse to the lower animal forms of being, before being makes the powerful leap to the spirit of the highest earthly creature, man."[89]

In both text and music the fourth and fifth movements are a pair of syzygial opposites. "What man tells me" is a through-composed setting of the midnight drunken song from Nietzsche's scriptural parody *Thus Spake Zarathustra*, which is launched by Zarathustra's famous pronouncement that "God is dead!"[90] In the two renditions of his midnight song, the prophet Zarathustra guardedly reveals and elaborates the doctrine of eternal recurrence (which Nietzsche had previously characterized as "the eternal hourglass of existence . . . turned upside down again and again, and you with it, speck of dust!").[91] Mahler's first-movement introductory material had foreshadowed this solemn and mysterious moment, which begins with undulating third relations followed by static pedals and modal ambiguity; very slowly the alto intones "O Mensch! Gib Acht!" (O Man, take heed), placing special emphasis on the word "deep" (*tief*). But interspersed in this (rehearsal no. 5) is a major-mode transformation of the "wailing youth" idea from the symphony's opening; this is strongly reminiscent of "Urlicht" from the *Resurrection* Symphony, and when the voice takes it up a bit later (four mm. before rehearsal no. 10), we get Mahler's point: "But all joyous desire [*Lust*] wills eternity, wants deep, deep eternity." Following eighteen bars of hushed orchestral commentary, the movement closes in irresolution on a dominant bass note.

Bimm-bamm morning bells with boys' and women's choirs singing *Wunderhorn* verse are Mahler's response to Nietzsche: "Es sungen drei Engel einen süßen Gesang" (Three angels sang a sweet song). Marked "Merry in tempo and cheeky in expression," this short movement is the closest of the six to "Das himmlische Leben," the child's celestial vision that was originally to conclude the Third Symphony. Moreover, the text of "Es sungen drei Engel" is explicitly Christian, ending thus:

> Die himmlische Freud' ist eine selige Stadt;
> Die himmlische Freud', die kein Ende mehr hat.
> Die himmlische Freude war Petro bereit't
> Durch Jesum und allen zur Seligkeit.

> Heavenly joy is a Blessed City;
> Heavenly joy has no end anymore.
> Heavenly joy was prepared through Jesus
> For Peter and everyone, for bliss.

Like "Das himmlische Leben," this is rather at odds with Zarathustra's teaching: "'To be sure: except ye become as little children, ye shall not enter into *that* kingdom of heaven.' (And Zarathustra pointed upward with his hands.) 'But we have no wish whatever to enter into the kingdom of heaven: we have become men—*so we want the earth*.'"[92] Thus, whatever inspiration he may have drawn from the later writing of Nietzsche, Mahler's point in the Third Symphony (and the Fourth) seems clear: Nietzsche's "unconditional and infinitely repeated circular course of all things"[93] was not, in his view, the highest level of finality.[94]

Instead, this musical cosmos concludes in a hymnic *adagio*, "What love tells me," the "liberating resolution" of all the previous movements, which stills the wheel of Ixion.[95] "I could almost also call the movement 'What God tells me!'" Mahler wrote, "And this in precisely the sense that God can only be comprehended as 'Love.'"[96] This notion, already apparent in the conclusion of the *Resurrection* Symphony, cropped up in Mahler's conversation countless times.[97] But the musical manifestation of it in the Third differs from anything he had ever written. This is his first genuine slow movement, and, in contrast to much of the "nature" music that precedes it, the texture is dominated by rich contrapuntal string writing (with cellos and violas frequently *divisi*); his inspiration for this may well have been the celestial slow movements of the late Beethoven quartets (especially Op. 135, and also the "Heiliger Dankgesang" of Op. 132). The finale's formal scheme is rondo-like, centered on periodic returns to D major (at rehearsal nos. 9, 21, and 26), while the thematic materials are reordered and varied as the piece proceeds. Each of the three tonic affirmations just noted resolves successively stronger recurrences of the "rigid shadow of nature" from the first movement, and only after the third of these subsides does Mahler deploy his full orchestral resources, "not with raw power," but rather with "saturated, noble tone" in the superabundantly bright D-major close of the work.[98]

The Fourth Symphony (1899–1900)

Each of Mahler's first three symphonies opens new musical territory through expansion and boldness: orchestral sonorities are intensified; raw or even vulgar ideas are ushered into symphonic discourse; the gravitational field of tonality is stretched, without being abandoned; and both individual movements and the symphonies as wholes become progressively longer—from about an hour for the First (including "Blumine") to an hour and a half for the Third. In addition, the performing forces needed for these symphonic worlds grew substantially, from the Brahms-size double-wind orchestra required in the earliest surviving version of the First Symphony to the quadruple winds, expanded brass—eight horns, four trumpets, four trombones (plus tuba)—plus enlarged percussion and two harps demanded in the Third. By comparison, Mahler's Fourth is a world apart in nearly all respects: it is his shortest symphony, lasting only about fifty minutes; three of its four movements are quite traditional in form (sonata, scherzo, variations), and all are taut and transparent in structure; the orchestration is restricted to triple winds (plus an extra flute-and-piccolo player), four horns, three trumpets, a battery of delicately deployed percussion, and the usual strings; the textures are contrapuntally richer than in the majority of his earlier music; moreover, the epic-dramatic, Faustian tone is all but gone. Mahler's Fourth is exquisitely stylized, refined, humorous, and almost neoclassical—in Nietzschean terms, an Apollonian rather than a Dionysian work. Its sophistication notwithstanding, the world of the Fourth is in many respects that of childhood, from the fool's bells of the opening to the naïve yet covertly mystical text of the vocal finale.[99] So far removed is this symphony from the First and Second (the Third had not yet been performed in full) that most early hearers thought it a scandalous hoax. From Munich to Berlin to Vienna, Mahler's first performances of the Fourth during the winter of 1901–2 were hissed by audiences and savaged by the press; evidently only Richard Strauss recognized the excellence of the work, which is today among the most favored of Mahler's symphonies.[100]

Part of its success is owing to the manner of its gestation: previously, what Mahler imagined would be a symphony turned out to be three times the normal length, whereas with the Fourth "I only wanted to write a symphonic humoresque, and out of it came the normal size of a symphony."[101] More significantly, the goal of this symphonic world was never in doubt: Mahler carefully crafted the first three movements as the setting for a gem—"Das himmlische Leben," the musical treasure he had brought forth from a *Wunderhorn* poem in early 1892. When the symphony was completed in 1900 Mahler characterized this child's vision of Heaven as "the tapering spire of the structure,"[102] and acknowledged that its close connection to the other movements of both the Third and Fourth gave it a special, all-encompassing meaning: "Indeed, you don't think about just how far the smallest, most intimate circle can, through radii that reach out beyond every circle, grow into concentric circles, for all of which, the widest as well as the narrowest, πr^2 is still just as valid."[103] The work thus concludes with a vocal finale, but one that differs radically from the grand apotheoses of Mahler's Second and Beethoven's Ninth: "Das himmlische Leben" is a strophic lied on a folklike poem to be sung "with bright childlike expression, entirely without parody."[104]

The texture of the first three movements is especially enlivened by motivic interplay and polyphony—"like in a kaleidoscope, the thousand-fold little specks of the picture often change, so that we can't recognize it again. As though a rainbow suddenly disintegrated before us into its dancing and ever-changing droplets, and its entire arc seemed to waver and dissolve itself."[105] Mahler had long recognized that the organic relation between structure and detail was essential to great symphonic music, and in his Fourth he achieved a new level in their synthesis. Overall, the basic tone of the entire symphony was to be "constant," like "the undifferentiated blue of the sky, which is more difficult to hit upon than all changing and contrasting tints."[106] The wrenching contrasts between and within movements that are frequently characteristic of his first three symphonies would be out of place here.

The Fourth begins "as though it couldn't count to three" with the motive for winds and bells that Mahler called "the jester's cap":[107] empty fifths in B minor decorated with rolling sixteenths. This gesture is drawn from the music accompanying the rather grislier lines of "Das himmlische Leben" (John the Baptist lets the lamb out for Herod to slaughter, etc.); thereby Mahler seems to acknowledge, as in the "Bruder Martin" movement of the First, that childhood is not all sweetness and light. The bell motive will mark all major moments of the first movement's sonata form; conveniently, its repeated eighths echo the traditional eighteenth-century *Trommelbaß* accompaniment, for which purpose Mahler will deploy his "jester's cap" in many other passages of the piece.

But in the opening the bells quietly yield to the easygoing main theme, which, although "childishly simple and unselfconscious," cost Mahler a good deal of effort to orchestrate.[108] The components of its graceful shape are rich in potential for development, as the composer himself noted: "On its first appearance it lies there as unpretentious as the dew drop on the blossom before the sun shines in upon it. But when the sun's ray falls upon the meadow, it breaks into a thousand lights and colors in every pearl of dew, from which an entire sea of light shines forth before us."[109] We hear this at once as the melody changes registers and colors, combines with its own inversion, extends its phrase length, and imitates itself at the octave, all within the first twenty bars. Here, and indeed throughout the exposition, Mahler projects an expectation of old-fashioned periodic phrasing that is neither entirely fulfilled nor fully brushed aside. The bridge to the dominant (marked "fresh," rehearsal no. 2) could pass for a tune from the nursery playground—yet this and the second theme it ushers in, like so much in the symphony, are subtly connected to the music of "Das himmlische Leben."

The second group is an extraordinary study in antecedent-consequent phrase timing and color changes—humorous in the lofty sense to which Mahler aspires in this work, yet growing increasingly warmer in tone. Then at rehearsal number 4 the kaleidoscope shifts somewhat unexpectedly, and we find ourselves in the midst of laconic, sparsely scored closing material derived from the main thematic group. There follows in classical manner the exposition's repeat (six mm. after rehearsal no. 5 ff.)—but it is varied, condensed, and deprived of both modulation and second theme, such that the whole first part trails off in the tonic, practically devoid of energy.

The jester's cap revives the proceedings, almost as though (as in many Classical symphonies) the constant eighth-note ticking had never really stopped. In the ensuing development section the virtuosic shuffling of ideas is intertwined with subtly modulated undulations in mood—from uneasiness that something awful might be just barely concealed by the

ILLUSTRATION 14.4. Mahler, autograph short-score draft for the Fourth
Symphony, first movement, mm. 198ff. (end of the development approaching the
reprise). The blue-crayon marking "Bum-bum" beneath the second system
probably refers to the tam-tam strokes (reinforced by bass instruments) that
punctuate this passage in the completed work, and may indicate its similarity to
the "bimm-bamm" morning bells of the Third Symphony (movt. 5). In the third
system the climax of the passage (= mm. 221ff.) is notated "impressionistically"
rather than precisely; at this stage of the movement's genesis the shape of the
gesture was evidently more important than the specific pitches. In the last three
bars of the third system the fourth staff includes pencil sketching for the fanfare
Mahler called "a sort of little roll call" (cf. also Ex. 14.6). Photograph courtesy of
the Newberry Library, Chicago.

fool's bells, to the sunny serenity of the first theme. The texture and the
ever-shifting coloration are more delicate than in any of Mahler's earlier
developments; full forces are deployed only for punctuation, and at the
climax. A "new" theme in A major at rehearsal number 10 temporarily af-
firms the brighter side of the affective spectrum, yet also adds a curious
tint: the tune is the opening of "Das himmlische Leben" played in pentatonic outline by oriental-sounding unison flutes in the high register—like
"children's instruments that no one ever heard," in Adorno's view.[110] Kernels of the pentatonic tune commingle with those of the main theme
through much of what follows, as the tonality becomes unsettled (four
mm. after rehearsal no. 11 ff.) and moves distinctly toward flat keys and
minor mode (E♭ minor at rehearsal no. 12, F minor at rehearsal no. 13).

The tension is subtle yet palpable, as though we could easily be transported from Elysian fields to the terrors of Tartarus.[111] The climax and reprise (rehearsal nos. 16–18) epitomize this aspect of the development as a whole: a brightly booming C-major passage of "himmlische Leben" and bridge material (enthusiastically marked "Bum-bum" in Mahler's sketches)[112] is quickly swamped by a shrieking dissonant outburst (rehearsal no. 17). In the ensuing disorientation the trumpet sounds "a kind of little roll call (complementing the great one in the Finale of the Second) . . . [Mahler said]: 'When the confusion and crowding of the troops, who initially came out in good order, becomes too severe, at a stroke an order from the commander assembles them again in the old formation under his banner'"[113] (see Ill. 14.4 and Ex. 14.6). In this gently farcical deus ex machina Mahler's humor is at its best: the thematic reprise begins as the tonal chaos is still receding (five mm. before rehearsal no. 18), and there is virtually no preparation of G major. The tonic simply appears in midphrase after a brief hold—the utter antithesis of powerful Beethovenian drive to the recapitulation. "They won't discover just how artful it is until later!" Mahler observed, doubtless tongue-in-cheek.[114]

EXAMPLE 14.6. Mahler, Fourth Symphony, movt. 1, mm. 227–33 (7 mm. after rehearsal no. 17ff.): "Der kleine Appell" (the little roll call) before the recapitulation

Once underway, the recapitulation immediately explores new contrapuntal and motivic transformations, for in Mahler's view "each repetition is already a lie. A work of art, like life, must always develop itself further."[115] The bridge material is expanded to review the development's "Bum-bum" passage, and the second theme group becomes vigorously "Schwungvoll" (full of enthusiasm). In the coda (six mm. after rehearsal no. 22 ff.) the veiled menace of the development returns briefly, to be calmed by a delicately soaring passage for strings ascending to the highest register and gradually ceasing all motion: this adumbrates the extraordinary final variant of the third movement (six mm. after rehearsal no. 11 ff.), just prior to the jubilant transition to "Das himmlische Leben." But that moment is not yet, and the first movement hesitantly regains its cheerful momentum, closing with a conventionally bright cadential flourish.

"That the third, and yet also the second movements are variations—will they find that out?" Mahler wondered.[116] The Fourth Symphony's C-minor scherzo begins with the fool's bells transformed, under harmonic influence of the first movement's development, and introduced by a fragment of its codetta.[117] As in the first movement, this motto-gesture will function as a sectional marker for the scherzo, which also contains numerous allusions to the work's finale. Formally, this is a scherzo with two appearances of the trio, à la Beethoven; topically, it is a *Ländler* frequently gone awry; and affectively, in Mahler's words, it is "so mystical, confused, and uncanny that it will make your hair stand on end. . . . [It's] nothing but cobwebs."[118] The tuned-up solo violin woven intermittently into this fine-spun fabric is intended to "sound raw and screeching, 'as though Death were striking up.'"[119] Death fiddling for the dance is the archetypal German folk figure Freund Hein, whose origins date to medieval legend, and who had been portrayed in the nineteenth century by numerous artists including Schwind and Böcklin, whom Mahler admired.[120] Yet this scherzo is not music of terror such as we encounter in Mahler's earlier (and later) works. Rather, as in fairy tales that children repeat endlessly without becoming distraught, its grimness is substantially concealed through artistic stylization; in addition, the trio sections provide lighter contrast. "Certainly in the Adagio that follows, where everything is resolved," Mahler said, "you'll see that no harm was meant."[121]

The slow movement, a double variation set (like the third movement of Beethoven's Ninth), is an extraordinary achievement; Mahler himself regarded it as the best thing he had yet written, and Richard Strauss declared that he could never write such an *adagio*.[122] Mahler's own poetic descriptions of it are worth repeating at length; he told Natalie Bauer-Lechner that:

"A divinely serene and deeply sad melody runs throughout, at which you will both smile and weep."
He also said that it bore the countenance of St. Ursula (who is sung about in the "Heavenly Life" of the fourth movement). And when I asked him whether he knew anything about this saint or were familiar with her legends, he replied: "No; otherwise I would certainly not have been in a position, or in the mood, to make such a distinct and splendid portrait of her."
At one point he also called the Andante the smile of St. Ursula, and said that in it there had hovered before him the face of his mother from childhood, with deep sadness, and as though smiling through tears; she suffered unendingly, yet always lovingly resolved and forgave everything.[123]

In conversation with Bruno Walter, Mahler again associated the movement with "the smile of St. Ursula":

> She smiles . . . like the monuments of the old knights and prelates with hands folded over their chests, which one sees when walking through old churches—they have the scarcely noticeable, peaceful smile of the slumbering, departed children of mankind: solemn, blessed peace, earnest, gentle cheerfulness is the character of this movement, which also includes deeply painful contrasts—if you wish, reminiscences of earthly life—as well as a buildup of the cheerfulness into liveliness.[124]

The main theme of the variations is introduced in a rich texture of divided lower strings over an ostinato bass rhythm; the serenely symmetrical phrases come to a half cadence in measure 16, which ushers in the first half of the theme again, now varied and with a countermelody. The same harmonic scheme precipitates two more variants: the third includes an extension (seven mm. after rehearsal no. 1 ff.) derived from the refrain of "Das himmlische Leben" (cf. Ex. 14.7a, b), while the fourth (thirteen

EXAMPLE 14.7.

a. Mahler, *Das himmlische Leben,* first occurrence of the refrain, mm. 36–38 (4 bars before rehearsal no. 3 ff.)

b. Mahler, Fourth Symphony, movt. 3, mm. 31–34 (7 bars after rehearsal no. 1 ff.)

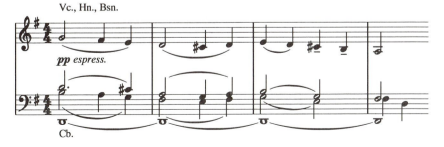

mm. after rehearsal no. 1) is a contour inversion of the opening. The first full cadence occurs only at the forty-fifth bar, which introduces a delicate closing section: Mahler's ongoing phrases, like those in the third movement of Beethoven's Ninth, reduce the static jingling often characteristic of variations by opening a broader span of musical time. The overall pattern of this first-theme group—three open-ended variants followed by contour inversion and closing—is maintained in the variations of it that follow.

The briefest of transitions leads to the second theme in E minor: the choice of relative (rather than parallel) minor bolsters the G–E third relation central to the symphony as a whole—for "Das himmlische Leben" will conclude in E major.[125] Indeed, the double-period second theme begins with an almost literal inversion of the song's cadential refrain, as shown in Example 14.8a, b. (The third appearance of the refrain in "Das himmlische Leben" is counterpointed by its own contour inversion, as shown in Ex. 14.8c.) This second thematic area also presents rather distinct allusions to "Saint Ursula herself smiles" (see Ex. 14.9). In addition, it provides our first hint of the "deeply painful contrasts" Mahler mentioned to Walter: both the cheerfulness and the sorrow of the movement

EXAMPLE 14.8.
a. Mahler, Fourth Symphony, movt. 3, second theme of the double variations, mm. 62–64 (rehearsal no. 2ff.)

b. Mahler, refrain of *Das himmlische Leben,* first occurrence (cf. Ex. 14.6.)

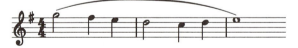

c. Mahler, *Das himmlische Leben,* third occurrence of refrain, mm. 106–08 (rehearsal no. 10ff.), with contour inversion in bass line

Sankt Mar - tha die Kö - chin muß sein!

are intensified during the subsequent variations of the two themes (beginning at rehearsal nos. 4 and 6 respectively).

As Mahler proudly pointed out, the rich mix of colors this yields is extraordinary indeed, as is the masterly polyphony.[126] The first group returns in triple time (rehearsal no. 9), and its pace increases unexpectedly from a hesitant *andante* to a dancing *allegretto*, reminding us that according to the *Wunderhorn* finale, St. Ursula's maidens actually dance in paradise. Again without warning, carnival music breaks out in the third variant of this section (rehearsal no. 10), first in E major, then in G (complete with carousel bells). This childlike mirth is brought to order as quickly as it arose by a variant on the first group's closing material (rehearsal no. 11), which leads to a final slow-paced presentation of the theme's inversion (accompanied by material from previous variations).

Just as it seems that the movement's energy is completely spent, Mahler introduces the most dramatic stroke of the symphony as a whole:

EXAMPLE 14.9.
a. Mahler, *Das himmlishce Leben*, mm. 151–53 (2 bars before rehearsal no. 14ff.), "Saint Ursula herself smiles about it!"

b. Mahler, Fourth Symphony, movt. 3, second theme, mm. 69–71 (8 bars after rehearsal no. 2ff.)

c. Mahler, Fourth Symphony, movt. 3, mm. 81–84, rehearsal no. 3ff.

d. Mahler, cadential refrain of *Das himmlische Leben*, mm. 36–38 (4 bars before rehearsal no. 3ff.)

"Das himmlische Leben" in a stunningly bright E-major fanfare—another Mahlerian breakthrough that sounds "as though it had fallen from heaven, as though it came from another world."[127] Once again, the influence of Beethoven's Ninth seems apparent: the closing of its slow movement is twice interrupted by arresting fanfares, which are often interpreted as summonses to a higher sphere. But Mahler's jubilant gesture expands into an extraordinary transition to the finale: as he described this passage, "the dying away at the close is like music of the spheres, an almost ecclesiastical, Catholic atmosphere."[128] And Mahler would later quote this celestial music in concluding two of his most personal compositions—the lied "Ich bin der Welt abhanden gekommen" (1901), which he characterized as "myself," and the well-known Adagietto of the Fifth Symphony (1901–2), which was almost certainly a declaration of love to his fiancée, Alma Schindler.[129]

Having been so thoroughly prepared, "Das himmlische Leben" seems like the inevitable conclusion to this symphony. Mahler completely reorchestrated the song for its symphonic role, yet did not alter its musical substance; thus, while it is stylistically less complex than the music he was capable of writing in 1900, its relative simplicity yields the effect of "tapering away" from the variations, which are the work's center of gravity. The four strophes of the song's text are clearly declaimed and punctuated by the archaic-sounding cadential refrain, yet none is a mere repetition: the musical kernels of the lied, which ultimately traverse such wide distances through concentric circles in Mahler's musical cosmos, begin to develop almost at once. The G major–E minor third-polarity adumbrated in the third movement is again manifest between the song's first and second stanzas; this is resolved into E major in the serene music of the closing strophe.

For Adorno, the Fourth Symphony is a work "composed within quotation marks"; the fool's bells with which it opens say "none of what you now hear is true."[130] But for Mahler it meant more. The voice of the child, the transformed voice of the Faustian symphonic hero, seems to assure us that there is more to the music of paradise than is dreamt of in Schopenhauer's philosophy; Mahler's tetralogy of early symphonies reaches its deepest peace in the low E of harp and contrabasses over which this singular vision of heavenly life fades away. The Fourth is thus the polar opposite of the Second Symphony: there Mahler's eschatology is monumentally declaimed by the most massive choral and orchestral forces he dared muster; here a folkish poem and the naïve, intimate perspective of a child suffice. Mahler would later compose a similar pair of opposites: his Eighth, the "Symphony of a Thousand," in which he finally set the celebrated conclusion of *Faust*, and *Das Lied von der Erde*, which uses two solo voices with orchestra (or piano) to project the inner world of a single persona at the moment of liminal transition from earthly life. But it was in the Fourth that he achieved a level of compositional mastery—almost a second maturity—that gave him the craft to produce the later master-pieces. While Mahler's first four symphonies are traditionally known as the *Wunderhorn* symphonies, from the standpoint of motivic and contra-puntal technique as well as large-scale control, the Fourth stands apart from the other three.

Yet from broader poetic and aesthetic perspectives, the Fourth in-deed caps Mahler's *Wunderhorn* years. Mahler never abandoned his long-ing to achieve the unfulfilled hopes of Romanticism. But in later works his perspective deepens, and he acknowledges the power of doubt, alien-ation, and despair to an extent that few, if any, artists previously had. Less than a year after the reorchestration of "Das himmlische Leben" was fin-ished, and months before the Fourth was first performed, Mahler penned three of the *Kindertotenlieder* (Songs on the death of children).[131] That same summer (1901) he began work on his Fifth Symphony, whose biting funeral march opens by quoting "the little roll call" from the first move-ment of the Fourth (cf. Exs. 14.6 and 14.10). Never again would he con-clude a work in the naïvely cheerful realm of "Das himmlische Leben."

EXAMPLE 14.10. Mahler, Fifth Symphony, movt. 1 ("Trauermarsch"), mm. 1–8

In gemessenem Schritt. Streng wie ein Kondukt

Thus the "Ixion wheel" of Mahler's own creativity continued to turn for the remainder of his career; as Bruno Walter sums it up,

> "For what" remained the agonizing question of his soul. From this arose the strongest spiritual impulses for his creativity, each of his works was a new attempt at an answer. And when he had won the answer for himself, the old question soon raised its unassuageable call of longing in him anew. He could not—such was his nature—hold fast to any achieved spiritual posi-tion, for he himself was not constant.[132]

Notes

1. *Gustav Mahler in den Erinnerungen von Natalie Bauer-Lechner*, ed. Herbert Killian, with annotations by Knud Martner (Hamburg, 1984), 35 (cited hereafter as *NBL2*), summer 1895; here and below, translations are by the present author unless otherwise noted. Bauer-Lechner was a violinist of professional caliber as well as a good amateur writer who, like Goethe's Eckermann, acted as self-appointed chronicler of Mahler's utterances, especially between 1893 and 1901; the reliability of her reportage has proven to be excellent. The surviving manuscripts of her diaries are in private hands, and Killian's edition (*NBL2*) is the most complete selection from them currently available. *Recollections of Gustav Mahler*, trans. Dika Newlin, ed. Peter Franklin (Cambridge, 1980) (cited hereafter as *NBLE*) is a useful English version based on earlier published excerpts, wherein the passage quoted above will be found on p. 40.

2. *NBL2*, 198 (*NBLE*, 178), 12 October 1901.

3. Bauer-Lechner, "Aus einem Tagebuch über Mahler," *Der Merker* 3/5 (1912): 184 (from July–August 1893). A slightly different version of this passage is found in *NBL2*, 26 (*NBLE*, 30, 231). "Truth and poetry" is undoubtedly an allusion to Goethe's autobiography, *Dichtung und Wahrheit*.

4. *NBL2*, 164 (*NBLE*, 154), 1 August 1900.

5. Mahler's programs are cited and discussed in appendix 3 of Henry-Louis de La Grange, *Mahler* (Garden City, NY, 1973) (hereafter *HLG*); more up-to-date is the French edition of de La Grange's biography, *Gustav Mahler: Chronique d'une vie*, vol. 1: *Les Chemins de la gloire (1860–1900)* (Paris, 1979) (hereafter *HLGF*). See also Hefling, "Mahler's 'Todtenfeier' and the Problem of Program Music," *19th-Century Music* 12 (1988): 27–53; n. 4 on p. 45 provides a concise bibliographical listing of Mahler's programmatic remarks concerning his first four symphonies.

6. See William J. McGrath, *Dionysian Art and Populist Politics in Austria* (New Haven, Conn., 1974), esp. chapters 2–4, as well as Hefling, *The Making of Mahler's "Todtenfeier": Program, Sketches, Analysis* (Lanham, MD, forthcoming), chapter 1.

7. Arthur Schopenhauer, *The World As Will and Representation*, trans. E. F. J. Payne (New York, 1966), 1:15, 14, 436, and passim.

8. Ibid. 2:196.

9. Ibid. 1:110.

10. Mann, "Freud and the Future," in *Essays of Three Decades*, trans. H. T. Lowe-Porter (New York, 1948), 417; see also L. J. Rather, *The Dream of Self-Destruction: Wagner's "Ring" and the Modern World* (Baton Rouge, LA, 1979), chapter 3.

11. Schopenhauer, *World* 1:196, 274–326.

12. Ibid. 1:378–412, esp. 404.

13. Ibid. 1:179, 184–85, 195–98.

14. Ibid. 1:257, 263.

15. Ibid. 1:261.

16. Wagner, "Beethoven," in *Richard Wagner's Prose Works*, trans. William Ashton Ellis (London, 1892ff.; rpt., New York, 1966), vol. 5: *Actors and Singers*, 65–72; see also McGrath, *Dionysian Art*, 122–24.

17. *Prose Works*, vol. 6: *Religion and Art*, esp. 247.

18. Nietzsche, *The Birth of Tragedy*, trans. Walter Kaufmann (New York, 1967), 37.

19. Ibid., 52; cf. also 141.

20. Ibid., 70.

21. Ibid., 104.

22. Ibid., 104–5.

23. Lipiner, *Der entfesselte Prometheus* (Leipzig, 1876); see also Helmut von Hartungen, *Der Dichter Siegfried Lipiner, 1856–1911* (Dr. Phil. dissertation, Munich, 1932 [mimeographed]), 14–20; McGrath, *Dionysian Art*, 62–120; and Constantin Floros, *Gustav Mahler*, vol. 1: *Die geistige Welt Gustav Mahlers in systematischer Darstellung* (Wiesbaden, 1977), 72–83.

24. Lipiner, *Über die Elemente einer Erneuerung religiöser Ideen in der Gegenwart* (Vienna, 1878), 4.

25. Ibid., 9.

26. Ibid., 11.

27. Ibid., 11–12.

28. Ferdinand Pfohl, *Gustav Mahler: Eindrücke und Erinnerungen aus den hamburger Jahren* (ca. 1924–29), ed. Knud Martner (Hamburg, 1973), 21; see also J. B. Foerster, *Der Pilger: Erinnerungen eines Musikers*, trans. Pavel Eisner (Prague, 1955), 383.

29. *NBL2*, 173 (*NBLE*, 157, 237, 239), November 1900.

30. Letter from Mahler to Max Marschalk, 26 March 1896, *Gustav Mahler Briefe*, rev. ed., ed. Herta Blaukopf (Vienna, 1982) (hereafter *GMB2*), no. 167; also found in *Selected Letters of Gustav Mahler*, ed. Knud Martner, trans. Eithne Wilkins, Ernst Kaiser, and Bill Hopkins (New York, 1979) (hereafter *GMBE*), no. 158.

31. Letter to Arthur Seidel, 17 February 1897, *GMB2*, no. 216 (*GMBE*, no. 205).

32. Bruno Walter, *Gustav Mahler* (Vienna, 1936), 76; in the English trans. by James Galston (New York, 1941; rpt., New York, 1973), 105.

33. See *HLG*, vol. 1, and *HLGF*, vol. 1, chapter 12, as well as Eduard Reeser, ed., *Gustav Mahler und Holland: Briefe* (Vienna, 1980), 88–91.

34. *GBM2*, no. 167 (*GMBE*, no. 158).

35. Concerning the original sources see *HLG* 1:746ff. and plates 46–47, opposite p. 574 (*HLGF* 1:965–72, and plates 19–20 and 27–28, opposite p. 566), *NBL2*, 172–76 (*NBLE*, 157–61), and *NBLE*, 236–41. The "fairy-tale illustration" has been identified as "Des Jägers Leichenbegägnis" by Moritz von Schwind, and is frequently reproduced (e.g., *HLG*, vol. 1, plate 34, opposite p. 478).

36. *NBL2*, 173 (*NBLE*, 157), November 1900.

37. The modulatory procedure between rehearsal nos. 18 and 20 comes directly from the second strophe of "Ging heut' morgens über's Feld," mm. 46ff.

38. Mahler told Bruno Walter that in the closing bars of the work "he saw before him Beethoven, who burst out laughing uproariously and then ran away." (Walter, *Gustav Mahler*, 79, trans. Galston, 110.)

39. Concerning "Blumine" see *HLG* 1:752–53 (*HLGF* 1:975–78), as well as Donald Mitchell, *Gustav Mahler: The Wunderhorn Years* (Boulder, CO, 1976), 217–24, and Jack Diether, "Notes on Some Mahler Juvenilia," *Chord and Discord* 3 (1969): 76–80, 84–100. A score of the movement was published by Theodore Presser (Bryn Mawr, PA) in 1968.

40. A manuscript fragment from Mahler's youth (now in US-NYpm) suggests that the scherzo of the First may originally have been drafted for piano four hands.

41. See *HLG* 1:203–7, 282–83, and 300–301 (*HLGF* 1:307–12, 432–34, and 458–61) as well as *NBL2*, 176 (*NBLE*, 160–61).

42. *NBL2*, 175–76 (*NBLE*, 159–60). Extraordinary though it is, Mahler never considered his orchestration to be of primary significance in his works; as he wrote to the critic and composer Max Marschalk, "*what* one writes has always seemed to me more important than what it is scored *for*" (*GMB2*, no. 198 [*GMBE*, no. 189], 4 December 1896).

43. Friedrich Löhr, note to *GMB2*, no. 85, 416, n. 55 (*GMBE*, no. 79, note on 483–84).

44. See also Constantin Floros, *Gustav Mahler*, vol. 3: *Die Symphonien* (Wiesbaden, 1985), 41–46. "Associative" tonality, frequently encountered in Mahler's works, dates back at least to Mozart (e.g., D minor in *Don Giovanni*) and is central to Wagner's music; see Robert Bailey, "The Structure of the *Ring* and Its Evolution," *19th-Century Music* 1 (1977): 48–61.

45. At twenty measures after rehearsal no. 44 Mahler originally wrote a full reprise of the opening outburst over the dominant of F; while formally logical, this move would seem psychologically redundant from the perspective of the symphonic hero, and in revising the work for the 1893–94 performances Mahler worked out the more ambivalent approach to the reprise we know today. Diether's "Notes on Some Mahler Juvenilia," plates V–VI, reproduces the first two pages of the deleted reprise as preserved in the 1893 autograph score.

46. *NBL2*, 27 (*NBLE*, 31), July–August 1893; as Floros has pointed out (*Gustav Mahler*, vol. 2: *Mahler und die Symphonik des 19. Jahrhunderts in neuer Deutung* [Wiesbaden, 1977], 256, 407), the passage is thematically related to the "Grail" motive of Wagner's *Parsifal*.

47. See *Gustav Mahler–Richard Strauss: Briefwechsel 1888–1911*, ed. Herta Blaukopf (Munich, 1980), no. M 19 (19 July 1894).

48. *NBL2*, 50 (*NBLE*, 53), April 1896. *Die drei Pintos*, Weber's unfinished opera, had been turned over to Mahler by Captain and Marion von Weber; Mahler arranged and completed the fragments, and his highly successful version of the opera was premiered on 20 January 1888.

49. Lipiner, "Einleitung" to *Poetische Werke von Adam Mickiewicz*, trans. Lipiner, vol. 2: *Todtenfeier (Dziady)* (Leipzig, 1887), vii, xiv, xix; see Hefling, "Mahler's 'Todtenfeier' and the Problem of Program Music."

50. *GMB2*, no. 167 (*GMBE*, no. 158).

51. For additional analysis of this movement see Hefling, "Mahler's 'Todtenfeier' and the Problem of Program Music," esp. pp. 35 and 40.

52. See *HLG*, vol. 1 (*HLGF*, vol. 1), chapters 13–15.

53. *NBL2*, 172 (not in *NBLE*), November 1900.

54. *Des Knaben Wunderhorn* (*From the Youth's Magic Horn*) is the well-known collection of German folk poetry published by Achim von Arnim and Clemens Brentano between 1805 and 1808. In *The Birth of Tragedy* (trans. Kaufmann, 53) Nietzsche claims that such folk poetry results from a union of the Apollonian and the Dionysian and, moreover, that melody generates the poetry: *Des Knaben Wunderhorn* contains "innumerable instances of the way the continuously generating melody scatters image sparks all around." Mahler composed twenty-four *Wunderhorn* lieder between c. 1887 and 1901.

55. In *HLG* 1:249–50 (*HLGF* 1:378) an unpublished letter from Mahler to his sister Justine is mistakenly interpreted to suggest that Mahler was planning as early as 1892 to incorporate "Das himmlische Leben" into his Third Symphony. (I

am grateful to Dr. Stephen McClatchie, Mahler-Rosé Collection, Music Library, University of London, Ontario, for a photocopy of the relevant passage from the autograph letter.)

56. *NBL2*, 184 (not in *NBLE*), 20 March–6 April 1901.

57. Peter (Nikolaus) Marcellin Sturm (1760–1812); see Ludwig Erk and Franz Böhme, *Deutscher Liederhort* (Leipzig, 1894), 3:551–52 (no. 1765); *Allgemeine deutsche Biographie*, vol. 37 (Leipzig, 1894; rpt., Berlin, 1971), s.v. "Sturm: Nikolaus (Marcelin)," by Hyac. Holland; and cf. also Fritz Egon Pamer, "Gustav Mahlers Lieder," In *Studien zur Musikwissenschaft*, vol. 16, *Beihefte der Denkmäler der Tonkunst in Österreich* (Vienna, 1929), 126.

58. *NBL2*, 172 (not in *NBLE*).

59. *NBL2*, 198 (*NBLE*, 178), 12 October 1901. Mahler's own piano roll of "Das himmlische Leben" has recently been reproduced in an excellent recording: *Mahler Plays Mahler: The Welte-Mignon Piano Rolls* (Golden Legacy Recorded Music GLRS 101).

60. Goethe, *Faust*, part 2, act V (Insel-Verlag Gesamtausgabe, 481).

61. *NBL2*, 27 (*NBLE*, 32), July–August 1893.

62. On programs for the Second Symphony, see *HLG* 1:780–86 (*HLGF* 1:101–22); *NBL2*, 40 (*NBLE*, 43–44); *GMB2*, no. 167 (*GMBE*, no. 158); and Alma Mahler, *Gustav Mahler: Memories and Letters*, 3d ed, ed. Donald Mitchell and Knud Martner, trans. Basil Creighton (Seattle, 1975), 213–17. A beautiful color facsimile of the autograph score has been published: *Symphony No. 2 in C minor, "Resurrection": Facsimile*, ed. Gilbert E. Kaplan (New York, 1986); this volume also reproduces numerous documents relating to the symphony's genesis.

63. *NBL2*, 40 (*NBLE*, 44), January 1896.

64. Fechner, *Das Büchlein vom Leben nach dem Tode* (1836), trans. Mary C. Wadsworth as *Life after Death* (New York, 1943), 33–35. That Mahler read Fechner during his Hamburg years is confirmed by Pfohl, *Gustav Mahler*, 20.

65. See *GMB2*, no. 216 (*GMBE*, no. 205), 17 February 1897.

66. *NBL2*, 168 (not in *NBLE*), October 1900. The precise moment Mahler had in mind is the stroke of the glockenspiel at rehearsal no. 3.

67. See *NBL2*, 133, 169 (*NBLE*, 127; second passage missing).

68. See Hefling, "'Variations *in nuce*': A Study of Mahler Sketches, and a Comment on Sketch Studies," in *Beiträge '79–81 der Österreichischen Gesellschaft für Musik: Gustav Mahler Kolloquium 1979* (Kassel, 1981), 121, n. 3, as well as Peter Franklin, *Mahler: Symphony No. 3*, Cambridge Handbooks in Music (Cambridge, 1991), 43–45.

69. There were at least eight versions of the programmatic titles for the Third; the best summary is *HLGF* 1:1033–40 (*HLG* 1:795–801). See also Edward R. Reilly, "A Re-examination of the Manuscripts of Mahler's Third Symphony," in *Colloque international Gustav Mahler 25. 26. 27. janvier 1985* (Paris, 1986), 62–72.

70. *GMB2*, no. 146 (*GMBE*, no. 137), 29 August 1895.

71. Fechner, *Life after Death*, 89.

72. *NBL2*, 59 (*NBLE*, 62), 4 July 1896; see also *NBL2*, 49 (*NBLE*, 53), 2–6 April 1896.

73. *NBL2*, 68 (*NBLE*, 67), August 1896.

74. *NBL2*, 56 (*NBLE*, 59), 22 June 1896.

75. *NBL2*, 59–60 (*NBLE*, 61–63), 4 July 1896.

76. Theodor W. Adorno, *Mahler: A Musical Physiognomy*, trans. Edmund Jephcott (Chicago, 1992), 79.

77. Ibid., 77, 78.

78. **US-NYpm** Lehman Deposit; cf. also Floros, *Mahler* 3:86.

79. *NBL2*, 56 (*NBLE*, 59), 22 June 1896.

80. Ibid.

81. *NBL2*, 60 (*NBLE*, 64), 4 July 1896.

82. Ibid.

83. *NBL2*, 61 (*NBLE*, 64), 4 July 1896.

84. "Whoever doesn't know the place . . . would almost have to recognize it from the piece, so singular is it in its loveliness, as though created to provide the impulse for such an inspiration" (*NBL2*, 49 [*NBLE*, 52], 2–6 April 1896).

85. Ibid.

86. *NBL2*, 136 (*NBLE*, 129), June–July 1899.

87. Adorno, 36–37; *HLG* 1:805 (*HLGF* 1:1046).

88. *NBL2*, 58 (*NBLE*, 61 and 201, n. 19); Floros, *Mahler* 3:94–95; see also Morten Solvik Olsen, "'Der Postillon': Eine Anmerkung zu Ernst Decseys Interpretation des Posthorn-Solos in Mahlers *Dritter Symphonie*," *Nachrichten zur Mahler-Forschunng*, no. 29 (March 1993): 3–7.

89. *NBL2*, 56 (*NBLE*, 59), 22 June 1896.

90. Nietzsche, *Also Sprach Zarathustra*, part 1, "Zarathustras Vorrede," §2, trans. Walter Kaufman as *Thus Spoke Zarathustra* in *The Portable Nietzsche* (New York, 1968), 124.

91. This concise formulation appears in Nietzsche, *Die fröliche Wissenschaft*, book 4, §341, trans. Walter Kaufman as *The Gay Science* (New York, 1974), 273.

92. Nietzsche, *Zarathustra*, part 4, "Das Eselfest," §2, trans. Kaufmann, 428.

93. This is Nietzsche's characterization of the eternal recurrence in *Ecce Homo*, "The Birth of Tragedy," §3, trans. Kaufmann (New York, 1969), 273–74.

94. See also Hefling, "The Making of Mahler's 'Todtenfeier': A Documentary and Analytical Study" (Ph.D. dissertation, Yale University, 1985), 1:334–40, as well as Floros, *Mahler* 3:82–84.

95. *NBL2*, 61, 68 (*NBLE*, 64, 67), 4 July and early August, 1896.

96. Letter of 1 July 1896 to Anna von Mildenburg, the famous singer with whom Mahler was then having an affair, *GMB2*, no. 181 (*GMBE*, no. 169).

97. Alfred Roller, *Die Bildnisse von Gustav Mahler* (Leipzig, 1922), 26; see also Floros, *Mahler* 1:125.

98. Fig. 32: "Nicht mit roher Kraft. Gesättigten, edlen Ton."

99. Cf. also Adorno, *Mahler*, 52–57.

100. *HLG* 1:648–62 (*HLGF*, vol. 2: *L'Age d'or de Vienne, 1900–1907* [Paris, 1983], 132–54); *NBL2*, 201–4 (*NBLE*, 182–85), November 1901–January 1902.

101. *NBL2*, 162 (*NBLE*, 151), 1 August 1900.

102. Ibid.

103. *NBL2*, 172 (November 1900); not in *NBLE*. This concentric expansion is apparent in the manifest thematic connections between "Das himmlische Leben" and the finale, only a few of which can be noted here. Three months before his death, Mahler wrote a letter responding to Georg Göhler's program notes for the Fourth Symphony: "I miss one thing: have you overlooked the thematic interconnections that are also so important for the idea of the work? . . . In any case, I ask you to look for just this in my work. Each of the first three movements is themati-

cally connected most intimately and significantly with the last." *GMB2*, no. 463 (*GMBE*, no. 443), 8 February 1911.

104. Mahler's annotation at rehearsal no. 1 in the score.

105. *NBL2*, 163 (*NBLE*, 152), 1 August 1900.

106. *NBL2*, 163, 162 (*NBLE*, 152).

107. *NBL2*, 164, 202 (*NBLE*, 154, 182), 1 August 1900 and November 1901.

108. *NBL2*, 179 (*NBLE*, 162), early January 1901.

109. Ibid.

110. Adorno, *Mahler*, 53.

111. Cf. *NBL2*, 161, 162–63 (*NBLE*, 150, 152), 1 August 1900.

112. **US-Cn** Case MS VM 1001.M21s4; see Ill. 14.4.

113. *NBL2*, 164 (*NBLE*, 154), 1 August 1900.

114. *NBL2*, 202 (*NBLE*, 183), late November 1901.

115. *NBL2*, 158 (*NBLE*, 147), 13 July 1900.

116. *NBL2*, 202 (*NBLE*, 182–83), late November 1901.

117. Cf. the recurring motive of three repeated quarter notes at nine mm. after rehearsal no. 15 ff. of the first movement, and also four mm. after rehearsal no. 5 ff. (mm. 70–72).

118. *NBL2*, 163, 179 (*NBLE*, 152, 161) 1 August 1900 and late December 1900.

119. *NBL2*, 179 (*NBLE*, 162), late December 1900. See also *Bruno Walter Briefe, 1894–1962*, ed. Lotte Walter Lindt (Frankfurt am Main, 1969), 52; and Mahler's comments recorded by Alphons Diepenbrock in *Gustav Mahler und Holland: Briefe*, ed. Reeser, 105: "It is Death who here strikes up the dance and wants to lure souls into his realm."

Mahler very likely got the idea for the *scordatura* violin from the works of the seventeenth-century Austrian composer Heinrich Biber (1644–1704), who frequently uses unusual tunings; through the efforts of his friend Guido Adler, the leading figure in Austrian musicology, Mahler was appointed to the board of the *Denkmäler der Tonkunst in Österreich*, which published Biber's 1681 collection of sonatas, ed. by Adler, in 1898 (*DTÖ* Jg. V/2, vol. 11). See also Edward R. Reilly, *Gustav Mahler and Guido Adler: Records of a Friendship* (Cambridge, 1982), 92–93.

120. See also Mitchell, *The Wunderhorn Years*, 237, 303, and *NBL2*, 182 (not in *NBLE*).

121. *NBL2*, 163 (*NBLE*, 152), 1 August 1900.

122. *NBL2*, 163, 203 (*NBLE*, 152, 184), 1 August 1900 and mid-December 1901.

123. *NBL2*, 163 (*NBLE*, 152–53).

124. *Bruno Walter Briefe*, 52.

125. Mahler made several revisions to bolster the G/E third pairing during the gestation of the third movement; see Hefling, "'Variations *in nuce*,'" esp. pp. 108 and 115–18.

126. See *NBL2*, 163 (*NBLE*, 153).

127. Cf. Mahler's comments on the D-major breakthrough in the finale of the First Symphony, cited earlier in this chapter.

128. *NBL2*, 163 (*NBLE*, 153).

129. See *NBL2*, 194 (*NBLE*, 174); Hefling, "The Composition of 'Ich bin der Welt abhanden gekommen,'" in *Gustav Mahler*, ed. Hermann Danuser, *Wege der Forschung*, vol. 653 (Darmstadt, 1992), 96–103, 157–58; cf. also Gilbert E. Kaplan,

ed., *Gustav Mahler, Adagietto: Facsimile, Documentation, Recording* (New York, 1992), 19–29.

130. Adorno, *Mahler*, 96, 56; cf. also Adorno, "Mahler: Centenary Address, Vienna 1960," in *Quasi una fantasia: Essays on Modern Music*, trans. Rodney Livingstone (London, 1992), 83.

131. Concerning the chronology of the *Kindertotenlieder*, see *HLGF* 2:1140–42, and especially Christopher O. Lewis, "On the Chronology of the *Kindertotenlieder*," *Revue Mahler Review* 1 (1987): 22–45.

132. Bruno Walter, *Gustav Mahler*, 90–91 (trans. Galston, 129).

Selected Bibliography

Adorno, Theodor W. *Mahler: A Musical Physiognomy*. Trans. Edmund Jephcott. Chicago, 1992.

Bauer-Lechner, Natalie. *Gustav Mahler in den Erinnerungen von Natalie Bauer-Lechner*. Ed. Herbert Killian, with annotations by Knud Martner. Hamburg, 1984. [*NBL2*]

———. *Recollections of Gustav Mahler*. Trans. Dika Newlin. Ed. Peter Franklin. Cambridge, 1980. [*NBLE*]

Bekker, Paul. *Gustav Mahlers Sinfonien*. Berlin, 1921. Reprint. Tutzing, 1969.

Blaukopf, Kurt, ed. and comp. *Mahler: A Documentary Study*. With contributions by Zoltan Roman. Trans. Paul Baker et al. New York, 1976.

———. *Gustav Mahler*. Vol. 2: *Vienna: The Years of Challenge (1897–1904)*. Oxford, 1995.

———. *Mahler*. Vol. 1. Garden City, NY, 1973. [*HLG*]

Filler, Susan M. *Gustav and Alma Mahler: A Guide to Research*. Garland Composer Resource Manuals, 28. New York, 1989.

Floros, Constantin. *Gustav Mahler*. 3 vols. Wiesbaden, 1977–85.

———. "Weltanschauung und Symphonik bei Mahler." In *Beiträge '79–80 der Österreichischen Gesellschaft für Musik: Gustav Mahler Kolloquium 1979*, 29–39. Kassel, 1981. Reprinted in *Gustav Mahler*, ed. Hermann Danuser, Wege der Forschung, vol. 653, 344–61. Darmstadt, 1992.

Franklin, Peter. *Mahler: Symphony No. 3*. Cambridge Music Handbooks. Cambridge, 1991.

Hefling, Stephen E. "The Composition of Mahler's 'Ich bin der Welt abhanden gekommen.'" In *Gustav Mahler*, ed. Hermann Danuser, Wege der Forschung. Vol. 653, 96–158. Darmstadt, 1992.

———. "Mahler's 'Todtenfeier' and the Problem of Program Music." *19th-Century Music* 12 (1988): 27–53.

———. "'Variations *in nuce*': A Study of Mahler Sketches and a Comment on Sketch Studies." In *Beiträge '79–80 der Österreichischen Gesellschaft für Musik: Gustav Mahler Kolloquium 1979*, 102–26. Kassel, 1981.

La Grange, Henry-Louis de. *Gustav Mahler: Chronique d'une vie*. 3 vols. Paris, 1979–84. [*HLGF*].

Lewis, Christopher O. "On the Chronology of the *Kindertotenlieder*." *Revue Mahler Review* 1 (1987): 22–45. Published by the Bibliothèque Musicale Gustav Mahler, Paris; publication suspended after first issue.

Mahler, Alma. *Gustav Mahler: Memories and Letters.* 3d ed. Rev. Donald Mitchell and Knud Martner. Trans. Basil Creighton. Seattle, 1975.

Mahler, Gustav. *Adagietto* [from the Fifth Symphony]: *Facsimile, Documentation, Recording.* Ed. Gilbert E. Kaplan. New York, 1992.

———. *Gustav Mahler Briefe.* Ed. Herta Blaukopf. Vienna, 1982. [*GMB2*]

———. *Gustav Mahler–Richard Strauss: Briefwechsel, 1888–1911.* Ed. Herta Blaukopf. Munich, 1980. Trans. Edmund Jephcott as *Gustav Mahler–Richard Strauss: Correspondence.* Chicago, 1984.

———. *Gustav Mahler und Holland: Briefe.* Ed. Eduard Reeser. Vienna, 1980.

———. *Mahler Plays Mahler: The Welte-Mignon Piano Rolls.* Produced by the Kaplan Foundation, 1993. Golden Legacy Recorded Music GLRS 101, licensed to Pickwick Group Ltd. An excellent recording from Mahler's 1905 piano rolls of the songs "Ging heut' morgens übers Feld," "Ich ging mit Lust durch einen grünen Wald," and "Das himmlische Leben" as well as the first movement of his Fifth Symphony.

———. *Mahler: The Resurrection Chorale.* Ed. Gilbert E. Kaplan. New York, 1994. Color facs. ed. of six sketch and ms. pages for the finale of the Second Symphony.

———. *Sämtliche Werke: Kritische Gesamtausgabe.* Ed. the Internationale Gustav Mahler Gesellschaft. Vienna, 1960– .

———. *Symphonic Movement: "Blumine."* Bryn Mawr, PA, 1968.

———. *Selected Letters of Gustav Mahler.* Ed. Knud Martner. Trans. Eithne Wilkins, Ernst Kaiser, and Bill Hopkins. New York, 1979. [*GMBE*]

———. *Symphony No. 2 in C Minor, "Resurrection": Facsimile.* Ed. Gilbert E. Kaplan. New York, 1986.

———. *Unbekannte Briefe.* Ed. Herta Blaukopf et al. Vienna, 1983. Trans. Richard Stokes as *Mahler's Unknown Letters.* London, 1986.

McGrath, William J. *Dionysian Art and Populist Politics in Austria.* New Haven, 1974.

Mitchell, Donald. *Gustav Mahler: The Early Years.* Ed. Paul Banks and David Matthews. Berkeley and Los Angeles, 1980.

———. *Gustav Mahler: The Wunderhorn Years.* Boulder, CO, 1976. Reprint. Berkeley and Los Angeles, 1980.

Nachrichten zur Mahler-Forschung / News About Mahler Research. Vienna, 1976– .

Namenwirth, Simon Michael. *Gustav Mahler: A Critical Bibliography.* 3 vols. Wiesbaden, 1987.

Nietzsche, Friedrich. *The Birth of Tragedy.* Trans. Walter Kaufmann. New York, 1967.

———. *Thus Spoke Zarathustra.* Trans. Walter Kaufmann in *The Portable Nietzsche.* New York, 1968.

Nikkels, Eveline. *"O Mensch! Gib Acht!" Friedrich Nietzsches Bedeutung für Gustav Mahler.* Amsterdam, 1989.

Nowack, Adolf. "Zur Deutung der Dritten und Vierten Sinfonie Gustav Mahlers." In *Religiöse Musik in nicht-liturgischen Werken von Beethoven bis Reger,* ed. Walter Wiora, Studien zur Musikgeschichte des 19. Jahrhunderts. Vol. 51, 185–94. Regensburg, 1978. Reprinted in *Gustav Mahler,* ed. Hermann Danuser, Wege der Forschung. Vol. 653, 191–205. Darmstadt, 1992.

Reilly, Edward R. "A Brief History of the Manuscripts." In Mahler, *Symphony No. 2 in C Minor, "Resurrection": Facsimile,* ed. Gilbert E. Kaplan. New York, 1986.

————. *Gustav Mahler and Guido Adler: Records of a Friendship*. Cambridge, 1982. Includes an English translation of Adler's 1916 monograph *Gustav Mahler*.

————. "A Re-examination of the Manuscripts of Mahler's Third Symphony." In *Colloque international Gustav Mahler 25. 26. 27. janvier 1985*. Paris, 1986.

Schopenhauer, Arthur. *The World As Will and Representation*. 2 vols. Trans. E. F. J. Payne. New York, 1966.

Wagner, Richard. "Beethoven [1870]." In *Richard Wagner's Prose Works*, trans. William Ashton Ellis. Vol. 5: *Actors and Singers*, 57–126. London, 1896. Reprint. New York, 1966.

Walter, Bruno. *Gustav Mahler*. Trans. James Galston. New York, 1941. Reprint. New York, 1973.

CHAPTER FIFTEEN

Sibelius

James Hepokoski

The generation of the "modern" European composers, those born in the years around 1860, was the first to come of age in a post–Wagnerian, post–Lisztian period of rapidly proliferating art-music enterprises—civic and private orchestras, conservatories and universities, music-publishing networks, stable outlets for criticism and commentary, and so on.[1] These recently secured, generally prosperous, and (at least outwardly) confident enterprises spawned a demand for new works to display alongside the canon that they had been formed to perpetuate. As shrines of liberal-humanist cultural memory, they also sought their own continued affirmation from succeeding generations. Among the essential functions of this perception of institutional continuity was its ability to serve as a sealant against the corrosive social and aesthetic forces that were beginning to eat away at the liberal consensus in the last decades of the nineteenth century.[2] Such considerations can help us to understand what Carl Dahlhaus called "the second age of the symphony," and what we may regard as its remarkable reinvigoration in a series of three or four generational waves.[3]

"The moderns" constituted the second of those waves, and it brought forth at least six major symphonic composers: Richard Strauss, Gustav Mahler, Edward Elgar, Jean Sibelius, Carl Nielsen, and Alexander Glazunov.[4] Notwithstanding the substantial differences among them (including the divergent cultural politics of their music's reception history), all six, probably along with a few others, are best considered as a group facing the same kinds of compositional problems.[5] Moreover, these six are only a fragment of a much larger, self-sustaining network—the multi-faceted institution of art music—which was shot through with ominous sociocultural tensions and aesthetic controversies.[6] Studies that encourage the examination of only a single "great" figure or work can mislead, particularly if they downplay the framing context for the competitive circulation of this music. The de facto precondition for the dissemination of Sibelius's music in larger Europe, for example, was his status as an exotic "outsider"—someone utterly different from "us"—an early advantage that before long turned into a curse.

And yet, considered less reductively, his grasp of essential symphonic problems proceeded incrementally: in each major work his grip tightened a notch further. Once past his training as a student, his compositional development took him through three interrelated but distinguishable phases. The first, lasting from the early 1890s through around 1902 or 1903, is indeed an emphatically Finnish political phase marked by his immersion into and gradual emergence out of the exclusively local and national. This phase ranges from the early, massive "symphonic poem" (with voice) *Kullervo* (1892) and the subsequent suite of Kalevalaic tone poems, *Four Legends* (1895–96, actually something of a programmatic symphony in E♭ major) to the First and Second Symphonies. In the second phase, from around 1904 to 1912, Sibelius shifted to a "modern-classical" strategy that strove to engage a larger public, that of the central musical marketplaces of Europe. To this end, he forged a modern musical language of renunciation and compression, one clearly evident in the Third and Fourth Symphonies. The third phase, from around 1912 to the early 1930s, was triggered both by his realization of the inevitable marketplace failure of the second and by the unforeseen emergence of the aggressive cultural politics surrounding the dissonant New Music of a younger generation. This final phase, which saw the compression, severity, and "strangeness" of his style pushed to their limits, is one of disillusioned withdrawal into a private world of symphonic meditation and nature mysticism. Its monuments are the Fifth, Sixth, and Seventh Symphonies and the tone poems *Luonnotar, The Oceanides,* and *Tapiola.* This phase concludes with the unknown (though much discussed) Eighth Symphony, which was never released and whose manuscript and various drafts, it seems, Sibelius eventually burned once and for all in the 1940s.[7] It is with characterizing these three phases that we shall be concerned in this essay.

National Romanticism

For the most part, Sibelius's early symphonic work was a local affair, caught up in the Finnish intellectual and artistic movement often referred to as National Romanticism or Karelianism. A closely knit movement both of self-assertion against the Swedish-language elite culture established by Finland's past and of political resistance to the harsh Russian control of its present, National Romanticism sought to touch and re-evoke what it regarded as the true springs of uncontaminated Finnish-ness. One source was the preindustrial culture of Karelia, the undeveloped region in the southeast, to which a reverent pilgrimage was de rigueur for virtually any Finnish artist of the period. (Since the 1939–40 "Winter War" with the Soviet Union it has been part of Russia, the region northwest of St. Petersburg.) Another source was the *Kalevala*, the Finnish—often Karelian—folk epic of gods, heroes (including Kullervo and Lemminkäinen), charms, and spells collected, stitched together, and published by Elias Lönnrot (1835, revised and enlarged 1849). Still another was Lönnrot's companion book of collected folk poetry, the *Kanteletar* (1840). Often accompanied by a bleak, unadorned realism, the brisk winds of 1890s Karelianism were felt not only in music but also, and in fact more primarily, in Finnish painting and literature. In painting Akseli Gallen-Kallela became the most celebrated figure, but Pekka Halonen, Juho Rissanen, and Eero Järnefelt (Sibelius's brother-in-law) also produced significant work; in literature we should note Juhani Aho's historical novel *Panu* (1897) and Eino Leino's collection of poems *Helkavirsiä* (1903).

The impact of all this on the young Sibelius is obvious enough: merely to list the programmatic titles of his major works from the 1890s would be sufficient. Still, when we confront the specifics of his early musical style—particularly as it had developed by the end of this period in the First and Second Symphonies, when he was emerging out of a merely local context to enter a more competitive, international marketplace—the issue is more complex. From the beginning this music embraced the risks of the new wave of European modernism, and it was driven by the search for a strongly individualized, willfully eccentric style. Sibelius's early style was an inseparable mixture of at least three different traditions: the Austro-Germanic, the "Nationalist" (especially the Scandinavian and Russian variants), and the primally Finnish. Each was a vital ingredient, but none should be given an absolute priority.

Two of these traditions were central elements of the institution of art music. The first, the hegemonic Austro-Germanic symphonic tradition, was grounded in a broader concept of musical metaphysics—music as *Geist*—and its adherents generally regarded rock-solid formal construction (as defined by Beethovenian models) and unswerving, motivic "musical logic"[8] as moral imperatives. This tradition was inescapable, and Sibelius had encountered it full-strength in his studies in Berlin and Vienna from 1889 to 1891. The key point, though, is that he seems to have regarded it with uncommon veneration. (Displaying the intense concentration and developmental motivic interconnectedness of his music is the most common strategy of Sibelius analysis.) Nor was his regard limited to the conservative or academic wing of the tradition: his early music rings with echoes or adaptations of Lisztian, Wagnerian, and Brucknerian gestures. As recent scholarship has suggested, for example, certain surface features of Bruckner's earlier symphonies seem to have had a particularly potent influence: multiple waves of static sound blocks (*Klangflächen*), reverberating ostinatos, craggy sequences, chasms of silence, cumulative climaxes, and so on.[9]

Related to this first tradition was one closer to home, the customary tradition to which a non-Germanic symphonist was expected to aspire: that of the eclectic "nationalists," who paid homage to the *Formenlehre* structures and their deformations but illuminated them with melodies, harmonies, and rhythms perceived as "national" or in touch with the "folk." For Sibelius this group included Grieg, Svendsen, and Sinding from Norway, yet surely the most prestigious models were those provided by the recent Russian schools—Tchaikovsky above all, but also the nearby Petersburg composers from Balakirev, Borodin, and Rimsky-Korsakov to Sibelius's contemporary, Glazunov.[10]

The third tradition was the Finnish folk idiom, in which Sibelius seems to have been determined to steep himself and whose premodern atmosphere, naïveté, and bluntness he wished to incorporate into his own compositions. As a budding Romantic Nationalist, for example—freshly home from Viennese training, and during the period of the composition of *Kullervo*—he traveled to Porvoo (Borgå) in December 1891 and was deeply impressed after hearing the woman who was the most celebrated *Kalevala* lament and rune singer of the time, Larin Paraske.[11] (Within the Karelian folk tradition the trochaic tetrameter poetic lines of the *Kalevala* runes—*runo* is Finnish for "poem"—were typically sung to "monotonous," conceptually endless repetitions of a characteristic two-phrase melody type. Its characteristics included an implied $\frac{5}{4}$ meter, persistently disposed as six eighth notes plus two quarter notes; an obsessive, narrowly circumscribed minor or "Dorian" mode; and a hypnotic, back-and-forth rocking of the two "antecedent-consequent" phrases, the first ending with the two quarter notes on the repeated second scale-step, the second on a repeated modal final or "tonic.")

A pilgrimage to Karelia itself would follow in summer 1892. Within a few years he was collecting and editing more rune melodies, some of which were published in 1895, the year of the *Four Legends*, in a book of *Kalevala* commentary. Perhaps most telling, on 25 November 1896 Sibelius delivered a lecture at Helsinki University, "Some Reflections on Folk Music and Its Influence on the Development of Art Music." Here he insisted that European art-music harmony was on the decline and could be regenerated only through an intermixing with the spiritual truth of the folk idiom. For a Finnish composer this meant a personal bonding with traditional Kalevalaic recitation formulas. He went on to insist that Finnish rune singing's core consisted of melody types bound together by a ruling minor pentachord, D–E–F–G–A (which could be expanded in various ways—for example, by transposition or by adding extra pitches for strongly emotional texts), and by delivery patterns of circular, varied-line, and stanza repetitions resembling the process of theme and variations. Finally, he argued the importance of finding non-normative, though instinctively and spiritually appropriate, harmonizations for pentachord-related melodies.[12]

At the turn of the century, perhaps spurred on by a Breitkopf contract in 1898 for the *King Christian II* Suite, followed by a performance of it in Leipzig the following year, Sibelius began to grope toward the exit of his first, Karelianist-local phase, to move toward a larger, more influential audience with his only slightly more abstract First and Second Symphonies.[13] Although the First (written in 1898–99 and revised in 1900, a year after its Helsinki premiere) is not explicitly programmatic, its clear allusion to, then deformation of, the standard *per aspera ad astra* symphonic plot nonetheless invites speculation along this line. (The deformation is that the expected *astra* conclusion is crushed.) Moreover, both Sibelius and his Finnish backers initially used the work for unabashedly political purposes. The new symphony was the centerpiece of the Helsinki Philharmonic's European tour in the summer of 1900, which aimed, in part, to marshal sympathy for a Finland suffering under the Bobrikov governorship and its policy of Russification, made most explicit in the notorious February Manifesto of 1899 (this deprived Finland of its political autonomy and severely limited the freedom of speech and assembly). The month-long tour, which included concerts in Lübeck, Berlin, Amsterdam, and Paris, was a volatile mixture of the new aesthetic of "elemental" Northern sound and subtle politics, and it was a pivotal moment in Sibelius's career.

Toward the end of this first compositional phase some of Sibelius's music became known in the musical power centers of Europe (Germany, France, and England). According to the existing terms of reception, it was heard under the sign of the exotic. Ernest Newman's response to the First Symphony in 1905 reminds us of how daringly primitive it could sound to its first non-Finnish listeners: "I have never listened to any music that took me away so completely from our usual Western life, and transported me into a quite new civilization. Every page of it breathes of another manner of thought, another way of living, even another landscape and seascape than ours."[14] Much of the First Symphony's exotic effect relies on the radicalism of its orchestration. Among the sources for this is Tchaikovsky, whose spirit and tone loom behind the work, for all of its rugged individuality. To a later generation of Northern modernists Tchaikovsky's nakedly direct, heartfelt intensity, his coloristic outbursts, and his unleashing of eruptive emotion—the very aspects that some Western European critics criticized as recklessness or barbaric transgressions of cultivated taste—represented a revolution of sonority that should not be undervalued. The young Sibelius embraced this liberated orchestral style and pushed it in even bolder directions.

From this perspective the "post–Tchaikovskian" First Symphony may be heard as a succession of contrasting, static timbre tableaux or sound sheets. Here we encounter bold patches of color laid onto the sonic canvas with the broad strokes of the palette knife, not the fine brush. Transitional material is minimized to permit rich chunks of primal sound to butt up against one another. Consider, for example, the harsh brass closes of the first and last movements; or the "cold" reprise of the first movement's second theme, whose phrases are passed back and forth among the clarinet, trumpet, horn, and flute; or the hammered timpani that ignite the scherzo's main theme. Or consider the characteristic intercutting of the horns at the beginning of the scherzo's trio (Ex. 15.1, mm. 4ff.). Here the *allegro* vigor, ostinato energy, modally inflected C tonality, and characteristic deep-string-based *Klang* of the scherzo are abruptly liquidated by a non sequitur, horn-bassoon-tuba slab of momentarily static, dissonant E-major wind color—an ephemeral E, as it turns out, that soon slips off toward G♯ minor. (Notice also the equal division of the octave by major thirds, C–E–G♯.) In the extremity of its contrasts and in its non-nuanced primitivism and directness the passage is quintessential early Sibelius.

The drama and abstract program of the First Symphony are driven by three principles: a novel treatment of symphonic tonality, a stringent "musical logic" carried out through the four movements, and the persistent recirculation of a limited collection of relatively static *Klänge*, or sound objects. Tonally, the symphony's reigning idea seems to be that its musical narrative is obliged to unfold in a negative tonic, E minor—apparently an "imposed" or oppressive tonic subjugating a more "ideal" tonic, G major. Within the context of this interpretation, much of the work is played out in an unnatural or false tonality: the E minor is a persistent, unwelcome distortion of a desired, but unsustainable, G major. Thus the slow movement's E♭ major relates primarily to the suppressed tonic, G major, as an escape into its flat submediant, a distant dream color, far from the symphony's E-minor reality. The scherzo on C (with its trio touching fleetingly on the also potentially redemptive E major: see Ex. 15.1) belongs both to the E and G complexes. The finale reimposes the negative E minor.

The underlying E minor/G major duality is established at the symphony's opening. In the introductory frame, *andante, ma non troppo,* Sibelius sets up the narrative to come with spare, lyrical lines that hover in the border zones between E minor and G major. Its final phrase, though, sounds on G minor, and the ensuing narrative proper, the *allegro energico,* begins with a shimmering upper-string dyad, g^2–b^2, that momentarily suggests a release into the "true" tonic, G major (Ex. 15.2). What is sought at this point is a stable $\frac{5}{3}$ triad above G, but with the subsequent theme (whose core is the g^2–$f\sharp^2$–e^2 descent) the expected $\frac{5}{3}$ decays instead into an implied $\frac{6}{3}$, whose "E-minor" connotations are then shored up with a bludgeoning root in measure 9, whereupon the process is immediately repeated. In a burst of frustration, measures 14–15, the G bass is reinstated, *fz*, and by degrees, moving back through the $\frac{6}{3}$ above G (m. 15), it man-

EXAMPLE 15.1. Sibelius, Symphony No. 1, movt. 3 (opening of trio)

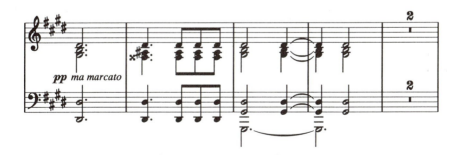

EXAMPLE 15.2. Sibelius, Symphony No. 1, movt. 1 (end of introduction and principal theme)

Andante, ma non troppo

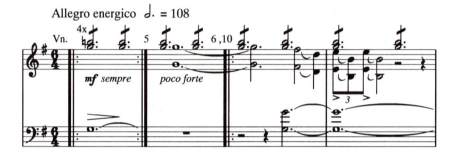

ages to secure the "ideal"—but still all too temporary—$\frac{5}{3}$ above G (mm. 19–20). The remainder of the principal theme, in which E minor ultimately predominates, may be easily read in terms of this struggle of internal self-assertion and external thwarting.[15] This is also true of both the movement and the symphony as a whole.

Example 15.2 also demonstrates several characteristic gestures and sonorities of this early phase of the Sibelius style. In addition to its clipped syntax and static G pedals in contrasting registers, we should notice the obsession with the brooding melodic descent, 3–2–1. Particularly in the minor mode, this figure serves throughout Sibelius's career as one of his most important "sonic ideograms," or objects for contemplative immersion. (It is probably best regarded as the lower segment of the minor pentachord that Sibelius emphasized as typically Finnish in his 1896 Helsinki University lecture.) In Example 15.2 the 3–2–1 ideogram appears as the B♭–A–G conclusion of the introductory frame; at the opening of the principal theme, as the 8–7–6 decay of G major into E minor (where it becomes 3–2–1); in measures 9 and 13, only inverted, e^2–$f\sharp^2$–g^2, as if in an impulsive attempt to undo the 8–7–6 E-minor decay; and in measures 14–15, b^2–a^2–g^2, anticipating the G-major triad established only in measures 19–20.

Its dissonant appearance in measures 14–15—manifestly recalling, though more violently, the middle section of the second movement of Tchaikovsky's *Pathétique* Symphony, one of the source-passages for early Sibelius[16]—is a recurring sonority of this symphony: a 3–2–1 (10–9–8) motion over a held bass, consisting of an accented upper neighbor resolving to a diminished seventh, which then moves to either an unstable $\frac{6}{3}$, as here (when further prolonged this last sonority produces the so-called Sibelian mediant pedal, although that term should probably be contested),[17] or a more stable $\frac{5}{3}$. A variant of the same "*Pathétique*" dissonance may be found in Example 15.1, at the beginning of the scherzo's trio. Here the more characteristic E pedal bass is underpinned at first by a low C, which evaporates with the dissonance's resolution, and that resolution is to a $\frac{5}{3}$, not a $\frac{6}{3}$. Nonetheless, its allusions to the first movement are unmistakable.

The dissonance also recurs prominently in the preceding slow movement (Ex. 15.3, mm. 4, 6, 12, 14, 19, and 21). Here it is linked with the closely related "Russian 5–♯5–6 shift," another meditative *Klang* object (involving a move from a $\frac{5}{3}$ to a $\frac{6}{3}$ sonority, and sometimes back again, through a chromatic passing tone) that sounds through so much of early Sibelius. In the passage shown in Example 15.3 Sibelius tracks through the 5–♯5–6–♭6–5 motion three times over the static E♭ bass: measures 3–8, 11–16, and 18–23. (The same chromatic shift is a prominent feature of the finale's second theme.) Whatever its pre-*kuchka* pedigree, there is little doubt that from Sibelius's perspective its most immediate derivation

EXAMPLE 15.3. Sibelius, Symphony No. 1, movt. 2, mm. 1–23

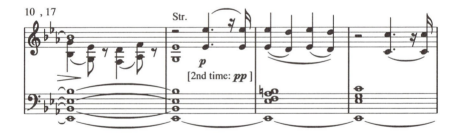

was Russian: it is one of the most commonly encountered "exotic" sounds of the Petersburg composers.[18] A model for the slow-movement theme might have been the similar main theme of the slow movement of Glazunov's Second Symphony (1889), one of the most celebrated "re-

EXAMPLE 15.4. Glazunov, Symphony No. 2, movt. 2, mm. 1–10

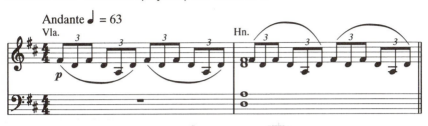

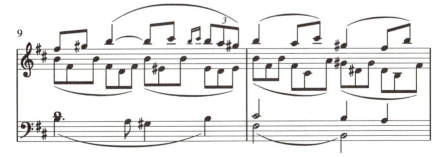

gional" symphonies of the time (Ex. 15.4). However tempting it might be to suggest that Sibelius's darker, more brooding theme was based on Glazunov's, it is probably safer to suppose that both exemplify a Petersburg theme type that Sibelius was adapting and Finnicizing.

EXAMPLE 15.5. Sibelius, Symphony No. 2, movt. 2, 5 mm. after rehearsal letter C

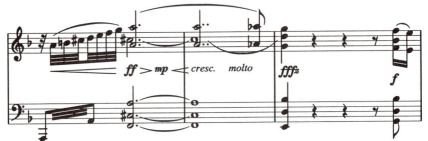

(*continued*)

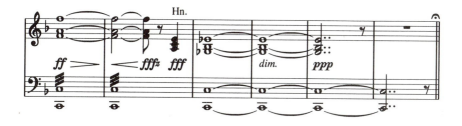

The concept of Northern sound object meditation also pervades the Second Symphony. While the Second, like the First, invited its audiences to perceive it primarily as a nationalistic symphony (its driving toward the circular folk reiterations of the finale's second theme is especially characteristic of the genre), Sibelius was now also beginning to reach out to a wider European audience. Correspondingly, allusions to the Germanic canon become more evident. In the famous eruptions of the slow movement, for instance (Ex. 15.5 shows the essential voices), the references to the *Tristan* chord, and indeed, to the sequential opening of *Tristan* itself are unmistakable. Among other things, this passage is a modern-primitivist reworking (or purposeful "misprision")[19] of Wagner that transmutes the original sign—that of erotic desire—into an anguished attempt to writhe free from the prison house of D minor, only to have the gates swing shut again in the powerful descent of measure 6–11. (Mm. 12–18 are best interpreted not as a positive shift away from D minor, but as the reactive, impotent aftermath of defeat: it leads to the movement's second part, the "Christus" passage in F♯ major.)[20] We may also recognize here reworked echoes of Bruckner and Strauss. The gaping silences of measures 8–10 suggest features of the former, while the "frustrated" two-chord conclusion in the horns seems adapted from the collapse at the end of the developmental space of *Tod und Verklärung* (after rehearsal letter W, mm. 364–66). Yet the Finnish core remains: the passage outlines three grim minor-pentachord descents (5–4–3–2–1 on E, A, and D minor) and the meditative 3–2–1 ideogram resounds in the bass in measures 10–11.

Modern Classicism

From about 1904 to 1912—beginning with revision of the Violin Concerto (1905), the incidental music to *Pelléas et Mélisande* (1905), and the Kalevalaic tone poem *Pohjola's Daughter* (1906, surely a response to Richard Strauss)—Sibelius turned his attention to carving out a space of distinction in larger, non-Scandinavian modernist markets. He now sought to compete for attention with such composers as Strauss, Mahler, Busoni, Pfitzner, Schillings, and Reger on their home territory. To this end he began to rethink, deepen, and expand his aesthetic beyond his earlier "modern nationalism" in order to address some of the ongoing modernist controversies in the pan-European—and particularly Germanic—mainstream. The problems that he faced in engaging the rapidly shifting cultural politics in Germany (and eventually in England) are not easily summarizable, although they are central to any thoughtful consideration of Sibelius as a twentieth-century composer.

The crux of the issue is that his entrée into the larger arena was the work of his earlier phase. While these compositions opened the larger European door for him, they simultaneously stamped his reception pattern so irrevocably that his subsequent works could never escape being collapsed into the facile, and ultimately (from the Germanic perspective) peripheral, category of "mere" nationalism. It was in these years that Sibelius's name began to appear in the German music journals. In 1904, for example, the Helsinki critic Karl Flodin skillfully played the nationalist gambit in Germany on Sibelius's behalf—the standard opening, though a simplistic one, in this cultural-political situation—reporting in a special Scandinavian issue of the influential Berlin journal *Die Musik* that Sibelius's music was the culmination of the "awakening of the national tone in Finland," that "the ancient Finnish sacred song lingers on him in the form of the antique modes," and that Sibelius, though clearly influenced by Tchaikovsky, was no mere nationalist of the old school—rather, this was music of keen "originality," "modern through and through," and so on.[21]

In January 1905 a Sibelius-conducted performance of the Second Symphony on one of Busoni's new-music concerts with the Berlin Philharmonic initiated a vigorous German debate about the composer. At first it was mostly positive, and we should note that Sibelius was greeted both as a nationalist and an emphatic modernist.[22] At this point all was promise in his career. This was confirmed a month later, when in February 1905 he turned away from his Helsinki publishers, Fazer and Westerlund, to sign a contract with Lienau (Schlesinger) in Berlin. It was confirmed further with his first trip to England in November and December 1905. This, too, was a decisive moment, signaling the onset of his "English connection."

For his part, Sibelius now seems to have decided to make his voice heard in the ongoing Germanic battles concerning the direction of modern instrumental music. At the heart of this controversy lay the perception that the leaders of *die neudeutsche Richtung* (especially Strauss, but also Mahler and others) had shifted their attention away from architectonic principle in favor of a hypertechnically advanced, decorative, or illustrative instrumental color. (Much of the debate centered on such seemingly episodic works as *Also sprach Zarathustra* and *Ein Heldenleben* and Mahler's Second and Third Symphonies.) For ardent partisans of *der moderne Geist*, such as Arthur Seidl, Hans Merian, and Max Graf, modernism was a liberation from shackles, an "emancipation of color" wedded to "free form," a post–Wagnerian, post–Lisztian leap into technique,

tone color, and monumentality, all carried out with the full modern orchestra for the sake of *Fortschritt,* or progress.[23] Others welcomed the liberation of color and technique but were unsettled by its potentially anar-
chic, centrifugal spinning away from the formal principle—all too easily
taken, perhaps, as a metaphor for the feared dissolution of the European
liberal-humanist consensus itself. Consequently, this century's first
decade heard a number of prominent calls for the introduction of a principle of restraint. If successful, the resulting new classicism would embrace modernism's color, boldness, and uncompromising character, but
would also shore up the eroding genre of the symphony—widely viewed
as the essentially German musical way of thinking—by renouncing its current tendency toward episodic looseness and trying to recover, on new
terms, its earlier compression of thought and rigorous musical logic.[24]
Thus emerged within the institution of art music the possibility of *Reak-
tion als Fortschritt* (as Rudolf Louis described it in 1909): something perceived as a needed course-correction or reconsolidation, but something
that was still undeniably "progressive."

By and large, this seems to have been Sibelius's view in his 1904–12,
"modern classical" period, represented above all by the Third and Fourth
Symphonies (1907 and 1911). Perfectly suited by temperament to the
task, he now set out to reconstitute the strictness and discipline of the
modern "symphony," to repudiate the reigning principle of monumentality, and to counter what he believed to be the surface sensationalism of
the leading Germanic modernists with the bracing purity of cold Northern water. By no means was he jettisoning his earlier "modern nationalist"
style; rather, he was trying to transform, deepen, and ultimately overwhelm it with a radical austerity that simultaneously addressed more internationally urgent, pan-European issues of symphonic construction. To
be sure, this was a risky strategy for an outsider in a volatile, prestige marketplace most responsive to heightened scandal and "the shock of the
new": after all, these were the *Salome* and *Elektra* years. Nonetheless, these
were the terms on which he now decided to compete.

This new phase saw a determined weeding-out of sounds and procedures that he considered inessential or indulgent. The result was a leaner,
sparer music. To avoid falling prey to the charges of naïveté or academicism, the new style correspondingly demanded the cultivation of compen-
sating techniques to heighten the impact, implications, and sheer
strangeness of the limited number of *Klang* objects that survived this process of critique. On the one hand, we may perceive his growing obsession
with the "severity and style [of the symphony] and the profound logic that
created an inner connection between all the motifs," as he remarked to
an apparently unimpressed Mahler in October 1907.[25] On the other
hand, Sibelius now embarked in earnest on the project that we might interpret as an attempt to draw out the hidden secrets of sound itself—to
give the impression of a phenomenological deep-sinking into its material-

ity and "being." To be sure, his music of this period is often stamped with puzzling, acerbic sonorities and brooding dissonances. (The Fourth Symphony is a case in point.) But it also strives to recover both the diatonic melodic fragment and the pure triad as meaningful modern utterances, to "defamiliarize" them so that their potential to speak might be disclosed anew. Given the European aesthetic environment in which it was proposed, this defamiliarization of the diatonic and the consonant was a daunting task, one easy for audiences to misconstrue, both then and now. Indeed, it is on this widely misunderstood feature that most of the subsequent Sibelius controversy of this century has pivoted.

A watershed in his career, the Third Symphony sets out the challenge in no uncertain terms: within an anti-monumental work to restore the possibility of experiencing the reality not merely of the major triad but of C major, its tonic, as a progressively deepening, revelatory event. Here one needs to grasp the trajectory of the whole symphony: the initial near-regularity of the first movement's C-major sonata arrangement moves forward through two complementary stages of gestational nurturing—the broad circular rotations of the second movement and the first, "scherzo" portion of the third movement (G♯ minor and a not fully complete or stable C major)—in order to bring forth the work's *telos*, an altogether new, gravitationally "heavier" C major, in the third movement's even more obsessively circular finale-conclusion. This is the procedure that would eventually become a central feature of Sibelius's final stylistic period: a progressive, teleological genesis (generation of climactic goal-statement) involving the process of formal rotations through gestational sound matrices (the process, i.e., of successive cyclings through a referential thematic pattern within which the *telos* idea is gradually nurtured and shaped); these sound matrices then decay away or are discarded once they have given birth to the *telos*.[26]

That the procedure has implications for a gendered reading of "alternative" musical process and structure is obvious. While any adequate consideration of these implications would lead us afield,[27] we should at least look more closely at its first appearance in the symphonies. In brief, following a preparatory, rotational second movement, whose deceptively simple surface conceals its generation of the crucial interval of the major third, from which the finale theme proper will grow,[28] the third movement's initial, "scherzo-character" section continues the process more forthrightly—and closer to C major—through a series of three broad rotations. The first (or expositional rotation)[29] subdivides into two areas: 1a in C major, leading to a fleeting, "off-tonic," and *rinforzando* triple enunciation of the descending major third (Ex. 15.6, mm. 4–5, or 2 mm. before rehearsal no. 2; notice also the characteristic 3–2–1 ideogram in the bass around rehearsal no. 2); and 1b, on A minor (beginning at rehearsal no. 2) and leading to even more emphatic descending thirds, C–A♭, eight measures after rehearsal number 3.

EXAMPLE 15.6. Sibelius, Symphony No. 3, movt. 3, 5 mm. before rehearsal no. 2

The complementary rotation 2a (beginning around rehearsal no. 4) returns to the material of 1a and readjusts the thirds at the end to sound the pitch classes E–C (after rehearsal no. 5). These thirds, that is, are being shaped toward the key of the finale theme. In rotation 2b (5 mm. after rehearsal no. 5), however, the tonal color shifts to F minor. Within five measures the prior third descents begin to take on the recognizable, though still incomplete, shape of the finale theme—its quickening within the womb or its drowsy awakening from slumber. But the stirrings subside (rehearsal no. 6) and rotation 2b continues, taking on extraordinary energy and driving to a shattering A♭ downbeat (rehearsal no. 8), which disperses the scattered motivic particles in all directions. Modulatory and "developmental," culminatory rotation 3 (beginning gradually between rehearsal nos. 8 and 9) seeks to reconfigure these particles and to trigger the emergence of the fully formed *telos* in the proper key. The finale theme is anticipated one last time, in the violas, *divisi*—still wrapped in the motives and timbres of surrounding matrix (6 mm. after rehearsal no. 12). It finally appears on its own, as the *telos* proper, four measures after rehearsal number 13, the beginning of the movement's finale portion (Ex. 15.7).

This obsessively circular *telos* music—confined to varied, accumulative rotations of a single theme and a single key—may be understood from differing perspectives. We may regard it as an exponentially distilled

EXAMPLE 15.7. Sibelius, Symphony No. 3, movt. 3, "finale theme," 4 mm. after rehearsal no. 13

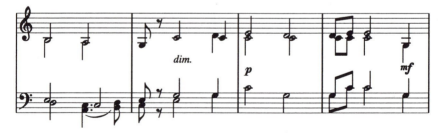

illustration of that type of "nationalist" symphony finale that featured circular "folk" reiterations as the *telos* of the whole work. Or we could hear it as occupying the substantially altered recapitulatory space of a bold sonata deformation encompassing both the scherzo and the finale portions of the third movement, conceived as a single, generative gesture. Or—perhaps most relevantly from our immediate perspective here—we may regard it as the production of a "supersaturated" C major whose sheer specific gravity, ever accruing, permits no escape (for instance, via its frequent "Lydian" fourth) to subordinate themes or keys. Even its two feints toward E minor, six measures after rehearsal number 15 and one measure before rehearsal number 18, are immediately undermined by a shift to a $\frac{6}{3}$ position above the E bass (the so-called C⁶ chord), and in each case the $\frac{5}{3}$ above a C bass is vigorously restored within a few bars. This progressive accumulation of concentration and weight on a single sonority is unique in the symphonic repertory. It drives toward a maximal-density, heavily weighted close, a sonorous black hole that excludes all other possibilities. Appropriately, it is capped at the end with an elemental, 5–3–1 C-major triadic affirmation, *ff*, in the brass.

Both the Third and the even more extreme Fourth Symphony—extreme especially in its obsession with dark sonority, aphoristic utterance, and bitter, spare astringency—can be understood as Sibelius's two principal attempts to find an individual symphonic voice in the larger European, and especially German, marketplace of art music. This voice was intended to be simultaneously "modern" and "classical." It was offered as a proposed advance in terms of orchestral sound, intellectual concentration, and compositional seriousness. Yet, as a protest against what he regarded as the "circus tricks" or musical indulgences of his principal competitors, it was also to be part of what he hoped would be a new wave of modern classicism.

But in marketplace terms the strategy was ineffective. Despite the existence of a few scattered champions, particularly in England, for the most part Sibelius's second-phase music proved to be only puzzling, to the degree that it was noticed at all. Since the composer had been largely ghettoized as a mere nationalist—not "one of us"—and worse, since he was frequently judged to have run out of the expected "grand-gesture," coloristically sensational, or inflated rhetoric that the Germanic and French marketplaces, in particular, expected from such "exotic" nationalists, his newer, more difficult works failed to achieve a widespread resonance. And as became increasingly clear, in the 1909–12 period the aesthetic debates over the direction of modernism were being eclipsed by the musical concerns of a radical new generation—that of Schoenberg and Stravinsky.

Late Style: Nature Mysticism and Content-Based Forms

In the years 1909–12 (those not only of his own Fourth Symphony but also of Mahler's death, the premiere of *Der Rosenkavalier*, and, above all, the growing public awareness of the dissonant New Music in France and Germany), Sibelius came painfully to terms with his own lukewarm reception in the modern Germanic and French institutions of art music, now veering off in directions with which he could not sympathize. These were years of personal artistic crisis and intense self-examination. Although convinced that he had forged an aesthetically responsible, high-density modern classicism, he was obliged to concede that the art-music world had changed. However his music might be welcomed in certain sectors of England and the United States (often touted, ominously, as a "healthy" antidote to the decadence of a younger generation's New Music), it had become clear that in Germany, Austria, and France, the markets he had originally sought to address, his own music now had little chance of being received sympathetically.

In his final, third phase, beginning around 1912, Sibelius chose to pursue his own path even more doggedly, but simultaneously to accept his irrelevance to "their" marketplace—and thus from "their" constructions of history. This psychological withdrawal was reinforced by the isolating conditions of World War I, which barred him from foreign travel, interfered with his music's distribution and performance in greater Europe, and ground significant publication to a near halt; it was further complicated by Finland's independence from the newly Bolshevik Russia in December 1917 and the subsequent Finnish civil war. In this period Sibelius embraced the inescapability of what he called his *Alleingefühl* (sense of solitude). Now secluded, with his family, for even longer stretches at Ainola, his rustic forest retreat in Järvenpää, he undertook an isolated, meditative project that has no parallel among his contemporary composers. "At Ainola," Sibelius would frequently remark, "this stillness speaks."[30] It is the still presence of nature—clean, cold Finnish lakes and towering, resinous pines, forest flowers, winds, stars, sun, snow, migrating swans, cranes, and wild geese—whose being he would seek to awaken in a contemplative music of mysticism and intuition. On 20 May 1918, while again revising the Fifth Symphony (an early version of which, with four separate movements, had received its first performance in December 1915, the centerpiece of the Helsinki celebration of his fiftieth birthday), he would write: "From everything I notice how my inner being has changed since the period of the Fourth Symphony. And these symphonies of mine are more confessions of faith than are my other works."[31]

Recent research into Sibelius diaries and sketches from the final period has established that its four major pieces after 1914 are conceptually interrelated: the Fifth, Sixth, and Seventh Symphonies and *Tapiola*. (Doubtless the destroyed Eighth Symphony would also have belonged in this group.) Each is an individual facet of an even larger project, that of uncovering nature's hidden voice by means of a correspondingly elemental musical process and *Klang*. Since the title of the 1926 tone poem seems (coincidentally?) to summarize the essence of this grand project, we may consider these four works as forming a closely knit "*Tapiola* complex" ("The Forest," or, more precisely, "The Place Where the God Tapio Dwells"). Appropriately enough, the complex was foreshadowed by the immediately preceding tone poems from 1913 and 1914, the creation myth *Luonnotar* ([Feminine] nature spirit) and *The Oceanides*.

So much is evident from the period's most important compositional process document, a forty-page thematic sketchbook (now preserved in the State Archives in Helsinki), whose first thirty-seven pages date from the beginning of Sibelius's wartime isolation, August 1914 through June 1915.[32] Although the sketchbook contains many entries for minor works and for pieces that he never brought to completion, this was the period dominated by melodies and thematic tables that he was encouraging to germinate into the Fifth Symphony. By around December 1914 the ideas for this work had multiplied to the point that he began also to nurture plans for an orchestral "Fantasia I." By January 1915 this seems to have changed into a projected Sixth Symphony, and a few of the themes originally planned for the Fifth migrated toward the Sixth, and vice versa. Moreover, in the 1920s Sibelius would rework two of the themes associated in late 1914 with the Fifth Symphony, but eventually set aside, into significant moments of the Seventh Symphony and *Tapiola*: an early version—in $\frac{7}{4}$ and B major!—of the Seventh's recurring "trombone theme" (first heard seven mm. after rehearsal no. C);[33] and the main idea for the staccato music at G of *Tapiola*, the beginning of the second large rotation (which may also be heard as the onset of the developmental space).[34]

From all this it is clear that the sketchbook illuminates a ten- or eleven-month period that was unusually rich in the creation of raw materials. Much of Sibelius's final period would be spent sorting out these ideas, determining their optimal contexts, reshaping them, and surrounding them with related music. Thus, in a famous diary remark from 10 April 1915 regarding his struggle with the Fifth Symphony: "Arrangement of the themes. . . . It's as if God the Father had thrown down the tiles of a mosaic from heaven's floor and asked me to determine what kind of picture it was. Maybe [this is] a good definition of 'composing.' Maybe not. How would I know?"[35] It is important to realize that some of the 1914–15 sketchbook jottings were more than mere themes. Several were eventually situated in mid- and late-movement contexts as spotlighted "nature-mystical" moments, synthesis passages, or the bearers of musical arrival points of one sort or another. These became the core ideas into which the works or movements in which they were incorporated may be heard as growing. Not only does the 1914–15 sketchbook demonstrate the interrelationships among the *Tapiola*-complex works; it is also an essential component of any informed study of their musical processes.

The earliest sketchbook idea ultimately retained in the Fifth Symphony, for instance, is the "splitting apart" of the finale's second theme (the wedgelike melodic line shown in Ex. 15.8, from the movement's culminatory [third] rotation, rehearsal letter P). It was this distortion of the second theme, not the theme proper (first sounded one m. after rehearsal letter D), that was the generating seed of the Fifth. In the completed symphony this passage takes the decisive step into the work's final gateway; filled with pain and trembling, it initiates the process leading to the *telos*, the concluding set of emphatic cadences.[36] In April 1915, while still planning the work, Sibelius linked this expanding version of the theme with his sighting at Ainola of "16 [migrating] swans. One of my greatest experiences! Lord God, that beauty! They circled over me for a long time. Disappeared into the solar haze like a gleaming, silver ribbon. . . . Nature mysticism and life's *Angst!*"[37] The swan reference was significant. Henceforth in Sibelius's private circles it seems to have been linked with the differing versions of the finale's second theme. On 15 December 1916, for example, his friend Axel Carpelan referred to the theme in correspondence with the composer as "that swan hymn beyond compare."[38]

EXAMPLE 15.8. Sibelius, Symphony No. 5, finale, rehearsal letter P

Occasionally the 1914–15 sketchbook directs our attention to things we might otherwise overlook. The only extended portion found in it of the Fifth's second movement (*andante mosso, quasi allegretto*), for instance, is located in the second-movement section of a thematic table for the Sixth Symphony. In the final version of the Fifth the corresponding passage is found beginning fourteen measures after rehearsal letter E (Ex. 15.9). Seemingly retransitional, this is actually the movement's first arrival point: its intervals are replicated within the subsequent finale's opening theme. Similarly, the Swan Hymn emerges briefly in the bass shortly thereafter (five mm. after rehearsal letter F) as the movement's second goal. The sketches help us to notice that generating these two themes for the finale—or calling them forth—is the point of the second movement's many rotations; immediately after their generation the rotational processes, no longer needed, begin to decay. A later, separate sketch helps to confirm this reading (Ex. 15.10): here we may observe that part

EXAMPLE 15.9. Sibelius, Symphony No. 5, movt. 2, 14 mm. after rehearsal letter E

EXAMPLE 15.10. Sibelius, Sketch for Symphony No. 5, movt. 2

EXAMPLE 15.11. Sibelius, Symphony No. 6, finale, rehearsal letter D

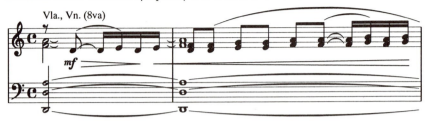

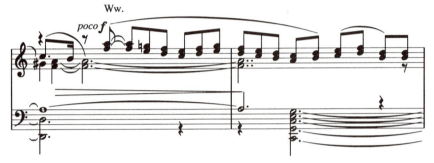

of the second movement's main theme was planned as a counterpoint to the (normally unstated) Swan Hymn.[39]

In addition, the 1914–15 sketchbook contains two versions of a theme, initially suggested for the Fifth Symphony, that would become the generating idea of the Sixth. In the completed Sixth it emerges in the middle of the finale (Ex. 15.11, from rehearsal letter D, slightly simplified), although once given the sketchbook clue, one may easily see how the rest of that symphony both sprang from it and consequently, in performance, grows inevitably toward it as a *telos*. Particularly telling are the tonic-subtonic chordal oscillation (d–C, suggesting parallel triads), the melodic parallel thirds (for instance, compare Ex. 15.11, m. 3, with the opening of the first movement), the prominent "Finnish" A–D pentachord and its various scalar segments and transpositions (again recalling the composer's 1896 Helsinki University lecture), the 3–2–1 ideogram (c^3–b^2–a^2), and so on.[40]

The final compositional period witnesses Sibelius's most radical experiments with symphonic architecture. As several related diary entries from 1912 indicate, his aim had become to rethink the concept of form by allowing certain nature-mystical core ideas to ramify "naturally" or meditatively, as though they had a separate volition not to be thwarted by the habits of traditional practice. Thus on 8 May 1912: "I intend to let the musical thoughts and their development determine their own form in my soul."[41] This resulted in what I have called Sibelius's "content-based forms," a concept relatable to A. B. Marx's mid-nineteenth-century description of the fantasia. (Indeed, while composing each of the last three symphonies, Sibelius wondered whether the title "fantasia" might not be more apt. The Seventh, for example, was first performed in 1924 under the title *Fantasia sinfonica*.)

The most characteristic of these content-based forms took their cue from the procedure encountered at the end of the Third Symphony: some sort of rotational form (a set of freely varied recyclings through a musical pattern, itself dominated by a closely knit "musical logic") simultaneously serving as a gestational matrix for the nurturing, and ultimately the full production, of a separate, decisive idea embedded and growing within it. A further complication—a major one for anyone seeking simple answers—is that many of these "new" structures were also in dialogue with the sonata-deformational practices so characteristic of the second wave of modernists. Thus one is normally obliged to confront the structures of these late works on at least two levels: primarily on that of rotational form merged with the process of teleological genesis; and secondarily in terms of allusions to the standard types of sonata deformation. This is the case, for example, with the first and last movements of the Fifth Symphony, with the first movement of the Sixth,[42] and with the tone poems *Luonno-*

tar (climactic *telos* in the third rotation, at rehearsal letter I, anticipated twice earlier), *The Oceanides,* and *Tapiola* (*telos* beginning thirteen mm. after rehearsal letter Q, anticipated several times earlier), and it is one reason why it is so difficult to deal with those pieces nonreductively.

Occasionally Sibelius's rotational/teleological structures seem to unfold without significant reference to sonata-deformational procedures. The second movement of the Fifth Symphony (striving to generate the finale themes as suggested above) is one of the clearest examples; the broad span of the entire Seventh Symphony—perhaps the most remarkable (and elusive) instance of a multimovement form in a single movement ever composed—is surely the most complex. Also noteworthy is the unorthodox finale of the Sixth, which may be heard as nine rotations apparently succeeding one another to articulate what seems to be a metaphor of birth/blossoming/full-flower/decay/death. Particularly telling in this reading of the movement—apart from Sibelius's provocative use of mode and key, which would require a much more expanded study—are the differing appearances of the *telos* (Ex. 15.11) in rotations 3, 4, and 5. Rotation 3, for example (from five mm. before rehearsal letter C to two mm. after rehearsal letter E) presents us with a pre-*telos* figure (five mm. after rehearsal letter C), the *telos* itself in seemingly full flower (one m. after rehearsal letter D: see Ex. 15.11), and an anacrusis figure or spur (four mm. before rehearsal letter E; Ex. 15.11, mm. 6–10) into the next rotation. In rotation 4 (from one m. after rehearsal letter E to seven mm. after rehearsal letter G) all this is recycled more intensely, in even fuller flower. In rotation 5, however (from seven mm. after rehearsal letter G to two mm. after rehearsal letter J), the process becomes "overripe" and decay begins to set in: the pre-*telos music* (rehearsal letter I) begins to decenter, triggering a *fff* crisis *telos* (rehearsal letter J)—one broken off after only two bars—whereupon everything thereafter, in subsequent rotations, becomes autumnal or valedictory. While motivically related to the movement, the final rotation 9 (beginning five mm. after rehearsal letter O, *doppio più lento*) seems more a separate *envoi* to the cyclical process of birth, flourishing, and decay that the movement, and indeed the whole symphony, has embodied.[43]

In his major works of the final period—conceived in isolation, split off from the tumult of the marketplace that he had once sought to engage, and subjected to increasingly severe self-criticism—Sibelius brought the central tropes of the "modern" symphony to an unforeseen concentration and musical cohesion. To be sure, brilliant new reconceptions of the symphonic genres, particularly heavily ironized ones facing even more decisive cultural erosions, would continue to emerge throughout the twentieth century. But perhaps the greatest irony is that it was with Sibelius—the perpetual outsider—that the grand heritage of the modern symphony took its most idiosyncratic and uncompromisingly inward turn.

Notes

1. For this sense of the complex and variously defined term *modern* see Carl Dahlhaus, "Modernism As a Period in Music History," in *Nineteenth-Century Music*, trans. J. Bradford Robinson (Berkeley and Los Angeles, 1989), 332–39. See also Dahlhaus's earlier remarks, "Musikalische Moderne und Neue Musik," *Melos/Neue Zeitschrift für Musik* 2 (1976): 90. My own view of this modernist wave encompasses composers born from about 1854 to 1866.

2. This topic of the enormous social and ideological changes that began to gather speed in Europe in the later nineteenth century has been treated by innumerable historians. For a provocative overview that stresses the model of institutional self-protection and increasing social challenge—one that centers on the dialectic of bourgeois triumphalism and self-celebration on the one hand and pervasive cultural pessimism on the other—see Eric Hobsbawm, *The Age of Empire: 1875–1914* (New York, 1989). Hobsbawm persuasively argues that "more generally, the 'high' arts were ill at ease in society. Somehow, in the field of culture as elsewhere, the results of bourgeois society and historical progress, long conceived as a co-ordinated forward march of the human mind, were different from what had been expected" (226).

3. Dahlhaus, *Nineteenth-Century Music*, 265–76. See also pp. 360–68, and cf. n. 1 above.

4. Two clarifications. First, I am concerned at this point with composers who identified themselves emphatically with the institution of the liberal-bourgeois public concert and with genres explicitly labeled and received by the audiences as symphonies or, in the case of Strauss, extended symphonic poems (which could function as modern substitutes for symphonies). Thus Puccini and Debussy, for example—both central modern composers—do not appear on this list (although at least one of the latter's works, *La Mer*, could in some senses be considered a symphony, just as the earlier orchestral *Nocturnes* could be heard as engaging in a dialogue with the tradition of the standard four-movement symphony, here shorn of its first movement). Other candidates for the list, though, would certainly include such figures as Dukas (1865) and Busoni (1866).

Second, in this model the first wave comprises symphonic composers who, at differing ages, launched most of their symphonic output in the recently stabilized international musical marketplaces of the later 1860s or 1870s. This wave brings together composers born between about 1825 and 1850, and it includes Bruckner, Brahms, Bruch, Saint-Saëns, Franck, Dvořák, Borodin, and Tchaikovsky. A third generational wave, consisting, roughly, of composers born in the 1870–85 period, reacted to the de facto institution of art music (n. 6 below) and the public that supported it in various ways, thus precipitating a sharp division within the institution and forcing a socioaesthetic crisis. Here we encounter such diverse figures as Schoenberg, Stravinsky, Ravel, Rachmaninoff, and Scriabin. The model proposed above argues that in a period of rapid social change each generational wave established a different set of relationships with the evolving aesthetic, cultural, and economic structures that supported the circulation of art music.

5. The first chapter of Hepokoski, *Sibelius: Symphony No. 5* (Cambridge, 1993), elaborates several of the concepts alluded to in the present essay.

6. By "institution of art music" I mean the complex social and economic network that makes that concept of "art music" possible and sets the terms of its

apprehension and circulation. The term is adapted from such writings as Peter Bürger, *Theory of the Avant-Garde* (1974), trans. Michael Shaw (Minneapolis, 1984); Peter Bürger, "The Institution of 'Art' As a Category in the Sociology of Literature," trans. Michael Shaw, *Cultural Critique* 2 (1985–86): 5–33, reprinted in Peter and Christa Bürger, *The Institutions of Art*, trans. Loren Kruger (Lincoln, NE, 1992), 3–30; Christa Bürger, *Der Ursprung der bürgerlichen Institution Kunst im höfischen Weimar: Literatursoziologische Untersuchungen zum klassischen Goethe* (Frankfurt, 1977); and Peter Uwe Hohendahl, "Introduction: The Institution of Literature," in *Building a National Literature: The Case of Germany, 1830–1870*, trans. Renate Baron Franciscono (Ithaca, NY, 1989), 1–43.

7. Erik Tawaststjerna, "Sibelius's Eighth Symphony: An Insoluble Mystery," *Finnish Music Quarterly* (1985): 61–70, 92–101.

8. On "musical logic" as a source of value and validation within that tradition see, e.g., Carl Dahlhaus, "Musical Logic and Speech Character," in *The Idea of Absolute Music*, trans. Roger Lustig (Chicago, 1989), 103–16; and Dahlhaus, the section on "Musikalische Logik" in the essay "Musikkritik als Sprachkritik," in *Klassische und romantische Musikästhetik* (Laaber, 1988), 283–84.

9. Bruckner's Third Symphony made "an enormous impression" on the young Sibelius, as he reported to his fiancée, Aino Järnefelt, from Vienna on 21 December 1890. See, e.g., Erik Tawaststjerna, *Sibelius*, trans. Robert Layton (Berkeley and Los Angeles, 1976 and 1986), 1:77–78, 109–11. For the remark on *Klangflächen* I am indebted to Peter Revers, "Jean Sibelius and the Viennese Musical Tradition," paper delivered at the First International Jean Sibelius Conference, 25 August 1990. A much larger study of the issue is that of Philip Coad, "Bruckner and Sibelius," (Ph.d. dissertation, University of Cambridge, 1985; available in book format, Cambridge University Library, Photographic Dept., 1990).

10. In "Perspectives on the Early Symphonies: The Russian Connection Redux," *Proceedings from the First International Sibelius Conference: Helsinki, August 1990*, ed. Eero Tarasti (Helsinki, 1995), 21–30, Malcolm Brown casts a skeptical eye on the often-adduced Russian influences on the young Sibelius and pointed out that several of the most prominent Russian critics of Sibelius—including Taneyev and Rimsky-Korsakov—judged his style as very foreign and non-Russian. Brown's argument effectively challenges the many casual Russian "influences"—thematic resemblances and the like—that have been found in Sibelius. (For some of the most superficial, see Cecil Gray and Gerald Abraham's comparison of Sibelius and Borodin, in, e.g., "The Symphonies," *The Music of Sibelius*, ed. Abraham [New York, 1947], 15–19).

While I agree with many of Brown's general remarks, it still seems undeniable that the young Sibelius adapted certain characteristically Russian sounds and musical procedures, although he adapted them in such personalized ways as also to make them his own. (Perhaps, needless to say, the debate here concerns the presence of seemingly "Russian" sounds as foregrounded, local events on the acoustic surface of the music; clearly, Sibelius's middleground and background procedures—his larger structural concerns—seem more idiosyncratic, less informed by Russian precedent.) The internal evidence for these dabs of Russian color (both Tchaikovskian and Petersburgian) is overwhelming, and I shall mention some of it in the discussion below. In addition, it is likely that the negative Russian criticism around 1900 was fraught with the politics of the period. We should keep in mind, for example, that some of these critics were associated with the highly polished, smooth, and elegant perspective of the Petersburg school at the turn of the century. Centering on Rimsky-Korsakov and his protegé Glazunov, the so-called *Belyayevtsï* were all too aware of their own "unrefined" *kuchka* past, which (though revered as a crucial spiritual source) they hoped had been transcended by the opalescent wizardry and technical progressivism of the present. Another group of critics spoke on behalf the glittering Moscow virtuosi. It is hardly surprising that Sibelius's broad-brushed musical "primitivism"—emerging, moreover, from a presumably "backward" outpost of the Russian empire—would have been something tempting to disavow. (See also the mixed reviews cited in Tawaststjerna, *Sibelius*, trans. Layton, 1:293).

11. Tawaststjerna's brief account of this in *Sibelius*, trans. Layton, 1:97–98, was expanded in the second Finnish edition of the book, which remains untranslated: *Jean Sibelius*, 2d ed. (Helsinki, 1989), 213–18, and in two new appendices to that book, "Larin Paraske ja runonlaulu" (Larin Paraske and rune song), 287–99, and "Nuori Sibelius: Duuri-molli tonaalisuudesta modaalisten ja duuri-molli tonaalisten ainesten synteesiin" (Young Sibelius: From major-minor tonality to a synthesis of modal and major-minor tonal elements"), 301–15. This last article, however, has appeared in a German translation, "Der junge Sibelius: Von Dur-Moll-Tonalität zu einer Synthese von modalen and Dur-Moll tonalen Elementen," in *Das musikalische Kunstwerk: Geschichte, Ästhetik, Theorie: Festschrift Carl Dahlhaus zum 60. Geburtstag*, ed. H. Danuser, L. de la Motte-Haber, S. Leopold, and N. Miller (Laaber, 1988), 639–50.

12. The main source regarding Sibelius's lecture, his thoughts on the pentachord and its harmonizations, and his publication of the folk songs has not been translated into English: Jouko Tolonen, "Jean Sibeliuksen koelunto ja mollipentakordin soinnutus" (Jean Sibelius's examination-lecture and the harmonization of the minor pentachord), in *Juhlakirja Erik Tawaststjernalle 10 X 1976*, ed. Erkki Salmenhaara (Helsinki, 1976), 79–92. Tolonen provides excerpts from the lecture itself in the original Swedish. For a brief account of other aspects of this lecture, see Tawaststjerna, *Sibelius*, trans. Layton, 1:190–91.

13. Some of what follows is adapted from notes written by the author for the recording of the First Symphony by Leonard Bernstein and the Vienna Philharmonic (1992): Deutsche Grammophon Compact Disc 435 351-2.

14. From the *Manchester Guardian*, 4 December 1905, quoted in Tawaststjerna, *Sibelius*, trans. Layton, 2:41–42.

15. Moreover, once the G-major/E-minor struggle is grasped, the semiotic sense of the generally parallel conclusions of the first movement (notice especially the strained E–F♯–G ascent in the cello and bassoon in the last seven measures) and the finale could scarcely be clearer.

16. This has been noted by, among others, Tawaststjerna, *Sibelius*, trans. Layton, 1:209–11. I should add that the ancestry of the the "*Pathétique* dissonance" may be traced back further, at least to Wagner's *Tannhäuser*. It occurs in the opening lines of act 1, "Naht euch dem Strande!," etc., one of the most celebrated—and imitated—sonorities of the second half of the century. For an argument on behalf of another allusion to it, see David Brodbeck, "Brahms, the Third Symphony, and the New German School," in *Brahms and His World*, ed. Walter Frisch (Princeton, NJ, 1990), 65–78.

17. A better case may be made, for instance, that prolonged $\frac{6}{3}$ sonorities in Sibelius are often not "first inversions" proper but rather expressive or decorative

alternatives to a more stable $^5_3$ chord, which may or may not be sounded nearby. In these cases the bass is not a true chordal mediant—and, of course, when the $^6_3$ sonority is prolonged one may at times question whether the implied tonal center is that of the supposed "root" or the actual bass. (For example, taken in the context of what follows, mm. 3–6 and 9–20 of the "B minor" *Tapiola* of 1926 express not "G♯^{6}"—that is, a momentary "tonality" of G♯ minor—but rather a $^6_3$ sonority above a static B bass. This sonority soon stabilizes (m. 26) into a $^5_3$ chord, a "B minor" that before long is provided with a further "Dorian" color. In brief, mm. 1–25 are probably best considered shifting color sonorities over an implied or actual B bass, leading to the $^5_3$ arrival point in m. 26.) One might add that the same issue arises with the two sources for the pre-Sibelian "mediant pedal" effect: the middle section of the second movement of Tchaikovsky's *Pathétique* Symphony (a section over a D pedal that I would prefer not to interpret as being "in B minor") and the trio of the scherzo of Schumann's "Rhenish" Symphony (arguably a somewhat clearer mediant pedal, because of the cadence at its end).

18. Some examples: the second theme of Balakirev's *Islamey*, the opening theme of the third movement of Rimsky-Korsakov's *Scheherazade*, the beginning of Borodin's String Quartet No. 2, and so on.

19. Often borrowed in current discussions of influence, the term is taken from Harold Bloom, *The Anxiety of Influence: A Theory of Poetry* (New York, 1973), and *A Map of Misreading* (New York, 1975).

20. For Sibelius's labeling of the "Christus" theme and for other labels given at early stages of the sketching see Tawaststjerna, *Sibelius*, trans. Layton, 1:250–52. (Tawaststjerna also hears an allusion to *Götterdämmerung* in the movement.)

21. Flodin, "Die Erweckung des nationalen Tones in der Finnischen Musik," *Die Musik* 3 (1903–4): 287–89. Cf. Flodin's two earlier reports, "Die neue Symphonie von Jean Sibelius," *Die Musik* 1 (1902): 1302 (in this article concerning the Second Symphony he mentions that the First is "already known, also in Germany"); and "Die Entwickelung der Musik in Finnland," *Die Musik* 2 (1903): 355–62. In Germany, Flodin's positives would be often recast negatively, as limitations, most notably by the influential writer Walter Niemann.

22. Tawaststjerna, *Sibelius*, trans. Layton, 2:22–24. This was Sibelius's second appearance on his friend Busoni's Berlin series; the first was in November 1902, conducting *En saga*.

23. See, e.g., Seidl, *Moderner Geist in der deutschen Tonkunst* (Berlin, 1901) ("Emanzipation der Farbe" adduced as a *Schlagwort*, 59); Merian, *Richard Strauß' Tondichtung "Also sprach Zarathustra": Eine Studie über die moderne Programmsymphonie* (Leipzig, 1899), esp. p. 9; Graf, "Gedanken über das Moderne in der Musik," *Die Musik* 3 (1903): 21–26 ("die freie Form," 22).

24. See, e.g., the clear appeal at the close of Karl Schmalz, "Richard Strauss' 'Also sprach Zarathustra' und 'Ein Heldenleben': Ein Vergleich," *Die Musik* 4 (1905); 102–23—which Sibelius, in Berlin at the time of its publication (and an avid reader of *Die Musik*), is likely to have read; Rudolf Louis, *Die deutsche Musik der Gegenwart* (Munich and Leipzig, 1909); Otto Klauwell, *Geschichte der Programmusik von ihren Anfangen bis zur Gegenwart* (Leipzig, 1910), 5–8; and the persistent echoes of such thought in, e.g., Walter Niemann, *Die Musik der Gegenwart* (Berlin, 1913), 172–97 ("[In modern music] the sense of musical economy is evaporating," etc., 196). See also the discussion of this point, including the possible impact of Busoni's thought on Sibelius (or vice versa) at this time, in chapters 1 and 2 of Hepokoski, *Sibelius: Symphony No. 5*.

25. This famous remark was reported by Sibelius much later to Karl Ekman, *Jean Sibelius: His Life and Personality*, trans. Edward Birse (London, 1936), 176. According to the composer, Mahler's response—the precisely opposite view—was, "No! [the] symphony must be like the world. It must embrace everything." For another overview of this encounter, see Tawaststjerna, *Sibelius*, trans. Layton, 2:76–77.

26. Hepokoski, *Sibelius: Symphony No. 5*, chapters 3 and 5.

27. I pursue some of these issues in an essay on Sibelius's *Luonnotar*, forthcoming in *The Sibelius Companion*, ed. Glenda Dawn Goss (New York, 1997).

28. The third is embedded in the theme itself, of course, and the frequency of phrases ending with a descending major third is particularly telling. One should not oversimplify this complex movement, but it might also be suggested that its G♯ minor probably alludes to the common procedure of moving to ♭VI for a slow movement. Here, however, the expected C common tone (of A♭ major, that is) is shifted to C♯ (enharmonically B♮), which momentarily blocks out the "C character" of this movement. The reemergence of this C character, along with the further, more developed gestation of the third, is one of the central features of the initial scherzo portion of the subsequent movement and helps to define it as a step further in the process of teleological genesis.

29. For more on the terms *expositional, complementary*, and *culminatory rotation*, see my *Sibelius: Symphony No. 5*, 28–29 and chapter 5, passim.

30. "Ainolassa tämä hiljaisuus puhuu": from, e.g., Sibelius's radio interview on 8 December 1948. This recorded interview dates from well into his retirement, and in it he seems to have wished to document several of the key sentences of his life. A short excerpt from this interview (in Finnish), concluding with these words, was released on the recording *Music of Jean Sibelius*, Finlandia Records, FA 003 (1984).

31. Letter to Axel Carpelan, 20 May 1918; Tawaststjerna, *Jean Sibelius*, vol. 4 (Helsinki, 1978), 290 (in Finnish).

32. In the still untranslated fourth volume of his *Jean Sibelius* Tawaststjerna provides plates of fifteen pages of the sketchbook (following p. 176). The sketchbook's final three pages date from Summer 1916.

33. For transcriptions of some of the pre-Seventh-Symphony versions of the theme see Tawaststjerna, *Jean Sibelius* 4:60; Hepokoski, *Sibelius: Symphony No. 5*, 34, 38; and Kari Kilpeläinen, "Sibelius's Seventh Symphony: An Introduction to the Manuscript and Printed Sources," trans. James Hepokoski and Sari Rönnholm, forthcoming in *The Sibelius Companion*. Tawaststjerna further suggests (4:22) that this theme may be related to Sibelius's 10 October 1914 diary entry: "*Alleingefühl* again. Alone and strong. . . . The autumn sun is shining. Nature in its farewell colors. My heart sings sadly—'The shadows lengthen.' Fifth Symphony Adagio? That such a poor being as I can have such rich moments!" And according to Kilpeläinen, a later sketch suggests that at one point Sibelius considered incorporating a version of it into a projected multimovement tone poem, *Kuutar* ([Feminine] moon spirit); subsequent sketches for this never-completed piece indicate that he may have intended it for a D-major section called "Tähtölä" (Where the stars dwell).

34. In the 1914–15 sketchbook the "*Tapiola* theme" is explicitly joined to a version of Fifth Symphony finale's second theme, that is, to the "Swan Hymn" in its expanding-interval form (see below); see Tawaststjerna *Jean Sibelius*, vol. 4, plate 4, following 176. For a transcription see my *Sibelius: Symphony No. 5*, 37.

448   *Sibelius*

35. Tawaststjerna, *Jean Sibelius* 4:55.

36. Hepokoski, *Sibelius: Symphony No. 5*, 59–60, 83–84.

37. Translation (and fuller quotation of the diary entry) in Hepokoski, *Sibelius: Symphony No. 5*, 36.

38. "Tuo joutsenhymni vailla vertaa," in Tawaststjerna, *Jean Sibelius* 4:195. See also Hepokoski, *Sibelius: Symphony No. 5*, 37, 53. This differs markedly from Tovey's often quoted remark about this theme and its preparations: "The bustling introduction provides a rushing wind, through which Thor can enjoy swinging his hammer" (1935–39, rpt. in *Essays in Musical Analysis*, vol. 1: *Symphonies and Other Orchestral Works* [Oxford, 1989], 499.) Sibelius's original swan image and Tovey's Thor, however, do share a crucial feature: the "rushing wind" that offers resistance to a spiritual object moving forward through it.

39. Undated sketch, numbered as A/0339 in Kari Kilpeläinen, *The Jean Sibelius Musical Manuscripts at Helsinki University Library: A Complete Catalogue* (Wiesbaden, 1991).

40. For the 1914–15 sketches see Tawaststjerna, *Jean Sibelius*, vol. 4, plates 11 (the theme in E♭ minor) and 13 (in D minor), following p. 176.

41. This and related diary entries are provided in my *Sibelius: Symphony No. 5*, chapter 3.

42. The first movement of the Sixth Symphony is also in dialogue with a number of sonata-deformational procedures, including, perhaps most obviously, that of the nonresolving recapitulation. (On this procedure, see my essay on Elgar in the present volume.)

43. Interpretations may differ both on the number of rotations and on their precise boundaries in this closely integrated movement. I hear the nine rotations as follows: 1 (mm. 1–16, an antiphonal hymn or nature epiphany; notice especially the second phrase pair's consequent, mm. 13–16, which anticipates the intervals of the *telos*, as transcribed in Ex. 15.11); 2 (mm. 17–52, a further germinating of the idea, leading to a "spur" onward at rehearsal letter B); 3 (mm. 52–82, near-full flower); 4 (mm. 83–113, fullest flower); 5 (mm. 114–47, "overripening" and crisis); 6 (mm. 148–64, showing the decay that has set into the ideas first exposed in rotation 1); 7 (mm. 165–188, one ♭ signature [!], D minor and F major [!], and onset of "coda" tone); 8 (mm. 189–224, recycling the "coda" ideas); 9 (mm. 224–256, *envoi*: farewell to the entire process).

Some prior analyses have heard the C-major "spur" near the end of my rotation 2 (rehearsal letter B, m. 49) as the beginning of a second theme. I hear it, however, not as a conceptually accented thematic incipit but as an anacrusis or transition into the next rotation: this seems even more clearly its function in rotations 3 and 4. Within this "nature-contemplative" work—and there can be little doubt of this fundamental status—the transition-spur in rotation 2 would seem to be analogous to something on the order of the sudden appearance of any one of a number of forest fauna (avian? leporine? but surely specifics cannot matter), startled, then fluttering (scampering?) off into the wider D-minor-modal "nature-space," which correspondingly opens up into availability with the onset of rotation 3.

Selected Bibliography

Abraham, Gerald. "The Symphonies." In *The Music of Sibelius*, ed. Gerald Abraham, 14–37. New York, 1947.

Cherniavsky, David. "Sibelius's Tempo Corrections." *Music and Letters* 31 (1950): 53–55.

Coad, Philip N. "Bruckner and Sibelius." Dissertation, Queen's College, Cambridge, 1985. Available in book format, Cambridge, 1990.

Dahlström, Fabian. *The Works of Jean Sibelius*. Helsinki, 1987.

Hepokoski, James. *Sibelius: Symphony No. 5*. Cambridge, 1993.

———. "The Essence of Sibelius: Creation Myths and Rotational Cycles in *Luonnotar*. In *The Sibelius Companion*, ed. Glenda Dawn Goss. New York. Forthcoming 1997.

Howell, Tim. *Jean Sibelius: Progressive Techniques in the Symphonies and Tone Poems*. New York and London, 1989.

Jalas, Jussi. *Kirjoituksia Sibeliuksen sinfonioista: Sinfonian eetinin pakko*. Helsinki, 1988.

Kilpeläinen, Kari. "Sibelius's Seventh Symphony: An Introduction to the Manuscript and Printed Sources." Ed. and trans. James Hepokoski and Sari Rönnholm. In *The Sibelius Companion*, ed. Glenda Dawn Goss. New York. Forthcoming 1997.

———. *The Jean Sibelius Musical Manuscripts at Helsinki University Library: A Complete Catalogue*. Wiesbaden, 1991.

Krohn, Ilmari. *Der Formenbau in den Symphonien von Jean Sibelius*. Helsinki, 1942.

Layton, Robert. *Sibelius*. Rev. ed. New York, 1992.

Luyken, Lorenz. *". . . aus dem Nichtigen eine Welt Schaffen . . ."*: Studien zur Dramaturgie im symphonischen Spätwerk von Jean Sibelius. Kölner Beiträge zur Musikforschung 190. Kassel, 1995.

Murtomäki, Veijo. *Symphonic Unity: The Development of Formal Thinking in the Symphonies of Sibelius*. Helsinki, 1993.

Parmet, Simon. *The Symphonies of Sibelius. A Study in Musical Appreciation*. Trans. Kingsley A. Hart. London, 1959.

Pike, Lionel A. *Beethoven, Sibelius, and the "Profound Logic."* London, 1978.

Ringbom, Nils-Eric. *Jean Sibelius: A Master and His Work*. Trans. G. I. C. de Courcy. Norman, OK, 1954.

Roiha, Eino. *Die Symphonien von Jean Sibelius: Eine form-analytische Studie*. Jyväskylä, 1941.

Salmenhaara, Erkki. *Jean Sibelius*. Helsinki, 1984. In Finnish.

Simpson, Robert. *Carl Nielsen: Symphonist*. Rev. ed. London, 1979.

Tammarro, Ferruccio. *Le sinfonie de Sibelius*. Turin, 1982.

Tanzberger, Ernst. *Jean Sibelius: Eine Monographie*. Wiesbaden, 1962.

Tawaststjerna, Erik. *Jean Sibelius*. 5 vols. Helsinki, 1965–88. In Finnish, trans. from the original Swedish by Tuomas Anhava, Raija Mattila, and Erkki Salmenhaara.

———. *Sibelius*. 2 vols. Abridged translation of vols. 1–3 of the above—from the original Swedish—by Robert Layton. London, 1976, 1986. The third volume, encompassing the original vols. 4–5, is forthcoming.

———. "Sibelius's Eighth Symphony—An Insoluble Mystery." *Finnish Music Quarterly* (1985): 61–70, 92–101.

Tarasti, Eero, ed. *Proceedings from the First International Jean Sibelius Conference* [1990]. Helsinki, 1995.

Tovey, Donald Francis. *Essays in Musical Analysis: Symphonies and Other Orchestral Works*. Oxford, 1989.

Vignal, Marc. *Jean Sibelius: L'homme et son œuvre*. Paris, 1965.

Index

[Note: Italic page numeration indicates the main entry for the indexed item.]